The
Oxford Book
Of English Verse
1250–1918

Chosen and Edited by
Sir Arthur Quiller-Couch

Second Edition

Oxford   New York
OXFORD UNIVERSITY PRESS

Oxford University Press, Walton Street, Oxford OX2 6DP

Oxford New York
Athens Auckland Bangkok Bombay
Calcutta Cape Town Dar es Salaam Delhi
Florence Hong Kong Istanbul Karachi
Kuala Lumpur Madras Madrid Melbourne
Mexico City Nairobi Paris Singapore
Taipei Tokyo Toronto

and associated companies in
Berlin Ibadan

Oxford is a trade mark of Oxford University Press

First published 1900 by Oxford University Press
Second edition first published 1939

Reprinted 1943, 1948, 1949, 1953, 1955 (with corrections), 1957,
1961, 1966, 1968, 1971, 1973, 1974, 1979, 1983, 1984, 1985,
1987, 1988, 1989, 1991, 1992, 1994

ISBN 0-19-812107-5

Printed and bound in Great Britain by
Clays Ltd
Bungay, Suffolk

PREFACE TO THE FIRST EDITION

FOR this Anthology I have tried to range over the whole field of English Verse from the beginning, or from the Thirteenth Century to this closing year of the Nineteenth, and to choose the best. Nor have I sought in these Islands only, but wheresoever the Muse has followed the tongue which among living tongues she most delights to honour. To bring home and render so great a spoil compendiously has been my capital difficulty. It is for the reader to judge if I have so managed it as to serve those who already love poetry and to implant that love in some young minds not yet initiated.

My scheme is simple. I have arranged the poets as nearly as possible in order of birth, with such groupings of anonymous pieces as seemed convenient. For convenience, too, as well as to avoid a dispute-royal, I have gathered the most of the Ballads into the middle of the Seventeenth Century; where they fill a languid interval between two winds of inspiration—the Italian dying down with Milton and the French following at the heels of the restored Royalists. For convenience, again, I have set myself certain rules of spelling. In the very earliest poems inflection and spelling are structural, and to modernize is to destroy. But as old inflections fade into modern the old spelling becomes less and less vital, and has been brought (not, I hope, too abruptly) into line with that sanctioned by use and familiar. To do this seemed wiser than to discourage many readers for the sake of diverting others by a scent of antiquity which—to be essential—should breathe of something rarer than an odd arrangement of type. But there are scholars whom I cannot expect to agree with me; and to conciliate them I have excepted Spenser and Milton from the rule.

Glosses of archaic and otherwise difficult words are given at the foot of the page: but the text has not been disfigured with reference-marks. And rather than make the book unwieldy I have eschewed notes—reluctantly when some obscure passage or allusion seemed to ask for a timely word; with more equanimity when the temptation was to criticize or 'appreciate'. For the function of the anthologist includes criticizing in silence.

Care has been taken with the texts. But I have sometimes thought it consistent with the aim of the book to prefer the more beautiful to the better attested reading. I have often excised weak or superfluous stanzas when sure that excision would improve; and have not hesitated to extract a few stanzas from a long poem when persuaded that they could stand alone as a lyric. The apology for such experiments can only lie in their success: but the risk is one which, in my judgement, the anthologist ought to take. A few small corrections have been made, but only when they were quite obvious.

The numbers chosen are either lyrical or epigrammatic. Indeed I am mistaken if a single epigram included fails to preserve at least some faint thrill of the emotion through which it had to pass before the Muse's lips let it fall, with however exquisite deliberation. But the lyrical spirit is volatile and notoriously hard to bind with definitions; and seems to grow wilder with the years. With the anthologist—as with the fisherman who knows the fish at the end of his sea-line—the gift, if he have it, comes by sense, improved by practice. The definition, if he be clever enough to frame one, comes by after-thought. I don't know that it helps, and am sure that it may easily mislead.

Having set my heart on choosing the best, I resolved not to be dissuaded by common objections against anthologies—that they repeat one another until the proverb δὶς ἢ τρὶς τὰ καλά loses all application—or perturbed if my judgement should often agree with that of good critics. The best is the best, though a hundred judges have declared it so; nor had it been any feat to search out and insert the second-rate merely because it happened to be recondite. To be sure, a man must come to such a task as mine haunted by his youth and the favourites he loved in days when he had much enthusiasm but little reading.

> A deeper import
> Lurks in the legend told my infant years
> Than lies upon that truth we live to learn.

Few of my contemporaries can erase—or would wish to erase—the dye their minds took from the late Mr. Palgrave's *Golden Treasury*: and he who has returned to it again and again with an affection born of companionship on many journeys must remember not only what the *Golden Treasury* includes, but the moment when this or that poem appealed to him, and even how it lies on the page. To Mr. Bullen's *Lyrics from the Elizabethan Song Books* and his other treasuries I own a more advised debt. Nor am I free of obligation to anthologies even more recent—to Archbishop Trench's *Household Book of Poetry*, Mr. Locker-Lampson's *Lyra Elegantiarum*, Mr. Miles' *Poets and Poetry of the Century*, Mr. Beeching's *Paradise of English Poetry*, Mr. Henley's *English Lyrics*, Mrs. Sharp's *Lyra Celtica*, Mr. Yeats' *Book of*

Irish Verse, and Mr. Churton Collins' *Treasury of Minor British Poetry*: though my rule has been to consult these after making my own choice. Yet I can claim that the help derived from them—though gratefully owned—bears but a trifling proportion to the labour, special and desultory, which has gone to the making of my book.

For the anthologist's is not quite the *dilettante* business for which it is too often and ignorantly derided. I say this, and immediately repent; since my wish is that the reader should in his own pleasure quite forget the editor's labour, which too has been pleasant: that, standing aside, I may believe this book has made the Muses' access easier when, in the right hour, they come to him to uplift or to console—

ἄκλητος μὲν ἔγωγε μένοιμί κεν· ἐς δὲ καλεύντων
θαρσήσας Μοίσαισι σὺν ἀμετέραισιν ἱκοίμαν.

October, 1900

PREFACE TO SECOND EDITION

BY favour of the Public, *The Oxford Book of English Verse* has held its own in request for close upon forty years. The editor would stand convicted of dullness indeed if in these years he had not learnt, revising his judgement, to regret some inclusions and omissions of indolence; the industry of scholars having rescued to light meanwhile many gems long hidden away in libraries, miscellanies, even scrap-books. In this new edition, therefore, I have risked repairing the old structure with a stone here, a tile there, and hope to have left it as weather-proof as when it was first built.

I have added a hundred-odd pages, and close upon Armistice Day 1918, admitting a few later numbers by poets who, whether consciously or not, had indicated before that date the trend of their genius. I shrank, of course, from making the book unwieldy; but in fact also I felt my judgement insecure amid post-War poetry. Although I cannot dispute against Time, this is not to admit a charge of crabbed age: since it has been my good fortune to spend the most part of these later years with the young and to share—even in some measure to encourage—their zest for experiment. The Muses' house has many mansions: their hospitality has outlived many policies of State, more than a few religions, countless heresies—*tamen usque recurret Apollo*—and it were profane to misdoubt the Nine as having forsaken these so long favoured islands. Of experiment I still hold myself fairly competent to judge. But, writing in 1939, I am at a loss what to do with a fashion of morose disparagement; of sneering at things long by catholic consent accounted beautiful; of scorning at 'Man's unconquerable mind' and hanging up (without benefit of laundry) our common humanity as a rag on a clothes-line. Be it allowed that these present times are dark. Yet what are our poets of use—what are they *for*—if they cannot hearten the crew with auspices of daylight? In a time no less perilous Wordsworth could write

> In our halls is hung
> Armoury of the invincible knights of old:

—'armoury', not museum-pieces, still less tear-bottles. 'Agincourt, Agincourt, know ye not Agincourt?'

The reader, turning the pages of this book, will find this note of valiancy—of the old Roman 'virtue' mated with cheerfulness—dominant throughout, if in many curious moods. He may trace it back, if he care, far behind Chaucer to the rudest beginnings of English Song. It is indigenous, proper to our native spirit, and it will endure.   A. Q.-C.

Whitsun, 1939

ACKNOWLEDGEMENTS

GRATEFUL acknowledgement is here made for permission given during their lifetime to include poems by the following authors now deceased: H. C. Beeching (for two poems of his own and for his redaction of *Quia Amore Langueo*); Hilaire Belloc; A. C. Benson; Laurence Binyon; Edmund Blunden; Gordon Bottomley; Robert Bridges; J. A. Chapman; Padraic Colum; John Davidson; W. H. Davies; Walter de la Mare; Aubrey de Vere; Austin Dobson; Lord Alfred Douglas; Mary Duclaux (Darmesteter); Oliver St. John Gogarty; Sir Edmund Gosse; Bret Harte; W. E. Henley; Catherine Tynan Hinkson; Ralph Hodgson; W. D. Howells; Dr Douglas Hyde; James Joyce; Andrew Lang; Richard Le Gallienne; John Masefield; George Meredith; Alice Meynell; Thomas Sturge Moore; Sir Henry Newbolt; Alfred Noyes; Herbert Palmer; Sir Gilbert Parker; Eden Phillpotts; Earnest Rhys; T. W. Rolleston; G. W. Russell ('Æ'); Siegfried Sassoon; Mrs. Clement Shorter (Dora Sigerson); James Stephens; A. C. Swinburne; Francis Thompson; Sir William Watson; Charles Williams; Margaret Louisa Woods; W. B. Yeats.

The editor's thanks are also due to publishers and others for kind permission to include copyright poems by the following.

Lascelles Abercrombie: Messrs. John Lane the Bodley Head, Ltd.
William Allingham: the late Mrs. Allingham.
William Barnes: the executors.
Hilaire Belloc: Peters Fraser & Dunlop Group Ltd.
Laurence Binyon: Mrs. Nicolette Gray and the Society of Authors on behalf of the Laurence Binyon Estate.

ACKNOWLEDGEMENTS

Edmund Blunden: Peters Fraser & Dunlop Group Ltd.

Wilfrid Scawen Blunt: Sir Sydney Cockerell.

Gordon Bottomley: the executors.

F. W. Bourdillon: the executors.

Robert Bridges: Clarendon Press.

Rupert Brooke (from *Poems*): the author's representatives; Messrs. Sidgwick & Jackson; Messrs. Dodd, Mead & Co., New York; Messrs. McClelland & Stewart, Toronto.

T. E. Brown (from *Collected Poems of T. E. Brown*): the author's representatives; Messrs. Macmillan & Co., Ltd.; the Macmillan Co., New York.

Bliss Carman: the executors.

Mrs. Browning: the proprietors of Mr. and Mrs. Browning's copyrights and Messrs. Smith, Elder & Co., Ltd.

J. A. Chapman: the executors.

G. K. Chesterton: Miss Collins, Messrs. Methuen & Co., Ltd., and Messrs. Dodd, Mead & Co., New York (for 'The Rolling English Road'); Messrs. J. M. Dent & Co., Ltd. (for 'The Donkey').

Mary Coleridge (from *Poems*): Sir Francis Newbolt and the executors of the late Sir Henry Newbolt; Messrs. Elkin Mathews.

Padraic Colum: the executors and the Macmillan Co., New York.

W. H. Davies: the executors; Messrs. Jonathan Cape, Ltd.; Oxford University Press, New York.

Walter de la Mare: the Literary Trustees of Walter de la Mare and the Society of Authors as their representative.

Lord Alfred Douglas (from *Sonnets*): the Lord Alfred Douglas Literary Estate.

Ernest Dowson: Messrs. John Lane the Bodley Head, Ltd.

Mary Duclaux (Darmesteter; from *Collected Poems*): T. Fisher Unwin, now part of A. C. Black.

George du Maurier: Lady du Maurier.

Sir Samuel Ferguson: the late Lady Ferguson.

Edward FitzGerald: the late William Aldis Wright and Messrs. Macmillan & Co., Ltd.

James Elroy Flecker: Messrs. Martin Secker & Warburg, Ltd.

Norman Gale: Mr. Gale.

Oliver St. John Gogarty (from *Collected Poems*): Copyright by

ACKNOWLEDGEMENTS

Devin-Adair, Publishers Inc., Old Greenwich, Connecticut 06870. All rights reserved.

Julian Grenfell: Lord and Lady Desborough.

Thomas Hardy: the executrix; Messrs. Macmillan & Co., Ltd.; the Macmillan Co., New York.

Ralph Hodgson: the executors; Messrs. Macmillan & Co., Ltd; the Macmillan Co., New York.

G. M. Hopkins: Oxford University Press.

Lord Houghton: the Marquis of Crewe.

A. E. Housman (from *Last Poems* and *A Shropshire Lad*): the literary executors and Messrs. Henry Holt, Inc., New York.

Dr. Douglas Hyde: the executors.

Selwyn Image: the executors.

Jean Ingelow: Messrs. Longmans, Green & Co., Ltd.

Lionel Johnson: Messrs. Elkin Mathews & Marrot, Ltd.

James Joyce (from *Collected Poems*): the executors; Messrs. Faber & Faber, Ltd.; Viking Press, New York.

Rudyard Kipling (from *Rewards and Fairies*): Mrs. Kipling; Messrs. Macmillan & Co., Ltd.; Messrs. Doubleday Doran & Co.; the Macmillan Co. of Canada, Ltd.

Hon. Emily Lawless: Hon. Kathleen Lawless.

Richard Le Gallienne: The Society of Authors as the literary representative of the Estate of Richard Le Gallienne.

John Masefield (from *The Collected Poems of John Masefield*): The Society of Authors as the literary representative of the Estate of John Masefield. Messrs. Wm. Heinemann, Ltd.; the Macmillan Co., New York.

George Meredith: Messrs. Constable & Co., Ltd., and Messrs. Charles Scribner's Sons, New York.

Thomas Sturge Moore: the executors.

William Morris: Sir Sydney Cockerell.

Sir Henry Newbolt (from *Poems New and Old*): Sir Francis Newbolt and the executors of the late Sir Hery Newbolt.

Alfred Noyes: the executors.

Arthur O'Shaugnessy: Messrs. Chatto & Windus, Ltd.

Wilfrid Owen: Mrs. Owen; Messrs. Chatto & Windus, Ltd.; Viking Press, New York.

H. E. Palmer: Phoebe Hesketh.

ACKNOWLEDGEMENTS

Stephen Phillips: Messrs. John Lane the Bodley Head, Ltd.

Eden Phillpotts: the executors.

William Philpot: the executor.

W. B. Rands: Messrs. John Lane the Bodley Head, Ltd.

Ernest Rhys: J. M. Dent & Sons Ltd. Publishers.

Christina Rossetti: Messrs. Macmillan & Co., Ltd.

John Ruskin: Mr. George Allen.

George William Russell ('Æ'): Messrs. Macmillan & Co., Ltd.; the Macmillan Co., New York.

Siegfried Sassoon: G. T. Sassoon; Messrs. Wm. Heinemann, Ltd.

W. B. Scott: the executors.

Walter C. Smith: Messrs. Jackson, Son, & Co., Ltd., Glasgow.

Charles Sorley: Mrs. Sorley and the Cambridge University Press.

James Stephens: The Society of Authors on behalf of the copyright holder Mrs. Iris Wise; Messrs. Macmillan & Co., Ltd.; the Macmillan Co., New York.

R. L. Stevenson: the executors; Messrs. Chatto & Windus, Ltd.; Messrs. Charles Scribner's Sons, New York.

A. C. Swinburne: Messrs. Wm. Heinemann, Ltd.

Frederick Tennyson: the executors.

Lord Tennyson (from *Works of Alfred Tennyson*): the author's representative; Messrs. Macmillan & Co., Ltd.; the Macmillan Co., New York.

Edward Thomas (from *Collected Poems of Edward Thomas*): Mrs. Edward Thomas and Messrs. Faber & Faber, Ltd.

Francis Thompson: Mr. Wilfrid Meynell.

James Thomson: the late Bertram Dobell.

Thomas Traherne: the late Bertram Dobell.

F. Herbert Trench: Messrs. Jonathan Cape, Ltd.

C. T. Turner: Sir Franklyn Lushington.

Charles Williams: David Higham Associates and Oxford University Press.

Margaret Louisa Woods (from *Collected Poems*): Random House UK Limited.

W. B. Yeats (from *Collected Poems*): Messrs. Macmillan & Co., Ltd.

CONTENTS

CONTENTS

CONTENTS

CONTENTS

CONTENTS

CONTENTS

CONTENTS

xxiv

CONTENTS

CONTENTS

CONTENTS

LIST OF AUTHORS

The references are to the numbers of the poems

xxviii

LIST OF AUTHORS

LIST OF AUTHORS

LIST OF AUTHORS

LIST OF AUTHORS

ANONYMOUS

1 · *Cuckoo Song*

c. 1226

SUMER is icumen in,
   Lhude sing cuccu!
Groweth sed, and bloweth med,
   And springeth the wude nu—
          Sing cuccu!

Awe bleteth after lomb,
   Lhouth after calve cu;
Bulluc sterteth, bucke verteth,
   Murie sing cuccu!

Cuccu, cuccu, well singes thu, cuccu:
   Ne swike thu naver nu;
Sing cuccu, nu, sing cuccu,
   Sing cuccu, sing cuccu, nu!

2 · *The Irish Dancer*

c. 1300

ICH am of Irlaunde,
   Ant of the holy londe
     Of Irlande.
Gode sire, pray ich the,
For of saynte charité,
Come ant daunce wyth me
     In Irlaunde.

1 lhude] loud.   awe] ewe.   lhouth] loweth.   sterteth] leaps. swike] cease.

Alison

c. 1300

BYTUENE Mershe and Averil
　When spray biginneth to springe,
The lutel foul hath hire wyl
　On hyre lud to synge:
Ich libbe in love-longinge
For semlokest of alle thynge,
He may me blisse bringe,
　Ich am in hire baundoun.
An hendy hap ichabbe y-hent,
Ichot from hevene it is me sent,
From alle wymmen my love is lent
　And lyht on Alysoun.

On heu hire her is fayr ynoh,
　Hire browe broune, hire eye blake;
With lossum chere he on me loh;
　With middel smal and wel y-make;
Bote he me wolle to hire take
For to buen hire owen make,
Long to lyven ichulle forsake
　And feye fallen adoun.
An hendy hap, etc.

Nihtes when I wende and wake,
　For-thi myn wonges waxeth won,

on hyre lud] in her language.　ich libbe] I live.　semlokest]
seemliest.　he] she.　baundoun] thraldom.　hendy] gracious.
y-hent] received.　ichot] I wot　lyht] alighted.　hire her]
her hair.　lossum chere] lovely face.　loh] smiled.　bote
he] unless she.　buen] be.　make] mate.　feye] like to die.
nihtes] at night.　wende] turn.　for-thi] on that account.
wonges waxeth won] cheeks grow wan.

Levedi, al for thine sake
  Longinge is y-lent me on.
In world nis non so wyter mon
That al hire bounté telle con;
Hire swyre is whittore than the swon,
  And feyrest may in toune.
An hendy hap, etc.

Ich am for wowyng al for-wake,
  Wery so water in wore;
Lest eny reve me my make
  Ichabbe y-yerned yore.
Betere is tholien whyle sore
Then mournen evermore.
Geynest under gore,
  Herkne to my roun.
An hendy hap, etc.

4   *Spring-tide*

c. 1300

LENTEN ys come with love to toune,
  With blosmen and with briddes roune,
That al this blisse bryngeth;
Dayes-eyes in this dales,
Notes suete of nyhtegales,
  Uch foul song singeth;

3 levedi] lady.   y-lent me on] come upon me.   so wyter
mon] so wise a man.   swyre] neck.   may] maid.   for-wake]
worn out with vigils.   so water in wore] as water in a weir.
reve] rob.   y-yerned yore] long desired.   tholien] to endure.
geynest under gore] comeliest under robe.   roun] voice.
  4 toune] the dwellings of men.

3

ANONYMOUS

The threstelcoc him threteth oo,
Away is huere wynter wo,
When woderove springeth;
Thise foules singeth ferly fele,
Ant wlyteth on huere wunne wele,
That al the wode ryngeth.

The rose rayleth hire rode,
The leves on the lyhte wode
Waxen al with wille;
The mone mandeth hire bleo,
The lilie is lossom to seo,
The fenyl and the fille;
Wowes thise wilde drakes,
Miles murgeth huere makes
Ase strem that striketh stille.
Mody meneth; so doth mo
(Ichot ych am on of tho)
For loue that likes ille.

The mone mandeth hire lyht,
So doth the semly sonne bryht,
When briddes singeth breme;

him threteth oo] is aye chiding.   huere] their.   wode-
rove] woodruff.   ferly fele] marvellous many.   wlyteth etc.]
whistle, in their wealth of joy.   rayleth hire rode] clothes
herself in red.   mandeth hire bleo] sends forth her light.
lossom to seo] lovesome to see   fille] thyme.   wowes]
woo.   murgeth] make merry.   makes] mates   striketh]
flows.   mody meneth] the passionate man makes moan.   so
doth mo] so do others.   on of tho] one of them.   breme]
lustily.

4

Deawes donketh the dounes,
Deores with huere derne rounes
   Domes for to deme;
Wormes woweth under cloude,
Wymmen waxeth wounder proude,
   So wel hit wol hem seme,
Yef me shal wonte wille of on,
This wunne weole y wole forgon
   Ant wyht in wode be fleme.

5   *Blow, Northern Wind*

c. 1300

ICHOT a burde in boure bryht,
  That fully semly is on syht,
Menskful maiden of myht;
   Feir ant fre to fonde;
In al this wurhliche won
A burde of blod ant of bon
Never yete y nuste non
   Lussomore in londe.
      Blow northerne wynd!
      Send thou me my suetyng!
      Blow northerne wynd! blow, blow, blow!

4 deawes] dews.   donketh] make dank.   deores] animals.   huere derne rounes] their secret cries.   domes for to deme] whereby they converse.   cloude] clod. wunne weole] wealth of joy.   fleme] fugitive.

5 Ichot] I know.   burde] maiden.   menskful] worshipful. feir] fair.   fonde] deal with.   wurhliche] noble.   won] multitude.   y nuste] I knew not.   lussomore in londe] lovelier on earth.   suetyng] sweetheart.

With lokkes lefliche ant longe,
With frount ant face feir to fonge,
With murthes monie mote heo monge,
    That brid so breme in boure.
With lossom eye grete ant gode,
With browen blysfol under hode,
He that reste him on the rode,
    That leflych lyf honoure.
      Blow northerne wynd, etc.

Hire lure lumes liht,
Ase a launterne a-nyht,
Hire bleo blykyeth so bryht,
    So feyr heo is ant fyn.
A suetly swyre heo hath to holde,
With armes, shuldre ase mon wolde,
Ant fingres feyre for to folde,
    God wolde hue were myn!
      Blow northerne wynd, etc.

Heo is coral of godnesse,
Heo is rubie of ryhtfulnesse,
Heo is cristal of clannesse,
    Ant baner of bealté.
Heo is lilie of largesse,
Heo is parvenke of prouesse,
Heo is solsecle of suetnesse,
    Ant lady of lealté.

lefliche] lovely.   fonge] take between hands.   murthes]
mirths, joys.   mote heo monge] may she mingle.   brid] bird.
breme] glorious.   rode] the Cross.   lure] face.   lumes]
beams.   bleo] colour.   suetly swyre] darling neck.
hue, heo] she.   clannesse] cleanness, purity.   parvenke]
periwinkle.   solsecle] sunflower.

6

For hire love y carke ant care,
For hire love y droupne ant dare,
For hire love my blisse is bare
   Ant al ich waxe won.
For hire love in slep y slake,
For hire love al nyht ich wake,
For hire love mournynge y make
   More then eny mon.
     Blow northerne wynd!
     Send thou me my suetyng!
     Blow northerne wynd! blou, blou, blou!

6   *Lines from Love Letters*

(i)

De Amico ad Amicam

A CELUY que pluys eyme en mounde,
  Of alle tho that I have founde
    Carissima,
Saluz od treyé amour,
With grace and joye and alle honoure,
    Dulcissima.

Sachez bien, pleysant et beele,
That I am right in goode heele
    Laus Christo!
Et moun amour doné vous ay,
And also thine owene, night and day
    In cisto.

5 dare] am in dismay.   won] wan.

ANONYMOUS

Ma tres duce et tres amé,
Night and day for love of thee
    Suspiro.
Soyez permanent et leal;
Love me so that I it fele,
    Requiro.

A vous jeo suy tut doné;
Mine herte is full of love to thee
    Presento;
Et pur ceo jeo vous pry,
Sweting, for thin curtesy,
    Memento.

Jeo vous pry par charité
The wordes that here wreten be
    Tenete;
And turne thy herte me toward
O à Dieu que vous gard!
    Valete!

(ii)

Responcio

A SOUN tres chere et special,
Fer and ner and overal
    In mundo,
Que soy ou saltz et gré
With mouth, word and herte free
    Jocundo.

ANONYMOUS

Jeo vous pry sans debat
That ye wolde of myn estat
   Audire;
Sertfyés a vous jeo fay
I wil in time whan I may
   Venire.

Pur vostre amour, allas, allas!
I am werse than I was
   Per multa:
Jeo suy dolourouse en tut manere,
Woulde God in youre armes I were
   Sepulta!

Vous estes ma morte et ma vye,
I preye you for your curteisie
   Amate,
Cestes maundés jeo vous pry
In youre herté stedefastly
   Notate.

7   *This World's Joy*

c. 1300

WYNTER wakeneth al my care,
  Nou thise leves waxeth bare;
Ofte I sike and mourne sare
  When hit cometh in my thoht
  Of this worldes joie, hou hit geth al to noht.

  7 this leves] these leaves.   sike] sigh.

Nou hit is, and nou hit nys,
Al so hit ner nere, ywys;
That moni mon seith, soth hit ys:
    Al goth bote Godes wille:
    Alle we shule deye, thah us like ylle.

Al that gren me graveth grene,
Nou hit faleweth al bydene:
Jehsu, help that hit be sene
    And shild us from helle!
For y not whider y shal, ne hou longe her duelle.

8   *Our Lady's Song*

c. 1375

IESU, swete sone dere!
  On porful bed list thou here,
And that me greveth sore;
For thi cradel is ase a bere,
Oxe and asse beth thi fere:
    Weepe ich mai tharfore.

Iesu, swete, beo noth wroth,
Thou ich nabbe clout ne cloth
    The on for to folde,
    The on to folde ne to wrappe,
For ich nabbe clout ne lappe;
Bote ley thou thi fet to my pappe,
    And wite the from the colde.

7 nys] is not.   al so hit ner nere] as though it had never been.
soth] sooth.   thah] though.   faleweth] fadeth.   al bydene]
forthwith.   y not whider] I know not whither.   her
duelle] here dwell.
8 bere] byre.   fere] companion.   lappe] fold of
garment.   wite] keep.

10

ANONYMOUS

9 *A Hymn to the Virgin*

c. 1300

OF on that is so fayr and bright
    Velut maris stella,
Brighter than the day is light,
    Parens et puella:
Ic crie to the, thou see to me,
Levedy, preye thi Sone for me,
    Tam pia,
That ic mote come to thee
    Maria.

Al this world was for-lore
    Eva peccatrice,
Tyl our Lord was y-bore
    De te genetrice.
With *ave* it went away
Thuster nyth and cometh the day
    Salutis;
The welle springeth ut of the
    Virtutis.

Levedy, flour of alle thing,
    Rosa sine spina,
Thu bere Jhesu, hevene king,
    Gratia divina:
Of alle thu berst the pris,
Levedy, quene of paradys
    Electa:
Mayde milde, Moder *es*
    Effecta.

on] one.   levedy] lady.   thuster] dark.   pris] prize.

10 *Of a rose, a lovely rose,*
Of a rose is al myn song.

c. 1400

LESTENYT, lordynges, both elde and yinge,
How this rose began to sprynge;
Swych a rose to myn lykynge
    In al this word ne knowe I non.

The aungil came fro hevene tour
To grete Marye with gret honour,
And seyde sche xuld bere the flour
    That xulde breke the fyndes bond.

The flour sprong in heye Bedlem,
That is bothe bryht and schen:
The rose is Mary, hevene qwen,
    Out of here bosum the blosme sprong.

The ferste braunche is ful of myht,
That sprong on Cyrstemesse nyht,
The sterre schon over Bedlem bryht
    That is bothe brod and long.

The secunde braunche sprong to helle,
The fendys power doun to felle:
Therein myht non sowle dwelle;
    Blyssid be the time the rose sprong!

The thredde braunche is good and swote,
It sprang to hevene, crop and rote,
Therein to dwellyn and ben our bote;
    Every day it schewit in prystes hond.

lestenyt] listen. word] world. xuld] was to. fyndes] Devil's.
schen] beautiful. hevene qwen] heaven's queen. bote] salvation.

ANONYMOUS

Prey we to here with gret honour,
She that bar the blyssid flowr,
She be our helpe and our socour
  And schyld us fro the fyndes bond.

ROBERT MANNYNG OF BRUNNE

1288–1338

11   *Praise of Women*

NO thyng is to man so dere
  As wommanys love in gode manere.
A gode womman is mannys blys,
There here love right and stedfast is.
There is no solas under hevene,
Of alle that a man may nevene,
That shuld a man do so moche glew
As a gode womman that loveth trew.
Ne derer is none in Goddys hurde
Than a chaste womman with lovely worde.

WILLIAM LANGLAND

?1332–?1400

12   *Piers the Plowman*

FOR trewthe telleth that loue · is triacle of hevene;
  May no synne be on him sene · that useth that spise,
And alle his werkes he wrou3te · with loue as him liste;
And lered it Moises for the levest thing · and moste like to
    heuene,

11 nevene] name.   glew] gladness.   hurde] flock.
12 triacle] sovereign remedy.   as him liste] as seemed good
to him (Christ).   lered] taught.   levest] most pleasing.

13

And also the plante of pees · moste precious of vertues.

    For hevene myghte noughte holden it · it was so hevy of hym-self,

Tyl it hadde of the erthe · yeten his fylle,

    And whan it haved of this folde · flesshe and blode taken,

Was neuere leef upon lynde · lighter ther-after,

And portatyf and persant · as the poynt of a nedle,

That myghte non armure it lette · ne none heigh walles.

    For-thi is love leder · of the lordes folke of hevene,

And a mene, as the maire is · bitwene the kyng and the comune;

Right so is love a ledere · and the lawe shapeth,

Upon man for his mysdedes · the merciment he taxeth.

And for to knowe it kyndely · it comseth bi myght,

And in the herte, there is the hevede · and the heigh welle.

JOHN BARBOUR

1316?–1395

13   *Freedom*

A! Fredome is a noble thing!
   Fredome mays man to haiff liking;
Fredome all solace to man giffis,
He levys at ese that frely levys!
A noble hart may haiff nane ese,
Na ellys nocht that may him plese,
Gyff fredome fail; for fre liking
Is yarnyt our all othir thing.
Na he that ay has levyt fre
May nocht knaw weill the propyrtè,

   12 yeten] eaten.   lynde] lime tree.   portatyf] quick-moving.
lette] prevent.   mene] mediator.   merciment] fine.
kyndely] properly.

   13 liking] pleasure.   na ellys nocht] nor aught else.   yarnyt]
yearned for.   our] above.

JOHN BARBOUR

The angyr, na the wretchyt dome
That is couplyt to foule thyrldome.
Bot gyff he had assayit it,
Than all perquer he suld it wyt;
And suld think fredome mar to prise
Than all the gold in warld that is.
Thus contrar thingis evirmar
Discoweryngis off the tothir ar.

GEOFFREY CHAUCER

1340?–1400

14   *The Complaint of Troilus*

'O PALEYS, whylom croune of houses alle,
   Enlumined with sonne of alle blisse!
O ring, fro which the ruby is out-falle,
O cause of wo, that cause hast been of lisse!
Yet, sin I may no bet, fayn wolde I kisse
Thy colde dores, dorste I for this route;
And fare-wel shryne, of which the seynt is oute!'

Fro thennesforth he rydeth up and doun,
And every thing com him to remembraunce
As he rood forth by places of the toun
In whiche he whylom hadde al his plesaunce.
'Lo, yond saugh I myn owene lady daunce;
And in that temple, with hir eyen clere,
Me caughte first my righte lady dere.

And yonder have I herd ful lustily
My dere herte laughe, and yonder pleye

13 perquer] thoroughly, by heart.
14 paleys] palace.   lisse] joy.   sin I may no bet] since
I can do nothing better.   route] company.

Saugh I hir ones eek ful blisfully.
And yonder ones to me gan she seye,
"Now goode swete, love me wel, I preye."
And yond so goodly gan she me biholde,
That to the deeth myn herte is to hir holde.

And at that corner, in the yonder hous,
Herde I myn alderlevest lady dere
So wommanly, with voys melodious,
Singen so wel, so goodly, and so clere,
That in my soule yet me thinketh I here
The blisful soun; and, in that yonder place,
My lady first me took un-to hir grace.'

'O sterre, of which I lost have al the light,
With herte soor wel oughte I to bewayle,
That ever derk in torment, night by night,
Toward my deeth with wind in stere I sayle;
For which the tenthe night if that I fayle
The gyding of thy bemes brighte an houre,
My ship and me Caribdis wol devoure.'

15 *The Love Unfeigned*

O YONGE fresshe folkes, he or she,
  In which that love up groweth with your age,
Repeyreth hoom from worldly vanitee,
And of your herte up-casteth the visage
To thilke god that after his image
Yow made, and thinketh al nis but a fayre
This world, that passeth sone as floures fayre.

14 ones] once.   alderlevest] dearest of all
15 repeyreth] repair ye.

16

And loveth him, the which that right for love
Upon a cros, our soules for to beye,
First starf, and roos, and sit in hevene a-bove;
For he nil falsen no wight, dar I seye,
That wol his herte al hoolly on him leye.
And sin he best to love is, and most meke,
What nedeth feyned loves for to seke?

16 *Balade*

HYD, Absolon, thy gilte tresses clere;
Ester, ley thou thy meknesse al a-doun;
Hyd, Jonathas, al thy frendly manere;
Penalopee, and Marcia Catoun,
Mak of your wyfhod no comparisoun;
Hyde ye your beautes, Isoude and Eleyne;
My lady cometh, that al this may disteyne.

Thy faire body, lat hit nat appere,
Lavyne; and thou, Lucresse of Rome toun,
And Polixene, that boghten love so dere,
And Cleopatre, with al thy passioun,
Hyde ye your trouthe of love and your renoun;
And thou, Tisbe, that hast of love swich peyne;
My lady cometh, that al this may disteyne.

Herro, Dido, Laudomia, alle y-fere,
And Phyllis, hanging for thy Demophoun,
And Canace, espyed by thy chere,
Ysiphile, betraysed with Jasoun,
Maketh of your trouthe neyther boost ne soun;
Nor Ypermistre or Adriane, ye tweyne;
My lady cometh, that all this may distevne.

   15 starf] died.   *16* y-fere] together.

THOMAS HOCCLEVE

1368–9?–1450?

17   *Lament for Chaucer*

ALLAS! my worthi maister honorable,
  This landes verray tresor and richesse!
Deth by thy deth hath harme irreparable
Unto us done: hir vengeable duresse
Dispoiled hath this londe of the swetnesse
Of rethoryk; for unto Tullius
Was never man so like amonges us.

Also who was hier in philosophie
To Aristotle in our tonge but thou?
The steppes of Virgile in poesie
Thou folwedest eeke, men wot wel ynow.
That combre-world that thee my maister slow—
Wolde I slayne were!—Deth, was to hastyfe
To renne on thee and reve the thi lyfe . . .

She myght han taried hir vengeaunce a while
Til that som man had egal to the be;
Nay, lat be that! sche knew wel that this yle
May never man forth brynge like to the,
And hir office nedes do mot she:
God bade hir so, I truste as for the beste;
O maister, maister, God thy soule reste!

hier] heir.   combre-world] encumberer of earth.
slow] slew.

18

JOHN LYDGATE

1370?–1450?

18 *Vox ultima Crucis*

TARYE no lenger; toward thyn herytage
　　Hast on thy weye, and be of ryght good chere.
Go eche day onward on thy pylgrymage;
Thynke howe short tyme thou hast abyden here.
Thy place is bygged above the sterres clere,
Noon erthly palys wrought in so statly wyse.
Come on, my frend, my brother most entere!
For the I offered my blood in sacryfice.

KING JAMES I OF SCOTLAND

1394–1437

19 *Spring Song of the Birds*

WORSCHIPPE ye that loveris bene this May,
　　For of your blisse the Kalendis are begonne,
And sing with us, Away, Winter, away!
　　Cum, Somer, cum, the suete sesoùn and sonne!
　　Awake for schame! that have your hevynnis wonne,
　　　　And amorously lift up your hedis all,
　　　　Thank Lufe that list you to his merci call!

18 bygged] built.　　　palys] palace.　　　*19* suete] sweet.
Lufe] Love.

ROBERT HENRYSON

1425-1500

Robin and Makyne

20

ROBIN sat on gude green hill,
   Kepand a flock of fe:
Mirry Makyne said him till
   'Robin, thou rew on me:
I haif thee luvit, loud and still,
   Thir yeiris twa or thre;
My dule in dern bot gif thou dill,
   Doutless but dreid I de.'

Robin answerit 'By the Rude
   Na thing of luve I knaw,
But keipis my scheip undir yon wud:
   Lo, quhair they raik on raw.
Quhat has marrit thee in thy mude,
   Makyne, to me thou shaw;
Or quhat is luve, or to be lude?
   Fain wald I leir that law.'

'At luvis lair gif thou will leir
   Tak thair ane A B C;
Be heynd, courtass, and fair of feir,
   Wyse, hardy, and free:

kepand] keeping.   fe] sheep, cattle.   him till] to him.
dule in dern] sorrow in secret.   dill] soothe.   but dreid I de]
I shall certainly die.   raik on raw] range in row.
lude] loved.   leir] learn.   lair] lore.   heynd] gentle.
feir] demeanour.

So that no danger do thee deir
   Quhat dule in dern thou dre;
Preiss thee with pain at all poweir
   Be patient and previe.'

Robin answerit hir agane,
   'I wat nocht quhat is luve;
But I haif mervel in certaine
   Quhat makis thee this wanrufe:
The weddir is fair, and I am fain;
   My scheip gois haill aboif;
And we wald play us in this plane,
   They wald us baith reproif.'

'Robin, tak tent unto my tale,
   And wirk all as I reid,
And thou sall haif my heart all haill,
   Eik and my maiden-heid:
Sen God sendis bute for baill,
   And for murnyng remeid,
In dern with thee bot gif I daill
   Dowtles I am bot deid.'

'Makyne, to-morn this ilka tyde
   And ye will meit me heir,
Peraventure my scheip may gang besyde,
   Quhyll we haif liggit full neir;

danger] disdain.   deir] harm.   dre] endure.   preiss]
endeavour.   wanrufe] unrest.   haill] healthy, whole.
aboif] up yonder.   and] if.   tak tent] give heed.
reid] advise.   bute for baill] remedy for hurt.   bot gif]
but if, unless.

But mawgré haif I and I byde,
    Fra they begin to steir;
Quhat lyis on heart I will nocht hyd;
    Makyn, then mak gude cheir.'

'Robin, thou reivis me roiff and rest;
    I luve bot thee allane.'
'Makyne, adieu! the sone gois west,
    The day is neir-hand gane.'
'Robin, in dule I am so drest
    That luve will be my bane.'
'Ga luve, Makyne, quhair-evir thow list,
    For lemman I luve nane.'

'Robin, I stand in sic a styll,
    I sicht, and that full sair.'
'Makyne, I haif been here this quhyle;
    At hame God gif I wair.'
'My huny, Robin, talk ane quhyll,
    Gif thow will do na mair.'
'Makyn, sum uthir man begyle,
    For hamewart I will fair.'

Robin on his wayis went
    As light as leif of tre;
Makyne murnit in hir intent,
    And trowd him nevir to se.

  mawgré haif I and] I am uneasy if.   reivis] robbest.   roiff]
quiet.   drest] beset.   lemman] mistress.   styll] plight.
sicht] sigh.   in hir intent] in her inward thought.

Robin brayd attour the bent;
    Then Makyne cryit on hie,
'Now may thow sing, for I am schent!
    Quhat alis lufe at me?'

Makyne went hame withowttin fail,
    Full wery eftir cowth weip;
Then Robin in a ful fair daill
    Assemblit all his scheip.
Be that sum part of Makynis aill
    Out-throw his hairt cowd creip;
He fallowit hir fast thair till assaill,
    And till her tuke gude keip.

'Abyd, abyd, thow fair Makyne,
    A word for ony thing;
For all my luve, it sal be thyne,
    Withowttin departing.
All haill thy harte for till haif myne
    Is all my cuvating;
My scheip to-morn, quhyll houris nyne,
    Will neid of no keping.'

'Robin, thow hes hard soung and say,
    In gestis and storeis auld,
The man that will nocht quhen he may
    Sall haif nocht quhen he wald.

brayd] strode.   bent] coarse grass.   schent] destroyed.
alis] ails.   cowth] did.   be that] by the time that.
till] to.   tuke keip] paid attention.   hard] heard.
gestis] romances.

I pray to Jesu every day,
 Mot eik thair cairis cauld
That first preissis with thee to play
 Be firth, forrest, or fawld.'

'Makyne, the nicht is soft and dry,
 The weddir is warme and fair,
And the grene woid rycht neir us by
 To walk attour all quhair:
Thair ma na janglour us espy,
 That is to lufe contrair;
Thairin, Makyne, baith ye and I,
 Unsene we ma repair.'

'Robin, that warld is all away,
 And quyt brocht till ane end:
And nevir agane thereto, perfay,
 Sall it be as thow wend;
For of my pane thow maid it play;
 And all in vane I spend:
As thow hes done, sa sall I say,
 "Murne on, I think to mend." '

'Makyne, the howp of all my heill,
 My hairt on thee is sett;
And evirmair to thee be leill
 Quhill I may leif but lett;
Never to faill as utheris feill,
 Quhat grace that evir I gett.'
'Robin, with thee I will nocht deill;
 Adew! for thus we mett.'

mot eik] may add to be] by. janglour] talebearer.
wend] weened. howp] hope. but lett] without hindrance.

ROBERT HENRYSON

Makyne went hame blyth anneuche
    Attour the holttis hair;
Robin murnit, and Makyne leuche;
    Scho sang, he sichit sair:
And so left him baith wo and wreuch,
    In dolour and in cair,
Kepand his hird under a huche
    Amangis the holtis hair.

WILLIAM DUNBAR

1465–1520?

21   *To a Lady*

SWEET rois of vertew and of gentilness,
  Delytsum lily of everie lustynes,
    Richest in bontie and in bewtie clear,
    And everie vertew that is wenit dear,
Except onlie that ye are mercyless,

Into your garth this day I did persew;
There saw I flowris that fresche were of hew;
    Baith quhyte and reid most lusty were to seyne,
    And halesome herbis upon stalkis greene;
Yet leaf nor flowr find could I nane of rew.

I doubt that Merche, with his cauld blastis keyne,
Has slain this gentil herb, that I of mene;
    Quhois piteous death dois to my heart sic paine
    That I would make to plant his root againe,—
So confortand his levis unto me bene.

20 anneuche] enough.   holttis hair] grey woodlands.
leuche] laughed.   wreuch] peevish.   huche] cliff.
  21 rois] rose.   wenit] weened, esteemed.   garth] garden-
close.   to seyne] to see.   that I of mene] that I complain of,
mourn for.

22 *In Honour of the City of London*

LONDON, thou art of townes *A per se.*
  Soveraign of cities, seemliest in sight,
Of high renoun, riches and royaltie;
    Of lordis, barons, and many a goodly knyght;
    Of most delectable lusty ladies bright;
Of famous prelatis, in habitis clericall;
    Of merchauntis full of substaunce and of myght:
London, thou art the flour of Cities all.

Gladdith anon, thou lusty Troynovaunt,
    Citie that some tyme cleped was New Troy;
In all the erth, imperiall as thou stant,
    Pryncesse of townes, of pleasure and of joy,
    A richer restith under no Christen roy;
For manly power, with craftis naturall,
    Fourmeth none fairer sith the flode of Noy:
London, thou art the flour of Cities all.

Gemme of all joy, jasper of jocunditie,
    Most myghty carbuncle of vertue and valour;
Strong Troy in vigour and in strenuytie;
    Of royall cities rose and geraflour;
    Empress of townes, exalt in honour;
In beawtie beryng the crone imperiall;
    Swete paradise precelling in pleasure;
London, thou art the flour of Cities all.

gladdith] rejoice.   Troynovaunt] Troja nova or
Trinovantum.   sith] since.   geraflour]
gillyflower.

26

Above all ryvers thy Ryver hath renowne,
   Whose beryall stremys, pleasaunt and preclare,
Under thy lusty wallys renneth down,
   Where many a swan doth swymme with wyngis fair;
   Where many a barge doth saile and row with are;
Where many a ship doth rest with top-royall.
   O, towne of townes! patrone and not compare,
London, thou art the flour of Cities all.

Upon thy lusty Brigge of pylers white
   Been merchauntis full royall to behold;
Upon thy stretis goeth many a semely knyght
   In velvet gownes and in cheynes of gold.
   By Julyus Cesar thy Tour founded of old
May be the hous of Mars victoryall,
   Whose artillary with tonge may not be told:
London, thou art the flour of Cities all.

Strong be thy wallis that about thee standis;
   Wise be the people that within thee dwellis;
Fresh is thy ryver with his lusty strandis;
   Blith be thy chirches, wele sownyng be thy bellis;
   Rich be thy merchauntis in substaunce that excellis;
Fair be their wives, right lovesom, white and small;
   Clere be thy virgyns, lusty under kellis:
London, thou art the flour of Cities all.

Thy famous Maire, by pryncely governaunce,
   With sword of justice thee ruleth prudently.
No Lord of Parys, Venyce, or Floraunce
   In dignitye or honour goeth to hym nigh.

are] oar.   compare] compeer.   small] slender.
kellis] hoods, head-dresses.

He is exampler, loode-ster, and guye;
Principall patrone and rose orygynalle,
　　Above all Maires as maister most worthy:
London, thou art the flour of Cities all.

23　　　　*On the Nativity of Christ*

*R*ORATE *coeli desuper!*
　　Hevins, distil your balmy schouris!
For now is risen the bricht day-ster,
　　Fro the rose Mary, flour of flouris:
　　The cleir Sone, quhom no cloud devouris,
Surmounting Phebus in the Est,
　　Is cumin of his hevinly touris:
　　　　Et nobis Puer natus est.

Archangellis, angellis, and dompnationis,
　　Tronis, potestatis, and marteiris seir,
And all ye hevinly operationis,
　　Ster, planeit, firmament, and spheir,
　　Fire, erd, air, and water cleir,
To Him gife loving, most and lest,
　　That come in to so meik maneir;
　　　　Et nobis Puer natus est.

Synnaris be glad, and penance do,
　　And thank your Maker hairtfully;
For he that ye micht nocht come to
　　To you is cumin full humbly

22 guye] guide.　　　*23* schouris] showers.　.　　cumin]
come, entered.　　seir] various.　　erd] earth.　　lest] least.
synnaris] sinners.

28

Your soulis with his blood to buy
And loose you of the fiendis arrest—
    And only of his own mercy;
        Pro nobis Puer natus est.

All clergy do to him inclyne,
    And bow unto that bairn benyng,
And do your observance divyne
    To him that is of kingis King:
    Encense his altar, read and sing
In holy kirk, with mind degest,
    Him honouring attour all thing
        Qui nobis Puer natus est.

Celestial foulis in the air,
    Sing with your nottis upon hicht,
In firthis and in forrestis fair
    Be myrthful now at all your mycht;
    For passit is your dully nicht,
Aurora has the cloudis perst,
    The Son is risen with glaidsum licht,
        Et nobis Puer natus est.

Now spring up flouris fra the rute,
    Revert you upward naturaly,
In honour of the blissit frute
    That raiss up fro the rose Mary;
    Lay out your levis lustily,
Fro deid take life now at the lest
    In wirschip of that Prince worthy
        Qui nobis Puer natus est.

benyng] benign.   attour] over, above.   perst] pierced.
raiss] rose.

Sing, hevin imperial, most of hicht!
  Regions of air mak armony!
All fish in flud and fowl of flicht
  Be mirthful and mak melody!
    All *Gloria in excelsis* cry!
Heaven, erd, se, man, bird, and best,—
  He that is crownit abone the sky
    Pro nobis Puer natus est!

24   *Lament for the Makers*

I THAT in heill was and gladnèss
  Am trublit now with great sickness
And feblit with infirmitie:—
    Timor Mortis conturbat me.

Our plesance here is all vain glory,
This fals world is but transitory,
The flesh is bruckle, the Feynd is slee:—
    Timor Mortis conturbat me.

The state of man does change and vary,
Now sound, now sick, now blyth, now sary,
Now dansand mirry, now like to die:—
    Timor Mortis conturbat me.

No state in Erd here standis sicker;
As with the wynd wavis the wicker
So wannis this world's vanitie:—
    Timor Mortis conturbat me.

23 best] beast.   **24** heill] health.   bruckle] brittle,
feeble.   slee] sly.   dansand] dancing.   sicker] sure.
wicker] willow.   wannis] wanes.

WILLIAM DUNBAR

Unto the ded gois all Estatis,
Princis, Prelatis, and Potestatis,
Baith rich and poor of all degree:—
Timor Mortis conturbat me.

He takis the knichtis in to the field
Enarmit under helm and scheild;
Victor he is at all mellie:—
Timor Mortis conturbat me.

That strong unmerciful tyrand
Takis, on the motheris breast sowkand,
The babe full of benignitie:—
Timor Mortis conturbat me.

He takis the campion in the stour,
The captain closit in the tour,
The lady in bour full of bewtie:—
Timor Mortis conturbat me.

He spairis no lord for his piscence,
Na clerk for his intelligence;
His awful straik may no man flee:—
Timor Mortis conturbat me.

Art-magicianis and astrologgis,
Rethoris, logicianis, and theologgis,
Them helpis no conclusionis slee:—
Timor Mortis conturbat me.

In medecine the most practicianis,
Leechis, surrigianis, and physicianis,
Themself fra ded may not supplee:—
Timor Mortis conturbat me.

mellie] mellay.   sowkand] sucking.   campion] champion.
stour] fight. piscence] puissance. straik] stroke. supplee] save.

WILLIAM DUNBAR

I see that makaris amang the lave
Playis here their padyanis, syne gois to grave;
Sparit is nocht their facultie:—
  Timor Mortis conturbat me.

He has done petuously devour
The noble Chaucer, of makaris flour,
The Monk of Bury, and Gower, all three:—
  Timor Mortis conturbat me.

The good Sir Hew of Eglintoun,
Ettrick, Heriot, and Wintoun,
He has tane out of this cuntrie:—
  Timor Mortis conturbat me.

That scorpion fell has done infeck
Maister John Clerk, and James Afflek,
Fra ballat-making and tragedie:—
  Timor Mortis conturbat me.

Holland and Barbour he has berevit;
Alas! that he not with us levit
Sir Mungo Lockart of the Lee:—
  Timor Mortis conturbat me.

Clerk of Tranent eke he has tane,
That made the anteris of Gawaine;
Sir Gilbert Hay endit has he:—
  Timor Mortis conturbat me.

He has Blind Harry and Sandy Traill
Slain with his schour of mortal hail,
Quhilk Patrick Johnstoun might nought flee:—
  Timor Mortis conturbat me.

makaris] poets. the lave] the leave, the rest. padyanis]
pageants. anteris] adventures. schour] shower.

He has reft Merseir his endite,
That did in luve so lively write,
So short, so quick, of sentence hie:—
  Timor Mortis conturbat me.

He has tane Rowll of Aberdene,
And gentill Rowll of Corstorphine;
Two better fallowis did no man see:—
  Timor Mortis conturbat me.

In Dumfermline he has done roun
With Maister Robert Henrysoun;
Sir John the Ross enbrast has he:—
  Timor Mortis conturbat me.

And he has now tane, last of a,
Good gentil Stobo and Quintin Shaw,
Of quhom all wichtis hes pitie:—
  Timor Mortis conturbat me.

Good Maister Walter Kennedy
In point of Death lies verily;
Great ruth it were that so suld be:—
  Timor Mortis conturbat me.

Sen he has all my brether tane,
He will naught let me live alane;
Of force I man his next prey be:—
  Timor Mortis conturbat me.

Since for the Death remeid is none,
Best is that we for Death dispone,
After our death that live may we:—
  Timor Mortis conturbat me.

endite] inditing.   fallowis] fellows.   wichtis] wights, persons.   man] must.   dispone] make disposition.

25 *May in the Green-Wood*

IN somer when the shawes be sheyne,
   And leves be large and long,
Hit is full merry in feyre foreste
   To here the foulys song.

To se the dere draw to the dale
   And leve the hilles hee,
And shadow him in the leves grene
   Under the green-wode tree.

Hit befell on Whitsontide
   Early in a May mornyng,
The Sonne up faire can shyne,
   And the briddis mery can syng.

'This is a mery mornyng,' said Litulle Johne,
   'Be Hym that dyed on tre;
A more mery man than I am one
   Lyves not in Christiantè.

'Pluk up thi hert, my dere mayster,'
   Litulle Johne can say,
'And thynk hit is a fulle fayre tyme
   In a mornynge of May.'

26 *Carol*

I SING of a maiden
   That is makeles;
King of all kings
   To her son she ches.

25 sheyne] bright.   26 makeles] matchless.   ches] chose.

He came al so still
    There his mother was,
As dew in April
    That falleth on the grass.

He came al so still
    To his mother's bour,
As dew in April
    That falleth on the flour.

He came al so still
    There his mother lay,
As dew in April
    That falleth on the spray.

Mother and maiden
    Was never none but she;
Well may such a lady
    Goddes mother be.

27   *Towneley Plays. The Shepherds' Play, II.*

Primus Pastor

Haylle, comly and clene! Haylle, yong child!
Haylle, maker, as I meyne, of a madn so mylde!
Thou has waryd, I weyne the warlo so wylde;
The fals gyler of teyn, now goys he begylde.
    Lo, he merys;
Lo, he laghys, my swetyng,
A wel fare metyng,
I have holden my hetyng;
    Have a bob of cherys.

27 waryd] cursed.   warlo] warlock, sorcerer.   hetyng] promise.

35

Secundus Pastor

Haylle, sufferan savyoure! for thou has us soght;
Haylle, frely foyde and floure that all thyng has wroght!
Haylle, full of favoure that made all of noght!
Haylle! I kneyll and I cowre. A byrd haue I broght
    To my barne.
Haylle, lytylle tyné mop!
Of oure crede thou art crop;
I wold drynk on thy cop,
    Lytyll day starne.

Tertius Pastor

Haylle, derlyng dere, full of godhede!
I pray the be nere when that I have nede.
Haylle! swete is thy chere! my hert wold blede
To se the sytt here in so poore wede,
    With no pennys.
Haylle! put furth thy dalle!
I bryng the bot a balle:
Have and play the with-alle,
    And go to the tenys.

28   *The Knight of the Grail*

Early 16th Cent.

LULLY, lulley; lully, lulley;
   The fawcon hath born my mak away.

He bare hym vp, he bare hym down;
He bare hym into an orchard brown.

In that orchard ther was an hall,
That was hangid with purpill and pall.

27 **frely foyde**] goodly child.   **mop**] baby.   **dalle**] little hand.

And in that hall ther was a bede;
Hit was hangid with gold so rede.

And yn that bed ther lythe a knyght,
His wowndes bledyng day and nyght.

By that bedes side ther kneleth a may,
And she wepeth both nyght and day.

And by that beddes side ther stondith a ston,
'Corpus Christi' wretyn theron.

29   *Quia Amore Langueo*

14th Cent.

IN a valley of this restles mind
I sought in mountain and in mead,
Trusting a true love for to find.
Upon an hill then took I heed;
A voice I heard (and near I yede)
In great dolour complaining tho:
See, dear soul, how my sides bleed
    Quia amore langueo.

Upon this hill I found a tree,
Under a tree a man sitting;
From head to foot wounded was he;
His hearte blood I saw bleeding:
A seemly man to be a king,
A gracious face to look unto.
I askèd why he had paining;
    Quia amore langueo.

29 yede] went.

37

I am true love that false was never;
My sister, man's soul, I loved her thus.
Because we would in no wise dissever
I left my kingdom glorious.
I purveyed her a palace full precious;
She fled, I followed, I loved her so
That I suffered this pain piteous
  Quia amore langueo.

My fair love and my spouse bright!
I saved her from beating, and she hath me bet;
I clothed her in grace and heavenly light;
This bloody shirt she hath on me set;
For longing of love yet would I not let;
Sweet strokes are these: lo!
I have loved her ever as I her het
  Quia amore langueo.

I crowned her with bliss and she me with thorn;
I led her to chamber and she me to die;
I brought her to worship and she me to scorn;
I did her reverence and she me villany.
To love that loveth is no maistry;
Her hate made never my love her foe
Ask me then no question why—
  Quia amore langueo.

Look unto mine handes, man!
These gloves were given me when I her sought;
They be not white, but red and wan;
Embroidered with blood my spouse them brought.
They will not off; I loose hem nought:

                het] promised.

I woo her with hem wherever she go.
These hands for her so friendly fought
  Quia amore langueo.

Marvel not, man, though I sit still.
See, love hath shod me wonder strait:
Buckled my feet, as was her will,
With sharp nails (well thou may'st wait!)
In my love was never desait;
All my membres I have opened her to;
My body I made her herte's bait
  Quia amore langueo.

In my side I have made her nest;
Look in, how wet a wound is here!
This is her chamber, here shall she rest,
That she and I may sleep in fere.
Here may she wash, if any filth were;
Here is seat for all her woe;
Come when she will, she shall have cheer
  Quia amore langueo.

I will abide till she be ready,
I will her sue if she say nay;
If she be retchless I will be greedy,
If she be dangerous I will her pray;
If she weep, then bide I ne may:
Mine arms ben spread to clip her me to.
Cry once, I come: now, soul, assay!
  Quia amore langueo.

Fair love, let us go play:
Apples ben ripe in my gardayne.

bait] resting-place.   in fere] together.   dangerous]
disdainful.

I shall thee clothe in a new array,
Thy meat shall be milk, honey and wine.
Fair love, let us go dine:
Thy sustenance is in my crippe, lo!
Tarry thou not, my fair spouse mine,
  Quia amore langueo.

If thou be foul, I shall thee make clean;
If thou be sick, I shall thee heal;
If thou mourn ought, I shall thee mene;
Why wilt thou not, fair love, with me deal?
Foundest thou ever love so leal?
What wilt thou, soul, that I shall do?
I may not unkindly thee appeal,
  Quia amore langueo.

What shall I do now with my spouse
But abide her of my gentleness,
Till that she look out of her house
Of fleshly affection? love mine she is;
Her bed is made, her bolster is bliss,
Her chamber is chosen; is there none mo.
Look out on me at the window of kindeness,
  Quia amore langueo.

My love is in her chamber: hold your peace!
Make ye no noise, but let her sleep.
My babe I would not were in disease,
I may not hear my dear child weep.
With my pap I shall her keep;
Ne marvel ye not though I tend her to:
This wound in my side had ne'er been so deep
  But Quia amore langueo.

crippe] scrip.   mene] care for.

Long thou for love never so high,
My love is more than thine may be.
Thou weepest, thou gladdest, I sit thee by:
Yet wouldst thou once, love, look unto me!
Should I always feede thee
With children meat? Nay, love, not so!
I will prove thy love with adversitè,
   Quia amore langueo.

Wax not weary, mine own wife!
What mede is aye to live in comfort?
In tribulation I reign more rife
Ofter times than in disport.
In weal and in woe I am aye to support:
Mine own wife, go not me fro!
Thy mede is marked, when thou art mort:
   Quia amore langueo.

30   *Snatches*

[? Wm. Cornish]

(i)

Latet Anguis

16th Century

YOU and I and Amyas,
   Amyas and you and I,
To the green-wood must we go, alas!
You and I, my lyf, and Amyas

(ii)

Bridal Morning

15th–16th Cent.

The maidens came
When I was in my mother's bower;
  I had all that I would.
  The bailey beareth the bell away
  The lily, the rose, the rose I lay.

The silver is white, red is the gold;
The robes they lay in fold.
  The bailey beareth the lull away;
  The lily, the rose, the rose I lay.

And thro the glass window shines the sun.
How should I love, and I so young?
  The bailey beareth the lull away;
  The lily, the rose, the rose I lay.

31   *The Lover in Winter Plaineth for*
          the Spring

16th Cent. (?)

WESTERN wind, when will thou blow
    The small rain down can rain?
Christ, if my love were in my arms
And I in my bed again!

32   *The Nut-Brown Maid*

15th Cent.

He.   *B**E it right or wrong, these men among*
          On women do complain;
        Affirming this, how that it is
        A labour spent in vain

            32 among] sometimes.

42

ANONYMOUS

To love them wele; for never a dele
 They love a man again:
For let a man do what he can
 Their favour to attain,
Yet if a new to them pursue,
 Their first true lover than
Laboureth for naught; for from her thought
 He is a banished man.

She.   *I say not nay, but that all day*
 It is both written and said
That woman's faith is, as who saith,
 All utterly decayed:
But nevertheless, right good witness
 In this case might be laid
That they love true and continue:
 Record the Nut-brown Maid,
Which, when her love came her to prove,
 To her to make his moan,
Would not depart; for in her heart
 She loved but him alone.

He.   *Then between us let us discuss*
 What was all the manere
Between them two: we will also
 Tell all the pain in fere
That she was in. Now I began,
 So that ye me answere:

never a dele] never a bit.   than] then.   in fere] in company together.

43

ANONYMOUS

Wherefore all ye that present be,
   I pray you, give an ear.
I am the Knight. I come by night,
   As secret as I can,
Saying, Alas! thus standeth the case,
   I am a banished man.

She.   *And I your will for to fulfil*
     In this will not refuse
   Trusting to show, in wordes few,
     That men have an ill use—
   To their own shame—women to blame,
     And causeless them accuse.
   Therefore to you I answer now,
     All women to excuse—
   Mine own heart dear, with you what cheer?
     I pray you, tell anone;
   For, in my mind, of all mankind
     I love but you alone.

He.   It standeth so: a deed is do
     Whereof great harm shall grow:
   My destiny is for to die
     A shameful death, I trow;
   Or else to flee. The t' one must be:
     None other way I know
   But to withdraw as an outlàw,
     And take me to my bow.
   Wherefore adieu, mine own heart true!
     None other rede I can:
   For I must to the green-wood go,
     Alone, a banished man.

        rede I can] counsel I know.

She.   O Lord, what is this worldis bliss,
     That changeth as the moon!
My summer's day in lusty May
     Is darked before the noon.
I hear you say, farewell: Nay, nay,
     We dèpart not so soon.
Why say ye so? whither will ye go?
     Alas! what have ye done?
All my welfàre to sorrow and care
     Should change, if ye were gone:
For, in my mind, of all mankind
     I love but you alone.

He.   I can believe it shall you grieve,
     And somewhat you distrain;
But afterward, your paines hard
     Within a day or twain
Shall soon aslake; and ye shall take
     Comfort to you again.
Why should ye nought? for, to take thought,
     Your labour were in vain.
And thus I do; and pray you to,
     As hartely as I can:
For I must to the green-wood go,
     Alone, a banished man.

She.   Now, sith that ye have showed to me
     The secret of your mind,
I shall be plain to you again,
     Like as ye shall me find.
Sith it is so that ye will go,
     I will not leve behind.

Shall never be said the Nut-brown Maid
   Was to her love unkind.
Make you readỳ, for so am I,
   Although it were anone:
For, in my mind, of all mankind
   I love but you alone.

He.   Yet I you rede to take good heed
      What men will think and say:
Of young, of old, it shall be told
   That ye be gone away
Your wanton will for to fulfil,
   In green-wood you to play;
And that ye might for your delight
   No longer make delay
Rather than ye should thus for me
   Be called an ill womàn
Yet would I to the green-wood go,
   Alone, a banished man.

She.   Though it be sung of old and young
      That I should be to blame,
Theirs be the charge that speak so large
   In hurting of my name:
For I will prove that faithful love
   It is devoid of shame;
In your distress and heaviness
   To part with you the same:
And sure all tho that do not so
   True lovers are they none:
For, in my mind, of all mankind
   I love but you alone.

     part with] share with.   tho] those.

ANONYMOUS

He.　I counsel you, Remember how
　　　　It is no maiden's law
　　　Nothing to doubt, but to run out
　　　　To wood with an outlàw.
　　　For ye must there in your hand bear
　　　　A bow readỳ to draw;
　　　And as a thief thus must you live
　　　　Ever in dread and awe;
　　　Whereby to you great harm might grow!
　　　　Yet had I liever than
　　　That I had to the green-wood go,
　　　　Alone, a banished man.

She.　I think not nay, but as ye say;
　　　　It is no maiden's lore;
　　　But love may make me for your sake,
　　　　As I have said before,
　　　To come on foot, to hunt and shoot,
　　　　To get us meat and store;
　　　For so that I your company
　　　　May have, I ask no more.
　　　From which to part it maketh my heart
　　　　As cold as any stone;
　　　For, in my mind, of all mankind
　　　　I love but you alone.

He.　For an outlàw this is the law,
　　　　That men him take and bind:
　　　Without pitie, hangèd to be,
　　　　And waver with the wind.
　　　If I had need (as God forbede !)
　　　　What socours could ye find?

Forsooth I trow, you and your bow
   For fear would draw behind.
And no mervail; for little avail
   Were in your counsel than:
Wherefore I'll to the green-wood go,
   Alone, a banished man.

She.   Right well know ye that women be
   But feeble for to fight;
No womanhede it is, indeed,
   To be bold as a knight:
Yet in such fear if that ye were
   With enemies day and night,
I would withstand, with bow in hand,
   To grieve them as I might,
And you to save; as women have
   From death men many one:
For, in my mind, of all mankind
   I love but you alone.

He.   Yet take good hede; for ever I drede
   That ye could not sustain
The thorny ways, the deep vallèys,
   The snow, the frost, the rain,
The cold, the heat; for dry or wete,
   We must lodge on the plain;
And, us above, no other roof
   But a brake bush or twain:
Which soon should grieve you, I believe:
   And ye would gladly than
That I had to the green-wood go,
   Alone, a banished man.

She. Sith I have here been partynere
  With you of joy and bliss,
I must alsò part of your woe
  Endure, as reason is:
Yet I am sure of one pleasùre,
  And shortly it is this—
That where ye be, me seemeth, pardé,
  I could not fare amiss.
Without more speech I you beseech
  That we were shortly gone;
For, in my mind, of all mankind
  I love but you alone.

He. If ye go thyder, ye must consider,
  When ye have lust to dine,
There shall no meat be for to gete,
  Nether bere, ale, ne wine,
Ne shetès clean, to lie between,
  Made of thread and twine;
None other house, but leaves and boughs,
  To cover your head and mine.
Lo, mine heart sweet, this ill diète
  Should make you pale and wan:
Wherefore I'll to the green-wood go,
  Alone, a banished man.

She. Among the wild deer such an archère,
  As men say that ye be,
Ne may not fail of good vitayle
  Where is so great plentè:
And water clear of the rivere
  Shall be full sweet to me;

With which in hele I shall right wele
  Endure, as ye shall see;
And, or we go, a bed or two
  I can provide anone;
For, in my mind, of all mankind
  I love but you alone.

He. Lo yet, before, ye must do more,
    If ye will go with me:
As, cut your hair up by your ear,
    Your kirtle by the knee;
With bow in hand for to withstand
    Your enemies, if need be:
And this same night, before daylight,
    To woodward will I flee.
If that ye will all this fulfil,
    Do it shortly as ye can:
Else will I to the green-wood go,
    Alone, a banished man.

She. I shall as now do more for you
    Than 'longeth to womanhede;
To short my hair, a bow to bear,
    To shoot in time of need.
O my sweet mother! before all other
    For you I have most drede!
But now, adieu! I must ensue
    Where fortune doth me lead.
All this make ye: Now let us flee;
    The day cometh fast upon:
For, in my mind, of all mankind
    I love but you alone.

        hele] health.

He.   Nay, nay, not so; ye shall not go,
       And I shall tell you why—
     Your appetite is to be light
       Of love, I well espy:
     For, right as ye have said to me,
       In likewise hardily
     Ye would answere whosoever it were,
       In way of companỳ:
     It is said of old, Soon hot, soon cold;
       And so is a womàn:
     Wherefore I to the wood will go,
       Alone, a banished man.

She.   If ye take heed, it is no need
       Such words to say to me;
     For oft ye prayed, and long assayed,
       Or I loved you, pardè:
     And though that I of ancestry
       A baron's daughter be,
     Yet have you proved how I you loved,
       A squire of low degree;
     And ever shall, whatso befall,
       To die therefore anone;
     For, in my mind, of all mankind
       I love but you alone.

He.   A baron's child to be beguiled,
       It were a cursèd deed!
     To be felàw with an outlaw—
       Almighty God forbede!
     Yet better were the poor squyere
       Alone to forest yede

          yede] should go.

Than ye shall say another day
   That by my cursèd rede
Ye were betrayed. Wherefore, good maid,
   The best rede that I can,
Is, that I to the green-wood go,
   Alone, a banished man.

She. Whatever befall, I never shall
   Of this thing be upbraid:
But if ye go, and leave me so,
   Then have ye me betrayed.
Remember you wele, how that ye dele;
   For if ye, as ye said,
Be so unkind to leave behind
   Your love, the Nut-brown Maid,
Trust me trulỳ that I shall die
   Soon after ye be gone:
For, in my mind, of all mankind
   I love but you alone.

He. If that ye went, ye should repent;
   For in the forest now
I have purveyed me of a maid
   Whom I love more than you:
Another more fair than ever ye were
   I dare it well avow;
And of you both each should be wroth
   With other, as I trow:
It were mine ease to live in peace;
   So will I, if I can:
Wherefore I to the wood will go,
   Alone, a banished man.

She. Though in the wood I understood
    Ye had a paramour,
All this may nought remove my thought,
    But that I will be your':
And she shall find me soft and kind
    And courteis every hour;
Glad to fulfil all that she will
    Command me, to my power:
For had ye, lo, an hundred mo,
    Yet would I be that one:
For, in my mind, of all mankind
    I love but you alone.

He. Mine own dear love, I see the prove
    That ye be kind and true;
Of maid, of wife, in all my life,
    The best that ever I knew.
Be merry and glad; be no more sad;
    The case is changèd new;
For it were ruth that for your truth
    Ye should have cause to rue.
Be not dismayed, whatsoever I said
    To you when I began:
I will not to the green-wood go;
    I am no banished man.

She. These tidings be more glad to me
    Than to be made a queen,
If I were sure they should endure;
    But it is often seen
When men will break promise they speak
    The wordis on the splene.

      on the splene] in jest.

Ye shape some wile me to beguile,
    And steal from me, I ween:
Then were the case worse than it was,
    And I more wo-begone:
For, in my mind, of all mankind
    I love but you alone.

He.   Ye shall not nede further to drede:
    I will not disparàge
You (God defend), sith you descend
    Of so great a linàge.
Now understand: to Westmoreland,
    Which is my heritage,
I will you bring; and with a ring,
    By way of marriàge
I will you take, and lady make,
    As shortly as I can:
Thus have you won an Earles son,
    And not a banished man.

Here may ye see that women be
    In love meek, kind, and stable;
Let never man reprove them than,
    Or call them variable;
But rather pray God that we may
    To them be comfortable;
Which sometime proveth such as He loveth,
    If they be charitable.
For sith men would that women should
    Be meek to them each one;
Much more ought they to God obey,
    And serve but Him alone.

33

Cradle Song

16th Cent.

O MY deir hert, young Jesus sweit,
 Prepare thy creddil in my spreit,
And I sall rock thee in my hert
And never mair from thee depart.

But I sall praise thee evermoir
With sangis sweit unto thy gloir;
The knees of my hert sall I bow,
And sing that richt *Balulalow!*

34

As ye came from the Holy Land

16th Cent.

AS ye came from the holy land
 Of Walsinghame,
Met you not with my true love
 By the way as you came?

How should I know your true love,
 That have met many a one
As I came from the holy land,
 That have come, that have gone?

She is neither white nor brown,
 But as the heavens fair;
There is none hath her form divine
 In the earth or the air.

Such a one did I meet, good sir,
 Such an angelic face,
Who like a nymph, like a queen, did appear
 In her gait, in her grace.

ANONYMOUS

She hath left me here alone
  All alone, as unknown,
Who sometime did me lead with herself,
  And me loved as her own.

What's the cause that she leaves you alone
  And a new way doth take,
That sometime did love you as her own,
  And her joy did you make?

I have loved her all my youth,
  But now am old, as you see:
Love likes not the falling fruit,
  Nor the withered tree.

Know that Love is a careless child,
  And forgets promise past:
He is blind, he is deaf when he list,
  And in faith never fast.

His desire is a dureless content,
  And a trustless joy;
He is won with a world of despair,
  And is lost with a toy.

Of womenkind such indeed is the love,
  Or the word love abusèd,
Under which many childish desires
  And conceits are excusèd.

But true love is a durable fire,
  In the mind ever burning,
Never sick, never dead, never cold,
  From itself never turning.

Balow

35

BALOW, my babe, lie still and sleep!
It grieves me sore to see thee weep.
Wouldst thou be quiet I'se be glad,
Thy mourning makes my sorrow sad:
Balow my boy, thy mother's joy,
Thy father breeds me great annoy—
Balow, la-low!

When he began to court my love,
And with his sugred words me move,
His fainings false and flattering cheer
To me that time did not appear:
But now I see most cruelly
He cares not for my babe nor me—
Balow, la-low!

Lie still, my darling, sleep awhile,
And when thou wak'st thou'le sweetly smile:
But smile not as thy father did,
To cozen maids: nay, God forbid!
But yet I fear thou wilt go near
Thy father's heart and face to bear—
Balow, la-low!

I cannot choose but ever will
Be loving to thy father still;
Where'er he go, where'er he ride,
My love with him doth still abide;
In weal or woe, where'er he go,
My heart shall ne'er depart him fro—
Balow, la-low!

But do not, do not, pretty mine,
To fainings false thy heart incline!
Be loyal to thy lover true,
And never change her for a new:
If good or fair, of her have care
For women's banning's wondrous sare—
   Balow, la-low!

Bairn, by thy face I will beware;
Like Sirens' words, I'll come not near;
My babe and I together will live;
He'll comfort me when cares do grieve.
My babe and I right soft will lie,
And ne'er respect man's cruelty—
   Balow, la-low!

Farewell, farewell, the falsest youth
That ever kist a woman's mouth!
I wish all maids be warn'd by me
Never to trust man's curtesy;
For if we do but chance to bow,
They'll use us then they care not how—
   Balow, la-low!

36   *The Old Cloak* 16th Cent. (?)

THIS winter's weather it waxeth cold,
 And frost it freezeth on every hill,
And Boreas blows his blast so bold
 That all our cattle are like to spill.
Bell, my wife, she loves no strife;
 She said unto me quietly,
Rise up, and save cow Crumbock's life!
 Man, put thine old cloak about thee!

ANONYMOUS

He. O Bell my wife, why dost thou flyte?
     Thou kens my cloak is very thin:
It is so bare and over worn,
     A cricket thereon cannot renn.
Then I'll no longer borrow nor lend;
     For once I'll new apparell'd be;
To-morrow I'll to town and spend;
     For I'll have a new cloak about me.

She. Cow Crumbock is a very good cow:
     She has been always true to the pail;
She has helped us to butter and cheese, I trow,
     And other things she will not fail.
I would be loth to see her pine.
     Good husband, counsel take of me:
It is not for us to go so fine—
     Man, take thine old cloak about thee!

He. My cloak it was a very good cloak,
     It hath been always true to the wear;
But now it is not worth a groat:
     I have had it four and forty year'.
Sometime it was of cloth in grain:
     'Tis now but a sigh clout, as you may see:
It will neither hold out wind nor rain;
     And I'll have a new cloak about me.

She. It is four and forty years ago
     Sine the one of us the other did ken;
And we have had, betwixt us two,
     Of children either nine or ten:

flyte] scold.   cloth in grain] scarlet cloth.   sigh clout]
a rag for straining.

We have brought them up to women and men:
   In the fear of God I trow they be.
And why wilt thou thyself misken?
   Man, take thine old cloak about thee!

He. O Bell my wife, why dost thou flyte?
   Now is now, and then was then:
Seek now all the world throughout,
   Thou kens not clowns from gentlemen:
They are clad in black, green, yellow and blue,
   So far above their own degree.
Once in my life I'll take a view;
   For I'll have a new cloak about me.

She. King Stephen was a worthy peer;
   His breeches cost him but a crown;
He held them sixpence all too dear,
   Therefore he called the tailor 'lown'.
He was a king and wore the crown,
   And thou'se but of a low degree:
It's pride that puts this country down:
   Man, take thy old cloak about thee!

He. Bell my wife, she loves not strife,
   Yet she will lead me, if she can;
And to maintain an easy life
   I oft must yield, though I'm goodman.
It's not for a man with a woman to threap,
   Unless he first give o'er the plea:
As we began, so will we keep,
   And I'll take my old cloak about me.

threap] argue.

1460?–1529

37 *To Mistress Margery Wentworth*

WITH margerain gentle,
   The flower of goodlihead,
Embroidered the mantle
   Is of your maidenhead.
Plainly I cannot glose;
   Ye be, as I divine,
The pretty primrose,
   The goodly columbine.

Benign, courteous, and meek,
   With wordes well devised;
In you, who list to seek,
   Be virtues well comprised.
With margerain gentle,
   The flower of goodlihead,
Embroidered the mantle
   Is of your maidenhead.

38 *To Mistress Isabell Pennell*

BY saint Mary, my lady,
   Your mammy and your daddy
Brought forth a goodly baby!
   My maiden Isabel,
Reflaring rosabel,
The flagrant camamel;
   The ruddy rosary,
The sovereign rosemary,
The pretty strawberry;

   37 margerain] marjoram.

The columbine, the nept,
The gilliflower well set,
The proper violet;
Ennewed your colour
Is like the daisy flower
After the April shower;
Star of the morrow gray,
The blossom on the spray,
The freshest flower of May;
Maidenly demure,
Of womanhood the lure;
Wherefore I make you sure,
It were an hevenly health,
It were an endless wealth,
A life for God himself,
To hear this nightingale,
Among the birds smale,
Warbling in the vale,
Dug, dug,
Iug, iug.
Good year and good luck,
With chuck, chuck, chuck, chuck!

39 *To Mistress Margaret Hussey*

MERRY Margaret
As midsummer flower,
Gentle as falcon
Or hawk of the tower:
With solace and gladness,
Much mirth and no madness,
All good and no badness;

38 nept] catamint.   ennewed] fresh-tinted.

JOHN SKELTON

So joyously,
So maidenly,
So womanly
Her demeaning
In every thing,
Far, far passing
That I can indite,
Or suffice to write
Of Merry Margaret
As midsummer flower
Gentle as falcon
Or hawk of the tower.
As patient and still
And as full of good will
As fair Isaphill,
Coliander,
Sweet pomander,
Good Cassander;
Steadfast of thought,
Well made, well wrought,
Far may be sought,
Ere that ye can find
So courteous, so kind
As merry Margaret,
This midsummer flower,
Gentle as falcon
Or hawk of the tower.

Isaphill] Hypsipyle.   coliander] coriander seed, an
aromatic.   pomander] a ball of perfume.   Cassander]
Cassandra.

STEPHEN HAWES

d. 1523

40 *The True Knight*

FOR knighthood is not in the feats of war,
  As for to fight in quarrel right or wrong,
But in a cause which truth can not defar:
  He ought himself for to make sure and strong,
  Justice to keep mixt with mercỳ among:
    And no quarrel a knight ought to take
    But for a truth, or for the common's sake.

41 *An Epitaph*

O MORTAL folk, you may behold and see
  How I lie here, sometime a mighty knight;
The end of joy and all prosperity
  Is death at last, thorough his course and might:
  After the day there cometh the dark night,
    For though the day be never so long,
    At last the bells ringeth to evensong.

SIR THOMAS WYATT

1503–1542

42 *Forget not yet*

*The Lover Beseecheth his Mistress not to Forget his
Steadfast Faith and True Intent*

FORGET not yet the tried entent
  Of such a truth as I have meant;
My great travail so gladly spent,
  Forget not yet!

  40 defar] undo.

Forget not yet when first began
The weary life ye know, since whan
The suit, the service, none tell can;
Forget not yet!

Forget not yet the great assays,
The cruel wrong, the scornful ways,
The painful patience in denays,
Forget not yet!

Forget not, yet forget not this—
How long ago hath been, and is,
The mind that never meant amiss—
Forget not yet!

Forget not then thine own approved,
The which so long hath thee so loved,
Whose steadfast faith yet never moved:
Forget not this!

43   *The Appeal*

*An Earnest Suit to his Unkind Mistress, not to
Forsake him*

AND wilt thou leave me thus?
    Say nay, say nay, for shame!
—To save thee from the blame
Of all my grief and grame.
And wilt thou leave me thus?
    Say nay! say nay!

42 denays] refusals.   *43* grame] sorrow.

And wilt thou leave me thus,
That hath loved thee so long
In wealth and woe among:
And is thy heart so strong
As for to leave me thus?
　Say nay! say nay!

And wilt thou leave me thus,
That hath given thee my heart
Never for to depart
Neither for pain nor smart:
And wilt thou leave me thus?
　Say nay! say nay!

And wilt thou leave me thus,
And have no more pity
Of him that loveth thee?
Alas, thy cruelty!
And wilt thou leave me thus?
　Say nay! say nay!

44　　　　　　　　*A Revocation*

WHAT should I say?
　—Since Faith is dead,
And Truth away
　From you is fled?
　Should I be led
　　With doubleness?
　Nay! nay! mistress.

I promised you,
    And you promised me,
To be as true
    As I would be.
    But since I see
        Your double heart,
        Farewell my part!

Thought for to take
    'Tis not my mind;
But to forsake
    One so unkind;
    And as I find
        So will I trust.
        Farewell, unjust!

Can ye say nay
    But that you said
That I alway
    Should be obeyed?
    And—thus betrayed
        Or that I wist!
        Farewell, unkist!

45   *Vixi Puellis Nuper Idoneus . . .*

THEY flee from me that sometime did me seek,
    With naked foot stalking in my chamber:
I have seen them gentle, tame, and meek,
    That now are wild, and do not once remember
    That sometime they have put themselves in danger
To take bread at my hand; and now they range,
Busily seeking with a continual change.

Thanked be fortune, it hath been otherwise
   Twenty times better; but once, in special,
In thin array, after a pleasant guise,
   When her loose gown from her shoulders did fall,
   And she me caught in her arms long and small,
Therewith all sweetly did me kiss,
And softly said, *'Dear heart, how like you this?'*

It was no dream; I lay broad waking:
   But all is turned, thorough my gentleness,
Into a strange fashion of forsaking;
   And I have leave to go, of her goodness;
   And she also to use new-fangleness.
But since that I unkindely so am served,
'How like you this?'—what hath she now deserved?

46   *To His Lute*

MY lute, awake! perform the last
   Labour that thou and I shall waste,
   And end that I have now begun;
For when this song is sung and past,
   My lute, be still, for I have done.

As to be heard where ear is none,
As lead to grave in marble stone,
   My song may pierce her heart as soon:
Should we then sing, or sigh, or moan?
   No, no, my lute! for I have done.

The rocks do not so cruelly
Repulse the waves continually,
   As she my suit and affection;
So that I am past remedy:
   Whereby my lute and I have done.

SIR THOMAS WYATT

Proud of the spoil that thou hast got
Of simple hearts thorough Love's shot,
   By whom, unkind, thou hast them won;
Think not he hath his bow forgot,
   Although my lute and I have done.

Vengeance shall fall on thy disdain,
That makest but game on earnest pain:
   Think not alone under the sun
Unquit to cause thy lover's plain,
   Although my lute and I have done.

Perchance thee lie withered and old
The winter nights that are so cold,
   Plaining in vain unto the moon:
Thy wishes then dare not be told:
   Care then who list! for I have done.

And then may chance thee to repent
The time that thou hast lost and spent
   To cause thy lover's sigh and swoon:
Then shalt thou know beauty but lent,
   And wish and want, as I have done.

Now cease, my lute! this is the last
Labour that thou and I shall waste,
   And ended is that we begun:
Now is this song both sung and past—
   My lute, be still, for I have done.

HENRY HOWARD, EARL OF SURREY

1516–1547

47 *Description of Spring*

Wherein each thing renews, save only the Lover

THE soote season, that bud and bloom forth brings,
   With green hath clad the hill and eke the vale:
The nightingale with feathers new she sings;
The turtle to her make hath told her tale.
Summer is come, for every spray now springs:
The hart hath hung his old head on the pale;
The buck in brake his winter coat he flings;
The fishes flete with new repairèd scale.
The adder all her slough away she slings;
The swift swallow pursueth the flies smale;
The busy bee her honey now she mings;
Winter is worn that was the flowers' bale.

And thus I see among these pleasant things
Each care decays, and yet my sorrow springs.

48 *Complaint of the Absence of Her Lover*
being upon the Sea

O HAPPY dames! that may embrace
   The fruit of your delight,
Help to bewail the woful case
   And eke the heavy plight
Of me, that wonted to rejoice
The fortune of my pleasant choice:
Good ladies, help to fill my mourning voice.

47 make] mate.   mings] mingles, mixes.

HENRY HOWARD, EARL OF SURREY

In ship, freight with rememberance
    Of thoughts and pleasures past,
He sails that hath in governance
    My life while it will last:
With scalding sighs, for lack of gale,
Furthering his hope, that is his sail,
Toward me, the sweet port of his avail.

Alas! how oft in dreams I see
    Those eyes that were my food;
Which sometime so delighted me,
    That yet they do me good:
Wherewith I wake with his return
Whose absent flame did make me burn:
But when I find the lack, Lord! how I mourn!

When other lovers in arms across
    Rejoice their chief delight,
Drownèd in tears, to mourn my loss
    I stand the bitter night
In my window where I may see
Before the winds how the clouds flee:
Lo! what a mariner love hath made me!

And in green waves when the salt flood
    Doth rise by rage of wind,
A thousand fancies in that mood
    Assail my restless mind.
Alas! now drencheth my sweet foe,
That with the spoil of my heart did go,
And left me; but alas! why did he so?

        drencheth] is drowned.

And when the seas wax calm again
  To chase fro me annoy,
My doubtful hope doth cause me plain;
  So dread cuts off my joy.
Thus is my wealth mingled with woe
And of each thought a doubt doth grow;
—Now he comes! Will he come? Alas! no, no.

49 *The Means to attain Happy Life*

MARTIAL, the things that do attain
  The happy life be these, I find:
The richesse left, not got with pain;
  The fruitful ground, the quiet mind;

The equal friend; no grudge, no strife;
  No charge of rule, nor governance;
Without disease, the healthful life;
  The household of continuance;

The mean diet, no delicate fare;
  True wisdom join'd with simpleness;
The night dischargèd of all care,
  Where wine the wit may not oppress.

The faithful wife, without debate;
  Such sleeps as may beguile the night:
Contented with thine own estate
  Ne wish for death, ne fear his might.

NICHOLAS GRIMALD

1519–1562

50   *A True Love*

WHAT sweet relief the showers to thirsty plants we see,
    What dear delight the blooms to bees, my true love is
    to me!
As fresh and lusty Ver foul Winter doth exceed—
As morning bright, with scarlet sky, doth pass the evening's
    weed—
As mellow pears above the crabs esteemèd be—
So doth my love surmount them all, whom yet I hap to see!
The oak shall olives bear, the lamb the lion fray,
The owl shall match the nightingale in tuning of her lay.
Or I my love let slip out of mine entire heart,
So deep reposèd in my breast is she for her desart!
For many blessèd gifts, O happy, happy land!
Where Mars and Pallas strive to make their glory most to stand!
Yet, land, more is thy bliss that, in this cruel age,
A Venus' imp thou hast brought forth, so steadfast and so sage.
Among the Muses Nine a tenth if Jove would make,
And to the Graces Three a fourth, her would Apollo take.
Let some for honour hunt, and hoard the massy gold:
With her so I may live and die, my weal cannot be told.

ALEXANDER SCOTT

1525?–1584?

51   *A Bequest of His Heart*

HENCE, heart, with her that must depart,
    And hald thee with thy soverane!
For I had liever want ane heart,
    Nor have the heart that dois me pain.

    50 fray] affright.   *51* hald] keep.

Therefore, go, with thy luve remain,
And let me leif thus unmolest;
   And see that thou come not again,
But bide with her thou luvis best.

Sen she that I have servit lang
   Is to depart so suddenly,
Address thee now, for thou sall gang
   And bear thy lady company.
   Fra she be gone, heartless am I,
For quhy? thou art with her possest.
   Therefore, my heart, go hence in high,
And bide with her thou luvis best.

Though this belappit body here
   Be bound to servitude and thrall,
My faithful heart is free entier
   And mind to serve my lady at all.
   Would God that I were perigall
Under that redolent rose to rest!
   Yet at the least, my heart, thou sall
Abide with her thou luvis best.

Sen in your garth the lily quhyte
   May not remain amang the laif,
Adieu the flower of whole delite!
   Adieu the succour that may me saif!
   Adieu the fragrant balme suaif,
And lamp of ladies lustiest!
   My faithful heart she shall it haif
To bide with her it luvis best.

sen] since.   belappit] downtrodden.   perigall] made
equal to, privileged.   garth] garden-close.   laif] rest.

Deploir, ye ladies cleir of hue,
    Her absence, sen she must depart!
And, specially, ye luveris true
    That wounded bene with Luvis dart.
    For some of you sall want ane heart
As well as I; therefore at last
    Do go with mine, with mind inwart,
And bide with her thou luvis best!

52   *A Rondel of Love*

    LO, quhat it is to love
      Learn ye that list to prove,
By me, I say, that no ways may
    The ground of grief remove,
But still decay both nicht and day:
    Lo, quhat it is to love!

    Love is ane fervent fire
    Kindlit without desire,
Short pleasour, long displeasour,
    Repentance is the hire;
Ane pure tressour without measour;
    Love is ane fervent fire.

    To love and to be wise,
    To rage with good advice;
Now thus, now than, so gois the game,
    Incertain is the dice;
There is no man, I say, that can
    Both love and to be wise.

51 with mind inwart] with inner mind, i.e. in spirit.

ALEXANDER SCOTT

Flee always from the snare,
Learn at me to beware;
It is ane pain, and double trane
Of endless woe and care;
For to refrain that danger plain,
Flee always from ane snare.

ROBERT WEVER

c. 1550

53   *In Youth is Pleasure*

IN a harbour grene aslepe whereas I lay,
The byrdes sang swete in the middes of the day,
I dreamèd fast of mirth and play:
    In youth is pleasure, in youth is pleasure.

Methought I walked still to and fro,
And from her company I could not go—
But when I waked it was not so:
    In youth is pleasure, in youth is pleasure.

Therefore my hart is surely pyght
Of her alone to have a sight
Which is my joy and hartes delight:
    In youth is pleasure, in youth is pleasure.

RICHARD EDWARDES

1523–1566

54   *Amantium Irae*

IN going to my naked bed as one that would have slept,
I heard a wife sing to her child, that long before had wept;
She sighèd sore and sang full sweet, to bring the babe to rest,
That would not cease but crièd still, in sucking at her breast.

RICHARD EDWARDES

She was full weary of her watch, and grievèd with her child,
She rockèd it and rated it, till that on her it smiled.
Then did she say, Now have I found this proverb true to prove,
The falling out of faithful friends renewing is of love.

Then took I paper, pen, and ink, this proverb for to write,
In register for to remain of such a worthy wight:
As she proceeded thus in song unto her little brat,
Much matter utter'd she of weight, in place whereas she sat:
And provèd plain there was no beast, nor creature bearing life,
Could well be known to live in love without discord and strife:
Then kissèd she her little babe, and sware by God above,
The falling out of faithful friends renewing is of love.

She said that neither king nor prince nor lord could live aright,
Until their puissance they did prove, their manhood and their
    might.
When manhood shall be matchèd so that fear can take no
    place,
Then weary works make warriors each other to embrace,
And left their force that failèd them, which did consume the
    rout,
That might before have lived their time, their strength and
    nature out:
Then did she sing as one that thought no man could her
    reprove,
The falling out of faithful friends renewing is of love.

She said she saw no fish nor fowl, nor beast within her haunt,
That met a stranger in their kind, but could give it a taunt:
Since flesh might not endure, but rest must wrath succeed,
And force the fight to fall to play in pasture where they feed,

So noble nature can well end the work she hath begun,
And bridle well that will not cease her tragedy in some:
Thus in song she oft rehearsed, as did her well behove,
The falling out of faithful friends renewing is of love.

I marvel much pardy (quoth she) for to behold the rout,
To see man, woman, boy and beast, to toss the world about:
Some kneel, some crouch, some beck, some check, and some
    can smoothly smile,
And some embrace others in arm, and there think many a wile,
Some stand aloof at cap and knee, some humble and some stout,
Yet are they never friends in deed until they once fall out:
Thus ended she her song and said, before she did remove,
The falling out of faithful friends renewing is of love.

GEORGE GASCOIGNE

1525?–1577

55   *A Lover's Lullaby*

SING lullaby, as women do,
   Wherewith they bring their babes to rest;
And lullaby can I sing too,
   As womanly as can the best.
With lullaby they still the child;
And if I be not much beguiled,
Full many a wanton babe have I,
Which must be still'd with lullaby.

First lullaby my youthful years,
   It is now time to go to bed:
For crookèd age and hoary hairs
   Have won the haven within my head.

With lullaby, then, youth be still;
With lullaby content thy will;
Since courage quails and comes behind,
Go sleep, and so beguile thy mind!

Next lullaby my gazing eyes,
   Which wonted were to glance apace;
For every glass may now suffice
   To show the furrows in thy face.
With lullaby then wink awhile;
With lullaby your looks beguile;
Let no fair face, nor beauty bright,
Entice you eft with vain delight.

And lullaby my wanton will;
   Let reason's rule now reign thy thought;
Since all too late I find by skill
   How dear I have thy fancies bought;
With lullaby now take thine ease,
With lullaby thy doubts appease;
For trust to this, if thou be still,
My body shall obey thy will.

Thus lullaby my youth, mine eyes,
   My will, my ware, and all that was:
I can no more delays devise;
   But welcome pain, let pleasure pass.
With lullaby now take your leave;
With lullaby your dreams deceive;
And when you rise with waking eye,
Remember then this lullaby.

               wink] slumber.

1540?-1610?

56 *The Night is Near Gone*

HEY! now the day dawis;
    The jolly cock crawis;
Now shroudis the shawis
    Thro' Nature anon.
The thissel-cock cryis
On lovers wha lyis:
Now skaillis the skyis;
    The nicht is neir gone.

The fieldis ouerflowis
With gowans that growis,
Quhair lilies like low is
    As red as the rone.
The turtle that true is,
With notes that renewis,
Her pairty pursuis:
    The nicht is neir gone.

Now hairtis with hindis
Conform to their kindis,
Hie tursis their tyndis
    On ground quhair they grone.
Now hurchonis, with hairis,
Aye passis in pairis;
Quhilk duly declaris
    The nicht is neir gone.

shroudis] dress themselves.   shawis] woods.   skaillis]
clears.   gowans] daisies.   low] flame.   rone] rowan.
pairty] partner, mate.   tursis] thrust.   tyndis] antlers.
grone] utter their rutting cry.   hurchonis] hedgehogs, 'urchins.'

80

The season excellis
Through sweetness that smellis;
Now Cupid compellis
   Our hairtis echone
On Venus wha waikis,
To muse on our maikis,
Syne sing for their saikis—
   'The nicht is neir gone!'

All courageous knichtis
Aganis the day dichtis
The breist-plate that bright is
   To fight with their fone.
The stonèd steed stampis
Through courage, and crampis,
Syne on the land lampis:
   The nicht is neir gone.

The freikis on feildis
That wight wapins weildis
With shyning bright shieldis
   At Titan in trone;
Stiff speiris in reistis
Ouer corseris crestis
Are broke on their breistis:
   The nicht is neir gone.

So hard are their hittis,
Some sweyis, some sittis,
And some perforce flittis
   On ground quhile they grone.

maikis] mates.   fone] foes.   stonèd steed] stallion.
crampis] prances.   lampis] gallops.   freikis] men, warriors.
wight wapins] stout weapons.   at Titan] over against Titan
(the sun), or read 'as'.   flittis] are cast.

Syne groomis that gay is
On blonkis that brayis
With swordis assayis:—
    The nicht is neir gone.

WILLIAM STEVENSON

1530?–1575

57   *Jolly Good Ale and Old*

I CANNOT eat but little meat,
  My stomach is not good;
But sure I think that I can drink
  With him that wears a hood.
Though I go bare, take ye no care,
  I nothing am a-cold;
I stuff my skin so full within
  Of jolly good ale and old.
      Back and side go bare, go bare;
      Both foot and hand go cold;
      But, belly, God send thee good ale enough,
      Whether it be new or old.

I love no roast but a nut-brown toast,
  And a crab laid in the fire;
A little bread shall do me stead;
  Much bread I not desire.
No frost nor snow, no wind, I trow,
  Can hurt me if I wold;
I am so wrapp'd and thoroughly lapp'd
  Of jolly good ale and old.
      Back and side go bare, go bare, &c.

    56 blonkis] white palfreys.

WILLIAM STEVENSON

And Tib, my wife, that as her life
  Loveth well good ale to seek,
Full oft drinks she till ye may see
  The tears run down her cheek:
Then doth she trowl to me the bowl
  Even as a maltworm should,
And saith, 'Sweetheart, I took my part
  Of this jolly good ale and old.'
      Back and side go bare, go bare, &c.

Now let them drink till they nod and wink,
  Even as good fellows should do;
They shall not miss to have that bliss
  Good ale doth bring men to;
And all poor souls that have scour'd bowls
  Or have them lustily troll'd,
God save the lives of them and their wives,
  Whether they be young or old.
      Back and side go bare, go bare;
      Both foot and hand go cold;
      But, belly, God send thee good ale enough,
      Whether it be new or old.

ANONYMOUS (SCOTTISH)

16th Cent.

58   *When Flora had O'erfret the Firth*

QUHEN Flora had o'erfret the firth
  In May of every moneth queen;
Quhen merle and mavis singis with mirth
  Sweet melling in the shawis sheen;

58 o'erfret] adorned.   shawis] woods.   sheen] beautiful.

ANONYMOUS (SCOTTISH)

Quhen all luvaris rejoicit bene
And most desirous of their prey,
   I heard a lusty luvar mene
   —'I luve, but I dare nocht assay!

'Strong are the pains I daily prove,
   But yet with patience I sustene,
I am so fetterit with the luve
   Only of my lady sheen,
   Quhilk for her beauty micht be queen,
Nature so craftily alway
   Has done depaint that sweet serene:
   —Quhom I luve I dare nocht assay.

'She is so bricht of hyd and hue,
   I luve but her alone, I ween;
Is none her luve that may eschew,
   That blinkis of that dulce amene;
   So comely cleir are her twa een
That she mae luvaris dois affray
   Than ever of Greece did fair Helene:
   —Quhom I luve I dare nocht assay!'

59   *Lusty May*

16th Cent.

O LUSTY May, with Flora queen!
   The balmy dropis from Phoebus sheen
Preluciand beams before the day:
By that Diana growis green
   Through gladness of this lusty May.

58 mene] mourn.   hyd] skin.   blinkis] gets a glimpse.
dulce amene] gentle and pleasant one.   mae] more.
  59 sheen] bright.

ANONYMOUS (SCOTTISH)

Then Esperus, that is so bricht,
Til woful hairtis castis his light,
   With bankis that bloomis on every brae;
And schouris are shed forth of their sicht
   Through gladness of this lusty May.

Birdis on bewis of every birth,
Rejoicing notis makand their mirth
   Richt plesantly upon the spray,
With flourishingis o'er field and firth
   Through gladness of this lusty May.

All luvaris that are in care
To their ladies they do repair
   In fresh mornings before the day,
And are in mirth ay mair and mair
   Through gladness of this lusty May.

60   *My Heart is High Above*
                       16th Cent.

MY heart is high above, my body is full of bliss,
   For I am set in luve as well as I would wiss
I luve my lady pure and she luvis me again,
I am her serviture, she is my soverane;
She is my very heart, I am her howp and heill,
She is my joy invart, I am her luvar leal;
I am her bond and thrall, she is at my command;
I am perpetual her man, both foot and hand;

59 til] into.   bewis] boughs.   birth] kind.   60 wiss]
wish.   heill] health.   invart] inward.

ANONYMOUS (SCOTTISH)

The thing that may her please my body sall fulfil;
Quhatever her disease, it does my body ill.
My bird, my bonny ane, my tender babe venust,
My luve, my life alane, my liking and my lust!
We interchange our hairtis in others armis soft,
Spriteless we twa depairtis, usand our luvis oft.
We mourn when licht day dawis, we plain the nicht is short,
We curse the cock that crawis, that hinderis our disport.
I glowffin up aghast, quhen I her miss on nicht,
And in my oxter fast I find the bowster richt;
Then languor on me lies like Morpheus the mair,
Quhilk causes me uprise and to my sweet repair.
And then is all the sorrow forth of remembrance
That ever I had a-forrow in luvis observance.
Thus never I do rest, so lusty a life I lead,
Quhen that I list to test the well of womanheid.
Luvaris in pain, I pray God send you sic remeid
As I have nicht and day, you to defend from deid!
Therefore be ever true unto your ladies free,
And they will on you rue as mine has done on me.

venust] delightful.   glowffin] blink on awaking.   oxter]
armpit.   a-forrow] aforetime.

ELIZABETHAN MISCELLANIES AND SONG-BOOKS

BY UNNAMED OR UNCERTAIN AUTHORS

61   *A Praise of His Lady*

Tottel's Miscellany, 1557

GIVE place, you ladies, and begone!
  Boast not yourselves at all!
For here at hand approacheth one
  Whose face will stain you all.

The virtue of her lively looks
  Excels the precious stone;
I wish to have none other books
  To read or look upon.

In each of her two crystal eyes
  Smileth a naked boy;
It would you all in heart suffice
  To see that lamp of joy.

I think Nature hath lost the mould
  Where she her shape did take;
Or else I doubt if Nature could
  So fair a creature make.

She may be well compared
  Unto the Phoenix kind,
Whose like was never seen or heard,
  That any man can find.

ANONYMOUS

In life she is Diana chaste,
    In troth Penelopey;
In word and eke in deed steadfast.
    —What will you more we say?

If all the world were sought so far,
    Who could find such a wight?
Her beauty twinkleth like a star
    Within the frosty night.

Her rosial colour comes and goes
    With such a comely grace,
More ruddier, too, than doth the rose,
    Within her lively face.

At Bacchus' feast none shall her meet,
    Ne at no wanton play,
Nor gazing in an open street,
    Nor gadding as a stray.

The modest mirth that she doth use
    Is mix'd with shamefastness;
All vice she doth wholly refuse,
    And hateth idleness.

O Lord! it is a world to see
    How virtue can repair,
And deck in her such honesty,
    Whom Nature made so fair.

Truly she doth so far exceed
    Our women nowadays,
As doth the jeliflower a weed;
    And more a thousand ways.

ANONYMOUS

How might I do to get a graff
    Of this unspotted tree?
—For all the rest are plain but chaff,
    Which seem good corn to be.

This gift alone I shall her give;
    When death doth what he can,
Her honest fame shall ever live
    Within the mouth of man.

? by John Heywood

62   *To Her Sea-faring Lover*

Tottel's Miscellany, 1557

SHALL I thus ever long, and be no whit the neare?
    And shall I still complain to thee, the which me will not
        hear?
    Alas! say nay! say nay! and be no more so dumb,
But open thou thy manly mouth and say that thou wilt come:
    Whereby my heart may think, although I see not thee,
That thou wilt come—thy word so sware—if thou a live
        man be.
    The roaring nugy waves they threaten my poor ghost,
And toss thee up and down the seas in danger to be lost.
    Shall they not make me fear that they have swallowed thee?
—But as thou art most sure alive, so wilt thou come to me.
    Whereby I shall go see thy ship ride on the strand,
And think and say *Lo where he comes* and *Sure here will he
        land:*
    And then I shall lift up to thee my little hand,
And thou shalt think thine heart in ease, in health to see me
        stand.

62 neare] nearer.

89

And if thou come indeed (as Christ thee send to do!)
Those arms which miss thee now shall then embrace [and
    hold] thee to:
Each vein to every joint the lively blood shall spread
Which now for want of thy glad sight doth show full pale and
    dead.
But if thou slip thy troth, and do not come at all,
As minutes in the clock do strike so call for death I shall:
    To please both thy false heart and rid myself from woe,
That rather had to die in troth than live forsaken so!

63   *The Faithless Shepherdess*

William Byrd's *Songs of
Sundry Natures*, 1589

WHILE that the sun with his beams hot
    Scorchèd the fruits in vale and mountain,
Philon the shepherd, late forgot,
    Sitting beside a crystal fountain
        In shadow of a green oak tree,
        Upon his pipe this song play'd he:
Adieu, Love, adieu, Love, untrue Love!
Untrue Love, untrue Love, adieu, Love!
Your mind is light, soon lost for new love.

So long as I was in your sight
    I was your heart, your soul, your treasure;
And evermore you sobb'd and sigh'd
    Burning in flames beyond all measure:
        —Three days endured your love to me,
        And it was lost in other three!
Adieu, Love, adieu, Love, untrue Love!
Untrue Love, untrue Love, adieu, Love!
Your mind is light, soon lost for new love.

Another shepherd you did see,
    To whom your heart was soon enchainèd;
Full soon your love was leapt from me,
    Full soon my place he had obtainèd.
        Soon came a third your love to win,
        And we were out and he was in.
Adieu, Love, adieu, Love, untrue Love!
Untrue Love, untrue Love, adieu, Love!
Your mind is light, soon lost for new love.

Sure you have made me passing glad
    That you your mind so soon removèd,
Before that I the leisure had
    To choose you for my best belovèd:
        For all my love was pass'd and done
        Two days before it was begun.
Adieu, Love, adieu, Love, untrue Love!
Untrue Love, untrue Love, adieu, Love!
Your mind is light, soon lost for new love.

64   *Crabbed Age and Youth*

The Passionate Pilgrim, 1599

CRABBÈD Age and Youth
    Cannot live together:
Youth is full of pleasance,
Age is full of care;
Youth like summer morn,
Age like winter weather;
Youth like summer brave,
Age like winter bare.

Youth is full of sport,
Age's breath is short;
Youth is nimble, Age is lame;
Youth is hot and bold,
Age is weak and cold;
Youth is wild, and Age is tame.
Age, I do abhor thee;
Youth, I do adore thee;
O, my Love, my Love is young!
Age, I do defy thee:
O, sweet shepherd, hie thee!
For methinks thou stay'st too long.

? by William Shakespeare

65 *Phyllida's Love-Call*

England's Helicon, 1600

Phyllida. CORYDON, arise, my Corydon!
         Titan shineth clear.
Corydon. Who is it that calleth Corydon?
         Who is it that I hear?
Phyl. Phyllida, thy true love, calleth thee,
         Arise then, arise then,
             Arise and keep thy flock with me!
Cor. Phyllida, my true love, is it she?
         I come then, I come then,
             I come and keep my flock with thee.

Phyl. Here are cherries ripe for my Corydon;
         Eat them for my sake.
Cor. Here's my oaten pipe, my lovely one,
         Sport for thee to make.

Phyl. Here are threads, my true love, fine as silk,
    To knit thee, to knit thee,
      A pair of stockings white as milk.
 Cor. Here are reeds, my true love, fine and neat,
    To make thee, to make thee,
      A bonnet to withstand the heat.

Phyl. I will gather flowers, my Corydon,
    To set in thy cap.
 Cor. I will gather pears, my lovely one,
    To put in thy lap.
Phyl. I will buy my true love garters gay,
    For Sundays, for Sundays,
      To wear about his legs so tall.
 Cor. I will buy my true love yellow say,
    For Sundays, for Sundays,
      To wear about her middle small.

Phyl. When my Corydon sits on a hill
    Making melody—
 Cor. When my lovely one goes to her wheel,
    Singing cheerily—
Phyl. Sure methinks my true love doth excel
    For sweetness, for sweetness,
      Our Pan, that old Arcadian knight.
 Cor. And methinks my true love bears the bell
    For clearness, for clearness,
      Beyond the nymphs that be so bright.

Phyl. Had my Corydon, my Corydon,
    Been, alack! her swain—
 Cor. Had my lovely one, my lovely one,
    Been in Ida plain—

        say] *soie*, silk.

ANONYMOUS

Phyl. Cynthia Endymion had refused,
   Preferring, preferring,
    My Corydon to play withal.

Cor. The Queen of Love had been excused
   Bequeathing, bequeathing,
    My Phyllida the golden ball.

Phyl. Yonder comes my mother, Corydon!
   Whither shall I fly?

Cor. Under yonder beech, my lovely one,
   While she passeth by.

Phyl. Say to her thy true love was not here;
   Remember, remember,
    To-morrow is another day.

Cor. Doubt me not, my true love, do not fear;
   Farewell then, farewell then!
    Heaven keep our loves alway!

66   *A Pedlar*

John Dowland's *Second Book of
Songs or Airs,* 1600

FINE knacks for ladies! cheap, choice, brave, and new,
 Good pennyworths—but money cannot move:
I keep a fair but for the Fair to view—
 A beggar may be liberal of love.
Though all my wares be trash, the heart is true,
    The heart is true.

Great gifts are guiles and look for gifts again;
 My trifles come as treasures from my mind:
It is a precious jewel to be plain;
 Sometimes in shell the orient'st pearls we find:—
Of others take a sheaf, of me a grain!
    Of me a grain!

67 *Hey nonny no!*

Christ Church MS.

HEY nonny no!
    Men are fools that wish to die!
Is't not fine to dance and sing
When the bells of death do ring?
Is't not fine to swim in wine,
And turn upon the toe,
And sing hey nonny no!
When the winds blow and the seas flow?
Hey nonny no!

68 *Heart's Music*

Campian's *First Book of Airs*

TUNE thy music to thy heart;
    Sing thy joy with thanks, and so thy sorrow.
    Though devotion needs not art,
Sometime of the poor the rich may borrow.

    Strive not yet for curious ways;
Concord pleaseth more the less 'tis strainèd.
    Zeal affects not outward praise,
Only strives to show a love unfeignèd.

    Love can wondrous things effect,
Sweetest sacrifice all wrath appeasing.
    Love the Highest doth respect;
Love alone to Him is ever pleasing.

69 *Preparations*

Christ Church MS.

YET if His Majesty, our sovereign lord,
    Should of his own accord
Friendly himself invite,
And say 'I'll be your guest to-morrow night,'

ANONYMOUS

How should we stir ourselves, call and command
All hands to work! 'Let no man idle stand!

'Set me fine Spanish tables in the hall;
See they be fitted all;
Let there be room to eat
And order taken that there want no meat.
See every sconce and candlestick made bright,
That without tapers they may give a light.

'Look to the presence: are the carpets spread,
The dazie o'er the head,
The cushions in the chairs,
And all the candles lighted on the stairs?
Perfume the chambers, and in any case
Let each man give attendance in his place!'

Thus, if a king were coming, would we do;
And 'twere good reason too;
For 'tis a duteous thing
To show all honour to an earthly king,
And after all our travail and our cost,
So he be pleased, to think no labour lost.

But at the coming of the King of Heaven
All's set at six and seven;
We wallow in our sin,
Christ cannot find a chamber in the inn.
We entertain Him always like a stranger,
And, as at first, still lodge Him in the manger.

ANONYMOUS

The New Jerusalem

Song of Mary the Mother of
Christ (London: E. Allde), 1601

HIERUSALEM, my happy home,
  When shall I come to thee?
When shall my sorrows have an end,
  Thy joys when shall I see?

O happy harbour of the Saints!
  O sweet and pleasant soil!
In thee no sorrow may be found,
  No grief, no care, no toil.

There lust and lucre cannot dwell,
  There envy bears no sway;
There is no hunger, heat, nor cold,
  But pleasure every way.

Thy walls are made of precious stones,
  Thy bulwarks diamonds square;
Thy gates are of right orient pearl,
  Exceeding rich and rare.

Thy turrets and thy pinnacles
  With carbuncles do shine;
Thy very streets are paved with gold,
  Surpassing clear and fine.

Ah, my sweet home, Hierusalem,
  Would God I were in thee!
Would God my woes were at an end,
  Thy joys that I might see!

Thy gardens and thy gallant walks
   Continually are green;
There grows such sweet and pleasant flowers
   As nowhere else are seen.

Quite through the streets, with silver sound,
   The flood of Life doth flow;
Upon whose banks on every side
   The wood of Life doth grow.

There trees for evermore bear fruit,
   And evermore do spring;
There evermore the angels sit,
   And evermore do sing.

Our Lady sings *Magnificat*
   With tones surpassing sweet;
And all the virgins bear their part,
   Sitting about her feet.

Hierusalem, my happy home,
   Would God I were in thee!
Would God my woes were at an end,
   Thy joys that I might see!

71   *Icarus*

Robert Jones's *Second Book of
Songs and Airs*, 1601

LOVE wing'd my Hopes and taught me how to fly
  Far from base earth, but not to mount too high:
     For true pleasure
     Lives in measure,
     Which if men forsake,
Blinded they into folly run and grief for pleasure take.

But my vain Hopes, proud of their new-taught flight,
Enamour'd sought to woo the sun's fair light,
      Whose rich brightness
      Moved their lightness
      To aspire so high
That, all scorch'd and consumed with fire, now drown'd in
  woe they lie.

And none but Love their woeful hap did rue,
For Love did know that their desires were true;
      Though Fate frownèd,
      And now drownèd
      They in sorrow dwell,
It was the purest light of heav'n for whose fair love they fell.

72   *Madrigal*

                 Davison's *Poetical Rhapsody*, 1602

M Y Love in her attire doth show her wit,
   It doth so well become her;
For every season she hath dressings fit,
  For Winter, Spring, and Summer.
    No beauty she doth miss
      When all her robes are on:
     But Beauty's self she is
      When all her robes are gone.

73 *How can the Heart forget her?*

Davison's *Poetical Rhapsody,* 1602

AT her fair hands how have I grace entreated
  With prayers oft repeated!
Yet still my love is thwarted:
Heart, let her go, for she'll not be converted—
    Say, shall she go?
    O no, no, no, no, no!
She is most fair, though she be marble-hearted.

How often have my sighs declared my anguish,
Wherein I daily languish!
Yet still she doth procure it:
Heart, let her go, for I can not endure it—
    Say, shall she go?
    O no, no, no, no, no!
She gave the wound, and she alone must cure it.

But shall I still a true affection owe her,
Which prayers, sighs, tears do show her,
And shall she still disdain me?
Heart, let her go, if they no grace can gain me—
    Say, shall she go?
    O no, no, no, no, no!
She made me hers, and hers she will retain me.

But if the love that hath and still doth burn me
No love at length return me,
Out of my thoughts I'll set her:
Heart, let her go, O heart I pray thee, let her!
    Say, shall she go?
    O no, no, no, no, no!
Fix'd in the heart, how can the heart forget her?

74

Tears

John Dowland's *Third and Last*
Book of Songs or Airs, 1603

WEEP you no more, sad fountains;
    What need you flow so fast?
Look how the snowy mountains
    Heaven's sun doth gently waste!
But my Sun's heavenly eyes
      View not your weeping,
      That now lies sleeping
Softly, now softly lies
      Sleeping.

Sleep is a reconciling,
    A rest that peace begets;
Doth not the sun rise smiling
    When fair at even he sets?
Rest you then, rest, sad eyes!
      Melt not in weeping,
      While she lies sleeping
Softly, now softly lies
      Sleeping.

75

My Lady's Tears

John Dowland's *Third and Last*
Book of Songs or Airs, 1603

I SAW my Lady weep,
    And Sorrow proud to be advancèd so
In those fair eyes where all perfections keep.
    Her face was full of woe;
But such a woe (believe me) as wins more hearts
Than Mirth can do with her enticing parts.

ANONYMOUS

Sorrow was there made fair,
And Passion wise; Tears a delightful thing;
Silence beyond all speech, a wisdom rare:
    She made her sighs to sing,
And all things with so sweet a sadness move
As made my heart at once both grieve and love.

    O fairer than aught else
The world can show, leave off in time to grieve!
Enough, enough: your joyful look excels:
    Tears kill the heart, believe.
O strive not to be excellent in woe,
Which only breeds your beauty's overthrow.

76   *Sister, Awake!*

Thomas Bateson's *First Set of*
English Madrigals, 1604

SISTER, awake! close not your eyes!
    The day her light discloses,
And the bright morning doth arise
    Out of her bed of roses.

See the clear sun, the world's bright eye,
    In at our window peeping:
Lo, how he blusheth to espy
    Us idle wenches sleeping!

Therefore awake! make haste, I say,
    And let us, without staying,
All in our gowns of green so gay
    Into the Park a-maying!

77 *Devotion*

Captain Tobias Hume's *The First
Part of Airs, &c.,* 1605

FAIN would I change that note
 To which fond Love hath charm'd me
Long, long to sing by rote,
Fancying that that harm'd me:
Yet when this thought doth come,
'Love is the perfect sum
    Of all delight,'
I have no other choice
Either for pen or voice
    To sing or write.

O Love! they wrong thee much
That say thy sweet is bitter,
When thy rich fruit is such
As nothing can be sweeter.
Fair house of joy and bliss,
Where truest pleasure is,
    I do adore thee:
I know thee what thou art,
I serve thee with my heart,
    And fall before thee.

78 *Since First I saw your Face*

Thomas Ford's *Music of
Sundry Kinds,* 1607

SINCE first I saw your face I resolved to honour and
 renown ye;
If now I be disdainèd I wish my heart had never known ye.
What? I that loved and you that liked, shall we begin to
    wrangle?
No, no, no, my heart is fast, and cannot disentangle.

If I admire or praise you too much, that fault you may forgive
    me;
Or if my hands had stray'd but a touch, then justly might
    you leave me.
I ask'd you leave, you bade me love; is 't now a time to chide
    me?
No, no, no, I'll love you still what fortune e'er betide me.

The Sun, whose beams most glorious are, rejecteth no
    beholder,
And your sweet beauty past compare made my poor eyes the
    bolder:
Where beauty moves and wit delights and signs of kindness
    bind me,
There, O there, where'er I go I'll leave my heart behind me!

79   *There is a Lady sweet and kind*

Thomas Ford's *Music of
Sundry Kinds,* 1607

THERE is a Lady sweet and kind,
    Was never face so pleased my mind;
I did but see her passing by,
And yet I love her till I die.

Her gesture, motion, and her smiles,
Her wit, her voice my heart beguiles,
Beguiles my heart, I know not why,
And yet I love her till I die.

Cupid is wingèd and doth range,
Her country so my love doth change:
But change she earth, or change she sky,
Yet will I love her till I die.

80   *Love not me for comely grace*

John Wilbye's *Second Set of Madrigals,* 1609

LOVE not me for comely grace,
For my pleasing eye or face,
Nor for any outward part,
No, nor for a constant heart:
　　For these may fail or turn to ill,
　　So thou and I shall sever:
Keep, therefore, a true woman's eye,
And love me still but know not why—
　　So hast thou the same reason still
　　To doat upon me ever!

81   *The Wakening*

John Attye's *First Book of Airs,* 1622

ON a time the amorous Silvy
Said to her shepherd, 'Sweet, how do ye?
Kiss me this once and then God be wi' ye,
　　　　My sweetest dear!
Kiss me this once and then God be wi' ye,
For now the morning draweth near.'

With that, her fairest bosom showing,
Op'ning her lips, rich perfumes blowing,
She said, 'Now kiss me and be going,
　　　　My sweetest dear!
Kiss me this once and then be going,
For now the morning draweth near.'

With that the shepherd waked from sleeping,
And spying where the day was peeping,
He said, 'Now take my soul in keeping,
          My sweetest dear!
Kiss me and take my soul in keeping,
Since I must go, now day is near.'

NICHOLAS BRETON

1542–1626

82   *Phillida and Coridon*

IN the merry month of May,
  In a morn by break of day,
Forth I walk'd by the wood-side
When as May was in his pride:
There I spièd all alone
Phillida and Coridon.
Much ado there was, God wot!
He would love and she would not.
She said, Never man was true;
He said, None was false to you.
He said, He had loved her long;
She said, Love should have no wrong.
Coridon would kiss her then;
She said, Maids must kiss no men
Till they did for good and all;
Then she made the shepherd call
All the heavens to witness truth
Never loved a truer youth.
Thus with many a pretty oath,
Yea and nay, and faith and troth,

Such as silly shepherds use
When they will not Love abuse,
Love, which had been long deluded,
Was with kisses sweet concluded;
And Phillida, with garlands gay,
Was made the Lady of the May.

NICHOLAS BRETON?

83

A Cradle Song

*The Arbor of Amorous
Devices*, 1593–4

COME little babe, come silly soul,
   Thy father's shame, thy mother's grief,
Born as I doubt to all our dole,
And to thyself unhappy chief:
   Sing lullaby, and lap it warm,
   Poor soul that thinks no creature harm.

Thou little think'st and less dost know
The cause of this thy mother's moan;
Thou want'st the wit to wail her woe,
And I myself am all alone:
   Why dost thou weep? why dost thou wail?
   And know'st not yet what thou dost ail.

Come, little wretch—ah, silly heart!
Mine only joy, what can I more?
If there be any wrong thy smart,
That may the destinies implore:
   'Twas I, I say, against my will,
   I wail the time, but be thou still.

NICHOLAS BRETON?

And dost thou smile? O, thy sweet face!
Would God Himself He might thee see!—
No doubt thou wouldst soon purchase grace,
I know right well, for thee and me:
> But come to mother, babe, and play,
> For father false is fled away.

Sweet boy, if it by fortune chance
Thy father home again to send,
If death do strike me with his lance,
Yet mayst thou me to him commend:
> If any ask thy mother's name,
> Tell how by love she purchased blame.

Then will his gentle heart soon yield:
I know him of a noble mind:
Although a lion in the field,
A lamb in town thou shalt him find:
> Ask blessing, babe, be not afraid,
> His sugar'd words hath me betray'd.

Then mayst thou joy and be right glad;
Although in woe I seem to moan,
Thy father is no rascal lad,
A noble youth of blood and bone:
> His glancing looks, if he once smile,
> Right honest women may beguile.

Come, little boy, and rock asleep;
Sing lullaby and be thou still;
I, that can do naught else but weep,
Will sit by thee and wail my fill:
> God bless my babe, and lullaby
> From this thy father's quality.

1552–1618

84

The Silent Lover

(i)

PASSIONS are liken'd best to floods and streams:
　　The shallow murmur, but the deep are dumb;
So, when affection yields discourse, it seems
　　The bottom is but shallow whence they come.
They that are rich in words, in words discover
That they are poor in that which makes a lover.

85

(ii)

WRONG not, sweet empress of my heart,
　　The merit of true passion,
With thinking that he feels no smart,
　　That sues for no compassion.

Silence in love bewrays more woe
　　Than words, though ne'er so witty:
A beggar that is dumb, you know,
　　May challenge double pity.

Then wrong not, dearest to my heart,
　　My true, though secret passion;
He smarteth most that hides his smart,
　　And sues for no compassion.

86

His Pilgrimage

GIVE me my scallop-shell of quiet,
   My staff of faith to walk upon,
My scrip of joy, immortal diet,
   My bottle of salvation,
My gown of glory, hope's true gage;
And thus I'll take my pilgrimage.

Blood must be my body's balmer;
   No other balm will there be given;
Whilst my soul, like quiet palmer,
   Travelleth towards the land of heaven;
Over the silver mountains,
Where spring the nectar fountains;
         There will I kiss
         The bowl of bliss;
         And drink mine everlasting fill
         Upon every milken hill.
         My soul will be a-dry before;
         But, after, it will thirst no more.

87

The Conclusion

EVEN such is Time, that takes in trust
   Our youth, our joys, our all we have,
And pays us but with earth and dust;
   Who in the dark and silent grave,
When we have wander'd all our ways,
Shuts up the story of our days;
But from this earth, this grave, this dust,
My God shall raise me up, I trust.

EDMUND SPENSER

1552-1599

88 *Whilst it is prime*

FRESH Spring, the herald of loves mighty king,
  In whose cote-armour richly are displayd
All sorts of flowers, the which on earth do spring,
In goodly colours gloriously arrayd—
Goe to my love, where she is carelesse layd,
Yet in her winters bowre not well awake;
Tell her the joyous time wil not be staid,
Unlesse she doe him by the forelock take;
Bid her therefore her selfe soone ready make,
To wayt on Love amongst his lovely crew;
Where every one, that misseth then her make,
Shall be by him amearst with penance dew.
    Make hast, therefore, sweet love, whilest it is prime;
    For none can call againe the passèd time.

89 *A Ditty*

In praise of Eliza, Queen of the Shepherds

SEE where she sits upon the grassie greene,
    (O seemely sight!)
Yclad in Scarlot, like a mayden Queene,
    And ermines white:
Upon her head a Cremosin coronet
With Damaske roses and Daffadillies set:
    Bay leaves betweene,
    And primroses greene,
Embellish the sweete Violet.

88 make] mate.

Tell me, have ye seene her angelick face
      Like Phœbe fayre?
Her heavenly haveour, her princely grace,
      Can you well compare?
The Redde rose medled with the White yfere,
In either cheeke depeincten lively chere:
      Her modest eye,
      Her Majestie,
Where have you seene the like but there?

I see Calliope speede her to the place,
      Where my Goddesse shines;
And after her the other Muses trace
      With their Violines.
Bene they not Bay braunches which they do beare,
All for Eliza in her hand to weare?
      So sweetely they play,
      And sing all the way,
That it a heaven is to heare.

Lo, how finely the Graces can it foote
      To the Instrument:
They dauncen deffly, and singen soote,
      In their meriment.
Wants not a fourth Grace to make the daunce even?
Let that rowne to my Lady be yeven.
      She shal be a Grace,
      To fyll the fourth place,
And reigne with the rest in heaven.

medled] mixed.   yfere] together.   soote] sweet.

Bring hether the Pincke and purple Cullambine,
    With Gelliflowers;
Bring Coronations, and Sops-in-wine
    Worne of Paramoures:
Strowe me the ground with Daffadowndillies,
And Cowslips, and Kingcups, and lovèd Lillies:
    The pretie Pawnce,
    And the Chevisaunce,
Shall match with the fayre flowre Delice.

Now ryse up, Elisa, deckèd as thou art
    In royall aray;
And now ye daintie Damsells may depart
    Eche one her way.
I feare I have troubled your troupes to longe:
Let dame Elisa thanke you for her song:
    And if you come hether
    When Damsines I gether,
I will part them all you among.

90   *Iambicum Trimetrum*

UNHAPPY Verse, the witnesse of my unhappie state,
  Make thy selfe fluttring wings of thy fast flying
Thought, and fly forth unto my Love, whersoever she be:
Whether lying reastlesse in heavy bed, or else
  Sitting so cheerelesse at the cheerfull boord, or else
  Playing alone carelesse on her heavenlie Virginals.
If in Bed, tell her that my eyes can take no rest;

89 coronations] carnations.   sops-in-wine] striped pinks.
pawnce] pansy.   chevisaunce] wallflower.   flowre delice] iris.

If at Boord, tell her that my mouth can eat no meate;
If at her Virginals, tell her I can heare no mirth.
Asked why? say, Waking Love suffereth no sleepe;
　　Say that raging Love doth appall the weak stomacke;
　　Say that lamenting Love marreth the Musicall.
Tell her that her pleasures were wonte to lull me asleepe;
　　Tell her that her beautie was wonte to feede mine eyes;
　　Tell her that her sweete Tongue was wont to make me mirth.
Nowe do I nightly waste, wanting my kindely rest;
　　Nowe do I dayly starve, wanting my lively food?
　　Nowe do I alwayes dye, wanting thy timely mirth.
And if I waste, who will bewaile my heavy chaunce?
　　And if I starve, who will record my cursed end?
　　And if I dye, who will saye, *this was Immerito?*

91　　　　　　*Prothalamion*

CALME was the day, and through the trembling ayre
　　Sweete-breathing Zephyrus did softly play
A gentle spirit, that lightly did delay
Hot Titans beames, which then did glyster fayre;
When I, (whom sullein care,
Through discontent of my long fruitlesse stay
In Princes Court, and expectation vayne
Of idle hopes, which still doe fly away,
Like empty shaddowes, did afflict my brayne,)
Walkt forth to ease my payne
Along the shoare of silver streaming Themmes;
Whose rutty Bancke, the which his River hemmes,
Was paynted all with variable flowers,
And all the meades adornd with daintie gemmes
Fit to decke maydens bowres,

114

And crowne their Paramours
Against the Brydale day, which is not long:
   Sweete Themmes! runne softly, till I end my Song.

There, in a Meadow, by the Rivers side,
A Flocke of Nymphes I chauncèd to espy,
All lovely Daughters of the Flood thereby,
With goodly greenish locks, all loose untyde,
As each had bene a Bryde;
And each one had a little wicker basket,
Made of the twigs, entraylèd curiously,
In which they gathered flowers to fill their flasket,
And with fine Fingers crept full feateously
The tender stalkes on hye.
Of every sort, which in that Meadow grew,
They gathered some; the Violet, pallid blew,
The little Dazie, that at evening closes,
The virgin Lillie, and the Primrose trew,
With store of vermeil Roses,
To decke their Bridegromes posies
Against the Brydale day, which was not long:
   Sweete Themmes! runne softly, till I end my Song.

With that I saw two Swannes of goodly hewe
Come softly swimming downe along the Lee;
Two fairer Birds I yet did never see;
The snow, which doth the top of Pindus strew,
Did never whiter shew;
Nor Jove himselfe, when he a Swan would be
For love of Leda, whiter did appeare;
Yet Leda was (they say) as white as he,
Yet not so white as these, nor nothing neare;
So purely white they were,

That even the gentle streame, the which them bare,
Seem'd foule to them, and bad his billowes spare
To wet their silken feathers, least they might
Soyle their fayre plumes with water not so fayre,
And marre their beauties bright,
That shone as heavens light,
Against their Brydale day, which was not long:
   Sweete Themmes! runne softly, till I end my Song.

Eftsoones the Nymphes, which now had Flowers their fill,
Ran all in haste to see that silver brood,
As they came floating on the Christal Flood;
Whom when they sawe, they stood amazèd still,
Their wondring eyes to fill;
Them seem'd they never saw a sight so fayre,
Of Fowles, so lovely, that they sure did deeme
Them heavenly borne, or to be that same payre
Which through the Skie draw Venus silver Teeme;
For sure they did not seeme
To be begot of any earthly Seede,
But rather Angels, or of Angels breede;
Yet were they bred of Somers-heat, they say,
In sweetest Season, when each Flower and weede
The earth did fresh aray;
So fresh they seem'd as day,
Even as their Brydale day, which was not long:
   Sweete Themmes! runne softly, till I end my Song.

Then forth they all out of their baskets drew
Great store of Flowers, the honour of the field,
That to the sense did fragrant odours yield,
All which upon those goodly Birds they threw
And all the Waves did strew,

116

Whose want too well now feeles my freendles case;
But ah! here fits not well
Olde woes, but joyes, to tell
Against the Brydale daye, which is not long:
   Sweete Themmes! runne softly, till I end my Song.

Yet therein now doth lodge a noble Peer,
Great Englands glory, and the World wide wonder,
Whose dreadfull name late through all Spaine did thunder,
And Hercules two pillors standing neere
Did make to quake and feare:
Faire branch of Honor, flower of Chevalrie!
That fillest England with thy triumphs fame,
Joy have thou of thy noble victorie,
And endlesse happinesse of thine owne name
That promiseth the same;
That through thy prowesse, and victorious armes,
Thy country may be freed from forraine harmes;
And great Elisaes glorious name may ring
Through al the world, fil'd with thy wide Alarmes,
Which some brave muse may sing
To ages following,
Upon the Brydale day, which is not long:
   Sweete Themmes! runne softly till I end my Song.

From those high Towers this noble Lord issuing,
Like Radiant Hesper, when his golden hayre
In th' Ocean billowes he hath bathèd fayre,
Descended to the Rivers open vewing,
With a great traine ensuing.
Above the rest were goodly to bee seene
Two gentle Knights of lovely face and feature,
Beseeming well the bower of anie Queene,

With gifts of wit, and ornaments of nature,
Fit for so goodly stature,
That like the twins of Jove they seem'd in sight,
Which decke the Bauldricke of the Heavens bright;
They two, forth pacing to the Rivers side,
Received those two faire Brides, their Loves delight;
Which, at th' appointed tyde,
Each one did make his Bryde
Against their Brydale day, which is not long:
    Sweete Themmes! runne softly, till I end my Song.

92   *Epithalamion*

YE learnèd sisters, which have oftentimes
    Beene to me ayding, others to adorne,
Whom ye thought worthy of your gracefull rymes,
That even the greatest did not greatly scorne
To heare theyr names sung in your simple layes,
But joyèd in theyr praise;
And when ye list your owne mishaps to mourne,
Which death, or love, or fortunes wreck did rayse,
Your string could soone to sadder tenor turne,
And teach the woods and waters to lament
Your dolefull dreriment:
Now lay those sorrowfull complaints aside;
And, having all your heads with girlands crownd,
Helpe me mine owne loves prayses to resound;
Ne let the same of any be envide:
So Orpheus did for his owne bride!
So I unto my selfe alone will sing;
    The woods shall to me answer, and my Eccho ring.

EDMUND SPENSER

Early, before the worlds light-giving lampe
His golden beame upon the hils doth spred,
Having disperst the nights unchearefull dampe,
Doe ye awake; and, with fresh lusty-hed,
Go to the bowre of my belovèd love,
My truest turtle dove;
Bid her awake; for Hymen is awake,
And long since ready forth his maske to move,
With his bright Tead that flames with many a flake,
And many a bachelor to waite on him,
In theyr fresh garments trim.
Bid her awake therefore, and soone her dight,
For lo! the wishèd day is come at last,
That shall, for all the paynes and sorrowes past,
Pay to her usury of long delight:
And, whylest she doth her dight,
Doe ye to her of joy and solace sing,
That all the woods may answer, and your eccho ring.

Bring with you all the Nymphes that you can heare
Both of the rivers and the forrests greene,
And of the sea that neighbours to her neare:
Al with gay girlands goodly wel beseene.
And let them also with them bring in hand
Another gay girland
For my fayre love, of lillyes and of roses,
Bound truelove wize, with a blew silke riband.
And let them make great store of bridale poses,
And let them eeke bring store of other flowers,
To deck the bridale bowers.
And let the ground whereas her foot shall tread,

tead] torch.

For feare the stones her tender foot should wrong,
Be strewed with fragrant flowers all along,
And diapred lyke the discolored mead.
Which done, doe at her chamber dore awayt,
For she will waken strayt;
The whiles doe ye this song unto her sing,
The woods shall to you answer, and your Eccho ring.

Ye Nymphes of Mulla, which with carefull heed
The silver scaly trouts doe tend full well,
And greedy pikes which use therein to feed;
(Those trouts and pikes all others doo excell;)
And ye likewise, which keepe the rushy lake,
Where none doo fishes take;
Bynd up the locks the which hang scatterd light,
And in his waters, which your mirror make,
Behold your faces as the christall bright,
That when you come whereas my love doth lie,
No blemish she may spie.
And eke, ye lightfoot mayds, which keepe the deere,
That on the hoary mountayne used to towre;
And the wylde wolves, which seeke them to devoure,
With your steele darts doo chace from comming neer;
Be also present heere,
To helpe to decke her, and to help to sing,
That all the woods may answer, and your eccho ring.

Wake now, my love, awake! for it is time;
The Rosy Morne long since left Tithones bed,
All ready to her silver coche to clyme;
And Phœbus gins to shew his glorious hed.
Hark! how the cheerefull birds do chaunt theyr laies
And carroll of Loves praise.

EDMUND SPENSER

The merry Larke hir mattins sings aloft;
The Thrush replyes; the Mavis descant playes;
The Ouzell shrills; the Ruddock warbles soft;
So goodly all agree, with sweet consent,
To this dayes merriment.
Ah! my deere love, why doe ye sleepe thus long?
When meeter were that ye should now awake,
T' awayt the comming of your joyous make,
And hearken to the birds love-learnèd song,
The deawy leaves among!
Nor they of joy and pleasance to you sing,
That all the woods them answer, and theyr eccho ring.

My love is now awake out of her dreames,
And her fayre eyes, like stars that dimmèd were
With darksome cloud, now shew theyr goodly beams
More bright then Hesperus his head doth rere.
Come now, ye damzels, daughters of delight,
Helpe quickly her to dight:
But first come ye fayre houres, which were begot
In Joves sweet paradice of Day and Night;
Which doe the seasons of the yeare allot,
And al, that ever in this world is fayre,
Doe make and still repayre:
And ye three handmayds of the Cyprian Queene,
The which doe still adorne her beauties pride,
Helpe to addorne my beautifullest bride:
And, as ye her array, still throw betweene
Some graces to be seene;
And, as ye use to Venus, to her sing,
The whiles the woods shal answer, and your eccho ring.

ruddock] redbreast.

EDMUND SPENSER

Now is my love all ready forth to come:
Let all the virgins therefore well awayt:
And ye fresh boyes, that tend upon her groome,
Prepare your selves; for he is comming strayt.
Set all your things in seemely good aray,
Fit for so joyfull day:
The joyfulst day that ever sunne did see.
Faire Sun! shew forth thy favourable ray,
And let thy lifull heat not fervent be,
For feare of burning her sunshyny face,
Her beauty to disgrace.
O fayrest Phœbus! father of the Muse!
If ever I did honour thee aright,
Or sing the thing that mote thy mind delight,
Doe not thy servants simple boone refuse;
But let this day, let this one day, be myne;
Let all the rest be thine.
Then I thy soverayne prayses loud wil sing,
That all the woods shal answer, and theyr eccho ring.

Harke! how the Minstrils gin to shrill aloud
Their merry Musick that resounds from far,
The pipe, the tabor, and the trembling Croud,
That well agree withouten breach or jar.
But, most of all, the Damzels doe delite
When they their tymbrels smyte,
And thereunto doe daunce and carrol sweet,
That all the sences they doe ravish quite;
The whyles the boyes run up and downe the street,
Crying aloud with strong confusèd noyce,
As if it were one voyce,

        croud] violin.

Hymen, iö Hymen, Hymen, they do shout;
That even to the heavens theyr shouting shrill
Doth reach, and all the firmament doth fill;
To which the people standing all about,
As in approvance, doe thereto applaud,
And loud advaunce her laud;
And evermore they Hymen, Hymen sing,
That al the woods them answer, and theyr eccho ring.

Loe! where she comes along with portly pace,
Lyke Phœbe, from her chamber of the East,
Arysing forth to run her mighty race,
Clad all in white, that seemes a virgin best.
So well it her beseemes, that ye would weene
Some angell she had beene.
Her long loose yellow locks lyke golden wyre,
Sprinckled with perle, and perling flowres atweene,
Doe lyke a golden mantle her attyre;
And, being crownèd with a girland greene,
Seeme lyke some mayden Queene.
Her modest eyes, abashèd to behold
So many gazers as on her do stare,
Upon the lowly ground affixèd are;
Ne dare lift up her countenance too bold,
But blush to heare her prayses sung so loud,
So farre from being proud.
Nathlesse doe ye still loud her prayses sing,
That all the woods may answer, and your eccho ring.

Tell me, ye merchants daughters, did ye see
So fayre a creature in your towne before;
So sweet, so lovely, and so mild as she,
Adorned with beautyes grace and vertues store?

Her goodly eyes lyke Saphyres shining bright,
Her forehead yvory white,
Her cheekes lyke apples which the sun hath rudded,
Her lips lyke cherryes charming men to byte,
Her brest like to a bowle of creame uncrudded,
Her paps lyke lyllies budded,
Her snowie necke lyke to a marble towre;
And all her body like a pallace fayre,
Ascending up, with many a stately stayre,
To honors seat and chastities sweet bowre.
Why stand ye still ye virgins in amaze,
Upon her so to gaze,
While ye forget your former lay to sing,
To which the woods did answer, and your eccho ring?

But if ye saw that which no eyes can see,
The inward beauty of her lively spright,
Garnisht with heavenly guifts of high degree,
Much more then would ye wonder at that sight,
And stand astonisht lyke to those which red
Medusaes mazeful hed.
There dwels sweet love, and constant chastity,
Unspotted fayth, and comely womanhood,
Regard of honour, and mild modesty;
There vertue raynes as Queene in royal throne,
And giveth lawes alone,
The which the base affections doe obay,
And yeeld theyr services unto her will;
Ne thought of thing uncomely ever may
Thereto approch to tempt her mind to ill.
Had ye once seene these her celestial threasures,
And unrevealèd pleasures,

Then would ye wonder, and her prayses sing,
That al the woods should answer, and your echo ring.

Open the temple gates unto my love,
Open them wide that she may enter in,
And all the postes adorne as doth behove,
And all the pillours deck with girlands trim,
For to receyve this Saynt with honour dew,
That commeth in to you.
With trembling steps, and humble reverence,
She commeth in, before th' Almighties view;
Of her ye virgins learne obedience,
When so ye come into those holy places,
To humble your proud faces:
Bring her up to th' high altar, that she may
The sacred ceremonies there partake,
The which do endlesse matrimony make;
And let the roring Organs loudly play
The praises of the Lord in lively notes;
The whiles, with hollow throates,
The Choristers the joyous Antheme sing,
That al the woods may answere, and their eccho ring.

Behold, whiles she before the altar stands,
Hearing the holy priest that to her speakes,
And blesseth her with his two happy hands,
How the red roses flush up in her cheekes,
And the pure snow, with goodly vermill stayne
Like crimsin dyde in grayne:
That even th' Angels, which continually
About the sacred Altare doe remaine,

Forget their service and about her fly,
Ofte peeping in her face, that seems more fayre,
The more they on it stare.
But her sad eyes, still fastened on the ground.
Are governèd with goodly modesty,
That suffers not one looke to glaunce awry,
Which may let in a little thought unsownd.
Why blush ye, love, to give to me your hand,
The pledge of all our band!
Sing, ye sweet Angels, Alleluya sing,
That all the woods may answere, and your eccho ring.

Now al is done: bring home the bride againe;
Bring home the triumph of our victory:
Bring home with you the glory of her gaine;
With joyance bring her and with jollity.
Never had man more joyfull day then this,
Whom heaven would heape with blis,
Make feast therefore now all this live-long day;
This day for ever to me holy is.
Poure out the wine without restraint or stay,
Poure not by cups, but by the belly full,
Poure out to all that wull,
And sprinkle all the postes and wals with wine,
That they may sweat, and drunken be withall.
Crowne ye God Bacchus with a coronall,
And Hymen also crowne with wreathes of vine;
And let the Graces daunce unto the rest,
For they can doo it best:
The whiles the maydens doe theyr carroll sing,
To which the woods shall answer, and theyr eccho ring.

Ring ye the bels, ye yong men of the towne,
And leave your wonted labors for this day:
This day is holy; doe ye write it downe,
That ye for ever it remember may.
This day the sunne is in his chiefest hight,
With Barnaby the bright,
From whence declining daily by degrees,
He somewhat loseth of his heat and light,
When once the Crab behind his back he sees.
But for this time it ill ordainèd was,
To chose the longest day in all the yeare,
And shortest night, when longest fitter weare:
Yet never day so long, but late would passe.
Ring ye the bels, to make it weare away,
And bonefiers make all day;
And daunce about them, and about them sing,
That all the woods may answer, and your eccho ring.

Ah! when will this long weary day have end,
And lende me leave to come unto my love?
How slowly do the houres theyr numbers spend!
How slowly does sad Time his feathers move!
Hast thee, O fayrest Planet, to thy home,
Within the Westerne fome:
Thy tyrèd steedes long since have need of rest.
Long though it be, at last I see it gloome,
And the bright evening-star with golden creast
Appeare out of the East.
Fayre childe of beauty! glorious lampe of love!
That all the host of heaven in ranks doost lead,
And guydest lovers through the nights sad dread,
How chearefully thou lookest from above,

And seemest to laugh atweene thy twinkling light,
As joying in the sight
Of these glad many, which for joy doe sing,
That all the woods them answer, and their echo ring!

Now ceasse, ye damsels, your delights fore-past;
Enough it is that all the day was youres:
Now day is doen, and night is nighing fast,
Now bring the Bryde into the brydall boures.
The night is come, now soon her disaray,
And in her bed her lay;
Lay her in lillies and in violets,
And silken courteins over her display,
And odourd sheetes, and Arras coverlets.
Behold how goodly my faire love does ly,
In proud humility!
Like unto Maia, when as Jove her took
In Tempe, lying on the flowry gras,
Twixt sleepe and wake, after she weary was,
With bathing in the Acidalian brooke.
Now it is night, ye damsels may be gon,
And leave my love alone,
And leave likewise your former lay to sing:
The woods no more shall answere, nor your echo ring.

Now welcome, night! thou night so long expected,
That long daies labour doest at last defray,
And all my cares, which cruell Love collected
Hast sumd in one, and cancellèd for aye:
Spread thy broad wing over my love and me,
That no man may us see;
And in thy sable mantle us enwrap,

From feare of perrill and foule horror free.
Let no false treason seeke us to entrap,
Nor any dread disquiet once annoy
The safety of our joy;
But let the night be calme, and quietsome,
Without tempestuous storms or sad afray:
Lyke as when Jove with fayre Alcmena lay,
When he begot the great Tirynthian groome:
Or lyke as when he with thy selfe did lie
And begot Majesty.
And let the mayds and yong men cease to sing;
Ne let the woods them answer nor theyr eccho ring.

Let no lamenting cryes, nor dolefull teares,
Be heard all night within, nor yet without:
Ne let false whispers, breeding hidden feares,
Breake gentle sleepe with misconceivèd dout.
Let no deluding dreames, nor dreadfull sights,
Make sudden sad affrights;
Ne let house-fyres, nor lightnings helpelesse harmes,
Ne let the Pouke, nor other evill sprights,
Ne let mischivous witches with theyr charmes,
Ne let hob Goblins, names whose sence we see not,
Fray us with things that be not:
Let not the shriech Oule nor the Storke be heard,
Nor the night Raven, that still deadly yels;
Nor damnèd ghosts, cald up with mighty spels,
Nor griesly vultures, make us once affeard:
Ne let th' unpleasant Quyre of Frogs still croking
Make us to wish theyr choking.
Let none of these theyr drery accents sing;
Ne let the woods them answer, nor theyr eccho ring.

But let stil Silence trew night-watches keepe,
That sacred Peace may in assurance rayne,
And tymely Sleep, when it is tyme to sleepe,
May poure his limbs forth on your pleasant playne;
The whiles an hundred little wingèd loves,
Like divers-fethered doves,
Shall fly and flutter round about your bed,
And in the secret darke, that none reproves,
Their prety stealthes shal worke, and snares shal spread
To filch away sweet snatches of delight,
Conceald through covert night.
Ye sonnes of Venus, play your sports at will!
For greedy pleasure, carelesse of your toyes,
Thinks more upon her paradise of joyes,
Then what ye do, albe it good or ill.
All night therefore attend your merry play,
For it will soone be day:
Now none doth hinder you, that say or sing;
Ne will the woods now answer, nor your Eccho ring.

Who is the same, which at my window peepes?
Or whose is that faire face that shines so bright?
Is it not Cinthia, she that never sleepes,
But walkes about high heaven al the night?
O! fayrest goddesse, do thou not envy
My love with me to spy:
For thou likewise didst love, though now unthought,
And for a fleece of wooll, which privily
The Latmian shepherd once unto thee brought,
His pleasures with thee wrought.
Therefore to us be favorable now;
And sith of wemens labours thou hast charge,

And generation goodly dost enlarge,
Encline thy will t'effect our wishfull vow,
And the chast wombe informe with timely seed
That may our comfort breed:
Till which we cease our hopefull hap to sing;
Ne let the woods us answere, nor our Eccho ring.

And thou, great Juno! which with awful might
The lawes of wedlock still dost patronize;
And the religion of the faith first plight
With sacred rites hast taught to solemnize;
And eeke for comfort often callèd art
Of women in their smart;
Eternally bind thou this lovely band,
And all thy blessings unto us impart.
And thou, glad Genius! in whose gentle hand
The bridale bowre and geniall bed remaine,
Without blemish or staine;
And the sweet pleasures of theyr loves delight
With secret ayde doest succour and supply,
Till they bring forth the fruitfull progeny;
Send us the timely fruit of this same night.
And thou, fayre Hebe! and thou, Hymen free!
Grant that it may so be.
Til which we cease your further prayse to sing;
Ne any woods shall answer, nor your Eccho ring.

And ye high heavens, the temple of the gods,
In which a thousand torches flaming bright
Doe burne, that to us wretched earthly clods
In dreadful darknesse lend desirèd light
And all ye powers which in the same remayne,
More then we men can fayne!

Poure out your blessing on us plentiously,
And happy influence upon us raine,
That we may raise a large posterity,
Which from the earth, which they may long possesse
With lasting happinesse,
Up to your haughty pallaces may mount;
And, for the guerdon of theyr glorious merit,
May heavenly tabernacles there inherit,
Of blessèd Saints for to increase the count.
So let us rest, sweet love, in hope of this,
And cease till then our tymely joyes to sing:
The woods no more us answer, nor our eccho ring!

Song! made in lieu of many ornaments,
With which my love should duly have been dect,
Which cutting off through hasty accidents,
Ye would not stay your dew time to expect,
But promist both to recompens;
Be unto her a goodly ornament,
And for short time an endlesse moniment.

93.   *From 'Daphnaïda'*

An Elegy

SHE fell away in her first ages spring,
  Whil'st yet her leafe was greene, and fresh her rinde,
And whil'st her braunch faire blossomes foorth did bring,
She fell away against all course of kinde.
For age to dye is right, but youth is wrong;
She fel away like fruit blowne downe with winde.
Weepe, Shepheard! weepe, to make my undersong.

EDMUND SPENSER

Yet fell she not as one enforst to dye,
Ne dyde with dread and grudging discontent,
But as one toyld with travaile downe doth lye,
So lay she downe, as if to sleepe she went,
And closde her eyes with carelesse quietnesse;
The whiles soft death away her spirit hent,
And soule assoyld from sinfull fleshlinesse.

How happie was I when I saw her leade
The Shepheards daughters dauncing in a rownd!
How trimly would she trace and softly tread
The tender grasse, with rosie garland crownd!
And when she list advance her heavenly voyce,
Both Nymphes and Muses nigh she made astownd,
And flocks and shepheards causèd to rejoyce.

But now, ye Shepheard lasses! who shall lead
Your wandring troupes, or sing your virelayes?
Or who shall dight your bowres, sith she is dead
That was the Lady of your holy-dayes?
Let now your blisse be turnèd into bale,
And into plaints convert your joyous playes,
And with the same fill every hill and dale.

For I will walke this wandring pilgrimage,
Throughout the world from one to other end,
And in affliction wast my better age:
My bread shall be the anguish of my mind,
My drink the teares which fro mine eyes do raine,
My bed the ground that hardest I may finde;
So will I wilfully increase my paine.

Ne sleepe (the harbenger of wearie wights)
Shall ever lodge upon mine ey-lids more;
Ne shall with rest refresh my fainting sprights,
Nor failing force to former strength restore:
But I will wake and sorrow all the night
With Philumene, my fortune to deplore;
With Philumene, the partner of my plight.

And ever as I see the starres to fall,
And under ground to goe to give them light
Which dwell in darknes, I to minde will call
How my fair Starre (that shinde on me so bright)
Fell sodainly and faded under ground;
Since whose departure, day is turned to night,
And night without a Venus starre is found.

And she, my love that was, my Saint that is,
When she beholds from her celestiall throne
(In which she joyeth in eternall blis)
My bitter penance, will my case bemone,
And pitie me that living thus doo die;
For heavenly spirits have compassion
On mortall men, and rue their miserie.

So when I have with sorowe satisfide
Th' importune fates, which vengeance on me seeke,
And th' heavens with long languor pacifide,
She, for pure pitie of my sufferance meeke,
Will send for me; for which I daylie long:
And will till then my painful penance eeke.
Weep, Shepheard! weep, to make my undersong!

EDMUND SPENSER

94   *Easter*

MOST glorious Lord of Lyfe! that, on this day,
   Didst make Thy triumph over death and sin;
And, having harrowd hell, didst bring away
Captivity thence captive, us to win:
This joyous day, deare Lord, with joy begin;
And grant that we, for whom thou diddest dye,
Being with Thy deare blood clene washt from sin,
May live for ever in felicity!
And that Thy love we weighing worthily,
May likewise love Thee for the same againe;
And for Thy sake, that all lyke deare didst buy,
With love may one another entertayne!
   So let us love, deare Love, lyke as we ought,
   —Love is the lesson which the Lord us taught.

JOHN LYLY   1553–1606

95   *Cards and Kisses*

CUPID and my Campaspe play'd
   At cards for kisses—Cupid paid:
He stakes his quiver, bow, and arrows,
His mother's doves, and team of sparrows;
Loses them too; then down he throws
The coral of his lips, the rose
Growing on's cheek (but none knows how);
With these, the crystal of his brow,
And then the dimple of his chin:
All these did my Campaspe win.
At last he set her both his eyes—
She won, and Cupid blind did rise.
   O Love! has she done this for thee?
   What shall, alas! become of me?

JOHN LYLY

96

Spring's Welcome

WHAT bird so sings, yet so does wail?
  O 'tis the ravish'd nightingale.
Jug, jug, jug, jug, tereu! she cries,
And still her woes at midnight rise.
Brave prick-song! Who is't now we hear?
None but the lark so shrill and clear;
Now at heaven's gate she claps her wings,
The morn not waking till she sings.
Hark, hark, with what a pretty throat
Poor robin redbreast tunes his note!
Hark how the jolly cuckoos sing
Cuckoo! to welcome in the spring!
Cuckoo! to welcome in the spring!

ANTHONY MUNDAY

1553–1633

97

Beauty Bathing

BEAUTY sat bathing by a spring,
  Where fairest shades did hide her;
The winds blew calm, the birds did sing,
  The cool streams ran beside her.
My wanton thoughts enticed mine eye
  To see what was forbidden:
But better memory said Fie;
  So vain desire was chidden—
            Hey nonny nonny O!
            Hey nonny nonny!

Into a slumber then I fell,
　　And fond imagination
Seemèd to see, but could not tell,
　　Her feature or her fashion:
But ev'n as babes in dreams do smile,
　　And sometimes fall a-weeping,
So I awaked as wise that while
　　As when I fell a-sleeping.

SIR PHILIP SIDNEY

1554–1586

98　　*The Bargain*

MY true love hath my heart, and I have his,
　　By just exchange one for another given:
I hold his dear, and mine he cannot miss,
　　There never was a better bargain driven:
　　　　My true love hath my heart, and I have his.

His heart in me keeps him and me in one,
　　My heart in him his thoughts and senses guides:
He loves my heart, for once it was his own,
　　I cherish his because in me it bides:
　　　　My true love hath my heart, and I have his.

99　　*Song*

WHO hath his fancy pleasèd
　　With fruits of happy sight,
Let here his eyes be raisèd
　　On Nature's sweetest light;
A light which doth dissever
　　And yet unite the eyes,
A light which, dying never,
　　Is cause the looker dies.

SIR PHILIP SIDNEY

She never dies, but lasteth
　In life of lover's heart;
He ever dies that wasteth
　In love his chiefest part:
Thus is her life still guarded
　In never-dying faith;
Thus is his death rewarded,
　Since she lives in his death.

Look then, and die! The pleasure
　Doth answer well the pain:
Small loss of mortal treasure,
　Who may immortal gain!
Immortal be her graces,
　Immortal is her mind;
They, fit for heavenly places—
　This, heaven in it doth bind.

But eyes these beauties see not,
　Nor sense that grace descries;
Yet eyes deprivèd be not
　From sight of her fair eyes—
Which, as of inward glory
　They are the outward seal,
So may they live still sorry,
　Which die not in that weal.

But who hath fancies pleasèd
　With fruits of happy sight,
Let here his eyes be raisèd
　On Nature's sweetest light!

100 *Voices at the Window*

WHO is it that, this dark night,
  Underneath my window plaineth?
It is one who from thy sight
  Being, ah, exiled, disdaineth
Every other vulgar light.

Why, alas, and are you he?
  Be not yet those fancies changèd?
Dear, when you find change in me,
  Though from me you be estrangèd,
Let my change to ruin be.

Well, in absence this will die:
  Leave to see, and leave to wonder.
Absence sure will help, if I
  Can learn how myself to sunder
From what in my heart doth lie.

But time will these thoughts remove;
  Time doth work what no man knoweth.
Time doth as the subject prove:
  With time still the affection groweth
In the faithful turtle-dove.

What if you new beauties see?
  Will not they stir new affection?
I will think they pictures be
  (Image-like, of saint's perfection)
Poorly counterfeiting thee.

leave] cease.

But your reason's purest light
  Bids you leave such minds to nourish.
Dear, do reason no such spite!
  Never doth thy beauty flourish
More than in my reason's sight.

101 *Philomela*

THE Nightingale, as soon as April bringeth
  Unto her rested sense a perfect waking,
While late-bare Earth, proud of new clothing, springeth,
  Sings out her woes, a thorn her song-book making;
    And mournfully bewailing,
    Her throat in tunes expresseth
    What grief her breast oppresseth,
For Tereus' force on her chaste will prevailing.

  O Philomela fair, O take some gladness
  That here is juster cause of plaintful sadness!
    Thine earth now springs, mine fadeth;
  Thy thorn without, my thorn my heart invadeth.

Alas! she hath no other cause of anguish
  But Tereus' love, on her by strong hand wroken;
Wherein the suffering, all her spirits languish,
  Full womanlike complains her will was broken
    But I, who, daily craving,
    Cannot have to content me,
    Have more cause to lament me,
Since wanting is more woe than too much having.

  O Philomela fair, O take some gladness
  That here is juster cause of plaintful sadness!
    Thine earth now springs, mine fadeth;
  Thy thorn without, my thorn my heart invadeth.

102   *The Highway*

HIGHWAY, since you my chief Parnassus be,
    And that my Muse, to some ears not unsweet,
Tempers her words to trampling horses' feet
More oft than to a chamber-melody,—
Now blessèd you bear onward blessèd me
To her, where I my heart, safe-left, shall meet;
My Muse and I must you of duty greet
With thanks and wishes, wishing thankfully;
Be you still fair, honour'd by public heed;
By no encroachment wrong'd, nor time forgot;
Nor blamed for blood, nor shamed for sinful deed;
And that you know I envy you no lot
    Of highest wish, I wish you so much bliss,
    Hundreds of years you Stella's feet may kiss!

103   *His Lady's Cruelty*

WITH how sad steps, O moon, thou climb'st the skies!
    How silently, and with how wan a face!
What! may it be that even in heavenly place
That busy archer his sharp arrows tries?
Sure, if that long-with-love-acquainted eyes
Can judge of love, thou feel'st a lover's case:
I read it in thy looks; thy languish'd grace
To me, that feel the like, thy state descries.
Then, even of fellowship, O Moon, tell me,
Is constant love deem'd there but want of wit?
Are beauties there as proud as here they be?
Do they above love to be loved, and yet
    Those lovers scorn whom that love doth possess?
    Do they call 'virtue' there—ungratefulness?

104 *Sleep*

COME, Sleep; O Sleep! the certain knot of peace.
The baiting-place of wit, the balm of woe,
The poor man's wealth, the prisoner's release,
Th' indifferent judge between the high and low;
With shield of proof shield me from out the prease
Of those fierce darts Despair at me doth throw:
O make in me those civil wars to cease;
I will good tribute pay, if thou do so.
Take thou of me smooth pillows, sweetest bed,
A chamber deaf to noise and blind of light,
A rosy garland and a weary head;
And if these things, as being thine by right,
    Move not thy heavy grace, thou shalt in me,
    Livelier than elsewhere, Stella's image see.

105 *Splendidis longum valedico Nugis*

LEAVE me, O Love, which reachest but to dust,
And thou, my mind, aspire to higher things!
Grow rich in that which never taketh rust:
Whatever fades, but fading pleasure brings.
Draw in thy beams, and humble all thy might
To that sweet yoke where lasting freedoms be;
Which breaks the clouds and opens forth the light
That doth both shine and give us sight to see.
O take fast hold! let that light be thy guide
In this small course which birth draws out to death,
And think how evil becometh him to slide
Who seeketh Heaven, and comes of heavenly breath.
    Then farewell, world! thy uttermost I see:
    Eternal Love, maintain thy life in me!

104 prease] press.

FULKE GREVILLE, LORD BROOKE

1554–1628

Myra

I, WITH whose colours Myra dress'd her head,
   I, that ware posies of her own hand-making,
I, that mine own name in the chimneys read
   By Myra finely wrought ere I was waking:
Must I look on, in hope time coming may
With change bring back my turn again to play?

I, that on Sunday at the church-stile found,
   A garland sweet with true-love-knots in flowers,
Which I to wear about mine arms was bound
   That each of us might know that all was ours:
Must I lead now an idle life in wishes,
And follow Cupid for his loaves and fishes?

I, that did wear the ring her mother left,
   I, for whose love she gloried to be blamèd,
I, with whose eyes her eyes committed theft,
   I, who did make her blush wh-n I was namèd:
Must I lose ring, flowers, blush, theft, and go naked,
Watching with sighs till dead love be awakèd?

Was it for this that I might Myra see
   Washing the water with her beauty's white?
Yet would she never write her love to me.
   Thinks wit of change when thoughts are in delight?
Mad girls may safely love as they may leave;
No man can *print* a kiss: lines may deceive.

chimneys] *cheminées*, chimney-screens of tapestry work,
deceive] betray.

THOMAS LODGE

1556?–1625

107 *Rosalind's Madrigal*

LOVE in my bosom like a bee
    Doth suck his sweet:
Now with his wings he plays with me,
    Now with his feet.
Within mine eyes he makes his nest,
His bed amidst my tender breast;
My kisses are his daily feast,
And yet he robs me of my rest:
    Ah! wanton, will ye?

And if I sleep, then percheth he
    With pretty flight,
And makes his pillow of my knee
    The livelong night.
Strike I my lute, he tunes the string;
He music plays if so I sing;
He lends me every lovely thing,
Yet cruel he my heart doth sting:
    Whist, wanton, still ye!

Else I with roses every day
    Will whip you hence,
And bind you, when you long to play,
    For your offence.
I'll shut mine eyes to keep you in;
I'll make you fast it for your sin;
I'll count your power not worth a pin.
—Alas! what hereby shall I win
    If he gainsay me?

What if I beat the wanton boy
  With many a rod?
He will repay me with annoy,
  Because a god.
Then sit thou safely on my knee;
Then let thy bower my bosom be;
Lurk in mine eyes, I like of thee;
O Cupid, so thou pity me,
  Spare not, but play thee!

108 *Phillis* 1

MY Phillis hath the morning sun
 At first to look upon her;
And Phillis hath morn-waking birds
 Her risings still to honour.
My Phillis hath prime-feather'd flowers,
 That smile when she treads on them;
And Phillis hath a gallant flock,
 That leaps since she doth own them.
But Phillis hath too hard a heart,
 Alas that she should have it!
It yields no mercy to desert,
 Nor grace to those that crave it.

109 *Phillis* 2

LOVE guards the roses of thy lips
 And flies about them like a bee;
If I approach he forward skips,
 And if I kiss he stingeth me.

Love in thine eyes doth build his bower,
  And sleeps within their pretty shine;
And if I look the boy will lower,
  And from their orbs shoot shafts divine.

Love works thy heart within his fire,
  And in my tears doth firm the same;
And if I tempt it will retire,
  And of my plaints doth make a game.

Love, let me cull her choicest flowers;
  And pity me, and calm her eye;
Make soft her heart, dissolve her lowers
  Then will I praise thy deity.

But if thou do not, Love, I'll truly serve her
In spite of thee, and by firm faith deserve her.

110   *Rosaline*

LIKE to the clear in highest sphere
    Where all imperial glory shines,
Of selfsame colour is her hair
    Whether unfolded or in twines:
        Heigh ho, fair Rosaline!
Her eyes are sapphires set in snow,
    Resembling heaven by every wink;
The gods do fear whenas they glow,
    And I do tremble when I think
        Heigh ho, would she were mine!

Her cheeks are like the blushing cloud
    That beautifies Aurora's face,
Or like the silver crimson shroud
    That Phœbus' smiling looks doth grace.
        Heigh ho, fair Rosaline!

THOMAS LODGE

Her lips are like two budded roses
　　Whom ranks of lilies neighbour nigh,
Within whose bounds she balm encloses
　　Apt to entice a deity:
　　　　Heigh ho, would she were mine!

Her neck like to a stately tower
　　Where Love himself imprison'd lies,
To watch for glances every hour
　　From her divine and sacred eyes:
　　　　Heigh ho, fair Rosaline!
Her paps are centres of delight,
　　Her breasts are orbs of heavenly frame,
Where Nature moulds the dew of light
　　To feed perfection with the same:
　　　　Heigh ho, would she were mine!

With orient pearl, with ruby red,
　　With marble white, with sapphire blue,
Her body every way is fed,
　　Yet soft to touch and sweet in view:
　　　　Heigh ho, fair Rosaline!
Nature herself her shape admires;
　　The gods are wounded in her sight;
And Love forsakes his heavenly fires
　　And at her eyes his brand doth light:
　　　　Heigh ho, would she were mine!

Then muse not, Nymphs, though I bemoan
　　The absence of fair Rosaline,
Since for a fair there's fairer none,
　　Nor for her virtues so divine:
　　　　Heigh ho, fair Rosaline!
Heigh ho, my heart! would God that she were mine!

1558?–1597

III   *Fair and Fair*

 Œnone. FAIR and fair, and twice so fair,
    As fair as any may be;
    The fairest shepherd on our green,
    A love for any lady.

 Paris. Fair and fair, and twice so fair,
    As fair as any may be;
    Thy love is fair for thee alone
    And for no other lady.

 Œnone. My love is fair, my love is gay,
    As fresh as bin the flowers in May
    And of my love my roundelay,
    My merry, merry, merry roundelay,
    Concludes with Cupid's curse,—
    'They that do change old love for new
    Pray gods they change for worse!'

Ambo Simul. They that do change old love for new,
    Pray gods they change for worse!

 Œnone. Fair and fair, etc.
 Paris. Fair and fair, etc.
    Thy love is fair, etc.

 Œnone. My love can pipe, my love can sing,
    My love can many a pretty thing,
    And of his lovely praises ring
    My merry, merry, merry roundelays
    Amen to Cupid's curse,—
    'They that do change,' etc.

 Paris. They that do change, etc.
 Ambo. Fair and fair, etc.

112 *A Summer Song*

WHEN as the rye reach to the chin,
   And chopcherry, chopcherry ripe within,
Strawberries swimming in the cream,
And school-boys playing in the stream;
   Then O, then O, then O my true love said,
      Till that time come again,
   She could not live a maid.

113 *A Farewell to Arms*

(TO QUEEN ELIZABETH)

HIS golden locks Time hath to silver turn'd;
   O Time too swift, O swiftness never ceasing!
His youth 'gainst time and age hath ever spurn'd,
   But spurn'd in vain; youth waneth by increasing:
Beauty, strength, youth, are flowers but fading seen;
Duty, faith, love, are roots, and ever green.

His helmet now shall make a hive for bees;
   And, lovers' sonnets turn'd to holy psalms,
A man-at-arms must now serve on his knees,
   And feed on prayers, which are Age his alms:
But though from court to cottage he depart,
His Saint is sure of his unspotted heart.

And when he saddest sits in homely cell,
   He'll teach his swains this carol for a song,—
'Blest be the hearts that wish my sovereign well.
   Curst be the souls that think her any wrong.'
Goddess, allow this agèd man his right
To be your beadsman now that was your knight.

151

1560–1592

114

Samela

LIKE to Diana in her summer weed,
  Girt with a crimson robe of brightest dye,
    Goes fair Samela.
Whiter than be the flocks that straggling feed
  When wash'd by Arethusa faint they lie,
    Is fair Samela.
As fair Aurora in her morning grey,
  Deck'd with the ruddy glister of her love
    Is fair Samela;
Like lovely Thetis on a calmèd day
  Whenas her brightness Neptune's fancy move,
    Shines fair Samela.

Her tresses gold, her eyes like glassy streams,
  Her teeth are pearl, the breasts are ivory
    Of fair Samela;
Her cheeks like rose and lily yield forth gleams;
  Her brows bright arches framed of ebony.
    Thus fair Samela
Passeth fair Venus in her bravest hue,
  And Juno in the show of majesty
    (For she's Samela!),
Pallas in wit,—all three, if you well view,
  For beauty, wit, and matchless dignity,
    Yield to Samela.

115 *Fawnia*

AH! were she pitiful as she is fair,
Or but as mild as she is seeming so,
Then were my hopes greater than my despair,
Then all the world were heaven, nothing woe.
Ah! were her heart relenting as her hand,
That seems to melt even with the mildest touch,
Then knew I where to seat me in a land
Under wide heavens, but yet there is not such.
So as she shows she seems the budding rose,
Yet sweeter far than is an earthly flower;
Sovran of beauty, like the spray she grows;
Compass'd she is with thorns and canker'd flower.
   Yet were she willing to be pluck'd and worn,
   She would be gather'd, though she grew on thorn.

Ah! when she sings, all music else be still,
For none must be comparèd to her note;
Ne'er breathed such glee from Philomela's bill,
Nor from the morning-singer's swelling throat.
Ah! when she riseth from her blissful bed
She comforts all the world as doth the sun,
And at her sight the night's foul vapour 's fled;
When she is set the gladsome day is done.
   O glorious sun, imagine me the west,
   Shine in my arms, and set thou in my breast!

116 *Sephestia's Lullaby*

WEEP not, my wanton, smile upon my knee;
When thou art old there's grief enough for thee.
   Mother's wag, pretty boy,
   Father's sorrow, father's joy;

ROBERT GREENE

When thy father first did see
Such a boy by him and me,
He was glad, I was woe;
Fortune changèd made him so,
When he left his pretty boy,
Last his sorrow, first his joy.

Weep not, my wanton, smile upon my knee;
When thou art old there 's grief enough for thee.
Streaming tears that never stint,
Like pearl-drops from a flint,
Fell by course from his eyes,
That one another's place supplies;
Thus he grieved in every part,
Tears of blood fell from his heart,
When he left his pretty boy,
Father's sorrow, father's joy.

Weep not, my wanton, smile upon my knee;
When thou art old there 's grief enough for thee.
The wanton smiled, father wept,
Mother cried, baby leapt;
More he crow'd, more we cried,
Nature could not sorrow hide:
He must go, he must kiss
Child and mother, baby bliss,
For he left his pretty boy,
Father's sorrow, father's joy.

Weep not, my wanton, smile upon my knee,
When thou art old there 's grief enough for thee.

GEORGE CHAPMAN

1560–1634

117 *Bridal Song*

O COME, soft rest of cares! come, Night!
　Come, naked Virtue's only tire,
The reapèd harvest of the light
　　Bound up in sheaves of sacred fire.
　　　Love calls to war:
　　　　Sighs his alarms,
　　　Lips his swords are,
　　　　The field his arms.

Come, Night, and lay thy velvet hand
　On glorious Day's outfacing face;
And all thy crownèd flames command
　　For torches to our nuptial grace.
　　　Love calls to war:
　　　　Sighs his alarms,
　　　Lips his swords are,
　　　　The field his arms.

ROBERT SOUTHWELL

1561?–1595

118 *Of the Blessed Sacrament of the Altar*

THE angels' eyes, whom veils cannot deceive,
　Might best disclose that best they do discern;
Men must with sound and silent faith receive
　More than they can by sense or reason learn;
God's power our proofs, His works our wit exceed,
The doer's might is reason of His deed.

ROBERT SOUTHWELL

A body is endued with ghostly rights;
  And Nature's work from Nature's law is free;
In heavenly sun lie hid eternal lights,
  Lights clear and near, yet them no eye can see;
Dead forms a never-dying life do shroud;
A boundless sea lies in a little cloud.

The God of Hosts in slender host doth dwell,
  Yea, God and man with all to either due,
That God that rules the heavens and rifled hell,
  That man whose death did us to life renew:
That God and man that is the angels' bliss,
In form of bread and wine our nurture is.

Whole may His body be in smallest bread,
  Whole in the whole, yea whole in every crumb;
With which be one or be ten thousand fed,
  All to each one, to all but one doth come;
And though each one as much as all receive.
Not one too much, nor all too little have.

One soul in man is all in every part;
  One face at once in many mirrors shines;
One fearful noise doth make a thousand start;
  One eye at once of countless things defines;
If proofs of one in many Nature frame,
God may in stranger sort perform the same.

God present is at once in every place,
  Yet God in every place is ever one;
So may there be by gifts of ghostly grace,
  One man in many rooms, yet filling none;
Since angels may effects of bodies shew,
God angels' gifts on bodies may bestow.

119   *The Burning Babe*

AS I in hoary winter's night
    Stood shivering in the snow,
Surprised I was with sudden heat
    Which made my heart to glow;
And lifting up a fearful eye
    To view what fire was near,
A pretty babe all burning bright
    Did in the air appear;
Who, scorchèd with excessive heat,
    Such floods of tears did shed,
As though His floods should quench His flames,
    Which with His tears were bred:
'Alas!' quoth He, 'but newly born
    In fiery heats I fry,
Yet none approach to warm their hearts
    Or feel my fire but I!

'My faultless breast the furnace is;
    The fuel, wounding thorns;
Love is the fire, and sighs the smoke;
    The ashes, shames and scorns;
The fuel Justice layeth on,
    And Mercy blows the coals,
The metal in this furnace wrought
    Are men's defilèd souls:
For which, as now on fire I am
    To work them to their good,
So will I melt into a bath,
    To wash them in my blood.'

With this He vanish'd out of sight
And swiftly shrunk away,
And straight I callèd unto mind
That it was Christmas Day.

HENRY CONSTABLE

1562?–1613?

120   *On the Death of Sir Philip Sidney*

GIVE pardon blessèd soul, to my bold cries,
  If they, importune, interrupt thy song,
Which now with joyful notes thou sing'st among
The angel-quiristers of th' heavenly skies.
Give pardon eke, sweet soul, to my slow eyes,
That since I saw thee now it is so long,
And yet the tears that unto thee belong
To thee as yet they did not sacrifice.
I did not know that thou wert dead before;
I did not feel the grief I did sustain;
The greater stroke astonisheth the more;
Astonishment takes from us sense of pain;
  I stood amazed when others' tears begun,
  And now begin to weep when they have done.

SAMUEL DANIEL

1562–1619

121   *Love is a Sickness*

LOVE is a sickness full of woes,
  All remedies refusing;
A plant that with most cutting grows,
  Most barren with best using.
          Why so?

More we enjoy it, more it dies;
If not enjoy'd, it sighing cries—
                    Heigh ho!

Love is a torment of the mind,
    A tempest everlasting;
And Jove hath made it of a kind
    Not well, nor full nor fasting.
            Why so?
More we enjoy it, more it dies;
If not enjoy'd, it sighing cries—
                    Heigh ho!

122   *Ulysses and the Siren*

Siren. COME, worthy Greek! Ulysses, come,
        Possess these shores with me:
    The winds and seas are troublesome,
        And here we may be free.
    Here may we sit and view their toil
        That travail in the deep,
    And joy the day in mirth the while,
        And spend the night in sleep.

Ulysses. Fair Nymph, if fame or honour were
        To be attain'd with ease,
    Then would I come and rest me there,
        And leave such toils as these.
    But here it dwells, and here must I
        With danger seek it forth:
    To spend the time luxuriously
        Becomes not men of worth.

Siren.   Ulysses, O be not deceived
      With that unreal name;
  This honour is a thing conceived,
      And rests on others' fame:
  Begotten only to molest
      Our peace, and to beguile
  The best thing of our life—our rest,
      And give us up to toil.

Ulysses.   Delicious Nymph, suppose there were
      No honour nor report,
  Yet manliness would scorn to wear
      The time in idle sport:
  For toil doth give a better touch
      To make us feel our joy,
  And ease finds tediousness as much
      As labour yields annoy.

Siren.   Then pleasure likewise seems the shore
      Whereto tends all your toil,
  Which you forgo to make it more,
      And perish oft the while.
  Who may disport them diversely
      Find never tedious day,
  And ease may have variety
      As well as action may.

Ulysses.   But natures of the noblest frame
      These toils and dangers please;
  And they take comfort in the same
      As much as you in ease;

And with the thought of actions past
    Are recreated still:
When Pleasure leaves a touch at last
    To show that it was ill.

Siren. That doth *Opinion* only cause
    That 's out of *Custom* bred,
Which makes us many other laws
    Than ever *Nature* did.
No widows wail for our delights,
    Our sports are without blood;
The world we see by warlike wights
    Receives more hurt than good.

Ulysses. But yet the state of things require
    These motions of unrest:
And these great Spirits of high desire
    Seem born to turn them best:
To purge the mischiefs that increase
    And all good order mar:
For oft we see a wicked peace
    To be well changed for war.

Siren. Well, well, Ulysses, then I see
    I shall not have thee here:
And therefore I will come to thee,
    And take my fortune there.
I must be won, that cannot win,
    Yet lost were I not won;
For beauty hath created been
    T' undo, or be undone.

123   *Beauty, Time, and Love*

SONNETS. I

FAIR is my Love and cruel as she 's fair;
    Her brow-shades frown, although her eyes are sunny.
Her smiles are lightning, though her pride despair,
And her disdains are gall, her favours honey:
A modest maid, deck'd with a blush of honour,
Whose feet do tread green paths of youth and love;
The wonder of all eyes that look upon her,
Sacred on earth, design'd a Saint above.
Chastity and Beauty, which were deadly foes,
Live reconcilèd friends within her brow;
And had she Pity to conjoin with those,
Then who had heard the plaints I utter now?
   For had she not been fair, and thus unkind,
   My Muse had slept, and none had known my mind.

II

My spotless love hovers with purest wings,
About the temple of the proudest frame,
Where blaze those lights, fairest of earthly things,
Which clear our clouded world with brightest flame.
My ambitious thoughts, confinèd in her face,
Affect no honour but what she can give;
My hopes do rest in limits of her grace;
I weigh no comfort unless she relieve.
For she, that can my heart imparadise,
Holds in her fairest hand what dearest is;
My Fortune's wheel 's the circle of her eyes,
Whose rolling grace deign once a turn of bliss.
   All my life's sweet consists in her alone;
   So much I love the most Unloving one.

III

And yet I cannot reprehend the flight
Or blame th' attempt presuming so to soar;
The mounting venture for a high delight
Did make the honour of the fall the more.
For who gets wealth, that puts not from the shore?
Danger hath honour, great designs their fame;
Glory doth follow, courage goes before;
And though th' event oft answers not the same—
Suffice that high attempts have never shame.
The mean observer, whom base safety keeps,
Lives without honour, dies without a name,
And in eternal darkness ever sleeps.—
    And therefore, *Delia*, 'tis to me no blot
      To have attempted, tho' attain'd thee not.

IV

When men shall find thy flow'r, thy glory, pass,
And thou with careful brow, sitting alone,
Receivèd hast this message from thy glass,
That tells the truth and says that *All is gone;*
Fresh shalt thou see in me the wounds thou mad'st,
Though spent thy flame, in me the heat remaining:
I that have loved thee thus before thou fad'st—
My faith shall wax, when thou art in thy waning.
The world shall find this miracle in me,
That fire can burn when all the matter's spent:
Then what my faith hath been thyself shalt see,
And that thou wast unkind thou may'st repent.—
    Thou may'st repent that thou hast scorn'd my tears,
      When Winter snows upon thy sable hairs.

SAMUEL DANIEL

V

Beauty, sweet Love, is like the morning dew,
Whose short refresh upon the tender green
Cheers for a time, but till the sun doth show,
And straight 'tis gone as it had never been.
Soon doth it fade that makes the fairest flourish,
Short is the glory of the blushing rose;
The hue which thou so carefully dost nourish,
Yet which at length thou must be forced to lose.
When thou, surcharged with burthen of thy years,
Shalt bend thy wrinkles homeward to the earth;
And that, in Beauty's Lease expired, appears
The Date of Age, the Calends of our Death—
    But ah, no more!—this must not be foretold,
    For women grieve to think they must be old.

VI

I must not grieve my Love, whose eyes would read
Lines of delight, whereon her youth might smile;
Flowers have time before they come to seed,
And she is young, and now must sport the while.
And sport, Sweet Maid, in season of these years,
And learn to gather flowers before they wither;
And where the sweetest blossom first appears,
Let Love and Youth conduct thy pleasures thither.
Lighten forth smiles to clear the clouded air,
And calm the tempest which my sighs do raise;
Pity and smiles do best become the fair;
Pity and smiles must only yield thee praise.
    Make me to say when all my griefs are gone,
    Happy the heart that sighed for such a one!

VII

Let others sing of Knights and Paladines
In agèd accents and untimely words,
Paint shadows in imaginary lines,
Which well the reach of their high wit records:
But I must sing of thee, and those fair eyes
Authentic shall my verse in time to come;
When yet th' unborn shall say, *Lo, where she lies!*
Whose beauty made him speak, that else was dumb!
These are the arcs, the trophies I erect,
That fortify thy name against old age;
And these thy sacred virtues must protect
Against the Dark, and Time's consuming rage.
  Though th' error of my youth in them appear,
  Suffice, they show I lived, and loved thee dear.

MARK ALEXANDER BOYD   1563–1601

124 *Sonet*

FRA bank to bank, fra wood to wood I rin,
    Ourhailit with my feeble fantasie;
  Like til a leaf that fallis from a tree,
Or til a reed ourblawin with the win.

Twa gods guides me: the ane of tham is blin,
    Yea and a bairn brocht up in vanitie;
  The next a wife ingenrit of the sea,
And lichter nor a dauphin with her fin.

Unhappy is the man for evermair
    That tills the sand and sawis in the air;
  But twice unhappier is he, I lairn,
That feidis in his hairt a mad desire,
And follows on a woman throw the fire,
    Led by a blind and teachit by a bairn.

JOSHUA SYLVESTER

1561–1618

125   *Ubique*

WERE I as base as is the lowly plain,
    And you, my Love, as high as heaven above,
Yet should the thoughts of me, your humble swain,
Ascend to heaven in honour of my love.
Were I as high as heaven above the plain,
And you, my Love, as humble and as low
As are the deepest bottoms of the main,
Wheresoe'r you were, with you my love should go.
Were you the earth, dear Love, and I the skies,
My love should shine on you like to the Sun,
And look upon you with ten thousand eyes,
Till heaven wax'd blind, and till the world were done.
    Whereso'er I am,—below, or else above you—
    Whereso'er you are, my heart shall truly love you.

MICHAEL DRAYTON

1563–1631

126   *To His Coy Love*

I PRAY thee, leave, love me no more,
    Call home the heart you gave me!
I but in vain that saint adore
    That can but will not save me.
These poor half-kisses kill me quite—
Was ever man thus servèd?
Amidst an ocean of delight
    For pleasure to be starvèd?

Show me no more those snowy breasts
   With azure riverets branchèd,
Where, whilst mine eye with plenty feasts,
   Yet is my thirst not stanchèd;
O Tantalus, thy pains ne'er tell!
   By me thou art prevented:
'Tis nothing to be plagued in Hell,
   But thus in Heaven tormented.

Clip me no more in those dear arms,
   Nor thy life's comfort call me,
O these are but too powerful charms,
   And do but more enthral me!
      But see how patient I am grown
       In all this coil about thee:
        Come, nice thing, let thy heart alone,
        I cannot live without thee!

127   *The Parting*

SINCE there's no help, come let us kiss and part—
  Nay, I have done, you get no more of me;
And I am glad, yea, glad with all my heart,
That thus so cleanly I myself can free.
Shake hands for ever, cancel all our vows,
And when we meet at any time again,
Be it not seen in either of our brows
That we one jot of former love retain.
Now at the last gasp of Love's latest breath,
When, his pulse failing, Passion speechless lies,
When Faith is kneeling by his bed of death,
And Innocence is closing up his eyes,
  —Now if thou wouldst, when all have given him over,
  From death to life thou might'st him yet recover.

MICHAEL DRAYTON

Sirena

NEAR to the silver *Trent*
　　SIRENA dwelleth;
She to whom Nature lent
　　All that excelleth;
By which the Muses late
　　And the neat Graces
Have for their greater state
　　Taken their places;
Twisting an anadem
　　Wherewith to crown her,
As it belong'd to them
　　Most to renown her.
　　　　　On thy bank,
　　　　　In a rank,
　　　　　　Let thy swans sing her,
　　　　　And with their music
　　　　　　Along let them bring her.

Tagus and *Pactolus*
　　Are to thee debtor,
Nor for their gold to us
　　Are they the better:
Henceforth of all the rest
　　Be thou the River
Which, as the daintiest,
　　Puts them down ever.
For as my precious one
　　O'er thee doth travel,
She to pearl paragon
　　Turneth thy gravel.
　　　　　On thy bank . . .

MICHAEL DRAYTON

Our mournful Philomel,
　That rarest tuner,
Henceforth in Aperil
　Shall wake the sooner,
And to her shall complain
　From the thick cover,
Redoubling every strain
　Over and over:
For when my Love too long
　Her chamber keepeth,
As though it suffer'd wrong,
　The Morning weepeth.
　　　　On thy bank . . .

Oft have I seen the Sun,
　To do her honour,
Fix himself at his noon
　To look upon her;
And hath gilt every grove,
　Every hill near her,
With his flames from above
　Striving to cheer her:
And when she from his sight
　Hath herself turnèd,
He, as it had been night,
　In clouds hath mournèd.
　　　　On thy bank . . .

The verdant meads are seen,
　When she doth view them,
In fresh and gallant green
　Straight to renew them;

And every little grass
  Broad itself spreadeth,
Proud that this bonny lass
  Upon it treadeth:
Nor flower is so sweet
  In this large cincture,
But it upon her feet
  Leaveth some tincture.
        On thy bank . . .

The fishes in the flood,
  When she doth angle,
For the hook strive a-good
  Them to entangle;
And leaping on the land,
  From the clear water,
Their scales upon the sand
  Lavishly scatter;
Therewith to pave the mould
  Whereon she passes,
So herself to behold
  As in her glasses.
        On thy bank . . .

When she looks out by night,
  The stars stand gazing,
Like comets to our sight
  Fearfully blazing;
As wond'ring at her eyes
  With their much brightness,
Which so amaze the skies,
  Dimming their lightness.

MICHAEL DRAYTON

The raging tempests are calm
   When she speaketh,
Such most delightsome balm
   From her lips breaketh.
       On thy bank . . .

In all our *Brittany*
   There 's not a fairer,
Nor can you fit any
   Should you compare her.
Angels her eyelids keep,
   All hearts surprising;
Which look whilst she doth sleep
   Like the sun's rising:
She alone of her kind
   Knoweth true measure,
And her unmatchèd mind
   Is heaven's treasure.
       On thy bank . . .

Fair *Dove* and *Darwen* clear,
   Boast ye your beauties,
To *Trent* your mistress here
   Yet pay your duties:
My Love was higher born
   Tow'rds the full fountains,
Yet she doth moorland scorn
   And the *Peak* mountains;
Nor would she none should dream
   Where she abideth,
Humble as is the stream
   Which by her slideth.
       On thy bank . . .

Yet my poor rustic Muse
  Nothing can move her,
Nor the means I can use,
  Though her true lover:
Many a long winter's night
  Have I waked for her,
Yet this my piteous plight
  Nothing can stir her.
All thy sands, silver *Trent*,
  Down to the *Humber*,
The sighs that I have spent
  Never can number.
      On thy bank,
      In a rank,
        Let thy swans sing her,
      And with their music
        Along let them bring her.

129   *Agincourt*

FAIR stood the wind for France
    When we our sails advance,
Nor now to prove our chance
    Longer will tarry;
But putting to the main,
At Caux, the mouth of Seine,
With all his martial train
    Landed King Harry.

And taking many a fort,
Furnish'd in warlike sort,
Marcheth tow'rds Agincourt
    In happy hour;

MICHAEL DRAYTON

Skirmishing day by day
With those that stopp'd his way,
Where the French gen'ral lay
    With all his power.

Which, in his height of pride,
King Henry to deride,
His ransom to provide
    Unto him sending;
Which he neglects the while
As from a nation vile,
Yet with an angry smile
    Their fall portending.

And turning to his men,
Quoth our brave Henry then,
'Though they to one be ten
    Be not amazèd:
Yet have we well begun;
Battles so bravely won
Have ever to the sun
    By fame been raisèd.

'And for myself (quoth he):
This my full rest shall be:
England ne'er mourn for me
    Nor more esteem me:
Victor I will remain
Or on this earth lie slain,
Never shall she sustain
    Loss to redeem me.

'Poitiers and Cressy tell,
When most their pride did swell,

MICHAEL DRAYTON

Under our swords they fell:
   No less our skill is
Than when our grandsire great,
Claiming the regal seat,
By many a warlike feat
   Lopp'd the French lilies.'

The Duke of York so dread
The eager vaward led;
With the main Henry sped
   Among his henchmen.
Excester had the rear,
A braver man not there;
O Lord, how hot they were
   On the false Frenchmen!

They now to fight are gone,
Armour on armour shone,
Drum now to drum did groan,
   To hear was wonder;
That with the cries they make
The very earth did shake:
Trumpet to trumpet spake,
   Thunder to thunder.

Well it thine age became,
O noble Erpingham,
Which didst the signal aim
   To our hid forces!
When from a meadow by,
Like a storm suddenly
The English archery
   Stuck the French horses.

MICHAEL DRAYTON

With Spanish yew so strong,
Arrows a cloth-yard long
That like to serpents stung,
    Piercing the weather;
None from his fellow starts,
But playing manly parts,
And like true English hearts
    Stuck close together.

When down their bows they threw,
And forth their bilbos drew,
And on the French they flew,
    Not one was tardy;
Arms were from shoulders sent,
Scalps to the teeth were rent,
Down the French peasants went—
    Our men were hardy!

This while our noble king,
His broadsword brandishing,
Down the French host did ding
    As to o'erwhelm it;
And many a deep wound lent,
His arms with blood besprent,
And many a cruel dent
    Bruisèd his helmet.

Gloster, that duke so good,
Next of the royal blood,
For famous England stood
    With his brave brother;

    bilbos] swords, from Bilboa.

Clarence, in steel so bright,
Though but a maiden knight,
Yet in that furious fight
    Scarce such another.

Warwick in blood did wade,
Oxford the foe invade,
And cruel slaughter made
    Still as they ran up;
Suffolk his axe did ply,
Beaumont and Willoughby
Bare them right doughtily,
    Ferrers and Fanhope.

Upon Saint Crispin's Day
Fought was this noble fray,
Which fame did not delay
    To England to carry.
O when shall English men
With such acts fill a pen?
Or England breed again
    Such a King Harry?

130   *To the Virginian Voyage*

YOU brave heroic minds
    Worthy your country's name,
That honour still pursue;
    Go and subdue!
Whilst loitering hinds
    Lurk here at home with shame.

MICHAEL DRAYTON

Britons, you stay too long:
   Quickly aboard bestow you,
     And with a merry gale
     Swell your stretch'd sail
With vows as strong
   As the winds that blow you.

Your course securely steer,
   West and by south forth keep
     Rocks, lee-shores, nor shoals
     When Eolus scowls
You need not fear;
   So absolute the deep.

And cheerfully at sea
   Success you still entice
     To get the pearl and gold,
     And ours to hold
Virginia,
   Earth's only paradise.

Where nature hath in store
   Fowl, venison, and fish,
     And the fruitfull'st soil
     Without your toil
Three harvests more,
   All greater than your wish.

And the ambitious vine
   Crowns with his purple mass
     The cedar reaching high
     To kiss the sky,
The cypress, pine,
   And useful sassafras.

MICHAEL DRAYTON

To whom the Golden Age
   Still nature's laws doth give,
      No other cares attend,
      But them to defend
From winter's rage,
   That long there doth not live.

When as the luscious smell
   Of that delicious land
      Above the seas that flows
      The clear wind throws,
Your hearts to swell
   Approaching the dear strand;

In kenning of the shore
   (Thanks to God first given)
      O you the happiest men,
      Be frolic then!
Let cannons roar,
   Frighting the wide heaven.

And in regions far,
   Such heroes bring ye forth
      As those from whom we came;
      And plant our name
Under that star
   Not known unto our North.

And as there plenty grows
   Of laurel everywhere—
      Apollo's sacred tree—
      You it may see
A poet's brows
   To crown, that may sing there.

Thy *Voyages* attend,
  Industrious Hakluyt,
    Whose reading shall inflame
    Men to seek fame,
And much commend
  To after times thy wit.

CHRISTOPHER MARLOWE

1564–1593

131 *The Passionate Shepherd to His Love*

COME live with me and be my Love,
  And we will all the pleasures prove
That hills and valleys, dales and fields,
Or woods or steepy mountain yields.

And we will sit upon the rocks,
And see the shepherds feed their flocks
By shallow rivers, to whose falls
Melodious birds sing madrigals.

And I will make thee beds of roses
And a thousand fragrant posies;
A cap of flowers, and a kirtle
Embroider'd all with leaves of myrtle.

A gown made of the finest wool
Which from our pretty lambs we pull;
Fair-linèd slippers for the cold,
With buckles of the purest gold.

A belt of straw and ivy-buds
With coral clasps and amber studs:
And if these pleasures may thee move,
Come live with me and be my Love.

The shepherd swains shall dance and sing
For thy delight each May morning:
If these delights thy mind may move,
Then live with me and be my Love.

132 *Her Reply*

(WRITTEN BY SIR WALTER RALEIGH)

IF all the world and love were young,
    And truth in every shepherd's tongue,
These pretty pleasures might me move
To live with thee and be thy Love.

But Time drives flocks from field to fold;
When rivers rage and rocks grow cold;
And Philomel becometh dumb;
The rest complains of cares to come.

The flowers do fade, and wanton fields
To wayward Winter reckoning yields:
A honey tongue, a heart of gall,
Is fancy's spring, but sorrow's fall.

Thy gowns, thy shoes, thy beds of roses,
Thy cap, thy kirtle, and thy posies,
Soon break, soon wither—soon forgotten,
In folly ripe, in reason rotten.

Thy belt of straw and ivy-buds,
Thy coral clasps and amber studs,—
All these in me no means can move
To come to thee and be thy Love.

But could youth last, and love still breed,
Had joys no date, nor age no need,
Then these delights my mind might move
To live with thee and be thy Love.

WILLIAM SHAKESPEARE

133   *Silvia*

WHO is Silvia? What is she?
    That all our swains commend her?
Holy, fair, and wise is she;
    The heaven such grace did lend her,
That she might admirèd be.

Is she kind as she is fair?
    For beauty lives with kindness:
Love doth to her eyes repair,
    To help him of his blindness;
And, being help'd, inhabits there.

Then to Silvia let us sing,
    That Silvia is excelling;
She excels each mortal thing
    Upon the dull earth dwelling:
To her let us garlands bring.

134   *The Blossom*

ON a day—alack the day!—
    Love, whose month is ever May,
Spied a blossom passing fair
Playing in the wanton air:
Through the velvet leaves the wind
All unseen 'gan passage find;
That the lover, sick to death,
Wish'd himself the heaven's breath.
Air, quoth he, thy cheeks may blow;
Air, would I might triumph so!

But, alack, my hand is sworn
Ne'er to pluck thee from thy thorn:
Vow, alack, for youth unmeet;
Youth so apt to pluck a sweet!
Do not call it sin in me
That I am forsworn for thee;
Thou for whom e'en Jove would swear
Juno but an Ethiop were;
And deny himself for Jove,
Turning mortal for thy love.

135   *Spring and Winter*

(i)

WHEN daisies pied and violets blue,
  And lady-smocks all silver-white,
And cuckoo-buds of yellow hue
  Do paint the meadows with delight,
The cuckoo then, on every tree,
Mocks married men; for thus sings he,
      Cuckoo!
Cuckoo, cuckoo!—O word of fear,
Unpleasing to a married ear!

When shepherds pipe on oaten straws,
  And merry larks are ploughmen's clocks,
When turtles tread, and rooks, and daws,
  And maidens bleach their summer smocks
The cuckoo then, on every tree,
Mocks married men; for thus sings he,
      Cuckoo!
Cuckoo, cuckoo!—O word of fear,
Unpleasing to a married ear!

136

(ii)

WHEN icicles hang by the wall,
    And Dick the shepherd blows his nail.
And Tom bears logs into the hall,
    And milk comes frozen home in pail,
When blood is nipp'd and ways be foul,
Then nightly sings the staring owl,
                To-whit!
To-who!—a merry note,
While greasy Joan doth keel the pot.

When all aloud the wind doth blow,
    And coughing drowns the parson's saw,
And birds sit brooding in the snow,
    And Marian's nose looks red and raw,
When roasted crabs hiss in the bowl,
Then nightly sings the staring owl,
                To-whit!
To-who!—a merry note,
While greasy Joan doth keel the pot.

137   *Fairy Land*

(i)

OVER hill, over dale,
    Thorough bush, thorough brier,
Over park, over pale,
    Thorough flood, thorough fire,
    I do wander everywhere,
    Swifter than the moonè's sphere;

        136 keel] skim.

And I serve the fairy queen,
To dew her orbs upon the green:
The cowslips tall her pensioners be;
In their gold coats spots you see;
Those be rubies, fairy favours,
In those freckles live their savours:
I must go seek some dew-drops here,
And hang a pearl in every cowslip's ear.

138   (*ii*)

YOU spotted snakes with double tongue,
  Thorny hedgehogs, be not seen;
Newts and blind-worms, do no wrong;
  Come not near our fairy queen.

    Philomel, with melody,
    Sing in our sweet lullaby;
  Lulla, lulla, lullaby; lulla, lulla, lullaby!
      Never harm,
      Nor spell nor charm,
    Come our lovely lady nigh;
    So, good night, with lullaby.

Weaving spiders, come not here;
  Hence, you long-legg'd spinners, hence!
Beetles black, approach not near;
  Worm nor snail, do no offence.

    Philomel, with melody,
    Sing in our sweet lullaby;
  Lulla, lulla, lullaby; lulla, lulla, lullaby!
      Never harm,
      Nor spell nor charm,
    Come our lovely lady nigh;
    So, good night, with lullaby!

139 (*iii*)

COME unto these yellow sands,
  And then take hands:
Court'sied when you have, and kiss'd,—
  The wild waves whist,—
Foot it featly here and there;
And, sweet sprites, the burthen bear.
      Hark, hark!
        Bow, wow,
        The watch-dogs bark:
        Bow, wow.
        Hark, hark! I hear
      The strain of strutting chanticleer
    Cry, Cock-a-diddle-dow!

140 (*iv*)

WHERE the bee sucks, there suck I:
  In a cowslip's bell I lie;
There I couch when owls do cry.
On the bat's back I do fly
After summer merrily:
  Merrily, merrily, shall I live now,
  Under the blossom that hangs on the bough.

141 (*v*)

FULL fathom five thy father lies;
  Of his bones are coral made;
Those are pearls that were his eyes:
  Nothing of him that doth fade,

But doth suffer a sea-change
Into something rich and strange.
Sea-nymphs hourly ring his knell:
                        Ding-dong.
   Hark! now I hear them—
                        Ding-dong, bell!

142   *Love*

T ELL me where is Fancy bred,
   Or in the heart or in the head?
How begot, how nourishèd?
        Reply, reply.
It is engender'd in the eyes,
With gazing fed; and Fancy dies
In the cradle where it lies.
        Let us all ring Fancy's knell:
        I'll begin it,—Ding, dong, bell!
All. Ding, dong, bell!

143   *Sweet-and-Twenty*

O MISTRESS mine, where are you roaming?
   O, stay and hear! your true love's coming,
   That can sing both high and low:
Trip no further, pretty sweeting;
Journeys end in lovers meeting,
   Every wise man's son doth know.
   What is love? 'tis not hereafter;
   Present mirth hath present laughter;
      What's to come is still unsure:
   In delay there lies no plenty;
   Then come kiss me, sweet-and-twenty!
      Youth's a stuff will not endure.

144   *Dirge*

COME away, come away, death,
　　And in sad cypres let me be laid;
Fly away, fly away, breath;
　I am slain by a fair cruel maid.
My shroud of white, stuck all with yew,
　　　　O prepare it!
My part of death, no one so true
　　　　Did share it.

Not a flower, not a flower sweet,
　On my black coffin let there be strown;
Not a friend, not a friend greet
　My poor corse, where my bones shall be thrown:
A thousand thousand sighs to save,
　　　　Lay me, O, where
Sad true lover never find my grave
　　　　To weep there!

145   *Under the Greenwood Tree*

Amiens sings:

UNDER the greenwood tree,
　　Who loves to lie with me,
And turn his merry note
Unto the sweet bird's throat,
Come hither, come hither, come hither:
　　　Here shall he see
　　　No enemy
But winter and rough weather.

144 cypres] crape.

Who doth ambition shun,
And loves to live i' the sun,
Seeking the food he eats,
And pleased with what he gets,
Come hither, come hither, come hither:
Here shall he see
No enemy
But winter and rough weather.

Jaques replies:
If it do come to pass
That any man turn ass,
Leaving his wealth and ease
A stubborn will to please,
Ducdamè, ducdamè, ducdamè:
Here shall he see
Gross fools as he,
An if he will come to me.

146   *Blow, blow, thou Winter Wind*

BLOW, blow, thou winter wind,
Thou art not so unkind
As man's ingratitude;
Thy tooth is not so keen,
Because thou art not seen,
Although thy breath be rude.
Heigh ho! sing, heigh ho! unto the green holly:
Most friendship is feigning, most loving mere folly:
Then heigh ho, the holly!
This life is most jolly.

Freeze, freeze, thou bitter sky,
That dost not bite so nigh
    As benefits forgot:
Though thou the waters warp,
Thy sting is not so sharp
    As friend remember'd not.
Heigh ho! sing, heigh ho! unto the green holly:
Most friendship is feigning, most loving mere folly:
    Then heigh ho, the holly!
    This life is most jolly.

147   *It was a Lover and his Lass*

IT was a lover and his lass,
    With a hey, and a ho, and a hey nonino,
That o'er the green corn-field did pass,
    In the spring time, the only pretty ring time,
When birds do sing, hey ding a ding, ding;
Sweet lovers love the spring.

Between the acres of the rye,
    With a hey, and a ho, and a hey nonino,
These pretty country folks would lie,
    In the spring time, the only pretty ring time,
When birds do sing, hey ding a ding, ding;
Sweet lovers love the spring.

This carol they began that hour,
    With a hey, and a ho, and a hey nonino,
How that life was but a flower
    In the spring time, the only pretty ring time,
When birds do sing, hey ding a ding, ding;
Sweet lovers love the spring.

And, therefore, take the present time
　　With a hey, and a ho, and a hey nonino,
For love is crownèd with the prime
　　In the spring time, the only pretty ring time,
When birds do sing, hey ding a ding, ding;
Sweet lovers love the spring.

148　　*Take, O take those Lips away*

TAKE, O take those lips away,
　　That so sweetly were forsworn;
And those eyes, the break of day,
　　Lights that do mislead the morn!
But my kisses bring again,
　　　　　　Bring again;
Seals of love, but seal'd in vain,
　　　　　· Seal'd in vain!

149　　*Aubade*

HARK! hark! the lark at heaven's gate sings,
　　And Phœbus 'gins arise,
His steeds to water at those springs
　　On chaliced flowers that lies;
And winking Mary-buds begin
　　To ope their golden eyes:
With everything that pretty bin,
　　My lady sweet, arise!
　　　　Arise, arise!

150　　*Fidele*

FEAR no more the heat o' the sun,
　　Nor the furious winter's rages;
Thou thy worldly task hast done,
　　Home art gone, and ta'en thy wages:

Golden lads and girls all must,
As chimney-sweepers, come to dust.

Fear no more the frown o' the great,
   Thou art past the tyrant's stroke;
Care no more to clothe and eat;
   To thee the reed is as the oak:
The sceptre, learning, physic, must
All follow this, and come to dust.

Fear no more the lightning-flash,
   Nor the all-dreaded thunder-stone;
Fear not slander, censure rash;
   Thou hast finish'd joy and moan:
All lovers young, all lovers must
Consign to thee, and come to dust.

No exorciser harm thee!
Nor no witchcraft charm thee!
Ghost unlaid forbear thee!
Nothing ill come near thee!
Quiet consummation have;
And renownèd be thy grave!

151   *Bridal Song*

ROSES, their sharp spines being gone,
   Not royal in their smells alone,
    But in their hue;
Maiden pinks, of odour faint,
Daisies smell-less, yet most quaint,
   And sweet thyme true;

Primrose, firstborn child of Ver;
Merry springtime's harbinger,
   With harebells dim;
Oxlips in their cradles growing,
Marigolds on death-beds blowing,
   Larks'-heels trim;

All dear Nature's children sweet
Lie 'fore bride and bridegroom's feet,
   Blessing their sense!
Not an angel of the air,
Bird melodious or bird fair,
   Be absent hence!

The crow, the slanderous cuckoo, nor
The boding raven, nor chough hoar,
   Nor chattering pye,
May on our bride-house perch or sing,
Or with them any discord bring,
   But from it fly!

             ? or John Fletcher.

152   *Dirge of the Three Queens*

URNS and odours bring away!
   Vapours, sighs, darken the day!
Our dole more deadly looks than dying;
   Balms and gums and heavy cheers,
   Sacred vials fill'd with tears,
And clamours through the wild air flying!

   Come, all sad and solemn shows,
   That are quick-eyed Pleasure's foes!
   We convènt naught else but woes.

             ? or John Fletcher.

152 dole] lamentation.   convent] summon.

153 *Orpheus*

ORPHEUS with his lute made trees
　　And the mountain tops that freeze
　Bow themselves when he did sing:
To his music plants and flowers
Ever sprung; as sun and showers
　There had made a lasting spring.

Every thing that heard him play,
Even the billows of the sea,
　Hung their heads and then lay by.
In sweet music is such art,
　Killing care and grief of heart
　Fall asleep, or, hearing, die.

　　　　　　　　　　? or John Fletcher.

154 *The Phœnix and the Turtle*

LET the bird of loudest lay
　　On the sole Arabian tree,
　Herald sad and trumpeʋ be,
To whose sound chaste wings obey.

But thou shrieking harbinger,
　Foul precurrer of the fiend,
　Augur of the fever's end,
To this troop come thou not near.

From this session interdict
　Every fowl of tyrant wing
　Save the eagle, feather'd king.
Keep the obsequy so strict.

WILLIAM SHAKESPEARE

Let the priest in surplice white
    That defunctive music can,
    Be the death-divining swan,
Lest the requiem lack his right

And thou, treble-dated crow,
    That thy sable gender mak'st
    With the breath thou giv'st and tak'st,
'Mongst our mourners shalt thou go.

Here the anthem doth commence:—
    Love and constancy is dead;
    Phœnix and the turtle fled
In a mutual flame from hence.

So they loved, as love in twain
    Had the essence but in one;
    Two distincts, division none;
Number there in love was slain.

Hearts remote, yet not asunder;
    Distance, and no space was seen
    'Twixt the turtle and his queen:
But in them it were a wonder.

So between them love did shine,
    That the turtle saw his right
    Flaming in the phœnix' sight;
Either was the other's mine.

Property was thus appall'd,
    That the self was not the same;
    Single nature's double name
Neither two nor one was call'd.

        can] knows.

Reason, in itself confounded,
   Saw division grow together;
   To themselves yet either neither;
Simple were so well compounded,

That it cried, 'How true a twain
   Seemeth this concordant one!
   Love hath reason, reason none
If what parts can so remain.'

Whereupon it made this threne
   To the phœnix and the dove,
   Co-supremes and stars of love,
As chorus to their tragic scene.

THRENOS

BEAUTY, truth, and rarity,
   Grace in all simplicity,
Here enclosed in cinders lie.

Death is now the phœnix' nest;
And the turtle's loyal breast
To eternity doth rest,

Leaving no posterity:
'Twas not their infirmity,
It was married chastity.

Truth may seem, but cannot be;
Beauty brag, but 'tis not she;
Truth and beauty buried be.

To this urn let those repair
That are either true or fair;
For these dead birds sigh a prayer.

WILLIAM SHAKESPEARE

Sonnets

(i)

155

SHALL I compare thee to a Summer's day?
   Thou art more lovely and more temperate:
Rough winds do shake the darling buds of May,
And Summer's lease hath all too short a date:
Sometime too hot the eye of heaven shines,
And often is his gold complexion dimm'd;
And every fair from fair sometime declines,
By chance or nature's changing course untrimm'd:
But thy eternal Summer shall not fade
Nor lose possession of that fair thou owest;
Nor shall Death brag thou wanderest in his shade,
When in eternal lines to time thou growest:
   So long as men can breathe, or eyes can see,
   So long lives this, and this gives life to thee.

(ii)

156

WHEN, in disgrace with Fortune and men's eyes,
   I all alone beweep my outcast state,
And trouble deaf heaven with my bootless cries,
And look upon myself, and curse my fate,
Wishing me like to one more rich in hope,
Featured like him, like him with friends possest,
Desiring this man's art and that man's scope,
With what I most enjoy contented least;
Yet in these thoughts myself almost despising—
Haply I think on thee: and then my state,
Like to the Lark at break of day arising
From sullen earth, sings hymns at Heaven's gate;
   For thy sweet love rememb'red such wealth brings
   That then I scorn to change my state with Kings.

157   (*iii*)

WHEN to the Sessions of sweet silent thought
    I summon up remembrance of things past,
I sigh the lack of many a thing I sought,
And with old woes new wail my dear time's waste:
Then can I drown an eye, unused to flow,
For precious friends hid in death's dateless night,
And weep afresh love's long-since-cancell'd woe,
And moan th' expense of many a vanish'd sight:
Then can I grieve at grievances foregone,
And heavily from woe to woe tell o'er
The sad account of fore-bemoanèd moan,
Which I new pay as if not paid before.
    But if the while I think on thee, dear friend,
    All losses are restored and sorrows end.

158   (*iv*)

THY bosom is endearèd with all hearts
    Which I, by lacking, have supposèd dead:
And there reigns Love, and all Love's loving parts,
And all those friends which I thought burièd.
How many a holy and obsequious tear
Hath dear religious love stol'n from mine eye,
As interest of the dead!—which now appear
But things removed that hidden in thee lie.
Thou art the grave where buried love doth live,
Hung with the trophies of my lovers gone,
Who all their parts of me to thee did give:
—That due of many now is thine alone:
    Their images I loved I view in thee,
    And thou, all they, hast all the all of me.

159   (*v*)

WHAT is your substance, whereof are you made,
   That millions of strange shadows on you tend?
Since every one hath, every one, one shade,
And you, but one, can every shadow lend.
Describe Adonis, and the counterfeit
Is poorly imitated after you;
On Helen's cheek all art of beauty set,
And you in Grecian tires are painted new:
Speak of the spring and foison of the year,
The one doth shadow of your beauty show,
The other as your bounty doth appear;
And you in every blessèd shape we know.
   In all external grace you have some part,
   But you like none, none you, for constant heart.

160   (*vi*)

O HOW much more doth beauty beauteous seem
   By that sweet ornament which truth doth give!
The Rose looks fair, but fairer we it deem
For that sweet odour which doth in it live.
The Canker-blooms have full as deep a dye
As the perfumèd tincture of the Roses,
Hang on such thorns, and play as wantonly
When summer's breath their maskèd buds discloses:
But—for their virtue only is their show—
They live unwoo'd and unrespected fade,
Die to themselves. Sweet Roses do not so;
Of their sweet deaths are sweetest odours made.
   And so of you, beauteous and lovely youth,
   When that shall vade, my verse distils your truth.

159 foison] plenty.

161 *(vii)*

BEING your slave, what should I do but tend
Upon the hours and times of your desire?
I have no precious time at all to spend,
Nor services to do, till you require.
Nor dare I chide the world-without-end hour
Whilst I, my sovereign, watch the clock for you,
Nor think the bitterness of absence sour
When you have bid your servant once adieu;
Nor dare I question with my jealous thought
Where you may be, or your affairs suppose,
But, like a sad slave, stay and think of nought
Save, where you are how happy you make those!
   So true a fool is love, that in your Will,
   Though you do any thing, he thinks no ill.

162 *(viii)*

THAT time of year thou may'st in me behold
When yellow leaves, or none, or few, do hang
Upon those boughs which shake against the cold—
Bare ruin'd choirs where late the sweet birds sang.
In me thou see'st the twilight of such day
As after Sunset fadeth in the West,
Which by and by black night doth take away,
Death's second self, that seals up all in rest.
In me thou see'st the glowing of such fire
That on the ashes of his youth doth lie,
As the death-bed whereon it must expire,
Consumed with that which it was nourish'd by.
   This thou perceiv'st, which makes thy love more strong
   To love that well which thou must leave ere long.

163   *(ix)*

FAREWELL! thou art too dear for my possessing,
   And like enough thou know'st thy estimate:
The charter of thy worth gives thee releasing;
My bonds in thee are all determinate.
For how do I hold thee but by thy granting?
And for that riches where is my deserving?
The cause of this fair gift in me is wanting,
And so my patent back again is swerving.
Thyself thou gav'st, thy own worth then not knowing,
Or me, to whom thou gav'st it, else mistaking;
So thy great gift, upon misprision growing,
Comes home again, on better judgment making.
    Thus have I had thee, as a dream doth flatter
    In sleep a King; but waking, no such matter.

164   *(x)*

THEN hate me when thou wilt; if ever, now;
   Now, while the world is bent my deeds to cross,
Join with the spite of fortune, make me bow,
And do not drop in for an after loss:
Ah! do not, when my heart hath 'scaped this sorrow,
Come in the rearward of a conquer'd woe;
Give not a windy night a rainy morrow,
To linger out a purposed overthrow.
If thou wilt leave me, do not leave me last,
When other petty griefs have done their spite,
But in the onset come: so shall I taste
At first the very worst of fortune's might;
    And other strains of woe, which now seem woe,
    Compared with loss of thee will not seem so!

165 (*xi*)

THEY that have power to hurt and will do none,
That do not do the thing they most do show,
Who, moving others, are themselves as stone,
Unmovèd, cold, and to temptation slow—
They rightly do inherit Heaven's graces,
And husband Nature's riches from expense;
They are the Lords and owners of their faces,
Others, but stewards of their excellence.
The Summer's flower is to the Summer sweet,
Though to itself it only live and die;
But if that flower with base infection meet,
The basest weed outbraves his dignity:
    For sweetest things turn sourest by their deeds;
    Lilies that fester smell far worse than weeds.

166 (*xii*)

HOW like a Winter hath my absence been
From thee, the pleasure of the fleeting year!
What freezings have I felt, what dark days seen,
What old December's bareness everywhere!
And yet this time removed was summer's time;
The teeming Autumn, big with rich increase,
Bearing the wanton burden of the prime
Like widow'd wombs after their Lord's decease:
Yet this abundant issue seem'd to me
But hope of orphans and unfather'd fruit;
For Summer and his pleasures wait on thee,
And, thou away, the very birds are mute:
    Or if they sing, 'tis with so dull a cheer
    That leaves look pale, dreading the Winter's near.

167 *(xiii)*

FROM you have I been absent in the spring,
  When proud-pied April, dress'd in all his trim,
Hath put a spirit of youth in everything,
That heavy Saturn laugh'd and leap'd with him.
Yet nor the lays of birds, nor the sweet smell
Of different flowers in odour and in hue,
Could make me any summer's story tell,
Or from their proud lap pluck them where they grew;
Nor did I wonder at the Lily's white,
Nor praise the deep vermilion in the Rose;
They were but sweet, but figures of delight,
Drawn after you, you pattern of all those.
    Yet seem'd it Winter still, and, you away,
    As with your shadow I with these did play.

168 *(xiv)*

MY love is strengthen'd, though more weak in seeming;
  I love not less, though less the show appear:
That love is merchandised whose rich esteeming
The owner's tongue doth publish everywhere.
Our love was new, and then but in the spring,
When I was wont to greet it with my lays;
As Philomel in Summer's front doth sing
And stops her pipe in growth of riper days:
Not that the Summer is less pleasant now
Than when her mournful hymns did hush the night,
But that wild music burthens every bough,
And sweets grown common lose their dear delight.
    Therefore, like her, I sometime hold my tongue,
    Because I would not dull you with my song.

169 (xv)

TO me, fair friend, you never can be old;
　For as you were when first your eye I eyed,
Such seems your beauty still. Three Winters cold
Have from the forests shook three Summers' pride;
Three beauteous Springs to yellow Autumn turn'd
In process of the seasons have I seen,
Three April perfumes in three hot Junes burn'd,
Since first I saw you fresh, which yet are green,
Ah! yet doth beauty, like a dial-hand,
Steal from his figure, and no pace perceived;
So your sweet hue, which methinks still doth stand,
Hath motion, and mine eye may be deceived:
　For fear of which, hear this, thou age unbred:
　Ere you were born was beauty's Summer dead.

170 (xvi)

WHEN in the chronicle of wasted time
　I see descriptions of the fairest wights,
And beauty making beautiful old rime
In praise of Ladies dead and lovely Knights;
Then, in the blazon of sweet beauty's best,
Of hand, of foot, of lip, of eye, of brow,
I see their antique pen would have exprest
Even such a beauty as you master now.
So all their praises are but prophecies
Of this our time, all you prefiguring;
And for they look'd but with divining eyes,
They had not skill enough your worth to sing:
　For we, which now behold these present days,
　Have eyes to wonder, but lack tongues to praise.

171   (*xvii*)

O NEVER say that I was false of heart,
    Though absence seem'd my flame to qualify!
As easy might I from myself depart,
As from my soul, which in thy breast doth lie:
That is my home of love; if I have ranged,
Like him that travels I return again,
Just to the time, not with the time exchanged,
So that myself bring water for my stain.
Never believe, though in my nature reign'd
All frailties that besiege all kinds of blood,
That it could so prepost'rously be stain'd,
To leave for nothing all thy sum of good:
    For nothing this wide Universe I call,
    Save thou, my Rose; in it thou art my all.

172   (*xviii*)

LET me not to the marriage of true minds
    Admit impediments. Love is not love
Which alters when it alteration finds,
Or bends with the remover to remove:
O, no! it is an ever-fixèd mark,
That looks on tempests and is never shaken;
It is the star to every wand'ring bark,
Whose worth's unknown, although his height be taken.
Love's not Time's fool, though rosy lips and cheeks
Within his bending sickle's compass come;
Love alters not with his brief hours and weeks,
But bears it out even to the edge of doom:—
    If this be error and upon me proved,
    I never writ, nor no man ever loved.

173   (*xix*)

TH' expense of Spirit in a waste of shame
   Is lust in action; and till action, lust
Is perjured, murderous, bloody, full of blame,
Savage, extreme, rude, cruel, not to trust;
Enjoy'd no sooner but despisèd straight;
Past reason hunted; and, no sooner had,
Past reason hated, as a swallow'd bait
On purpose laid to make the taker mad:
Mad in pursuit, and in possession so;
Had, having, and in quest to have, extreme;
A bliss in proof, and proved, a very woe;
Before, a joy proposed; behind, a dream.
   All this the world well knows; yet none knows well
   To shun the heaven that leads men to this hell.

174   (*xx*)

POOR soul, the centre of my sinful earth—
   My sinful earth, these rebel powers array—
Why dost thou pine within and suffer dearth,
Painting thy outward walls so costly gay?
Why so large cost, having so short a lease,
Dost thou upon thy fading mansion spend?
Shall worms, inheritors of this excess,
Eat up thy charge? Is this thy body's end?
Then, soul, live thou upon thy servant's loss,
And let that pine to aggravate thy store;
Buy terms divine in selling hours of dross;
Within be fed, without be rich no more:
   So shalt thou feed on Death, that feeds on men;
   And Death once dead, there's no more dying then.

1565–1630?

Lullaby

UPON my lap my sovereign sits
 And sucks upon my breast;
Meantime his love maintains my life
And gives my sense her rest.
　　Sing lullaby, my little boy,
　　Sing lullaby, mine only joy!

When thou hast taken thy repast,
Repose, my babe, on me;
So may thy mother and thy nurse
Thy cradle also be.
　　Sing lullaby, my little boy,
　　Sing lullaby, mine only joy!

I grieve that duty doth not work
All that my wishing would;
Because I would not be to thee
But in the best I should.
　　Sing lullaby, my little boy,
　　Sing lullaby, mine only joy!

Yet as I am, and as I may,
I must and will be thine,
Though all too little for thyself
Vouchsafing to be mine.
　　Sing lullaby, my little boy,
　　Sing lullaby, mine only joy!

THOMAS NASHE

1567–1601

176 *Spring*

SPRING, the sweet Spring, is the year's pleasant king;
  Then blooms each thing, then maids dance in a ring,
Cold doth not sting, the pretty birds do sing—
  Cuckoo, jug-jug, pu-we, to-witta-woo!

The palm and may make country houses gay,
Lambs frisk and play, the shepherds pipe all day,
And we hear aye birds tune this merry lay—
  Cuckoo, jug-jug, pu-we, to-witta-woo!

The fields breathe sweet, the daisies kiss our feet,
Young lovers meet, old wives a-sunning sit,
In every street these tunes our ears do greet—
  Cuckoo, jug-jug, pu-we, to-witta-woo!
    Spring, the sweet Spring!

177 *In Time of Pestilence*
1593

ADIEU, farewell earth's bliss!
  This world uncertain is:
Fond are life's lustful joys,
Death proves them all but toys.
None from his darts can fly;
I am sick, I must die—
      Lord, have mercy on us!

  Rich men, trust not in wealth,
  Gold cannot buy you health;
  Physic himself must fade;
  All things to end are made;

THOMAS NASHE

The plague full swift goes by;
I am sick, I must die—
  Lord, have mercy on us!

Beauty is but a flower
Which wrinkles will devour;
Brightness falls from the air;
Queens have died young and fair;
Dust hath closed Helen's eye;
I am sick, I must die—
  Lord, have mercy on us!

Strength stoops unto the grave,
Worms feed on Hector brave;
Swords may not fight with fate;
Earth still holds ope her gate;
Come, come! the bells do cry;
I am sick, I must die—
  Lord, have mercy on us!

Wit with his wantonness
Tasteth death's bitterness;
Hell's executioner
Hath no ears for to hear
What vain art can reply;
I am sick, I must die—
  Lord, have mercy on us!

Haste therefore each degree
To welcome destiny;
Heaven is our heritage,
Earth but a player's stage.
Mount we unto the sky;
I am sick, I must die—
  Lord, have mercy on us!

1567?–1619

178 *Cherry-Ripe*

THERE is a garden in her face
　Where roses and white lilies blow;
A heavenly paradise is that place,
　Wherein all pleasant fruits do flow:
　　There cherries grow which none may buy
　　Till 'Cherry-ripe' themselves do cry.

Those cherries fairly do enclose
　Of orient pearls a double row,
Which when her lovely laughter shows,
　They look like rose-buds fill'd with snow;
　　Yet them nor peer nor prince can buy
　　Till 'Cherry-ripe' themselves do cry.

Her eyes like angels watch them still;
　Her brows like bended bows do stand,
Threat'ning with piercing frowns to kill
　All that attempt with eye or hand
　　Those sacred cherries to come nigh,
　　Till 'Cherry-ripe' themselves do cry.

179 *Laura*

ROSE-CHEEK'D *Laura*, come;
　Sing thou smoothly with thy beauty's
Silent music, either other
　Sweetly gracing.

Lovely forms do flow
From concent divinely framèd:
Heaven is music, and thy beauty's
    Birth is heavenly.

These dull notes we sing
Discords need for helps to grace them;
Only beauty purely loving
    Knows no discord;

But still moves delight,
Like clear springs renew'd by flowing,
Ever perfect, ever in them-
    selves eternal.

180   *Devotion*
(i)

FOLLOW thy fair sun, unhappy shadow!
   Though thou be black as night,
  And she made all of light,
Yet follow thy fair sun, unhappy shadow!

Follow her, whose light thy light depriveth!
   Though here thou liv'st disgraced,
  And she in heaven is placed,
Yet follow her whose light the world reviveth!

Follow those pure beams, whose beauty burneth!
   That so have scorchèd thee
  As thou still black must be,
Till her kind beams thy black to brightness turneth

Follow her, while yet her glory shineth!
   There comes a luckless night
   That will dim all her light;
And this the black unhappy shade divineth.

Follow still, since so thy fates ordainèd!
   The sun must have his shade,
   Till both at once do fade,—
The sun still proud, the shadow still disdainèd.

181   (*ii*)

FOLLOW your saint, follow with accents sweet!
Haste you, sad notes, fall at her flying feet!
There, wrapt in cloud of sorrow, pity move,
And tell the ravisher of my soul I perish for her love:
But if she scorns my never-ceasing pain,
Then burst with sighing in her sight, and ne'er return again!

All that I sung still to her praise did tend;
Still she was first, still she my songs did end;
Yet she my love and music both doth fly,
The music that her echo is and beauty's sympathy:
Then let my notes pursue her scornful flight!
It shall suffice that they were breathed and died for her delight.

182   *Vobiscum est Iope*

WHEN thou must home to shades of underground,
And there arrived, a new admirèd guest,
The beauteous spirits do engirt thee round,
White Iope, blithe Helen, and the rest,
To hear the stories of thy finish'd love
From that smooth tongue whose music hell can move;

Then wilt thou speak of banqueting delights,
Of masques and revels which sweet youth did **make,**
Of tourneys and great challenges of knights,
And all these triumphs for thy beauty's sake:
When thou hast told these honours done to thee,
Then tell, O tell, how thou didst murder me!

183   *A Hymn in Praise of Neptune*

OF Neptune's empire let us sing,
   At whose command the waves obey;
To whom the rivers tribute pay,
Down the high mountains sliding:
To whom the scaly nation yields
Homage for the crystal fields
    Wherein they dwell:
And every sea-god pays a gem
Yearly out of his wat'ry cell
To deck great Neptune's diadem.

The Tritons dancing in a ring
Before his palace gates do make
The water with their echoes quake,
Like the great thunder sounding:
The sea-nymphs chant their accents shrill,
And the sirens, taught to kill
    With their sweet voice,
Make ev'ry echoing rock reply
Unto their gentle murmuring noise
The praise of Neptune's empery.

184 *Winter Nights*

NOW winter nights enlarge
 The number of their hours,
And clouds their storms discharge
 Upon the airy towers.
Let now the chimneys blaze
 And cups o'erflow with wine;
Let well-tuned words amaze
 With harmony divine.
Now yellow waxen lights
 Shall wait on honey love,
While youthful revels, masques, and courtly sights
 Sleep's leaden spells remove.

This time doth well dispense
 With lovers' long discourse;
Much speech hath some defence,
 Though beauty no remorse.
All do not all things well;
 Some measures comely tread,
Some knotted riddles tell,
 Some poems smoothly read.
The summer hath his joys,
 And winter his delights;
Though love and all his pleasures are but toys,
 They shorten tedious nights.

185 *Integer Vitae*

THE man of life upright,
 Whose guiltless heart is free
From all dishonest deeds,
 Or thought of vanity;

THOMAS CAMPION

The man whose silent days
  In harmless joys are spent,
Whom hopes cannot delude,
  Nor sorrow discontent;

That man needs neither towers
  Nor armour for defence,
Nor secret vaults to fly
  From thunder's violence:

He only can behold
  With unaffrighted eyes
The horrors of the deep
  And terrors of the skies.

Thus, scorning all the cares
  That fate or fortune brings,
He makes the heaven his book,
  His wisdom heavenly things;

Good thoughts his only friends,
  His wealth a well-spent age,
The earth his sober inn
  And quiet pilgrimage.

186   *O come quickly!*

NEVER weather-beaten sail more willing bent to shore,
  Never tirèd pilgrim's limbs affected slumber more,
Than my wearied sprite now longs to fly out of my troubled
    breast:
O come quickly, sweetest Lord, and take my soul to rest!

THOMAS CAMPION

Ever blooming are the joys of heaven's high Paradise,
Cold age deafs not there our ears nor vapour dims our eyes:
Glory there the sun outshines; whose beams the Blessèd only
    see:
O come quickly, glorious Lord, and raise my sprite to Thee!

JOHN REYNOLDS

16th Cent.

187   *A Nosegay*

SAY, crimson Rose and dainty Daffodil,
        With Violet blue;
Since you have seen the beauty of my saint,
        And eke her view;
Did not her sight (fair sight!) you lonely fill,
        With sweet delight
Of goddess' grace and angels' sacred teint
        In fine, most bright?

Say, golden Primrose, sanguine Cowslip fair,
        With Pink most fine;
Since you beheld the visage of my dear,
        And eyes divine;
Did not her globy front, and glistering hair,
        With cheeks most sweet,
So gloriously like damask flowers appear,
        The gods to greet?

Say, snow-white Lily, speckled Gillyflower,
        With Daisy gay;
Since you have viewed the Queen of my desire,
        In her array;

      187 teint] tint, hue.

JOHN REYNOLDS

Did not her ivory paps, fair Venus' bower,
    With heavenly glee,
A Juno's grace, conjure you to require
    Her face to see?

Say Rose, say Daffodil, and Violet blue,
    With Primrose fair,
Since ye have seen my nymph's sweet dainty face
    And gesture rare,
Did not (bright Cowslip, blooming Pink) her view
    (White Lily) shine—
(Ah, Gillyflower, ah Daisy!) with a grace
    Like stars divine?

SIR HENRY WOTTON   1568–1639

188   *Elizabeth of Bohemia*

YOU meaner beauties of the night,
    That poorly satisfy our eyes
More by your number than your light,
    You common people of the skies;
    What are you when the moon shall rise?

You curious chanters of the wood,
    That warble forth Dame Nature's lays,
Thinking your passions understood
    By your weak accents; what's your praise
    When Philomel her voice shall raise?

You violets that first appear,
    By your pure purple mantles known
Like the proud virgins of the year,
    As if the spring were all your own;
    What are you when the rose is blown?

So, when my mistress shall be seen
  In form and beauty of her mind,
By virtue first, then choice, a Queen,
  Tell me, if she were not design'd
  Th' eclipse and glory of her kind

189   *The Character of a Happy Life*

HOW happy is he born and taught
  That serveth not another's will;
Whose armour is his honest thought,
  And simple truth his utmost skill!

Whose passions not his masters are;
  Whose soul is still prepared for death,
Untied unto the world by care
  Of public fame or private breath;

Who envies none that chance doth raise,
  Nor vice; who never understood
How deepest wounds are given by praise;
  Nor rules of state, but rules of good;

Who hath his life from rumours freed;
  Whose conscience is his strong retreat;
Whose state can neither flatterers feed,
  Nor ruin make oppressors great;

Who God doth late and early pray
  More of His grace than gifts to lend;
And entertains the harmless day
  With a religious book or friend;

—This man is freed from servile bands
  Of hope to rise or fear to fall:
Lord of himself, though not of lands,
  And having nothing, yet hath all.

SIR HENRY WOTTON

190   *Upon the Death of Sir Albert
Morton's Wife*

HE first deceased; she for a little tried
To live without him, liked it not, and died.

SIR JOHN DAVIES

1569–1626

191   *Man*

I KNOW my soul hath power to know all things,
Yet she is blind and ignorant in all
I know I'm one of Nature's little kings,
Yet to the least and vilest things am thrall.

I know my life's a pain and but a span;
I know my sense is mock'd in everything;
And, to conclude, I know myself a Man—
Which is a proud and yet a wretched thing.

SIR ROBERT AYTON

1570–1638

192   *To His Forsaken Mistress*

I DO confess thou'rt smooth and fair,
  And I might have gone near to love thee,
Had I not found the slightest prayer
  That lips could move, had power to move thee;
But I can let thee now alone
As worthy to be loved by none.

I do confess thou'rt sweet; yet find
  Thee such an unthrift of thy sweets,
Thy favours are but like the wind
  That kisseth everything it meets:

And since thou canst with more than one,
Thou'rt worthy to be kiss'd by none.

The morning rose that untouch'd stands
  Arm'd with her briers, how sweet she smells!
But pluck'd and strain'd through ruder hands,
  Her sweets no longer with her dwells:
But scent and beauty both are gone,
And leaves fall from her, one by one.

Such fate ere long will thee betide
  When thou hast handled been awhile,
With sere flowers to be thrown aside;
  And I shall sigh, while some will smile,
To see thy love to every one
Hath brought thee to be loved by none.

193   *To an Inconstant One*

I LOVED thee once; I'll love no more—
  Thine be the grief as is the blame;
Thou art not what thou wast before,
  What reason I should be the same?
    He that can love unloved again,
    Hath better store of love than brain:
  God send me love my debts to pay,
  While unthrifts fool their love away!

Nothing could have my love o'erthrown
  If thou hadst still continued mine;
Yea, if thou hadst remain'd thy own,
  I might perchance have yet been thine.

But thou thy freedom didst recall
  That it thou might elsewhere enthral:
And then how could I but disdain
  A captive's captive to remain?

When new desires had conquer'd thee
  And changed the object of thy will,
It had been lethargy in me,
    Not constancy, to love thee still.
      Yea, it had been a sin to go
      And prostitute affection so:
    Since we are taught no prayers to say
    To such as must to others pray.

Yet do thou glory in thy choice—
  Thy choice of his good fortune boast;
I'll neither grieve nor yet rejoice
    To see him gain what I have lost:
      The height of my disdain shall be
      To laugh at him, to blush for thee;
    To love thee still, but go no more
    A-begging at a beggar's door.

BEN JONSON

1573–1637

194   *Hymn to Diana*

QUEEN and huntress, chaste and fair,
    Now the sun is laid to sleep,
Seated in thy silver chair,
    State in wonted manner keep:
      Hesperus entreats thy light,
      Goddess excellently bright.

Earth, let not thy envious shade
    Dare itself to interpose;
Cynthia's shining orb was made
    Heaven to clear when day did close:
      Bless us then with wishèd sight,
      Goddess excellently bright.

Lay thy bow of pearl apart,
    And thy crystal-shining quiver;
Give unto the flying hart
    Space to breathe, how short soever:
      Thou that mak'st a day of night—
      Goddess excellently bright.

195   *To Celia*

DRINK to me only with thine eyes,
    And I will pledge with mine;
Or leave a kiss but in the cup
    And I'll not look for wine.
The thirst that from the soul doth rise
    Doth ask a drink divine;
But might I of Jove's nectar sup,
    I would not change for thine.

I sent thee late a rosy wreath,
    Not so much honouring thee
As giving it a hope that there
    It could not wither'd be;
But thou thereon didst only breathe,
    And sent'st it back to me;
Since when it grows, and smells, I swear,
    Not of itself but thee!

196 *Simplex Munditiis*

STILL to be neat, still to be drest,
  As you were going to a feast;
Still to be powder'd, still perfumed:
Lady, it is to be presumed,
Though art's hid causes are not found,
All is not sweet, all is not sound.

Give me a look, give me a face
That makes simplicity a grace;
Robes loosely flowing, hair as free:
Such sweet neglect more taketh me
Than all th' adulteries of art;
They strike mine eyes, but not my heart.

197 *The Shadow*

FOLLOW a shadow, it still flies you;
  Seem to fly it, it will pursue:
So court a mistress, she denies you;
  Let her alone, she will court you.
    Say, are not women truly, then,
    Styled but the shadows of us men?

At morn and even, shades are longest;
  At noon they are or short or none:
So men at weakest, they are strongest,
  But grant us perfect, they're not known.
    Say, are not women truly, then,
    Styled but the shadows of us men?

A Nymph's Secret

I LOVE, and He loves me again,
    Yet dare I not tell, Who;
For if the Nymphs should know my Swain,
    I fear they'd love him too!
    Yet if it be not known;
The pleasure is as good as none;
For that's a narrow joy, is but our own.

I'll tell! that, if they be not glad,
    They may yet envy me;
But then, if I grow jealous mad,
    And of them, pitied be,
    It were a plague 'bove scorn;
And yet it cannot be forborne,
Unless my heart would, as my thought, be torn.

He is (if they can find him) fair,
    And fresh and fragrant too
As summer's sky, or purgèd air,
    And looks as lilies do
    That are, this morning, blown.
Yet, yet, I doubt, he is not known;
And fear much more, that more of him be shown.

But he hath eyes so round and bright,
    As make away my doubt,
Where Love may all his torches light,
    Though hate had put them out.
    But then, t' increase my fears,
What Nymph soe'er, his voice but hears,
Will be my rival, though she have but ears.

I'll tell no more, and yet I love,
    And he loves me. Yet no
One unbecoming thought doth move
    From either heart, I know;
    But so exempt from blame
As it would be to each a fame,
If love, or fear, would let me tell his name.

199   *The Triumph*

SEE the Chariot at hand here of Love,
    Wherein my Lady rideth!
Each that draws is a swan or a dove,
    And well the car Love guideth.
As she goes, all hearts do duty
        Unto her beauty;
And enamour'd do wish, so they might
        But enjoy such a sight,
That they still were to run by her side,
Thorough swords, thorough seas, whither she would ride.

Do but look on her eyes, they do light
    All that Love's world compriseth!
Do but look on her hair, it is bright
    As Love's star when it riseth!
Do but mark, her forehead's smoother
        Than words that soothe her;
And from her arch'd brows such a grace
        Sheds itself through the face,
As alone there triumphs to the life
All the gain, all the good, of the elements' strife.

Have you seen but a bright lily grow
　　Before rude hands have touch'd it?
Have you mark'd but the fall of the snow
　　Before the soil hath smutch'd it?
Have you felt the wool of beaver,
　　　　　Or swan's down ever?
Or have smelt o' the bud o' the brier,
　　　　　Or the nard in the fire?
Or have tasted the bag of the bee?
O so white, O so soft, O so sweet is she!

200　　　　　　*An Elegy*

THOUGH beauty be the mark of praise,
　And yours of whom I sing be such
　As not the world can praise too much,
Yet 'tis your Virtue now I raise.

A virtue, like allay so gone
　Throughout your form as, though that move
　And draw and conquer all men's love,
This subjects you to love of one.

Wherein you triumph yet—because
　'Tis of your flesh, and that you use
　The noblest freedom, not to choose
Against or faith or honour's laws.

But who should less expect from you?
　In whom alone Love lives again:
　By whom he is restored to men,
And kept and bred and brought up true.

200 allay] alloy.

His falling temples you have rear'd,
  The wither'd garlands ta'en away;
  His altars kept from that decay
That envy wish'd, and nature fear'd:

And on them burn so chaste a flame,
  With so much loyalty's expense,
  As Love to acquit such excellence
Is gone himself into your name.

And you are he—the deity
  To whom all lovers are design'd
  That would their better objects find;
Among which faithful troop am I—

Who as an off'ring at your shrine
  Have sung this hymn, and here entreat
  One spark of your diviner heat
To light upon a love of mine:

Which if it kindle not, but scant
  Appear, and that to shortest view;
  Yet give me leave to adore in you
What I in her am grieved to want!

201　　　*The Noble Balm*

HIGH-SPIRITED friend,
  I send nor balms nor cor'sives to your wound:
    Your fate hath found
A gentler and more agile hand to tend
The cure of that which is but corporal;
And doubtful days, which were named critical,

Have made their fairest flight
And now are out of sight.
Yet doth some wholesome physic for the mind
Wrapp'd in this paper lie,
Which in the taking if you misapply,
You are unkind.

Your covetous hand,
Happy in that fair honour it hath gain'd,
Must now be rein'd.
True valour doth her own renown command
In one full action; nor have you now more
To do, than be a husband of that store.
Think but how dear you bought
This fame which you have caught:
Such thoughts will make you more in love with truth.
'Tis wisdom, and that high,
For men to use their fortune reverently,
Even in youth.

Epitaphs

202   (i) On Elizabeth L. H.

WOULDST thou hear what Man can say
In a little? Reader, stay.
Underneath this stone doth lie
As much Beauty as could die:
Which in life did harbour give
To more Virtue than doth live.
If at all she had a fault,
Leave it buried in this vault.

One name was *Elizabeth,*
The other, let it sleep with death:
Fitter, where it died, to tell
Than that it lived at all. Farewell.

203   *(ii) On Salathiel Pavy*

A child of Queen Elizabeth's Chapel

WEEP with me, all you that read
  This little story;
And know, for whom a tear you shed
  Death's self is sorry.
'Twas a child that so did thrive
  In grace and feature,
As Heaven and Nature seem'd to strive
  Which own'd the creature.
Years he number'd scarce thirteen
  When Fates turn'd cruel,
Yet three fill'd zodiacs had he been
  The Stage's jewel;
And did act (what now we moan)
  Old men so duly,
As sooth the Parcae thought him one,
  He play'd so truly.
So, by error, to his fate
  They all consented;
But, viewing him since, alas, too late!
  They have repented;
And have sought, to give new birth,
  In baths to steep him;
But, being so much too good for earth,
  Heaven vows to keep him.

204　　　　　　*A Part of an Ode*

To the Immortal Memory and Friendship of that noble pair,
Sir Lucius Cary and Sir H. Morison

IT is not growing like a tree
　　In bulk, doth make man better be;
Or standing long an oak, three hundred year,
To fall a log at last, dry, bald, and sere:
　　　　　A lily of a day
　　　　　Is fairer far in May,
　　Although it fall and die that night;
　　It was the plant and flower of light.
In small proportions we just beauties see;
And in short measures, life may perfect be.

　　Call, noble *Lucius*, then for wine,
　　　And let thy looks with gladness shine:
Accept this garland, plant it on thy head,
And think—nay, know—thy *Morison*'s not dead.
　　　　　He leap'd the present age,
　　　　　Possest with holy rage
　　To see that bright eternal Day
　　Of which we Priests and Poets say
Such truths as we expect for happy men;
And there he lives with memory—and *Ben*

　　Jonson: who sung this of him, ere he went
　　　　　Himself to rest,
　　Or tast a part of that full joy he meant
　　　　　To have exprest

229

BEN JONSON

In this bright Asterism,
Where it were friendship's schism—
Were not his *Lucius* long with us to tarry—
To separate these twy
Lights, the Dioscuri,
And keep the one half from his *Harry*.
But fate doth so alternate the design,
Whilst that in Heav'n, this light on earth must shine.

And shine as you exalted are!
Two names of friendship, but one star:
Of hearts the union: and those not by chance
Made, or indenture, or leased out to advance
The profits for a time.
No pleasures vain did chime
Of rimes or riots at your feasts,
Orgies of drink or feign'd protests;
But simple love of greatness and of good,
That knits brave minds and manners more than blood.

This made you first to know the *Why
You liked*, then after, to apply
That liking, and approach so one the t'other
Till either grew a portion of the other:
Each stylèd by his end
The copy of his friend.
You lived to be the great surnames
And titles by which all made claims
Unto the Virtue—nothing perfect done
But as a *CARY* or a *MORISON*.

And such the force the fair example had
    As they that saw
The good, and durst not practise it, were glad
    That such a law
    Was left yet to mankind,
    Where they might read and find
FRIENDSHIP indeed was written, not in words,
    And with the heart, not pen,
    Of two so early men,
Whose lines her rules were and records:
Who, ere the first down bloomèd on the chin,
Had sow'd these fruits, and got the harvest in.

JOHN DONNE

1573-1631

205   *'Daybreak'*

STAY, O sweet, and do not rise!
  The light that shines comes from thine eyes;
The day breaks not: it is my heart,
    Because that you and I must part.
    Stay! or else my joys will die
    And perish in their infancy.

206   *Song*

GO and catch a falling star,
  Get with child a mandrake root,
Tell me where all past years are,
    Or who cleft the Devil's foot;

Teach me to hear mermaids singing,
Or to keep off envy's stinging,
        And find
        What wind
Serves to advance an honest mind.

If thou be'st born to strange sights,
    Things invisible to see,
Ride ten thousand days and nights
    Till Age snow white hairs on thee;
Thou, when thou return'st, wilt tell me
All strange wonders that befell thee,
        And swear
        No where
Lives a woman true and fair.

If thou find'st one, let me know;
    Such a pilgrimage were sweet.
Yet do not; I would not go,
    Though at next door we might meet.
Though she were true when you met her,
And last till you write your letter,
        Yet she
        Will be
False, ere I come, to two or three.

207   *The Apparition*

WHEN by thy scorn, O murd'ress I am dead,
        And that thou thinkst thee free
From all solicitation from me,
Then shall my ghost come to thy bed,
And thee, fain'd vestal, in worse arms shall see;

Then thy sick taper will begin to wink,
And he, whose thou art then, being tired before,
Will, if thou stir, or pinch to wake him, think
      Thou call'st for more,
And in false sleep will from thee shrink,
And then poor aspen wretch, neglected thou
Bath'd in a cold quicksilver sweat wilt lie
      A verier ghost than I;
What I will say I will not tell thee now,
Lest that preserve thee; and since my love is spent,
I had rather thou shouldst painfully repent,
Than by my threat'nings rest still innocent.

208   *The Ecstasy*

WHERE, like a pillow on a bed,
    A pregnant bank swell'd up, to rest
The violet's reclining head,
    Sat we two, one another's best.
Our hands were firmly cèmented
    By a fast balm which thence did spring;
Our eye-beams twisted, and did thread
    Our eyes upon one double string.
So to engraft our hands, as yet
    Was all the means to make us one;
And pictures in our eyes to get
    Was all our propagation.
As 'twixt two equal armies Fate
    Suspends uncertain victory,
Our souls—which to advance their state
    Were gone out—hung 'twixt her and me.

And whilst our souls negotiate there,
   We like sepulchral statues lay;
All day the same our postures were,
   And we said nothing, all the day.
If any, so by love refined,
   That he soul's language understood,
And by good love were grown all mind,
   Within convenient distance stood,
He (though he knew not which soul spake,
   Because both meant, both spake the same)
Might thence a new concoction take,
   And part far purer than he came.
This Ecstasy doth unperplex
   (We said) and tell us what we love,
We see by this, it was not sex,
   We see, we saw not what did move:
But as all several souls contain
   Mixture of things, they know not what,
Love, these mixed souls doth mix again,
   And makes both one, each this and that.
A single violet transplant,
   The strength, the colour, and the size
(All which before was poor and scant)
   Redoubles still, and multiplies.
When love, with one another so
   Interinanimates two souls,
That abler soul, which thence doth flow,
   Defects of loneliness controls.
We then, who are this new soul, know,
   Of what we are composed and made,
For th'Atomies of which we grow,
   Are souls, whom no change can invade.

But O alas, so long, so far
　　Our bodies why do we forbear?
They are ours, though they are not we, We are
　　The intelligences, they the sphere.
We owe them thanks, because they thus,
　　Did us, to us, at first convey,
Yielded their forces, sense, to us,
　　Nor are dross to us, but allay.
On man heavens' influence works not so,
　　But that it first imprints the air,
So soul into the soul may flow,
　　Though it to body first repair.
As our blood labours to beget
　　Spirits, as like souls as it can,
Because such fingers need to knit
　　That subtle knot, which makes us man,
So must pure lovers' souls descend
　　T' affections, and to faculties,
Which sense may reach and apprehend,
　　Else a great Prince in prison lies.
To our bodies turn we then, that so
　　Weak men on love revealed may look;
Love's mysteries in souls do grow,
　　But yet the body is his book.
And if some lover, such as we,
　　Have heard this dialogue of one,
Let him still mark us, he shall see
　　Small change, when we are to bodies gone.

The Dream

D EAR love, for nothing less than thee
    Would I have broke this happy dream,
        It was a theme
For reason, much too strong for fantasy.
Therefore thou waked'st me wisely; yet
My dream thou brok'st not, but continued'st it.
Thou art so true that thoughts of thee suffice
To make dreams truths and fables histories;
Enter these arms, for since thou thought'st it best
Not to dream all my dream, let's act the rest.

As lightning, or a taper's light,
Thine eyes, and not thy noise, waked me;
        Yet I thought thee—
For thou lov'st truth—an angel, at first sight;
But when I saw thou saw'st my heart,
And knew'st my thoughts beyond an angel's art,
When thou knew'st what I dreamt, when thou knew'st when
Excess of joy would wake me, and cam'st then,
I must confess it could not choose but be
Profane to think thee anything but thee.

Coming and staying show'd thee thee,
But rising makes me doubt that now
        Thou art not thou.
That Love is weak where Fear's as strong as he;
'Tis not all spirit pure and brave
If mixture it of Fear, Shame, Honour have.
Perchance as torches, which must ready be,
Men light and put out, so thou deal'st with me.
Thou cam'st to kindle, go'st to come: then I
Will dream that hope again, but else would die.

210   *The Funeral*

WHOEVER comes to shroud me, do not harm
            Nor question much
That subtle wreath of hair about mine arm;
The mystery, the sign you must not touch,
            For 'tis my outward soul,
Viceroy to that which, unto heav'n being gone,
            Will leave this to control
And keep these limbs, her provinces, from dissolution.

For if the sinewy thread my brain lets fall
            Through every part
Can tie those parts, and make me one of all,
Those hairs, which upward grew, and strength and art
            Have from a better brain,
Can better do't: except she meant that I
            By this should know my pain,
As prisoners then are manacled, when they're condemn'd to
      die.

Whate'er she meant by 't, bury it with me,
            For since I am
Love's martyr, it might breed idolatry
If into other hands these reliques came.
            As 'twas humility
T' afford to it all that a soul can do,
            So 'tis some bravery
That, since you would have none of me, I bury some of
      you.

JOHN DONNE

Death

DEATH, be not proud, though some have callèd thee
   Mighty and dreadful, for thou art not so:
For those whom thou think'st thou dost overthrow
Die not, poor Death; nor yet canst thou kill me.
From Rest and Sleep, which but thy picture be,
Much pleasure, then from thee much more must flow;
And soonest our best men with thee do go—
Rest of their bones and souls' delivery!
Thou'rt slave to fate, chance, kings, and desperate men,
And dost with poison, war, and sickness dwell;
And poppy or charms can make us sleep as well
And better than thy stroke. Why swell'st thou then?
  One short sleep past, we wake eternally,
  And Death shall be no more: Death, thou shalt die!

RICHARD BARNEFIELD

1574–1627

Philomel

AS it fell upon a day
  In the merry month of May,
Sitting in a pleasant shade
Which a grove of myrtles made,
Beasts did leap and birds did sing,
Trees did grow and plants did spring;
Everything did banish moan
Save the Nightingale alone:
She, poor bird, as all forlorn
Lean'd her breast up-till a thorn,
And there sung the dolefull'st ditty,
That to hear it was great pity.

RICHARD BARNEFIELD

Fie, fie, fie! now would she cry;
Tereu, Tereu! by and by;
That to hear her so complain
Scarce I could from tears refrain;
For her griefs so lively shown
Made me think upon mine own.
Ah! thought I, thou mourn'st in vain,
None takes pity on thy pain:
Senseless trees they cannot hear thee,
Ruthless beasts they will not cheer thee:
King Pandion he is dead,
All thy friends are lapp'd in lead;
All thy fellow birds do sing
Careless of thy sorrowing:
Even so, poor bird, like thee,
None alive will pity me.

THOMAS DEKKER

1575-1641

213   *Sweet Content*

ART thou poor, yet hast thou golden slumbers?
        O sweet content!
Art thou rich, yet is thy mind perplex'd?
        O punishment!
Dost thou laugh to see how fools are vex'd
To add to golden numbers golden numbers?
        O sweet content! O sweet, O sweet content!
Work apace, apace, apace, apace;
Honest labour bears a lovely face;
Then hey nonny nonny—hey nonny nonny!

THOMAS DEKKER

Canst drink the waters of the crispèd spring?
> O sweet content!

Swim'st thou in wealth, yet sink'st in thine own tears?
> O punishment!

Then he that patiently want's burden bears,
No burden bears, but is a king, a king!
> O sweet content! O sweet, O sweet content!

Work apace, apace, apace, apace;
Honest labour bears a lovely face;
Then hey nonny nonny—hey nonny nonny!

THOMAS HEYWOOD

1575?–1650

214 *Matin Song*

PACK, clouds, away! and welcome, day!
  With night we banish sorrow.
Sweet air, blow soft; mount, lark, aloft
  To give my Love good-morrow!
Wings from the wind to please her mind,
  Notes from the lark I'll borrow:
Bird, prune thy wing! nightingale, sing!
  To give my Love good-morrow!
    To give my Love good-morrow
    Notes from them all I'll borrow.

Wake from thy nest, robin red-breast!
  Sing, birds, in every furrow!
And from each bill let music shrill
  Give my fair Love good-morrow!
Blackbird and thrush in every bush,
  Stare, linnet, and cocksparrow,

214 stare] starling.

THOMAS HEYWOOD

You pretty elves, among yourselves
  Sing my fair Love good-morrow!
    To give my Love good-morrow!
    Sing, birds, in every furrow!

JOHN FLETCHER

1579-1625

215   *Bridal Song*

CYNTHIA, to thy power and thee
        We obey.
Joy to this great company!
      And no day
Come to steal this night away
    Till the rites of love are ended,
And the lusty bridegroom say,
    Welcome, light, of all befriended!

Pace out, you watery powers below;
        Let your feet,
Like the galleys when they row,
        Even beat;
Let your unknown measures, set
    To the still winds, tell to all
That gods are come, immortal, great,
    To honour this great nuptial!

216   *Aspatia's Song*

LAY a garland on my herse
    Of the dismal yew;
Maidens, willow branches bear;
    Say, I died true.

My love was false, but I was firm
 From my hour of birth.
Upon my buried body lie
 Lightly, gentle earth!

217   *Hymn to Pan*

SING his praises that doth keep
 Our flocks from harm,
Pan, the father of our sheep;
 And arm in arm
Tread we softly in a round,
Whilst the hollow neighbouring ground
Fills the music with her sound.

Pan, O great god Pan, to thee
 Thus do we sing!
Thou who keep'st us chaste and free
 As the young spring:
Ever be thy honour spoke
From that place the morn is broke
To that place day doth unyoke!

218   *Away, Delights*

AWAY, delights! go seek some other dwelling,
  For I must die.
Farewell, false love! thy tongue is ever telling
  Lie after lie.
For ever let me rest now from thy smarts;
  Alas, for pity go
  And fire their hearts
That have been hard to thee! Mine was not so.

Never again deluding love shall know me,
    For I will die;
And all those griefs that think to overgrow me
    Shall be as I:
For ever will I sleep, while poor maids cry—
      'Alas, for pity stay,
      And let us die
With thee! Men cannot mock us in the clay.'

219   *Love's Emblems*

NOW the lusty spring is seen;
    Golden yellow, gaudy blue,
  Daintily invite the view:
Everywhere on every green
Roses blushing as they blow
  And enticing men to pull,
Lilies whiter than the snow,
    Woodbines of sweet honey full:
      All love's emblems, and all cry,
      'Ladies, if not pluck'd, we die.'

Yet the lusty spring hath stay'd;
  Blushing red and purest white
  Daintily to love invite
Every woman, every maid:
Cherries kissing as they grow,
  And inviting men to taste,
Apples even ripe below,
    Winding gently to the waist:
      All love's emblems, and all cry,
      'Ladies, if not pluck'd, we die.'

220   *Hear, ye Ladies*

HEAR, ye ladies that despise
    What the mighty Love has done;
Fear examples and be wise:
    Fair Callisto was a nun;
Leda, sailing on the stream
    To deceive the hopes of man,
Love accounting but a dream,
    Doted on a silver swan;
        Danaë, in a brazen tower,
        Where no love was, loved a shower.

Hear, ye ladies that are coy,
    What the mighty Love can do;
Fear the fierceness of the boy:
    The chaste Moon he makes to woo;
Vesta, kindling holy fires,
    Circled round about with spies,
Never dreaming loose desires,
    Doting at the altar dies;
        Ilion, in a short hour, higher
        He can build, and once more fire.

221   *God Lyaeus*

GOD Lyaeus, ever young,
    Ever honour'd, ever sung,
Stain'd with blood of lusty grapes,
In a thousand lusty shapes
Dance upon the mazer's brim,
In the crimson liquor swim;

    221 mazer] a bowl of maple-wood.

From thy plenteous hand divine
Let a river run with wine:
   God of youth, let this day here
   Enter neither care nor fear.

222   *Beauty Clear and Fair*

BEAUTY clear and fair,
    Where the air
Rather like a perfume dwells;
   Where the violet and the rose
    Their blue veins and blush disclose,
And come to honour nothing else:

    Where to live near
    And planted there
Is to live, and still live new;
   Where to gain a favour is
    More than light, perpetual bliss—
Make me live by serving you!

Dear, again back recall
    To this light,
A stranger to himself and all!
   Both the wonder and the story
   Shall be yours, and eke the glory;
I am your servant, and your thrall.

223   *Melancholy*

HENCE, all you vain delights,
   As short as are the nights
    Wherein you spend your folly!
There 's naught in this life sweet,

If men were wise to see 't,
　　But only melancholy—
　　O sweetest melancholy!
Welcome, folded arms and fixèd eyes,
A sight that piercing mortifies,
A look that 's fasten'd to the ground,
A tongue chain'd up without a sound!

Fountain-heads and pathless groves,
Places which pale passion loves!
Moonlight walks, when all the fowls
Are warmly housed, save bats and owls!
　　A midnight bell, a parting groan—
　　These are the sounds we feed upon:
Then stretch our bones in a still gloomy valley,
Nothing 's so dainty sweet as lovely melancholy.

224　　　　　　*Weep no more*

WEEP no more, nor sigh, nor groan,
　　Sorrow calls no time that 's gone:
Violets pluck'd, the sweetest rain
Makes not fresh nor grow again.
Trim thy locks, look cheerfully;
Fate's hid ends eyes cannot see.
Joys as wingèd dreams fly fast,
Why should sadness longer last?
Grief is but a wound to woe;
Gentlest fair, mourn, mourn no moe.

1580?–1630?

225 *A Dirge*

CALL for the robin-redbreast and the wren,
  Since o'er shady groves they hover,
And with leaves and flowers do cover
The friendless bodies of unburied men.
Call unto his funeral dole
The ant, the field-mouse, and the mole,
To rear him hillocks that shall keep him warm,
And (when gay tombs are robb'd) sustain no harm;
But keep the wolf far thence, that's foe to men,
For with his nails he'll dig them up again.

226 *The Shrouding of the Duchess of Malfi*

HARK! Now everything is still,
  The screech-owl and the whistler shrill,
Call upon our dame aloud,
And bid her quickly don her shroud!

Much you had of land and rent;
Your length in clay's now competent:
A long war disturb'd your mind;
Here your perfect peace is sign'd.

Of what is't fools make such vain keeping?
Sin their conception, their birth weeping,
Their life a general mist of error,
Their death a hideous storm of terror.
Strew your hair with powders sweet,
Don clean linen, bathe your feet,

      225 dole] lamentation.

And—the foul fiend more to check—
A crucifix let bless your neck:
'Tis now full tide 'tween night and day;
End your groan and come away.

227 *Vanitas Vanitatum*

ALL the flowers of the spring
  Meet to perfume our burying;
These have but their growing prime,
And man does flourish but his time:
Survey our progress from our birth—
We are set, we grow, we turn to earth.
Courts adieu, and all delights,
All bewitching appetites!
Sweetest breath and clearest eye
Like perfumes go out and die;
And consequently this is done
As shadows wait upon the sun.
Vain the ambition of kings
Who seek by trophies and dead things
To leave a living name behind,
And weave but nets to catch the wind.

WILLIAM ALEXANDER, EARL OF STIRLING
580?–1640

228 *Aurora*

O HAPPY Tithon! if thou know'st thy hap,
  And valuest thy wealth, as I my want,
  Then need'st thou not—which ah! I grieve to grant—
Repine at Jove, lull'd in his leman's lap:

That golden shower in which he did repose—
    One dewy drop it stains
    Which thy Aurora rains
    Upon the rural plains,
When from thy bed she passionately goes.

Then, waken'd with the music of the merles,
    She not remembers Memnon when she mourns:
    That faithful flame which in her bosom burns
From crystal conduits throws those liquid pearls:
    Sad from thy sight so soon to be removed,
        She so her grief delates.
        —O favour'd by the fates
        Above the happiest states,
Who art of one so worthy well-beloved!

PHINEAS FLETCHER

1580–1650

229

A Litany

DROP, drop, slow tears,
    And bathe those beauteous feet
Which brought from Heaven
    The news and Prince of Peace;
Cease not, wet eyes,
    His mercy to entreat;
To cry for vengeance
    Sin doth never cease.
In your deep floods
    Drown all my faults and fears;
Nor let His eye
    See sin, but through my tears.

1583–1648

230   *Elegy over a Tomb*

MUST I then see, alas! eternal night
   Sitting upon those fairest eyes,
And closing all those beams, which once did rise
   So radiant and bright,
That light and heat in them to us did prove
    Knowledge and Love?

Oh, if you did delight no more to stay
   Upon this low and earthly stage,
But rather chose an endless heritage,
   Tell us at least, we pray,
Where all the beauties that those ashes ow'd
   Are now bestow'd?

Doth the Sun now his light with yours renew?
   Have Waves the curling of your hair?
Did you restore unto the Sky and Air,
   The red, and white, and blue?
Have you vouchsafed to flow'rs since your death
   That sweetest breath?

Had not Heav'ns Lights else in their houses slept,
   Or to some private life retir'd?
Must not the Sky and Air have else conspir'd?
   And in their Regions wept?
Must not each flower else the earth could breed
   Have been a weed?

250

But thus enrich'd may we not yield some cause
      Why they themselves lament no more?
That must have changed the course they held before,
      And broke their proper Laws,
Had not your beauties giv'n this second birth
      To Heaven and Earth?

Tell us—for Oracles must still ascend,
      For those that crave them at your tomb—
Tell us, where are those beauties now become,
      And what they now intend:
Tell us, alas, that cannot tell our grief,
      Or hope relief.

SIR JOHN BEAUMONT   1583–1627

231   *Of his Dear Son, Gervase*

DEAR Lord, receive my son, whose winning love
    To me was like a friendship, far above
The course of nature or his tender age;
Whose looks could all my bitter griefs assuage:
Let his pure soul, ordain'd seven years to be
In that frail body which was part of me,
Remain my pledge in Heaven, as sent to show
How to this port at every step I go.

WILLIAM DRUMMOND, OF HAWTHORNDEN
1585–1649

232   *Invocation*

PHŒBUS, arise!
    And paint the sable skies
With azure, white, and red;
Rouse Memnon's mother from her Tithon's bed,

That she thy càreer may with roses spread;
The nightingales thy coming each-where sing;
Make an eternal spring!
Give life to this dark world which lieth dead;
Spread forth thy golden hair
In larger locks than thou wast wont before,
And emperor-like decore
With diadem of pearl thy temples fair:
Chase hence the ugly night
Which serves but to make dear thy glorious light.
This is that happy morn,
That day, long wishèd day
Of all my life so dark
(If cruel stars have not my ruin sworn
And fates not hope betray),
Which, only white, deserves
A diamond for ever should it mark:
This is the morn should bring into this grove
My Love, to hear and recompense my love.
Fair King, who all preserves,
But show thy blushing beams,
And thou two sweeter eyes
Shalt see than those which by Penèus' streams
Did once thy heart surprise:
Nay, suns, which shine as clear
As thou when two thou did to Rome appear.
Now, Flora, deck thyself in fairest guise:
If that ye, winds, would hear
A voice surpassing far Amphion's lyre,
Your stormy chiding stay;
Let zephyr only breathe
And with her tresses play,

Kissing sometimes these purple ports of death.
The winds all silent are;
And Phœbus in his chair
Ensaffroning sea and air
Makes vanish every star:
Night like a drunkard reels
Beyond the hills to shun his flaming wheels:
The fields with flowers are deck'd in every hue,
The clouds bespangle with bright gold their blue:
Here is the pleasant place—
And everything, save Her, who all should grace.

233 *Madrigal*

LIKE the Idalian queen,
    Her hair about her eyne,
With neck and breast's ripe apples to be seen,
    At first glance of the morn
In Cyprus' gardens gathering those fair flow'rs
    Which of her blood were born,
I saw, but fainting saw, my paramours.
The Graces naked danced about the place,
    The winds and trees amazed
    With silence on her gazed,
The flowers did smile, like those upon her face;
And as their aspen stalks those fingers band,
    That she might read my case,
A hyacinth I wish'd me in her hand.

233 paramours] = sing. paramour.   band] bound.

234 *Spring Bereaved 1*

THAT zephyr every year
     So soon was heard to sigh in forests here,
It was for her: that wrapp'd in gowns of green
     Meads were so early seen,
That in the saddest months oft sung the merles,
It was for her; for her trees dropp'd forth pearls.
     That proud and stately courts
Did envy those our shades and calm resorts,
It was for her; and she is gone, O woe!
     Woods cut again do grow,
Bud doth the rose and daisy, winter done;
But we, once dead, no more do see the sun.

235 *Spring Bereaved 2*

SWEET Spring, thou turn'st with all thy goodly **train**,
     Thy head with flames, thy mantle bright with flow'rs:
The zephyrs curl the green locks of the plain,
The clouds for joy in pearls weep down their show'rs.
Thou turn'st, sweet youth, but ah! my pleasant hours
And happy days with thee come not again;
The sad memorials only of my pain
Do with thee turn, which turn my sweets in sours.
Thou art the same which still thou wast before,
Delicious, wanton, amiable, fair;
But she, whose breath embalm'd thy wholesome **air**,
Is gone—nor gold nor gems her can restore.
     Neglected virtue, seasons go and come,
     While thine forgot lie closèd in a tomb.

236   *Spring Bereaved* 3

ALEXIS, here she stay'd; among these pines,
    Sweet hermitress, she did alone repair;
Here did she spread the treasure of her hair,
More rich than that brought from the Colchian mines.
She set her by these muskèd eglantines,
—The happy place the print seems yet to bear:
Her voice did sweeten here thy sugar'd lines,
To which winds, trees, beasts, birds, did lend their ear.
Me here she first perceived, and here a morn
Of bright carnations did o'erspread her face;
Here did she sigh, here first my hopes were born,
And I first got a pledge of promised grace:
    But ah! what served it to be happy so?
    Sith passèd pleasures double but new woe?

237   *Her Passing*

THE beauty and the life
    Of life's and beauty's fairest paragon
—O tears! O grief!—hung at a feeble thread
To which pale Atropos had set her knife;
    The soul with many a groan
    Had left each outward part,
And now did take his last leave of the heart:
Naught else did want, save death, ev'n to be dead;
When the afflicted band about her bed,
Seeing so fair him come in lips, cheeks, eyes,
Cried, '*Ah! and can Death enter Paradise?*'

238   *Inexorable*

M Y thoughts hold mortal strife;
    I do detest my life,
And with lamenting cries
Peace to my soul to bring
Oft call that prince which here doth monarchise:
    —But he, grim-grinning King,
Who caitiffs scorns, and doth the blest surprise,
Late having deck'd with beauty's rose his tomb,
Disdains to crop a weed, and will not come.

239   *Change should breed Change*

N EW doth the sun appear,
    The mountains' snows decay,
Crown'd with frail flowers forth comes the baby year.
    My soul, time posts away;
    And thou yet in that frost
    Which flower and fruit hath lost,
As if all here immortal were, dost stay.
    For shame! thy powers awake,
Look to that Heaven which never night makes black,
And there at that immortal sun's bright rays,
Deck thee with flowers which fear not rage of days!

240   *Saint John Baptist*

THE last and greatest Herald of Heaven's King,
    Girt with rough skins, hies to the deserts wild,
Among that savage brood the woods forth bring,
Which he than man more harmless found and mild.
His food was locusts, and what young doth spring
With honey that from virgin hives distill'd;
Parch'd body, hollow eyes, some uncouth thing
Made him appear, long since from earth exiled.
There burst he forth: 'All ye, whose hopes rely
On God, with me amidst these deserts mourn;
Repent, repent, and from old errors turn!'
—Who listen'd to his voice, obey'd his cry?
    Only the echoes, which he made relent,
    Rung from their marble caves 'Repent! Repent!

GILES FLETCHER

1588?–1623

241   *Wooing Song*

LOVE is the blossom where there blows
    Every thing that lives or grows:
Love doth make the Heav'ns to move,
And the Sun doth burn in love:
Love the strong and weak doth yoke,
And makes the ivy climb the oak,
Under whose shadows lions wild,
Soften'd by love, grow tame and mild:
Love no med'cine can appease,
He burns the fishes in the seas:

Not all the skill his wounds can stench,
Not all the sea his fire can quench.
Love did make the bloody spear
Once a leavy coat to wear,
While in his leaves there shrouded lay
Sweet birds, for love that sing and play
And of all love's joyful flame
I the bud and blossom am.

    Only bend thy knee to me,
    Thy wooing shall thy winning be

See, see the flowers that below
Now as fresh as morning blow;
And of all the virgin rose
That as bright Aurora shows;
How they all unleavèd die,
Losing their virginity!
Like unto a summer shade,
But now born, and now they fade.
Every thing doth pass away;
There is danger in delay:
Come, come, gather then the rose,
Gather it, or it you lose!
All the sand of Tagus' shore
Into my bosom casts his ore:
All the valleys' swimming corn
To my house is yearly borne:
Every grape of every vine
Is gladly bruised to make me wine:
While ten thousand kings, as proud,
To carry up my train have bow'd,
And a world of ladies send me

In my chambers to attend me:
All the stars in Heav'n that shine,
And ten thousand more, are mine:
    Only bend thy knee to me,
    Thy wooing shall thy winning be!

FRANCIS BEAUMONT

1586-1616

242   *On the Tombs in Westminster Abbcy*

MORTALITY, behold and fear!
   What a change of flesh is here!
Think how many royal bones
Sleep within this heap of stones:
Here they lie had realms and lands,
Who now want strength to stir their hands:
Where from their pulpits seal'd with dust
They preach, 'In greatness is no trust.'
Here's an acre sown indeed
With the richest, royall'st seed
That the earth did e'er suck in
Since the first man died for sin:
Here the bones of birth have cried—
'Though gods they were, as men they died.'
Here are sands, ignoble things,
Dropt from the ruin'd sides of kings;
Here's a world of pomp and state,
Buried in dust, once dead by fate.

243 *Dawn*

FLY hence, shadows, that do keep
  Watchful sorrows charm'd in sleep!
Tho' the eyes be overtaken,
Yet the heart doth ever waken
Thoughts chain'd up in busy snares
Of continual woes and cares:
Love and griefs are so exprest
As they rather sigh than rest.
    Fly hence, shadows, that do keep
    Watchful sorrows charm'd in sleep!

244 *I loved a Lass*

I LOVED a lass, a fair one,
  As fair as e'er was seen;
She was indeed a rare one,
  Another Sheba Queen:
But, fool as then I was,
  I thought she loved me too:
But now, alas! she's left me,
  Falero, lero, loo!

Her hair like gold did glister,
  Each eye was like a star,
She did surpass her sister,
  Which pass'd all others far;

GEORGE WITHER

She would me 'honey' call,
   She'd—O she'd kiss me too!
But now, alas! she's left me,
   Falero, lero, loo!

In summer time to Medley
   My love and I would go;
The boatmen there stood read'ly
   My love and me to row.
For cream there would we call,
   For cakes and for prunes too;
But now, alas! she's left me,
   Falero, lero, loo!

Her cheeks were like the cherry,
   Her skin was white as snow;
When she was blithe and merry
   She angel-like did show;
Her waist exceeding small,
   The fives did fit her shoe:
But now, alas! she's left me,
   Falero, lero, loo!

In summer time or winter
   She had her heart's desire;
I still did scorn to stint her
   From sugar, sack, or fire;
The world went round about,
   No cares we ever knew:
But now, alas! she's left me,
   Falero, lero, loo!

To maidens' vows and swearing
  Henceforth no credit give;
You may give them the hearing,
  But never them believe;
They are as false as fair,
  Unconstant, frail, untrue:
For mine, alas! hath left me,
  Falero, lero, loo!

245   *The Lover's Resolution*

SHALL I, wasting in despair,
  Die because a woman's fair?
Or make pale my cheeks with care
'Cause another's rosy are?
Be she fairer than the day,
Or the flow'ry meads in May,
  If she think not well of me,
  What care I how fair she be?

Shall my silly heart be pined
'Cause I see a woman kind?
Or a well disposèd nature
Joinèd with a lovely feature?
Be she meeker, kinder, than
Turtle-dove or pelican,
  If she be not so to me,
  What care I how kind she be?

Shall a woman's virtues move
Me to perish for her love?
Or her well-deservings known
Make me quite forget my own?
Be she with that goodness blest

Which may merit name of Best,
  If she be not such to me,
    What care I how good she be?

'Cause her fortune seems too high,
Shall I play the fool and die?
She that bears a noble mind,
If not outward helps she find,
Thinks what with them he would do
That without them dares her woo;
  And unless that mind I see,
    What care I how great she be?

Great, or good, or kind, or fair,
I will ne'er the more despair;
If she love me, this believe,
I will die ere she shall grieve;
If she slight me when I woo,
I can scorn and let her go;
  For if she be not for me,
    What care I for whom she be?

246   *The Choice*

ME so oft my fancy drew
  Here and there, that I ne'er knew
Where to place desire before
So that range it might no more;
But as he that passeth by
Where, in all her jollity,
Flora's riches in a row
Do in seemly order grow,
And a thousand flowers stand
Bending as to kiss his hand;

Out of which delightful store
One he may take and no more;
Long he pausing doubteth whether
Of those fair ones he should gather.

First the Primrose courts his eyes,
Then the Cowslip he espies;
Next the Pansy seems to woo him,
Then Carnations bow unto him;
Which whilst that enamour'd swain
From the stalk intends to strain,
(As half-fearing to be seen)
Prettily her leaves between
Peeps the Violet, pale to see
That her virtues slighted be;
Which so much his liking wins
That to seize her he begins.

Yet before he stoop'd so low
He his wanton eye did throw
On a stem that grew more high,
And the Rose did there espy.
Who, beside her previous scent,
To procure his eyes content
Did display her goodly breast,
Where he found at full exprest
All the good that Nature showers
On a thousand other flowers;
Wherewith he affected takes it,
His belovèd flower he makes it,
And without desire of more
Walks through all he saw before.

GEORGE WITHER

So I wand'ring but erewhile
Through the garden of this Isle,
Saw rich beauties, I confess,
And in number numberless:
Yea, so differing lovely too,
That I had a world to do
Ere I could set up my rest,
Where to choose and choose the best.

Thus I fondly fear'd, till Fate
(Which I must confess in that
Did a greater favour to me
Than the world can malice do me)
Show'd to me that matchless flower,
Subject for this song of our;
Whose perfection having eyed,
Reason instantly espied
That Desire, which ranged abroad,
There would find a period:
And no marvel if it might,
For it there hath all delight,
And in her hath nature placed
What each several fair one graced.

Let who list, for me, advance
The admirèd flowers of France,
Let who will praise and behold
The reservèd Marigold;
Let the sweet-breath'd Violet now
Unto whom she pleaseth bow;
And the fairest Lily spread
Where she will her golden head;

I have such a flower to wear
That for those I do not care.

Let the young and happy swains
Playing on the Britain plains
Court unblamed their shepherdesses,
And with their gold curlèd tresses
Toy uncensured, until I
Grudge at their prosperity.
Let all times, both present, past,
And the age that shall be last,
Vaunt the beauties they bring forth.
I have found in one such worth,
That content I neither care
What the best before me were;
Nor desire to live and see
Who shall fair hereafter be;
For I know the hand of Nature
Will not make a fairer creature.

247   *A Widow's Hymn*

HOW near me came the hand of Death,
    When at my side he struck my dear,
And took away the precious breath
    Which quicken'd my belovèd peer!
        How helpless am I thereby made!
        By day how grieved, by night how sad!
And now my life's delight is gone,
—Alas! how am I left alone!

247 peer] companion.

GEORGE WITHER

The voice which I did more esteem
   Than music in her sweetest key,
Those eyes which unto me did seem
   More comfortable than the day;
     Those now by me, as they have been,
     Shall never more be heard or seen;
But what I once enjoy'd in them
Shall seem hereafter as a dream.

Lord! keep me faithful to the trust
   Which my dear spouse reposed in me:
To him now dead preserve me just
   In all that should performèd be!
     For though our being man and wife
     Extendeth only to this life,
Yet neither life nor death should end
The being of a faithful friend.

WILLIAM BROWNE, OF TAVISTOCK

1588–1643

248   *A Welcome*

WELCOME, welcome! do I sing,
   Far more welcome than the spring;
He that parteth from you never
Shall enjoy a spring for ever.

He that to the voice is near
   Breaking from your iv'ry pale,
Need not walk abroad to hear
   The delightful nightingale.
         Welcome, welcome, then . . .

267

He that looks still on your eyes,
    Though the winter have begun
To benumb our arteries,
    Shall not want the summer's sun.
            Welcome, welcome, then . . .

He that still may see your cheeks,
    Where all rareness still reposes,
Is a fool if e'er he seeks
    Other lilies, other roses.
            Welcome, welcome, then . . .

He to whom your soft lip yields,
    And perceives your breath in kissing,
All the odours of the fields
    Never, never shall be missing.
            Welcome, welcome, then . . .

He that question would anew
    What fair Eden was of old,
Let him rightly study you,
    And a brief of that behold.
            Welcome, welcome, then . . .

249   *The Sirens' Song*

STEER, hither steer your wingèd pines,
    All beaten mariners!
Here lie Love's undiscover'd mines,
    A prey to passengers—
Perfumes far sweeter than the best
Which make the Phœnix' urn and nest.

Fear not your ships,
Nor any to oppose you save our lips;
 But come on shore,
Where no joy dies till Love hath gotten more.

For swelling waves our panting breasts,
 Where never storms arise,
Exchange, and be awhile our guests:
 For stars gaze on our eyes.
The compass Love shall hourly sing,
And as he goes about the ring,
 We will not miss
To tell each point he nameth with a kiss.
 —Then come on shore,
Where no joy dies till Love hath gotten more.

250   *The Rose*

A ROSE, as fair as ever saw the North,
 Grew in a little garden all alone;
A sweeter flower did Nature ne'er put forth,
Nor fairer garden yet was never known:
The maidens danced about it morn and noon,
And learnèd bards of it their ditties made;
The nimble fairies by the pale-faced moon
Water'd the root and kiss'd her pretty shade.
But well-a-day!—the gardener careless grew;
The maids and fairies both were kept away,
And in a drought the caterpillars threw
Themselves upon the bud and every spray.
 God shield the stock! If heaven send no supplies,
 The fairest blossom of the garden dies.

251 *Song*

FOR her gait, if she be walking;
Be she sitting, I desire her
For her state's sake; and admire her
For her wit if she be talking;
Gait and state and wit approve her;
For which all and each I love her.

Be she sullen, I commend her
For a modest. Be she merry,
For a kind one her prefer I.
Briefly, everything doth lend her
So much grace, and so approve her,
That for everything I love her.

252 *Memory*

SO shuts the marigold her leaves
At the departure of the sun;
So from the honeysuckle sheaves
The bee goes when the day is done;
So sits the turtle when she is but one,
And so all woe, as I since she is gone.

To some few birds kind Nature hath
Made all the summer as one day:
Which once enjoy'd, cold winter's wrath
As night they sleeping pass away.
Those happy creatures are, that know not yet
The pain to be deprived or to forget.

WILLIAM BROWNE

I oft have heard men say there be
　　Some that with confidence profess
The helpful Art of Memory:
　　But could they teach Forgetfulness,
I'd learn; and try what further art could do
To make me love her and forget her too.

Epitaphs

253　　*In Obitum M.S. X° Maij, 1614*

MAY! Be thou never graced with birds that sing,
　　　　Nor Flora's pride!
In thee all flowers and roses spring,
　　　　Mine only died.

254　　*On the Countess Dowager of Pembroke*

UNDERNEATH this sable herse
　　Lies the subject of all verse:
Sidney's sister, Pembroke's mother:
Death, ere thou hast slain another
Fair and learn'd and good as she,
Time shall throw a dart at thee.

ROBERT HERRICK

1591-1674

255　　*Corinna's going a-Maying*

GET up, get up for shame! The blooming morn
　　Upon her wings presents the god unshorn.
See how Aurora throws her fair
Fresh-quilted colours through the air:

ROBERT HERRICK

Get up, sweet slug-a-bed, and see
  The dew bespangling herb and tree!
Each flower has wept and bow'd toward the east
Above an hour since, yet you not drest;
  Nay! not so much as out of bed?
  When all the birds have matins said
  And sung their thankful hymns, 'tis sin,
  Nay, profanation, to keep in,
Whereas a thousand virgins on this day
Spring sooner than the lark, to fetch in May.

Rise and put on your foliage, and be seen
To come forth, like the spring-time, fresh and green,
  And sweet as Flora. Take no care
  For jewels for your gown or hair:
  Fear not; the leaves will strew
  Gems in abundance upon you:
Besides, the childhood of the day has kept,
Against you come, some orient pearls unwept.
  Come, and receive them while the light
  Hangs on the dew-locks of the night:
  And Titan on the eastern hill
  Retires himself, or else stands still
Till you come forth! Wash, dress, be brief in praying:
Few beads are best when once we go a-Maying.

Come, my Corinna, come; and coming, mark
How each field turns a street, each street a park,
  Made green and trimm'd with trees! see how
  Devotion gives each house a bough

    beads] prayers.

Or branch! each porch, each door, ere this,
    An ark, a tabernacle is,
Made up of white-thorn neatly interwove,
As if here were those cooler shades of love.
    Can such delights be in the street
    And open fields, and we not see't?
    Come, we'll abroad: and let's obey
    The proclamation made for May,
And sin no more, as we have done, by staying;
But, my Corinna, come, let's go a-Maying.

There's not a budding boy or girl this day
But is got up and gone to bring in May.
    A deal of youth ere this is come
    Back, and with white-thorn laden home.
    Some have dispatch'd their cakes and cream,
    Before that we have left to dream:
And some have wept and woo'd, and plighted troth,
And chose their priest, ere we can cast off sloth:
    Many a green-gown has been given,
    Many a kiss, both odd and even:
    Many a glance, too, has been sent
    From out the eye, love's firmament:
Many a jest told of the keys betraying
This night, and locks pick'd: yet we're not a-Maying!

Come, let us go, while we are in our prime,
And take the harmless folly of the time!
    We shall grow old apace, and die
    Before we know our liberty.

      green-gown] tumble on the grass.

Our life is short, and our days run
As fast away as does the sun.
And, as a vapour or a drop of rain,
Once lost, can ne'er be found again,
So when or you or I are made
A fable, song, or fleeting shade,
All love, all liking, all delight
Lies drown'd with us in endless night.
Then, while time serves, and we are but decaying,
Come, my Corinna, come, let's go a-Maying.

256 *To the Virgins, to make much of Time*

GATHER ye rosebuds while ye may,
Old Time is still a-flying:
And this same flower that smiles to-day
To-morrow will be dying.

The glorious lamp of heaven, the sun,
The higher he's a-getting,
The sooner will his race be run,
And nearer he's to setting.

That age is best which is the first,
When youth and blood are warmer;
But being spent, the worse, and worst
Times still succeed the former.

Then be not coy, but use your time,
And while ye may, go marry:
For having lost but once your prime,
You may for ever tarry.

257
To the Western Wind

SWEET western wind, whose luck it is,
  Made rival with the air,
To give Perenna's lip a kiss,
  And fan her wanton hair:

Bring me but one, I'll promise thee,
  Instead of common showers,
Thy wings shall be embalm'd by me,
  And all beset with flowers.

258
To Electra

I DARE not ask a kiss,
  I dare not beg a smile,
Lest having that, or this,
  I might grow proud the while.

No, no, the utmost share
  Of my desire shall be
Only to kiss that air
  That lately kissèd thee.

259
To Violets

WELCOME, maids of honour!
    You do bring
    In the spring,
And wait upon her.

She has virgins many,
    Fresh and fair;
    Yet you are
More sweet than any.

You're the maiden posies,
    And so graced
    To be placed
'Fore damask roses.

Yet, though thus respected,
    By-and-by
    Ye do lie,
Poor girls, neglected.

260   *To Daffodils*

FAIR daffodils, we weep to see
    You haste away so soon;
As yet the early-rising sun
    Has not attain'd his noon.
        Stay, stay
      Until the hasting day
        Has run
      But to the evensong;
And, having pray'd together, we
    Will go with you along.

We have short time to stay, as you,
    We have as short a spring;
As quick a growth to meet decay,
    As you, or anything.
        We die
      As your hours do, and dry
        Away
      Like to the summer's rain;
Or as the pearls of morning's dew,
    Ne'er to be found again.

261 *To Blossoms*

FAIR pledges of a fruitful tree,
  Why do ye fall so fast?
Your date is not so past
But you may stay yet here awhile
  To blush and gently smile,
    And go at last.

What! were ye born to be
  An hour or half's delight,
  And so to bid good night?
'Twas pity Nature brought you forth
  Merely to show your worth
    And lose you quite.

But you are lovely leaves, where we
  May read how soon things have
  Their end, though ne'er so brave:
And after they have shown their pride
  Like you awhile, they glide
    Into the grave.

262 *The Primrose*

ASK me why I send you here
  This sweet Infanta of the year?
Ask me why I send to you
This primrose, thus bepearl'd with dew?
I will whisper to your ears:—
The sweets of love are mix'd with tears.

Ask me why this flower does show
So yellow-green, and sickly too?
Ask me why the stalk is weak
And bending (yet it doth not break)?
I will answer:—These discover
What fainting hopes are in a lover.

263   *The Funeral Rites of the Rose*

THE Rose was sick and smiling died;
    And, being to be sanctified,
About the bed there sighing stood
The sweet and flowery sisterhood:
Some hung the head, while some did bring,
To wash her, water from the spring;
Some laid her forth, while others wept,
But all a solemn fast there kept:
The holy sisters, some among,
The sacred dirge and trental sung.
But ah! what sweets smelt everywhere,
As Heaven had spent all perfumes there.
At last, when prayers for the dead
And rites were all accomplishèd,
They, weeping, spread a lawny loom,
And closed her up as in a tomb.

264   *Cherry-Ripe*

CHERRY-RIPE, ripe, ripe, I cry,
    Full and fair ones; come and buy.
If so be you ask me where
They do grow, I answer: There

263 trental] services for the dead, of thirty masses.

Where my Julia's lips do smile;
There's the land, or cherry-isle,
Whose plantations fully show
All the year where cherries grow.

265   *A Meditation for his Mistress*

YOU are a tulip seen to-day,
But, dearest, of so short a stay
That where you grew scarce man can say.

You are a lovely July-flower,
Yet one rude wind or ruffling shower
Will force you hence, and in an hour.

You are a sparkling rose i' th' bud,
Yet lost ere that chaste flesh and blood
Can show where you or grew or stood.

You are a full-spread, fair-set vine,
And can with tendrils love entwine,
Yet dried ere you distil your wine.

You are like balm enclosèd well
In amber or some crystal shell,
Yet lost ere you transfuse your smell.

You are a dainty violet,
Yet wither'd ere you can be set
Within the virgin's coronet.

You are the queen all flowers among;
But die you must, fair maid, ere long,
As he, the maker of this song.

266   *Delight in Disorder*

A SWEET disorder in the dress
   Kindles in clothes a wantonness:
A lawn about the shoulders thrown
Into a fine distraction:
An erring lace, which here and there
Enthrals the crimson stomacher:
A cuff neglectful, and thereby
Ribbands to flow confusedly:
A winning wave, deserving note,
In the tempestuous petticoat:
A careless shoe-string, in whose tie
I see a wild civility:
Do more bewitch me than when art
Is too precise in every part.

267   *Upon Julia's Clothes*

W HENAS in silks my Julia goes,
   Then, then, methinks, how sweetly flows
The liquefaction of her clothes!

Next, when I cast mine eyes and see
That brave vibration each way free,
—O how that glittering taketh me!

268   *The Bracelet: To Julia*

W HY I tie about thy wrist,
   Julia, this silken twist;
For what other reason is't
But to show thee how, in part,
Thou my pretty captive art?
But thy bond-slave is my heart:

'Tis but silk that bindeth thee,
Knap the thread and thou art free;
But 'tis otherwise with me:
—I am bound and fast bound, so
That from thee I cannot go;
If I could, I would not so.

269   *To Daisies, not to shut so soon*

SHUT not so soon; the dull-eyed night
Has not as yet begun
To make a seizure on the light,
   Or to seal up the sun.

No marigolds yet closèd are,
   No shadows great appear;
Nor doth the early shepherd's star
   Shine like a spangle here.

Stay but till my Julia close
   Her life-begetting eye,
And let the whole world then dispose
   Itself to live or die.

270   *The Night-piece: To Julia*

HER eyes the glow-worm lend thee,
   The shooting stars attend thee;
      And the elves also,
      Whose little eyes glow
Like the sparks of fire, befriend thee.

No Will-o'-the-wisp mislight thee,
Nor snake or slow-worm bite thee;
    But on, on thy way
    Not making a stay,
Since ghost there's none to affright thee.

Let not the dark thee cumber:
What though the moon does slumber?
    The stars of the night
    Will lend thee their light
Like tapers clear without number.

Then, Julia, let me woo thee,
Thus, thus to come unto me;
    And when I shall meet
    Thy silv'ry feet,
My soul I'll pour into thee.

271   *To Music, to becalm his Fever*

CHARM me asleep, and melt me so
    With thy delicious numbers,
That, being ravish'd, hence I go
    Away in easy slumbers.
      Ease my sick head,
      And make my bed,
    Thou power that canst sever
      From me this ill,
      And quickly still,
      Though thou not kill
        My fever.

Thou sweetly canst convert the same
  From a consuming fire
Into a gentle licking flame,
  And make it thus expire.
     Then make me weep
     My pains asleep;
  And give me such reposes
    That I, poor I,
    May think thereby
    I live and die
     'Mongst roses.

Fall on me like the silent dew,
  Or like those maiden showers
Which, by the peep of day, do strew
  A baptim o'er the flowers.
     Melt, melt my pains
     With thy soft strains;
  That, having ease me given,
    With full delight
    I leave this light,
    And take my flight
     For Heaven.

272   *To Dianeme*

SWEET, be not proud of those two eyes
  Which starlike sparkle in their skies;
Nor be you proud that you can see
All hearts your captives, yours yet free;
Be you not proud of that rich hair
Which wantons with the love-sick air;

Whenas that ruby which you wear,
Sunk from the tip of your soft ear,
Will last to be a precious stone
When all your world of beauty's gone.

273   *To Œnone*

WHAT conscience, say, is it in thee,
    When I a heart had one,
To take away that heart from me,
    And to retain thy own?

For shame or pity now incline
    To play a loving part;
Either to send me kindly thine,
    Or give me back my heart.

Covet not both; but if thou dost
    Resolve to part with neither,
Why, yet to show that thou art just,
    Take me and mine together!

274   *To Anthea, who may command*
             him Anything

BID me to live, and I will live
    Thy Protestant to be;
Or bid me love, and I will give
    A loving heart to thee.

A heart as soft, a heart as kind,
    A heart as sound and free
As in the whole world thou canst find;
    That heart I'll give to thee.

Bid that heart stay, and it will stay
    To honour thy decree:
Or bid it languish quite away,
    And 't shall do so for thee.

Bid me to weep, and I will weep
    While I have eyes to see:
And, having none, yet will I keep
    A heart to weep for thee.

Bid me despair, and I'll despair
    Under that cypress-tree:
Or bid me die, and I will dare
    E'en death to die for thee.

Thou art my life, my love, my heart,
    The very eyes of me:
And hast command of every part
    To live and die for thee.

275   *To the Willow-tree*

THOU art to all lost love the best,
    The only true plant found,
Wherewith young men and maids distrest,
    And left of love, are crown'd.

When once the lover's rose is dead,
    Or laid aside forlorn:
Then willow-garlands 'bout the head
    Bedew'd with tears are worn.

When with neglect, the lovers' bane,
   Poor maids rewarded be
For their love lost, their only gain
   Is but a wreath from thee.

And underneath thy cooling shade,
   When weary of the light,
The love-spent youth and love-sick maid
   Come to weep out the night.

276   *The Mad Maid's Song*

GOOD-MORROW to the day so fair,
   Good-morning, sir, to you;
Good-morrow to mine own torn hair
   Bedabbled with the dew.

Good-morning to this primrose too,
   Good-morrow to each maid
That will with flowers the tomb bestrew
   Wherein my love is laid.

Ah! woe is me, woe, woe is me!
   Alack and well-a-day!
For pity, sir, find out that bee
   Which bore my love away.

I'll seek him in your bonnet brave,
   I'll seek him in your eyes;
Nay, now I think they've made his grave
   I' th' bed of strawberries.

I'll seek him there; I know ere this
   The cold, cold earth doth shake him;
But I will go, or send a kiss
   By you, sir, to awake him.

Pray hurt him not; though he be dead,
  He knows well who do love him,
And who with green turfs rear his head,
  And who do rudely move him.

He's soft and tender (pray take heed);
  With bands of cowslips bind him,
And bring him home—but 'tis decreed
  That I shall never find him!

277   *Comfort to a Youth that had lost
        his Love*

WHAT needs complaints,
    When she a place
Has with the race
    Of saints?

In endless mirth
She thinks not on
What's said or done
    In Earth.

She sees no tears,
Or any tone
Of thy deep groan
    She hears:

Nor does she mind
Or think on't now
That ever thou
    Wast kind;

But changed above,
She likes not there,
As she did here,
    Thy love.

Forbear therefore,
And lull asleep
Thy woes, and weep
    No more.

278   *To Meadows*

YE have been fresh and green,
    Ye have been fill'd with flowers,
And ye the walks have been
    Where maids have spent their hours.

You have beheld how they
    With wicker arks did come
To kiss and bear away
    The richer cowslips home.

You've heard them sweetly sing,
    And seen them in a round:
Each virgin like a spring,
    With honeysuckles crown'd.

But now we see none here
    Whose silv'ry feet did tread
And with dishevell'd hair
    Adorn'd this smoother mead.

Like unthrifts, having spent
    Your stock and needy grown,
You're left here to lament
    Your poor estates, alone.

279   *A Child's Grace*

HERE a little child I stand
    Heaving up my either hand;
Cold as paddocks though they be,
Here I lift them up to Thee,
For a benison to fall
On our meat and on us all. Amen.

280   *Epitaph*
upon a Child that died

HERE she lies, a pretty bud,
    Lately made of flesh and blood:
Who as soon fell fast asleep
As her little eyes did peep.
Give her strewings, but not stir
The earth that lightly covers her.

281   *Another*

HERE a pretty baby lies
    Sung asleep with lullabies:
Pray be silent and not stir
Th' easy earth that covers her.

282   *His Winding-sheet*

COME thou, who art the wine and wit
    Of all I've writ:
The grace, the glory, and the best
    Piece of the rest.

279 paddocks] frogs.

ROBERT HERRICK

Thou art of what I did intend
    The all and end;
And what was made, was made to meet
    Thee, thee, my sheet.
Come then and be to my chaste side
    Both bed and bride:
We two, as reliques left, will have
    One rest, one grave:
And hugging close, we will not fear
    Lust entering here:
Where all desires are dead and cold
    As is the mould;
And all affections are forgot,
    Or trouble not.
Here, here, the slaves and prisoners be
    From shackles free:
And weeping widows long oppress'd
    Do here find rest.
The wrongèd client ends his laws
    Here, and his cause.
Here those long suits of Chancery lie
    Quiet, or die:
And all Star-Chamber bills do cease
    Or hold their peace.
Here needs no Court for our Request
    Where all are best,
All wise, all equal, and all just
    Alike i' th' dust.
Nor need we here to fear the frown
    Of Court or Crown:
Where fortune bears no sway o'er things,
    There all are Kings.

In this securer place we'll keep
    As lull'd asleep;
Or for a little time we'll lie
    As robes laid by;
To be another day re-worn,
    Turn'd, but not torn:
Or like old testaments engross'd,
    Lock'd up, not lost.
And for a while lie here conceal'd,
    To be reveal'd
Next at the great Platonick year,
    And then meet here.

283   *Litany to the Holy Spirit*

IN the hour of my distress,
  When temptations me oppress,
And when I my sins confess,
    Sweet Spirit, comfort me!

When I lie within my bed,
Sick in heart and sick in head,
And with doubts discomforted,
    Sweet Spirit, comfort me!

When the house doth sigh and weep,
And the world is drown'd in sleep,
Yet mine eyes the watch do keep,
    Sweet Spirit, comfort me!

282 Platonick year] the perfect or cyclic year, when the sun, moon, and five planets end their revolutions together and start anew. See *Timaeus*, 39.

ROBERT HERRICK

When the passing bell doth toll,
And the Furies in a shoal
Come to fright a parting soul,
  Sweet Spirit, comfort me!

When the tapers now burn blue,
And the comforters are few,
And that number more than true,
  Sweet Spirit, comfort me!

When the priest his last hath pray'd,
And I nod to what is said,
'Cause my speech is now decay'd,
  Sweet Spirit, comfort me!

When, God knows, I'm toss'd about
Either with despair or doubt;
Yet before the glass be out,
  Sweet Spirit, comfort me!

When the tempter me pursu'th
With the sins of all my youth,
And half damns me with untruth,
  Sweet Spirit, comfort me!

When the flames and hellish cries
Fright mine ears and fright mine eyes,
And all terrors me surprise,
  Sweet Spirit, comfort me!

When the Judgment is reveal'd,
And that open'd which was seal'd,
When to Thee I have appeal'd,
  Sweet Spirit, comfort me!

FRANCIS QUARLES[1]

284   *A Divine Rapture*

E'EN like two little bank-dividing brooks,
 That wash the pebbles with their wanton streams,
And having ranged and search'd a thousand nooks,
 Meet both at length in silver-breasted Thames,
  Where in a greater current they conjoin:
So I my Best-belovèd's am; so He is mine.

E'en so we met; and after long pursuit,
 E'en so we joined; we both became entire;
No need for either to renew a suit,
 For I was flax, and He was flames of fire:
  Our firm-united souls did more than twine;
So I my Best-belovèd's am; so He is mine.

If all those glittering Monarchs, that command
 The servile quarters of this earthly ball,
Should tender in exchange their shares of land,
 I would not change my fortunes for them all:
  Their wealth is but a counter to my coin:
The world's but theirs; but my Belovèd's mine.

285   *Epigram*

Respice Finem

MY soul, sit thou a patient looker-on;
 Judge not the play before the play is done:
Her plot hath many changes; every day
Speaks a new scene; the last act crowns the play.

[1] See Rochester, p. 492.

286 *A Contemplation upon Flowers*

BRAVE flowers—that I could gallant it like you,
    And be as little vain!
You come abroad, and make a harmless show,
    And to your beds of earth again.
You are not proud: you know your birth:
For your embroider'd garments are from earth.

You do obey your months and times, but I
    Would have it ever Spring:
My fate would know no Winter, never die,
    Nor think of such a thing.
O that I could my bed of earth but view
And smile, and look as cheerfully as you!

O teach me to see Death and not to fear,
    But rather to take truce!
How often have I seen you at a bier,
    And there look fresh and spruce!
You fragrant flowers! then teach me, that my breath
Like yours may sweeten and perfume my death.

287 *A Renunciation*

WE, that did nothing study but the way
    To love each other, with which thoughts the day
Rose with delight to us and with them set,
Must learn the hateful art, how to forget.

HENRY KING

We, that did nothing wish that Heaven could give
Beyond ourselves, nor did desire to live
Beyond that wish, all these now cancel must,
As if not writ in faith, but words and dust.
Yet witness those clear vows which lovers make,
Witness the chaste desires that never brake
Into unruly heats; witness that breast
Which in thy bosom anchor'd his whole rest—
'Tis no default in us: I dare acquite
Thy maiden faith, thy purpose fair and white
As thy pure self. Cross planets did envỳ
Us to each other, and Heaven did untie
Faster than vows could bind. Oh, that the stars,
When lovers meet, should stand opposed in wars!

Since then some higher Destinies command,
Let us not strive, nor labour to withstand
What is past help. The longest date of grief
Can never yield a hope of our relief:
Fold back our arms; take home our fruitless loves,
That must new fortunes try, like turtle-doves
Dislodgèd from their haunts. We must in tears
Unwind a love knit up in many years.
In this last kiss I here surrender thee
Back to thyself.—So, thou again art free:
Thou in another, sad as that, re-send
The truest heart that lover e'er did lend.
Now turn from each: so fare our sever'd hearts
As the divorced soul from her body parts.

Exequy on his Wife

ACCEPT, thou shrine of my dead saint,
    Instead of dirges this complaint;
And for sweet flowers to crown thy herse
Receive a strew of weeping verse
From thy grieved friend, whom thou might'st see
Quite melted into tears for thee.

    Dear loss! since thy untimely fate,
My task hath been to meditate
On thee, on thee! Thou art the book,
The library whereon I look,
Tho' almost blind. For thee, loved clay,
I languish out, not live, the day. . . .
Thou hast benighted me; thy set
This eve of blackness did beget,
Who wast my day (tho' overcast
Before thou hadst thy noontide past):
And I remember must in tears
Thou scarce hadst seen so many years
As day tells hours. By thy clear sun
My love and fortune first did run;
But thou wilt never more appear
Folded within my hemisphere,
Since both thy light and motion,
Like a fled star, is fall'n and gone,
And 'twixt me and my soul's dear wish
The earth now interposèd is. . . .

    I could allow thee for a time
To darken me and my sad clime;
Were it a month, a year, or ten,
I would thy exile live till then,

And all that space my mirth adjourn—
So thou wouldst promise to return,
And putting off thy ashy shroud
At length disperse this sorrow's cloud.

   But woe is me! the longest date
Too narrow is to calculate
These empty hopes: never shall I
Be so much blest as to descry
A glimpse of thee, till that day come
Which shall the earth to cinders doom,
And a fierce fever must calcine
The body of this world—like thine,
My little world! That fit of fire
Once off, our bodies shall aspire
To our souls' bliss: then we shall rise
And view ourselves with clearer eyes
In that calm region where no night
Can hide us from each other's sight.

   Meantime thou hast her, Earth: much good
May my harm do thee! Since it stood
With Heaven's will I might not call
Her longer mine, I give thee all
My short-lived right and interest
In her whom living I loved best.
Be kind to her, and prithee look
Thou write into thy Doomsday book
Each parcel of this rarity
Which in thy casket shrined doth lie,
As thou wilt answer Him that lent—
Not gave—thee my dear monument.
So close the ground, and 'bout her shade
Black curtains draw: my bride is laid.

HENRY KING

Sleep on, my Love, in thy cold bed
Never to be disquieted!
My last good-night! Thou wilt not wake
Till I thy fate shall overtake:
Till age, or grief, or sickness must
Marry my body to that dust
It so much loves; and fill the room
My heart keeps empty in thy tomb.
Stay for me there: I will not fail
To meet thee in that hollow vale.
And think not much of my delay:
I am already on the way,
And follow thee with all the speed
Desire can make, or sorrows breed.
Each minute is a short degree
And every hour a step towards thee. . . .
    'Tis true—with shame and grief I yield—
Thou, like the van, first took'st the field;
And gotten hast the victory
In thus adventuring to die
Before me, whose more years might crave
A just precedence in the grave.
But hark! my pulse, like a soft drum,
Beats my approach, tells thee I come;
And slow howe'er my marches be
I shall at last sit down by thee.
    The thought of this bids me go on
And wait my dissolution
With hope and comfort. Dear—forgive
The crime—I am content to live
Divided, with but half a heart,
Till we shall meet and never part.

289   *Virtue*

SWEET day, so cool, so calm, so bright!
The bridal of the earth and sky—
The dew shall weep thy fall to-night;
         For thou must die.

Sweet rose, whose hue angry and brave
Bids the rash gazer wipe his eye,
Thy root is ever in its grave,
         And thou must die.

Sweet spring, full of sweet days and roses,
A box where sweets compacted lie,
My music shows ye have your closes,
         And all must die.

Only a sweet and virtuous soul,
Like season'd timber, never gives;
But though the whole world turn to coal,
         Then chiefly lives.

290   *Easter*

I GOT me flowers to straw Thy way,
I got me boughs off many a tree;
But Thou wast up by break of day,
         And brought'st Thy sweets along with Thee.

Yet though my flowers be lost, they say
A heart can never come too late;
Teach it to sing Thy praise this day,
         And then this day my life shall date.

Discipline

THROW away Thy rod,
  Throw away Thy wrath;
    O my God,
Take the gentle path!

For my heart's desire
Unto Thine is bent:
    I aspire
To a full consent.

Not a word or look
I affect to own,
    But by book,
And Thy Book alone.

Though I fail, I weep;
Though I halt in pace,
    Yet I creep
To the Throne of Grace.

Then let wrath remove;
Love will do the deed:
    For with Love
Stony hearts will bleed.

Love is swift of foot;
Love's a man of war,
    And can shoot,
And can hit from far.

Who can 'scape his bow?
That which wrought on Thee,
    Brought Thee low,
Needs must work on me.

Throw away Thy rod;
Though man frailties hath,
  Thou art God:
Throw away Thy wrath!

292   *A Dialogue*

Man. SWEETEST Saviour, if my soul
           Were but worth the having,
       Quickly should I then control
           Any thought of waving.
       But when all my care and pains
       Cannot give the name of gains
       To Thy wretch so full of stains,
       What delight or hope remains?

Saviour. What, child, is the balance thine,
              Thine the poise and measure?
          If I say, 'Thou shalt be Mine,'
              Finger not My treasure.
          What the gains in having thee
          Do amount to, only He
          Who for man was sold can see
          That transferr'd th' accounts to Me.

Man. But as I can see no merit
          Leading to this favour,
       So the way to fit me for it
          Is beyond my savour.
       As the reason, then, is Thine,
       So the way is none of mine;
       I disclaim the whole design;
       Sin disclaims and I resign.

       292 savour] savoir, knowing.

Saviour. That is all: if that I could
   Get without repining;
  And My clay, My creature, would
   Follow My resigning;
  That as I did freely part
  With My glory and desert,
  Left all joys to feel all smart——

Man. Ah, no more! Thou break'st my heart!

293   *The Pulley*

WHEN God at first made Man,
  Having a glass of blessings standing by—
Let us (said He) pour on him all we can;
Let the world's riches, which dispersèd lie,
  Contract into a span.

  So strength first made a way,
Then beauty flow'd, then wisdom, honour, pleasure:
When almost all was out, God made a stay,
Perceiving that, alone of all His treasure,
  Rest in the bottom lay.

  For if I should (said He)
Bestow this jewel also on My creature,
He would adore My gifts instead of Me,
And rest in Nature, not the God of Nature:
  So both should losers be.

  Yet let him keep the rest,
But keep them with repining restlessness;
Let him be rich and weary, that at least,
If goodness lead him not, yet weariness
  May toss him to My breast.

294   *Love*

LOVE bade me welcome; yet my soul drew back,
    Guilty of dust and sin.
But quick-eyed Love, observing me grow slack
    From my first entrance in,
Drew nearer to me, sweetly questioning
    If I lack'd anything.

'A guest,' I answer'd, 'worthy to be here:'
    Love said, 'You shall be he.'
'I, the unkind, ungrateful? Ah, my dear,
    I cannot look on Thee.'
Love took my hand and smiling did reply,
    'Who made the eyes but I?'

'Truth, Lord; but I have marr'd them: let my shame
    Go where it doth deserve.'
'And know you not,' says Love, 'Who bore the blame?'
    'My dear, then I will serve.'
'You must sit down,' says Love, 'and taste my meat.'
    So I did sit and eat.

JAMES SHIRLEY

1596–1666

295   *Piping Peace*

YOU virgins that did late despair
    To keep your wealth from cruel men,
Tie up in silk your careless hair:
    Soft peace is come again.

Now lovers' eyes may gently shoot
    A flame that will not kill;
The drum was angry, but the lute
    Shall whisper what you will.

Sing Io, Io! for his sake
 That hath restored your drooping heads;
With choice of sweetest flowers make
 A garden where he treads;

Whilst we whole groves of laurel bring,
 A pretty triumph for his brow,
Who is the Master of our spring
 And all the bloom we owe.

296   *Death the Leveller*

THE glories of our blood and state
 Are shadows, not substantial things;
There is no armour against Fate;
 Death lays his icy hand on kings:
   Sceptre and Crown
   Must tumble down,
And in the dust be equal made
With the poor crookèd scythe and spade.

Some men with swords may reap the field,
 And plant fresh laurels where they kill:
But their strong nerves at last must yield;
 They tame but one another still:
   Early or late
   They stoop to fate,
And must give up their murmuring breath
When they, pale captives, creep to death.

The garlands wither on your brow;
 Then boast no more your mighty deeds!
Upon Death's purple altar now
 See where the victor-victim bleeds.

   295 owe] own.

JAMES SHIRLEY

  Your heads must come
  To the cold tomb:
Only the actions of the just
Smell sweet and blossom in their dust.

THOMAS CAREW

1595 ?–1639 ?

297   *Song*

ASK me no more where Jove bestows,
 When June is past, the fading rose;
For in your beauty's orient deep
These flowers, as in their causes, sleep.

Ask me no more whither do stray
The golden atoms of the day;
For in pure love heaven did prepare
Those powders to enrich your hair.

Ask me no more whither doth haste
The nightingale when May is past;
For in your sweet dividing throat
She winters and keeps warm her note.

Ask me no more where those stars 'light
That downwards fall in dead of night;
For in your eyes they sit, and there
Fixèd become as in their sphere.

Ask me no more if east or west
The Phœnix builds her spicy nest;
For unto you at last she flies,
And in your fragrant bosom dies.

298   *Persuasions to Joy: a Song*

IF the quick spirits in your eye
   Now languish and anon must die;
If every sweet and every grace
Must fly from that forsaken face;
     Then, Celia, let us reap our joys
     Ere Time such goodly fruit destroys.

Or if that golden fleece must grow
For ever free from agèd snow;
If those bright suns must know no shade,
Nor your fresh beauties ever fade;
     Then fear not, Celia, to bestow
     What, still being gather'd, still must grow.

Thus either Time his sickle brings
In vain, or else in vain his wings.

299   *To His Inconstant Mistress*

WHEN thou, poor Excommunicate
   From all the joys of Love, shalt see
The full reward and glorious fate
   Which my strong faith shall purchase me,
   Then curse thine own inconstancy!

A fairer hand than thine shall cure
   That heart which thy false oaths did wound;
And to my soul a soul more pure
   Than thine shall by Love's hand be bound,
   And both with equal glory crown'd.

306

Then shalt thou weep, entreat, complain
  To Love, as I did once to thee;
When all thy tears shall be as vain
  As mine were then: for thou shalt be
  Damn'd for thy false apostasy.

300   *The Unfading Beauty*

HE that loves a rosy cheek,
    Or a coral lip admires,
Or from star-like eyes doth seek
  Fuel to maintain his fires:
As old Time makes these decay,
So his flames must waste away.

But a smooth and steadfast mind,
  Gentle thoughts and calm desires,
Hearts with equal love combined,
  Kindle never-dying fires.
Where these are not, I despise
Lovely cheeks or lips or eyes.

301   *Ingrateful Beauty threatened*

KNOW, Celia, since thou art so proud,
    'Twas I that gave thee thy renown.
Thou hadst in the forgotten crowd
  Of common beauties lived unknown,
Had not my verse extoll'd thy name,
And with it imp'd the wings of Fame.

  301 imp'd] grafted with new feathers.

That killing power is none of thine;
 I gave it to thy voice and eyes;
Thy sweets, thy graces, all are mine;
 Thou art my star, shin'st in my skies;
Then dart not from thy borrow'd sphere
Lightning on him that fix'd thee there.

Tempt me with such affrights no more,
 Lest what I made I uncreate;
Let fools thy mystic form adore,
 I know thee in thy mortal state.
Wise poets, that wrapt Truth in tales,
Knew her themselves through all her veils.

302   *Epitaph*

On the Lady Mary Villiers

THE Lady Mary Villiers lies
 Under this stone; with weeping eyes
The parents that first gave her birth,
And their sad friends, laid her in earth.
If any of them, Reader, were
Known unto thee, shed a tear;
Or if thyself possess a gem
As dear to thee, as this to them,
Though a stranger to this place,
Bewail in theirs thine own hard case:
 For thou perhaps at thy return
 May'st find thy Darling in an urn.

THOMAS CAREW

Another

THIS little vault, this narrow room,
　Of Love and Beauty is the tomb;
The dawning beam, that 'gan to clear
Our clouded sky, lies darken'd here,
For ever set to us: by Death
Sent to enflame the World Beneath.
　'Twas but a bud, yet did contain
More sweetness than shall spring again;
A budding Star, that might have grown
Into a Sun when it had blown.
This hopeful Beauty did create
New life in Love's declining state;
But now his empire ends, and we
From fire and wounding darts are free;
　　His brand, his bow, let no man fear:
　　The flames, the arrows, all lie here.

JASPER MAYNE

1604–1672

Time

TIME is the feather'd thing,
　And, whilst I praise
The sparklings of thy looks and call them rays,
　　Takes wing,
　Leaving behind him as he flies
An unperceivèd dimness in thine eyes.
　His minutes, whilst they're told,
　　Do make us old;
　And every sand of his fleet glass,
　Increasing age as it doth pass,

JASPER MAYNE

Insensibly sows wrinkles there
Where flowers and roses do appear.
Whilst we do speak, our fire
Doth into ice expire,
    Flames turn to frost;
    And ere we can
Know how our crow turns swan,
Or how a silver snow
Springs there where jet did grow,
Our fading spring is in dull winter lost.

    Since then the Night hath hurl'd
        Darkness, Love's shade,
    Over its enemy the Day, and made
        The world
    Just such a blind and shapeless thing
As 'twas before light did from darkness spring,
    Let us employ its treasure
    And make shade pleasure:
Let's number out the hours by blisses,
And count the minutes by our kisses;
    Let the heavens new motions feel
    And by our embraces wheel;
    And whilst we try the way
    By which Love doth convey
        Soul unto soul,
        And mingling so
    Makes them such raptures know
    As makes them entranced lie
        In mutual ecstasy,
Let the harmonious spheres in music roll!

WILLIAM HABINGTON

1605-1654

305   *To Roses in the Bosom of Castara*

YE blushing virgins happy are
   In the chaste nunnery of her breasts—
For he'd profane so chaste a fair,
   Whoe'er should call them Cupid's nests.

Transplanted thus how bright ye grow!
   How rich a perfume do ye yield!
In some close garden cowslips so
   Are sweeter than i' th' open field.

In those white cloisters live secure
   From the rude blasts of wanton breath!—
Each hour more innocent and pure,
   Till you shall wither into death.

Then that which living gave you room,
   Your glorious sepulchre shall be.
There wants no marble for a tomb
   Whose breast hath marble been to me.

306   *Nox Nocti Indicat Scientiam*

WHEN I survey the bright
   Celestial sphere;
So rich with jewels hung, that Night
   Doth like an Ethiop bride appear:

My soul her wings doth spread
     And heavenward flies,
Th' Almighty's mysteries to read
   In the large volumes of the skies.

WILLIAM HABINGTON

For the bright firmament
　　　Shoots forth no flame
So silent, but is eloquent
　　　In speaking the Creator's name.

No unregarded star
　　　Contracts its light
Into so small a character,
　　　Removed far from our human sight,

But if we steadfast look
　　　We shall discern
In it, as in some holy book,
　　　How man may heavenly knowledge learn.

It tells the conqueror
　　　That far-stretch'd power,
Which his proud dangers traffic for,
　　　Is but the triumph of an hour:

That from the farthest North,
　　　Some nation may,
Yet undiscover'd, issue forth,
　　　And o'er his new-got conquest sway:

Some nation yet shut in
　　　With hills of ice
May be let out to scourge his sin,
　　　Till they shall equal him in vice.

And then they likewise shall
　　　Their ruin have;
For as yourselves your empires fall,
　　　And every kingdom hath a grave.

WILLIAM HABINGTON

Thus those celestial fires,
    Though seeming mute,
The fallacy of our desires
    And all the pride of life confute:—

For they have watch'd since first
    The World had birth:
And found sin in itself accurst,
    And nothing permanent on Earth.

THOMAS RANDOLPH

1605–1635

307 *A Devout Lover*

I HAVE a mistress, for perfections rare
  In every eye, but in my thoughts most fair.
Like tapers on the altar shine her eyes;
Her breath is the perfume of sacrifice;
And wheresoe'er my fancy would begin,
Still her perfection lets religion in.
We sit and talk, and kiss away the hours
As chastely as the morning dews kiss flowers:
I touch her, like my beads, with devout care,
And come unto my courtship as my prayer.

308 *An Ode to Master Anthony Stafford*
to hasten Him into the Country

COME, spur away,
  I have no patience for a longer stay,
But must go down
And leave the chargeable noise of this great town:
  I will the country see,
  Where old simplicity,

THOMAS RANDOLPH

Though hid in gray,
Doth look more gay
Than foppery in plush and scarlet clad.
Farewell, you city wits, that are
Almost at civil war—
'Tis time that I grow wise, when all the world grows mad.

More of my days
I will not spend to gain an idiot's praise;
Or to make sport
For some slight Puisne of the Inns of Court.
Then, worthy Stafford, say,
How shall we spend the day?
With what delights
Shorten the nights?
When from this tumult we are got secure,
Where mirth with all her freedom goes,
Yet shall no finger lose;
Where every word is thought, and every thought is pure?

There from the tree
We'll cherries pluck, and pick the strawberry;
And every day
Go see the wholesome country girls make hay,
Whose brown hath lovelier grace
Than any painted face
That I do know
Hyde Park can show:
Where I had rather gain a kiss than meet
(Though some of them in greater state
Might court my love with plate)
The beauties of the Cheap, and wives of Lombard Street.

But think upon
Some other pleasures: these to me are none.
Why do I prate
Of women, that are things against my fate!
I never mean to wed
That torture to my bed:
My Muse is she
My love shall be.
Let clowns get wealth and heirs: when I am gone
And that great bugbear, grisly Death,
Shall take this idle breath,
If I a poem leave, that poem is my son.

Of this no more!
We'll rather taste the bright Pomona's store.
No fruit shall 'scape
Our palates, from the damson to the grape.
Then, full, we'll seek a shade,
And hear what music's made;
How Philomel
Her tale doth tell,
And how the other birds do fill the quire;
The thrush and blackbird lend their throats,
Warbling melodious notes;
We will all sports enjoy which others but desire.

Ours is the sky,
Where, at what fowl we please, our hawk shall fly:
Nor will we spare
To hunt the crafty fox or timorous hare;
But let our hounds run loose
In any ground they'll choose;

THOMAS RANDOLPH

The buck shall fall,
The stag, and all.
Our pleasures must from their own warrants be,
For to my Muse, if not to me,
I'm sure all game is free:
Heaven, earth, are all but parts of her great royalty.

And when we mean
To taste of Bacchus' blessings now and then,
And drink by stealth
A cup or two to noble Barkley's health,
I'll take my pipe and try
The Phrygian melody;
Which he that hears,
Lets through his ears
A madness to distemper all the brain:
Then I another pipe will take
And Doric music make,
To civilize with graver notes our wits again.

SIR WILLIAM DAVENANT

1606–1668

309   *Aubade*

THE lark now leaves his wat'ry nest,
  And climbing shakes his dewy wings.
He takes this window for the East,
  And to implore your light he sings—
Awake, awake! the morn will never rise
Till she can dress her beauty at your eyes.

The merchant bows unto the seaman's star,
　　The ploughman from the sun his season takes;
But still the lover wonders what they are
　　Who look for day before his mistress wakes.
Awake, awake! break thro' your veils of lawn!
Then draw your curtains, and begin the dawn!

310　　　*To a Mistress Dying*

Lover.　Y OUR beauty, ripe and calm and fresh
　　　　　As eastern summers are,
　　　Must now, forsaking time and flesh,
　　　　　Add light to some small star.

Philosopher.　Whilst she yet lives, were stars decay'd,
　　　　　Their light by hers relief might find;
　　　But Death will lead her to a shade
　　　　　Where Love is cold and Beauty blind.

Lover.　Lovers, whose priests all poets are,
　　　　　Think every mistress, when she dies,
　　　Is changed at least into a star:
　　　　　And who dares doubt the poets wise?

Philosopher.　But ask not bodies doom'd to die
　　　　　To what abode they go;
　　　Since Knowledge is but Sorrow's spy,
　　　　　It is not safe to know.

311　　　*Praise and Prayer*

P RAISE is devotion fit for mighty minds,
　　The diff'ring world's agreeing sacrifice;
Where Heaven divided faiths united finds:
　　But Prayer in various discord upward flies.

For Prayer the ocean is where diversely
 Men steer their course, each to a sev'ral coast;
Where all our interests so discordant be
 That half beg winds by which the rest are lost.

By Penitence when we ourselves forsake,
 'Tis but in wise design on piteous Heaven;
In Praise we nobly give what God may take,
 And are, without a beggar's blush, forgiven.

EDMUND WALLER   1606–1687

312 *On a Girdle*

THAT which her slender waist confined
 Shall now my joyful temples bind;
No monarch but would give his crown
His arms might do what this has done.

It was my Heaven's extremest sphere,
The pale which held that lovely deer:
My joy, my grief, my hope, my love,
Did all within this circle move.

A narrow compass! and yet there
Dwelt all that's good, and all that's fair!
Give me but what this ribband bound,
Take all the rest the sun goes round!

313   *Go, lovely Rose*

GO, lovely Rose—
 Tell her that wastes her time and me,
  That now she knows,
 When I resemble her to thee,
 How sweet and fair she seems to be.

Tell her that 's young,
And shuns to have her graces spied,
That hadst thou sprung
In deserts where no men abide,
Thou must have uncommended died.

Small is the worth
Of beauty from the light retired:
Bid her come forth,
Suffer herself to be desired,
And not blush so to be admired.

Then die—that she
The common fate of all things rare
May read in thee;
How small a part of time they share
That are so wondrous sweet and fair!

314 *Old Age*

THE seas are quiet when the winds give o'er;
So calm are we when passions are no more.
For then we know how vain it was to boast
Of fleeting things, so certain to be lost.
Clouds of affection from our younger eyes
Conceal that emptiness which age descries.

The soul's dark cottage, batter'd and decay'd,
Lets in new light through chinks that Time hath made:
Stronger by weakness, wiser men become
As they draw near to their eternal home.
Leaving the old, both worlds at once they view
That stand upon the threshold of the new.

JOHN MILTON

1608–1674

315 *Hymn on the Morning of Christ's Nativity*

IT was the Winter wilde,
   While the Heav'n-born-childe,
   All meanly wrapt in the rude manger lies;
Nature in aw to him
Had doff't her gawdy trim,
   With her great Master so to sympathize:
It was no season then for her
To wanton with the Sun her lusty Paramour.

Only with speeches fair
She woo's the gentle Air
   To hide her guilty front with innocent Snow,
And on her naked shame,
Pollute with sinfull blame,
   The Saintly Vail of Maiden white to throw,
Confounded, that her Makers eyes
Should look so neer her foul deformities.

But he her fears to cease,
Sent down the meek-eyd Peace,
   She crown'd with Olive green, came softly sliding
Down through the turning sphear
His ready Harbinger,
   With Turtle wing the amorous clouds dividing,
And waving wide her mirtle wand,
She strikes a universall Peace through Sea and Land.

No War, or Battails sound
Was heard the World around,

320

The idle spear and shield were high up hung;
The hookèd Chariot stood
Unstain'd with hostile blood,
  The Trumpet spake not to the armèd throng,
And Kings sate still with awfull eye,
As if they surely knew their sovran Lord was by.

But peacefull was the night
Wherin the Prince of light
  His raign of peace upon the earth began:
The Windes with wonder whist,
Smoothly the waters kist,
  Whispering new joyes to the milde Ocean,
Who now hath quite forgot to rave,
While Birds of Calm sit brooding on the charmèd wave,

The Stars with deep amaze
Stand fixt in stedfast gaze,
  Bending one way their pretious influence,
And will not take their flight,
For all the morning light,
  Or Lucifer that often warn'd them thence;
But in their glimmering Orbs did glow,
Untill their Lord himself bespake, and bid them go.

And though the shady gloom
Had given day her room,
  The Sun himself with-held his wonted speed,
And hid his head for shame,
As his inferiour flame,
  The new enlightn'd world no more should need;
He saw a greater Sun appear
Then his bright Throne, or burning Axletree could bear.

Then] than.

JOHN MILTON

The Shepherds on the Lawn,
Or ere the point of dawn,
  Sate simply chatting in a rustick row;
Full little thought they than,
That the mighty Pan
  Was kindly com to live with them below;
Perhaps their loves, or els their sheep,
Was all that did their silly thoughts so busie keep.

When such musick sweet
Their hearts and ears did greet,
  As never was by mortall finger strook,
Divinely-warbled voice
Answering the stringèd noise,
  As all their souls in blisfull rapture took.
The Air such pleasure loth to lose,
With thousand echo's still prolongs each heav'nly close.

Nature that heard such sound
Beneath the hollow round
  Of Cynthia's seat, the Airy region thrilling,
Now was almost won
To think her part was don,
  And that her raign had here its last fulfilling;
She knew such harmony alone
Could hold all Heav'n and Earth in happier union.

At last surrounds their sight
A Globe of circular light,
  That with long beams the shame-fac't night array'd,
The helmèd Cherubim
And sworded Seraphim,
  Are seen in glittering ranks with wings displaid,

Harping in loud and solemn quire,
With unexpressive notes to Heav'ns new-born Heir.

Such musick (as 'tis said)
Before was never made,
    But when of old the sons of morning sung,
While the Creator Great
His constellations set,
    And the well-ballanc't world on hinges hung,
And cast the dark foundations deep,
And bid the weltring waves their oozy channel keep.

Ring out ye Crystall sphears,
Once bless our human ears,
    (If ye have power to touch our senses so)
And let your silver chime
Move in melodious time;
    And let the Base of Heav'ns deep Organ blow
And with your ninefold harmony
Make up full consort to th'Angelike symphony.

For if such holy Song
Enwarp our fancy long
    Time will run back, and fetch the age of gold,
And speckl'd vanity
Will sicken soon and die,
    And leprous sin will melt from earthly mould,
And Hell it self will pass away,
And leave her dolorous mansions to the peering day.

Yea Truth, and Justice then
Will down return to men,

Th'enameld Arras of the Rain-bow wearing,
And Mercy set between,
Thron'd in Celestiall sheen,
    With radiant feet the tissued clouds down stearing,
And Heav'n as at som festivall,
Will open wide the Gates of her high Palace Hall.

But wisest Fate sayes no,
This must not yet be so,
    The Babe lies yet in smiling Infancy,
That on the bitter cross
Must redeem our loss;
    So both himself and us to glorifie:
Yet first to those ychain'd in sleep,
The wakefull trump of doom must thunder through the deep,

With such a horrid clang
As on mount Sinai rang
    While the red fire, and smouldring clouds out brake:
The agèd Earth agast
With terrour of that blast,
    Shall from the surface to the center shake;
When at the worlds last session,
The dreadfull Judge in middle Air shall spread his throne.

And then at last our bliss
Full and perfect is,
    But now begins; for from this happy day
Th'old Dragon under ground
In straiter limits bound,
    Not half so far casts his usurpèd sway,
And wrath to see his Kingdom fail,
Swindges the scaly Horrour of his foulded tail.

The Oracles are dumm,
No voice or hideous humm
   Runs through the archèd roof in words deceiving.
Apollo from his shrine
Can no more divine,
   With hollow shreik the steep of Delphos leaving.
No nightly trance, or breathèd spell,
Inspire's the pale-ey'd Priest from the prophetic cell.

The lonely mountains o're,
And the resounding shore,
   A voice of weeping heard, and loud lament;
From haunted spring, and dale
Edg'd with poplar pale,
   The parting Genius is with sighing sent,
With flowre-inwov'n tresses torn
The Nimphs in twilight shade of tangled thickets mourn.

In consecrated Earth,
And on the holy Hearth,
   The Lars, and Lemures moan with midnight plaint,
In Urns, and Altars round,
A drear, and dying sound
   Affrights the Flamins at their service quaint;
And the chill Marble seems to sweat,
While each peculiar power forgoes his wonted seat.

Peor, and Baalim,
Forsake their Temples dim,
   With that twise-batter'd god of Palestine,
And moonèd Ashtaroth,
Heav'ns Queen and Mother both,
   Now sits not girt with Tapers holy shine,

325

The Libyc Hammon shrinks his horn,
In vain the Tyrian Maids their wounded Thamuz mourn.

And sullen Moloch fled,
Hath left in shadows dred,
   His burning Idol all of blackest hue,
In vain with Cymbals ring,
They call the grisly king,
   In dismall dance about the furnace blue;
The brutish gods of Nile as fast,
Isis and Orus, and the Dog Anubis hast.

Nor is Osiris seen
In Memphian Grove, or Green,
   Trampling the unshowr'd Grasse with lowings loud:
Nor can he be at rest
Within his sacred chest,
   Naught but profoundest Hell can be his shroud,
In vain with Timbrel'd Anthems dark
The sable-stolèd Sorcerers bear his worshipt Ark.

He feels from Juda's Land
The dredded Infants hand,
   The rayes of Bethlehem blind his dusky eyn;
Nor all the gods beside,
Longer dare abide,
   Not Typhon huge ending in snaky twine:
Our Babe to shew his Godhead true,
Can in his swadling bands controul the damnèd crew.

So when the Sun in bed,
Curtain'd with cloudy red,

Pillows his chin upon an Orient wave,
The flocking shadows pale,
Troop to th'infernall jail,
　　Each fetter'd Ghost slips to his severall grave,
And the yellow-skirted Fayes,
Fly after the Night-steeds, leaving their Moon-lov'd maze.

But see the Virgin blest,
Hath laid her Babe to rest.
　　Time is our tedious Song should here have ending,
Heav'ns youngest teemèd Star,
Hath fixt her polisht Car,
　　Her sleeping Lord with Handmaid Lamp attending:
And all about the Courtly Stable,
Bright-harnest Angels sit in order serviceable.

316 *On Time*

FLY envious Time, till thou run out thy race,
　　Call on the lazy leaden-stepping hours,
Whose speed is but the heavy Plummets pace;
And glut thy self with what thy womb devours,
Which is no more then what is false and vain,
And meerly mortal dross;
So little is our loss,
So little is thy gain.
For when as each thing bad thou hast entomb'd,
And last of all, thy greedy self consum'd,
Then long Eternity shall greet our bliss
With an individual kiss;
And Joy shall overtake us as a flood,
When every thing that is sincerely good

And perfectly divine,
With Truth, and Peace, and Love shall ever shine
About the supreme Throne
Of him, t'whose happy-making sight alone,
When once our heav'nly-guided soul shall clime,
Then all this Earthy grosnes quit,
Attir'd with Stars, we shall for ever sit,
    Triumphing over Death, and Chance, and thee O Time.

317   *At a Solemn Musick*

B LEST pair of Sirens, pledges of Heav'ns joy,
    Sphear-born harmonious Sisters, Voice, and Vers,
Wed your divine sounds, and mixt power employ
Dead things with inbreath'd sense able to pierce,
And to our high-rais'd phantasie present,
That undisturbèd Song of pure content,
Ay sung before the saphire-colour'd throne
To him that sits theron
With Saintly shout, and solemn Jubily,
Where the bright Seraphim in burning row
Their loud up-lifted Angel trumpets blow,
And the Cherubick host in thousand quires
Touch their immortal Harps of golden wires,
With those just Spirits that wear victorious Palms,
Hymns devout and holy Psalms
Singing everlastingly;
That we on Earth with undiscording voice
May rightly answer that melodious noise;
As once we did, till disproportion'd sin
Jarr'd against natures chime, and with harsh din

328

Broke the fair musick that all creatures made
To their great Lord, whose love their motion sway'd
In perfect Diapason, whilst they stood
In first obedience, and their state of good.
O may we soon again renew that Song,
And keep in tune with Heav'n, till God ere long
To his celestial consort us unite,
To live with him, and sing in endles morn of light.

318 *L'Allegro*

HENCE loathèd Melancholy
    Of Cerberus and blackest midnight born,
In Stygian Cave forlorn
'Mongst horrid shapes, and shreiks, and sights unholy.
Find out som uncouth cell,
    Where brooding darknes spreads his jealous wings,
And the night-Raven sings;
    There, under Ebon shades, and low-brow'd Rocks,
As ragged as thy Locks,
    In dark Cimmerian desert ever dwell.
But com thou Goddes fair and free,
In Heav'n ycleap'd Euphrosyne,
And by men, heart-easing Mirth,
Whom lovely Venus, at a birth
With two sister Graces more
To Ivy-crownèd Bacchus bore;
Or whether (as som Sager sing)
The frolick Wind that breathes the Spring,
Zephir with Aurora playing,
As he met her once a Maying,

There on Beds of Violets blew,
And fresh-blown Roses washt in dew,
Fill'd her with thee a daughter fair,
So bucksom, blith, and debonair.
    Haste thee nymph, and bring with thee
Jest and youthful Jollity,
Quips and Cranks, and wanton Wiles,
Nods, and Becks, and Wreathèd Smiles,
Such as hang on Hebe's cheek,
And love to live in dimple sleek;
Sport that wrincled Care derides,
And Laughter holding both his sides.
Com, and trip it as ye go
On the light fantastick toe,
And in thy right hand lead with thee,
The Mountain Nymph, sweet Liberty;
And if I give thee honour due,
Mirth, admit me of thy crue
To live with her, and live with thee,
In unreprovèd pleasures free;
To hear the Lark begin his flight,
And singing startle the dull night,
From his watch-towre in the skies,
Till the dappled dawn doth rise;
Then to com in spight of sorrow,
And at my window bid good morrow,
Through the Sweet-Briar, or the Vine,
Or the twisted Eglantine.
While the Cock with lively din,
Scatters the rear of darknes thin,
And to the stack, or the Barn dore,
Stoutly struts his Dames before.

Oft list'ning how the Hounds and horn
Chearly rouse the slumbring morn,
From the side of som Hoar Hill,
Through the high wood echoing shrill.
Som time walking not unseen
By Hedge-row Elms, on Hillocks green,
Right against the Eastern gate,
Wher the great Sun begins his state,
Rob'd in flames, and Amber light,
The clouds in thousand Liveries dight.
While the Plowman neer at hand,
Whistles ore the Furrow'd Land,
And the Milkmaid singeth blithe,
And the Mower whets his sithe,
And every Shepherd tells his tale
Under the Hawthorn in the dale.
Streit mine eye hath caught new pleasures
Whilst the Lantskip round it measures,
Russet Lawns, and Fallows Gray,
Where the nibling flocks do stray,
Mountains on whose barren brest
The labouring clouds do often rest:
Meadows trim with Daisies pide,
Shallow Brooks, and Rivers wide.
Towers, and Battlements it sees
Boosom'd high in tufted Trees,
Wher perhaps som beauty lies,
The Cynosure of neighbouring eyes.
Hard by, a Cottage chimney smokes,
From betwixt two agèd Okes,
Where Corydon and Thyrsis met,
Are at their savory dinner set

Of Hearbs, and other Country Messes,
Which the neat-handed Phillis dresses;
And then in haste her Bowre she leaves,
With Thestylis to bind the Sheaves;
Or if the earlier season lead
To the tann'd Haycock in the Mead,
Som times with secure delight
The up-land Hamlets will invite,
When the merry Bells ring round,
And the jocond rebecks sound
To many a youth, and many a maid,
Dancing in the Chequer'd shade;
And young and old com forth to play
On a Sunshine Holyday,
Till the live-long day-light fail,
Then to the Spicy Nut-brown Ale,
With stories told of many a feat,
How Faery Mab the junkets eat,
She was pincht, and pull'd she sed,
And he by Friars Lanthorn led
Tells how the drudging Goblin swet,
To ern his Cream-bowle duly set,
When in one night, ere glimps of morn,
His shadowy Flale hath thresh'd the Corn
That ten day-labourers could not end,
Then lies him down the Lubbar Fend,
And stretch'd out all the Chimney's length,
Basks at the fire his hairy strength;
And Crop-full out of dores he flings,
Ere the first Cock his Mattin rings.
Thus don the Tales, to bed they creep,
By whispering Windes soon lull'd asleep.

JOHN MILTON

Towred Cities please us then,
And the busie humm of men,
Where throngs of Knights and Barons bold,
In weeds of Peace high triumphs hold,
With store of Ladies, whose bright eies
Rain influence, and judge the prise
Of Wit, or Arms, while both contend
To win her Grace, whom all commend.
There let Hymen oft appear
In Saffron robe, with Taper clear,
And pomp, and feast, and revelry,
With mask, and antique Pageantry,
Such sights as youthfull Poets dream
On Summer eeves by haunted stream.
Then to the well-trod stage anon,
If Jonsons learnèd Sock be on,
Or sweetest Shakespear fancies childe,
Warble his native Wood-notes wilde,
And ever against eating Cares,
Lap me in soft Lydian Aires,
Married to immortal verse
Such as the meeting soul may pierce
In notes, with many a winding bout
Of linckèd sweetnes long drawn out,
With wanton heed, and giddy cunning,
The melting voice through mazes running;
Untwisting all the chains that ty
The hidden soul of harmony.
That Orpheus self may heave his head
From golden slumber on a bed
Of heapt Elysian flowres, and hear
Such streins as would have won the ear

Of Pluto, to have quite set free
His half regain'd Eurydice.
These delights, if thou canst give,
Mirth with thee, I mean to live.

319   *Il Penseroso*

HENCE vain deluding joyes,
   The brood of folly without father bred,
How little you bested,
   Or fill the fixèd mind with all your toyes;
Dwell in som idle brain,
   And fancies fond with gaudy shapes possess,
As thick and numberless
   As the gay motes that people the Sun Beams,
Or likest hovering dreams
   The fickle Pensioners of Morpheus train.
But hail thou Goddes, sage and holy,
Hail divinest Melancholy,
Whose Saintly visage is too bright
To hit the Sense of human sight;
And therfore to our weaker view,
Ore laid with black staid Wisdoms hue.
Black, but such as in esteem,
Prince Memnons sister might beseem,
Or that Starr'd Ethiope Queen that strove
To set her beauties praise above
The Sea Nymphs, and their powers offended.
Yet thou art higher far descended,
Thee bright-hair'd Vesta long of yore,
To solitary Saturn bore;

His daughter she (in Saturns raign,
Such mixture was not held a stain)
Oft in glimmering Bowres, and glades
He met her, and in secret shades
Of woody Ida's inmost grove,
Whilst yet there was no fear of Jove.
Com pensive Nun, devout and pure,
Sober, stedfast, and demure,
All in a robe of darkest grain,
Flowing with majestick train,
And sable stole of Cipres Lawn,
Over thy decent shoulders drawn.
Com, but keep thy wonted state,
With eev'n step, and musing gate,
And looks commercing with the skies,
Thy rapt soul sitting in thine eyes:
There held in holy passion still,
Forget thy self to Marble, till
With a sad Leaden downward cast,
Thou fix them on the earth as fast.
And joyn with thee calm Peace, and Quiet,
Spare Fast, that oft with gods doth diet,
And hears the Muses in a ring,
Ay round about Joves Altar sing.
And adde to these retirèd Leasure,
That in trim Gardens takes his pleasure;
But first, and chiefest, with thee bring,
Him that yon soars on golden wing,
Guiding the fiery-wheelèd throne,
The Cherub Contemplation,
And the mute Silence hist along,
'Less Philomel will daign a Song,

JOHN MILTON

In her sweetest, saddest plight,
Smoothing the rugged brow of night,
While Cynthia checks her Dragon yoke,
Gently o're th'accustom'd Oke;
Sweet Bird that shunn'st the noise of folly,
Most musicall, most melancholy!
Thee Chauntress oft the Woods among,
I woo to hear thy eeven-Song;
And missing thee, I walk unseen
On the dry smooth-shaven Green,
To behold the wandring Moon,
Riding neer her highest noon,
Like one that had bin led astray
Through the Heav'ns wide pathles way;
And oft, as if her head she bow'd,
Stooping through a fleecy cloud.
Oft on a Plat of rising ground,
I hear the far-off Curfeu sound,
Over som wide-water'd shoar,
Swinging slow with sullen roar;
Or if the Ayr will not permit,
Some still removèd place will fit,
Where glowing Embers through the room
Teach light to counterfeit a gloom,
Far from all resort of mirth,
Save the Cricket on the hearth,
Or the Belmans drousie charm,
To bless the dores from nightly harm:
Or let my Lamp at midnight hour,
Be seen in som high lonely Towr,
Where I may oft out-watch the Bear,
With thrice great Hermes, or unsphear

JOHN MILTON

The spirit of Plato to unfold
What Worlds, or what vast Regions hold
The immortal mind that hath forsook
Her mansion in this fleshly nook:
And of those Dæmons that are found
In fire, air, flood, or under ground,
Whose power hath a true consent
With Planet, or with Element.
Som time let Gorgeous Tragedy
In Scepter'd Pall com sweeping by,
Presenting Thebs, or Pelops line,
Or the tale of Troy divine.
Or what (though rare) of later age,
Ennoblèd hath the Buskind stage.

But, O sad Virgin, that thy power
Might raise Musæus from his bower
Or bid the soul of Orpheus sing
Such notes as warbled to the string.
Drew Iron tears down Pluto's cheek,
And made Hell grant what Love did seek.
Or call up him that left half told
The story of Cambuscan bold,
Of Camball, and of Algarsife,
And who had Canace to wife,
That own'd the vertuous Ring and Glass,
And of the wondrous Hors of Brass,
On which the Tartar King did ride;
And if ought els, great Bards beside,
In sage and solemn tunes have sung,
Of Turneys and of Trophies hung;
Of Forests, and inchantments drear,
Where more is meant then meets the ear.

Thus night oft see me in thy pale career,
Till civil-suited Morn appeer,
Not trickt and frounc't as she was wont,
With the Attick Boy to hunt,
But Cherchef't in a comly Cloud,
While rocking Winds are Piping loud,
Or usher'd with a shower still,
When the gust hath blown his fill,
Ending on the russling Leaves,
With minute drops from off the Eaves.
And when the Sun begins to fling
His flaring beams, me Goddes bring
To archèd walks of twilight groves,
And shadows brown that Sylvan loves,
Of Pine, or monumental Oake,
Where the rude Ax with heavèd stroke,
Was never heard the Nymphs to daunt,
Or fright them from their hallow'd haunt.
There in close covert by som Brook,
Where no profaner eye may look,
Hide me from Day's garish eie,
While the Bee with Honied thie,
That at her flowry work doth sing,
And the Waters murmuring
With such consort as they keep,
Entice the dewy-feather'd Sleep;
And let som strange mysterious dream,
Wave at his Wings in Airy stream,
Of lively portrature display'd,
Softly on my eye-lids laid.
And as I wake, sweet musick breath
Above, about, or underneath,

Sent by som spirit to mortals good,
Or th'unseen Genius of the Wood.
   But let my due feet never fail,
To walk the studious Cloysters pale,
And love the high embowèd Roof,
With antick Pillars massy proof,
And storied Windows richly dight,
Casting a dimm religious light.
There let the pealing Organ blow,
To the full voic'd Quire below,
In Service high, and Anthems cleer,
As may with sweetnes, through mine ear,
Dissolve me into extasies,
And bring all Heav'n before mine eyes.
And may at last my weary age
Find out the peacefull hermitage,
The Hairy Gown and Mossy Cell,
Where I may sit and rightly spell
Of every Star that Heav'n doth shew,
And every Herb that sips the dew;
Till old experience do attain
To somthing like Prophetic strain.
These pleasures Melancholy give,
And I with thee will choose to live.

320   *From 'Arcades'*

O'RE the smooth enameld green
　　Where no print of step hath been,
　　Follow me as I sing,
　　And touch the warbled string.

Under the shady roof
Of branching Elm Star-proof,
    Follow me,
I will bring you where she sits
Clad in splendor as befits
    Her deity.
Such a rural Queen
All Arcadia hath not seen.

321   *From 'Comus'*
              (i)

THE Star that bids the Shepherd fold,
    Now the top of Heav'n doth hold,
And the gilded Car of Day,
His glowing Axle doth allay
In the steep Atlantick stream,
And the slope Sun his upward beam
Shoots against the dusky Pole,
Pacing toward the other gole
Of his Chamber in the East.
Mean while welcom Joy, and Feast,
Midnight shout, and revelry,
Tipsie dance, and Jollity.
Braid your Locks with rosie Twine
Dropping odours, dropping Wine.
Rigor now is gon to bed,
And Advice with scrupulous head,
Strict Age, and sowre Severity,
With their grave Saws in slumber ly.
We that are of purer fire
Imitate the Starry Quire,

Who in their nightly watchfull Sphears,
Lead in swift round the Months and Years.
The Sounds, and Seas with all their finny drove
Now to the Moon in wavering Morrice move,
And on the Tawny Sands and Shelves,
Trip the pert Fairies and the dapper Elves;
By dimpled Brook, and Fountain brim,
The Wood-Nymphs deckt with Daisies trim,
Their merry wakes and pastimes keep:
What hath night to do with sleep?
Night hath better sweets to prove,
Venus now wakes, and wak'ns Love. . . .
Com, knit hands, and beat the ground,
In a light fantastick round.

322   *(ii)*

ECHO

SWEET Echo, sweetest Nymph that liv'st unseen
  Within thy airy shell
   By slow Meander's margent green,
  And in the violet imbroider'd vale
   Where the love-lorn Nightingale
Nightly to thee her sad Song mourneth well.
Canst thou not tell me of a gentle Pair
   That likest thy Narcissus are?
    O if thou have
   Hid them in som flowry Cave,
    Tell me but where
  Sweet Queen of Parly, Daughter of the Sphear!
  So maist thou be translated to the skies,
And give resounding grace to all Heav'ns Harmonies!

323 (*iii*)

SABRINA

The Spirit sings:

SABRINA fair
 Listen where thou art sitting
Under the glassie, cool, translucent wave,
 In twisted braids of Lillies knitting
The loose train of thy amber-dropping hair,
 Listen for dear honour's sake,
 Goddess of the silver lake,
      Listen and save !

Listen and appear to us,
In name of great Oceanus,
By the earth-shaking Neptune's mace,
And Tethys grave majestick pace,
By hoary Nereus wrincled look,
And the Carpathian wisards hook,
By scaly Tritons winding shell,
And old sooth-saying Glaucus spell,
By Leucothea's lovely hands,
And her son that rules the strands,
By Thetis tinsel-slipper'd feet,
And the Songs of Sirens sweet,
By dead Parthenope's dear tomb,
And fair Ligea's golden comb,
Wherwith she sits on diamond rocks
Sleeking her soft alluring locks,
By all the Nymphs that nightly dance
Upon thy streams with wily glance,
Rise, rise, and heave thy rosie head
From thy coral-pav'n bed,

And bridle in thy headlong wave,
Till thou our summons answered have.

Listen and save!

Sabrina replies:

By the rushy fringèd bank,
Where grows the Willow and the Osier dank,
My sliding Chariot stayes,
Thick set with Agat, and the azurn sheen
Of Turkis blew, and Emrauld green
That in the channell strayes,
Whilst from off the waters fleet
Thus I set my printless feet
O're the Cowslips Velvet head,
That bends not as I tread,
Gentle swain at thy request
I am here.

324 (*iv*)

The Spirit epiloguizes:

TO the Ocean now I fly,
And those happy climes that ly
Where day never shuts his eye,
Up in the broad fields of the sky:
There I suck the liquid ayr
All amidst the Gardens fair
Of Hesperus, and his daughters three
That sing about the golden tree:
Along the crispèd shades and bowres
Revels the spruce and jocond Spring,
The Graces, and the rosie-boosom'd Howres,
Thither all their bounties bring,

That there eternal Summer dwels,
And West winds, with musky wing
About the cedar'n alleys fling
Nard, and Cassia's balmy smels.
Iris there with humid bow,
Waters the odorous banks that blow
Flowers of more mingled hew
Than her purfl'd scarf can shew,
And drenches with Elysian dew
(List mortals, if your ears be true)
Beds of Hyacinth, and roses
Where young Adonis oft reposes,
Waxing well of his deep wound
In slumber soft, and on the ground
Sadly sits th' Assyrian Queen;
But far above in spangled sheen
Celestial Cupid her fam'd son advanc't,
Holds his dear Psyche sweet intranc't
After her wandring labours long,
Till free consent the gods among
Make her his eternal Bride,
And from her fair unspotted side
Two blissful twins are to be born,
Youth and Joy; so Jove hath sworn.

But now my task is smoothly don,
I can fly, or I can run
Quickly to the green earths end,
Where the bow'd welkin slow doth bend,
And from thence can soar as soon
To the corners of the Moon.

Mortals that would follow me,
Love vertue, she alone is free.

She can teach ye how to clime
Higher then the Spheary chime;
Or if Vertue feeble were,
Heav'n it self would stoop to her.

325   *Lycidas*

*A Lament for a friend drowned in his passage from Chester
on the Irish Seas,* 1637

YET once more, O ye Laurels, and once more
Ye Myrtles brown, with Ivy never-sear,
I com to pluck your Berries harsh and crude,
And with forc'd fingers rude,
Shatter your leaves before the mellowing year.
Bitter constraint, and sad occasion dear,
Compels me to disturb your season due:
For Lycidas is dead, dead ere his prime
Young Lycidas, and hath not left his peer:
Who would not sing for Lycidas? he knew
Himself to sing, and build the lofty rhyme.
He must not flote upon his watry bear
Unwept, and welter to the parching wind,
Without the meed of som melodious tear.
   Begin, then, Sisters of the sacred well,
That from beneath the seat of Jove doth spring,
Begin, and somwhat loudly sweep the string.
Hence with denial vain, and coy excuse,
So may som gentle Muse
With lucky words favour my destin'd Urn,
And as he passes turn,
And bid fair peace be to my sable shrowd.

For we were nurst upon the self-same hill,
Fed the same flock, by fountain, shade, and rill.

 Together both, ere the high Lawns appear'd
Under the opening eye-lids of the morn,
We drove a field, and both together heard
What time the Gray-fly winds her sultry horn,
Batt'ning our flocks with the fresh dews of night,
Oft till the Star that rose, at Ev'ning, bright
Towards Heav'ns descent had slop'd his westering wheel.
Mean while the Rural ditties were not mute,
Temper'd to th'Oaten Flute;
Rough Satyrs danc'd, and Fauns with clov'n heel,
From the glad sound would not be absent long,
And old Damætas lov'd to hear our song.

 But O the heavy change, now thou art gon,
Now thou art gon, and never must return!
Thee Shepherd, thee the Woods, and desert Caves,
With wilde Thyme and the gadding Vine o'regrown,
And all their echoes mourn.
The Willows, and the Hazle Copses green,
Shall now no more be seen,
Fanning their joyous Leaves to thy soft layes.
As killing as the Canker to the Rose,
Or Taint-worm to the weanling Herds that graze,
Or Frost to Flowers, that their gay wardrop wear,
When first the White thorn blows;
Such, Lycidas, thy loss to Shepherds ear.

 Where were ye Nymphs when the remorseless deep
Clos'd o'er the head of your lov'd Lycidas?
For neither were ye playing on the steep,
Where your old Bards, the famous Druids ly,
Nor on the shaggy top of Mona high,

Nor yet where Deva spreads her wisard stream:
Ay me, I fondly dream!
Had ye bin there—for what could that have don?
What could the Muse her self that Orpheus bore,
The Muse her self, for her inchanting son
Whom Universal nature did lament,
When by the rout that made the hideous roar,
His goary visage down the stream was sent,
Down the swift Hebrus to the Lesbian shore.

    Alas! what boots it with uncessant care
To tend the homely slighted Shepherds trade,
And strictly meditate the thankles Muse,
Were it not better don as others use,
To sport with Amaryllis in the shade,
Or with the tangles of Neæra's hair?
Fame is the spur that the clear spirit doth raise
(That last infirmity of Noble mind)
To scorn delights, and live laborious dayes;
But the fair Guerdon when we hope to find,
And think to burst out into sudden blaze,
Comes the blind Fury with th'abhorrèd shears,
And slits the thin spun life. But not the praise,
Phœbus repli'd, and touch'd my trembling ears;
Fame is no plant that grows on mortal soil,
Nor in the glistering foil
Set off to th'world, nor in broad rumour lies,
But lives and spreds aloft by those pure eyes,
And perfet witnes of all judging Jove;
As he pronounces lastly on each deed,
Of so much fame in Heav'n expect thy meed.

with the tangles] ? withe, plait, the tangles (R. W. Chapman's conjecture).

347

JOHN MILTON

O fountain Arethuse, and thou honour'd floud,
Smooth-sliding Mincius, crown'd with vocall reeds,
That strain I heard was of a higher mood:
But now my Oate proceeds,
And listens to the Herald of the Sea
That came in Neptune's plea,
He ask'd the Waves, and ask'd the Fellon winds,
What hard mishap hath doom'd this gentle swain?
And question'd every gust of rugged wings
That blows from off each beakèd Promontory,
They knew not of his story,
And sage Hippotades their answer brings,
That not a blast was from his dungeon stray'd,
The Ayr was calm, and on the level brine,
Sleek Panope with all her sisters play'd.
It was that fatall and perfidious Bark
Built in th'eclipse, and rigg'd with curses dark,
That sunk so low that sacred head of thine.

Next Camus, reverend Sire, went footing slow,
His Mantle hairy, and his Bonnet sedge,
Inwrought with figures dim, and on the edge
Like to that sanguine flower inscrib'd with woe.
Ah; Who hath reft (quoth he) my dearest pledge?
Last came, and last did go,
The Pilot of the Galilean lake,
Two massy Keyes he bore of metals twain,
(The Golden opes, the Iron shuts amain)
He shook his Miter'd locks, and stern bespake,
How well could I have spar'd for thee, young swain,
Anow of such as for their bellies sake,
Creep and intrude, and climb into the fold?
Of other care they little reck'ning make,

Then how to scramble at the shearers feast,
And shove away the worthy bidden guest.
Blind mouthes! that scarce themselves know how to hold
A Sheep-hook, or have learn'd ought els the least
That to the faithfull Herdmans art belongs!
What recks it them? What need they? They are sped;
And when they list, their lean and flashy songs
Grate on their scrannel Pipes of wretched straw,
The hungry Sheep look up, and are not fed,
But swoln with wind, and the rank mist they draw,
Rot inwardly, and foul contagion spread:
Besides what the grim Woolf with privy paw
Daily devours apace, and nothing sed,
But that two-handed engine at the door,
Stands ready to smite once, and smite no more.
   Return Alpheus, the dread voice is past,
That shrunk thy streams; Return Sicilian Muse,
And call the Vales, and bid them hither cast
Their Bels, and Flourets of a thousand hues.
Ye valleys low where the milde whispers use,
Of shades and wanton winds, and gushing brooks,
On whose fresh lap the swart Star sparely looks,
Throw hither all your quaint enameld eyes,
That on the green terf suck the honied showres,
And purple all the ground with vernal flowres.
Bring the rathe Primrose that forsaken dies,
The tufted Crow-toe, and pale Gessamine,
The white Pink, and the Pansie freakt with jeat,
The glowing Violet.
The Musk-rose, and the well attir'd Woodbine.
With Cowslips wan that hang the pensive hed,
And every flower that sad embroidery wears:

Bid Amaranthus all his beauty shed,
And Daffadillies fill their cups with tears,
To strew the Laureat Herse where Lycid lies.
For so to interpose a little ease,
Let our frail thoughts dally with false surmise.
Ay me! Whilst thee the shores, and sounding Seas
Wash far away, where ere thy bones are hurld,
Whether beyond the stormy Hebrides,
Where thou perhaps under the whelming tide
Visit'st the bottom of the monstrous world;
Or whether thou to our moist vows deny'd,
Sleep'st by the fable of Bellerus old,
Where the great vision of the guarded Mount
Looks toward Namancos and Bayona's hold;
Look homeward Angel now, and melt with ruth.
And, O ye Dolphins, waft the haples youth.

Weep no more, woful Shepherds weep no more,
For Lycidas your sorrow is not dead,
Sunk though he be beneath the watry floar,
So sinks the day-star in the Ocean bed,
And yet anon repairs his drooping head,
And tricks his beams, and with new spangled Ore,
Flames in the forehead of the morning sky:
So Lycidas sunk low, but mounted high,
Through the dear might of him that walk'd the waves
Where other groves, and other streams along,
With Nectar pure his oozy Lock's he laves,
And hears the unexpressive nuptiall Song,
In the blest Kingdoms meek of joy and love.
There entertain him all the Saints above,
In solemn troops, and sweet Societies
That sing, and singing in their glory move,

And wipe the tears for ever from his eyes.
Now Lycidas the Shepherds weep no more;
Hence forth thou art the Genius of the shore,
In thy large recompense, and shalt be good
To all that wander in that perilous flood.

Thus sang the uncouth Swain to th'Okes and rills,
While the still morn went out with Sandals gray,
He touch'd the tender stops of various Quills,
With eager thought warbling his Dorick lay:
And now the Sun had stretch'd out all the hills,
And now was dropt into the Western bay;
At last he rose, and twitch'd his Mantle blew:
To morrow to fresh Woods, and Pastures new.

326   *To the Lady Margaret Ley*

DAUGHTER to that good Earl, once President
Of Englands Counsel, and her Treasury,
Who liv'd in both, unstain'd with gold or fee,
And left them both, more in himself content,
Till the sad breaking of that Parlament
Broke him, as that dishonest victory
At Chæronèa, fatal to liberty
Kil'd with report that Old man eloquent,
Though later born, then to have known the dayes
Wherin your Father flourisht, yet by you
Madam, me thinks I see him living yet;
So well your words his noble vertues praise,
That all both judge you to relate them true,
And to possess them, Honour'd Margaret.

JOHN MILTON

On His Blindness

WHEN I consider how my light is spent,
 E're half my days, in this dark world and wide,
And that one Talent which is death to hide,
Lodg'd with me useless, though my Soul more bent
To serve therewith my Maker, and present
 My true account, least he returning chide,
 Doth God exact day-labour, light deny'd,
 I fondly ask; But patience to prevent
That murmur, soon replies, God doth not need
 Either man's work or his own gifts, who best
 Bear his milde yoak, they serve him best, his State
Is Kingly. Thousands at his bidding speed
 And post o're Land and Ocean without rest:
They also serve who only stand and waite.

To Mr. Lawrence

LAWRENCE of vertuous Father vertuous Son,
 Now that the Fields are dank, and ways are mire,
 Where shall we sometimes meet, and by the fire
 Help wast a sullen day; what may be won
From the hard Season gaining: time will run
 On smoother, till Favonius re-inspire
 The frozen earth; and cloth in fresh attire
 The Lillie and Rose, that neither sow'd nor spun.
What neat repast shall feast us, light and choice,
 Of Attick tast, with Wine, whence we may rise
 To hear the Lute well toucht, or artfull voice
Warble immortal Notes and Tuskan Ayre?
 He who of those delights can judge, and spare
 To interpose them oft, is not unwise.

329 *To Cyriack Skinner*

CYRIACK, whose Grandsire on the Royal Bench
　Of Brittish Themis, with no mean applause
　Pronounc't and in his volumes taught our Lawes,
　Which others at their Barr so often wrench:
To day deep thoughts resolve with me to drench
　In mirth, that after no repenting drawes;
　Let Euclid rest and Archimedes pause,
　And what the Swede intend, and what the French.
To measure life, learn thou betimes, and know
　Toward solid good what leads the nearest way;
　For other things mild Heav'n a time ordains,
And disapproves that care, though wise in show,
　That with superfluous burden loads the day,
　And when God sends a cheerful hour, refrains.

330 *On His Deceased Wife*

METHOUGHT I saw my late espousèd Saint
　Brought to me like Alcestis from the grave,
　Whom Joves great Son to her glad Husband gave,
　Rescu'd from death by force though pale and faint,
Mine as whom washt from spot of child-bed taint,
　Purification in the old Law did save,
　And such, as yet once more I trust to have
　Full sight of her in Heaven without restraint,
Came vested all in white, pure as her mind:
　Her face was vail'd, yet to my fancied sight,
　Love, sweetness, goodness, in her person shin'd
So clear, as in no face with more delight.
　But O as to embrace me she enclin'd
　I wak'd, she fled, and day brought back my night.

331 *Light*

HAIL holy light, ofspring of Heav'n first-born,
Or of th' Eternal Coeternal beam
May I express thee unblam'd? since God is light,
And never but in unapproachèd light
Dwelt from Eternitie, dwelt then in thee,
Bright effluence of bright essence increate.
Or hear'st thou rather pure Ethereal stream,
Whose Fountain who shall tell? before the Sun,
Before the Heavens thou wert, and at the voice
Of God, as with a Mantle didst invest
The rising world of waters dark and deep,
Won from the void and formless infinite.
Thee I re-visit now with bolder wing,
Escap't the Stygian Pool, though long detain'd
In that obscure sojourn, while in my flight
Through utter and through middle darkness borne
With other notes then to th' Orphean Lyre
I sung of Chaos and Eternal Night,
Taught by the heav'nly Muse to venture down
The dark descent, and up to reascend,
Though hard and rare: thee I revisit safe,
And feel thy sovran vital Lamp; but thou
Revisit'st not these eyes, that rowle in vain
To find thy piercing ray, and find no dawn;
So thick a drop serene hath quencht thir Orbs,
Or dim suffusion veild. Yet not the more
Cease I to wander where the Muses haunt
Cleer Spring, or shadie Grove, or Sunnie Hill,
Smit with the love of sacred song; but chief
Thee *Sion* and the flowrie Brooks beneath

That wash thy hallowd feet, and warbling flow,
Nightly I visit: nor somtimes forget
Those other two equal'd with me in Fate,
So were I equal'd with them in renown.
Blind Thamyris and blind Mæonides,
And Tiresias and Phineus Prophets old.
Then feed on thoughts, that voluntarie move
Harmonious numbers; as the wakeful Bird
Sings darkling, and in shadiest Covert hid
Tunes her nocturnal Note. Thus with the Year
Seasons return, but not to me returns
Day, or the sweet approach of Ev'n or Morn,
Or sight of vernal bloom, or Summers Rose,
Or flocks, or herds, or human face divine;
But cloud in stead, and ever-during dark
Surrounds me, from the chearful waies of men
Cut off, and for the Book of knowledg fair
Presented with a Universal blanc
Of Natures works to mee expung'd and ras'd,
And wisdome at one entrance quite shut out.
So much the rather thou Celestial light
Shine inward, and the mind through all her powers
Irradiate, there plant eyes, all mist from thence
Purge and disperse, that I may see and tell
Of things invisible to mortal sight.

332   (i) From 'Samson Agonistes'

OH how comely it is and how reviving
     To the Spirits of just men long opprest!
When God into the hands of thir deliverer
Puts invincible might

To quell the mighty of the Earth, th' oppressour,
The brute and boist'rous force of violent men
Hardy and industrious to support
Tyrannic power, but raging to pursue
The righteous and all such as honour Truth;
He all thir Ammunition
And feats of War defeats
With plain Heroic magnitude of mind
And celestial vigour arm'd,
Thir Armories and Magazins contemns,
Renders them useless, while
With wingèd expedition
Swift as the lightning glance he executes
His errand on the wicked, who surpris'd
Lose thir defence distracted and amaz'd.

333   (*ii*)

ALL is best, though we oft doubt,
   What th' unsearchable dispose
Of highest wisdom brings about,
And ever best found in the close.
Oft he seems to hide his face,
But unexpectedly returns
And to his faithful Champion hath in place
Bore witness gloriously; whence Gaza mourns
And all that band them to resist
His uncontroulable intent.
His servants he with new acquist
Of true experience from this great event
With peace and consolation hath dismist,
And calm of mind all passion spent.

334   *A Doubt of Martyrdom*

O FOR some honest lover's ghost,
  Some kind unbodied post
    Sent from the shades below!
    I strangely long to know
Whether the noble chaplets wear
Those that their mistress' scorn did bear
    Or those that were used kindly.

For whatsoe'er they tell us here
  To make those sufferings dear,
    'Twill there, I fear, be found
    That to the being crown'd
T' have loved alone will not suffice,
Unless we also have been wise
    And have our loves enjoy'd.

What posture can we think him in
  That, here unloved, again
    Departs, and 's thither gone
    Where each sits by his own?
Or how can that Elysium be
Where I my mistress still must see
    Circled in other's arms?

For there the judges all are just,
  And Sophonisba must
    Be his whom she held dear,
    Not his who loved her here.

The sweet Philoclea, since she died,
Lies by her Pirocles his side,
   Not by Amphialus.

Some bays, perchance, or myrtle bough
  For difference crowns the brow
    Of those kind souls that were
    The noble martyrs here:
And if that be the only odds
(As who can tell?), ye kinder gods,
    Give me the woman here!

335
The Constant Lover

OUT upon it, I have loved
   Three whole days together!
And am like to love three more,
  If it prove fair weather.

Time shall moult away his wings
  Ere he shall discover
In the whole wide world again
  Such a constant lover.

But the spite on 't is, no praise
  Is due at all to me:
Love with me had made no stays,
  Had it any been but she.

Had it any been but she,
  And that very face,
There had been at least ere this
  A dozen dozen in her place.

336   *Why so Pale and Wan?*

WHY so pale and wan, fond lover?
     Prithee, why so pale?
Will, when looking well can't move her,
     Looking ill prevail?
     Prithee, why so pale?

Why so dull and mute, young sinner?
     Prithee, why so mute?
Will, when speaking well can't win her,
     Saying nothing do 't?
     Prithee, why so mute?

Quit, quit for shame! This will not move;
     This cannot take her.
If of herself she will not love,
     Nothing can make her:
     The devil take her!

337   *When, Dearest, I but think of Thee*

WHEN, dearest I but think of thee,
     Methinks all things that lovely be
Are present, and my soul delighted:
For beauties that from worth arise
Are like the grace of deities,
     Still present with us, tho' unsighted.

Thus while I sit and sigh the day
With all his borrow'd lights away,
     Till night's black wings do overtake me,
Thinking on thee, thy beauties then,
As sudden lights do sleepy men,
     So they by their bright rays awake me.

SIR JOHN SUCKLING

Thus absence dies, and dying proves
No absence can subsist with loves
    That do partake of fair perfection:
Since in the darkest night they may
By love's quick motion find a way
    To see each other by reflection.

The waving sea can with each flood
Bathe some high promont that hath stood
    Far from the main up in the river:
O think not then but love can do
As much! for that's an ocean too,
    Which flows not every day, but ever!

SIR RICHARD FANSHAWE

1608–1666

338   *A Rose*

BLOWN in the morning, thou shalt fade ere noon.
    What boots a life which in such haste forsakes thee?
Thou'rt wondrous frolic, being to die so soon,
And passing proud a little colour makes thee.
If thee thy brittle beauty so deceives,
Know then the thing that swells thee is thy bane;
For the same beauty doth, in bloody leaves,
The sentence of thy early death contain.
Some clown's coarse lungs will poison thy sweet flower,
If by the careless plough thou shalt be torn;
And many Herods lie in wait each hour
To murder thee as soon as thou art born—
    Nay, force thy bud to blow—their tyrant breath
    Anticipating life, to hasten death!

WILLIAM CARTWRIGHT

1611–1643

339   *To Chloe*

Who for his sake wished herself younger

THERE are two births; the one when light
  First strikes the new awaken'd sense;
The other when two souls unite,
  And we must count our life from thence:
When you loved me and I loved you
Then both of us were born anew.

Love then to us new souls did give
  And in those souls did plant new powers;
Since when another life we live,
  The breath we breathe is his, not ours:
Love makes those young whom age doth chill,
And whom he finds young keeps young still.

340   *Falsehood*

STILL do the stars impart their light
  To those that travel in the night;
Still time runs on, nor doth the hand
Or shadow on the dial stand;
The streams still glide and constant are:
        Only thy mind
        Untrue I find,
        Which carelessly
        Neglects to be
Like stream or shadow, hand or star.

Fool that I am! I do recall
My words, and swear thou'rt like them all,
Thou seem'st like stars to nourish fire,
But O how cold is thy desire!
And like the hand upon the brass
　　　Thou point'st at me
　　　In mockery;
　　　If I come nigh
　　　Shade-like thou'lt fly,
And as the stream with murmur pass.

341　*On the Queen's Return from the Low
Countries*

HALLOW the threshold, crown the posts anew!
　　The day shall have its due.
Twist all our victories into one bright wreath,
　　On which let honour breathe;
Then throw it round the temples of our Queen!
'Tis she that must preserve those glories green.

When greater tempests than on sea before
　　Received her on the shore;
When she was shot at 'for the King's own good'
　　By legions hired to blood;
How bravely did she do, how bravely bear!
And show'd, though they durst rage, she durst not fear.

Courage was cast about her like a dress
　　Of solemn comeliness:
A gather'd mind and an untroubled face
　　Did give her dangers grace:
Thus, arm'd with innocence, secure they move
Whose highest 'treason' is but highest love.

362

WILLIAM CARTWRIGHT

342   *On a Virtuous Young Gentlewoman that died suddenly*

SHE who to Heaven more Heaven doth annex,
   Whose lowest thought was above all our sex,
Accounted nothing death but t' be reprieved,
And died as free from sickness as she lived.
Others are dragg'd away, or must be driven,
She only saw her time and stept to Heaven;
Where seraphims view all her glories o'er,
As one return'd that had been there before.
For while she did this lower world adorn,
Her body seem'd rather assumed than born;
So rarified, advanced, so pure and whole,
That body might have been another's soul;
And equally a miracle it were
That she could die, or that she could live here.

JAMES GRAHAM, MARQUIS OF MONTROSE

1612–165c

343   *I'll never love Thee more*

MY dear and only Love, I pray
   That little world of thee
Be govern'd by no other sway
   Than purest monarchy;
For if confusion have a part
   (Which virtuous souls abhor),
And hold a synod in thine heart,
   I'll never love thee more.

JAMES GRAHAM

Like Alexander I will reign,
  And I will reign alone;
My thoughts did evermore disdain
  A rival on my throne.
He either fears his fate too much,
  Or his deserts are small,
That dares not put it to the touch,
  To gain or lose it all.

And in the empire of thine heart,
  Where I should solely be,
If others do pretend a part
  Or dare to vie with me,
Or if *Committees* thou erect,
  And go on such a score,
I'll laugh and sing at thy neglect,
  And never love thee more.

But if thou wilt prove faithful then,
  And constant of thy word,
I'll make thee glorious by my pen
  And famous by my sword;
I'll serve thee in such noble ways
  Was never heard before;
I'll crown and deck thee all with bays,
  And love thee more and more.

THOMAS JORDAN

1612?–1685

344 *Coronemus nos Rosis antequam marcescant*

LET us drink and be merry, dance, joke, and rejoice,
With claret and sherry, theorbo and voice!
The changeable world to our joy is unjust,
    All treasure's uncertain,
    Then down with your dust!
In frolics dispose your pounds, shillings, and pence,
For we shall be nothing a hundred years hence.

We'll sport and be free with Moll, Betty, and Dolly,
Have oysters and lobsters to cure melancholy:
Fish-dinners will make a lass spring like a flea,
    Dame Venus, love's lady,
    Was born of the sea;
With her and with Bacchus we'll tickle the sense,
For we shall be past it a hundred years hence.

Your most beautiful bride who with garlands is crown'd
And kills with each glance as she treads on the ground,
Whose lightness and brightness doth shine in such splendour
    That none but the stars
    Are thought fit to attend her,
Though now she be pleasant and sweet to the sense,
Will be damnable mouldy a hundred years hence.

Then why should we turmoil in cares and in fears,
Turn all our tranquill'ty to sighs and to tears?
Let's eat, drink, and play till the worms do corrupt us,
    'Tis certain, *Post mortem*
    Nulla voluptas.
For health, wealth and beauty, wit, learning and sense,
Must all come to nothing a hundred years hence.

RICHARD CRASHAW

1613?–1649

345 *Wishes to His Supposed Mistress*

WHOE'ER she be—
  That not impossible She
That shall command my heart and me:

Where'er she lie,
Lock'd up from mortal eye
In shady leaves of destiny:

Till that ripe birth
Of studied Fate stand forth,
And teach her fair steps to our earth:

Till that divine
Idea take a shrine
Of crystal flesh, through which to shine:

Meet you her, my Wishes,
Bespeak her to my blisses,
And be ye call'd my absent kisses.

I wish her Beauty,
That owes not all its duty
To gaudy tire, or glist'ring shoe-tie:

Something more than
Taffata or tissue can,
Or rampant feather, or rich fan.

A Face, that's best
By its own beauty drest,
And can alone commend the rest.

RICHARD CRASHAW

A Face, made up
Out of no other shop
Than what Nature's white hand sets ope.

A Cheek, where youth
And blood, with pen of truth,
Write what the reader sweetly ru'th.

A Cheek, where grows
More than a morning rose,
Which to no box his being owes.

Lips, where all day
A lover's kiss may play,
Yet carry nothing thence away.

Looks, that oppress
Their richest tires, but dress
And clothe their simplest nakedness.

Eyes, that displace
The neighbour diamond, and outface
That sunshine by their own sweet grace.

Tresses, that wear
Jewels but to declare
How much themselves more precious are:

Whose native ray
Can tame the wanton day
Of gems that in their bright shades play.

Each ruby there,
Or pearl that dare appear,
Be its own blush, be its own tear.

RICHARD CRASHAW

A well-tamed Heart,
For whose more noble smart
Love may be long choosing a dart.

Eyes, that bestow
Full quivers on love's bow,
Yet pay less arrows than they owe.

Smiles, that can warm
The blood, yet teach a charm,
That chastity shall take no harm.

Blushes, that bin
The burnish of no sin,
Nor flames of aught too hot within.

Joys, that confess
Virtue their mistress,
And have no other head to dress.

Fears, fond and slight
As the coy bride's, when night
First does the longing lover right.

Days, that need borrow
No part of their good-morrow
From a fore-spent night of sorrow.

Days, that in spite
Of darkness, by the light
Of a clear mind, are day all night.

Nights, sweet as they,
Made short by lovers' play,
Yet long by th' absence of the day.

RICHARD CRASHAW

Life, that dares send
A challenge to his end,
And when it comes, say, 'Welcome, friend!'

Sydneian showers
Of sweet discourse, whose powers
Can crown old Winter's head with flowers.

Soft silken hours,
Open suns, shady bowers;
'Bove all, nothing within that lowers.

Whate'er delight
Can make Day's forehead bright,
Or give down to the wings of Night.

I wish her store
Of worth may leave her poor
Of wishes; and I wish—no more.

Now, if Time knows
That Her, whose radiant brows
Weave them a garland of my vows;

Her, whose just bays
My future hopes can raise,
A trophy to her present praise;

Her, that dares be
What these lines wish to see;
I seek no further, it is She.

'Tis She, and here,
Lo! I unclothe and clear
My Wishes' cloudy character.

369

May she enjoy it
Whose merit dare apply it,
But modesty dares still deny it!

Such worth as this is
Shall fix my flying Wishes,
And determine them to kisses.

Let her full glory,
My fancies, fly before ye;
Be ye my fictions—but her story.

346 *The Weeper*

HAIL, sister springs,
Parents of silver-footed rills!
Ever bubbling things,
Thawing crystal, snowy hills!
    Still spending, never spent; I mean
    Thy fair eyes, sweet Magdalene.

Heavens thy fair eyes be;
Heavens of ever-falling stars;
'Tis seed-time still with thee,
And stars thou sow'st whose harvest dares
    Promise the earth to countershine
    Whatever makes Heaven's forehead fine.

Every morn from hence
A brisk cherub something sips
Whose soft influence
Adds sweetness to his sweetest lips;
    Then to his music: and his song
    Tastes of this breakfast all day long.

RICHARD CRASHAW

When some new bright guest
Takes up among the stars a room,
  And Heaven will make a feast,
Angels with their bottles come,
      And draw from these full eyes of thine
      Their Master's water, their own wine.

The dew no more will weep
The primrose's pale cheek to deck;
  The dew no more will sleep
Nuzzled in the lily's neck:
      Much rather would it tremble here,
      And leave them both to be thy tear.

When sorrow would be seen
In her brightest majesty,
  —For she is a Queen—
Then is she drest by none but thee:
      Then and only then she wears
      Her richest pearls—I mean thy tears.

Not in the evening's eyes,
When they red with weeping are
  For the Sun that dies,
Sits Sorrow with a face so fair.
      Nowhere but here did ever meet
      Sweetness so sad, sadness so sweet.

Does the night arise?
Still thy tears do fall and fall.
  Does night lose her eyes?
Still the fountain weeps for all.
      Let day and night do what they will,
      Thou hast thy task, thou weepest still.

371

Not *So long she lived*
Will thy tomb report of thee;
  But *So long she grieved*:
Thus must we date thy memory.
    Others by days, by months, by years,
    Measure their ages, thou by tears.

  Say, ye bright brothers,
The fugitive sons of those fair eyes
  Your fruitful mothers,
What make you here? What hopes can 'tice
    You to be born? What cause can borrow
    You from those nests of noble sorrow?

  Whither away so fast
For sure the sordid earth
  Your sweetness cannot taste,
Nor does the dust deserve your birth.
    Sweet, whither haste you then? O say,
    Why you trip so fast away?

  We go not to seek
The darlings of Aurora's bed,
  The rose's modest cheek,
Nor the violet's humble head.
    No such thing: we go to meet
    A worthier object—our Lord's feet.

347   *A Hymn to the Name and Honour*
       of the Admirable Saint Teresa

LOVE, thou art absolute, sole Lord
  Of life and death. To prove the word,
We'll now appeal to none of all
Those thy old soldiers, great and tall,

Ripe men of martyrdom, that could reach down
With strong arms their triumphant crown:
Such as could with lusty breath
Speak loud, unto the face of death,
Their great Lord's glorious name; to none
Of those whose spacious bosoms spread a throne
For love at large to fill. Spare blood and sweat:
We'll see Him take a private seat,
And make His mansion in the mild
And milky soul of a soft child.

Scarce has she learnt to lisp a name
Of martyr, yet she thinks it shame
Life should so long play with that breath
Which spent can buy so brave a death.
She never undertook to know
What death with love should have to do.
Nor has she e'er yet understood
Why, to show love, she should shed blood;
Yet, though she cannot tell you why,
She can love, and she can die.
Scarce has she blood enough to make
A guilty sword blush for her sake;
Yet has a heart dares hope to prove
How much less strong is death than love. . . .

Since 'tis not to be had at home,
She'll travel for a martyrdom.
No home for her, confesses she,
But where she may a martyr be.
She'll to the Moors, and trade with them
For this unvalued diadem;

She offers them her dearest breath,
With Christ's name in 't, in change for death:
She'll bargain with them, and will give
Them God, and teach them how to live
In Him; or, if they this deny,
For Him she'll teach them how to die.
So shall she leave amongst them sown
Her Lord's blood, or at least her own.

Farewell then, all the world, adieu!
Teresa is no more for you.
Farewell all pleasures, sports, and joys,
Never till now esteemèd toys!
Farewell whatever dear may be—
Mother's arms, or father's knee!
Farewell house, and farewell home!
She 's for the Moors and Martyrdom.

Sweet, not so fast; lo! thy fair spouse,
Whom thou seek'st with so swift vows,
Calls thee back, and bids thee come
T' embrace a milder martyrdom. . . .

O how oft shalt thou complain
Of a sweet and subtle pain!
Of intolerable joys!
Of a death, in which who dies
Loves his death, and dies again,
And would for ever so be slain;
And lives and dies, and knows not why
To live, but that he still may die!
How kindly will thy gentle heart
Kiss the sweetly-killing dart!
And close in his embraces keep

RICHARD CRASHAW

Those delicious wounds, that weep
Balsam, to heal themselves with thus,
When these thy deaths, so numerous,
Shall all at once die into one,
And melt thy soul's sweet mansion;
Like a soft lump of incense, hasted
By too hot a fire, and wasted
Into perfuming clouds, so fast
Shalt thou exhale to heaven at last
In a resolving sigh, and then,—
O what? Ask not the tongues of men.

Angels cannot tell; suffice,
Thyself shalt feel thine own full joys,
And hold them fast for ever there.
So soon as thou shalt first appear,
The moon of maiden stars, thy white
Mistress, attended by such bright
Souls as thy shining self, shall come,
And in her first ranks make thee room;
Where, 'mongst her snowy family,
Immortal welcomes wait for thee.
O what delight, when she shall stand
And teach thy lips heaven, with her hand,
On which thou now may'st to thy wishes
Heap up thy consecrated kisses!
What joy shall seize thy soul, when she,
Bending her blessèd eyes on thee,
Those second smiles of heaven, shall dart
Her mild rays through thy melting heart!

Angels, thy old friends, there shall greet thee,
Glad at their own home now to meet thee.

All thy good works which went before,
And waited for thee at the door,
Shall own thee there; and all in one
Weave a constellation
Of crowns, with which the King, thy spouse,
Shall build up thy triumphant brows.
All thy old woes shall now smile on thee,
And thy pains sit bright upon thee:
All thy sorrows here shall shine,
And thy sufferings be divine,
Tears shall take comfort, and turn gems,
And wrongs repent to diadems.
Even thy deaths shall live, and new
Dress the soul which late they slew.
Thy wounds shall blush to such bright scars
As keep account of the Lamb's wars.

Those rare works, where thou shalt leave writ
Love's noble history, with wit
Taught thee by none but Him, while here
They feed our souls, shall clothe thine there.
Each heavenly word by whose hid flame
Our hard hearts shall strike fire, the same
Shall flourish on thy brows, and be
Both fire to us and flame to thee;
Whose light shall live bright in thy face
By glory, in our hearts by grace.
Thou shalt look round about, and see
Thousands of crown'd souls throng to be
Themselves thy crown, sons of thy vows,
The virgin-births with which thy spouse
Made fruitful thy fair soul; go now,

And with them all about thee bow
To Him; put on, He'll say, put on,
My rosy Love, that thy rich zone,
Sparkling with the sacred flames
Of thousand souls, whose happy names
Heaven keeps upon thy score: thy bright
Life brought them first to kiss the light
That kindled them to stars; and so
Thou with the Lamb, thy Lord, shalt go.
And, wheresoe'er He sets His white
Steps, walk with Him those ways of light,
Which who in death would live to see,
Must learn in life to die like thee.

348 *Upon the Book and Picture of the*
Seraphical Saint Teresa

O THOU undaunted daughter of desires!
   By all thy dower of lights and fires;
By all the eagle in thee, all the dove;
By all thy lives and deaths of love;
By thy large draughts of intellectual day,
And by thy thirsts of love more large than they;
By all thy brim-fill'd bowls of fierce desire,
By thy last morning's draught of liquid fire;
By the full kingdom of that final kiss
That seized thy parting soul, and seal'd thee His;
By all the Heav'n thou hast in Him
(Fair sister of the seraphim!);
By all of Him we have in thee;
Leave nothing of myself in me.
Let me so read thy life, that I
Unto all life of mine may die!

377

349 *Verses from the Shepherd's Hymn*

WE saw Thee in Thy balmy nest,
　　Young dawn of our eternal day;
We saw Thine eyes break from the East,
　　And chase the trembling shades away:
We saw Thee, and we blest the sight,
We saw Thee by Thine own sweet light.

Poor world, said I, what wilt thou do
　　To entertain this starry stranger?
Is this the best thou canst bestow—
　　A cold and not too cleanly manger?
Contend, the powers of heaven and earth,
To fit a bed for this huge birth.

Proud world, said I, cease your contest,
　　And let the mighty Babe alone;
The phœnix builds the phœnix' nest,
　　Love's architecture is His own.
The Babe, whose birth embraves this morn,
Made His own bed ere He was born.

I saw the curl'd drops, soft and slow,
　　Come hovering o'er the place's head,
Off'ring their whitest sheets of snow,
　　To furnish the fair infant's bed.
Forbear, said I, be not too bold;
Your fleece is white, but 'tis too cold.

I saw th' obsequious seraphim
　　Their rosy fleece of fire bestow,
For well they now can spare their wings,
　　Since Heaven itself lies here below.
Well done, said I; but are you sure
Your down, so warm, will pass for pure?

No, no, your King's not yet to seek
   Where to repose His royal head;
See, see how soon His new-bloom'd cheek
   'Twixt mother's breasts is gone to bed!
Sweet choice, said we; no way but so,
Not to lie cold, yet sleep in snow!

She sings Thy tears asleep, and dips
   Her kisses in Thy weeping eye;
She spreads the red leaves of Thy lips,
   That in their buds yet blushing lie.
She 'gainst those mother diamonds tries
The points of her young eagle's eyes.

Welcome—tho' not to those gay flies,
   Gilded i' th' beams of earthly kings,
Slippery souls in smiling eyes—
   But to poor shepherds, homespun things,
Whose wealth 's their flocks, whose wit 's to be
Well read in their simplicity.

Yet, when young April's husband show'rs
   Shall bless the fruitful Maia's bed.
We'll bring the first-born of her flowers,
   To kiss Thy feet and crown Thy head.
To Thee, dread Lamb! whose love must keep
The shepherds while they feed their sheep.

To Thee, meek Majesty, soft King
   Of simple graces and sweet loves!
Each of us his lamb will bring,
   Each his pair of silver doves!
At last, in fire of Thy fair eyes,
Ourselves become our own best sacrifice!

350 *Christ Crucified*

THY restless feet now cannot go
    For us and our eternal good,
As they were ever wont. What though
    They swim, alas! in their own flood?

Thy hands to give Thou canst not lift,
    Yet will Thy hand still giving be;
It gives, but O, itself's the gift!
    It gives tho' bound, tho' bound 'tis free!

351 *An Epitaph upon Husband and Wife*
Who died and were buried together

TO these whom death again did wed
    This grave's the second marriage-bed.
For though the hand of Fate could force
'Twixt soul and body a divorce,
It could not sever man and wife,
Because they both lived but one life.
Peace, good reader, do not weep;
Peace, the lovers are asleep.
They, sweet turtles, folded lie
In the last knot that love could tie.
Let them sleep, let them sleep on,
Till the stormy night be gone,
And the eternal morrow dawn;
Then the curtains will be drawn,
And they wake into a light
Whose day shall never die in night.

RICHARD LOVELACE

1618–1658

352   *To Lucasta, going to the Wars*

TELL me not, Sweet, I am unkind,
    That from the nunnery
Of thy chaste breast and quiet mind
    To war and arms I fly.

True, a new mistress now I chase,
    The first foe in the field;
And with a stronger faith embrace
    A sword, a horse, a shield.

Yet this inconstancy is such
    As thou too shalt adore;
I could not love thee, Dear, so much,
    Loved I not Honour more.

353   *To Lucasta, going beyond the Seas*

IF to be absent were to be
    Away from thee;
    Or that when I am gone
    You or I were alone;
    Then, my Lucasta, might I crave
Pity from blustering wind or swallowing wave.

But I'll not sigh one blast or gale
    To swell my sail,
    Or pay a tear to 'suage
    The foaming blue god's rage;
    For whether he will let me pass
Or no, I'm still as happy as I was.

Though seas and land betwixt us both,
　　Our faith and troth,
　　　Like separated souls,
　　　All time and space controls:
　　Above the highest sphere we meet
Unseen, unknown; and greet as Angels greet.

So then we do anticipate
　　Our after-fate,
　　　And are alive i' the skies,
　　　If thus our lips and eyes
　　Can speak like spirits unconfined
In Heaven, their earthy bodies left behind.

354　　　　*Gratiana Dancing*

SHE beat the happy pavèment—
　　By such a star made firmament,
　　　Which now no more the roof envìes!
　　　But swells up high, with Atlas even,
　　　Bearing the brighter nobler heaven,
　　And, in her, all the deities.

Each step trod out a Lover's thought,
And the ambitious hopes he brought
　　Chain'd to her brave feet with such arts,
　　　Such sweet command and gentle awe,
　　　As, when she ceased, we sighing saw
　　The floor lay paved with broken hearts.

355 *To Amarantha, that she would dishevel her Hair*

AMARANTHA sweet and fair,
  Ah, braid no more that shining hair!
As my curious hand or eye
Hovering round thee, let it fly!

Let it fly as unconfined
As its calm ravisher the wind,
Who hath left his darling, th' East,
To wanton o'er that spicy nest.

Every tress must be confest,
But neatly tangled at the best;
Like a clew of golden thread
Most excellently ravellèd.

Do not then wind up that light
In ribbands, and o'ercloud in night,
Like the Sun in 's early ray;
But shake your head, and scatter day!

356 *The Grasshopper*

O THOU that swing'st upon the waving hair
  Of some well-fillèd oaten beard,
Drunk every night with a delicious tear
  Dropt thee from heaven, where thou wert rear'd!

The joys of earth and air are thine entire,
  That with thy feet and wings dost hop and fly;
And when thy poppy works, thou dost retire
  To thy carved acorn-bed to lie.

Up with the day, the Sun thou welcom'st then,
  Sport'st in the gilt plaits of his beams,
And all these merry days mak'st merry men,
  Thyself, and melancholy streams.

357   *To Althea, from Prison*

WHEN Love with unconfinèd wings
    Hovers within my gates,
And my divine Althea brings
  To whisper at the grates;
When I lie tangled in her hair
  And fetter'd to her eye,
The birds that wanton in the air
  Know no such liberty.

When flowing cups run swiftly round
  With no allaying Thames,
Our careless heads with roses bound,
  Our hearts with loyal flames;
When thirsty grief in wine we steep,
  When healths and draughts go free—
Fishes that tipple in the deep
  Know no such liberty.

When, like committed linnets, I
  With shriller throat shall sing
The sweetness, mercy, majesty,
  And glories of my King;
When I shall voice aloud how good
  He is, how great should be,
Enlargèd winds, that curl the flood,
  Know no such liberty.

Stone walls do not a prison make,
    Nor iron bars a cage;
Minds innocent and quiet take
    That for an hermitage;
If I have freedom in my love
    And in my soul am free,
Angels alone, that soar above,
    Enjoy such liberty.

ABRAHAM COWLEY

1618–1667

358

Anacreontics

1. Drinking

THE thirsty earth soaks up the rain,
    And drinks and gapes for drink again;
The plants suck in the earth, and are
With constant drinking fresh and fair;
The sea itself (which one would think
Should have but little need of drink)
Drinks twice ten thousand rivers up,
So fill'd that they o'erflow the cup.
The busy Sun (and one would guess
By 's drunken fiery face no less)
Drinks up the sea, and when he 's done,
The Moon and Stars drink up the Sun:
They drink and dance by their own light,
They drink and revel all the night:
Nothing in Nature 's sober found,
But an eternal health goes round.
Fill up the bowl, then, fill it high,
Fill all the glasses there—for why
Should every creature drink but I?
Why, man of morals, tell me why?

2. *The Epicure*

UNDERNEATH this myrtle shade,
On flowery beds supinely laid,
With odorous oils my head o'erflowing,
And around it roses growing,
What should I do but drink away
The heat and troubles of the day?
In this more than kingly state
Love himself on me shall wait.
Fill to me, Love! nay, fill it up!
And mingled cast into the cup
Wit and mirth and noble fires,
Vigorous health and gay desires.
The wheel of life no less will stay
In a smooth than rugged way:
Since it equally doth flee,
Let the motion pleasant be.
Why do we precious ointments shower?—
Nobler wines why do we pour?—
Beauteous flowers why do we spread
Upon the monuments of the dead?
Nothing they but dust can show,
Or bones that hasten to be so.
Crown me with roses while I live,
Now your wines and ointments give:
After death I nothing crave,
Let me alive my pleasures have:
All are Stoics in the grave.

3. *The Swallow*

FOOLISH prater, what dost thou
  So early at my window do?
Cruel bird, thou'st ta'en away
A dream out of my arms to-day;
A dream that ne'er must equall'd be
By all that waking eyes may see.
Thou this damage to repair
Nothing half so sweet and fair,
Nothing half so good, canst bring,
Tho' men say thou bring'st the Spring.

361   *On the Death of Mr. William Hervey*

IT was a dismal, and a fearful night,
  Scarce could the Morn drive on th' unwilling Light,
When Sleep, Death's image, left my troubled breast
      By something liker Death possest.
My eyes with tears did uncommanded flow,
      And on my soul hung the dull weight
      Of some intolerable fate.
What bell was that? Ah me! too much I know!

My sweet companion, and my gentle peer,
Why hast thou left me thus unkindly here,
Thy end for ever, and my life to moan?
      O thou hast left me all alone!
Thy soul and body, when death's agony
      Besieged around thy noble heart,
      Did not with more reluctance part
Than I, my dearest Friend, do part from thee.

My dearest Friend, would I had died for thee!
Life and this world henceforth will tedious be:
Nor shall I know hereafter what to do
  If once my griefs prove tedious too.
Silent and sad I walk about all day,
  As sullen ghosts stalk speechless by
  Where their hid treasures lie;
Alas! my treasure's gone; why do I stay?

Say, for you saw us, ye immortal lights,
How oft unwearied have we spent the nights,
Till the Ledæan stars, so famed for love,
  Wonder'd at us from above!
We spent them not in toys, in lusts, or wine;
  But search of deep Philosophy,
  Wit, Eloquence, and Poetry—
Arts which I loved, for they, my Friend, were thine.

Ye fields of Cambridge, our dear Cambridge, say,
Have ye not seen us walking every day?
Was there a tree about which did not know
  The love betwixt us two?
Henceforth, ye gentle trees, for ever fade;
  Or your sad branches thicker join,
  And into darksome shades combine,
Dark as the grave wherein my Friend is laid!

Large was his soul; as large a soul as e'er
Submitted to inform a body here;
High as the place 'twas shortly in Heaven to have,
  But low and humble as his grave;

So high that all the virtues there did come,
    As to their chiefest seat
    Conspicuous and great;
So low, that for me too it made a room.

Knowledge he only sought, and so soon caught,
As if for him Knowledge had rather sought;
Nor did more learning ever crowded lie
    In such a short mortality.
Whene'er the skilful youth discoursed or writ,
    Still did the notions throng
    About his eloquent tongue,
Nor could his ink flow faster than his wit.

His mirth was the pure spirits of various wit,
Yet never did his God or friends forget;
And when deep talk and wisdom came in view,
    Retired, and gave to them their due.
For the rich help of books he always took,
    Though his own searching mind before
    Was so with notions written o'er,
As if wise Nature had made that her book.

With as much zeal, devotion, piety,
He always lived, as other saints do die.
Still with his soul severe account he kept,
    Weeping all debts out ere he slept.
Then down in peace and innocence he lay,
    Like the sun's laborious light,
    Which still in water sets at night,
Unsullied with his journey of the day.

But happy Thou, ta'en from this frantic age,
Where ignorance and hypocrisy does rage!
A fitter time for Heaven no soul e'er chose—
    The place now only free from those.
There 'mong the blest thou dost for ever shine,
      And wheresoe'er thou casts thy view
      Upon that white and radiant crew,
See'st not a soul clothed with more light than thine.

362   *The Wish*

WELL then! I now do plainly see
    This busy world and I shall ne'er agree.
The very honey of all earthly joy
Does of all meats the soonest cloy;
    And they, methinks, deserve my pity
Who for it can endure the stings,
The crowd, and buzz, and murmurings,
    Of this great hive, the city.

Ah, yet, ere I descend to the grave,
May I a small house and large garden have;
And a few friends, and many books, both true,
Both wise, and both delightful too!
    And since love ne'er will from me flee,
A Mistress moderately fair,
And good as guardian angels are,
    Only beloved and loving me.

O fountains! when in you shall I
Myself eased of unpeaceful thoughts espy?
O fields! O woods! when, when shall I be made
The happy tenant of your shade?

ABRAHAM COWLEY

Here 's the spring-head of Pleasure's flood:
Here 's wealthy Nature's treasury,
Where all the riches lie that she
    Has coin'd and stamp'd for good.

Pride and ambition here
Only in far-fetch'd metaphors appear;
Here nought but winds can hurtful murmurs scatter,
And nought but Echo flatter.
    The gods, when they descended, hither
From heaven did always choose their way:
And therefore we may boldly say
    That 'tis the way too thither.

How happy here should I
And one dear She live, and embracing die!
She who is all the world, and can exclude
In deserts solitude.
    I should have then this only fear:
Lest men, when they my pleasures see,
Should hither throng to live like me,
    And so make a city here.

ALEXANDER BROME
1620-1666

363

The Resolve

TELL me not of a face that 's fair,
    Nor lip and cheek that 's red,
Nor of the tresses of her hair,
    Nor curls in order laid,
Nor of a rare seraphic voice
    That like an angel sings;
Though if I were to take my choice
    I would have all these things:

But if that thou wilt have me love,
   And it must be a she,
'The only argument can move
   Is that she will love me.

The glories of your ladies be
   But metaphors of things,
And but resemble what we see
   Each common object brings.
Roses out-red their lips and cheeks,
   Lilies their whiteness stain;
What fool is he that shadows seeks
   And may the substance gain?
Then if thou'lt have me love a lass,
   Let it be one that's kind:
Else I'm a servant to the glass
   That's with Canary lined.

ANDREW MARVELL

1621–1678

364 *An Horatian Ode*

upon Cromwell's Return from Ireland

THE forward youth that would appear
   Must now forsake his Muses dear,
     Nor in the shadows sing
     His numbers languishing.

'Tis time to leave the books in dust,
And oil the unused armour's rust,
     Removing from the wall
     The corslet of the hall.

So restless Cromwell could not cease
In the inglorious arts of peace,
 But through adventurous war
 Urgèd his active star:

And like the three-fork'd lightning, first
Breaking the clouds where it was nurst,
 Did thorough his own side
 His fiery way divide:

For 'tis all one to courage high,
The emulous, or enemy;
 And with such, to enclose
 Is more than to oppose.

Then burning through the air he went
And palaces and temples rent;
 And Caesar's head at last
 Did through his laurels blast.

'Tis madness to resist or blame
The face of angry Heaven's flame;
 And if we would speak true,
 Much to the man is due,

Who, from his private gardens, where
He lived reservèd and austere
 (As if his highest plot
 To plant the bergamot),

Could by industrious valour climb
To ruin the great work of time,
 And cast the Kingdoms old
 Into another mould;

ANDREW MARVELL

Though Justice against Fate complain,
And plead the ancient rights in vain—
    But those do hold or break
    As men are strong or weak—

Nature, that hateth emptiness,
Allows of penetration less,
    And therefore must make room
    Where greater spirits come.

What field of all the civil war
Where his were not the deepest scar?
    And Hampton shows what part
    He had of wiser art;

Where, twining subtle fears with hope,
He wove a net of such a scope
    That Charles himself might chase
    To Carisbrook's narrow case;

That thence the Royal actor borne
The tragic scaffold might adorn:
    While round the armèd bands
    Did clap their bloody hands.

He nothing common did or mean
Upon that memorable scene,
    But with his keener eye
    The axe's edge did try;

Nor call'd the Gods, with vulgar spite,
To vindicate his helpless right;
    But bow'd his comely head
    Down, as upon a bed.

ANDREW MARVELL

This was that memorable hour
Which first assured the forcèd power;
    So when they did design
    The Capitol's first line,

A Bleeding Head, where they begun,
Did fright the architects to run;
    And yet in that the State
    Foresaw its happy fate!

And now the Irish are ashamed
To see themselves in one year tamed;
    So much one man can do
    That does both act and know.

They can affirm his praises best,
And have, though overcome, confest
    How good he is, how just
    And fit for highest trust;

Nor yet grown stiffer with command,
But still in the Republic's hand—
    How fit he is to sway
    That can so well obey!

He to the Commons' feet presents
A Kingdom for his first year's rents,
    And, what he may, forbears
    His fame, to make it theirs:

And has his sword and spoils ungirt
To lay them at the public's skirt.
    So when the falcon high
    Falls heavy from the sky,

She, having kill'd, no more does search
But on the next green bough to perch,
    Where, when he first does lure,
    The falconer has her sure.

What may not then our Isle presume
While victory his crest does plume?
    What may not others fear,
    If thus he crowns each year?

As Caesar he, ere long, to Gaul,
To Italy an Hannibal,
    And to all States not free
    Shall climacteric be.

The Pict no shelter now shall find
Within his particolour'd mind,
    But, from this valour, sad
    Shrink underneath the plaid,

Happy, if in the tufted brake
The English hunter him mistake,
    Nor lay his hounds in near
    The Caledonian deer.

But thou, the War's and Fortune's son,
March indefatigably on;
    And for the last effect,
    Still keep the sword erect:

Besides the force it has to fright
The spirits of the shady night,
    The same arts that did gain
    A power, must it maintain.

365

A Garden

Written after the Civil Wars

SEE how the flowers, as at parade,
  Under their colours stand display'd:
Each regiment in order grows,
That of the tulip, pink, and rose.
But when the vigilant patrol
Of stars walks round about the pole,
Their leaves, that to the stalks are curl'd,
Seem to their staves the ensigns furl'd.
Then in some flower's belovèd hut
Each bee, as sentinel, is shut,
And sleeps so too; but if once stirr'd,
She runs you through, nor asks the word.

  O thou, that dear and happy Isle,
The garden of the world erewhile,
Thou Paradise of the four seas
Which Heaven planted us to please,
But, to exclude the world, did guard
With wat'ry, if not flaming, sword;
What luckless apple did we taste
To make us mortal and thee waste!
Unhappy! shall we never more
That sweet militia restore,
When gardens only had their towers,
And all the garrisons were flowers;
When roses only arms might bear,
And men did rosy garlands wear?

ANDREW MARVELL

The Definition of Love

MY Love is of a birth as rare
As 'tis for object strange and high:
It was begotten by Despair
Upon Impossibility.

Magnanimous Despair alone
Could show me so divine a thing,
Where feeble Hope could ne'r have flown
But vainly flapt its tinsel wing.

And yet I quickly might arrive
Where my extended Soul is fixt,
But Fate does iron wedges drive,
And always crowds it self betwixt.

For Fate with jealous eye does see
Two perfect Loves; nor lets them close:
Their union would her ruin be,
And her Tyrannic pow'r depose.

And therefore her Decrees of Steel
Us as the distant Poles have plac'd,
(Though Love's whole World on us doth wheel)
Not by themselves to be embrac'd.

Unless the giddy Heaven fall,
And Earth some new Convulsion tear;
And, us to join, the World should all
Be cramp'd into a *Planisphere*.

As Lines so Loves *oblique* may well
Themselves in every Angle greet:
But ours so truly *Parallel*,
Though infinite can never meet.

Therefore the Love which us doth bind
But Fate so enviously debars,
Is the Conjunction of the Mind,
And Opposition of the Stars.

367   *To His Coy Mistress*

HAD we but world enough, and time,
     This coyness, Lady, were no crime.
We would sit down and think which way
To walk and pass our long love's day.
Thou by the Indian Ganges' side
Shouldst rubies find: I by the tide
Of Humber would complain. I would
Love you ten years before the Flood,
And you should, if you please, refuse
Till the conversion of the Jews.
My vegetable love should grow
Vaster than empires, and more slow;
An hundred years should go to praise
Thine eyes and on thy forehead gaze;
Two hundred to adore each breast;
But thirty thousand to the rest;
An age at least to every part,
And the last age should show your heart;
For, Lady, you deserve this state,
Nor would I love at lower rate.
    But at my back I always hear
Time's wingèd chariot hurrying near;
And yonder all before us lie
Deserts of vast eternity.
Thy beauty shall no more be found,
Nor, in thy marble vault, shall sound

My echoing song: then worms shall try
That long preserved virginity,
And your quaint honour turn to dust,
And into ashes all my lust:
The grave's a fine and private place,
But none, I think, do there embrace.
    Now therefore, while the youthful hue
Sits on thy skin like morning dew,
And while thy willing soul transpires
At every pore with instant fires,
Now let us sport us while we may,
And now, like amorous birds of prey,
Rather at once our time devour
Than languish in his slow-chapt power.
Let us roll all our strength and all
Our sweetness up into one ball,
And tear our pleasures with rough strife
Thorough the iron gates of life:
Thus, though we cannot make our sun
Stand still, yet we will make him run.

368   *The Picture of Little T. C. in a
Prospect of Flowers*

S EE with what simplicity
   This nymph begins her golden days!
In the green grass she loves to lie,
And there with her fair aspect tames
The wilder flowers, and gives them names;

367 slow-chapt] slow-jawed, slowly devouring.

But only with the roses plays,
           And them does tell
What colour best becomes them, and what smell.

Who can foretell for what high cause
  This darling of the gods was born?
    Yet this is she whose chaster laws
The wanton Love shall one day fear,
And, under her command severe,
  See his bow broke and ensigns torn.
           Happy who can
Appease this virtuous enemy of man!

O then let me in time compound
  And parley with those conquering eyes,
    Ere they have tried their force to wound;
Ere with their glancing wheels they drive
In triumph over hearts that strive,
  And them that yield but more despise:
           Let me be laid,
Where I may see the glories from some shade.

Meantime, whilst every verdant thing
  Itself does at thy beauty charm,
    Reform the errors of the Spring;
Make that the tulips may have share
Of sweetness, seeing they are fair,
  And roses of their thorns disarm;
           But most procure
That violets may a longer age endure.

But O, young beauty of the woods,
  Whom Nature courts with fruits and flowers,
    Gather the flowers, but spare the buds;

Lest Flora, angry at thy crime
To kill her infants in their prime,
   Do quickly make th' example yours;
             And ere we see,
Nip in the blossom all our hopes and thee.

369   *Thoughts in a Garden*

HOW vainly men themselves amaze
   To win the palm, the oak, or bays,
And their uncessant labours see
Crown'd from some single herb or tree,
Whose short and narrow-vergèd shade
Does prudently their toils upbraid;
While all the flowers and trees do close
To weave the garlands of repose!

Fair Quiet, have I found thee here,
And Innocence thy sister dear?
Mistaken long, I sought you then
In busy companies of men:
Your sacred plants, if here below,
Only among the plants will grow:
Society is all but rude
To this delicious solitude.

No white nor red was ever seen
So amorous as this lovely green.
Fond lovers, cruel as their flame,
Cut in these trees their mistress' name:
Little, alas! they know or heed
How far these beauties hers exceed!
Fair trees! wheres'e'er your barks I wound,
No name shall but your own be found.

ANDREW MARVELL

When we have run our passions' heat,
Love hither makes his best retreat:
The gods, that mortal beauty chase,
Still in a tree did end their race;
Apollo hunted Daphne so
Only that she might laurel grow;
And Pan did after Syrinx speed
Not as a nymph, but for a reed.

What wondrous life in this I lead!
Ripe apples drop about my head;
The luscious clusters of the vine
Upon my mouth do crush their wine;
The nectarine and curious peach
Into my hands themselves do reach;
Stumbling on melons, as I pass,
Ensnared with flowers, I fall on grass.

Meanwhile the mind from pleasure less
Withdraws into its happiness;
The mind, that Ocean where each kind
Does straight its own resemblance find;
Yet it creates, transcending these,
Far other worlds, and other seas;
Annihilating all that's made
To a green thought in a green shade.

Here at the fountain's sliding foot,
Or at some fruit-tree's mossy root,
Casting the body's vest aside,
My soul into the boughs does glide;
There, like a bird, it sits and sings,
Then whets and combs its silver wings,

And, till prepared for longer flight,
Waves in its plumes the various light.

Such was that happy Garden-state
While man there walk'd without a mate:
After a place so pure and sweet,
What other help could yet be meet!
But 'twas beyond a mortal's share
To wander solitary there:
Two paradises 'twere in one,
To live in Paradise alone.

How well the skilful gard'ner drew
Of flowers and herbs this dial new!
Where, from above, the milder sun
Does through a fragrant zodiac run:
And, as it works, th' industrious bee
Computes its time as well as we.
How could such sweet and wholesome hours
Be reckon'd, but with herbs and flowers!

370   *Bermudas*

WHERE the remote Bermudas ride
        In the ocean's bosom unespied,
From a small boat that row'd along
The listening woods received this song:

  'What should we do but sing His praise
That led us through the watery maze
Unto an isle so long unknown,
And yet far kinder than our own?
Where He the huge sea-monsters wracks, ·
That lift the deep upon their backs,

ANDREW MARVELL

He lands us on a grassy stage,
Safe from the storms' and prelates' rage:
He gave us this eternal Spring
Which here enamels everything,
And sends the fowls to us in care
On daily visits through the air:
He hangs in shades the orange bright
Like golden lamps in a green night,
And does in the pomegranates close
Jewels more rich than Ormus shows:
He makes the figs our mouths to meet
And throws the melons at our feet;
But apples plants of such a price,
No tree could ever bear them twice.
With cedars chosen by His hand
From Lebanon He stores the land;
And makes the hollow seas that roar
Proclaim the ambergris on shore.
He cast (of which we rather boast)
The Gospel's pearl upon our coast;
And in these rocks for us did frame
A temple where to sound His name.
O, let our voice His praise exalt
Till it arrive at Heaven's vault,
Which thence (perhaps) rebounding may
Echo beyond the Mexique bay !'

Thus sung they in the English boat
A holy and a cheerful note:
And all the way, to guide their chime,
With falling oars they kept the time.

ANDREW MARVELL

An Epitaph

ENOUGH; and leave the rest to Fame!
'Tis to commend her, but to name.
Courtship which, living, she declined,
When dead, to offer were unkind:
Nor can the truest wit, or friend,
Without detracting, her commend.

To say—she lived a virgin chaste
In this age loose and all unlaced;
Nor was, when vice is so allowed,
Of virtue or ashamed or proud;
That her soul was on Heaven so bent,
No minute but it came and went;
That, ready her last debt to pay,
She summ'd her life up every day;
Modest as morn, as mid-day bright,
Gentle as evening, cool as night:
—'Tis true; but all too weakly said.
'Twas more significant, she's dead.

HENRY VAUGHAN

1621–1695

The Retreat

HAPPY those early days, when I
Shin'd in my Angel-infancy!
Before I understood this place
Appointed for my second race,
Or taught my soul to fancy aught
But a white celestial thought:
When yet I had not walk'd above
A mile or two from my first Love,

And looking back—at that short space—
Could see a glimpse of His bright face:
When on some gilded cloud, or flow'r,
My gazing soul would dwell an hour,
And in those weaker glories spy
Some shadows of eternity:
Before I taught my tongue to wound
My Conscience with a sinful sound,
Or had the black art to dispense
A several sin to ev'ry sense,
But felt through all this fleshly dress
Bright shoots of everlastingness.

O how I long to travel back,
And tread again that ancient track!
That I might once more reach that plain
Where first I left my glorious train;
From whence th' enlightned spirit sees
That shady City of Palm-trees.
But ah! my soul with too much stay
Is drunk, and staggers in the way!
Some men a forward motion love,
But I by backward steps would move;
And when this dust falls to the urn,
In that state I came, return.

373   *Peace*

MY soul, there is a country
   Far beyond the stars,
Where stands a wingèd sentry
   All skilful in the wars:

There, above noise and danger,
    Sweet Peace sits crown'd with smiles,
And One born in a manger
    Commands the beauteous files.
He is thy gracious Friend,
    And—O my soul, awake !—
Did in pure love descend
    To die here for thy sake.
If thou canst get but thither,
    There grows the flower of Peace,
The Rose that cannot wither,
    Thy fortress, and thy ease.
Leave then thy foolish ranges;
    For none can thee secure
But One who never changes—
    Thy God, thy life, thy cure.

374 *The Timber*

SURE thou didst flourish once ! and many springs,
    Many bright mornings, much dew, many showers,
Pass'd o'er thy head; many light hearts and wings,
    Which now are dead, lodg'd in thy living bowers.

And still a new succession sings and flies;
    Fresh groves grow up, and their green branches shoot
Towards the old and still enduring skies,
    While the low violet thrives at their root.

But thou beneath the sad and heavy line
    Of death, doth waste all senseless, cold, and dark;
Where not so much as dreams of light may shine, ·
    Nor any thought of greenness, leaf, or bark.

And yet—as if some deep hate and dissent,
  Bred in thy growth betwixt high winds and thee,
Were still alive—thou dost great storms resent
  Before they come, and know'st how near they be.

Else all at rest thou liest, and the fierce breath
  Of tempests can no more disturb thy ease;
But this thy strange resentment after death
  Means only those who broke—in life—thy peace.

375 *Friends Departed*

THEY are all gone into the world of light!
  And I alone sit ling'ring here;
Their very memory is fair and bright,
    And my sad thoughts doth clear.

It glows and glitters in my cloudy breast,
    Like stars upon some gloomy grove,
Or those faint beams in which this hill is drest
    After the sun's remove.

I see them walking in an air of glory,
    Whose light doth trample on my days:
My days, which are at best but dull and hoary,
    Mere glimmering and decays.

O holy Hope! and high Humility,
    High as the heavens above!
These are your walks, and you have show'd them me,
    To kindle my cold love.

Dear, beauteous Death! the jewel of the Just,
    Shining nowhere, but in the dark;
What mysteries do lie beyond thy dust,
    Could man outlook that mark!

He that hath found some fledg'd bird's nest may know,
    At first sight, if the bird be flown;
But what fair well or grove he sings in now,
      That is to him unknown.

And yet as Angels in some brighter dreams
    Call to the soul, when man doth sleep:
So some strange thoughts transcend our wonted themes,
      And into glory peep.

If a star were confin'd into a tomb,
    Her captive flames must needs burn there;
But when the hand that lock'd her up gives room,
      She'll shine through all the sphere.

O Father of eternal life, and all
    Created glories under Thee!
Resume Thy spirit from this world of thrall
      Into true liberty.

Either disperse these mists, which blot and fill
    My perspective still as they pass:
Or else remove me hence unto that hill,
      Where I shall need no glass.

376   *The Night*

John 2. 3.

THROUGH that pure Virgin-shrine,
    That sacred vail drawn o'er thy glorious noon
That men might look and live as Glow-worms shine,
      And face the Moon:
    Wise Nicodemus saw such light
    As made him know his God by night.

Were all my loud, evil days
Calm and unhaunted as is thy dark Tent,
Whose peace but by some Angels wing or voice
      Is seldom rent;
   Then I in Heaven all the long year
   Would keep, and never wander here.

     But living where the Sun
Doth all things wake, and where all mix and tyre
Themselves and others, I consent and run
      To ev'ry myre,
   And by this worlds ill-guiding light,
   Erre more then I can do by night.

     There is in God (some say)
A deep, but dazling darkness; as men here
Say it is late and dusky, because they
      See not all clear;
   O for that night! where I in him
   Might live invisible and dim.

377   *Nature, Man, Eternity*

(*i*)

The Bird

HITHER thou com'st: the busy wind all night
   Blew thro' thy lodging, where thy own warm wing
Thy pillow was. Many a sullen storm
(For which coarse man seems much the fitter born)
     Rained on thy bed
     And harmless head:

And now as fresh and cheerful as the light
Thy little heart in early hymns doth sing
Unto that Providence, whose unseen arm
Curbed them, and clothed thee well and warm.
      All things that be praise Him, and had
        Their lesson taught them when first made.

So hills and valleys into singing break;
And though poor stones have neither speech nor tongue,
While active winds and streams both run and speak,
Yet stones are deep in admiration.
      Thus praise and prayer here beneath the sun
        Make lesser mornings, when the great are done.

(ii)

Man

Weighing the steadfastness and state
    Of some mean things which here below reside,
Where birds like watchful clocks the noiseless date
    And intercourse of times divide,
Where bees at night get home and hive, and flowers
        Early as well as late,
Rise with the sun and set in the same bowers;

I would, said I, my God would give
    The staidness of these things to man! for these
To His divine appointments ever cleave,
    And no new business breaks their peace;
The birds nor sow nor reap, yet sup and dine,
        The flowers without clothes live,
     Yet Solomon was never drest so fine.

Man hath still either toys or care;
  He hath no root, nor to one place is tied,
But ever restless and irregular
  About the earth doth run and ride,
He knows he hath a home, but scarce knows where;
    He says it is so far
That he hath quite forgot how to get there.

He knocks at all doors, strays and roams;
  Nay hath not so much wit as some stones have
Which in the darkest nights point to their homes,
  By some hid sense their Maker gave;
Man is the shuttle to whose winding quest
    And passage through these looms
God ordered motion, but ordained no rest.

(iii)

Eternity

I saw Eternity the other night
Like a great Ring of pure and endless light,
    All calm, as it was bright,
And round beneath it, Time in hours, days, years
    Driv'n by the spheres
Like a vast shadow mov'd, In which the world
    And all her train were hurl'd;
The doting Lover in his quaintest strain
    Did there Complain,

    .   .   .   .   .   .

Yet some, who all this while did weep and sing,
And sing, and weep, soar'd up into the Ring,
    But most would use no wing.

413

HENRY VAUGHAN

O fools (said I,) thus to prefer dark night
    Before true light,
To live in grots, and caves, and hate the day
    Because it shews the way,
The way which from this dead and dark abode
    Leads up to God,
A way where you might tread the Sun, and be
    More bright than he.
But as I did their madness so discuss
    One whisper'd thus,
This Ring the Bride-groome did for none provide
    But for his bride.

JOHN BUNYAN   1628–1688

378   *The Shepherd Boy sings in the*
         Valley of Humiliation

HE that is down needs fear no fall,
    He that is low, no pride;
He that is humble ever shall
    Have God to be his guide.

I am content with what I have,
    Little be it or much:
And, Lord, contentment still I crave,
    Because Thou savest such.

Fullness to such a burden is
    That go on pilgrimage:
Here little, and hereafter bliss,
    Is best from age to age.

379   *Thomas the Rhymer*

TRUE Thomas lay on Huntlie bank;
  A ferlie he spied wi' his e'e;
And there he saw a ladye bright
  Come riding down by the Eildon Tree.

Her skirt was o' the grass-green silk,
  Her mantle o' the velvet fyne;
At ilka tett o' her horse's mane,
  Hung fifty siller bells and nine.

True Thomas he pu'd aff his cap,
  And louted low down on his knee:
'Hail to thee, Mary, Queen of Heaven!
  For thy peer on earth could never be.'

'O no, O no, Thomas,' she said,
  'That name does not belang to me;
I'm but the Queen o' fair Elfland,
  That am hither come to visit thee.

'Harp and carp, Thomas,' she said;
  'Harp and carp along wi' me;
And if ye dare to kiss my lips,
  Sure of your bodie I will be.'

ferlie] marvel.   tett] tuft, lock.   harp and carp] play
and recite (as a minstrel).

'Betide me weal, betide me woe,
　　That weird shall never daunten me.'
Syne he has kiss'd her rosy lips,
　　All underneath the Eildon Tree.

'Now ye maun go wi' me,' she said,
　　'True Thomas, ye maun go wi' me;
And ye maun serve me seven years,
　　Thro' weal or woe as may chance to be.'

She 's mounted on her milk-white steed,
　　She 's ta'en true Thomas up behind;
And aye, whene'er her bridle rang,
　　The steed gaed swifter than the wind.

O they rade on, and farther on,
　　The steed gaed swifter than the wind;
Until they reach'd a desert wide,
　　And living land was left behind.

'Light down, light down now, true Thomas,
　　And lean your head upon my knee;
Abide ye there a little space,
　　And I will show you ferlies three.

'O see ye not yon narrow road,
　　So thick beset wi' thorns and briers?
That is the Path of Righteousness,
　　Though after it but few inquires.

'And see ye not yon braid, braid road,
　　That lies across the lily leven?
That is the Path of Wickedness,
　　Though some call it the Road to Heaven.

　　　　leven] ? lawn.

'And see ye not yon bonny road
    That winds about the fernie brae?
That is the Road to fair Elfland,
    Where thou and I this night maun gae.

'But, Thomas, ye sall haud your tongue,
    Whatever ye may hear or see;
For speak ye word in Elfyn-land,
    Ye'll ne'er win back to your ain countrie.'

O they rade on, and farther on,
    And they waded rivers abune the knee;
And they saw neither sun nor moon,
    But they heard the roaring of the sea.

It was mirk, mirk night, there was nae starlight,
    They waded thro' red blude to the knee;
For a' the blude that 's shed on the earth
    Rins through the springs o' that countrie.

Syne they came to a garden green,
    And she pu'd an apple frae a tree:
'Take this for thy wages, true Thomas;
    It will give thee the tongue that can never lee.'

'My tongue is my ain,' true Thomas he said;
    'A gudely gift ye wad gie to me!
I neither dought to buy or sell
    At fair or tryst where I might be.

'I dought neither speak to prince or peer,
    Nor ask of grace from fair ladye !'—
'Now haud thy peace, Thomas,' she said,
    'For as I say, so must it be.'

          dought] could.

He has gotten a coat of the even cloth,
    And a pair o' shoon of the velvet green;
And till seven years were gane and past,
    True Thomas on earth was never seen.

380   *Tam Lin*

I

'O I forbid you, maidens a',
    That wear gowd on your hair,
To come or gae by Carterhaugh,
    For young Tam Lin is there.

II

'For even about that knight's middle
    O' siller bells are nine;
And nae maid comes to Carterhaugh
    And a maid returns again.'

III

Fair Janet sat in her bonny bower,
    Sewing her silken seam,
And wish'd to be in Carterhaugh
    Amang the leaves sae green.

IV

She's lat her seam fa' to her feet,
    The needle to her tae,
And she's awa' to Carterhaugh
    As fast as she could gae.

         380 tae] toe.

V

And she has kilted her green kirtle
  A little abune her knee;
And she has braided her yellow hair
  A little abune her bree;
And she has gaen for Carterhaugh
  As fast as she can hie.

VI

She hadna pu'd a rose, a rose,
  A rose but barely ane,
When up and started young Tam Lin;
  Says, 'Ladye, let alane.

VII

'What gars ye pu' the rose, Janet?
  What gars ye break the tree?
What gars ye come to Carterhaugh
  Without the leave o' me?'

VIII

'Weel may I pu' the rose,' she says,
  'And ask no leave at thee;
For Carterhaugh it is my ain,
  My daddy gave it me.'

IX

He's ta'en her by the milk-white hand,
  And by the grass-green sleeve,
He's led her to the fairy ground
  At her he ask'd nae leave.

bree] eye-brow.

X

Janet has kilted her green kirtle
   A little abune her knee,
And she has snooded her yellow hair
   A little abune her bree,
And she is to her father's ha'
   As fast as she can hie.

XI

But when she came to her father's ha',
   She look'd sae wan and pale,
They thought the lady had gotten a fright,
   Or with sickness she did ail.

XII

Four and twenty ladies fair
   Were playing at the ba',
And out then came fair Janet
   Ance the flower amang them a'.

XIII

Four and twenty ladies fair
   Were playing at the chess,
And out then came fair Janet
   As green as onie glass.

XIV

Out then spak' an auld grey knight
   Lay owre the Castle wa',
And says, 'Alas, fair Janet!
   For thee we'll be blamèd a'.'

XV

'Hauld your tongue, ye auld-faced knight,
 Some ill death may ye die!
Father my bairn on whom I will,
 I'll father nane on thee.

XVI

'O if my love were an earthly knight,
 As he is an elfin gay,
I wadna gie my ain true-love
 For nae laird that ye hae.

XVII

'The steed that my true-love rides on
 Is fleeter nor the wind;
Wi' siller he is shod before,
 Wi' burning gold behind.'

XVIII

Out then spak' her brither dear—
 He meant to do her harm:
'There grows an herb in Carterhaugh
 Will twine you an' the bairn.'

XIX

Janet has kilted her green kirtle
 A little abune her knee,
And she has snooded her yellow hair
 A little abune her bree,
And she's awa' to Carterhaugh
 As fast as she can hie.

twine] part, sunder.

XX

She hadna pu'd a leaf, a leaf,
  A leaf but only twae,
When up and started young Tam Lin,
  Says, 'Ladye, thou's pu' nae mae.

XXI

'How dar' ye pu' a leaf?' he says,
  'How dar' ye break the tree?
How dar' ye scathe my babe,' he says,
  'That's between you and me?'

XXII

'O tell me, tell me, Tam,' she says,
  'For His sake that died on tree,
If ye were ever in holy chapel
  Or sain'd in Christentie?'

XXIII

'The truth I'll tell to thee, Janet,
  Ae word I winna lee;
A knight me got, and a lady me bore,
  As well as they did thee.

XXIV

'Roxburgh he was my grandfather,
  Took me with him to bide;
And ance it fell upon a day,
  As hunting I did ride,

scathe] harm.   sain'd] blessed, baptized.

XXV

'There came a wind out o' the north,
  A sharp wind an' a snell,
A dead sleep it came over me
  And frae my horse I fell;
And the Queen o' Fairies she took me
  In yon green hill to dwell.

XXVI

'And pleasant is the fairy land
  For those that in it dwell,
But ay at end of seven years
  They pay a teind to hell;
I am sae fair and fu' o' flesh
  I'm fear'd 'twill be mysell.

XXVII

'But the night is Hallowe'en, Janet,
  The morn is Hallowday;
Then win me, win me, an ye will,
  For weel I wat ye may.

XXVIII

'The night it is gude Hallowe'en,
  The fairy folk do ride,
And they that wad their true-love win,
  At Miles Cross they maun bide.'—

XXIX

'But how should I you ken, Tam Lin,
  How should I borrow you,
Amang a pack of uncouth knights
  The like I never saw?'—

snell] keen, cold.   teind] tithe.   borrow] ransom.
uncouth] unknown.

423

XXX

'You'll do you down to Miles Cross
　　Between twel' hours and ane,
And fill your hands o' the holy water
　　And cast your compass roun'.

XXXI

'The first company that passes by,
　　Say na, and let them gae;
The neist company that passes by,
　　Say na, and do right sae;
The third company that passes by,
　　Then I'll be ane o' thae.

XXXII

'O first let pass the black, ladye,
　　And syne let pass the brown;
But quickly run to the milk-white steed,
　　Pu' ye his rider down.

XXXIII

'For some ride on the black, ladye,
　　And some ride on the brown;
But I ride on a milk-white steed,
　　A gowd star on my crown:
Because I was an earthly knight
　　They gie me that renown.

XXXIV

'My right hand will be gloved, ladye,
　　My left hand will be bare,
And thae's the tokens I gie thee:
　　Nae doubt I will be there.

ANONYMOUS

XXXV

'Ye'll tak' my horse then by the head
　　And let the bridle fa';
The Queen o' Elfin she'll cry out
　　"True Tam Lin he's awa'!"

XXXVI

'They'll turn me in your arms, ladye,
　　An aske but and a snake;
But hauld me fast, let me na gae,
　　To be your warldis make.

XXXVII

'They'll turn me in your arms, ladye,
　　But and a deer so wild;
But hauld me fast, let me na gae,
　　The father o' your child.

XXXVIII

'They'll shape me in your arms, ladye,
　　A hot iron at the fire;
But hauld me fast, let me na gae,
　　To be your heart's desire.

XXXIX

'They'll shape me last in your arms, Janet,
　　A mother-naked man;
Cast your green mantle over me,
　　And sae will I be won.'

aske] newt, lizard.　　　　make] mate, husband.

XL

Janet has kilted her green kirtle
   A little abune the knee;
And she has snooded her yellow hair
   A little abune her bree,
And she is on to Miles Cross
   As fast as she can hie.

XLI

About the dead hour o' the night
   She heard the bridles ring;
And Janet was as glad at that
   As any earthly thing.

XLII

And first gaed by the black, black steed,
   And syne gaed by the brown;
But fast she gript the milk-white steed
   And pu'd the rider down.

XLIII

She's pu'd him frae the milk-white steed,
   An' loot the bridle fa',
And up there rase an eldritch cry,
   'True Tam Lin he's awa'!'

XLIV

They shaped him in her arms twa
   An aske but and a snake;
But aye she grips and hau'ds him fast
   To be her warldis make.

    loot] let.   eldritch] unearthly.

XLV

They shaped him in her arms twa
    But and a deer sae wild;
But aye she grips and hau'ds him fast,
    The father o' her child.

XLVI

They shaped him in her arms twa
    A hot iron at the fire;
But aye she grips and hau'ds him fast
    To be her heart's desire.

XLVII

They shaped him in her arms at last
    A mother-naked man;
She cast her mantle over him,
    And sae her love she wan.

XLVIII

Up then spak' the Queen o' Fairies,
    Out o' a bush o' broom,
'She that has borrow'd young Tam Lin
    Has gotten a stately groom.'

XLIX

Out then spak' the Queen o' Fairies,
    And an angry woman was she,
'She's ta'en awa' the bonniest knight
    In a' my companie!

L

'But what I ken this night, Tam Lin,
    Gin I had kent yestreen,
I wad ta'en out thy heart o' flesh,
    And put in a heart o' stane.

LI

'And adieu, Tam Lin! But gin I had kent
  A ladye wad borrow'd thee,
I wad ta'en out thy twa grey e'en
  Put in twa e'en o' tree.

LII

'And had I the wit yestreen, yestreen,
  That I have coft this day,
I'd paid my teind seven times to hell
  Ere you had been won away!'

381   *Sir Patrick Spens*

1. *The Sailing*

THE king sits in Dunfermline town
  Drinking the blude-red wine;
'O whare will I get a skeely skipper
  To sail this new ship o' mine?'

O up and spak an eldern knight,
  Sat at the king's right knee;
'Sir Patrick Spens is the best sailor
  That ever sail'd the sea.'

Our king has written a braid letter,
  And seal'd it with his hand,
And sent it to Sir Patrick Spens,
  Was walking on the strand.

'To Noroway, to Noroway,
  To Noroway o'er the faem;
The king's daughter o' Noroway,
  'Tis thou must bring her hame.'

380 tree] wood.   coft] bought.   *381* skeely] skilful.

The first word that Sir Patrick read
   So loud, loud laugh'd he;
The neist word that Sir Patrick read
   The tear blinded his e'e.

'O wha is this has done this deed
   And tauld the king o' me,
To send us out, at this time o' year,
   To sail upon the sea?

'Be it wind, be it weet, be it hail, be it sleet,
   Our ship must sail the faem;
The king's daughter o' Noroway,
   'Tis we must fetch her hame.'

They hoysed their sails on Monenday morn
   Wi' a' the speed they may;
They hae landed in Noroway
   Upon a Wodensday.

II. *The Return*

'Mak ready, mak ready, my merry men a'!
   Our gude ship sails the morn.'
'Now ever alack, my master dear,
   I fear a deadly storm.

'I saw the new moon late yestreen
   Wi' the auld moon in her arm;
And if we gang to sea, master,
   I fear we'll come to harm.'

They hadna sail'd a league, a league,
   A league but barely three,
When the lift grew dark, and the wind blew loud,
   And gurly grew the sea.

        lift] sky.

The ankers brak, and the topmast lap,
    It was sic a deadly storm:
And the waves cam owre the broken ship
    Till a' her sides were torn.

'Go fetch a web o' the silken claith,
    Another o' the twine,
And wap them into our ship's side,
    And let nae the sea come in.'

They fetch'd a web o' the silken claith,
    Another o' the twine,
And they wapp'd them round that gude ship's side,
    But still the sea came in.

O laith, laith were our gude Scots lords
    To wet their cork-heel'd shoon!
But lang or a' the play was play'd
    They wat their hats aboon.

And mony was the feather bed
    That flatter'd on the faem;
And mony was the gude lord's son
    That never mair cam hame.

O lang, lang may the ladies sit,
    Wi' their fans into their hand,
Before they see Sir Patrick Spens
    Come sailing to the strand!

And lang, lang may the maidens sit
    Wi' their gowd kames in their hair,
A-waiting for their ain dear loves!
    For them they'll see nae mair.

lap] sprang.   flatter'd] tossed afloat.   kames] combs.

430

Half-owre, half-owre to Aberdour,
  'Tis fifty fathoms deep;
And there lies gude Sir Patrick Spens,
  Wi' the Scots lords at his feet!

382   *The Dowie Houms of Yarrow*

LATE at een, drinkin' the wine,
    And ere they paid the lawin',
They set a combat them between,
  To fight it in the dawin'.

'O stay at hame, my noble lord!
  O stay at hame, my marrow!
My cruel brother will you betray,
  On the dowie houms o' Yarrow.'

'O fare ye weel, my lady gay!
  O fare ye weel, my Sarah!
For I maun gae, tho' I ne'er return
  Frae the dowie banks o' Yarrow.'

She kiss'd his cheek, she kamed his hair,
  As she had done before, O;
She belted on his noble brand,
  An' he's awa to Yarrow.

O he's gane up yon high, high hill—
  I wat he gaed wi' sorrow—
An' in a den spied nine arm'd men,
  I' the dowie houms o' Yarrow.

382 **lawin'**] reckoning.   marrow] mate.   dowie]
doleful.   houms] water-meads.

'O are ye come to drink the wine,
    As ye hae doon before, O?
Or are ye come to wield the brand,
    On the dowie banks o' Yarrow?'

'I am no come to drink the wine,
    As I hae don before, O,
But I am come to wield the brand,
    On the dowie houms o' Yarrow.'

Four he hurt, an' five he slew,
    On the dowie houms o' Yarrow,
Till that stubborn knight came him behind,
    An' ran his body thorrow.

'Gae hame, gae hame, good brother John,
    An' tell your sister Sarah
To come an' lift her noble lord,
    Who's sleepin' sound on Yarrow.'

'Yestreen I dream'd a dolefu' dream;
    I ken'd there wad be sorrow;
I dream'd I pu'd the heather green,
    On the dowie banks o' Yarrow.'

She gaed up yon high, high hill—
    I wat she gaed wi' sorrow—
An' in a den spied nine dead men,
    On the dowie houms o' Yarrow.

She kiss'd his cheek, she kamed his hair,
    As oft she did before, O;
She drank the red blood frae him ran,
    On the dowie houms o' Yarrow.

'O haud your tongue, my douchter dear,
    For what needs a' this sorrow?
I'll wed you on a better lord
    Than him you lost on Yarrow.'

'O haud your tongue, my father dear,
    An' dinna grieve your Sarah;
A better lord was never born
    Than him I lost on Yarrow.

'Tak hame your ousen, tak hame your kye,
    For they hae bred our sorrow;
I wiss that they had a' gane mad
    Whan they cam first to Yarrow.'

383   *Clerk Saunders*

CLERK SAUNDERS and may Margaret
    Walk'd owre yon garden green;
And deep and heavy was the love
    That fell thir twa between.

'A bed, a bed,' Clerk Saunders said,
    'A bed for you and me!'
'Fye na, fye na,' said may Margaret,
    'Till anes we married be!'

'Then I'll take the sword frae my scabbard
    And slowly lift the pin;
And you may swear, and save your aith,
    Ye ne'er let Clerk Saunders in.

'Take you a napkin in your hand,
    And tie up baith your bonnie e'en,
And you may swear, and save your aith,
    Ye saw me na since late yestreen.'

It was about the midnight hour,
　　When they asleep were laid,
When in and came her seven brothers,
　　Wi' torches burning red:

When in and came her seven brothers,
　　Wi' torches burning bright:
They said, 'We hae but one sister,
　　And behold her lying with a knight!'

Then out and spake the first o' them,
　　'I bear the sword shall gar him die.'
And out and spake the second o' them,
　　'His father has nae mair but he.'

And out and spake the third o' them,
　　'I wot that they are lovers dear.'
And out and spake the fourth o' them,
　　'They hae been in love this mony a year.'

Then out and spake the fifth o' them,
　　'It were great sin true love to twain.'
And out and spake the sixth o' them,
　　'It were shame to slay a sleeping man.'

Then up and gat the seventh o' them,
　　And never a word spake he;
But he has striped his bright brown brand
　　Out through Clerk Saunders' fair bodye.

Clerk Saunders he started, and Margaret she turn'd
　　Into his arms as asleep she lay;
And sad and silent was the night
　　That was atween thir twae.

striped] thrust.

And they lay still and sleepit sound
   Until the day began to daw';
And kindly she to him did say,
   'It is time, true love, you were awa'.'

But he lay still, and sleepit sound,
   Albeit the sun began to sheen;
She look'd atween her and the wa',
   And dull and drowsie were his e'en.

Then in and came her father dear;
   Said, 'Let a' your mourning be;
I'll carry the dead corse to the clay,
   And I'll come back and comfort thee.'

'Comfort weel your seven sons,
   For comforted I will never be:
I ween 'twas neither knave nor loon
   Was in the bower last night wi' me.'

The clinking bell gaed through the town,
   To carry the dead corse to the clay;
And Clerk Saunders stood at may Margaret's window,
   I wot, an hour before the day.

'Are ye sleeping, Marg'ret?' he says,
   'Or are ye waking presentlie?
Give me my faith and troth again,
   I wot, true love, I gied to thee.'

'Your faith and troth ye sall never get,
   Nor our true love sall never twin,
Until ye come within my bower,
   And kiss me cheik and chin.'

          twin] part in two.

'My mouth it is full cold, Marg'ret;
  It has the smell, now, of the ground;
And if I kiss thy comely mouth,
  Thy days of life will not be lang.

'O cocks are crowing a merry midnight;
  I wot the wild fowls are boding day;
Give me my faith and troth again,
  And let me fare me on my way.'

'Thy faith and troth thou sallna get,
  And our true love sall never twin,
Until ye tell what comes o' women,
  I wot, who die in strong traivelling?'

'Their beds are made in the heavens high,
  Down at the foot of our good Lord's knee,
Weel set about wi' gillyflowers;
  I wot, sweet company for to see.

'O cocks are crowing a merry midnight;
  I wot the wild fowls are boding day;
The psalms of heaven will soon be sung,
  And I, ere now, will be miss'd away.'

Then she has taken a crystal wand,
  And she has stroken her troth thereon;
She has given it him at the shot-window,
  Wi' mony a sad sigh and heavy groan.

'I thank ye, Marg'ret; I thank ye, Marg'ret;
  And ay I thank ye heartilie;
Gin ever the dead come for the quick,
  Be sure, Marg'ret, I'll come for thee.'

ANONYMOUS

It's hosen and shoon, and gown alone,
   She climb'd the wall, and follow'd him,
Until she came to the green forest,
   And there she lost the sight o' him.

'Is there ony room at your head, Saunders?
   Is there ony room at your feet?
Or ony room at your side, Saunders,
   Where fain, fain, I wad sleep?'

'There's nae room at my head, Marg'ret,
   There's nae room at my feet;
My bed it is fu' lowly now,
   Amang the hungry worms I sleep.

'Cauld mould is my covering now,
   But and my winding-sheet;
The dew it falls nae sooner down
   Than my resting-place is weet.

'But plait a wand o' bonny birk,
   And lay it on my breast;
And shed a tear upon my grave,
   And wish my saul gude rest.'

Then up and crew the red, red cock,
   And up and crew the gray:
''Tis time, 'tis time, my dear Marg'ret,
   That you were going away.

'And fair Marg'ret, and rare Marg'ret,
   And Marg'ret o' veritie,
Gin e'er ye love another man,
   Ne'er love him as ye did me.'

437

384 *Edward, Edward*

'WHY does your brand sae drop wi' blude,
    Edward, Edward?
Why does your brand sae drop wi' blude,
    And why sae sad gang ye, O?'
'O I hae kill'd my hawk sae gude,
    Mither, mither;
O I hae kill'd my hawk sae gude,
    And I had nae mair but he, O.'

'Your hawk's blude was never sae red,
    Edward, Edward;
Your hawk's blude was never sae red,
    My dear son, I tell thee, O.'
'O I hae kill'd my red-roan steed,
    Mither, mither;
O I hae kill'd my red-roan steed,
    That erst was sae fair and free, O.'

'Your steed was auld, and ye hae got mair,
    Edward, Edward;
Your steed was auld, and ye hae got mair;
    Some other dule ye dree, O.'
'O I hae kill'd my father dear,
    Mither, mither;
O I hae kill'd my father dear,
    Alas, and wae is me, O!'

'And whatten penance will ye dree for that,
    Edward, Edward?
Whatten penance will ye dree for that?
    My dear son, now tell me, O.'

    dule ye dree] grief you suffer.

'I'll set my feet in yonder boat,
  Mither, mither;
I'll set my feet in yonder boat,
    And I'll fare over the sea, O.'

'And what will ye do wi' your tow'rs and your ha',
    Edward, Edward?
And what will ye do wi' your tow'rs and your ha',
    That were sae fair to see, O?'
'I'll let them stand till they doun fa',
    Mither, mither;
I'll let them stand till they doun fa',
    For here never mair maun I be, O.'

'And what will ye leave to your bairns and your wife,
    Edward, Edward?
And what will ye leave to your bairns and your wife,
    When ye gang owre the sea, O?'
'The warld's room: let them beg through life,
    Mither, mither;
The warld's room: let them beg through life;
    For them never mair will I see, O.'

'And what will ye leave to your ain mither dear,
    Edward, Edward?
And what will ye leave to your ain mither dear,
    My dear son, now tell me, O?'
'The curse of hell frae me sall ye bear,
    Mither, mither,
The curse of hell frae me sall ye bear:
    Sic counsels ye gave to me, O!'

385   *The Queen's Marie*

MARIE HAMILTON'S to the kirk gane,
    Wi' ribbons in her hair;
The King thought mair o' Marie Hamilton
    Than ony that were there.

Marie Hamilton's to the kirk gane
    Wi' ribbons on her breast;
The King thought mair o' Marie Hamilton
    Than he listen'd to the priest.

Marie Hamilton's to the kirk gane,
    Wi' gloves upon her hands;
The King thought mair o' Marie Hamilton
    Than the Queen and a' her lands.

She hadna been about the King's court
    A month, but barely one,
Till she was beloved by a' the King's court
    And the King the only man.

She hadna been about the King's court
    A month, but barely three,
Till frae the King's court Marie Hamilton,
    Marie Hamilton durstna be.

The King is to the Abbey gane,
    To pu' the Abbey tree,
To scale the babe frae Marie's heart;
    But the thing it wadna be.

O she has row'd it in her apron,
   And set it on the sea—
'Gae sink ye or swim ye, bonny babe,
   Ye'se get nae mair o' me.'

Word is to the kitchen gane,
   And word is to the ha',
And word is to the noble room
   Amang the ladies a',
That Marie Hamilton's brought to bed,
   And the bonny babe's miss'd and awa'.

Scarcely had she lain down again,
   And scarcely fa'en asleep,
When up and started our gude Queen
   Just at her bed-feet;
Saying—'Marie Hamilton, where's your babe?
   For I am sure I heard it greet.'

'O no, O no, my noble Queen!
   Think no sic thing to be;
'Twas but a stitch into my side,
   And sair it troubles me!'

'Get up, get up, Marie Hamilton:
   Get up and follow me;
For I am going to Edinburgh town,
   A rich wedding for to see.'

O slowly, slowly rase she up,
   And slowly put she on;
And slowly rade she out the way
   Wi' mony a weary groan.

   row'd] rolled, wrapped.   greet] cry.

ANONYMOUS

The Queen was clad in scarlet,
   Her merry maids all in green;
And every town that they cam to,
   They took Marie for the Queen.

'Ride hooly, hooly, gentlemen,
   Ride hooly now wi' me!
For never, I am sure, a wearier burd
   Rade in your companie.'—

But little wist Marie Hamilton,
   When she rade on the brown,
That she was gaen to Edinburgh,
   And a' to be put down.

'Why weep ye so, ye burgess wives,
   Why look ye so on me?
O I am going to Edinburgh town.
   A rich wedding to see.'

When she gaed up the Tolbooth stairs,
   The corks frae her heels did flee;
And lang or e'er she cam down again,
   She was condemn'd to die.

When she cam to the Netherbow port,
   She laugh'd loud laughters three;
But when she cam to the gallows foot
   The tears blinded her e'e.

           hooly] gently.

ANONYMOUS

'Yestreen the Queen had four Maries,
  The night she'll hae but three;
There was Marie Seaton, and Marie Beaton,
  And Marie Carmichael, and me.

'O often have I dress'd my Queen
  And put gowd upon her hair;
But now I've gotten for my reward
  The gallows to be my share.

'Often have I dress'd my Queen
  And often made her bed;
But now I've gotten for my reward
  The gallows tree to tread.

'I charge ye all, ye mariners,
  When ye sail owre the faem,
Let neither my father nor mother get wit
  But that I'm coming hame.

'I charge ye all, ye mariners,
  That sail upon the sea,
That neither my father nor mother get wit
  The dog's death I'm to die.

'For if my father and mother got wit,
  And my bold brethren three,
O mickle wad be the gude red blude
  This day wad be spilt for me!

'O little did my mother ken,
  The day she cradled me,
The lands I was to travel in
  Or the death I was to die!

Binnorie

THERE were twa sisters sat in a bour;
   Binnorie, O Binnorie!
There cam a knight to be their wooer,
   By the bonnie milldams o' Binnorie.

He courted the eldest with glove and ring,
But he lo'ed the youngest abune a' thing.

The eldest she was vexèd sair,
And sair envìed her sister fair.

Upon a morning fair and clear,
She cried upon her sister dear:

'O sister, sister, tak my hand,
And let's go down to the river-strand.'

She's ta'en her by the lily hand,
And led her down to the river-strand.

The youngest stood upon a stane,
The eldest cam and push'd her in.

'O sister, sister, reach your hand!
And ye sall be heir o' half my land:

'O sister, reach me but your glove!
And sweet William sall be your love.'

Sometimes she sank, sometimes she swam,
Until she cam to the miller's dam.

Out then cam the miller's son,
And saw the fair maid soummin' in.

     soummin'] swimming.

'O father, father, draw your dam!
There's either a mermaid or a milk-white swan.'

The miller hasted and drew his dam,
And there he found a drown'd womàn.

You couldna see her middle sma',
Her gowden girdle was sae braw.

You couldna see her lily feet,
Her gowden fringes were sae deep.

All amang her yellow hair
A string o' pearls was twisted rare.

You couldna see her fingers sma',
Wi' diamond rings they were cover'd a'.

And by there cam a harper fine,
That harpit to the king at dine.

And when he look'd that lady on,
He sigh'd and made a heavy moan.

He's made a harp of her breast-bane,
Whose sound wad melt a heart of stane.

He's ta'en three locks o' her yellow hair,
And wi' them strung his harp sae rare.

He went into her father's hall,
And there was the court assembled all.

He laid his harp upon a stane,
And straight it began to play by lane.

'O yonder sits my father, the King,
And yonder sits my mother, the Queen;

   by lane] alone, of itself.

'And yonder stands my brother Hugh,
But by him my William, sweet and true.'

But the last tune that the harp play'd then—
   Binnorie, O Binnorie!
Was, 'Woe to my sister, false Helèn!'
   By the bonnie milldams o' Binnorie.

387   *The Bonnie House o' Airlie*

IT fell on a day, and a bonnie simmer day,
   When green grew aits and barley,
That there fell out a great dispute
   Between Argyll and Airlie.

Argyll has raised an hunder men,
   An hunder harness'd rarely,
And he's awa' by the back of Dunkell,
   To plunder the castle of Airlie.

Lady Ogilvie looks o'er her bower-window,
   And O but she looks warely!
And there she spied the great Argyll,
   Come to plunder the bonnie house of Airlie.

'Come down, come down, my Lady Ogilvie,
   Come down and kiss me fairly':
'O I winna kiss the fause Argyll,
   If he shouldna leave a standing stane in Airlie.'

He hath taken her by the left shoulder,
   Says, 'Dame, where lies thy dowry?'
'O it's east and west yon wan water side,
   And it's down by the banks of the Airlie.'

They hae sought it up, they hae sought it down,
　　They hae sought it maist severely,
Till they fand it in the fair plum-tree
　　That shines on the bowling-green of Airlie.

He hath taken her by the middle sae small,
　　And O but she grat sairly!
And laid her down by the bonnie burn-side,
　　Till they plunder'd the castle of Airlie.

'Gif my gude lord war here this night,
　　As he is with King Charlie,
Neither you, nor ony ither Scottish lord,
　　Durst avow to the plundering of Airlie.

'Gif my gude lord war now at hame,
　　As he is with his king,
There durst nae a Campbell in a' Argyll
　　Set fit on Airlie green.

'Ten bonnie sons I have borne unto him,
　　The eleventh ne'er saw his daddy;
But though I had an hunder mair,
　　I'd gie them a' to King Charlie!'

388　　　*The Wife of Usher's Well*

THERE lived a wife at Usher's well,
　　And a wealthy wife was she;
She had three stout and stalwart sons,
　　And sent them o'er the sea.

447

They hadna been a week from her,
   A week but barely ane,
When word came to the carline wife
   That her three sons were gane.

They hadna been a week from her,
   A week but barely three,
When word came to the carline wife
   That her sons she'd never see.

'I wish the wind may never cease,
   Nor fashes in the flood,
Till my three sons come hame to me,
   In earthly flesh and blood!'

It fell about the Martinmas,
   When nights are lang and mirk,
The carline wife's three sons came hame,
   And their hats were o' the birk.

It neither grew in syke nor ditch,
   Nor yet in ony sheugh;
But at the gates o' Paradise
   That birk grew fair eneugh.

'Blow up the fire, my maidens!
   Bring water from the well!
For a' my house shall feast this night,
   Since my three sons are well.'

And she has made to them a bed,
   She's made it large and wide;
And she's ta'en her mantle her about,
   Sat down at the bedside.

carline] country.   fashes] troubles.   syke] marsh.
sheugh] trench.

Up then crew the red, red cock,
    And up and crew the gray;
The eldest to the youngest said.
    ''Tis time we were away.'

The cock he hadna craw'd but once,
    And clapp'd his wings at a',
When the youngest to the eldest said,
    'Brother, we must awa'.

'The cock doth craw, the day doth daw,
    The channerin' worm doth chide;
Gin we be miss'd out o' our place,
    A sair pain we maun bide.'

'Lie still, lie still but a little wee while,
    Lie still but if we may;
Gin my mother should miss us when she wakes,
    She'll go mad ere it be day.'

'Fare ye weel, my mother dear!
    Fareweel to barn and byre!
And fare ye weel, the bonny lass
    That kindles my mother's fire!'

389   *The Three Ravens*

THERE were three ravens sat on a tree,
    They were as black as they might be.

The one of them said to his make,
'Where shall we our breakfast take?'

'Down in yonder greene field
There lies a knight slain under his shield;

388 channerin'] fretting.   389 make] mate.

'His hounds they lie down at his feet,
So well they can their master keep;

'His hawks they flie so eagerly,
There's no fowl dare come him nigh.'

Down there comes a fallow doe
As great with young as she might goe.

She lift up his bloudy head
And kist his wounds that were so red.

She gat him up upon her back
And carried him to earthen lake.

She buried him before the prime,
She was dead herself ere evensong time.

God send every gentleman
Such hounds, such hawks, and such a leman.

390   *The Twa Corbies*

(SCOTTISH VERSION)

AS I was walking all alane
    I heard twa corbies making a mane:
The tane unto the tither did say,
'Whar sall we gang and dine the day?'

'—In behint yon auld fail dyke
I wot there lies a new-slain knight;
And naebody kens that he lies there
But his hawk, his hound, and his lady fair.

'His hound is to the hunting gane,
His hawk to fetch the wild-fowl hame,
His lady's ta'en anither mate,
So we may mak our dinner sweet.

   390 corbies] ravens.   fail] turf.

'Ye'll sit on his white hause-bane,
And I'll pike out his bonny blue e'en:
Wi' ae lock o' his gowden hair
We'll theek our nest when it grows bare.

'Mony a one for him maks mane,
But nane sall ken whar he is gane:
O'er his white banes, when they are bare,
The wind sall blaw for evermair.'

391   *A Lyke-Wake Dirge*

THIS ae nighte, this ae nighte,
  —*Every nighte and alle*,
Fire and fleet and candle-lighte,
  And Christe receive thy saule.

When thou from hence away art past,
  —*Every nighte and alle*,
To Whinny-muir thou com'st at last;
  And Christe receive thy saule.

If ever thou gavest hosen and shoon,
  —*Every nighte and alle*,
Sit thee down and put them on;
  And Christe receive thy saule.

If hosen and shoon thou ne'er gav'st nane
  —*Every nighte and alle*,
The whinnes sall prick thee to the bare bane;
  And Christe receive thy saule.

390 hause] neck.   theek] thatch.   391 fleet] house-room.

From Whinny-muir when thou may'st pass,
    —Every nighte and alle,
To Brig o' Dread thou com'st at last;
    And Christe receive thy saule.

From Brig o' Dread when thou may'st pass,
    —Every nighte and alle,
To Purgatory fire thou com'st at last;
    And Christe receive thy saule.

If ever thou gavest meat or drink,
    —Every nighte and alle,
The fire sall never make thee shrink;
    And Christe receive thy saule.

If meat or drink thou ne'er gav'st nane,
    —Every nighte and alle,
The fire will burn thee to the bare bane;
    And Christe receive thy saule.

This ae nighte, this ae nighte,
    —Every nighte and alle,
Fire and fleet and candle-lighte,
    And Christe receive thy saule.

392   *The Seven Virgins*

A CAROL

ALL under the leaves and the leaves of life
    I met with virgins seven,
And one of them was Mary mild,
    Our Lord's mother of Heaven.

'O what are you seeking, you seven fair maids,
    All under the leaves of life?
Come tell, come tell, what seek you
    All under the leaves of life?'

'We're seeking for no leaves, Thomas,
    But for a friend of thine;
We're seeking for sweet Jesus Christ,
    To be our guide and thine.'

'Go down, go down, to yonder town,
    And sit in the gallery,
And there you'll see sweet Jesus Christ
    Nail'd to a big yew-tree.'

So down they went to yonder town
    As fast as foot could fall,
And many a grievous bitter tear
    From the virgins' eyes did fall.

'O peace, Mother, O peace, Mother,
    Your weeping doth me grieve:
I must suffer this,' He said,
    'For Adam and for Eve.

'O Mother, take you John Evangelist
    All for to be your son,
And he will comfort you sometimes,
    Mother, as I have done.'

'O come, thou John Evangelist,
    Thou'rt welcome unto me;
But more welcome my own dear Son,
    Whom I nursed on my knee.'

453

Then He laid His head on His right shoulder,
    Seeing death it struck Him nigh—
'The Holy Ghost be with your soul,
    I die, Mother dear, I die.'

O the rose, the gentle rose,
    And the fennel that grows so green!
God give us grace in every place
    To pray for our king and queen.

Furthermore for our enemies all
    Our prayers they should be strong:
Amen, good Lord; your charity
    Is the ending of my song.

393   *Two Rivers*

SAYS Tweed to Till—
    'What gars ye rin sae still?'
Says Till to Tweed—
'Though ye rin with speed
    And I rin slaw,
For ae man that ye droon
    I droon twa.'

394   *The Call*

MY blood so red
    For thee was shed,
Come home again, come home again;
My own sweet heart, come home again!
    You've gone astray
    Out of your way,
Come home again, come home again!

ANONYMOUS

395

On Eleanor Freeman
who died 1650, *aged* 21

LET not Death boast his conquering power,
  She'll rise a star that fell a flower.

396

The Bonny Earl of Murray

YE Highlands and ye Lawlands,
  O where hae ye been?
They hae slain the Earl of Murray,
  And hae laid him on the green.

Now wae be to thee, Huntley!
  And whairfore did ye sae!
I bade you bring him wi' you.
  But forbade you him to slay.

He was a braw gallant,
  And he rid at the ring;
And the bonny Earl of Murray,
  O he might hae been a king!

He was a braw gallant,
  And he play'd at the ba';
And the bonny Earl of Murray
  Was the flower amang them a'!

He was a braw gallant,
  And he play'd at the gluve;
And the bonny Earl of Murray,
  O he was the Queen's luve!

O lang will his Lady
   Look owre the Castle Downe,
Ere she see the Earl of Murray
   Come sounding through the town!

397   *Helen of Kirconnell*

I WISH I were where Helen lies,
   Night and day on me she cries;
O that I were where Helen lies,
   On fair Kirconnell lea!

Curst be the heart that thought the thought,
And curst the hand that fired the shot,
When in my arms burd Helen dropt,
   And died to succour me!

O think na ye my heart was sair,
When my Love dropp'd and spak nae mair!
There did she swoon wi' meikle care,
   On fair Kirconnell lea.

As I went down the water side,
None but my foe to be my guide,
None but my foe to be my guide,
   On fair Kirconnell lea;

I lighted down my sword to draw,
I hackèd him in pieces sma',
I hackèd him in pieces sma',
   For her sake that died for me.

O Helen fair, beyond compare!
I'll mak a garland o' thy hair,
Shall bind my heart for evermair,
   Until the day I die!

O that I were where Helen lies!
Night and day on me she cries;
Out of my bed she bids me rise,
    Says, 'Haste, and come to me!'

O Helen fair! O Helen chaste!
If I were with thee, I'd be blest,
Where thou lies low and taks thy rest,
    On fair Kirconnell lea.

I wish my grave were growing green,
A winding-sheet drawn owre my e'en,
And I in Helen's arms lying,
    On fair Kirconnell lea.

I wish I were where Helen lies!
Night and day on me she cries;
And I am weary of the skies,
    For her sake that died for me.

398 *Waly, Waly*

O WALY, waly, up the bank,
    And waly, waly, doun the brae,
And waly, waly, yon burn-side,
    Where I and my Love wont to gae!
I lean'd my back unto an aik,
    I thocht it was a trustie tree;
But first it bow'd and syne it brak—
    Sae my true love did lichtlie me.

O waly, waly, gin love be bonnie
    A little time while it is new!
But when 'tis auld it waxeth cauld,
    And fades awa' like morning dew.

ANONYMOUS

O wherefore should I busk my heid,
    Or wherefore should I kame my hair?
For my true Love has me forsook,
    And says he'll never lo'e me mair.

Now Arthur's Seat sall be my bed,
    The sheets sall ne'er be 'filed by me;
Saint Anton's well sall be my drink;
    Since my true Love has forsaken me.
Marti'mas wind, when wilt thou blaw,
    And shake the green leaves aff the tree?
O gentle Death, when wilt thou come?
    For of my life I am wearie.

'Tis not the frost, that freezes fell,
    Nor blawing snaw's inclemencie,
'Tis not sic cauld that makes me cry;
    But my Love's heart grown cauld to me.
When we cam in by Glasgow toun,
    We were a comely sicht to see;
My Love was clad in the black velvèt,
    And I myself in cramasie.

But had I wist, before I kist,
    That love had been sae ill to win,
I had lock'd my heart in a case o' gowd.
    And pinn'd it wi' a siller pin.
And O! if my young babe were born,
    And set upon the nurse's knee;
And I mysel were dead and gane,
    And the green grass growing over me!

cramasie] crimson.

Barbara Allen's Cruelty

IN Scarlet town, where I was born,
   There was a fair maid dwellin',
Made every youth cry *Well-a-way!*
   Her name was Barbara Allen.

All in the merry month of May,
   When green buds they were swellin',
Young Jemmy Grove on his death-bed lay,
   For love of Barbara Allen.

He sent his man in to her then,
   To the town where she was dwellin',
'O haste and come to my master dear,
   If your name be Barbara Allen.'

So slowly, slowly rase she up,
   And slowly she came nigh him,
And when she drew the curtain by—
   'Young man, I think you're dyin'.'

'O it's I am sick and very very sick,
   And it's all for Barbara Allen.'
'O the better for me ye'se never be,
   Tho' your heart's blood were a-spillin'!

'O dinna ye mind, young man,' says she,
   'When the red wine ye were fillin',
That ye made the healths go round and round,
   And slighted Barbara Allen?'

He turn'd his face unto the wall,
   And death was with him dealin':
'Adieu, adieu, my dear friends all,
   And be kind to Barbara Allen!'

As she was walking o'er the fields,
    She heard the dead-bell knellin';
And every jow the dead-bell gave
    Cried 'Woe to Barbara Allen.'

'O mother, mother, make my bed,
    O make it saft and narrow:
My love has died for me to-day,
    I'll die for him to-morrow.

'Farewell,' she said, 'ye virgins all,
    And shun the fault I fell in:
Henceforth take warning by the fall
    Of cruel Barbara Allen.'

400   *Pipe and Can*

I

THE Indian weed witherèd quite;
    Green at morn, cut down at night;
Shows thy decay: all flesh is hay:
    Thus think, then drink Tobacco.

And when the smoke ascends on high,
Think thou behold'st the vanity
Of worldly stuff, gone with a puff:
    Thus think, then drink Tobacco.

But when the pipe grows foul within,
Think of thy soul defiled with sin,
And that the fire doth it require:
    Thus think, then drink Tobacco.

399 jow] beat, toll.

The ashes, that are left behind,
May serve to put thee still in mind
That unto dust return thou must:
    Thus think, then drink Tobacco.

II

WHEN as the chill Charokko blows,
  And Winter tells a heavy tale;
When pyes and daws and rooks and crows
Sit cursing of the frosts and snows;
    Then give me ale.

Ale in a Saxon rumkin then,
  Such as will make grimalkin prate;
Bids valour burgeon in tall men,
Quickens the poet's wit and pen,
    Despises fate.

Ale, that the absent battle fights,
  And frames the march of Swedish drum,
Disputes with princes, laws, and rights,
What's done and past tells mortal wights,
    And what's to come.

Ale, that the plowman's heart up-keeps
  And equals it with tyrants' thrones,
That wipes the eye that over-weeps,
And lulls in sure and dainty sleeps
    Th' o'er-wearied bones.

Charokko] Scirocco.

Grandchild of Ceres, Bacchus' daughter,
  Wine's emulous neighbour, though but stale,
Ennobling all the nymphs of water,
And filling each man's heart with laughter—
  Ha! give me ale!

401   *Love will find out the Way*

OVER the mountains
    And over the waves,
Under the fountains
    And under the graves;
Under floods that are deepest,
    Which Neptune obey,
Over rocks that are steepest,
    Love will find out the way.

When there is no place
    For the glow-worm to lie,
When there is no space
    For receipt of a fly;
When the midge dares not venture
    Lest herself fast she lay,
If Love come, he will enter
    And will find out the way.

You may esteem him
    A child for his might;
Or you may deem him
    A coward for his flight;
But if she whom Love doth honour
    Be conceal'd from the day—
Set a thousand guards upon her,
    Love will find out the way.

ANONYMOUS

Some think to lose him
    By having him confined;
And some do suppose him,
    Poor heart! to be blind;
But if ne'er so close ye wall him,
    Do the best that ye may,
Blind Love, if so ye call him,
    He will find out his way.

You may train the eagle
    To stoop to your fist;
Or you may inveigle
    The Phœnix of the east;
The lioness, you may move her
    To give over her prey;
But you'll ne'er stop a lover—
    He will find out the way.

If the earth it should part him,
    He would gallop it o'er;
If the seas should o'erthwart him,
    He would swim to the shore;
Should his Love become a swallow,
    Through the air to stray,
Love will lend wings to follow,
    And will find out the way.

There is no striving
    To cross his intent;
There is no contriving
    His plots to prevent;

But if once the message greet him
   That his True Love doth stay,
If Death should come and meet him,
   Love will find out the way!

402   *Phillada flouts Me*

O WHAT a plague is love!
    How shall I bear it?
She will inconstant prove,
   I greatly fear it.
She so torments my mind
   That my strength faileth,
And wavers with the wind
   As a ship saileth.
Please her the best I may,
She loves still to gainsay;
Alack and well-a-day!
   Phillada flouts me.

At the fair yesterday
   She did pass by me;
She look'd another way
   And would not spy me:
I woo'd her for to dine,
   But could not get her;
Will had her to the wine—
   He might entreat her.
With Daniel she did dance,
On me she look'd askance:
O thrice unhappy chance!
   Phillada flouts me.

ANONYMOUS

Fair maid, be not so coy,
    Do not disdain me!
I am my mother's joy:
    Sweet, entertain me!
She'll give me, when she dies,
    All that is fitting:
Her poultry and her bees,
    And her goose sitting,
A pair of mattrass beds,
And a bag full of shreds;
And yet, for all this guedes,
    Phillada flouts me!

She hath a clout of mine
    Wrought with blue coventry,
Which she keeps for a sign
    Of my fidelity:
But i' faith, if she flinch
    She shall not wear it;
To Tib, my t'other wench,
    I mean to bear it.
And yet it grieves my heart
So soon from her to part:
Death strike me with his dart!
    Phillada flouts me.

Thou shalt eat crudded cream
    All the year lasting,
And drink the crystal stream
    Pleasant in tasting;

guedes] goods, property of any kind.

Whig and whey whilst thou lust,
    And bramble-berries,
Pie-lid and pastry-crust,
    Pears, plums, and cherries.
Thy raiment shall be thin,
Made of a weevil's skin—
Yet all's not worth a pin!
    Phillada flouts me.

In the last month of May
    I made her posies;
I heard her often say
    That she loved roses.
Cowslips and gillyflowers
    And the white lily
I brought to deck the bowers
    For my sweet Philly.
But she did all disdain,
And threw them back again;
Therefore 'tis flat and plain
    Phillada flouts me.

Fair maiden, have a care,
    And in time take me;
I can have those as fair
    If you forsake me:
For Doll the dairy-maid
    Laugh'd at me lately,
And wanton Winifred
    Favours me greatly.

One throws milk on my clothes,
T'other plays with my nose;
What wanting signs are those?
   —Phillada flouts me!

I cannot work nor sleep
   At all in season:
Love wounds my heart so deep
   Without all reason.
I 'gin to pine away
   In my love's shadow,
Like as a fat beast may,
   Penn'd in a meadow.
I shall be dead, I fear,
Within this thousand year:
And all for that my dear
   Phillada flouts me.

403   *Suspiria*

O WOULD I were where I would be!
   There would I be where I am not:
For where I am would I not be,
   And where I would be I can not.

WILLIAM STRODE   1602–1645
404   *Chloris in the Snow*

I SAW fair Chloris walk alone,
   When feather'd rain came softly down,
As Jove descending from his Tower
To court her in a silver shower:

The wanton snow flew to her breast,
Like pretty birds into their nest,
But, overcome with whiteness there,
For grief it thaw'd into a tear:
> Thence falling on her garments' hem,
> To deck her, froze into a gem.

405   *In Commendation of Music*

WHEN whispering strains do softly steal
   With creeping passion through the heart
And when at every touch we feel
Our pulses beat and bear a part;
> When threads can make
> A heartstring shake
> Philosophy
> Can scarce deny
The soul consists of harmony.

When unto heavenly joy we feign
Whate'er the soul affecteth most,
Which only thus we can explain
By music of the wingèd host,
> Whose lays we think
> Make stars to wink,
> Philosophy
> Can scarce deny
Our souls consist of harmony.

O lull me, lull me, charming air,
My senses rock with wonder sweet;
Like snow on wool thy fallings are,
Soft, like a spirit's, are thy feet:

WILLIAM STRODE

Grief who need fear
That hath an ear?
Down let him lie
And slumbring die,
And change his soul for harmony.

THOMAS STANLEY

1625–1678

406 *The Relapse*

O TURN away those cruel eyes,
    The stars of my undoing!
Or death, in such a bright disguise,
    May tempt a second wooing.

Punish their blind and impious pride,
    Who dare contemn thy glory;
It was my fall that deified
    Thy name, and seal'd thy story.

Yet no new sufferings can prepare
    A higher praise to crown thee;
Though my first death proclaim thee fair,
    My second will unthrone thee.

Lovers will doubt thou canst entice
    No other for thy fuel,
And if thou burn one victim twice,
    Both think thee poor and cruel.

THOMAS D'URFEY

1653-1723

407 *Chloe Divine*

CHLOE's a Nymph in flowery groves,
  A Nereid in the streams;
Saint-like she in the temple moves,
  A woman in my dreams.

Love steals artillery from her eyes,
  The Graces point her charms;
Orpheus is rivall'd in her voice,
  And Venus in her arms.

Never so happily in one
  Did heaven and earth combine:
And yet 'tis flesh and blood alone
  That makes her so divine.

CHARLES COTTON

1630-1687

408 *To Cælia*

WHEN, Cælia, must my old day set,
  And my young morning rise
In beams of joy so bright as yet
  Ne'er bless'd a lover's eyes?
My state is more advanced than when
  I first attempted thee:
I sued to be a servant then,
  But now to be made free.

CHARLES COTTON

I've served my time faithful and true,
   Expecting to be placed
In happy freedom, as my due,
   To all the joys thou hast:
Ill husbandry in love is such
   A scandal to love's power,
We ought not to misspend so much
   As one poor short-lived hour.

Yet think not, sweet, I'm weary grown,
   That I pretend such haste;
Since none to surfeit e'er was known
   Before he had a taste:
My infant love could humbly wait
   When, young, it scarce knew how
To plead; but grown to man's estate,
   He is impatient now.

KATHERINE PHILIPS ('ORINDA')

1631–1664

409 *To One persuading a Lady to Marriage*

FORBEAR, bold youth; all's heaven here,
   And what you do aver
To others courtship may appear,
   'Tis sacrilege to her.
She is a public deity;
   And were't not very odd
She should dispose herself to be
   A petty household god?

First make the sun in private shine
And bid the world adieu,
That so he may his beams confine
In compliment to you:
But if of that you do despair,
Think how you did amiss
To strive to fix her beams which are
More bright and large than his.

THOMAS TRAHERNE

1637?–1674

410 *News*

NEWS from a foreign country came
As if my treasure and my wealth lay there;
So much it did my heart inflame,
'Twas wont to call my Soul into mine ear;
Which thither went to meet
The approaching sweet,
And on the threshold stood
To entertain the unknown Good.
It hover'd there
As if 'twould leave mine ear,
And was so eager to embrace
The joyful tidings as they came,
'Twould almost leave its dwelling-place
To entertain that same.

As if the tidings were the things,
My very joys themselves, my foreign treasure—
Or else did bear them on their wings—
With so much joy they came, with so much pleasure.

THOMAS TRAHERNE

My Soul stood at that gate
To recreate
Itself with bliss, and to
Be pleased with speed. A fuller view
It fain would take,
Yet journeys back would make
Unto my heart; as if 'twould fain
Go out to meet, yet stay within
To fit a place to entertain
And bring the tidings in.

What sacred instinct did inspire
My soul in childhood with a hope so strong?
What secret force moved my desire
To expect my joys beyond the seas, so young?
Felicity I knew
Was out of view,
And being here alone,
I saw that happiness was gone
From me! For this
I thirsted absent bliss,
And thought that sure beyond the seas,
Or else in something near at hand—
I knew not yet—since naught did please
I knew—my Bliss did stand.

But little did the infant dream
That all the treasures of the world were by:
And that himself was so the cream
And crown of all which round about did lie.
Yet thus it was: the Gem,
The Diadem,

THOMAS TRAHERNE

The ring enclosing all
That stood upon this earthly ball,
The Heavenly eye,
Much wider than the sky,
Wherein they all included were,
The glorious Soul, that was the King
Made to possess them, did appear
A small and little thing!

JOHN DRYDEN

1631–1700

411   *Ode*

*To the Pious Memory of the accomplished young lady, Mrs. Anne
Killigrew, excellent in the two sister arts of Poesy and
Painting*

THOU youngest virgin-daughter of the skies,
    Made in the last promotion of the blest;
Whose palms, new pluck'd from Paradise,
In spreading branches more sublimely rise,
    Rich with immortal green above the rest:
Whether, adopted to some neighbouring star,
Thou roll'st above us, in thy wandering race,
    Or, in procession fixt and regular,
    Mov'd with the heaven's majestic pace;
    Or, call'd to more superior bliss,
Thou tread'st with seraphims the vast abyss:
Whatever happy region is thy place,
Cease thy celestial song a little space;
Thou wilt have time enough for hymns divine,
    Since Heaven's eternal year is thine.

474

JOHN DRYDEN

Hear, then, a mortal Muse thy praise rehearse,
        In no ignoble verse;
But such as thy own voice did practise here,
When thy first-fruits of Poesy were given,
To make thyself a welcome inmate there;
    While yet a young probationer,
            And candidate of Heaven.

    If by traduction came thy mind,
    Our wonder is the less, to find
A soul so charming from a stock so good;
Thy father was transfus'd into thy blood:
So wert thou born into the tuneful strain,
An early, rich, and inexhausted vein.
    But if thy pre-existing soul
    Was form'd at first with myriads more,
It did through all the mighty poets roll
    Who Greek or Latin laurels wore,
And was that Sappho last, which once it was before.
    If so, then cease thy flight, O heaven-born mind!
    Thou hast no dross to purge from thy rich ore:
        Nor can thy soul a fairer mansion find,
    Than was the beauteous frame she left behind:
Return, to fill or mend the quire of thy celestial kind.

    May we presume to say, that, at thy birth,
New joy was sprung in heaven as well as here on earth?
    For sure the milder planets did combine
    On thy auspicious horoscope to shine,
    And even the most malicious were in trine.
        Thy brother-angels at thy birth
        Strung each his lyre, and tun'd it high,
        That all the people of the sky

Might know a poetess was born on earth;
    And then, if ever, mortal ears
    Had heard the music of the spheres.
    And if no clust'ring swarm of bees
On thy sweet mouth distill'd their golden dew,
    'Twas that such vulgar miraclès
    Heaven had not leisure to renew:
For all the blest fraternity of love
Solemniz'd there thy birth, and kept thy holiday above.

    O gracious God! how far have we
Profan'd thy heavenly gift of Poesy!
Made prostitute and profligate the Muse,
Debas'd to each obscene and impious use,
Whose harmony was first ordain'd above,
For tongues of angels and for hymns of love!
O wretched we! why were we hurried down
    This lubrique and adulterate age
(Nay, added fat pollutions of our own),
    To increase the streaming ordures of the stage?
What can we say to excuse our second fall?
Let this thy Vestal, Heaven, atone for all!
Her Arethusian stream remains unsoil'd,
    Unmixt with foreign filth, and undefil'd;
Her wit was more than man, her innocence a child.

    Art she had none, yet wanted none,
        For Nature did that want supply:
    So rich in treasures of her own,
        She might our boasted stores defy:
    Such noble vigour did her verse adorn,
    That it seem'd borrow'd, where 'twas only born.

Her morals, too, were in her bosom bred,
  By great examples daily fed,
What in the best of books, her father's life, she read.
  And to be read herself she need not fear;
  Each test, and every light, her Muse will bear,
  Though Epictetus with his lamp were there.
  Even love (for love sometimes her Muse exprest)
Was but a lambent flame which play'd about her breast,
  Light as the vapours of a morning dream;
  So cold herself, whilst she such warmth exprest,
  'Twas Cupid bathing in Diana's stream. . . .

  Now all those charms, that blooming grace,
The well-proportion'd shape, and beauteous face,
Shall never more be seen by mortal eyes;
In earth the much-lamented virgin lies.
Not wit, nor piety could Fate prevent;
Nor was the cruel Destiny content
To finish all the murder at a blow,
To sweep at once her life and beauty too;
But, like a harden'd felon, took a pride
  To work more mischievously slow,
  And plunder'd first, and then destroy'd.
O double sacrilege on things divine,
  To rob the relic, and deface the shrine!
      But thus Orinda died:
  Heaven, by the same disease, did both translate;
As equal were their souls, so equal was their fate.

  Meantime, her warlike brother on the seas
  His waving streamers to the winds displays,
And vows for his return, with vain devotion, pays.

477

Ah, generous youth! that wish forbear,
The winds too soon will waft thee here!
Slack all thy sails, and fear to come,
Alas, thou know'st not, thou art wreck'd at home!
No more shalt thou behold thy sister's face,
Thou hast already had her last embrace.
But look aloft, and if thou kenn'st from far,
Among the Pleiads a new kindl'd star,
If any sparkles than the rest more bright,
'Tis she that shines in that propitious light.

When in mid-air the golden trump shall sound,
    To raise the nations under ground;
When, in the Valley of Jehoshaphat,
The judging God shall close the book of Fate,
    And there the last assizes keep
    For those who wake and those who sleep;
    When rattling bones together fly
    From the four corners of the sky;
When sinews o'er the skeletons are spread,
Those cloth'd with flesh, and life inspires the dead;
The sacred Poets first shall hear the sound,
    And foremost from the tomb shall bound,
For they are cover'd with the lightest ground;
And straight, with inborn vigour, on the wing,
Like mounting larks, to the new morning sing.
There thou, sweet Saint, before the quire shalt go,
As harbinger of Heaven, the way to show,
The way which thou so well hast learn'd below.

412 *A Song for St. Cecilia's Day, 1687*

FROM harmony, from heavenly harmony,
    This universal frame began:
  When nature underneath a heap
    Of jarring atoms lay,
   And could not heave her head,
The tuneful voice was heard from high,
    'Arise, ye more than dead!'
Then cold, and hot, and moist, and dry,
  In order to their stations leap,
    And Music's power obey.
From harmony, from heavenly harmony,
    This universal frame began:
    From harmony to harmony
Through all the compass of the notes it ran,
The diapason closing full in Man.

What passion cannot Music raise and quell?
    When Jubal struck the chorded shell,
  His listening brethren stood around,
    And, wondering, on their faces fell
  To worship that celestial sound:
Less than a God they thought there could not dwell
    Within the hollow of that shell,
    That spoke so sweetly, and so well.
What passion cannot Music raise and quell?

    The trumpet's loud clangour
      Excites us to arms,
    With shrill notes of anger,
      And mortal alarms.

JOHN DRYDEN

The double double double beat
    Of the thundering drum
      Cries Hark! the foes come;
Charge, charge, 'tis too late to retreat!

  The soft complaining flute,
  In dying notes, discovers
  The woes of hopeless lovers,
Whose dirge is whisper'd by the warbling lute.

  Sharp violins proclaim
Their jealous pangs and desperation,
Fury, frantic indignation,
Depth of pains, and height of passion.
  For the fair, disdainful dame.

But O, what art can teach,
What human voice can reach,
   The sacred organ's praise?
Notes inspiring holy love,
Notes that wing their heavenly ways
  To mend the choirs above.

Orpheus could lead the savage race;
And trees unrooted left their place,
   Sequacious of the lyre;
But bright Cecilia rais'd the wonder higher:
When to her organ vocal breath was given,
  An angel heard, and straight appear'd
   Mistaking Earth for Heaven.

GRAND CHORUS
As from the power of sacred lays
  The spheres began to move,
And sung the great Creator's praise
  To all the Blest above;

So when the last and dreadful hour
This crumbling pageant shall devour,
The trumpet shall be heard on high,
The dead shall live, the living die,
And Music shall untune the sky!

413 *One Happy Moment*

NO, no, poor suff'ring Heart, no Change endeavour,
Choose to sustain the smart, rather than leave her;
My ravish'd eyes behold such charms about her,
I can die with her, but not live without her:
One tender Sigh of hers to see me languish,
Will more than pay the price of my past anguish:
Beware, O cruel Fair, how you smile on me,
'Twas a kind look of yours that has undone me.

Love has in store for me one happy minute,
And She will end my pain who did begin it;
Then no day void of bliss, or pleasure leaving,
Ages shall slide away without perceiving:
Cupid shall guard the door the more to please us,
And keep out Time and Death, when they would seize us:
Time and Death shall depart, and say in flying,
Love has found out a way to live, by dying.

414 *Hidden Flame*

I FEED a flame within, which so torments me
That it both pains my heart, and yet contents me:
'Tis such a pleasing smart, and I so love it,
That I had rather die than once remove it.

Yet he, for whom I grieve, shall never know it;
My tongue does not betray, nor my eyes show it.
Not a sigh, nor a tear, my pain discloses,
But they fall silently, like dew on roses.

Thus, to prevent my Love from being cruel,
My heart's the sacrifice, as 'tis the fuel;
And while I suffer this to give him quiet,
My faith rewards my love, though he deny it.

On his eyes will I gaze, and there delight me;
While I conceal my love no frown can fright me.
To be more happy I dare not aspire,
Nor can I fall more low, mounting no higher.

415   *Song to a Fair Young Lady, going
out of the Town in the Spring*

ASK not the cause why sullen Spring
    So long delays her flowers to bear;
Why warbling birds forget to sing,
    And winter storms invert the year:
Chloris is gone; and fate provides
To make it Spring where she resides.

Chloris is gone, the cruel fair;
    She cast not back a pitying eye:
But left her lover in despair
    To sigh, to languish, and to die:
Ah! how can those fair eyes endure
To give the wounds they will not cure!

JOHN DRYDEN

Great God of Love, why hast thou made
   A face that can all hearts command,
That all religions can invade,
   And change the laws of every land?
Where thou hadst plac'd such power before,
Thou shouldst have made her mercy more.

When Chloris to the temple comes,
   Adoring crowds before her fall;
She can restore the dead from tombs
   And every life but mine recall.
I only am by Love design'd
To be the victim for mankind.

CHARLES WEBBE

c. 1678

416   *Against Indifference*

MORE love or more disdain I crave,
   Sweet, be not still indifferent:
O send me quickly to my grave,
   Or else afford me more content!
Or love or hate me more or less,
For love abhors all lukewarmness.

Give me a tempest if 'twill drive
   Me to the place where I would be;
Or if you'll have me still alive,
   Confess you will be kind to me.
Give hopes of bliss or dig my grave:
More love or more disdain I crave.

SIR GEORGE ETHEREGE

417 *To a Lady asking him how long he
would love her*

IT is not, Celia, in our power
To say how long our love will last;
It may be we within this hour
    May lose those joys we now do taste;
The Blessèd, that immortal be,
From change in love are only free.

Then since we mortal lovers are,
    Ask not how long our love will last;
But while it does, let us take care
    Each minute be with pleasure past:
Were it not madness to deny
To live because we're sure to die?

THOMAS FLATMAN

1637-1688

418 *The Sad Day*

O THE sad day!
    When friends shall shake their heads, and say
Of miserable me—
'Hark, how he groans!
Look, how he pants for breath!
See how he struggles with the pangs of death!'
When they shall say of these dear eyes—
'How hollow, O how dim they be!
Mark how his breast doth rise and swell
Against his potent enemy!'
When some old friend shall step to my bedside,
Touch my chill face, and thence shall gently slide.

484

But—when his next companions say
'How does he do? What hopes?'—shall turn away,
Answering only, with a lift-up hand—
'Who can his fate withstand?'

Then shall a gasp or two do more
Than e'er my rhetoric could before:
Persuade the world to trouble me no more!

CHARLES SACKVILLE, EARL OF DORSET
1638–1706

419 *Song*

*Written at Sea, in the First Dutch War (1665), the night
before an Engagement*

TO all you ladies now at land
We men at sea indite;
But first would have you understand
How hard it is to write:
The Muses now, and Neptune too,
We must implore to write to you—
With a fa, la, la, la, la.

For though the Muses should prove kind,
And fill our empty brain,
Yet if rough Neptune rouse the wind
To wave the azure main,
Our paper, pen, and ink, and we,
Roll up and down our ships at sea—
With a fa, la, la, la, la.

485

Then if we write not by each post,
　　Think not we are unkind;
Nor yet conclude our ships are lost
　　By Dutchmen or by wind:
Our tears we'll send a speedier way,
The tide shall bring them twice a day—
　　　With a fa, la, la, la, la.

The King with wonder and surprise
　　Will swear the seas grow bold,
Because the tides will higher rise
　　Than e'er they did of old:
But let him know it is our tears
Bring floods of grief to Whitehall stairs—
　　　With a fa, la, la, la, la.

Should foggy Opdam chance to know
　　Our sad and dismal story,
The Dutch would scorn so weak a foe,
　　And quit their fort at Goree:
For what resistance can they find
From men who've left their hearts behind?—
　　　With a fa, la, la, la, la.

Let wind and weather do its worst,
　　Be you to us but kind;
Let Dutchmen vapour, Spaniards curse,
　　No sorrow we shall find:
'Tis then no matter how things go,
Or who's our friend, or who's our foe—
　　　With a fa, la, la, la, la.

CHARLES SACKVILLE, EARL OF DORSET

To pass our tedious hours away
 We throw a merry main,
Or else at serious ombre play;
 But why should we in vain
Each other's ruin thus pursue?
We were undone when we left you—
  With a fa, la, la, la, la.

But now our fears tempestuous grow
 And cast our hopes away;
Whilst you, regardless of our woe,
 Sit careless at a play:
Perhaps permit some happier man
To kiss your hand, or flirt your fan—
  With a fa, la, la, la, la.

When any mournful tune you hear,
 That dies in every note
As if it sigh'd with each man's care
 For being so remote,
Think then how often love we've made
To you, when all those tunes were play'd—
  With a fa, la, la, la, la.

In justice you cannot refuse
 To think of our distress,
When we for hopes of honour lose
 Our certain happiness:
All those designs are but to prove
Ourselves more worthy of your love—
  With a fa, la, la, la, la.

And now we've told you all our loves,
    And likewise all our fears,
In hopes this declaration moves
    Some pity for our tears:
Let's hear of no inconstancy—
We have too much of that at sea—
      With a fa, la, la, la, la.

420

Dorinda

DORINDA's sparkling wit, and eyes,
    Uniting cast too fierce a light,
Which blazes high, but quickly dies,
    Pains not the heart, but hurts the sight.

Love is a calmer, gentler joy,
    Smooth are his looks and soft his pace,
Her Cupid is a black-guard boy
    That runs his link full in your face.

SIR CHARLES SEDLEY

1639–1701

421

To Chloris

AH, Chloris! that I now could sit
    As unconcern'd as when
Your infant beauty could beget
    No pleasure, nor no pain!
When I the dawn used to admire,
    And praised the coming day,
I little thought the growing fire
    Must take my rest away.

Your charms in harmless childhood lay
    Like metals in the mine;
Age from no face took more away
    Than youth conceal'd in thine.
But as your charms insensibly
    To their perfection prest,
Fond love as unperceived did fly,
    And in my bosom rest.

My passion with your beauty grew,
    And Cupid at my heart,
Still as his Mother favour'd you,
    Threw a new flaming dart:
Each gloried in their wanton part;
    To make a lover, he
Employ'd the utmost of his art—
    To make a beauty, she.

422 *To Celia*

NOT, Celia, that I juster am
    Or better than the rest!
For I would change each hour, like them,
    Were not my heart at rest.

But I am tied to very thee
    By every thought I have;
Thy face I only care to see,
    Thy heart I only crave.

All that in woman is adored
    In thy dear self I find—
For the whole sex can but afford
    The handsome and the kind.

Why then should I seek further store,
    And still make love anew?
When change itself can give no more,
    'Tis easy to be true!

APHRA BEHN

1640–1689

423
Song

LOVE in fantastic triumph sate
    Whilst bleeding hearts around him flow'd,
For whom fresh pains he did create
    And strange tyrannic power he show'd:
From thy bright eyes he took his fires,
    Which round about in sport he hurl'd;
But 'twas from mine he took desires
    Enough t' undo the amorous world.

From me he took his sighs and tears,
    From thee his pride and cruelty;
From me his languishments and fears,
    And every killing dart from thee.
Thus thou and I the god have arm'd
    And set him up a deity;
But my poor heart alone is harm'd,
    Whilst thine the victor is, and free!

JOHN WILMOT, EARL OF ROCHESTER

1647–1680

424
Return

ABSENT from thee, I languish still;
    Then ask me not, When I return?
The straying fool 'twill plainly kill
    To wish all day, all night to mourn.

Dear, from thine arms then let me fly,
   That my fantastic mind may prove
The torments it deserves to try,
   That tears my fix'd heart from my love.

When, wearied with a world of woe,
   To thy safe bosom I retire,
Where love, and peace, and truth does flow,
   May I contented there expire!

Lest, once more wandering from that heaven,
   I fall on some base heart unblest;
Faithless to thee, false, unforgiven—
   And lose my everlasting rest.

425   *Love and Life*

ALL my past life is mine no more;
   The flying hours are gone,
Like transitory dreams given o'er,
Whose images are kept in store
   By memory alone.

The time that is to come is not;
   How can it then be mine?
The present moment's all my lot;
And that, as fast as it is got,
   Phillis, is only thine.

Then talk not of inconstancy,
   False hearts, and broken vows;
If I by miracle can be
This live-long minute true to thee,
   'Tis all that Heaven allows.

426 *Constancy*

I CANNOT change as others do,
 Though you unjustly scorn;
Since that poor swain that sighs for you
 For you alone was born.
No, Phillis, no; your heart to move
 A surer way I'll try;
And, to revenge my slighted love,
 Will still love on and die.

When kill'd with grief Amyntas lies,
 And you to mind shall call
The sighs that now unpitied rise,
 The tears that vainly fall—
That welcome hour, that ends this smart,
 Will then begin your pain;
For such a faithful tender heart
 Can never break in vain.

427 *To His Mistress*[1]

WHY dost thou shade thy lovely face? O why
 Does that eclipsing hand of thine deny
The sunshine of the Sun's enlivening eye?

Without thy light what light remains in me?
Thou art my life; my way, my light's in thee;
I live, I move, and by thy beams I see.

Thou art my life—if thou but turn away
My life's a thousand deaths. Thou art my way—
Without thee, Love, I travel not but stray.

 [1] Pilfered from Francis Quarles, and improved.

JOHN WILMOT, EARL OF ROCHESTER

My light thou art—without thy glorious sight
My eyes are darken'd with eternal night.
My Love, thou art my way, my life, my light.

Thou art my way; I wander if thou fly.
Thou art my light; if hid, how blind am I!
Thou art my life; if thou withdraw'st, I die.

My eyes are dark and blind, I cannot see:
To whom or whither should my darkness flee,
But to that light?—and who's that light but thee?

If I have lost my path, dear lover, say,
Shall I still wander in a doubtful way?
Love, shall a lamb of Israel's sheepfold stray?

My path is lost, my wandering steps do stray;
I cannot go, nor can I safely stay;
Whom should I seek but thee, my path, my way?

And yet thou turn'st thy face away and fly'st me!
And yet I sue for grace and thou deny'st me!
Speak, art thou angry, Love, or only try'st me?

Thou art the pilgrim's path, the blind man's eye,
The dead man's life. On thee my hopes rely:
If I but them remove, I surely die.

Dissolve thy sunbeams, close thy wings and stay!
See, see how I am blind, and dead, and stray!
—O thou that art my life, my light, my way!

Then work thy will! If passion bid me flee,
My reason shall obey, my wings shall be
Stretch'd out no farther than from me to thee!

JOHN SHEFFIELD, DUKE OF BUCKINGHAMSHIRE

1648–1721

428 *The Reconcilement*

COME, let us now resolve at last
　　To live and love in quiet;
We'll tie the knot so very fast
　　That Time shall ne'er untie it.

The truest joys they seldom prove
　　Who free from quarrels live:
'Tis the most tender part of love
　　Each other to forgive.

When least I seem'd concern'd, I took
　　No pleasure nor no rest;
And when I feign'd an angry look,
　　Alas! I loved you best.

Own but the same to me—you'll find
　　How blest will be our fate.
O to be happy—to be kind—
　　Sure never is too late!

429 *On One who died discovering her
Kindness*

SOME vex their souls with jealous pain,
　　While others sigh for cold disdain:
Love's various slaves we daily see—
Yet happy all compared with me!

494

JOHN SHEFFIELD

Of all mankind I loved the best
A nymph so far above the rest
That we outshined the Blest above;
In beauty she, as I in love.

And therefore They, who could not bear
To be outdone by mortals here,
Among themselves have placed her now,
And left me wretched here below.

All other fate I could have borne,
And even endured her very scorn;
But oh! thus all at once to find
That dread account—both dead and kind!
What heart can hold? If yet I live,
'Tis but to show how much I grieve.

THOMAS OTWAY

1652–1685

430   *The Enchantment*

I DID but look and love awhile,
  'Twas but for one half-hour;
Then to resist I had no will,
  And now I have no power.

To sigh and wish is all my ease;
  Sighs which do heat impart
Enough to melt the coldest ice,
  Yet cannot warm your heart.

O would your pity give my heart
  One corner of your breast,
'Twould learn of yours the winning art,
  And quickly steal the rest.

JOHN OLDHAM

1653-1683

431   *A Quiet Soul*

THY soul within such silent pomp did keep,
　　As if humanity were lull'd asleep;
So gentle was thy pilgrimage beneath,
　　Time's unheard feet scarce make less noise,
　　Or the soft journey which a planet goes:
Life seem'd all calm as its last breath.
　　A still tranquillity so hush'd thy breast,
　　　As if some Halcyon were its guest,
　　　And there had built her nest;
It hardly now enjoys a greater rest.

MATTHEW PRIOR

1664-1721

432   *The Question to Lisetta*

WHAT nymph should I admire or trust,
　　But Chloe beauteous, Chloe just?
What nymph should I desire to see,
But her who leaves the plain for me?
To whom should I compose the lay,
But her who listens when I play?
To whom in song repeat my cares,
But her who in my sorrow shares?
For whom should I the garland make,
But her who joys the gift to take,
And boasts she wears it for my sake?
In love am I not fully blest?
Lisetta, prithee tell the rest.

MATTHEW PRIOR

Sure Chloe just, and Chloe fair,
Deserves to be your only care;
But, when you and she to-day
Far into the wood did stray,
And I happen'd to pass by,
Which way did you cast your eye?
But, when your cares to her you sing,
You dare not tell her whence they spring;
Does it not more afflict your heart,
That in those cares she bears a part?
When you the flowers for Chloe twine,
Why do you to her garland join
The meanest bud that falls from mine?
Simplest of swains! the world may see
Whom Chloe loves, and who loves me.

433   *To a Child of Quality*
       Five Years Old, 1704. The Author then Forty

LORDS, knights, and squires, the numerous band
    That wear the fair Miss Mary's fetters,
Were summoned by her high command
    To show their passions by their letters.

My pen amongst the rest I took,
    Lest those bright eyes, that cannot read,
Should dart their kindling fire, and look
    The power they have to be obey'd.

Nor quality, nor reputation,
    Forbid me yet my flame to tell;
Dear Five-years-old befriends my passion,
    And I may write till she can spell.

For, while she makes her silkworms beds
 With all the tender things I swear;
Whilst all the house my passion reads,
 In papers round her baby's hair;

She may receive and own my flame,
 For, though the strictest prudes should know it,
She'll pass for a most virtuous dame,
 And I for an unhappy poet.

Then too, alas! when she shall tear
 The rhymes some younger rival sends,
She'll give me leave to write, I fear,
 And we shall still continue friends.

For, as our different ages move,
 'Tis so ordain'd (would Fate but mend it!),
That I shall be past making love
 When she begins to comprehend it.

434   *Song*

THE merchant, to secure his treasure,
 Conveys it in a borrow'd name:
Euphelia serves to grace my measure;
 But Chloe is my real flame.

My softest verse, my darling lyre,
 Upon Euphelia's toilet lay;
When Chloe noted her desire
 That I should sing, that I should play.

My lyre I tune, my voice I raise;
 But with my numbers mix my sighs:
And while I sing Euphelia's praise,
 I fix my soul on Chloe's eyes.

Fair Chloe blush'd: Euphelia frown'd:
  I sung, and gazed: I play'd, and trembled:
And Venus to the Loves around
  Remark'd, how ill we all dissembled.

435 *On My Birthday, July 21*

I MY dear, was born to-day—
  So all my jolly comrades say:
They bring me music, wreaths, and mirth,
And ask to celebrate my birth:
Little, alas! my comrades know
That I was born to pain and woe;
To thy denial, to thy scorn,
Better I had ne'er been born:
I wish to die, even whilst I say—
'I, my dear, was born to-day.'

I, my dear, was born to-day:
Shall I salute the rising ray,
Well-spring of all my joy and woe?
Clotilda, thou alone dost know.
Shall the wreath surround my hair?
Or shall the music please my ear?
Shall I my comrades' mirth receive,
And bless my birth, and wish to live?
Then let me see great Venus chase
Imperious anger from thy face;
Then let me hear thee smiling say—
'Thou, my dear, wert born to-day.'

436 *The Lady who offers her Looking-Glass to Venus*

VENUS, take my votive glass:
   Since I am not what I was,
What from this day I shall be,
Venus, let me never see.

437 *A Letter*

to Lady Margaret Cavendish Holles-Harley, when a Child

MY noble, lovely, little Peggy,
   Let this my First Epistle beg ye,
At dawn of morn, and close of even,
To lift your heart and hands to Heaven.
In double duty say your prayer:
Our Father first, then *Notre Père*.
And, dearest child, along the day,
In every thing you do and say,
Obey and please my lord and lady,
So God shall love and angels aid ye.

If to these precepts you attend,
No second letter need I send,
And so I rest your constant friend.

438 *Jinny the Just*

RELEAS'D from the noise of the butcher and baker
   Who, my old friends be thanked, did seldom forsake her,
And from the soft duns of my landlord the Quaker,

From chiding the footmen and watching the lasses,
From Nell that burn'd milk, and Tom that broke glasses
(Sad mischiefs thro' which a good housekeeper passes!)

From some real care but more fancied vexation,
From a life parti-colour'd half reason half passion,
Here lies after all the best wench in the nation.

From the Rhine to the Po, from the Thames to the Rhone,
Joanna or Janneton, Jinny or Joan,
'Twas all one to her by what name she was known.

For the idiom of words very little she heeded,
Provided the matter she drove at succeeded,
She took and gave languages just as she needed.

So for kitchen and market, for bargain and sale,
She paid English or Dutch or French down on the nail,
But in telling a story she sometimes did fail;

Then begging excuse as she happen'd to stammer,
With respect to her betters but none to her grammar,
Her blush helped her out and her jargon became her.

Her habit and mien she endeavor'd to frame
To the different *gout* of the place where she came;
Her outside still chang'd, but her inside the same:

At the Hague in her slippers and hair as the mode is,
At Paris all falbalow'd fine as a goddess,
And at censuring London in smock sleeves and bodice.

She order'd affairs that few people could tell
In what part about her that mixture did dwell
Of Frow, or Mistress, or Mademoiselle.

For her surname and race let the heralds e'en answer;
Her own proper worth was enough to advance her,
And he who liked her, little valued her grandsire.

But from what house so ever her lineage may come
I wish my own Jinny but out of her tomb,
Tho' all her relations were there in her room.

Of such terrible beauty she never could boast
As with absolute sway o'er all hearts rules the roast
When J—— bawls out to the chair for a toast;

But of good household features her person was made,
Nor by faction cried up nor of censure afraid,
And her beauty was rather for use than parade.

Her blood so well mix't and flesh so well pasted
That, tho' her youth faded, her comeliness lasted;
The blue was wore off, but the plum was well tasted.

Less smooth than her skin and less white than her breast
Was this polished stone beneath which she lies pressed:
Stop, reader, and sigh while thou thinkst on the rest.

With a just trim of virtue her soul was endued,
Not affectedly pious nor secretly lewd
She cut even between the coquette and the prude.

Her will with her duty so equally stood
That, seldom oppos'd, she was commonly good,
And did pretty well, doing just what she would.

Declining all power she found means to persuade,
Was then most regarded when most she obey'd,
The mistress in truth when she seem'd but the maid.

Such care of her own proper actions she took
That on other folk's lives she had no time to look,
So censure and praise were struck out of her book.

Her thought still confin'd to its own little sphere,
She minded not who did excel or did err
But just as the matter related to her.

Then too when her private tribunal was rear'd
Her mercy so mix'd with her judgment appear'd
That her foes were condemn'd and her friends always clear'd.

Her religion so well with her learning did suit
That in practice sincere, and in controverse mute,
She show'd she knew better to live than dispute.

Some parts of the Bible by heart she recited,
And much in historical chapters delighted,
But in points about Faith she was something short sighted;

So notions and modes she refer'd to the schools,
And in matters of conscience adher'd to two rules,
To advise with no bigots, and jest with no fools.

And scrupling but little, enough she believ'd,
By charity ample small sins she retriev'd,
And when she had new clothes she always receiv'd.

Thus still whilst her morning unseen fled away
In ord'ring the linen and making the tea
That she scarce could have time for the psalms of the day;

And while after dinner the night came so soon
That half she propos'd very seldom was done;
With twenty God bless me's, how this day is gone!—

While she read and accounted and paid and abated,
Eat and drank, play'd and work'd, laugh'd and cried, lov'd
    and hated,
As answer'd the end of her being created:

In the midst of her age came a cruel disease
Which neither her juleps nor receipts could appease;
So down dropp'd her clay—may her Soul be at peace!

Retire from this sepulchre all the profane,
You that love for debauch, or that marry for gain,
Retire lest ye trouble the Manes of J——.

But thou that know'st love above int'rest or lust,
Strew the myrtle and rose on this once belov'd dust,
And shed one pious tear upon Jinny the Just.

Tread soft on her grave, and do right to her honor,
Let neither rude hand nor ill tongue light upon her,
Do all the small favors that now can be done her.

And when what thou lik'd shall return to her clay,
For so I'm persuaded she must do one day
—Whatever fantastic J[ohn] Asgill may say—

When as I have done now, thou shalt set up a stone
For something however distinguished or known,
May some pious friend the misfortune bemoan,
And make thy concern by reflexion his own.

439   *For my own Monument*

AS doctors give physic by way of prevention,
    Mat, alive and in health, of his tombstone took care;
For delays are unsafe, and his pious intention
    May haply be never fulfill'd by his heir.

Then take Mat's word for it, the sculptor is paid;
    That the figure is fine, pray believe your own eye;
Yet credit but lightly what more may be said,
    For we flatter ourselves, and teach marble to lie.

Yet counting as far as to fifty his years,
   His virtues and vices as other men's were;
High hopes he conceived, and he smother'd great fears,
   In a life parti-colour'd, half pleasure, half care.

Nor to business a drudge, nor to faction a slave,
   He strove to make int'rest and freedom agree;
In public employments industrious and grave,
   And, alone with his friends, Lord ! how merry was he !

Now in equipage stately, now humbly on foot,
   Both fortunes he tried, but to neither would trust;
And whirl'd in the round as the wheel turn'd about,
   He found riches had wings, and knew man was but dust.

This verse, little polish'd, tho' mighty sincere,
   Sets neither his titles nor merit to view;
It says that his relics collected lie here,
   And no mortal yet knows too if this may be true.

Fierce robbers there are that infest the highway,
   So Mat may be kill'd, and his bones never found;
False witness at court, and fierce tempests at sea,
   So Mat may yet chance to be hang'd or be drown'd.

If his bones lie in earth, roll in sea, fly in air,
   To Fate we must yield, and the thing is the same;
And if passing thou giv'st him a smile or a tear,
   He cares not—yet, prithee, be kind to his fame.

WILLIAM WALSH

1663–1708

440 *Rivals*

O F all the torments, all the cares,
　　With which our lives are curst;
Of all the plagues a lover bears,
　　Sure rivals are the worst!
By partners in each other kind
　　Afflictions easier grow;
In love alone we hate to find
　　Companions of our woe.

Sylvia, for all the pangs you see
　　Are labouring in my breast,
I beg not you would favour me,
　　Would you but slight the rest!
How great soe'er your rigours are,
　　With them alone I'll cope;
I can endure my own despair,
　　But not another's hope.

LADY GRISEL BAILLIE

1665–1746

441 *Werena my Heart licht I wad dee*

T HERE ance was a may, and she lo'ed na men;
　　She biggit her bonnie bow'r doun in yon glen;
But now she cries, Dool and a well-a-day!
Come doun the green gait and come here away!

441 may] maid.　　biggit] built.　　gait] way, path.

LADY GRISEL BAILLIE

When bonnie young Johnnie cam owre the see,
He said he saw naething sae lovely as me;
He hecht me baith rings and mony braw things—
And werena my heart's licht, I wad dee.

He had a wee titty that lo'ed na me,
Because I was twice as bonnie as she;
She raised sic a pother 'twixt him and his mother
That werena my heart's licht, I wad dee.

The day it was set, and the bridal to be:
The wife took a dwam and lay doun to dee;
She maned and she graned out o' dolour and pain,
Till he vow'd he never wad see me again.

His kin was for ane of a higher degree,
Said—What had he do wi' the likes of me?
Appose I was bonnie, I wasna for Johnnie—
And werena my heart's licht, I wad dee.

They said I had neither cow nor calf,
Nor dribbles o' drink rins thro' the draff,
Nor pickles o' meal rins thro' the mill-e'e—
And werena my heart's licht, I wad dee.

His titty she was baith wylie and slee:
She spied me as I cam owre the lea;
And then she ran in and made a loud din—
Believe your ain e'en, an ye trow not me.

His bonnet stood ay fu' round on his brow,
His auld ane look'd ay as well as some's new:
But now he lets 't wear ony gait it will hing,
And casts himsel dowie upon the corn bing.

hecht] promised.　　　titty] sister.　　　dwam] sudden illness.
appose] suppose.　　pickles] small quantities.　　hing] hang.
dowie] dejectedly.

And now he gaes daund'ring about the dykes,
And a' he dow do is to hund the tykes:
The live-lang nicht he ne'er steeks his e'e—
And werena my heart's licht, I wad dee.

Were I but young for thee, as I hae been,
We should hae been gallopin' doun in yon green,
And linkin' it owre the lily-white lea—
And wow, gin I were but young for thee!

WILLIAM CONGREVE

1670–1729

442

False though She be

FALSE though she be to me and love,
   I'll ne'er pursue revenge;
For still the charmer I approve,
   Though I deplore her change.

In hours of bliss we oft have met:
   They could not always last;
And though the present I regret,
   I'm grateful for the past.

443   *A Hue and Cry after Fair Amoret*

FAIR Amoret is gone astray—
   Pursue and seek her, ev'ry lover;
I'll tell the signs by which you may
   The wand'ring Shepherdess discover.

441 hund the tykes] direct the dogs.   steeks] closes.
linkin'] tripping arm-in-arm.

Coquette and coy at once her air,
    Both studied, tho' both seem neglected;
Careless she is, with artful care,
    Affecting to seem unaffected.

With skill her eyes dart ev'ry glance,
    Yet change so soon you'd ne'er suspect them,
For she'd persuade they wound by chance,
    Tho' certain aim and art direct them.

She likes herself, yet others hates
    For that which in herself she prizes;
And, while she laughs at them, forgets
    She is the thing that she despises.

JOSEPH ADDISON

1672–1719

444

Hymn

THE spacious firmament on high,
    With all the blue ethereal sky,
And spangled heavens, a shining frame,
Their great Original proclaim.
Th' unwearied Sun from day to day
Does his Creator's power display;
And publishes to every land
The work of an Almighty hand.

Soon as the evening shades prevail.
The Moon takes up the wondrous tale;
And nightly to the listening Earth
Repeats the story of her birth:

509

Whilst all the stars that round her burn,
And all the planets in their turn,
Confirm the tidings as they roll,
And spread the truth from pole to pole.

What though in solemn silence all
Move round the dark terrestrial ball;
What though nor real voice nor sound
Amidst their radiant orbs be found?
In Reason's ear they all rejoice,
And utter forth a glorious voice;
For ever singing as they shine,
'The Hand that made us is divine.'

ISAAC WATTS

1674–1748

445   *The Day of Judgement*

WHEN the fierce North-wind with his airy forces
 Rears up the Baltic to a foaming fury;
And the red lightning with a storm of hail comes
            Rushing amain down;

How the poor sailors stand amazed and tremble,
While the hoarse thunder, like a bloody trumpet,
Roars a loud onset to the gaping waters
            Quick to devour them.

Such shall the noise be, and the wild disorder
(If things eternal may be like these earthly),
Such the dire terror when the great Archangel
            Shakes the creation;

Tears the strong pillars of the vault of Heaven,
Breaks up old marble, the repose of princes,
Sees the graves open, and the bones arising,
                  Flames all around them.

Hark, the shrill outcries of the guilty wretches!
Lively bright horror and amazing anguish
Stare thro' their eyelids, while the living worm lies
                  Gnawing within them.

Thoughts, like old vultures, prey upon their heart-strings,
And the smart twinges, when the eye beholds the
Lofty Judge frowning, and a flood of vengeance
                  Rolling afore him.

Hopeless immortals! how they scream and shiver,
While devils push them to the pit wide-yawning
Hideous and gloomy, to receive them headlong
                  Down to the centre!

Stop here, my fancy: (all away, ye horrid
Doleful ideas!) come, arise to Jesus,
How He sits God-like! and the saints around Him
                  Throned, yet adoring!

O may I sit there when He comes triumphant,
Dooming the nations! then ascend to glory,
While our Hosannas all along the passage
                  Shout the Redeemer!

446   *A Cradle Hymn*

HUSH! my dear, lie still and slumber,
    Holy angels guard thy bed!
Heavenly blessings without number
    Gently falling on thy head.

ISAAC WATTS

Sleep, my babe; thy food and raiment,
  House and home, thy friends provide;
All without thy care or payment:
  All thy wants are well supplied.

How much better thou'rt attended
  Than the Son of God could be,
When from heaven He descended
  And became a child like thee!

Soft and easy is thy cradle:
  Coarse and hard thy Saviour lay,
When His birthplace was a stable
  And His softest bed was hay.

Blessèd babe! what glorious features—
  Spotless fair, divinely bright!
Must He dwell with brutal creatures
  How could angels bear the sight?

Was there nothing but a manger
  Cursèd sinners could afford
To receive the heavenly stranger?
  Did they thus affront their Lord?

Soft, my child: I did not chide thee,
  Though my song might sound too hard;
'Tis thy mother sits beside thee,
  And her arms shall be thy guard.

Yet to read the shameful story
  How the Jews abused their King,
How they served the Lord of Glory,
  Makes me angry while I sing.

See the kinder shepherds round Him,
　　Telling wonders from the sky!
Where they sought Him, there they found Him,
　　With His Virgin mother by.

See the lovely babe a-dressing;
　　Lovely infant, how He smiled!
When He wept, the mother's blessing
　　Soothed and hush'd the holy child.

Lo, He slumbers in His manger,
　　Where the hornèd oxen fed:
Peace, my darling; here's no danger,
　　Here's no ox anear thy bed.

'Twas to save thee, child, from dying,
　　Save my dear from burning flame,
Bitter groans and endless crying,
　　That thy blest Redeemer came.

May'st thou live to know and fear Him,
　　Trust and love Him all thy days;
Then go dwell for ever near Him,
　　See His face, and sing His praise!

THOMAS PARNELL

1679–1718

447　　*Song*

WHEN thy beauty appears
　　In its graces and airs
All bright as an angel new dropp'd from the sky,
At distance I gaze and am awed by my fears:
　　So strangely you dazzle my eye!

But when without art
Your kind thoughts you impart,
When your love runs in blushes through every vein;
When it darts from your eyes, when it pants in your heart,
Then I know you're a woman again.

There's a passion and pride
In our sex (she replied),
And thus, might I gratify both, I would do:
Still an angel appear to each lover beside,
But still be a woman to you.

ALLAN RAMSAY

1686-1758

448   *Peggy*

MY Peggy is a young thing,
Just enter'd in her teens,
Fair as the day, and sweet as May,
Fair as the day, and always gay;
My Peggy is a young thing,
And I'm not very auld,
Yet well I like to meet her at
The wawking of the fauld.

My Peggy speaks sae sweetly
Whene'er we meet alane,
I wish nae mair to lay my care,
I wish nae mair of a' that's rare;

448 wawking] watching.

ALLAN RAMSAY

My Peggy speaks sae sweetly,
    To a' the lave I'm cauld,
But she gars a' my spirits glow
    At wawking of the fauld.

My Peggy smiles sae kindly
    Whene'er I whisper love,
That I look down on a' the town,
That I look down upon a crown;
    My Peggy smiles sae kindly,
        It makes me blyth and bauld,
And naething gi'es me sic delight
    As wawking of the fauld.

My Peggy sings sae saftly
    When on my pipe I play,
By a' the rest it is confest,
By a' the rest, that she sings best;
    My Peggy sings sae saftly,
        And in her sangs are tauld,
With innocence the wale of sense,
    At wawking of the fauld.

WILLIAM OLDYS

1687–1761

449   *On a Fly drinking out of his Cup*

BUSY, curious, thirsty fly!
   Drink with me and drink as I:
Freely welcome to my cup,
Couldst thou sip and sip it up:
Make the most of life you may,
Life is short and wears away.

  448 lave] rest.   wale] choice, best.

Both alike are mine and thine
Hastening quick to their decline:
Thine's a summer, mine's no more,
Though repeated to threescore.
Threescore summers, when they're gone,
Will appear as short as one!

JOHN GAY

1685–1732

450   *To a Lady*

WHEN I some antique Jar behold,
  Or white, or blue, or speck'd with gold,
Vessels so pure, and so refin'd
Appear the types of woman-kind:
Are they not valu'd for their beauty,
Too fair, too fine for household duty?
With flowers and gold and azure dy'd,
Of ev'ry house the grace and pride?
How white, how polish'd is their skin,
And valu'd most when only seen!
She who before was highest priz'd
Is for a crack or flaw despis'd;
I grant they're frail, yet they're so rare,
The treasure cannot cost too dear!
But Man is made of coarser stuff,
And serves convenience well enough;
He's a strong earthen vessel made,
For drudging, labour, toil and trade;
And when wives lose their other self,
With ease they bear the loss of Delf.

451   *On a certain Lady at Court*

I KNOW a thing that's most uncommon;
   (Envy, be silent and attend!)
I know a reasonable woman,
   Handsome and witty, yet a friend.

Not warp'd by passion, awed by rumour;
   Not grave through pride, nor gay through folly;
An equal mixture of good-humour
   And sensible soft melancholy.

'Has she no faults then (Envy says), Sir?'
   Yes, she has one, I must aver:
When all the world conspires to praise her,
   The woman's deaf, and does not hear.

452   *Elegy to the Memory of an
Unfortunate Lady*

WHAT beck'ning ghost, along the moonlight shade
   Invites my steps, and points to yonder glade?
'Tis she!—but why that bleeding bosom gored,
Why dimly gleams the visionary sword?
O, ever beauteous, ever friendly! tell,
Is it, in Heav'n, a crime to love too well?
To bear too tender or too firm a heart,
To act a lover's or a Roman's part?
Is there no bright reversion in the sky
For those who greatly think, or bravely die?

Why bade ye else, ye Pow'rs! her soul aspire
Above the vulgar flight of low desire?
Ambition first sprung from your blest abodes;
The glorious fault of angels and of gods;
Thence to their images on earth it flows,
And in the breasts of kings and heroes glows.
Most souls, 'tis true, but peep out once an age,
Dull sullen pris'ners in the body's cage:
Dim lights of life, that burn a length of years,
Useless, unseen, as lamps in sepulchres;
Like Eastern kings a lazy state they keep,
And close confined to their own palace, sleep.

From these perhaps (ere Nature bade her die)
Fate snatch'd her early to the pitying sky.
As into air the purer spirits flow,
And sep'rate from their kindred dregs below,
So flew the soul to its congenial place,
Nor left one virtue to redeem her race.

But thou, false guardian of a charge too good!
Thou, mean deserter of thy brother's blood!
See on these ruby lips the trembling breath,
These cheeks now fading at the blast of Death:
Cold is that breast which warm'd the world before,
And those love-darting eyes must roll no more.
Thus, if eternal Justice rules the ball,
Thus shall your wives, and thus your children fall;
On all the line a sudden vengeance waits,
And frequent hearses shall besiege your gates.
There passengers shall stand, and pointing say
(While the long fun'rals blacken all the way),
'Lo! these were they whose souls the Furies steel'd
And cursed with hearts unknowing how to yield.'

Thus unlamented pass the proud away,
The gaze of fools, and pageant of a day!
So perish all whose breast ne'er learn'd to glow
For others' good, or melt at others' woe!
    What can atone (O ever-injured shade!)
Thy fate unpitied, and thy rites unpaid?
No friend's complaint, no kind domestic tear
Pleased thy pale ghost, or graced thy mournful bier.
By foreign hands thy dying eyes were closed,
By foreign hands thy decent limbs composed,
By foreign hands thy humble grave adorn'd,
By strangers honour'd, and by strangers mourn'd!
What tho' no friends in sable weeds appear,
Grieve for an hour, perhaps, then mourn a year,
And bear about the mockery of woe
To midnight dances, and the public show?
What tho' no weeping Loves thy ashes grace,
Nor polish'd marble emulate thy face?
What tho' no sacred earth allow thee room,
Nor hallow'd dirge be mutter'd o'er thy tomb?
Yet shall thy grave with rising flow'rs be drest,
And the green turf lie lightly on thy breast:
There shall the morn her earliest tears bestow,
There the first roses of the year shall blow;
While angels with their silver wings o'ershade
The ground now sacred by thy reliques made.
    So peaceful rests, without a stone, a name,
What once had beauty, titles, wealth, and fame.
How loved, how honour'd once, avails thee not,
To whom related, or by whom begot;
A heap of dust alone remains of thee,
'Tis all thou art, and all the proud shall be!

Poets themselves must fall, like those they sung,
Deaf the praised ear, and mute the tuneful tongue.
Ev'n he, whose soul now melts in mournful lays,
Shall shortly want the gen'rous tear he pays;
Then from his closing eyes thy form shall part,
And the last pang shall tear thee from his heart;
Life's idle business at one gasp be o'er,
The Muse forgot, and thou beloved no more!

453   *The Dying Christian to his Soul*

VITAL spark of heav'nly flame!
   Quit, O quit this mortal frame:
Trembling, hoping, ling'ring, flying,
   O the pain, the bliss of dying!
Cease, fond Nature, cease thy strife,
And let me languish into life.

   Hark! they whisper; angels say,
   Sister Spirit, come away!
   What is this absorbs me quite?
   Steals my senses, shuts my sight,
Drowns my spirits, draws my breath?
Tell me, my soul, can this be death?

   The world recedes; it disappears!
   Heav'n opens on my eyes! my ears
    With sounds seraphic ring!
Lend, lend your wings! I mount! I fly!
O Grave! where is thy victory?
    O Death! where is thy sting?

454 *Winifreda*

AWAY; let nought to Love displeasing,
    My *Winifreda*, move your Care;
Let nought delay the heav'nly Blessing,
    Nor squeamish Pride, nor gloomy Fear.

What tho' no Grants of Royal Donors
    With pompous Titles grace our Blood?
We'll shine in more substantial Honours,
    And, to be Noble, we'll be good.

Through Youth and Age, in Love excelling,
    We'll hand in hand together tread;
Sweet-smiling Peace shall crown our dwelling,
    And babes, sweet-smiling babes, our bed.

And, when with envy Time transported
    Shall think to rob us of our Joys;
You'll, in your Girls, again be courted,
    And I'll go wooing in my Boys.

HENRY CAREY

1693?–1743

455 *Sally in our Alley*

OF all the girls that are so smart
    There's none like pretty Sally;
She is the darling of my heart,
    And she lives in our alley.
There is no lady in the land
    Is half so sweet as Sally;
She is the darling of my heart,
    And she lives in our alley.

HENRY CAREY

Her father he makes cabbage-nets,
    And through the streets does cry 'em;
Her mother she sells laces long
    To such as please to buy 'em:
But sure such folks could ne'er beget
    So sweet a girl as Sally!
She is the darling of my heart,
    And she lives in our alley.

When she is by, I leave my work,
    I love her so sincerely;
My master comes like any Turk,
    And bangs me most severely:
But let him bang his bellyful,
    I'll bear it all for Sally;
She is the darling of my heart,
    And she lives in our alley.

Of all the days that's in the week
    I dearly love but one day—
And that's the day that comes betwixt
    A Saturday and Monday;
For then I'm drest all in my best
    To walk abroad with Sally;
She is the darling of my heart,
    And she lives in our alley.

My master carries me to church,
    And often am I blamèd
Because I leave him in the lurch
    As soon as text is namèd;

I leave the church in sermon-time
 And slink away to Sally;
She is the darling of my heart,
 And she lives in our alley.

When Christmas comes about again,
 O, then I shall have money;
I'll hoard it up, and box it all,
 I'll give it to my honey:
I would it were ten thousand pound,
 I'd give it all to Sally;
She is the darling of my heart,
 And she lives in our alley.

My master and the neighbours all,
 Make game of me and Sally,
And, but for her, I'd better be
 A slave and row a galley;
But when my seven long years are out,
 O, then I'll marry Sally;
O, then we'll wed, and then we'll bed—
 But not in our alley!

456   *A Drinking-Song*

BACCHUS must now his power resign—
 I am the only God of Wine!
It is not fit the wretch should be
In competition set with me,
Who can drink ten times more than he.

Make a new world, ye powers divine!
Stock'd with nothing else but Wine:
Let Wine its only product be,
Let Wine be earth, and air, and sea—
And let that Wine be all for me!

WILLIAM BROOME

1689-1745

457

The Rosebud

QUEEN of fragrance, lovely Rose,
    The beauties of thy leaves disclose!
—But thou, fair Nymph, thyself survey
In this sweet offspring of a day.
That miracle of face must fail,
Thy charms are sweet, but charms are frail:
Swift as the short-lived flower they fly,
At morn they bloom, at evening die:
Though Sickness yet a while forbears,
Yet Time destroys what Sickness spares:
Now Helen lives alone in fame,
And Cleopatra's but a name:
Time must indent that heavenly brow,
And thou must be what they are now.

JAMES THOMSON

1700-1748

458 *On the Death of a particular Friend*

AS those we love decay, we die in part,
    String after string is sever'd from the heart;
Till loosen'd life, at last but breathing clay,
Without one pang is glad to fall away.

Unhappy he who latest feels the blow!
Whose eyes have wept o'er every friend laid low,
Dragg'd ling'ring on from partial death to death,
Till, dying, all he can resign is—breath.

CHARLES WESLEY

1707–1788

459   *Wrestling Jacob*

COME, O Thou Traveller unknown,
   Whom still I hold, but cannot see,
My company before is gone,
   And I am left alone with Thee,
With Thee all night I mean to stay,
And wrestle till the break of day.

I need not tell Thee who I am,
   My misery, or sin declare,
Thyself hast call'd me by my name,
   Look on thy hands, and read it there,
But who, I ask Thee, who art Thou?
Tell me thy name, and tell me now.

In vain Thou strugglest to get free,
   I never will unloose my hold:
Art Thou the Man that died for me?
   The secret of thy love unfold;
Wrestling I will not let Thee go,
Till I thy name, thy nature know.

'Tis all in vain to hold thy tongue,
   Or touch the hollow of my thigh:
Though every sinew be unstrung,
   Out of my arms Thou shalt not fly;
Wrestling I will not let Thee go,
Till I thy name, thy nature know.

CHARLES WESLEY

My strength is gone, my nature dies,
　I sink beneath thy weighty hand,
Faint to revive, and fall to rise;
　I fall, and yet by faith I stand,
I stand, and will not let Thee go,
Till I thy name, thy nature know.

Yield to me now—for I am weak;
　But confident in self-despair:
Speak to my heart, in blessings speak,
　Be conquer'd by my instant prayer,
Speak, or Thou never hence shalt move,
And tell me, if thy name is Love.

'Tis Love, 'tis Love! Thou diedst for me,
　I hear thy whisper in my heart.
The morning breaks, the shadows flee:
　Pure Universal Love Thou art,
To me, to all, thy bowels move,
Thy nature, and thy name is Love.

Contented now upon my thigh
　I halt, till life's short journey end;
All helplessness, all weakness I,
　On Thee alone for strength depend,
Nor have I power, from Thee, to move;
Thy nature, and thy name is Love.

Lame as I am, I take the prey,
　Hell, earth, and sin with ease o'ercome;
I leap for joy, pursue my way,
　And as a bounding hart fly home,
Thro' all eternity to prove
Thy nature, and thy name is Love.

SAMUEL JOHNSON

1709–1784

One-and-Twenty

LONG-EXPECTED one-and-twenty,
　Ling'ring year, at length is flown:
Pride and pleasure, pomp and plenty,
　Great * * * * * * *, are now your own.

Loosen'd from the minor's tether,
　Free to mortgage or to sell,
Wild as wind, and light as feather,
　Bid the sons of thrift farewell.

Call the Betsies, Kates, and Jennies,
　All the names that banish care;
Lavish of your grandsire's guineas,
　Show the spirit of an heir.

All that prey on vice and folly
　Joy to see their quarry fly:
There the gamester, light and jolly,
　There the lender, grave and sly.

Wealth, my lad, was made to wander,
　Let it wander as it will;
Call the jockey, call the pander,
　Bid them come and take their fill.

When the bonny blade carouses,
　Pockets full, and spirits high—
What are acres? What are houses?
　Only dirt, or wet or dry.

Should the guardian friend or mother
   Tell the woes of wilful waste,
Scorn their counsel, scorn their pother;—
   You can hang or drown at last!

461   *On the Death of Mr. Robert Levet,*
       a Practiser in Physic

CONDEMN'D to Hope's delusive mine,
   As on we toil from day to day,
By sudden blasts or slow decline
   Our social comforts drop away.

Well tried through many a varying year,
   See Levet to the grave descend,
Officious, innocent, sincere,
   Of every friendless name the friend.

Yet still he fills affection's eye,
   Obscurely wise and coarsely kind;
Nor, letter'd Arrogance, deny
   Thy praise to merit unrefined.

When fainting nature call'd for aid,
   And hov'ring death prepared the blow,
His vig'rous remedy display'd
   The power of art without the show.

In Misery's darkest cavern known,
   His useful care was ever nigh,
Where hopeless Anguish pour'd his groan,
   And lonely Want retired to die.

SAMUEL JOHNSON

No summons mock'd by chill delay,
  No petty gain disdain'd by pride;
The modest wants of every day
  The toil of every day supplied.

His virtues walk'd their narrow round,
  Nor made a pause, nor left a void;
And sure th' Eternal Master found
  The single talent well employ'd.

The busy day, the peaceful night,
  Unfelt, uncounted, glided by;
His frame was firm—his powers were bright,
  Though now his eightieth year was nigh.

Then with no fiery throbbing pain,
  No cold gradations of decay,
Death broke at once the vital chain,
  And freed his soul the nearest way.

RICHARD JAGO

1715–1781

462   *Absence*

WITH leaden foot Time creeps along
  While Delia is away:
With her, nor plaintive was the song,
  Nor tedious was the day.

Ah, envious Pow'r! reverse my doom;
  Now double thy career,
Strain ev'ry nerve, stretch ev'ry plume,
  And rest them when she's here!

ANONYMOUS

463 *Will he no come back again?*

ROYAL Charlie's now awa,
    Safely owre the friendly main;
Mony a heart will break in twa,
    Should he ne'er come back again.
        Will you no come back again?
        Will you no come back again?
        Better lo'ed you'll never be,
        And will you no come back again?

Sweet the lav'rock's note and lang,
    Lilting wildly up the glen;
And aye the o'erword o' the sang
    Is 'Will he no come back again?'
        Will he no come back again, &c.

WILLIAM SHENSTONE

1714–1763

464 *Written at an Inn at Henley*

TO thee, fair freedom! I retire
    From flattery, cards, and dice, and din:
Nor art thou found in mansions higher
    Than the low cott, or humble inn.

'Tis here, with boundless pow'r, I reign;
    And ev'ry health which I begin
Converts dull port to bright champaigne;
    Such freedom crowns it, at an inn.

Here, waiter! take my sordid ore,
  Which lacqueys else might hope to win;
It buys, what courts have not in store;
  It buys me freedom, at an inn.

And now once more I shape my way
  Thro' rain or shine, thro' thick or thin,
Secure to meet, at close of day,
  With kind reception, at an inn.

Whoe'er has travell'd life's dull round,
  Where'er his stages may have been,
May sigh to think he still has found
  The warmest welcome, at an inn.

THOMAS GRAY

1716–1771

465 *Elegy written in a Country Churchyard*

THE Curfew tolls the knell of parting day,
  The lowing herd wind slowly o'er the lea,
The plowman homeward plods his weary way,
  And leaves the world to darkness and to me.

Now fades the glimmering landscape on the sight,
  And all the air a solemn stillness holds,
Save where the beetle wheels his droning flight,
  And drowsy tinklings lull the distant folds;

Save that from yonder ivy-mantled tow'r
  The moping owl does to the moon complain
Of such as, wand'ring near her secret bow'r,
  Molest her ancient solitary reign.

531

THOMAS GRAY

Beneath those rugged elms, that yew-tree's shade,
    Where heaves the turf in many a mould'ring heap,
Each in his narrow cell for ever laid,
    The rude Forefathers of the hamlet sleep.

The breezy call of incense-breathing Morn,
    The swallow twitt'ring from the straw-built shed,
The cock's shrill clarion, or the echoing horn,
    No more shall rouse them from their lowly bed.

For them no more the blazing hearth shall burn,
    Or busy housewife ply her evening care:
No children run to lisp their sire's return,
    Or climb his knees the envied kiss to share.

Oft did the harvest to their sickle yield,
    Their furrow oft the stubborn glebe has broke:
How jocund did they drive their team afield!
    How bow'd the woods beneath their sturdy stroke!

Let not Ambition mock their useful toil,
    Their homely joys, and destiny obscure;
Nor Grandeur hear with a disdainful smile
    The short and simple annals of the poor.

The boast of heraldry, the pomp of pow'r,
    And all that beauty, all that wealth e'er gave,
Awaits alike th' inevitable hour:
    The paths of glory lead but to the grave.

Nor you, ye Proud, impute to These the fault,
    If Memory o'er their Tomb no Trophies raise,
Where through the long-drawn aisle and fretted ·vault
    The pealing anthem swells the note of praise.

Can storied urn or animated bust
   Back to its mansion call the fleeting breath?
Can Honour's voice provoke the silent dust,
   Or Flatt'ry soothe the dull cold ear of death?

Perhaps in this neglected spot is laid
   Some heart once pregnant with celestial fire;
Hands, that the rod of empire might have sway'd,
   Or waked to ecstasy the living lyre.

But Knowledge to their eyes her ample page
   Rich with the spoils of time did ne'er unroll;
Chill Penury repress'd their noble rage,
   And froze the genial current of the soul.

Full many a gem of purest ray serene
   The dark unfathom'd caves of ocean bear:
Full many a flower is born to blush unseen,
   And waste its sweetness on the desert air.

Some village Hampden that with dauntless breast
   The little tyrant of his fields withstood,
Some mute inglorious Milton, here may rest,
   Some Cromwell guiltless of his country's blood.

Th' applause of list'ning senates to command,
   The threats of pain and ruin to despise,
To scatter plenty o'er a smiling land,
   And read their history in a nation's eyes,

Their lot forbade: nor circumscribed alone
   Their growing virtues, but their crimes confined;
Forbade to wade through slaughter to a throne,
   And shut the gates of mercy on mankind,

The struggling pangs of conscious truth to hide,
　　To quench the blushes of ingenuous shame,
Or heap the shrine of Luxury and Pride
　　With incense kindled at the Muse's flame.

Far from the madding crowd's ignoble strife
　　Their sober wishes never learn'd to stray;
Along the cool sequester'd vale of life
　　They kept the noiseless tenor of their way.

Yet ev'n these bones from insult to protect
　　Some frail memorial still erected nigh,
With uncouth rhymes and shapeless sculpture deck'd,
　　Implores the passing tribute of a sigh.

Their name, their years, spelt by th' unletter'd muse,
　　The place of fame and elegy supply:
And many a holy text around she strews,
　　That teach the rustic moralist to die.

For who, to dumb Forgetfulness a prey,
　　This pleasing anxious being e'er resign'd,
Left the warm precincts of the cheerful day,
　　Nor cast one longing ling'ring look behind?

On some fond breast the parting soul relies,
　　Some pious drops the closing eye requires;
E'en from the tomb the voice of Nature cries,
　　E'en in our Ashes live their wonted Fires.

For thee, who, mindful of th' unhonour'd dead,
　　Dost in these lines their artless tale relate;
If chance, by lonely contemplation led,
　　Some kindred spirit shall inquire thy fate,

Haply some hoary-headed Swain may say,
   'Oft have we seen him at the peep of dawn
Brushing with hasty steps the dews away
   To meet the sun upon the upland lawn.

'There at the foot of yonder nodding beech
   That wreathes its old fantastic roots so high,
His listless length at noontide would he stretch,
   And pore upon the brook that babbles by.

'Hard by yon wood, now smiling as in scorn,
   Mutt'ring his wayward fancies he would rove,
Now drooping, woeful wan, like one forlorn,
   Or crazed with care, or cross'd in hopeless love.

'One morn I miss'd him on the custom'd hill,
   Along the heath and near his fav'rite tree;
Another came, nor yet beside the rill,
   Nor up the lawn, nor at the wood was he;

'The next with dirges due in sad array
   Slow through the church-way path we saw him borne.
Approach and read (for thou canst read) the lay
   Graved on the stone beneath yon aged thorn.'

THE EPITAPH

Here rests his head upon the lap of Earth
   A Youth to Fortune and to Fame unknown.
Fair Science frown'd not on his humble birth,
   And Melancholy mark'd him for her own.

Large was his bounty, and his soul sincere,
   Heav'n did a recompense as largely send:
He gave to Mis'ry all he had, a tear,
   He gain'd from Heav'n ('twas all he wish'd) a friend.

No farther seek his merits to disclose,
  Or draw his frailties from their dread abode,
(There they alike in trembling hope repose,)
  The bosom of his Father and his God.

466 *The Curse upon Edward*

WEAVE the warp, and weave the woof,
  The winding-sheet of Edward's race.
Give ample room, and verge enough
The characters of hell to trace.
Mark the year, and mark the night,
When Severn shall re-echo with affright
The shrieks of death, thro' Berkley's roofs that ring,
Shrieks of an agonizing King!
  She-wolf of France, with unrelenting fangs,
That tear'st the bowels of thy mangled mate,
  From thee be born, who o'er thy country hangs
The scourge of Heav'n. What terrors round him wait!
Amazement in his van, with Flight combined,
And Sorrow's faded form, and Solitude behind.

  Mighty Victor, mighty Lord!
Low on his funeral couch he lies!
  No pitying heart, no eye, afford
A tear to grace his obsequies.
Is the sable warrior fled?
Thy son is gone. He rests among the dead.
The swarm that in thy noon-tide beam were born?
Gone to salute the rising morn.

Fair laughs the morn, and soft the zephyr blows,
While proudly riding o'er the azure realm
In gallant trim the gilded vessel goes;
   Youth on the prow, and Pleasure at the helm;
Regardless of the sweeping whirlwind's sway,
That, hush'd in grim repose, expects his evening prey.

   Fill high the sparkling bowl,
The rich repast prepare;
   Reft of a crown, he yet may share the feast:
Close by the regal chair
   Fell Thirst and Famine scowl
   A baleful smile upon their baffled guest.
Heard ye the din of battle bray,
   Lance to lance, and horse to horse?
   Long years of havoc urge their destined course,
And thro' the kindred squadrons mow their way.
   Ye Towers of Julius, London's lasting shame,
With many a foul and midnight murder fed,
   Revere his consort's faith, his father's fame,
And spare the meek usurper's holy head.

Above, below, the rose of snow,
   Twined with her blushing foe, we spread:
The bristled boar in infant-gore
   Wallows beneath the thorny shade.
Now, brothers, bending o'er th' accursèd loom
Stamp we our vengeance deep, and ratify his doom.

   Edward, lo! to sudden Fate
(*Weave we the woof. The thread is spun*)
   Half of thy heart we consecrate.
(*The web is wove. The work is done.*)

467 *The Progress of Poesy*

A PINDARIC ODE

AWAKE, Æolian lyre, awake,
 And give to rapture all thy trembling strings.
From Helicon's harmonious springs
 A thousand rills their mazy progress take:
The laughing flowers, that round them blow,
Drink life and fragrance as they flow.
Now the rich stream of music winds along
Deep, majestic, smooth and strong,
Thro' verdant vales, and Ceres' golden reign:
Now rolling down the steep amain,
Headlong, impetuous see it pour;
The rocks and nodding groves rebellow to the roar.

 O Sovereign of the willing soul,
Parent of sweet and solemn-breathing airs,
Enchanting shell! the sullen Cares
 And frantic Passions hear thy soft controul.
On Thracia's hills the Lord of War
Has curb'd the fury of his car,
And dropp'd his thirsty lance at thy command.
Perching on the sceptred hand
Of Jove, thy magic lulls the feather'd king
With ruffled plumes and flagging wing:
Quench'd in dark clouds of slumber lie
The terror of his beak, and lightnings of his eye.

Thee the voice, the dance, obey,
Temper'd to thy warbled lay.
 O'er Idalia's velvet-green
 The rosy-crownèd Loves are seen

538

On Cytherea's day
    With antic Sports, and blue-eyed Pleasures,
    Frisking light in frolic measures;
Now pursuing, now retreating,
    Now in circling troops they meet:
To brisk notes in cadence beating,
    Glance their many-twinkling feet.
Slow melting strains their Queen's approach declares
    Where'er she turns the Graces homage pay.
With arms sublime, that float upon the air,
    In gliding state she wins her easy way:
O'er her warm cheek and rising bosom move
The bloom of young Desire and purple light of Love.

    Man's feeble race what ills await,
Labour, and Penury, the racks of Pain,
Disease, and Sorrow's weeping train,
    And Death, sad refuge from the storms of fate!
The fond complaint, my song, disprove,
And justify the laws of Jove.
Say, has he giv'n in vain the heav'nly Muse?
Night, and all her sickly dews,
Her spectres wan, and birds of boding cry,
He gives to range the dreary sky:
Till down the eastern cliffs afar
Hyperion's march they spy, and glitt'ring shafts of war.

    In climes beyond the solar road,
Where shaggy forms o'er ice-built mountains roam,
The Muse has broke the twilight gloom
    To cheer the shiv'ring native's dull abode.
And oft, beneath the od'rous shade
Of Chili's boundless forests laid,

She deigns to hear the savage youth repeat
In loose numbers wildly sweet
Their feather-cinctured chiefs, and dusky loves.
Her track, where'er the Goddess roves,
Glory pursue and generous Shame,
Th' unconquerable Mind, and Freedom's holy flame.

Woods, that wave o'er Delphi's steep,
Isles, that crown th' Ægean deep,
   Fields, that cool Ilissus laves,
   Or where Mæander's amber waves
In lingering lab'rinths creep,
   How do your tuneful echoes languish,
   Mute, but to the voice of anguish?
Where each old poetic mountain
   Inspiration breathed around:
Ev'ry shade and hallow'd fountain
   Murmur'd deep a solemn sound:
Till the sad Nine, in Greece's evil hour,
   Left their Parnassus for the Latian plains.
Alike they scorn the pomp of tyrant Power,
   And coward Vice, that revels in her chains.
When Latium had her lofty spirit lost,
They sought, O Albion! next thy sea-encircled coast.

Far from the sun and summer gale,
In thy green lap was Nature's darling laid,
What time, where lucid Avon stray'd,
   To Him the mighty mother did unveil
Her awful face: the dauntless child
Stretch'd forth his little arms, and smiled.
This pencil take (she said), whose colours clear
Richly paint the vernal year:

Thine too these golden keys, immortal boy!
This can unlock the gates of joy;
Of horror that, and thrilling fears,
Or ope the sacred source of sympathetic tears.

   Nor second he, that rode sublime
Upon the seraph-wings of Ecstasy,
The secrets of th' abyss to spy.
   He pass'd the flaming bounds of place and time:
The living Throne, the sapphire-blaze,
Where Angels tremble while they gaze,
He saw; but blasted with excess of light,
Closed his eyes in endless night.
Behold, where Dryden's less presumptuous car,
Wide o'er the fields of glory bear
Two coursers of ethereal race,
With necks in thunder clothed, and long-resounding pace.

Hark, his hands the lyre explore!
Bright-eyed Fancy hovering o'er
   Scatters from her pictured urn
   Thoughts that breathe, and words that burn.
But ah! 'tis heard no more——
   O Lyre divine! what daring Spirit
   Wakes thee now? Tho' he inherit
Nor the pride, nor ample pinion,
   That the Theban eagle bear
Sailing with supreme dominion
   Thro' the azure deep of air:
Yet oft before his infant eyes would run
   Such forms as glitter in the Muse's ray,

With orient hues, unborrow'd of the Sun:
 Yet shall he mount, and keep his distant way
Beyond the limits of a vulgar fate,
Beneath the Good how far—but far above the Great.

468 *On a Favourite Cat, Drowned in a*
     Tub of Gold Fishes

'TWAS on a lofty vase's side,
 Where China's gayest art had dyed
  The azure flowers that blow;
Demurest of the tabby kind,
The pensive Selima reclined,
  Gazed on the lake below.

Her conscious tail her joy declared;
The fair round face, the snowy beard,
  The velvet of her paws,
Her coat, that with the tortoise vies,
Her ears of jet, and emerald eyes,
  She saw; and purr'd applause.

Still had she gazed; but 'midst the tide
Two angel forms were seen to glide,
  The Genii of the stream:
Their scaly armour's Tyrian hue
Thro' richest purple to the view
  Betray'd a golden gleam.

The hapless Nymph with wonder saw:
A whisker first and then a claw,
  With many an ardent wish,
She stretch'd in vain to reach the prize.
What female heart can gold despise?
  What Cat's averse to fish?

THOMAS GRAY

Presumptuous Maid! with looks intent
Again she stretch'd, again she bent,
   Nor knew the gulf between.
(Malignant Fate sat by, and smiled.)
The slipp'ry verge her feet beguiled,
   She tumbled headlong in.

Eight times emerging from the flood
She mew'd to ev'ry wat'ry god,
   Some speedy aid to send.
No Dolphin came, no Nereid stirr'd:
Nor cruel *Tom*, nor *Susan* heard.
   A Fav'rite has no friend!

From hence, ye Beauties undeceived,
Know, one false step is ne'er retrieved,
   And be with caution bold.
Not all that tempts your wand'ring eyes
And heedless hearts, is lawful prize;
   Nor all that glisters, gold.

WILLIAM COLLINS

1721–1759

469   *Ode to Simplicity*

O THOU, by Nature taught
   To breathe her genuine thought
In numbers warmly pure and sweetly strong:
   Who first on mountains wild,
   In Fancy, loveliest child,
Thy babe and Pleasure's, nursed the pow'rs of song!

   Thou, who with hermit heart
   Disdain'st the wealth of art,

And gauds, and pageant weeds, and trailing pall:
  But com'st a decent maid,
  In Attic robe array'd,
O chaste, unboastful nymph, to thee I call!

  By all the honey'd store
  On Hybla's thymy shore,
By all her blooms and mingled murmurs dear,
  By her whose love-lorn woe,
  In evening musings slow,
Soothed sweetly sad Electra's poet's ear:

  By old Cephisus deep,
  Who spread his wavy sweep
In warbled wand'rings round thy green retreat;
  On whose enamell'd side,
  When holy Freedom died,
No equal haunt allured thy future feet!

  O sister meek of Truth,
  To my admiring youth
Thy sober aid and native charms infuse!
  The flow'rs that sweetest breathe,
  Though beauty cull'd the wreath,
Still ask thy hand to range their order'd hues.

  While Rome could none esteem,
  But virtue's patriot theme,
You loved her hills, and led her laureate band;
  But stay'd to sing alone
  To one distinguish'd throne,
And turn'd thy face, and fled her alter'd land.

  No more, in hall or bow'r,
  The passions own thy pow'r.

Love, only Love her forceless numbers mean;
    For thou hast left her shrine,
    Nor olive more, nor vine,
Shall gain thy feet to bless the servile scene.

    Though taste, though genius bless
    To some divine excess,
Faint's the cold work till thou inspire the whole;
    What each, what all supply,
    May court, may charm our eye,
Thou, only thou, canst raise the meeting soul!

    Of these let others ask,
    To aid some mighty task,
I only seek to find thy temperate vale;
    Where oft my reed might sound
    To maids and shepherds round,
And all thy sons, O Nature, learn my tale.

470   *How sleep the Brave*

HOW sleep the brave, who sink to rest
   By all their country's wishes blest!
When Spring, with dewy fingers cold,
Returns to deck their hallow'd mould,
She there shall dress a sweeter sod
Than Fancy's feet have ever trod.

By fairy hands their knell is rung;
By forms unseen their dirge is sung;
There Honour comes, a pilgrim grey,
To bless the turf that wraps their clay;
And Freedom shall awhile repair
To dwell, a weeping hermit, there!

471 *Ode to Evening*

IF aught of oaten stop, or pastoral song,
  May hope, chaste Eve, to soothe thy modest ear,
    Like thy own solemn springs,
    Thy springs and dying gales;

O nymph reserved, while now the bright-hair'd sun
Sits in yon western tent, whose cloudy skirts,
    With brede ethereal wove,
    O'erhang his wavy bed:

Now air is hush'd save where the weak-eyed bat
With short shrill shriek flits by on leathern wing,
    Or where the beetle winds
    His small but sullen horn,

As oft he rises, 'midst the twilight path
Against the pilgrim borne in heedless hum:
    Now teach me, maid composed,
    To breathe some soften'd strain,

Whose numbers, stealing through thy darkening vale,
May not unseemly with its stillness suit,
    As, musing slow, I hail
    Thy genial loved return!

For when thy folding-star arising shows
His paly circlet, at his warning lamp
    The fragrant hours, and elves
    Who slept in buds the day,

And many a nymph who wreathes her brows with sedge,
And sheds the freshening dew, and, lovelier still,
    The pensive pleasures sweet,
    Prepare thy shadowy car:

Then lead, calm votaress, where some sheety lake
Cheers the lone heath, or some time-hallow'd pile,
  Or upland fallows grey
  Reflect its last cool gleam.

Or if chill blustering winds, or driving rain,
Prevent my willing feet, be mine the hut
  That from the mountain's side
  Views wilds and swelling floods,

And hamlets brown, and dim-discover'd spires,
And hears their simple bell, and marks o'er all
  Thy dewy fingers draw
  The gradual dusky veil.

While Spring shall pour his show'rs, as oft he wont,
And bathe thy breathing tresses, meekest Eve!
  While Summer loves to sport
  Beneath thy lingering light;

While sallow Autumn fills thy lap with leaves,
Or Winter, yelling through the troublous air,
  Affrights thy shrinking train,
  And rudely rends thy robes:

So long, regardful of thy quiet rule,
Shall Fancy, Friendship, Science, rose-lipp'd Health
  Thy gentlest influence own,
  And hymn thy favourite name!

472   *Fidele*

To fair Fidele's grassy tomb
 Soft maids and village hinds shall bring
Each opening sweet of earliest bloom,
 And rifle all the breathing Spring.

WILLIAM COLLINS

No wailing ghost shall dare appear
    To vex with shrieks this quiet grove;
But shepherd lads assemble here,
    And melting virgins own their love.

No wither'd witch shall here be seen,
    No goblins lead their nightly crew;
The female fays shall haunt the green,
    And dress thy grave with pearly dew.

The redbreast oft at evening hours
    Shall kindly lend his little aid,
With hoary moss, and gather'd flowers,
    To deck the ground where thou art laid.

When howling winds, and beating rain,
    In tempests shake thy sylvan cell;
Or 'midst the chase, on every plain,
    The tender thought on thee shall dwell;

Each lonely scene shall thee restore,
    For thee the tear be duly shed;
Beloved, till life can charm no more;
    And mourn'd, till Pity's self be dead.

MARK AKENSIDE

1721-1770

Amoret

473

IF rightly tuneful bards decide,
  If it be fix'd in Love's decrees,
That Beauty ought not to be tried
  But by its native power to please,
Then tell me, youths and lovers, tell—
What fair can Amoret excel?

Behold that bright unsullied smile,
    And wisdom speaking in her mien:
Yet—she so artless all the while,
    So little studious to be seen—
We naught but instant gladness know,
Nor think to whom the gift we owe.

But neither music, nor the powers
    Of youth and mirth and frolic cheer,
Add half the sunshine to the hours,
    Or make life's prospect half so clear,
As memory brings it to the eye
From scenes where Amoret was by.

This, sure, is Beauty's happiest part;
    This gives the most unbounded sway;
This shall enchant the subject heart
    When rose and lily fade away;
And she be still, in spite of Time,
Sweet Amoret in all her prime.

474   *The Complaint*

AWAY! away!
    Tempt me no more, insidious Love:
Thy soothing sway
Long did my youthful bosom prove:
At length thy treason is discern'd,
At length some dear-bought caution earn'd:
Away! nor hope my riper age to move.

  I know, I see
Her merit. Needs it now be shown,
  Alas! to me?
How often, to myself unknown,
The graceful, gentle, virtuous maid
Have I admired! How often said—
What joy to call a heart like hers one's own!

  But, flattering god,
O squanderer of content and ease
  In thy abode
Will care's rude lesson learn to please?
O say, deceiver, hast thou won
Proud Fortune to attend thy throne,
Or placed thy friends above her stern decrees?

475   *The Nightingale*

TO-NIGHT retired, the queen of heaven
  With young Endymion stays;
And now to Hesper it is given
Awhile to rule the vacant sky,
Till she shall to her lamp supply
  A stream of brighter rays.

Propitious send thy golden ray,
  Thou purest light above!
Let no false flame seduce to stray
Where gulf or steep lie hid for harm;
But lead where music's healing charm
  May soothe afflicted love.

To them, by many a grateful song
  In happier seasons vow'd,
These lawns, Olympia's haunts, belong:
Oft by yon silver stream we walk'd,
Or fix'd, while Philomela talk'd,
  Beneath yon copses stood.

Nor seldom, where the beechen boughs
  That roofless tower invade,
We came, while her enchanting Muse
The radiant moon above us held:
Till, by a clamorous owl compell'd,
  She fled the solemn shade.

But hark! I hear her liquid tone!
  Now Hesper guide my feet!
Down the red marl with moss o'ergrown,
Through yon wild thicket next the plain,
Whose hawthorns choke the winding lane
  Which leads to her retreat.

See the green space: on either hand
  Enlarged it spreads around:
See, in the midst she takes her stand,
Where one old oak his awful shade
Extends o'er half the level mead,
  Enclosed in woods profound.

Hark! how through many a melting note
  She now prolongs her lays:
How sweetly down the void they float!
The breeze their magic path attends;
The stars shine out; the forest bends;
  The wakeful heifers graze.

MARK AKENSIDE

Whoe'er thou art whom chance may bring
    To this sequester'd spot,
If then the plaintive Siren sing,
O softly tread beneath her bower
And think of Heaven's disposing power,
    Of man's uncertain lot.

O think, o'er all this mortal stage
    What mournful scenes arise:
What ruin waits on kingly rage;
How often virtue dwells with woe;
How many griefs from knowledge flow;
    How swiftly pleasure flies!

O sacred bird! let me at eve,
    Thus wandering all alone,
Thy tender counsel oft receive,
Bear witness to thy pensive airs,
And pity Nature's common cares,
    Till I forget my own.

THOMAS OSBERT MORDAUNT

1730–1809

476   *The Call*

SOUND, sound the clarion, fill the fife!
    Throughout the sensual world proclaim,
One crowded hour of glorious life
    Is worth an age without a name.

JOHN SCOTT OF AMWELL 1730–1783

477 *Retort on the Foregoing*

I HATE that drum's discordant sound,
  Parading round, and round, and round:
To thoughtless youth it pleasure yields,
And lures from cities and from fields,
To sell their liberty for charms
Of tawdry lace, and glittering arms;
And when Ambition's voice commands,
To march, and fight, and fall, in foreign lands.

I hate that drum's discordant sound,
Parading round, and round, and round:
To me it talks of ravag'd plains,
And burning towns, and ruin'd swains,
And mangled limbs, and dying groans,
And widows' tears, and orphans' moans;
And all that Misery's hand bestows,
To fill the catalogue of human woes.

Poetical Works, 1782.

TOBIAS GEORGE SMOLLETT 1721–1771

478 *To Leven Water*

PURE stream, in whose transparent wave
  My youthful limbs I wont to lave;
No torrents stain thy limpid source,
No rocks impede thy dimpling course
Devolving from thy parent lake
A charming maze thy waters make
By bowers of birch and groves of pine
And edges flower'd with eglantine.

553

TOBIAS GEORGE SMOLLETT

Still on thy banks so gaily green
May numerous herds and flocks be seen,
And lasses chanting o'er the pail,
And shepherds piping in the dale,
And ancient faith that knows no guile,
And industry embrown'd with toil,
And hearts resolved and hands prepared
The blessings they enjoy to guard.

CHRISTOPHER SMART

1722-1770

479 *Song to David*

SUBLIME—invention ever young,
Of vast conception, tow'ring tongue
    To God th' eternal theme;
Notes from yon exaltations caught,
Unrivall'd royalty of thought
    O'er meaner strains supreme!

His muse, bright angel of his verse,
Gives balm for all the thorns that pierce,
    For all the pangs that rage;
Blest light still gaining on the gloom,
The more than Michal of his bloom,
    Th' Abishag of his age.

He sang of God—the mighty source
Of all things—the stupendous force
    On which all strength depends;
From whose right arm, beneath whose eyes,
All period, power, and enterprise
    Commences, reigns, and ends.

CHRISTOPHER SMART

Tell them, I AM, Jehovah said
To Moses; while earth heard in dread,
    And, smitten to the heart,
At once above, beneath, around,
All Nature, without voice or sound,
      Replied, O LORD, THOU ART.

The world, the clustering spheres, He made;
The glorious light, the soothing shade,
    Dale, champaign, grove, and hill;
The multitudinous abyss,
Where Secrecy remains in bliss,
      And Wisdom hides her skill.

The pillars of the Lord are seven,
Which stand from earth to topmost heaven;
    His Wisdom drew the plan;
His Word accomplish'd the design,
From brightest gem to deepest mine;
      From Christ enthroned, to Man.

For Adoration all the ranks
Of Angels yield eternal thanks,
    And David in the midst;
With God's good poor, which, last and least
In man's esteem, Thou to Thy feast,
      O blessèd Bridegroom, bidd'st!

For Adoration, David's Psalms
Lift up the heart to deeds of alms;
    And he, who kneels and chants,
Prevails his passions to control,
Finds meat and medicine to the soul,
      Which for translation pants.

555

CHRISTOPHER SMART

For Adoration, in the dome
Of Christ, the sparrows find a home,
    And on His olives perch:
The swallow also dwells with thee,
O man of God's humility,
      Within his Saviour's church.

Sweet is the dew that falls betimes,
And drops upon the leafy limes;
    Sweet, Hermon's fragrant air:
Sweet is the lily's silver bell,
And sweet the wakeful taper's smell
    That watch for early prayer.

Sweet the young nurse, with love intense,
Which smiles o'er sleeping innocence;
    Sweet, when the lost arrive:
Sweet the musician's ardour beats,
While his vague mind's in quest of sweets,
    The choicest flowers to hive.

Strong is the horse upon his speed;
Strong in pursuit the rapid glede,
    Which makes at once his game:
Strong the tall ostrich on the ground;
Strong through the turbulent profound
    Shoots Xiphias to his aim.

Strong is the lion—like a coal
His eyeball,—like a bastion's mole
    His chest against the foes:
Strong the gier-eagle on his sail;
Strong against tide th' enormous whale
    Emerges as he goes.

    glede] kite.   Xiphias] sword-fish.

But stronger still, in earth and air,
And in the sea, the man of prayer,
 And far beneath the tide:
And in the seat to faith assign'd,
Where ask is have, where seek is find,
 Where knock is open wide.

Precious the penitential tear;
And precious is the sigh sincere,
 Acceptable to God:
And precious are the winning flowers,
In gladsome Israel's feast of bowers
 Bound on the hallow'd sod.

Glorious the sun in mid career;
Glorious th' assembled fires appear;
 Glorious the comet's train:
Glorious the trumpet and alarm;
Glorious the Almighty's stretch'd-out arm;
 Glorious th' enraptured main:

Glorious the northern lights astream;
Glorious the song, when God's the theme;
 Glorious the thunder's roar:
Glorious Hosanna from the den;
Glorious the catholic Amen;
 Glorious the martyr's gore:

Glorious—more glorious—is the crown
Of Him that brought salvation down,
 By meekness call'd thy Son:
Thou that stupendous truth believed;—
And now the matchless deed's achieved,
 Determined, dared, and done!

480   *A Lament for Flodden*

I'VE heard them lilting at our ewe-milking,
    Lasses a' lilting before dawn o' day;
But now they are moaning on ilka green loaning—
    The Flowers of the Forest are a' wede away.

At bughts, in the morning, nae blythe lads are scorning,
    Lasses are lonely and dowie and wae;
Nae daffing, nae gabbing, but sighing and sabbing,
    Ilk ane lifts her leglin and hies her away.

In hairst, at the shearing, nae youths now are jeering,
    Bandsters are lyart, and runkled, and gray:
At fair or at preaching, nae wooing, nae fleeching—
    The Flowers of the Forest are a' wede away.

At e'en, in the gloaming, nae swankies are roaming
    'Bout stacks wi' the lasses at bogle to play;
But ilk ane sits eerie, lamenting her dearie—
    The Flowers of the Forest are a' wede away.

Dool and wae for the order sent our lads to the Border!
    The English, for ance, by guile wan the day;
The Flowers of the Forest, that fought aye the foremost,
    The prime of our land, lie cauld in the clay.

We'll hear nae mair lilting at our ewe-milking;
    Women and bairns are heartless and wae;
Sighing and moaning on ilka green loaning—
    The Flowers of the Forest are a' wede away.

loaning] lane, field-track.   wede] weeded.   bughts] sheep-folds.   daffing] joking.   leglin] milk-pail.   hairst] harvest. bandsters] binders.   lyart] gray-haired.   runkled] wrinkled. fleeching] coaxing.   swankies] lusty lads.   bogle] bogy, hide-and-seek.

OLIVER GOLDSMITH

1730-1774

481 *Woman*

WHEN lovely woman stoops to folly,
    And finds too late that men betray,
What charm can soothe her melancholy?
    What art can wash her tears away?

The only art her guilt to cover,
    To hide her shame from ev'ry eye,
To give repentance to her lover,
    And wring his bosom is—to die.

482 *Memory*

O MEMORY. thou fond deceiver,
    Still importunate and vain,
To former joys recurring ever,
    And turning all the past to pain:

Thou, like the world, th' oppress'd oppressing,
    Thy smiles increase the wretch's woe:
And he who wants each other blessing
    In thee must ever find a foe.

ROBERT CUNNINGHAME-GRAHAM OF GARTMORE

1735-1797

483 *If Doughty Deeds*

IF doughty deeds my lady please,
    Right soon I'll mount my steed;
And strong his arm and fast his seat,
    That bears frae me the meed.

I'll wear thy colours in my cap,
   Thy picture in my heart;
And he that bends not to thine eye
   Shall rue it to his smart!
     Then tell me how to woo thee, Love;
      O tell me how to woo thee!
     For thy dear sake nae care I'll take,
      Tho' ne'er another trow me.

If gay attire delight thine eye
   I'll dight me in array;
I'll tend thy chamber door all night,
   And squire thee all the day.
If sweetest sounds can win thine ear,
   These sounds I'll strive to catch;
Thy voice I'll steal to woo thysel',
   That voice that nane can match.
     Then tell me how to woo thee, Love . . ;

But if fond love thy heart can gain,
   I never broke a vow;
Nae maiden lays her skaith to me,
   I never loved but you.
For you alone I ride the ring,
   For you I wear the blue;
For you alone I strive to sing,
   O tell me how to woo!
     Then tell me how to woo thee, Love;
      O tell me how to woo thee!
     For thy dear sake nae care I'll take
      Tho' ne'er another trow me.

484   *To Mary Unwin*

MARY! I want a lyre with other strings,
    Such aid from Heaven as some have feign'd they drew,
An eloquence scarce given to mortals, new
And undebased by praise of meaner things;
That ere through age or woe I shed my wings,
I may record thy worth with honour due,
In verse as musical as thou art true,
And that immortalizes whom it sings:
But thou hast little need. There is a Book
By seraphs writ with beams of heavenly light,
On which the eyes of God not rarely look,
A chronicle of actions just and bright—
    There all thy deeds, my faithful Mary, shine;
    And since thou own'st that praise, I spare thee mine.

485   *My Mary*

THE twentieth year is wellnigh past
    Since first our sky was overcast;
Ah, would that this might be the last!
           My Mary!

Thy spirits have a fainter flow,
I see thee daily weaker grow;
'Twas my distress that brought thee low,
           My Mary!

Thy needles, once a shining store,
For my sake restless heretofore,
Now rust disused, and shine no more;
           My Mary!

For though thou gladly wouldst fulfil
The same kind office for me still,
Thy sight now seconds not thy will,
              My Mary!

But well thou play'dst the housewife's part,
And all thy threads with magic art
Have wound themselves about this heart,
              My Mary!

Thy indistinct expressions seem
Like language utter'd in a dream;
Yet me they charm, whate'er the theme,
              My Mary!

Thy silver locks, once auburn bright,
Are still more lovely in my sight
Than golden beams of orient light,
              My Mary!

For could I view nor them nor thee,
What sight worth seeing could I see?
The sun would rise in vain for me,
              My Mary!

Partakers of thy sad decline,
Thy hands their little force resign;
Yet, gently press'd, press gently mine,
              My Mary!

Such feebleness of limbs thou prov'st,
That now at every step thou mov'st
Upheld by two; yet still thou lov'st,
              My Mary!

And still to love, though press'd with ill,
In wintry age to feel no chill,
With me is to be lovely still,
                    My Mary!

But ah! by constant heed I know
How oft the sadness that I show
Transforms thy smiles to looks of woe,
                    My Mary!

And should my future lot be cast
With much resemblance of the past,
Thy worn-out heart will break at last—
                    My Mary!

JAMES BEATTIE

1735–1803

486   *An Epitaph*

LIKE thee I once have stemm'd the sea of life,
    Like thee have languish'd after empty joys,
Like thee have labour'd in the stormy strife,
    Been grieved for trifles, and amused with toys.

Forget my frailties; thou art also frail:
    Forgive my lapses; for thyself may'st fall:
Nor read unmoved my artless tender tale—
    I was a friend, O man, to thee, to all.

ISOBEL PAGAN

1740–1821

487   *Ca' the Yowes to the Knowes*

CA' the yowes to the knowes,
    Ca' them where the heather grows,
Ca' them where the burnie rows,
        My bonnie dearie.

487 yowes] ewes.   knowes] knolls, little hills.   rows] rolls.

ISOBEL PAGAN

As I gaed down the water side,
There I met my shepherd lad;
He row'd me sweetly in his plaid,
    And he ca'd me his dearie.

'Will ye gang down the water side,
And see the waves sae sweetly glide
Beneath the hazels spreading wide?
    The moon it shines fu' clearly.'

'I was bred up at nae sic school,
My shepherd lad, to play the fool,
And a' the day to sit in dool,
    And naebody to see me.'

'Ye sall get gowns and ribbons meet,
Cauf-leather shoon upon your feet,
And in my arms ye'se lie and sleep,
    And ye sall be my dearie.'

'If ye'll but stand to what ye've said,
I'se gang wi' you, my shepherd lad,
And ye may row me in your plaid,
    And I sall be your dearie.'

'While waters wimple to the sea,
While day blinks in the lift sae hie,
Till clay-cauld death sall blin' my e'e,
    Ye aye sall be my dearie!'

row'd] rolled, wrapped.   dool] dule, sorrow.   lift] sky.

ANNA LÆTITIA BARBAULD 1743-1825

Life

LIFE ! I know not what thou art,
  But know that thou and I must part;
And when, or how, or where we met,
I own to me's a secret yet.
But this I know, when thou art fled,
Where'er they lay these limbs, this head,
No clod so valueless shall be
As all that then remains of me.

O whither, whither dost thou fly?
Where bend unseen thy trackless course?
    And in this strange divorce,
Ah, tell where I must seek this compound I?
To the vast ocean of empyreal flame
    From whence thy essence came
Dost thou thy flight pursue, when freed
From matter's base encumbering weed?
    Or dost thou, hid from sight,
    Wait, like some spell-bound knight,
Through blank oblivious years th' appointed hour
To break thy trance and reassume thy power?
Yet canst thou without thought or feeling be?
O say, what art thou, when no more thou'rt thee?

Life! we have been long together,
Through pleasant and through cloudy weather;
  'Tis hard to part when friends are dear;
  Perhaps 'twill cost a sigh, a tear;—

Then steal away, give little warning,
    Choose thine own time;
Say not Good-night, but in some brighter clime
    Bid me Good-morning!

FANNY GREVILLE

18th cent.

489   *Prayer for Indifference*

I ASK no kind return of love,
    No tempting charm to please;
Far from the heart those gifts remove,
    That sighs for peace and ease.

Nor peace nor ease the heart can know,
    That, like the needle true,
Turns at the touch of joy or woe,
    But, turning, trembles too.

Far as distress the soul can wound,
    'Tis pain in each degree:
'Tis bliss but to a certain bound,
    Beyond is agony.

MICHAEL BRUCE

1740–1767

490   *To the Cuckoo*

HAIL, beauteous stranger of the grove!
    Thou messenger of Spring!
Now Heaven repairs thy rural seat,
    And woods thy welcome ring.

What time the daisy decks the green,
    Thy certain voice we hear:
Hast thou a star to guide thy path,
    Or mark the rolling year?

Delightful visitant! with thee
    I hail the time of flowers,
And hear the sound of music sweet
    From birds among the bowers.

The schoolboy, wand'ring through the wood
    To pull the primrose gay,
Starts, the new voice of Spring to hear,
    And imitates thy lay.

What time the pea puts on the bloom,
    Thou fli'st thy vocal vale,
An annual guest in other lands,
    Another Spring to hail.

Sweet bird! thy bower is ever green,
    Thy sky is ever clear;
Thou hast no sorrow in thy song,
    No Winter in thy year!

O could I fly, I'd fly with thee!
    We'd make, with joyful wing,
Our annual visit o'er the globe,
    Companions of the Spring.

LADY ANNE LINDSAY

1750–1825

491   *Auld Robin Gray*

WHEN the sheep are in the fauld, and the kye at hame,
    And a' the warld to rest are gane,
The waes o' my heart fa' in showers frae my e'e,
While my gudeman lies sound by me.

LADY ANNE LINDSAY

Young Jamie lo'ed me weel, and sought me for his bride;
But saving a croun he had naething else beside:
To make the croun a pund, young Jamie gaed to sea;
And the croun and the pund were baith for me.

He hadna been awa' a week but only twa,
When my father brak his arm, and the cow was stown awa';
My mother she fell sick,—and my Jamie at the sea—
And auld Robin Gray came a-courtin' me.

My father couldna work, and my mother couldna spin;
I toil'd day and night, but their bread I couldna win;
Auld Rob maintain'd them baith, and wi' tears in his e'e
Said, 'Jennie, for their sakes, O, marry me!'

My heart it said nay; I look'd for Jamie back;
But the wind it blew high, and the ship it was a wrack;
His ship it was a wrack—Why didna Jamie dee?
Or why do I live to cry, Wae's me!

My father urged me sair: my mother didna speak;
But she look'd in my face till my heart was like to break:
They gi'ed him my hand, tho' my heart was in the sea;
Sae auld Robin Gray he was gudeman to me.

I hadna been a wife a week but only four,
When mournfu' as I sat on the stane at the door,
I saw my Jamie's wraith,—for I couldna think it he,
Till he said, 'I'm come hame to marry thee.'

O sair, sair did we greet, and muckle did we say;
We took but ae kiss, and we tore ourselves away:
I wish that I were dead, but I'm no like to dee;
And why was I born to say, Wae's me!

LADY ANNE LINDSAY

I gang like a ghaist, and I carena to spin;
I daurna think on Jamie, for that wad be a sin;
But I'll do my best a gude wife aye to be,
For auld Robin Gray he is kind unto me.

SIR WILLIAM JONES

1746–1794

492   *Epigram*

O<small>N</small> parent knees, a naked new-born child,
   Weeping thou sat'st while all around thee smiled:
So live, that sinking to thy life's last sleep,
Calm thou may'st smile, whilst all around thee weep.

THOMAS CHATTERTON

1752–1770

493   *Song from Ælla*

O SING unto my roundelay,
   O drop the briny tear with me;
Dance no more at holyday,
Like a running river be:
    My love is dead,
    Gone to his death-bed
All under the willow-tree.

Black his cryne as the winter night,
White his rode as the summer snow,
Red his face as the morning light,
Cold he lies in the grave below:
    My love is dead,
    Gone to his death-bed
All under the willow-tree.

493 cryne] hair.   rode] complexion.

THOMAS CHATTERTON

Sweet his tongue as the throstle's note,
Quick in dance as thought can be,
Deft his tabor, cudgel stout;
O he lies by the willow-tree!
 My love is dead,
  Gone to his death-bed
All under the willow-tree.

Hark! the raven flaps his wing
In the brier'd dell below;
Hark! the death-owl loud doth sing
To the nightmares, as they go:
 My love is dead,
  Gone to his death-bed
All under the willow-tree.

See! the white moon shines on high;
Whiter is my true-love's shroud:
Whiter than the morning sky,
Whiter than the evening cloud:
 My love is dead,
  Gone to his death-bed
All under the willow-tree.

Here upon my true-love's grave
Shall the barren flowers be laid;
Not one holy saint to save
All the coldness of a maid:
 My love is dead,
  Gone to his death-bed
All under the willow-tree.

With my hands I'll dent the briers
Round his holy corse to gre:
Ouph and fairy, light your fires,
Here my body still shall be:
    My love is dead,
      Gone to his death-bed
All under the willow-tree.

Come, with acorn-cup and thorn,
Drain my heartès blood away;
Life and all its good I scorn,
Dance by night, or feast by day:
    My love is dead,
      Gone to his death-bed
All under the willow-tree.

GEORGE CRABBE

1754–1832

494   *Meeting*

MY Damon was the first to wake
The gentle flame that cannot die;
My Damon is the last to take
  The faithful bosom's softest sigh:
The life between is nothing worth,
  O cast it from thy thought away!
Think of the day that gave it birth,
  And this its sweet returning day.

Buried be all that has been done,
  Or say that naught is done amiss;
For who the dangerous path can shun
  In such bewildering world as this?

493 dent] fasten.   gre] grow.   ouph] elf.

But love can every fault forgive,
   Or with a tender look reprove;
And now let naught in memory live
   But that we meet, and that we love.

495   *Late Wisdom*

WE'VE trod the maze of error round,
   Long wandering in the winding glade;
And now the torch of truth is found,
   It only shows us where we strayed:
By long experience taught, we know—
   Can rightly judge of friends and foes;
Can all the worth of these allow,
   And all the faults discern in those.

Now, 'tis our boast that we can quell
   The wildest passions in their rage,
Can their destructive force repel,
   And their impetuous wrath assuage.—
Ah, Virtue! dost thou arm when now
   This bold rebellious race are fled?
When all these tyrants rest, and thou
   Art warring with the mighty dead?

496   *A Marriage Ring*

THE ring, so worn as you behold,
   So thin, so pale, is yet of gold:
The passion such it was to prove—
Worn with life's care, love yet was love.

1757–1827

497   *To the Muses*

WHETHER on Ida's shady brow
        Or in the chambers of the East,
The chambers of the Sun, that now
        From ancient melody have ceased;

Whether in heaven ye wander fair,
        Or the green corners of the earth,
Or the blue regions of the air
        Where the melodious winds have birth;

Whether on crystal rocks ye rove,
        Beneath the bosom of the sea,
Wandering in many a coral grove;
        Fair Nine, forsaking Poetry;

How have you left the ancient love
        That bards of old enjoy'd in you!
The languid strings do scarcely move,
        The sound is forced, the notes are few.

498   *To Spring*

O THOU with dewy locks, who lookest down
        Through the clear windows of the morning, turn
Thine angel eyes upon our western isle,
Which in full choir hails thy approach, O Spring!

The hills tell one another, and the listening
Valleys hear; all our longing eyes are turn'd
Up to thy bright pavilions: issue forth
And let thy holy feet visit our clime!

Come o'er the eastern hills, and let our winds
Kiss thy perfumèd garments; let us taste
Thy morn and evening breath; scatter thy pearls
Upon our lovesick land that mourns for thee.

O deck her forth with thy fair fingers; pour
Thy soft kisses on her bosom; and put
Thy golden crown upon her languish'd head,
Whose modest tresses are bound up for thee.

499   *Jerusalem* (*from* '*Milton*')

AND did those feet in ancient time
  Walk upon England's mountains green?
And was the holy Lamb of God
  On England's pleasant pastures seen?

And did the Countenance Divine
  Shine forth upon our clouded hills?
And was Jerusalem builded here
  Among these dark Satanic Mills?

Bring me my bow of burning gold!
  Bring me my arrows of desire!
Bring me my spear! O clouds, unfold!
  Bring me my chariot of fire!

I will not cease from mental fight,
  Nor shall my sword sleep in my hand,
Till we have built Jerusalem
  In England's green and pleasant land.

500 *Reeds of Innocence*

PIPING down the valleys wild,
   Piping songs of pleasant glee,
On a cloud I saw a child,
   And he laughing said to me:

'Pipe a song about a Lamb!'
   So I piped with merry cheer.
'Piper, pipe that song again;'
   So I piped: he wept to hear.

'Drop thy pipe, thy happy pipe;
   Sing thy songs of happy cheer!'
So I sung the same again,
   While he wept with joy to hear.

'Piper, sit thee down and write
   In a book that all may read.'
So he vanish'd from my sight;
   And I pluck'd a hollow reed,

And I made a rural pen,
   And I stain'd the water clear,
And I wrote my happy songs
   Every child may joy to hear.

501 *The Little Black Boy*

MY mother bore me in the southern wild,
   And I am black, but O, my soul is white!
White as an angel is the English child,
   But I am black, as if bereaved of light.

My mother taught me underneath a tree,
   And, sitting down before the heat of day,
She took me on her lap and kissèd me,
   And, pointing to the East, began to say:

'Look at the rising sun: there God does live,
   And gives His light, and gives His heat away,
And flowers and trees and beasts and men receive
   Comfort in morning, joy in the noonday.

'And we are put on earth a little space,
   That we may learn to bear the beams of love;
And these black bodies and this sunburnt face
   Are but a cloud, and like a shady grove.

'For when our souls have learn'd the heat to bear,
   The cloud will vanish, we shall hear His voice,
Saying, "Come out from the grove, my love and care,
   And round my golden tent like lambs rejoice." '

Thus did my mother say, and kissèd me,
   And thus I say to little English boy.
When I from black and he from white cloud free,
   And round the tent of God like lambs we joy,

I'll shade him from the heat till he can bear
   To lean in joy upon our Father's knee;
And then I'll stand and stroke his silver hair,
   And be like him, and he will then love me.

502   *Hear the Voice*

HEAR the voice of the Bard,
   Who present, past, and future, sees;
Whose ears have heard
The Holy Word
That walk'd among the ancient trees;

Calling the lapsèd soul,
And weeping in the evening dew;
That might control
The starry pole,
And fallen, fallen light renew!

'O Earth, O Earth, return!
Arise from out the dewy grass!
Night is worn,
And the morn
Rises from the slumbrous mass.

'Turn away no more;
Why wilt thou turn away?
The starry floor,
The watery shore,
Is given thee till the break of day.'

503 *The Tiger*

TIGER, tiger, burning bright
In the forests of the night,
What immortal hand or eye
Could frame thy fearful symmetry?

In what distant deeps or skies
Burnt the fire of thine eyes?
On what wings dare he aspire?
What the hand dare seize the fire?

And what shoulder and what art
Could twist the sinews of thy heart?
And, when thy heart began to beat,
What dread hand and what dread feet?

What the hammer? What the chain?
In what furnace was thy brain?
What the anvil? What dread grasp
Dare its deadly terrors clasp?

When the stars threw down their spears,
And water'd heaven with their tears,
Did He smile His work to see?
Did He who made the lamb make thee?

Tiger, tiger, burning bright
In the forests of the night,
What immortal hand or eye
Dare frame thy fearful symmetry?

504   *Cradle Song*

SLEEP, sleep, beauty bright,
    Dreaming in the joys of night;
Sleep, sleep; in thy sleep
Little sorrows sit and weep.

Sweet babe, in thy face
Soft desires I can trace,
Secret joys and secret smiles,
Little pretty infant wiles.

As thy softest limbs I feel,
Smiles as of the morning steal
O'er thy cheek, and o'er thy breast
Where thy little heart doth rest.

O the cunning wiles that creep
In thy little heart asleep!
When thy little heart doth wake,
Then the dreadful night shall break.

505 *Night*

THE sun descending in the west,
  The evening star does shine;
The birds are silent in their nest.
  And I must seek for mine.
      The moon, like a flower
      In heaven's high bower,
      With silent delight
      Sits and smiles on the night.

Farewell, green fields and happy grove,
  Where flocks have took delight:
Where lambs have nibbled, silent move
  The feet of angels bright;
      Unseen they pour blessing
      And joy without ceasing
      On each bud and blossom,
      On each sleeping bosom.

They look in every thoughtless nest
  Where birds are cover'd warm;
They visit caves of every beast,
  To keep them all from harm:
      If they see any weeping
      That should have been sleeping,
      They pour sleep on their head,
      And sit down by their bed.

When wolves and tigers howl for prey,
  They pitying stand and weep,
Seeking to drive their thirst away
  And keep them from the sheep.

But, if they rush dreadful,
The angels, most heedful,
Receive each mild spirit,
New worlds to inherit.

And there the lion's ruddy eyes
  Shall flow with tears of gold:
And pitying the tender cries,
  And walking round the fold:
    Saying, 'Wrath by His meekness,
    And, by His health, sickness,
    Are driven away
    From our immortal day.

'And now beside thee, bleating lamb,
  I can lie down and sleep,
Or think on Him who bore thy name,
  Graze after thee, and weep.
    For, wash'd in life's river,
    My bright mane for ever
    Shall shine like the gold
    As I guard o'er the fold.'

506   *Love's Secret*

NEVER seek to tell thy love,
  Love that never told can be;
For the gentle wind doth move
  Silently, invisibly.

I told my love, I told my love,
  I told her all my heart,
Trembling, cold, in ghastly fears.
  Ah! she did depart!

Soon after she was gone from me,
　　A traveller came by,
Silently, invisibly:
　　He took her with a sigh.

ROBERT BURNS

1759-1796

507　　*Mary Morison*

O MARY, at thy window be,
　　It is the wish'd, the trysted hour!
Those smiles and glances let me see,
　　That make the miser's treasure poor:
How blythely wad I bide the stour
　　A weary slave frae sun to sun,
Could I the rich reward secure,
　　The lovely Mary Morison!

Yestreen, when to the trembling string
　　The dance gaed thro' the lighted ha',
To thee my fancy took its wing,
　　I sat, but neither heard nor saw:
Tho' this was fair, and that was braw,
　　And yon the toast of a' the town,
I sigh'd, and said amang them a',
　　'Ye arena Mary Morison.'

O Mary, canst thou wreck his peace,
　　Wha for thy sake wad gladly die?
Or canst thou break that heart of his,
　　Whase only faut is loving thee?

　　　507 stour] dust, turmoil.

If love for love thou wiltna gie,
 At least be pity to me shown;
A thought ungentle canna be
 The thought o' Mary Morison.

508   *Jean*

OF a' the airts the wind can blaw,
 I dearly like the west,
For there the bonnie lassie lives,
 The lassie I lo'e best:
There wild woods grow, and rivers row,
 And monie a hill between;
But day and night my fancy's flight
 Is ever wi' my Jean.

I see her in the dewy flowers,
 I see her sweet and fair:
I hear her in the tunefu' birds,
 I hear her charm the air:
There's not a bonnie flower that springs
 By fountain, shaw, or green;
There's not a bonnie bird that sings,
 But minds me o' my Jean.

509   *Auld Lang Syne*

SHOULD auld acquaintance be forgot,
 And never brought to min'?
Should auld acquaintance be forgot,
 And days o' lang syne?

  508 airts] points of the compass.   row] roll.

We twa hae rin about the braes,
  And pu'd the gowans fine;
But we've wander'd monie a weary fit
  Sin' auld lang syne.

We twa hae paidl't i' the burn,
  Frae mornin' sun till dine;
But seas between us braid hae roar'd
  Sin' auld lang syne.

And here's a hand, my trusty fiere,
  And gie's a hand o' thine;
And we'll tak a right gude-willie-waught
  For auld lang syne.

And surely ye'll be your pint-stowp,
  And surely I'll be mine;
And we'll tak a cup o' kindness yet
  For auld lang syne!

      For auld lang syne, my dear,
        For auld lang syne,
      We'll tak a cup o' kindness yet
        For auld lang syne.

510   *My Bonnie Mary*

GO fetch to me a pint o' wine,
  An' fill it in a silver tassie,
That I may drink, before I go,
  A service to my bonnie lassie.
The boat rocks at the pier o' Leith,

509 gowans] daisies.   fit] foot.   dine] dinner-time.
fiere] partner.   gude-willie-waught] friendly draught.
  510 tassie] cup.

Fu' loud the wind blaws frae the ferry,
The ship rides by the Berwick-law,
  And I maun leave my bonnie Mary.

The trumpets sound, the banners fly,
  The glittering spears are rankèd ready;
The shouts o' war are heard afar,
  The battle closes thick and bloody;
But it's no the roar o' sea or shore
  Wad mak me langer wish to tarry;
Nor shout o' war that's heard afar—
  It's leaving thee, my bonnie Mary!

511   *John Anderson, my Jo*

JOHN ANDERSON, my jo, John,
    When we were first acquent,
Your locks were like the raven,
  Your bonnie brow was brent;
But now your brow is beld, John,
  Your locks are like the snow;
But blessings on your frosty pow,
  John Anderson, my jo!

John Anderson, my jo, John,
  We clamb the hill thegither;
And monie a canty day, John,
  We've had wi' ane anither:
Now we maun totter down, John,
  But hand in hand we'll go,
And sleep thegither at the foot,
  John Anderson, my jo.

511 jo] sweetheart.   brent] smooth, unwrinkled.   beld]
bald.   pow] pate.   canty] cheerful.

ROBERT BURNS

The Banks o' Doon

YE flowery banks o' bonnie Doon,
    How can ye blume sae fair!
How can ye chant, ye little birds,
    And I sae fu' o' care!

Thou'll break my heart, thou bonnie bird,
    That sings upon the bough;
Thou minds me o' the happy days
    When my fause luve was true.

Thou'll break my heart, thou bonnie bird,
    That sings beside thy mate;
For sae I sat, and sae I sang,
    And wistna o' my fate.

Aft hae I roved by bonnie Doon,
    To see the woodbine twine;
And ilka bird sang o' its luve,
    And sae did I o' mine.

Wi' lightsome heart I pu'd a rose
    Upon a morn in June;
And sae I flourish'd on the morn,
    And sae was pu'd or' noon.

Wi' lightsome heart I pu'd a rose
    Upon its thorny tree;
But my fause luver staw my rose,
    And left the thorn wi' me.

or'] ere.   staw] stole.

Ae Fond Kiss

AE fond kiss, and then we sever;
   Ae fareweel, alas, for ever!
Deep in heart-wrung tears I'll pledge thee,
Warring sighs and groans I'll wage thee!

Who shall say that Fortune grieves him
While the star of hope she leaves him?
Me, nae cheerfu' twinkle lights me,
Dark despair around benights me.

I'll ne'er blame my partial fancy;
Naething could resist my Nancy;
But to see her was to love her,
Love but her, and love for ever.

Had we never loved sae kindly,
Had we never loved sae blindly,
Never met—or never parted,
We had ne'er been broken-hearted.

Fare thee weel, thou first and fairest!
Fare thee weel, thou best and dearest!
Thine be ilka joy and treasure,
Peace, enjoyment, love, and pleasure!

Ae fond kiss, and then we sever!
Ae fareweel, alas, for ever!
Deep in heart-wrung tears I'll pledge thee,
Warring sighs and groans I'll wage thee!

      wage] stake, plight.

514

Bonnie Lesley

O SAW ye bonnie Lesley
　　As she gaed o'er the Border?
She's gane, like Alexander,
　　To spread her conquests farther.

To see her is to love her,
　　And love but her for ever;
For Nature made her what she is,
　　And ne'er made sic anither!

Thou art a queen, fair Lesley,
　　Thy subjects we, before thee:
Thou art divine, fair Lesley,
　　The hearts o' men adore thee.

The Deil he couldna scaith thee,
　　Or aught that wad belang thee;
He'd look into thy bonnie face
　　And say, 'I canna wrang thee!'

The Powers aboon will tent thee,
　　Misfortune sha'na steer thee:
Thou'rt like themsel' sae lovely,
　　That ill they'll ne'er let near thee.

Return again, fair Lesley,
　　Return to Caledonie!
That we may brag we hae a lass
　　There's nane again sae bonnie!

scaith] harm.　　　tent] watch.　　　steer] molest.

Highland Mary

515

YE banks and braes and streams around
  The castle o' Montgomery,
Green be your woods, and fair your flowers,
  Your waters never drumlie!
There simmer first unfauld her robes,
  And there the langest tarry;
For there I took the last fareweel
  O' my sweet Highland Mary.

How sweetly bloom'd the gay green birk,
  How rich the hawthorn's blossom,
As underneath their fragrant shade
  I clasp'd her to my bosom!
The golden hours on angel wings
  Flew o'er me and my dearie;
For dear to me as light and life
  Was my sweet Highland Mary.

Wi' monie a vow and lock'd embrace
  Our parting was fu' tender;
And, pledging aft to meet again,
  We tore oursels asunder;
But oh! fell Death's untimely frost,
  That nipt my flower sae early!
Now green's the sod, and cauld's the clay,
  That wraps my Highland Mary!

O pale, pale now, those rosy lips
  I aft hae kiss'd sae fondly!
And closed for aye the sparkling glance
  That dwelt on me sae kindly!

    drumlie] miry.

And mouldering now in silent dust
    That heart that lo'ed me dearly!
But still within my bosom's core
    Shall live my Highland Mary.

516   *O were my Love yon Lilac fair*

O WERE my Love yon lilac fair,
    Wi' purple blossoms to the spring,
And I a bird to shelter there,
    When wearied on my little wing;
How I wad mourn when it was torn
    By autumn wild and winter rude!
But I wad sing on wanton wing
    When youthfu' May its bloom renew'd.

O gin my Love were yon red rose
    That grows upon the castle wa',
And I mysel a drap o' dew,
    Into her bonnie breast to fa';
O there, beyond expression blest,
    I'd feast on beauty a' the night;
Seal'd on her silk-saft faulds to rest,
    Till fley'd awa' by Phœbus' light.

517   *A Red, Red Rose*

O MY Luve's like a red, red rose
    That's newly sprung in June:
O my Luve's like the melodie
    That's sweetly play'd in tune!

As fair art thou, my bonnie lass,
 So deep in luve am I:
And I will luve thee still, my dear,
 Till a' the seas gang dry:

Till a' the seas gang dry, my dear,
 And the rocks melt wi' the sun;
I will luve thee still, my dear,
 While the sands o' life shall run.

And fare thee weel, my only Luve,
 And fare thee weel a while!
And I will come again, my Luve,
 Tho' it were ten thousand mile.

518 *Lament for Culloden*

THE lovely lass o' Inverness,
 Nae joy nor pleasure can she see;
For e'en and morn she cries, 'Alas!'
 And aye the saut tear blin's her e'e:
'Drumossie moor, Drumossie day,
 A waefu' day it was to me!
For there I lost my father dear,
 My father dear and brethren three.

'Their winding-sheet the bluidy clay,
 Their graves are growing green to see;
And by them lies the dearest lad
 That ever blest a woman's e'e!
Now wae to thee, thou cruel lord,

A bluidy man I trow thou be;
For monie a heart thou hast made sair,
That ne'er did wrang to thine or thee.·

519 *The Farewell*

IT was a' for our rightfu' King
    We left fair Scotland's strand;
It was a' for our rightfu' King
    We e'er saw Irish land,
            My dear—
    We e'er saw Irish land.

Now a' is done that men can do,
    And a' is done in vain;
My love and native land, farewell,
    For I maun cross the main,
            My dear—
    For I maun cross the main.

He turn'd him right and round about
    Upon the Irish shore;
And gae his bridle-reins a shake,
    With, Adieu for evermore,
            My dear—
    With, Adieu for evermore!

The sodger frae the wars returns,
    The sailor frae the main;
But I hae parted frae my love,
    Never to meet again,
            My dear—
    Never to meet again.

When day is gane, and night is come,
  And a' folk bound to sleep,
I think on him that's far awa',
  The lee-lang night, and weep,
      My dear—
  The lee-lang night, and weep.

520   *Hark! the Mavis*

CA' the yowes to the knowes,
  Ca' them where the heather grows,
Ca' them where the burnie rows,
  My bonnie dearie.

Hark! the mavis' evening sang
Sounding Clouden's woods amang,
Then a-faulding let us gang,
  My bonnie dearie.

We'll gae down by Clouden side,
Through the hazels spreading wide,
O'er the waves that sweetly glide
  To the moon sae clearly.

Yonder Clouden's silent towers,
Where at moonshine midnight hours
O'er the dewy bending flowers
  Fairies dance sae cheery.

Ghaist nor bogle shalt thou fear;
Thou'rt to Love and Heaven sae dear,
Nocht of ill may come thee near,
  My bonnie dearie.

519 lee-lang] livelong.

Fair and lovely as thou art,
Thou hast stown my very heart;
I can die—but canna part,
    My bonnie dearie.

While waters wimple to the sea;
While day blinks in the lift sae hie;
Till clay-cauld death shall blin' my e'e,
    Ye shall be my dearie.

Ca' the yowes to the knowes ...

HENRY ROWE

1754–1819

521 *Sun*

ANGEL, king of streaming morn;
    Cherub, call'd by Heav'n to shine;
T' orient tread the waste forlorn;
Guide ætherial, pow'r divine;
    Thou, Lord of all within!

Golden spirit, lamp of day,
Host, that dips in blood the plain,
Bids the crimson'd mead be gay,
Bids the green blood burst the vein;
    Thou, Lord of all within!

Soul, that wraps the globe in light;
Spirit, beckoning to arise;
Drives the frowning brow of night,
Glory bursting o'er the skies;
    Thou, Lord of all within!

520 lift] sky.

Moon

THEE too, modest tressèd maid,
  When thy fallen stars appear;
When in lawn of fire array'd
  Sov'reign of yon powder'd sphere;
To thee I chant at close of day,
Beneath, O maiden Moon! thy ray.

Throned in sapphired ring supreme,
  Pregnant with celestial juice,
On silver wing thy diamond stream
  Gives what summer hours produce;
While view'd impearl'd earth's rich inlay,
Beneath, O maiden Moon! thy ray.

Glad, pale Cynthian wine I sip,
  Breathed the flow'ry leaves among;
Draughts delicious wet my lip;
  Drown'd in nectar drunk my song;
While tuned to Philomel the lay,
Beneath, O maiden Moon! thy ray.

Dew, that od'rous ointment yields,
  Sweets, that western winds disclose,
Bathing spring's more purpled fields,
  Soft's the band that winds the rose;
While o'er thy myrtled lawns I stray
Beneath, O maiden Moon! thy ray.

WILLIAM LISLE BOWLES

1762–1850

523　　　　*Time and Grief*

O TIME! who know'st a lenient hand to lay
　　Softest on sorrow's wound, and slowly thence
(Lulling to sad repose the weary sense)
The faint pang stealest unperceived away;
On thee I rest my only hope at last,
And think, when thou hast dried the bitter tear
That flows in vain o'er all my soul held dear,
I may look back on every sorrow past,
And meet life's peaceful evening with a smile:
As some lone bird, at day's departing hour,
Sings in the sunbeam, of the transient shower
Forgetful, though its wings are wet the while:—
　　Yet ah! how much must this poor heart endure,
　　Which hopes from thee, and thee alone, a cure!

JOANNA BAILLIE

1762–1851

524　　　　*The Outlaw's Song*

THE chough and crow to roost are gone,
　　The owl sits on the tree,
The hush'd wind wails with feeble moan,
　　Like infant charity.
The wild-fire dances on the fen,
　　The red star sheds its ray;
Uprouse ye then, my merry men!
　　It is our op'ning day.

JOANNA BAILLIE

Both child and nurse are fast asleep,
  And closed is every flower,
And winking tapers faintly peep
  High from my lady's bower;
Bewilder'd hinds with shorten'd ken
  Shrink on their murky way;
Uprouse ye then, my merry men!
  It is our op'ning day.

Nor board nor garner own we now,
  Nor roof nor latchèd door,
Nor kind mate, bound by holy vow
  To bless a good man's store;
Noon lulls us in a gloomy den,
  And night is grown our day;
Uprouse ye then, my merry men!
  And use it as ye may.

MARY LAMB

1765–1847

525

A Child

A CHILD's a plaything for an hour;
  Its pretty tricks we try
For that or for a longer space—
  Then tire, and lay it by.

But I knew one that to itself
  All seasons could control;
That would have mock'd the sense of pain
  Out of a grievèd soul.

Thou straggler into loving arms,
  Young climber-up of knees,
When I forget thy thousand ways
  Then life and all shall cease.

1766–1845

526   *The Land o' the Leal*

I'M wearin' awa', John,
  Like snaw-wreaths in thaw, John,
I'm wearin' awa'
    To the land o' the leal.

There's nae sorrow there, John,
There's neither cauld nor care, John,
The day is aye fair
    In the land o' the leal.

Our bonnie bairn's there, John,
She was baith gude and fair, John;
And O! we grudged her sair
    To the land o' the leal.

But sorrow's sel' wears past, John,
And joy's a-coming fast, John,
The joy that's aye to last
    In the land o' the leal.

Sae dear's the joy was bought, John,
Sae free the battle fought, John,
That sinfu' man e'er brought
    To the land o' the leal.

O, dry your glistening e'e, John!
My saul langs to be free, John,
And angels beckon me
    To the land o' the leal.

O, haud ye leal and true, John!
Your day it's wearin' through, John,
And I'll welcome you
 To the land o' the leal.

Now fare-ye-weel, my ain John,
This warld's cares are vain, John,
We'll meet, and we'll be fain,
 In the land o' the leal.

JAMES HOGG

1770–1835

527   *A Boy's Song*

WHERE the pools are bright and deep,
 Where the grey trout lies asleep,
Up the river and over the lea,
That's the way for Billy and me.

Where the blackbird sings the latest,
Where the hawthorn blooms the sweetest,
Where the nestlings chirp and flee,
That's the way for Billy and me.

Where the mowers mow the cleanest,
Where the hay lies thick and greenest,
There to track the homeward bee,
That's the way for Billy and me.

Where the hazel bank is steepest,
Where the shadow falls the deepest,
Where the clustering nuts fall free,
That's the way for Billy and me.

Why the boys should drive away
Little sweet maidens from the play,
Or love to banter and fight so well,
That's the thing I never could tell.

But this I know, I love to play
Through the meadow, among the hay;
Up the water and over the lea,
That's the way for Billy and me.

528 *Kilmeny*

BONNIE Kilmeny gaed up the glen;
 But it wasna to meet Duneira's men,
Nor the rosy monk of the isle to see,
For Kilmeny was pure as pure could be.
It was only to hear the yorlin sing,
And pu' the cress-flower round the spring;
The scarlet hypp and the hindberrye,
And the nut that hung frae the hazel tree;
For Kilmeny was pure as pure could be.
But lang may her minny look o'er the wa',
And lang may she seek i' the green-wood shaw;
Lang the laird o' Duneira blame,
And lang, lang greet or Kilmeny come hame!

When many a day had come and fled,
When grief grew calm, and hope was dead,
When mass for Kilmeny's soul had been sung,
When the bedesman had pray'd and the dead bell rung,

528 yorlin] the yellow-hammer.   hindberrye] bramble.
minny] mother.   greet] mourn.

Late, late in gloamin' when all was still,
When the fringe was red on the westlin hill,
The wood was sere, the moon i' the wane,
The reek o' the cot hung over the plain,
Like a little wee cloud in the world its lane;
When the ingle low'd wi' an eiry leme,
Late, late in the gloamin' Kilmeny came hame!

'Kilmeny, Kilmeny, where have you been?
Lang hae we sought baith holt and den;
By linn, by ford, and green-wood tree,
Yet you are halesome and fair to see.
Where gat you that joup o' the lily scheen?
That bonnie snood of the birk sae green?
And these roses, the fairest that ever were seen?
Kilmeny, Kilmeny, where have you been?'

Kilmeny look'd up with a lovely grace,
But nae smile was seen on Kilmeny's face;
As still was her look, and as still was her e'e,
As the stillness that lay on the emerant lea,
Or the mist that sleeps on a waveless sea.
For Kilmeny had been, she knew not where,
And Kilmeny had seen what she could not declare;
Kilmeny had been where the cock never crew,
Where the rain never fell, and the wind never blew.
But it seem'd as the harp of the sky had rung,
And the airs of heaven play'd round her tongue,
When she spake of the lovely forms she had seen,
And a land where sin had never been;

westlin] western.   its lane] alone, by itself.   low'd] flamed.
eiry leme] eery gleam.   linn] waterfall.   joup] mantle.

A land of love and a land of light,
Withouten sun, or moon, or night;
Where the river swa'd a living stream,
And the light a pure celestial beam;
The land of vision, it would seem,
A still, an everlasting dream.

In yon green-wood there is a waik,
And in that waik there is a wene,
And in that wene there is a maike,
That neither has flesh, blood, nor bane;
And down in yon green-wood he walks his lane.

In that green wene Kilmeny lay,
Her bosom happ'd wi' flowerets gay;
But the air was soft and the silence deep,
And bonnie Kilmeny fell sound asleep.
She kenn'd nae mair, nor open'd her e'e,
Till waked by the hymns of a far countrye.

She 'waken'd on a couch of the silk sae slim,
All striped wi' the bars of the rainbow's rim;
And lovely beings round were rife,
Who erst had travell'd mortal life;
And aye they smiled and 'gan to speer,
'What spirit has brought this mortal here?'—

'Lang have I journey'd, the world wide,'
A meek and reverend fere replied;
'Baith night and day I have watch'd the fair,
Eident a thousand years and mair.

swa'd] swelled.   waik] a row of deep damp grass.   wene]
♭whin, a bush.   maike] a mate, match, equal.   his lane]
alone, by himself.   happ'd] covered.   speer] inquire.   fere]
fellow.   eident] unintermittently.

Yes, I have watch'd o'er ilk degree,
Wherever blooms femenitye;
But sinless virgin, free of stain
In mind and body, fand I nane.
Never, since the banquet of time,
Found I a virgin in her prime,
Till late this bonnie maiden I saw
As spotless as the morning snaw:
Full twenty years she has lived as free
As the spirits that sojourn in this countrye:
I have brought her away frae the snares of men,
That sin or death she never may ken.'—

They clasp'd her waist and her hands sae fair,
They kiss'd her cheek and they kemed her hair,
And round came many a blooming fere,
Saying, 'Bonnie Kilmeny, ye're welcome here!
Women are freed of the littand scorn:
O blest be the day Kilmeny was born!
Now shall the land of the spirits see,
Now shall it ken what a woman may be!
Many a lang year, in sorrow and pain,
Many a lang year through the world we've gane,
Commission'd to watch fair womankind,
For it's they who nurice the immortal mind.
We have watch'd their steps as the dawning shone,
And deep in the green-wood walks alone;
By lily bower and silken bed,
The viewless tears have o'er them shed;
Have soothed their ardent minds to sleep,
Or left the couch of love to weep.

kemed] combed.

We have seen! we have seen! but the time must come,
And the angels will weep at the day of doom!

'O would the fairest of mortal kind
Aye keep the holy truths in mind,
That kindred spirits their motions see,
Who watch their ways with anxious e'e,
And grieve for the guilt of humanitye!
O, sweet to Heaven the maiden's prayer,
And the sigh that heaves a bosom sae fair!
And dear to Heaven the words of truth,
And the praise of virtue frae beauty's mouth!
And dear to the viewless forms of air,
The minds that kyth as the body fair!

'O bonnie Kilmeny! free frae stain,
If ever you seek the world again,
That world of sin, of sorrow and fear,
O tell of the joys that are waiting here;
And tell of the signs you shall shortly see;
Of the times that are now, and the times that shall be.'—
They lifted Kilmeny, they led her away,
And she walk'd in the light of a sunless day;
The sky was a dome of crystal bright,
The fountain of vision, and fountain of light:
The emerald fields were of dazzling glow,
And the flowers of everlasting blow.
Then deep in the stream her body they laid,
That her youth and beauty never might fade;
And they smiled on heaven, when they saw her lie
In the stream of life that wander'd bye.

kyth] show, appear.

And she heard a song, she heard it sung,
She kenn'd not where; but sae sweetly it rung,
It fell on the ear like a dream of the morn:
'O, blest be the day Kilmeny was born!
Now shall the land of the spirits see,
Now shall it ken what a woman may be!
The sun that shines on the world sae bright,
A borrow'd gleid frae the fountain of light;
And the moon that sleeks the sky sae dun,
Like a gouden bow, or a beamless sun,
Shall wear away, and be seen nae mair,
And the angels shall miss them travelling the air.
But lang, lang after baith night and day,
When the sun and the world have elyed away;
When the sinner has gane to his waesome doom,
Kilmeny shall smile in eternal bloom!'—

They bore her away, she wist not how,
For she felt not arm nor rest below;
But so swift they wain'd her through the light,
'Twas like the motion of sound or sight;
They seem'd to split the gales of air,
And yet nor gale nor breeze was there.
Unnumber'd groves below them grew,
They came, they pass'd, and backward flew,
Like floods of blossoms gliding on,
In moment seen, in moment gone.
O, never vales to mortal view
Appear'd like those o'er which they flew!
That land to human spirits given,
The lowermost vales of the storied heaven;

      gleid] spark, glow.   elyed] vanished.

From thence they can view the world below,
And heaven's blue gates with sapphires glow,
More glory yet unmeet to know.

They bore her far to a mountain green,
To see what mortal never had seen;
And they seated her high on a purple sward,
And bade her heed what she saw and heard,
And note the changes the spirits wrought,
For now she lived in the land of thought.
She look'd, and she saw nor sun nor skies,
But a crystal dome of a thousand dyes:
She look'd, and she saw nae land aright,
But an endless whirl of glory and light:
And radiant beings went and came,
Far swifter than wind, or the linkèd flame.
She hid her e'en frae the dazzling view;
She look'd again, and the scene was new.

She saw a sun on a summer sky,
And clouds of amber sailing bye;
A lovely land beneath her lay,
And that land had glens and mountains gray;
And that land had valleys and hoary piles,
And marlèd seas, and a thousand isles.
Its fields were speckled, its forests green,
And its lakes were all of the dazzling sheen,
Like magic mirrors, where slumbering lay
The sun and the sky and the cloudlet gray;
Which heaved and trembled, and gently swung,
On every shore they seem'd to be hung;

marled] variegated, parti-coloured.

For there they were seen on their downward plain
A thousand times and a thousand again;
In winding lake and placid firth,
Little peaceful heavens in the bosom of earth.

Kilmeny sigh'd and seem'd to grieve,
For she found her heart to that land did cleave;
She saw the corn wave on the vale,
She saw the deer run down the dale;
She saw the plaid and the broad claymore,
And the brows that the badge of freedom bore;
And she thought she had seen the land before.

She saw a lady sit on a throne,
The fairest that ever the sun shone on!
A lion lick'd her hand of milk,
And she held him in a leish of silk;
And a leifu' maiden stood at her knee,
With a silver wand and melting e'e;
Her sovereign shield till love stole in
And poison'd all the fount within.

Then a gruff untoward bedesman came,
And hundit the lion on his dame;
And the guardian maid wi' the dauntless e'e,
She dropp'd a tear, and left her knee;
And she saw till the queen frae the lion fled,
Till the bonniest flower of the world lay dead;
A coffin was set on a distant plain,
And she saw the red blood fall like rain;
Then bonnie Kilmeny's heart grew sair,
And she turn'd away, and could look nae mair.

leifu'] lone, wistful.

Then the gruff grim carle girn'd amain,
And they trampled him down, but he rose again;
And he baited the lion to deeds of weir,
Till he lapp'd the blood to the kingdom dear;
And weening his head was danger-preef,
When crown'd with the rose and clover leaf,
He gowl'd at the carle, and chased him away
To feed wi' the deer on the mountain gray.
He gowl'd at the carle, and geck'd at Heaven,
But his mark was set, and his arles given.
Kilmeny a while her e'en withdrew;
She look'd again, and the scene was new.

She saw before her fair unfurl'd
One half of all the glowing world,
Where oceans roll'd, and rivers ran,
To bound the aims of sinful man.
She saw a people, fierce and fell,
Burst frae their bounds like fiends of hell;
Their lilies grew, and the eagle flew;
And she herkèd on her ravening crew,
Till the cities and towers were wrapp'd in a blaze,
And the thunder it roar'd o'er the lands and the seas.
The widows they wail'd, and the red blood ran,
And she threaten'd an end to the race of man;
She never lened, nor stood in awe,
Till caught by the lion's deadly paw.
O, then the eagle swink'd for life,
And brainyell'd up a mortal strife;

girn'd] snarled.   weir] war.   gowl'd] howled.   geck'd]
mocked.   arles] money paid on striking a bargain: *fig.* a
beating.   lened] crouched.   swink'd] laboured.
brainyell'd] stirred, beat.

But flew she north, or flew she south,
She met wi' the gowl o' the lion's mouth.

With a mooted wing and waefu' maen,
The eagle sought her eiry again;
But lang may she cower in her bloody nest,
And lang, lang sleek her wounded breast,
Before she sey another flight,
To play wi' the norland lion's might.

But to sing the sights Kilmeny saw,
So far surpassing nature's law,
The singer's voice wad sink away,
And the string of his harp wad cease to play.
But she saw till the sorrows of man were bye,
And all was love and harmony;
Till the stars of heaven fell calmly away,
Like flakes of snaw on a winter day.

Then Kilmeny begg'd again to see
The friends she had left in her own countrye;
To tell of the place where she had been,
And the glories that lay in the land unseen;
To warn the living maidens fair,
The loved of Heaven, the spirits' care,
That all whose minds unmeled remain
Shall bloom in beauty when time is gane.

With distant music, soft and deep,
They lull'd Kilmeny sound asleep;
And when she awaken'd, she lay her lane,
All happ'd with flowers, in the green-wood wene.

mooted] moulted.   sey] essay.   unmeled] unblemished.
her lane] alone, by herself.

608

When seven lang years had come and fled,
When grief was calm, and hope was dead;
When scarce was remember'd Kilmeny's name,
Late, late in a gloamin' Kilmeny came hame!
And O, her beauty was fair to see,
But still and steadfast was her e'e!
Such beauty bard may never declare,
For there was no pride nor passion there;
And the soft desire of maiden's e'en
In that mild face could never be seen.
Her seymar was the lily flower,
And her cheek the moss-rose in the shower;
And her voice like the distant melodye,
That floats along the twilight sea.
But she loved to raike the lanely glen,
And keepèd afar frae the haunts of men;
Her holy hymns unheard to sing,
To suck the flowers, and drink the spring.
But wherever her peaceful form appear'd,
The wild beasts of the hill were cheer'd;
The wolf play'd blythly round the field,
The lordly byson low'd and kneel'd;
The dun deer woo'd with manner bland,
And cower'd aneath her lily hand.
And when at even the woodlands rung,
When hymns of other worlds she sung
In ecstasy of sweet devotion,
O, then the glen was all in motion!
The wild beasts of the forest came,
Broke from their bughts and faulds the tame,

seymar] cymar, a slight covering.   raike] range, wander.
bughts] milking-pens.

And goved around, charm'd and amazed;
Even the dull cattle croon'd and gazed,
And murmur'd and look'd with anxious pain
For something the mystery to explain.
The buzzard came with the throstle-cock;
The corby left her houf in the rock;
The blackbird alang wi' the eagle flew;
The hind came tripping o'er the dew;
The wolf and the kid their raike began,
And the tod, and the lamb, and the leveret ran;
The hawk and the hern attour them hung,
And the merle and the mavis forhooy'd their young;
And all in a peaceful ring were hurl'd;
It was like an eve in a sinless world!

When a month and a day had come and gane,
Kilmeny sought the green-wood wene;
There laid her down on the leaves sae green,
And Kilmeny on earth was never mair seen.
But O, the words that fell from her mouth
Were words of wonder, and words of truth!
But all the land were in fear and dread,
For they kendna whether she was living or dead.
It wasna her hame, and she couldna remain;
She left this world of sorrow and pain,
And return'd to the land of thought again.

goved] stared, gazed.   corby] raven.   houf] haunt.
raike] ramble.   tod] fox.   attour] out over.   forhooy'd]
neglected.

1770–1850

Lucy

(*i*)

STRANGE fits of passion have I known:
  And I will dare to tell,
But in the lover's ear alone,
  What once to me befell.

When she I loved look'd every day
  Fresh as a rose in June,
I to her cottage bent my way,
  Beneath an evening moon.

Upon the moon I fix'd my eye,
  All over the wide lea;
With quickening pace my horse drew nigh
  Those paths so dear to me.

And now we reach'd the orchard-plot;
  And, as we climb'd the hill,
The sinking moon to Lucy's cot
  Came near and nearer still.

In one of those sweet dreams I slept,
  Kind Nature's gentlest boon!
And all the while my eyes I kept
  On the descending moon.

My horse moved on; hoof after hoof
  He raised, and never stopp'd:
When down behind the cottage roof,
  At once, the bright moon dropp'd.

What fond and wayward thoughts will slide
 Into a lover's head!
'O mercy!' to myself I cried,
 'If Lucy should be dead!'

530   *(ii)*

SHE dwelt among the untrodden ways
 Beside the springs of Dove,
A Maid whom there were none to praise
 And very few to love:

A violet by a mossy stone
 Half hidden from the eye!
Fair as a star, when only one
 Is shining in the sky.

She lived unknown, and few could know
 When Lucy ceased to be;
But she is in her grave, and oh,
 The difference to me!

531   *(iii)*

I TRAVELL'D among unknown men,
 In lands beyond the sea;
Nor, England! did I know till then
 What love I bore to thee.

'Tis past, that melancholy dream!
 Nor will I quit thy shore
A second time; for still I seem
 To love thee more and more.

Among thy mountains did I feel
 The joy of my desire;
And she I cherish'd turn'd her wheel
 Beside an English fire.

Thy mornings show'd, thy nights conceal'd,
  The bowers where Lucy play'd;
And thine too is the last green field
  That Lucy's eyes survey'd.

532   *(iv)*

THREE years she grew in sun and shower;
  Then Nature said, 'A lovelier flower
   On earth was never sown;
This child I to myself will take;
She shall be mine, and I will make
   A lady of my own.

'Myself will to my darling be
Both law and impulse: and with me
   The girl, in rock and plain,
In earth and heaven, in glade and bower,
Shall feel an overseeing power
   To kindle or restrain.

'She shall be sportive as the fawn
That wild with glee across the lawn
   Or up the mountain springs;
And hers shall be the breathing balm,
And hers the silence and the calm
   Of mute insensate things.

'The floating clouds their state shall lend
To her; for her the willow bend;
   Nor shall she fail to see
Even in the motions of the storm
Grace that shall mould the maiden's form
   By silent sympathy.

'The stars of midnight shall be dear
To her; and she shall lean her ear
   In many a secret place
Where rivulets dance their wayward round,
And beauty born of murmuring sound
   Shall pass into her face.

'And vital feelings of delight
Shall rear her form to stately height,
   Her virgin bosom swell;
Such thoughts to Lucy I will give
While she and I together live
   Here in this happy dell.'

Thus Nature spake—The work was done—
How soon my Lucy's race was run!
   She died, and left to me
This heath, this calm and quiet scene;
The memory of what has been,
   And never more will be.

533   (*v*)

A SLUMBER did my spirit seal;
   I had no human fears:
She seem'd a thing that could not feel
   The touch of earthly years.

No motion has she now, no force;
   She neither hears nor sees;
Roll'd round in earth's diurnal course,
   With rocks, and stones, and trees.

534 *Upon Westminster Bridge*

EARTH has not anything to show more fair:
  Dull would he be of soul who could pass by
A sight so touching in its majesty:
This City now doth like a garment wear
The beauty of the morning; silent, bare,
  Ships, towers, domes, theatres, and temples lie
  Open unto the fields, and to the sky;
All bright and glittering in the smokeless air.
Never did sun more beautifully steep
  In his first splendour valley, rock, or hill;
Ne'er saw I, never felt, a calm so deep!
  The river glideth at his own sweet will:
Dear God! the very houses seem asleep;
  And all that mighty heart is lying still!

535 *Evening on Calais Beach*

IT is a beauteous evening, calm and free,
  The holy time is quiet as a Nun
  Breathless with adoration; the broad sun
Is sinking down in its tranquillity;
The gentleness of heaven broods o'er the sea:
  Listen! the mighty Being is awake,
  And doth with his eternal motion make
A sound like thunder—everlastingly.
Dear Child! dear Girl! that walkest with me here,
  If thou appear untouch'd by solemn thought,
  Thy nature is not therefore less divine:
Thou liest in Abraham's bosom all the year;
  And worshipp'st at the Temple's inner shrine,
  God being with thee when we know it not.

536 *On the Extinction of the Venetian
Republic, 1802*

ONCE did she hold the gorgeous East in fee;
        And was the safeguard of the West: the worth
    Of Venice did not fall below her birth,
Venice, the eldest Child of Liberty.
She was a maiden City, bright and free;
    No guile seduced, no force could violate;
    And, when she took unto herself a mate,
She must espouse the everlasting Sea.
And what if she had seen those glories fade,
    Those titles vanish, and that strength decay;
Yet shall some tribute of regret be paid
    When her long life hath reach'd its final day:
Men are we, and must grieve when even the Shade
    Of that which once was great is pass'd away.

537 *England, 1802 (i)*

O FRIEND! I know not which way I must look
        For comfort, being, as I am, opprest,
    To think that now our life is only drest
For show; mean handy-work of craftsman, cook,
Or groom!—We must run glittering like a brook
    In the open sunshine, or we are unblest:
    The wealthiest man among us is the best:
No grandeur now in nature or in book
Delights us. Rapine, avarice, expense,
    This is idolatry; and these we adore:
    Plain living and high thinking are no more:
    The homely beauty of the good old cause
Is gone; our peace, our fearful innocence,
    And pure religion breathing household laws.

538   *(ii)*

MILTON! thou shouldst be living at this hour:
   England hath need of thee: she is a fen
Of stagnant waters: altar, sword, and pen,
Fireside, the heroic wealth of hall and bower,
Have forfeited their ancient English dower
   Of inward happiness. We are selfish men;
   O raise us up, return to us again,
And give us manners, virtue, freedom, power!
Thy soul was like a Star, and dwelt apart;
   Thou hadst a voice whose sound was like the sea:
   Pure as the naked heavens, majestic, free,
   So didst thou travel on life's common way,
In cheerful godliness; and yet thy heart
   The lowliest duties on herself did lay.

539   *(iii)*

GREAT men have been among us; hands that penn'd
   And tongues that utter'd wisdom—better none:
The later Sidney, Marvel, Harrington,
Young Vane, and others who call'd Milton friend.
These moralists could act and comprehend:
   They knew how genuine glory was put on;
   Taught us how rightfully a nation shone
In splendour: what strength was, that would not bend
But in magnanimous meekness. France, 'tis strange,
   Hath brought forth no such souls as we had then.
Perpetual emptiness! unceasing change!
   No single volume paramount, no code,
   No master spirit, no determined road;
   But equally a want of books and men!

540   (iv)

IT is not to be thought of that the flood
   Of British freedom, which, to the open sea
   Of the world's praise, from dark antiquity
Hath flow'd, 'with pomp of waters, unwithstood,'—
Roused though it be full often to a mood
   Which spurns the check of salutary bands,—
   That this most famous stream in bogs and sands
Should perish; and to evil and to good
Be lost for ever. In our halls is hung
   Armoury of the invincible Knights of old:
We must be free or die, who speak the tongue
   That Shakespeare spake; the faith and morals hold
Which Milton held.—In everything we are sprung
   Of Earth's first blood, have titles manifold.

541   (v)

WHEN I have borne in memory what has tamed
   Great Nations, how ennobling thoughts depart
   When men change swords for ledgers, and desert
The student's bower for gold, some fears unnamed
I had, my Country—am I to be blamed?
   Now, when I think of thee, and what thou art,
   Verily, in the bottom of my heart,
Of those unfilial fears I am ashamed.
For dearly must we prize thee; we who find
   In thee a bulwark for the cause of men;
   And I by my affection was beguiled:
   What wonder if a Poet now and then,
Among the many movements of his mind,
   Felt for thee as a lover or a child!

The Solitary Reaper

BEHOLD her, single in the field,
  Yon solitary Highland Lass!
Reaping and singing by herself;
  Stop here, or gently pass!
Alone she cuts and binds the grain,
And sings a melancholy strain;
O listen! for the Vale profound
Is overflowing with the sound.

No Nightingale did ever chaunt
  More welcome notes to weary bands
Of travellers in some shady haunt,
  Among Arabian sands:
A voice so thrilling ne'er was heard
In spring-time from the Cuckoo-bird,
Breaking the silence of the seas
Among the farthest Hebrides.

Will no one tell me what she sings?—
  Perhaps the plaintive numbers flow
For old, unhappy, far-off things,
  And battles long ago:
Or is it some more humble lay,
Familiar matter of to-day?
Some natural sorrow, loss, or pain,
That has been, and may be again?

Whate'er the theme, the Maiden sang
  As if her song could have no ending;
I saw her singing at her work,
  And o'er the sickle bending;—

I listen'd, motionless and still;
And, as I mounted up the hill,
The music in my heart I bore,
Long after it was heard no more.

543 *Perfect Woman*

SHE was a phantom of delight
When first she gleam'd upon my sight;
A lovely apparition, sent
To be a moment's ornament;
Her eyes as stars of twilight fair;
Like twilight's, too, her dusky hair;
But all things else about her drawn
From May-time and the cheerful dawn;
A dancing shape, an image gay,
To haunt, to startle, and waylay.

I saw her upon nearer view,
A Spirit, yet a Woman too!
Her household motions light and free,
And steps of virgin liberty;
A countenance in which did meet
Sweet records, promises as sweet;
A creature not too bright or good
For human nature's daily food;
For transient sorrows, simple wiles,
Praise, blame, love, kisses, tears, and smiles.

And now I see with eye serene
The very pulse of the machine;

A being breathing thoughtful breath,
A traveller between life and death;
The reason firm, the temperate will,
Endurance, foresight, strength, and skill;
A perfect Woman, nobly plann'd,
To warn, to comfort, and command;
And yet a Spirit still, and bright
With something of angelic light.

544 *Daffodils*

I WANDER'D lonely as a cloud
  That floats on high o'er vales and hills,
When all at once I saw a crowd,
  A host, of golden daffodils;
Beside the lake, beneath the trees,
Fluttering and dancing in the breeze.

Continuous as the stars that shine
  And twinkle on the Milky Way,
They stretch'd in never-ending line
  Along the margin of a bay:
Ten thousand saw I at a glance,
Tossing their heads in sprightly dance.

The waves beside them danced, but they
  Out-did the sparkling waves in glee:
A poet could not but be gay,
  In such a jocund company:
I gazed—and gazed—but little thought
What wealth the show to me had brought:

For oft, when on my couch I lie
    In vacant or in pensive mood,
They flash upon that inward eye
    Which is the bliss of solitude;
And then my heart with pleasure fills,
And dances with the daffodils.

545   *Ode to Duty*

STERN Daughter of the Voice of God!
  O Duty! if that name thou love,
Who art a light to guide, a rod
To check the erring and reprove;
Thou, who art victory and law
When empty terrors overawe;
From vain temptations dost set free;
And calm'st the weary strife of frail humanity!

There are who ask not if thine eye
Be on them; who, in love and truth,
Where no misgiving is, rely
Upon the genial sense of youth:
Glad hearts! without reproach or blot;
Who do thy work, and know it not:
O, if through confidence misplaced
They fail, thy saving arms, dread Power! around them cast.

Serene will be our days and bright,
And happy will our nature be,
When love is an unerring light,
And joy its own security.

And they a blissful course may hold
Even now, who, not unwisely bold,
Live in the spirit of this creed;
Yet seek thy firm support, according to their need.

I, loving freedom, and untried;
No sport of every random gust,
Yet being to myself a guide,
Too blindly have reposed my trust:
And oft, when in my heart was heard
Thy timely mandate, I deferr'd
The task, in smoother walks to stray;
But thee I now would serve more strictly, if I may.

Through no disturbance of my soul,
Or strong compunction in me wrought,
I supplicate for thy control;
But in the quietness of thought.
Me this uncharter'd freedom tires;
I feel the weight of chance-desires;
My hopes no more must change their name,
I long for a repose that ever is the same.

Yet not the less would I throughout
Still act according to the voice
Of my own wish; and feel past doubt
That my submissiveness was choice:
Not seeking in the school of pride
For 'precepts over dignified,'
Denial and restraint I prize
No farther than they breed a second Will more wise.

Stern Lawgiver! yet thou dost wear
The Godhead's most benignant grace;
Nor know we anything so fair
As is the smile upon thy face:
Flowers laugh before thee on their beds,
And fragrance in thy footing treads;
Thou dost preserve the stars from wrong;
And the most ancient heavens, through Thee, are fresh and
    strong.

To humbler functions, awful Power!
I call thee: I myself commend
Unto thy guidance from this hour;
O, let my weakness have an end!
Give unto me, made lowly wise,
The spirit of self-sacrifice;
The confidence of reason give;
And in the light of truth thy bondman let me live!

546   *The Rainbow*

MY heart leaps up when I behold
    A rainbow in the sky:
So was it when my life began;
So is it now I am a man;
So be it when I shall grow old,
    Or let me die!
The Child is father of the Man;
And I could wish my days to be
Bound each to each by natural piety.

624

547 *The Sonnet* (*i*)

NUNS fret not at their convent's narrow room,
    And hermits are contented with their cells,
    And students with their pensive citadels;
Maids at the wheel, the weaver at his loom,
Sit blithe and happy; bees that soar for bloom,
    High as the highest peak of Furness fells,
    Will murmur by the hour in foxglove bells:
In truth the prison unto which we doom
Ourselves no prison is: and hence for me,
    In sundry moods, 'twas pastime to be bound
    Within the Sonnet's scanty plot of ground;
Pleased if some souls (for such there needs must be)
Who have felt the weight of too much liberty,
    Should find brief solace there, as I have found.

548 (*ii*)

SCORN not the Sonnet; Critic, you have frown'd,
    Mindless of its just honours; with this key
    Shakespeare unlock'd his heart; the melody
Of this small lute gave ease to Petrarch's wound;
A thousand times this pipe did Tasso sound;
    With it Camöens sooth'd an exile's grief;
    The Sonnet glitter'd a gay myrtle leaf
Amid the cypress with which Dante crown'd
His visionary brow: a glow-worm lamp,
    It cheer'd mild Spenser, call'd from Faery-land
To struggle through dark ways; and when a damp
    Fell round the path of Milton, in his hand
The Thing became a trumpet; whence he blew
Soul-animating strains—alas, too few!

549 *The World*

T HE world is too much with us; late and soon,
　Getting and spending, we lay waste our powers:
Little we see in Nature that is ours;
We have given our hearts away, a sordid boon!
This sea that bares her bosom to the moon;
　The winds that will be howling at all hours,
　And are up-gather'd now like sleeping flowers;
For this, for everything, we are out of tune;
It moves us not.—Great God! I'd rather be
　A Pagan suckled in a creed outworn;
So might I, standing on this pleasant lea,
　Have glimpses that would make me less forlorn;
Have sight of Proteus rising from the sea;
　Or hear old Triton blow his wreathèd horn.

550 *Ode*

*Intimations of Immortality from Recollections of
Early Childhood*

T HERE was a time when meadow, grove, and stream,
　The earth, and every common sight,
　　　To me did seem
　　Apparell'd in celestial light,
The glory and the freshness of a dream.
It is not now as it hath been of yore;—
　　　Turn wheresoe'er I may,
　　　By night or day,
The things which I have seen I now can see no more.

626

The rainbow comes and goes,
And lovely is the rose;
The moon doth with delight
Look round her when the heavens are bare;
Waters on a starry night
Are beautiful and fair;
The sunshine is a glorious birth;
But yet I know, where'er I go,
That there hath pass'd away a glory from the earth.

Now, while the birds thus sing a joyous song,
And while the young lambs bound
As to the tabor's sound,
To me alone there came a thought of grief:
A timely utterance gave that thought relief,
And I again am strong:
The cataracts blow their trumpets from the steep;
No more shall grief of mine the season wrong;
I hear the echoes through the mountains throng,
The winds come to me from the fields of sleep,
And all the earth is gay;
Land and sea
Give themselves up to jollity,
And with the heart of May
Doth every beast keep holiday;—
Thou Child of Joy,
Shout round me, let me hear thy shouts, thou happy Shepherd-
boy!

Ye blessèd creatures, I have heard the call
Ye to each other make; I see
The heavens laugh with you in your jubilee;
My heart is at your festival,

My head hath its coronal,
The fullness of your bliss, I feel—I feel it all.
O evil day! if I were sullen
While Earth herself is adorning,
This sweet May-morning,
And the children are culling
On every side,
In a thousand valleys far and wide,
Fresh flowers; while the sun shines warm,
And the babe leaps up on his mother's arm:—
I hear, I hear, with joy I hear!
—But there's a tree, of many, one,
A single field which I have look'd upon,
Both of them speak of something that is gone:
The pansy at my feet
Doth the same tale repeat:
Whither is fled the visionary gleam?
Where is it now, the glory and the dream?

Our birth is but a sleep and a forgetting:
The Soul that rises with us, our life's Star,
Hath had elsewhere its setting,
And cometh from afar:
Not in entire forgetfulness,
And not in utter nakedness,
But trailing clouds of glory do we come
From God, who is our home:
Heaven lies about us in our infancy!
Shades of the prison-house begin to close
Upon the growing Boy,
But he beholds the light, and whence it flows,
He sees it in his joy;

The Youth, who daily farther from the east
 Must travel, still is Nature's priest,
  And by the vision splendid
  Is on his way attended;
At length the Man perceives it die away,
And fade into the light of common day.

Earth fills her lap with pleasures of her own;
 Yearnings she hath in her own natural kind;
And, even with something of a mother's mind,
  And no unworthy aim,
 The homely nurse doth all she can
To make her foster-child, her inmate Man,
 Forget the glories he hath known,
And that imperial palace whence he came.

Behold the Child among his new-born blisses,
A six years' darling of a pigmy size!
See, where 'mid work of his own hand he lies,
Fretted by sallies of his mother's kisses,
With light upon him from his father's eyes!
See, at his feet, some little plan or chart,
Some fragment from his dream of human life,
Shaped by himself with newly-learnèd art;
  A wedding or a festival,
  A mourning or a funeral;
   And this hath now his heart,
  And unto this he frames his song:
   Then will he fit his tongue
To dialogues of business, love, or strife;
   But it will not be long
   Ere this be thrown aside,
   And with new joy and pride

The little actor cons another part;
Filling from time to time his 'humorous stage'
With all the Persons, down to palsied Age,
That Life brings with her in her equipage;
    As if his whole vocation
    Were endless imitation.

Thou, whose exterior semblance doth belie
    Thy soul's immensity;
Thou best philosopher, who yet dost keep
Thy heritage, thou eye among the blind,
That, deaf and silent, read'st the eternal deep,
Haunted for ever by the eternal mind,—
    Mighty prophet! Seer blest!
    On whom those truths do rest,
Which we are toiling all our lives to find,
In darkness lost, the darkness of the grave;
Thou, over whom thy Immortality
Broods like the Day, a master o'er a slave,
A presence which is not to be put by;
Thou little Child, yet glorious in the might
Of heaven-born freedom on thy being's height,
Why with such earnest pains dost thou provoke
The years to bring the inevitable yoke,
Thus blindly with thy blessedness at strife?
Full soon thy soul shall have her earthly freight,
And custom lie upon thee with a weight,
Heavy as frost, and deep almost as life!

    O joy! that in our embers
    Is something that doth live,
    That nature yet remembers

What was so fugitive!
The thought of our past years in me doth breed
Perpetual benediction: not indeed
For that which is most worthy to be blest—
Delight and liberty, the simple creed
Of childhood, whether busy or at rest,
With new-fledged hope still fluttering in his breast:—
Not for these I raise
The song of thanks and praise;
But for those obstinate questionings
Of sense and outward things,
Fallings from us, vanishings;
Blank misgivings of a Creature
Moving about in worlds not realized,
High instincts before which our mortal Nature
Did tremble like a guilty thing surprised:
But for those first affections,
Those shadowy recollections,
Which, be they what they may,
Are yet the fountain-light of all our day,
Are yet a master-light of all our seeing;
Uphold us, cherish, and have power to make
Our noisy years seem moments in the being
Of the eternal Silence: truths that wake,
To perish never:
Which neither listlessness, nor mad endeavour,
Nor Man nor Boy,
Nor all that is at enmity with joy,
Can utterly abolish or destroy!
Hence in a season of calm weather
Though inland far we be,
Our souls have sight of that immortal sea

631

Which brought us hither,
Can in a moment travel thither,
And see the children sport upon the shore,
And hear the mighty waters rolling evermore.

Then sing, ye birds, sing, sing a joyous song!
And let the young lambs bound
As to the tabor's sound!
We in thought will join your throng,
Ye that pipe and ye that play,
Ye that through your hearts to-day
Feel the gladness of the May!
What though the radiance which was once so bright
Be now for ever taken from my sight,
Though nothing can bring back the hour
Of splendour in the grass, of glory in the flower;
We will grieve not, rather find
Strength in what remains behind;
In the primal sympathy
Which having been must ever be;
In the soothing thoughts that spring
Out of human suffering;
In the faith that looks through death,
In years that bring the philosophic mind.

And O ye Fountains, Meadows, Hills, and Groves,
Forebode not any severing of our loves!
Yet in my heart of hearts I feel your might;
I only have relinquish'd one delight
To live beneath your more habitual sway.

I love the brooks which down their channels fret,
Even more than when I tripp'd lightly as they;
The innocent brightness of a new-born Day
        Is lovely yet;
The clouds that gather round the setting sun
Do take a sober colouring from an eye
That hath kept watch o'er man's mortality;
Another race hath been, and other palms are won.
Thanks to the human heart by which we live,
Thanks to its tenderness, its joys, and fears,
To me the meanest flower that blows can give
Thoughts that do often lie too deep for tears.

551   *Desideria*

SURPRISED by joy—impatient as the Wind
   I turned to share the transport—O! with whom
   But Thee, deep buried in the silent tomb,
That spot which no vicissitude can find?
Love, faithful love, recall'd thee to my mind—
   But how could I forget thee? Through what power,
   Even for the least division of an hour,
Have I been so beguiled as to be blind
To my most grievous loss?—That thought's return
   Was the worst pang that sorrow ever bore,
Save one, one only, when I stood forlorn,
   Knowing my heart's best treasure was no more;
That neither present time, nor years unborn
   Could to my sight that heavenly face restore.

552 *Valedictory Sonnet to the River Duddon*

I THOUGHT of Thee, my partner and my guide,
  As being pass'd away.—Vain sympathies!
  For, backward, Duddon! as I cast my eyes,
I see what was, and is, and will abide;
Still glides the Stream, and shall for ever glide;
  The Form remains, the Function never dies;
  While we, the brave, the mighty, and the wise,
We Men, who in our morn of youth defied
The elements, must vanish;—be it so!
  Enough, if something from our hands have power
  To live, and act, and serve the future hour;
And if, as toward the silent tomb we go,   [dower,
  Through love, through hope, and faith's transcendent
We feel that we are greater than we know.

553 *Mutability*

FROM low to high doth dissolution climb,
  And sink from high to low, along a scale
  Of awful notes, whose concord shall not fail;
A musical but melancholy chime,
Which they can hear who meddle not with crime,
  Nor avarice, nor over-anxious care.
  Truth fails not; but her outward forms that bear
The longest date do melt like frosty rime,
That in the morning whiten'd hill and plain
And is no more; drop like the tower sublime
  Of yesterday, which royally did wear
His crown of weeds, but could not even sustain
  Some casual shout that broke the silent air,
  Or the unimaginable touch of Time.

554 *The Trosachs*

THERE 'S not a nook within this solemn Pass
But were an apt confessional for one
Taught by his summer spent, his autumn gone,
That Life is but a tale of morning grass
Wither'd at eve. From scenes of art which chase
That thought away, turn, and with watchful eyes
Feed it 'mid Nature's old felicities,
Rocks, rivers, and smooth lakes more clear than glass
Untouch'd, unbreathed upon. Thrice happy quest,
If from a golden perch of aspen spray
(October's workmanship to rival May)
The pensive warbler of the ruddy breast
That moral sweeten by a heaven-taught lay,
Lulling the year, with all its cares, to rest!

555 *Speak!*

WHY art thou silent! Is thy love a plant
Of such weak fibre that the treacherous air
Of absence withers what was once so fair?
Is there no debt to pay, no boon to grant?
Yet have my thoughts for thee been vigilant—
Bound to thy service with unceasing care,
The mind's least generous wish a mendicant
For naught but what thy happiness could spare.
Speak—though this soft warm heart, once free to hold
A thousand tender pleasures, thine and mine,
Be left more desolate, more dreary cold
Than a forsaken bird's-nest fill'd with snow
'Mid its own bush of leafless eglantine—
Speak, that my torturing doubts their end may know

1771–1832

556   *Proud Maisie*

PROUD Maisie is in the wood,
    Walking so early;
Sweet Robin sits on the bush,
    Singing so rarely.

'Tell me, thou bonny bird,
    When shall I marry me?'
—'When six braw gentlemen
    Kirkward shall carry ye.'

'Who makes the bridal bed,
    Birdie, say truly?'
—'The grey-headed sexton
    That delves the grave duly.

'The glow-worm o'er grave and stone
    Shall light thee steady;
The owl from the steeple sing
    Welcome, proud lady!'

557   *Brignall Banks*

O BRIGNALL banks are wild and fair,
    And Greta woods are green,
And you may gather garlands there,
    Would grace a summer queen:
And as I rode by Dalton Hall,
    Beneath the turrets high,
A Maiden on the castle wall
    Was singing merrily:—

SIR WALTER SCOTT

'O, Brignall banks are fresh and fair,
   And Greta woods are green!
I'd rather rove with Edmund there
   Than reign our English Queen.'

'If, Maiden, thou wouldst wend with me
   To leave both tower and town,
Thou first must guess what life lead we,
   That dwell by dale and down:
And if thou canst that riddle read,
   As read full well you may,
Then to the green-wood shalt thou speed
   As blithe as Queen of May.'

Yet sung she, 'Brignall banks are fair,
   And Greta woods are green!
I'd rather rove with Edmund there
   Than reign our English Queen.

'I read you by your bugle horn
   And by your palfrey good,
I read you for a Ranger sworn
   To keep the King's green-wood.'
'A Ranger, Lady, winds his horn,
   And 'tis at peep of light;
His blast is heard at merry morn,
   And mine at dead of night.'

Yet sung she, 'Brignall banks are fair,
   And Greta woods are gay!
I would I were with Edmund there,
   To reign his Queen of May!

637

'With burnish'd brand and musketoon
  So gallantly you come,
I read you for a bold Dragoon,
  That lists the tuck of drum.'
'I list no more the tuck of drum,
  No more the trumpet hear;
But when the beetle sounds his hum,
  My comrades take the spear.

'And O! though Brignall banks be fair,
  And Greta woods be gay,
Yet mickle must the maiden dare,
  Would reign my Queen of May!

'Maiden! a nameless life I lead,
  A nameless death I'll die;
The fiend whose lantern lights the mead
  Were better mate than I!
And when I'm with my comrades met
  Beneath the green-wood bough,
What once we were we all forget,
  Nor think what we are now.'

Chorus.   Yet Brignall banks are fresh and fair,
  And Greta woods are green,
And you may gather flowers there
  Would grace a summer queen.

558   *Lucy Ashton's Song*

LOOK not thou on beauty's charming;
  Sit thou still when kings are arming;
Taste not when the wine-cup glistens;
Speak not when the people listens;

638

Stop thine ear against the singer;
From the red gold keep thy finger;
Vacant heart and hand and eye,
Easy live and quiet die.

559 *The Rover's Adieu*

A WEARY lot is thine, fair maid,
   A weary lot is thine!
To pull the thorn thy brow to braid,
   And press the rue for wine.
A lightsome eye, a soldier's mien,
   A feather of the blue,
A doublet of the Lincoln green—
   No more of me ye knew,
      My Love!
No more of me ye knew.

'This morn is merry June, I trow,
   The rose is budding fain;
But she shall bloom in winter snow
   Ere we two meet again.'
—He turn'd his charger as he spake
   Upon the river shore,
He gave the bridle-reins a shake,
   Said 'Adieu for evermore,
      My Love!
And adieu for evermore.'

Patriotism

1. Innominatus

560

BREATHES there the man with soul so dead,
    Who never to himself hath said,
'This is my own, my native land!'
Whose heart hath ne'er within him burn'd
As home his footsteps he hath turn'd
    From wandering on a foreign strand?
If such there breathe, go, mark him well;
For him no Minstrel raptures swell;
High though his titles, proud his name,
Boundless his wealth as wish can claim;
Despite those titles, power, and pelf,
The wretch, concentred all in self,
Living, shall forfeit fair renown,
And, doubly dying, shall go down
To the vile dust from whence he sprung,
Unwept, unhonour'd, and unsung.

2. Nelson, Pitt, Fox

561

TO mute and to material things
    New life revolving summer brings;
The genial call dead Nature hears,
And in her glory reappears.
But oh, my Country's wintry state
What second spring shall renovate?
What powerful call shall bid arise
    The buried warlike and the wise;
The mind that thought for Britain's weal,
The hand that grasp'd the victor steel?

SIR WALTER SCOTT

The vernal sun new life bestows
Even on the meanest flower that blows;
But vainly, vainly may he shine
Where glory weeps o'er NELSON's shrine;
And vainly pierce the solemn gloom
That shrouds, O PITT, thy hallow'd tomb!

Deep graved in every British heart,
O never let those names depart!
Say to your sons,—Lo, here his grave,
Who victor died on Gadite wave!
To him, as to the burning levin,
Short, bright, resistless course was given.
Where'er his country's foes were found
Was heard the fated thunder's sound,
Till burst the bolt on yonder shore,
Roll'd, blazed, destroy'd—and was no more.

Nor mourn ye less his perish'd worth,
Who bade the conqueror go forth,
And launch'd that thunderbolt of war
On Egypt, Hafnia, Trafalgar;
Who, born to guide such high emprise,
For Britain's weal was early wise;
Alas! to whom the Almighty gave,
For Britain's sins, an early grave!
—His worth, who in his mightiest hour
A bauble held the pride of power,
Spurn'd at the sordid lust of pelf,
And served his Albion for herself;
Who, when the frantic crowd amain
Strain'd at subjection's bursting rein,

O'er their wild mood full conquest gain'd,
The pride he would not crush, restrain'd,
Show'd their fierce zeal a worthier cause,
And brought the freeman's arm to aid the freeman's laws.

Hadst thou but lived, though stripp'd of power,
A watchman on the lonely tower,
Thy thrilling trump had roused the land,
When fraud or danger were at hand;
By thee, as by the beacon-light,
Our pilots had kept course aright;
As some proud column, though alone,
Thy strength had propp'd the tottering throne.
Now is the stately column broke,
The beacon-light is quench'd in smoke,
The trumpet's silver voice is still,
The warder silent on the hill!

O think, how to his latest day,
When Death, just hovering, claim'd his prey,
With Palinure's unalter'd mood
Firm at his dangerous post he stood;
Each call for needful rest repell'd,
With dying hand the rudder held,
Till in his fall with fateful sway
The steerage of the realm gave way.
Then—while on Britain's thousand plains
One unpolluted church remains,
Whose peaceful bells ne'er sent around
The bloody tocsin's maddening sound,
But still upon the hallow'd day
Convoke the swains to praise and pray;

SIR WALTER SCOTT

While faith and civil peace are dear,
Grace this cold marble with a tear:—
He who preserved them, PITT, lies here!

Nor yet suppress the generous sigh,
Because his rival slumbers nigh;
Nor be thy *Requiescat* dumb
Lest it be said o'er Fox's tomb.
For talents mourn, untimely lost,
When best employ'd, and wanted most;
Mourn genius high, and lore profound,
And wit that loved to play, not wound;
And all the reasoning powers divine
To penetrate, resolve, combine;
And feelings keen, and fancy's glow—
They sleep with him who sleeps below:
And, if thou mourn'st they could not save
From error him who owns this grave,
Be every harsher thought suppress'd,
And sacred be the last long rest.
Here, where the end of earthly things
Lays heroes, patriots, bards, and kings;
Where stiff the hand, and still the tongue,
Of those who fought, and spoke, and sung;
Here, where the fretted vaults prolong
The distant notes of holy song,
As if some angel spoke agen,
'All peace on earth, good-will to men';
If ever from an English heart,
O, *here* let prejudice depart,
And, partial feeling cast aside,
Record that Fox a Briton died!

SIR WALTER SCOTT

When Europe crouch'd to France's yoke,
And Austria bent, and Prussia broke,
    And the firm Russian's purpose brave
Was barter'd by a timorous slave—
Even then dishonour's peace he spurn'd,
The sullied olive-branch return'd,
Stood for his country's glory fast,
And nail'd her colours to the mast!
Heaven, to reward his firmness, gave
A portion in this honour'd grave;
And ne'er held marble in its trust
Of two such wondrous men the dust.

With more than mortal powers endow'd,
How high they soar'd above the crowd!
Theirs was no common party race,
Jostling by dark intrigue for place;
Like fabled gods, their mighty war
Shook realms and nations in its jar;
Beneath each banner proud to stand,
Look'd up the noblest of the land,
Till through the British world were known
The names of PITT and Fox alone.
Spells of such force no wizard grave
E'er framed in dark Thessalian cave,
Though his could drain the ocean dry,
And force the planets from the sky.
These spells are spent, and, spent with these
The wine of life is on the lees.
Genius, and taste, and talent gone,
For ever tomb'd beneath the stone,

Where—taming thought to human pride!—
The mighty chiefs sleep side by side.
Drop upon Fox's grave the tear,
'Twill trickle to his rival's bier;
O'er PITT's the mournful requiem sound,
And Fox's shall the notes rebound.
The solemn echo seems to cry,
'Here let their discord with them die.
Speak not for those a separate doom
Whom fate made Brothers in the tomb;
But search the land of living men,
Where wilt thou find their like agen?'

SAMUEL TAYLOR COLERIDGE

1772–1834

562   The Rime of the Ancient Mariner

PART I

IT is an ancient Mariner,
And he stoppeth one of three.
'By thy long grey beard and glittering eye,
Now wherefore stopp'st thou me?

An ancient
Mariner
meeteth three
gallants
bidden to a
wedding feast,
and detaineth
one.

The Bridegroom's doors are open'd wide,
And I am next of kin;
The guests are met, the feast is set:
May'st hear the merry din.'

He holds him with his skinny hand,
'There was a ship,' quoth he.
'Hold off! unhand me, grey-beard loon!'
Eftsoons his hand dropt he.

645

The Wedding-Guest is spell-bound by the eye of the old seafaring man, and constrained to hear his tale.

He holds him with his glittering eye—
The Wedding-Guest stood still,
And listens like a three years' child:
The Mariner hath his will.

The Wedding-Guest sat on a stone:
He cannot choose but hear;
And thus spake on that ancient man,
The bright-eyed Mariner.

'The ship was cheer'd, the harbour clear'd,
Merrily did we drop
Below the kirk, below the hill,
Below the lighthouse top.

The Mariner tells how the ship sailed southward with a good wind and fair weather, till it reached the Line.

The Sun came up upon the left,
Out of the sea came he!
And he shone bright, and on the right
Went down into the sea.

Higher and higher every day,
Till over the mast at noon——'
The Wedding-Guest here beat his breast,
For he heard the loud bassoon.

The Wedding-Guest heareth the bridal music; but the Mariner continueth his tale.

The bride hath paced into the hall,
Red as a rose is she;
Nodding their heads before her goes
The merry minstrelsy.

The Wedding-Guest he beat his breast,
Yet he cannot choose but hear;
And thus spake on that ancient man,
The bright-eyed Mariner.

'And now the Storm-blast came, and he
Was tyrannous and strong:
He struck with his o'ertaking wings,
And chased us south along.

With sloping masts and dipping prow,
As who pursued with yell and blow
Still treads the shadow of his foe,
And forward bends his head,
The ship drove fast, loud roar'd the blast,
And southward aye we fled.

And now there came both mist and snow,
And it grew wondrous cold:
And ice, mast-high, came floating by,
As green as emerald.

And through the drifts the snowy clifts
Did send a dismal sheen:
Nor shapes of men nor beasts we ken—
The ice was all between.

The ice was here, the ice was there,
The ice was all around:
It crack'd and growl'd, and roar'd and howl'd,
Like noises in a swound!

At length did cross an Albatross,
Thorough the fog it came;
As if it had been a Christian soul,
We hail'd it in God's name.

It ate the food it ne'er had eat,
And round and round it flew.
The ice did split with a thunder-fit;
The helmsman steer'd us through!

The ship driven by a storm toward the South Pole.

The land of ice, and of fearful sounds, where no living thing was to be seen.

Till a great sea-bird, called the Albatross, came through the snow-fog, and was received with great joy and hospitality.

SAMUEL TAYLOR COLERIDGE

And lo! the Albatross proveth a bird of good omen, and followeth the ship as it returned northward through fog and floating ice.

And a good south wind sprung up behind;
The Albatross did follow,
And every day, for food or play,
Came to the mariners' hollo!

In mist or cloud, on mast or shroud,
It perch'd for vespers nine;
Whiles all the night, through fog-smoke white,
Glimmer'd the white moonshine.'

The ancient Mariner inhospitably killeth the pious bird of good omen.

'God save thee, ancient Mariner,
From the fiends, that plague thee thus!—
Why look'st thou so?'—'With my crossbow
I shot the Albatross.

Part II

'The Sun now rose upon the right:
Out of the sea came he,
Still hid in mist, and on the left
Went down into the sea.

And the good south wind still blew behind,
But no sweet bird did follow,
Nor any day for food or play
Came to the mariners' hollo!

His shipmates cry out against the ancient Mariner for killing the bird of good luck.

And I had done a hellish thing,
And it would work 'em woe:
For all averr'd I had kill'd the bird
That made the breeze to blow.
Ah wretch! said they, the bird to slay,
That made the breeze to blow!

648

Nor dim nor red, like God's own head,
The glorious Sun uprist:
Then all averr'd I had kill'd the bird
That brought the fog and mist.
'Twas right, said they, such birds to slay,
That bring the fog and mist.

> But when the fog cleared off, they justify the same, and thus make themselves accomplices in the crime.

The fair breeze blew, the white foam flew,
The furrow follow'd free;
We were the first that ever burst
Into that silent sea.

> The fair breeze continues; the ship enters the Pacific Ocean, and sails northward, even till it reaches the Line.

Down dropt the breeze, the sails dropt down,
'Twas sad as sad could be;
And we did speak only to break
The silence of the sea!

> The ship hath been suddenly becalmed.

All in a hot and copper sky,
The bloody Sun, at noon,
Right up above the mast did stand,
No bigger than the Moon.

Day after day, day after day,
We stuck, nor breath nor motion;
As idle as a painted ship
Upon a painted ocean.

Water, water, everywhere,
And all the boards did shrink;
Water, water, everywhere
Nor any drop to drink.

> And the Albatross begins to be avenged.

The very deep did rot: O Christ!
That ever this should be!
Yea, slimy things did crawl with legs
Upon the slimy sea.

649

About, about, in reel and rout
The death-fires danced at night;
The water, like a witch's oils,
Burnt green, and blue, and white.

A Spirit had followed them, one of the invisible inhabitants of this planet, neither departed souls nor angels; concerning whom

And some in dreams assurèd were
Of the Spirit that plagued us so;
Nine fathom deep he had follow'd us
From the land of mist and snow.

the learned Jew, Josephus, and the Platonic Constantinopolitan, Michael Psellus, may be consulted. They are very numerous, and there is no climate or element without one or more.

And every tongue, through utter drought,
Was wither'd at the root;
We could not speak, no more than if
We had been choked with soot.

The shipmates in their sore distress, would fain throw the whole guilt on the ancient Mariner in sign whereof they hang the dead sea-bird round his neck.

Ah! well a-day! what evil looks
Had I from old and young!
Instead of the cross, the Albatross
About my neck was hung.

PART III

'There passed a weary time. Each throat
Was parch'd, and glazed each eye.
A weary time! a weary time!
How glazed each weary eye!

The ancient Mariner beholdeth a sign in the element afar off.

When, looking westward, I beheld
A something in the sky.

At first it seem'd a little speck,
And then it seem'd a mist;
It moved and moved, and took at last
A certain shape, I wist.

SAMUEL TAYLOR COLERIDGE

A speck, a mist, a shape, I wist!
And still it near'd and near'd:
As if it dodged a water-sprite,
It plunged, and tack'd and veer'd.

With throats unslaked, with black lips baked,
We could nor laugh nor wail;
Through utter drought all dumb we stood!
I bit my arm, I suck'd the blood,
And cried, A sail! a sail!

At its nearer approach, it seemeth him to be a ship; and at a dear ransom he freeth his speech from the bonds of thirst.

With throats unslaked, with black lips baked,
Agape they heard me call:
Gramercy! they for joy did grin,
And all at once their breath drew in,
As they were drinking all.

A flash of joy;

See! see! (I cried) she tacks no more!
Hither to work us weal—
Without a breeze, without a tide,
She steadies with upright keel!

And horror follows. For can it be a ship that comes onward without wind or tide?

The western wave was all aflame,
The day was wellnigh done!
Almost upon the western wave
Rested the broad, bright Sun;
When that strange shape drove suddenly
Betwixt us and the Sun.

And straight the Sun was fleck'd with bars
(Heaven's Mother send us grace!),
As if through a dungeon-grate he peer'd
With broad and burning face.

It seemeth him but the skeleton of a ship.

Alas! (thought I, and my heart beat loud)
How fast she nears and nears!
Are those her sails that glance in the Sun,
Like restless gossameres?

And its ribs are seen as bars on the face of the setting Sun. The Spectre-Woman and her Death-mate, and no other, on board the skeleton ship. Like vessel, like crew!

Are those her ribs through which the Sun
Did peer, as through a grate?
And is that Woman all her crew
Is that a Death? and are there two?
Is Death that Woman's mate?

Her lips were red, her looks were free,
Her locks were yellow as gold:
Her skin was as white as leprosy,
The Nightmare Life-in-Death was she,
Who thicks man's blood with cold.

Death and Life-in-Death have diced for the ship's crew, and she (the latter) winneth the ancient Mariner.

The naked hulk alongside came,
And the twain were casting dice;
"The game is done! I've won! I've won!"
Quoth she, and whistles thrice.

No twilight within the courts of the Sun.

The Sun's rim dips; the stars rush out:
At one stride comes the dark;
With far-heard whisper, o'er the sea,
Off shot the spectre-bark.

We listen'd and look'd sideways up!
Fear at my heart, as at a cup,
My life-blood seem'd to sip!
The stars were dim, and thick the night,
The steersman's face by his lamp gleam'd white;
From the sails the dew did drip—

Till clomb above the eastern bar
The hornèd Moon, with one bright star
Within the nether tip.

At the rising
of the Moon,

One after one, by the star-dogg'd Moon,
Too quick for groan or sigh,
Each turn'd his face with a ghastly pang,
And cursed me with his eye.

One after
another,

Four times fifty living men
(And I heard nor sigh nor groan),
With heavy thump, a lifeless lump,
They dropp'd down one by one.

His shipmates
drop down
dead.

The souls did from their bodies fly—
They fled to bliss or woe!
And every soul, it pass'd me by
Like the whizz of my crossbow!'

But Life-in-
Death begins
her work on
the ancient
Mariner.

PART IV

'I fear thee, ancient Mariner!
I fear thy skinny hand!
And thou art long, and lank, and brown,
As is the ribb'd sea-sand.

The Wedding-
Guest feareth
that a spirit
is talking to
him.

I fear thee and thy glittering eye,
And thy skinny hand so brown.'—
'Fear not, fear not, thou Wedding-Guest!
This body dropt not down.

But the an-
cient Mariner
assureth him
of his bodily
life, and pro-
ceedeth to re-
late his horrible
penance.

Alone, alone, all, all alone
Alone on a wide, wide sea!
And never a saint took pity on
My soul in agony.

SAMUEL TAYLOR COLERIDGE

He despiseth the creatures of the calm.

The many men, so beautiful!
And they all dead did lie:
And a thousand thousand slimy things
Lived on; and so did I.

And envieth that they should live, and so many lie dead.

I look'd upon the rotting sea,
And drew my eyes away;
I look'd upon the rotting deck,
And there the dead men lay.

I look'd to heaven, and tried to pray;
But or ever a prayer had gusht,
A wicked whisper came, and made
My heart as dry as dust.

I closed my lids, and kept them close,
And the balls like pulses beat;
But the sky and the sea, and the sea and the sky,
Lay like a load on my weary eye,
And the dead were at my feet.

But the curse liveth for him in the eye of the dead men.

The cold sweat melted from their limbs,
Nor rot nor reek did they:
The look with which they look'd on me
Had never pass'd away.

An orphan's curse would drag to hell
A spirit from on high;
But oh! more horrible than that
Is the curse in a dead man's eye!
Seven days, seven nights, I saw that curse,
And yet I could not die.

SAMUEL TAYLOR COLERIDGE

The moving Moon went up the sky,
And nowhere did abide;
Softly she was going up,
And a star or two beside—

sojourn, yet still move onward; and everywhere the blue sky belongs to them,
and is their appointed rest and their native country and their own natural homes,
which they enter unannounced, as lords that are certainly expected, and yet
there is a silent joy at their arrival.

Her beams bemock'd the sultry main,
Like April hoar-frost spread;
But where the ship's huge shadow lay,
The charmèd water burnt alway
A still and awful red.

Beyond the shadow of the ship,
I watch'd the water-snakes:
They moved in tracks of shining white,
And when they rear'd, the elfish light
Fell off in hoary flakes.

Within the shadow of the ship
I watch'd their rich attire:
Blue, glossy green, and velvet black,
They coil'd and swam; and every track
Was a flash of golden fire.

O happy living things! no tongue
Their beauty might declare:
A spring of love gush'd from my heart,
And I bless'd them unaware:
Sure my kind saint took pity on me,
And I bless'd them unaware.

655

The spell
begins to
break.
The selfsame moment I could pray;
And from my neck so free
The Albatross fell off, and sank
Like lead into the sea.

Part V

'O sleep! it is a gentle thing,
Beloved from pole to pole!
To Mary Queen the praise be given!
She sent the gentle sleep from Heaven,
That slid into my soul.

By grace of
the holy
Mother, the
ancient
Mariner is
refreshed
with rain.
The silly buckets on the deck,
That had so long remain'd,
I dreamt that they were fill'd with dew;
And when I awoke, it rain'd.

My lips were wet, my throat was cold.
My garments all were dank;
Sure I had drunken in my dreams,
And still my body drank.

I moved, and could not feel my limbs:
I was so light—almost
I thought that I had died in sleep,
And was a blessèd ghost.

He heareth
sounds and
seeth strange
sights and
commotions
in the sky and
the element.
And soon I heard a roaring wind:
It did not come anear;
But with its sound it shook the sails,
That were so thin and sere.

The upper air burst into life;
And a hundred fire-flags sheen;
To and fro they were hurried about!
And to and fro, and in and out,
The wan stars danced between.

And the coming wind did roar more loud,
And the sails did sigh like sedge;
And the rain pour'd down from one black cloud;
The Moon was at its edge.

The thick black cloud was cleft, and still
The Moon was at its side;
Like waters shot from some high crag,
The lightning fell with never a jag,
A river steep and wide.

The loud wind never reach'd the ship,
Yet now the ship moved on!
Beneath the lightning and the Moon
The dead men gave a groan.

The bodies of the ship's crew are inspired, and the ship moves on;

They groan'd, they stirr'd, they all uprose,
Nor spake, nor moved their eyes;
It had been strange, even in a dream,
To have seen those dead men rise.

The helmsman steer'd, the ship moved on;
Yet never a breeze up-blew;
The mariners all 'gan work the ropes,
Where they were wont to do;
They raised their limbs like lifeless tools—
We were a ghastly crew.

4210

The body of my brother's son
Stood by me, knee to knee:
The body and I pull'd at one rope,
But he said naught to me.'

But not by
the souls of
the men, nor
by demons of
earth or middle
air, but by a
blessed troop
of angelic
spirits, sent
down by the
invocation of
the guardian
saint.

'I fear thee, ancient Mariner!'
'Be calm, thou Wedding-Guest:
'Twas not those souls that fled in pain,
Which to their corses came again,
But a troop of spirits blest:

For when it dawn'd—they dropp'd their arms,
And cluster'd round the mast;
Sweet sounds rose slowly through their mouths,
And from their bodies pass'd.

Around, around, flew each sweet sound,
Then darted to the Sun;
Slowly the sounds came back again,
Now mix'd, now one by one.

Sometimes a-dropping from the sky
I heard the skylark sing;
Sometimes all little birds that are,
How they seem'd to fill the sea and air
With their sweet jargoning!

And now 'twas like all instruments,
Now like a lonely flute;
And now it is an angel's song,
That makes the Heavens be mute.

It ceased; yet still the sails made on
A pleasant noise till noon,
A noise like of a hidden brook
In the leafy month of June,
That to the sleeping woods all night
Singeth a quiet tune.

Till noon we quietly sail'd on,
Yet never a breeze did breathe:
Slowly and smoothly went the ship,
Moved onward from beneath.

Under the keel nine fathom deep,
From the land of mist and snow,
The Spirit slid: and it was he
That made the ship to go.
The sails at noon left off their tune,
And the ship stood still also.

The lonesome Spirit from the South Pole carries on the ship as far as the Line, in obedience to the angelic troop, but still requireth vengeance.

The Sun, right up above the mast,
Had fix'd her to the ocean:
But in a minute she 'gan stir,
With a short uneasy motion—
Backwards and forwards half her length
With a short uneasy motion.

Then like a pawing horse let go,
She made a sudden bound:
It flung the blood into my head,
And I fell down in a swound.

The Polar
Spirit's fellow
demons, the
invisible inhabi-
tants of the
element, take
part in his
wrong; and
two of them
relate, one to
the other, that
penance long
and heavy for
the ancient
Mariner hath
been accorded
to the Polar
Spirit, who
returneth
southward.

How long in that same fit I lay,
I have not to declare;
But ere my living life return'd,
I heard, and in my soul discern'd
Two voices in the air.

"Is it he?" quoth one, "is this the man?
By Him who died on cross,
With his cruel bow he laid full low
The harmless Albatross.

The Spirit who bideth by himself
In the land of mist and snow,
He loved the bird that loved the man
Who shot him with his bow."

The other was a softer voice,
As soft as honey-dew:
Quoth he, "The man hath penance done,
And penance more will do."

Part VI

First Voice:

' "But tell me, tell me! speak again,
Thy soft response renewing—
What makes that ship drive on so fast?
What is the Ocean doing?"

Second Voice:

"Still as a slave before his lord,
The Ocean hath no blast;
His great bright eye most silently
Up to the Moon is cast—

If he may know which way to go;
For she guides him smooth or grim.
See, brother, see! how graciously
She looketh down on him."

First Voice:

"But why drives on that ship so fast,
Without or wave or wind?"

Second Voice:

"The air is cut away before,
And closes from behind.

Fly, brother, fly! more high, more high!
Or we shall be belated:
For slow and slow that ship will go,
When the Mariner's trance is abated."

I woke, and we were sailing on
As in a gentle weather:
'Twas night, calm night, the Moon was high;
The dead men stood together.

All stood together on the deck,
For a charnel-dungeon fitter:
All fix'd on me their stony eyes,
That in the Moon did glitter.

The pang, the curse, with which they died,
Had never pass'd away:
I could not draw my eyes from theirs,
Nor turn them up to pray.

And now this spell was snapt: once more
I viewed the ocean green,
And look'd far forth, yet little saw
Of what had else been seen—

The Mariner hath been cast into a trance; for the angelic power causeth the vessel to drive northward faster than human life could endure.

The supernatural motion is retarded; the Mariner awakes, and his penance begins anew.

The curse is finally expiated.

661

Like one that on a lonesome road
Doth walk in fear and dread,
And having once turn'd round, walks on,
And turns no more his head;
Because he knows a frightful fiend
Doth close behind him tread.

But soon there breathed a wind on me,
Nor sound nor motion made:
Its path was not upon the sea,
In ripple or in shade.

It raised my hair, it fann'd my cheek
Like a meadow-gale of spring—
It mingled strangely with my fears,
Yet it felt like a welcoming.

Swiftly, swiftly flew the ship,
Yet she sail'd softly too:
Sweetly, sweetly blew the breeze—
On me alone it blew.

And the ancient Mariner beholdeth his native country. O dream of joy! is this indeed
The lighthouse top I see?
Is this the hill? is this the kirk?
Is this mine own countree?

We drifted o'er the harbour-bar,
And I with sobs did pray—
O let me be awake, my God!
Or let me sleep alway.

The harbour-bay was clear as glass,
So smoothly it was strewn!
And on the bay the moonlight lay,
And the shadow of the Moon.

The rock shone bright, the kirk no less
That stands above the rock:
The moonlight steep'd in silentness
The steady weathercock.

And the bay was white with silent light
Till rising from the same,
Full many shapes, that shadows were,
In crimson colours came.

The angelic
spirits leave the
dead bodies,

A little distance from the prow
Those crimson shadows were:
I turn'd my eyes upon the deck—
O Christ! what saw I there!

And appear in
their own forms
of light.

Each corse lay flat, lifeless and flat,
And, by the holy rood!
A man all light, a seraph-man,
On every corse there stood.

This seraph-band, each waved his hand:
It was a heavenly sight!
They stood as signals to the land,
Each one a lovely light;

This seraph-band, each waved his hand,
No voice did they impart—
No voice; but O, the silence sank
Like music on my heart.

But soon I heard the dash of oars,
I heard the Pilot's cheer;
My head was turn'd perforce away,
And I saw a boat appear.

663

The Pilot and the Pilot's boy,
I heard them coming fast:
Dear Lord in Heaven! it was a joy
The dead men could not blast.

I saw a third—I heard his voice:
It is the Hermit good!
He singeth loud his godly hymns
That he makes in the wood.
He'll shrieve my soul, he'll wash away
The Albatross's blood.

Part VII

The Hermit
of the Wood.

'This hermit good lives in that wood
Which slopes down to the sea.
How loudly his sweet voice he rears!
He loves to talk with marineres
That come from a far countree.

He kneels at morn, and noon, and eve—
He hath a cushion plump.
It is the moss that wholly hides
The rotted old oak-stump.

The skiff-boat near'd: I heard them talk,
"Why, this is strange, I trow!
Where are those lights so many and fair,
That signal made but now?"

Approacheth
the ship with
wonder.

"Strange, by my faith!" the Hermit said—
"And they answer'd not our cheer!
The planks look warp'd! and see those sails
How thin they are and sere!
I never saw aught like to them,
Unless perchance it were

Brown skeletons of leaves that lag
My forest-brook along;
When the ivy-tod is heavy with snow,
And the owlet whoops to the wolf below,
That eats the she-wolf's young."

"Dear Lord! it hath a fiendish look—
(The Pilot made reply)
I am a-fear'd."—"Push on, push on!"
Said the Hermit cheerily.

The boat came closer to the ship,
But I nor spake nor stirr'd;
The boat came close beneath the ship,
And straight a sound was heard.

Under the water it rumbled on   The ship sud-
Still louder and more dread: denly sinketh.
It reach'd the ship, it split the bay;
The ship went down like lead

Stunn'd by that loud and dreadful sound,   The ancient
Which sky and ocean smote,   Mariner is
Like one that hath been seven days drown'd   saved in the
My body lay afloat;   Pilot's boat.
But swift as dreams, myself I found
Within the Pilot's boat.

Upon the whirl, where sank the ship,
The boat spun round and round;
And all was still, save that the hill
Was telling of the sound.

I moved my lips—the Pilot shriek'd
And fell down in a fit;
The holy Hermit raised his eyes,
And pray'd where he did sit.

I took the oars: the Pilot's boy,
Who now doth crazy go,
Laugh'd loud and long, and all the while
His eyes went to and fro.
"Ha! ha!" quoth he, "full plain I see
The Devil knows how to row."

The ancient Mariner earnestly entreateth the Hermit to shrieve him; and the penance of life falls on him.

And now, all in my own countree,
I stood on the firm land!
The Hermit stepp'd forth from the boat,
And scarcely he could stand.

"O shrieve me, shrieve me, holy man!"
The Hermit cross'd his brow.
"Say quick," quoth he, "I bid thee say—
What manner of man art thou?"

And ever and anon throughout his future life an agony constraineth him to travel from land to land;

Forthwith this frame of mine was wrench'd
With a woful agony,
Which forced me to begin my tale;
And then it left me free.

Since then, at an uncertain hour,
That agony returns:
And till my ghastly tale is told,
This heart within me burns.

I pass, like night, from land to land;
I have strange power of speech;

666

That moment that his face I see,
I know the man that must hear me:
To him my tale I teach.

What loud uproar bursts from that door!
The wedding-guests are there:
But in the garden-bower the bride
And bride-maids singing are:
And hark, the little vesper bell,
Which biddeth me to prayer!

O Wedding-Guest! this soul hath been
Alone on a wide, wide sea:
So lonely 'twas, that God Himself
Scarce seemèd there to be.

O sweeter than the marriage-feast,
'Tis sweeter far to me,
To walk together to the kirk
With a goodly company!—

To walk together to the kirk,
And all together pray,
While each to his great Father bends,
Old men, and babes, and loving friends,
And youths and maidens gay!

Farewell, farewell! but this I tell
To thee, thou Wedding-Guest!
He prayeth well, who loveth well
Both man and bird and beast.

And to teach, by his own example, love and reverence to all things that God made and loveth.

He prayeth best, who loveth best
All things both great and small;
For the dear God who loveth us,
He made and loveth all.'

The Mariner, whose eye is bright,
Whose beard with age is hoar,
Is gone: and now the Wedding-Guest
Turn'd from the bridegroom's door.

He went like one that hath been stunn'd,
And is of sense forlorn:
A sadder and a wiser man
He rose the morrow morn.

563 *Kubla Khan*

IN Xanadu did Kubla Khan
A stately pleasure-dome decree:
Where Alph, the sacred river, ran
Through caverns measureless to man
   Down to a sunless sea.
So twice five miles of fertile ground
   With walls and towers were girdled round:
And there were gardens bright with sinuous rills
Where blossom'd many an incense-bearing tree;
And here were forests ancient as the hills,
Enfolding sunny spots of greenery.

But O, that deep romantic chasm which slanted
Down the green hill athwart a cedarn cover!
A savage place! as holy and enchanted
As e'er beneath a waning moon was haunted
By woman wailing for her demon-lover!
And from this chasm, with ceaseless turmoil seething,
As if this earth in fast thick pants were breathing,
A mighty fountain momently was forced;

Amid whose swift half-intermitted burst
Huge fragments vaulted like rebounding hail,
Or chaffy grain beneath the thresher's flail:
And 'mid these dancing rocks at once and ever
It flung up momently the sacred river.
Five miles meandering with a mazy motion
Through wood and dale the sacred river ran,
Then reach'd the caverns measureless to man,
And sank in tumult to a lifeless ocean:
And 'mid this tumult Kubla heard from far
Ancestral voices prophesying war!

     The shadow of the dome of pleasure
       Floated midway on the waves;
     Where was heard the mingled measure
       From the fountain and the caves.
  It was a miracle of rare device,
  A sunny pleasure-dome with caves of ice!

  A damsel with a dulcimer
    In a vision once I saw:
  It was an Abyssinian maid,
    And on her dulcimer she play'd,
  Singing of Mount Abora.
  Could I revive within me,
    Her symphony and song,
To such a deep delight 'twould win me,
That with music loud and long,
I would build that dome in air,
That sunny dome! those caves of ice!
And all who heard should see them there,
And all should cry, Beware! Beware!
His flashing eyes, his floating hair!

Weave a circle round him thrice,
　　And close your eyes with holy dread,
　　For he on honey-dew hath fed,
And drunk the milk of Paradise.

564　　*Love*

ALL thoughts, all passions, all delights,
　　Whatever stirs this mortal frame,
All are but ministers of Love,
　　And feed his sacred flame.

Oft in my waking dreams do I
Live o'er again that happy hour,
When midway on the mount I lay,
　　Beside the ruin'd tower.

The moonshine, stealing o'er the scene,
Had blended with the lights of eve;
And she was there, my hope, my joy,
　　My own dear Genevieve!

She lean'd against the armèd man,
The statue of the armèd Knight;
She stood and listen'd to my lay,
　　Amid the lingering light.

Few sorrows hath she of her own,
My hope! my joy! my Genevieve!
She loves me best whene'er I sing
　　The songs that make her grieve.

I play'd a soft and doleful air;
I sang an old and moving story—
An old rude song, that suited well
　　That ruin wild and hoary.

She listen'd with a flitting blush,
With downcast eyes and modest grace;
For well she knew I could not choose
 But gaze upon her face.

I told her of the Knight that wore
Upon his shield a burning brand;
And that for ten long years he woo'd
 The Lady of the Land.

I told her how he pined: and ah!
The deep, the low, the pleading tone
With which I sang another's love,
 Interpreted my own.

She listen'd with a flitting blush,
With downcast eyes, and modest grace;
And she forgave me, that I gazed
 Too fondly on her face!

But when I told the cruel scorn
That crazed that bold and lovely Knight,
And that he cross'd the mountain-woods,
 Nor rested day nor night;

That sometimes from the savage den,
And sometimes from the darksome shade,
And sometimes starting up at once
 In green and sunny glade—

There came and look'd him in the face
An angel beautiful and bright;
And that he knew it was a Fiend,
 This miserable Knight!

And that, unknowing what he did,
He leap'd amid a murderous band,
And saved from outrage worse than death
    The Lady of the Land;—

And how she wept and clasp'd his knees;
And how she tended him in vain—
And ever strove to expiate
    The scorn that crazed his brain;—

And that she nursed him in a cave;
And how his madness went away,
When on the yellow forest leaves
    A dying man he lay;—

His dying words—but when I reach'd
That tenderest strain of all the ditty,
My faltering voice and pausing harp
    Disturb'd her soul with pity!

All impulses of soul and sense
Had thrill'd my guileless Genevieve;
The music and the doleful tale,
    The rich and balmy eve;

And hopes, and fears that kindle hope,
An undistinguishable throng,
And gentle wishes long subdued,
    Subdued and cherish'd long!

She wept with pity and delight,
She blush'd with love and virgin shame;
And like the murmur of a dream,
    I heard her breathe my name.

Her bosom heaved—she stepp'd aside,
As conscious of my look she stept—
Then suddenly, with timorous eye
    She fled to me and wept.

She half enclosed me with her arms,
She press'd me with a meek embrace;
And bending back her head, look'd up,
    And gazed upon my face.

'Twas partly love, and partly fear,
And partly 'twas a bashful art,
That I might rather feel, than see,
    The swelling of her heart.

I calm'd her fears, and she was calm,
And told her love with virgin pride;
And so I won my Genevieve,
    My bright and beauteous Bride.

565   *Youth and Age*

VERSE, a breeze 'mid blossoms straying,
   Where Hope clung feeding, like a bee—
Both were mine! Life went a-maying
With Nature, Hope, and Poesy,
           When I was young!
When I was young?—Ah, woful When!
Ah! for the change 'twixt Now and Then!
This breathing house not built with hands,
This body that does me grievous wrong,
O'er aery cliffs and glittering sands,
How lightly then it flash'd along—
Like those trim skiffs, unknown of yore,

On winding lakes and rivers wide,
That ask no aid of sail or oar,
That fear no spite of wind or tide!
Naught cared this body for wind or weather
When Youth and I lived in 't together.

Flowers are lovely! Love is flower-like;
Friendship is a sheltering tree;
O the joys, that came down shower-like,
Of Friendship, Love, and Liberty,
                              Ere I was old!

Ere I was old? Ah, woful Ere,
Which tells me, Youth's no longer here!
O Youth! for years so many and sweet,
'Tis known that thou and I were one;
I'll think it but a fond conceit—
It cannot be that thou art gone!
Thy vesper-bell hath not yet toll'd—
And thou wert aye a masker bold!
What strange disguise hast now put on,
To make believe that thou art gone?
I see these locks in silvery slips,
This drooping gait, this alter'd size:
But springtide blossoms on thy lips,
And tears take sunshine from thine eyes!
Life is but thought: so think I will
That Youth and I are housemates still.

Dewdrops are the gems of morning,
But the tears of mournful eve!
Where no hope is, life 's a warning
That only serves to make us grieve,
                              When we are old!

That only serves to make us grieve
With oft and tedious taking-leave,
Like some poor nigh-related guest
That may not rudely be dismist.
Yet hath outstay'd his welcome while,
And tells the jest without the smile.

566 *Time, Real and Imaginary*

AN ALLEGORY

ON the wide level of a mountain's head
   (I knew not where, but 'twas some faery place),
Their pinions, ostrich-like, for sails outspread,
Two lovely children run an endless race,
     A sister and a brother!
     This far outstripp'd the other;
Yet ever runs she with reverted face,
And looks and listens for the boy behind:
     For he, alas! is blind!
O'er rough and smooth with even step he pass'd,
And knows not whether he be first or last.

567 *Work without Hope*

ALL Nature seems at work. Slugs leave their lair—
  The bees are stirring—birds are on the wing—
And Winter, slumbering in the open air,
Wears on his smiling face a dream of Spring!
And I, the while, the sole unbusy thing,
Nor honey make, nor pair, nor build, nor sing.

Yet well I ken the banks where amaranths blow,
Have traced the fount whence streams of nectar flow.

Bloom, O ye amaranths! bloom for whom ye may,
For me ye bloom not! Glide, rich streams, away!
With lips unbrighten'd, wreathless brow, I stroll:
And would you learn the spells that drowse my soul?
Work without Hope draws nectar in a sieve,
And Hope without an object cannot live.

568 *Glycine's Song*

A SUNNY shaft did I behold,
  From sky to earth it slanted:
And poised therein a bird so bold—
  Sweet bird, thou wert enchanted!

He sank, he rose, he twinkled, he troll'd
  Within that shaft of sunny mist;
His eyes of fire, his beak of gold,
  All else of amethyst!

And thus he sang: 'Adieu! adieu!
Love's dreams prove seldom true.
The blossoms, they make no delay:
The sparkling dew-drops will not stay.
    Sweet month of May,
      We must away;
    Far, far away!
      To-day! to-day!'

ROBERT SOUTHEY

1774-1843

569 *His Books*

M Y days among the Dead are past;
  Around me I behold,
Where'er these casual eyes are cast,
  The mighty minds of old:

ROBERT SOUTHEY

My never-failing friends are they,
With whom I converse day by day.

With them I take delight in weal
   And seek relief in woe;
And while I understand and feel
   How much to them I owe,
My cheeks have often been bedew'd
With tears of thoughtful gratitude.

My thoughts are with the Dead; with them
   I live in long-past years,
Their virtues love, their faults condemn,
   Partake their hopes and fears;
And from their lessons seek and find
Instruction with an humble mind.

My hopes are with the Dead; anon
   My place with them will be,
And I with them shall travel on
   Through all Futurity;
Yet leaving here a name, I trust,
That will not perish in the dust.

WALTER SAVAGE LANDOR

1775–1864

570   *Corinna, from Athens, to Tanagra*

TANAGRA! think not I forget
   Thy beautifully-storey'd streets;
Be sure my memory bathes yet
   In clear Thermodon, and yet greets

WALTER SAVAGE LANDOR

The blythe and liberal shepherd boy,
Whose sunny bosom swells with joy
When we accept his matted rushes
Upheaved with sylvan fruit; away he bounds, and blushes.

I promise to bring back with me
    What thou with transport wilt receive,
The only proper gift for thee,
    Of which no mortal shall bereave
In later times thy mouldering walls,
Until the last old turret falls;
A crown, a crown from Athens won!
A crown no god can wear, beside Latona's son.

There may be cities who refuse
    To their own child the honours due,
And look ungently on the Muse;
    But ever shall those cities rue
The dry, unyielding, niggard breast,
Offering no nourishment, no rest,
To that young head which soon shall rise
Disdainfully, in might and glory, to the skies.

Sweetly where cavern'd Dirce flows
    Do white-arm'd maidens chaunt my lay,
Flapping the while with laurel-rose
    The honey-gathering tribes away;
And sweetly, sweetly, Attick tongues
Lisp your Corinna's early songs;
To her with feet more graceful come
The verses that have dwelt in kindred breasts at home

O let thy children lean aslant
    Against the tender mother's knee,
And gaze into her face, and want
    To know what magic there can be
In words that urge some eyes to dance,
While others as in holy trance
Look up to heaven; be such my praise!
Why linger? I must haste, or lose the Delphick bays.

571   *The Maid's Lament*

I LOVED him not; and yet now he is gone,
    I feel I am alone.
I check'd him while he spoke; yet, could he speak,
    Alas! I would not check.
For reasons not to love him once I sought,
    And wearied all my thought
To vex myself and him; I now would give
    My love, could he but live
Who lately lived for me, and when he found
    'Twas vain, in holy ground
He hid his face amid the shades of death.
    I waste for him my breath
Who wasted his for me; but mine returns,
    And this lorn bosom burns
With stifling heat, heaving it up in sleep,
    And waking me to weep
Tears that had melted his soft heart: for years
    Wept he as bitter tears.
Merciful God!' such was his latest prayer,
    'These may she never share!'

Quieter is his breath, his breast more cold
    Than daisies in the mould,
Where children spell, athwart the churchyard gate,
    His name and life's brief date.
Pray for him, gentle souls, whoe'er you be,
    And, O, pray too for me!

572   *Rose Aylmer*

AH, what avails the sceptred race!
    Ah, what the form divine!
What every virtue, every grace!
    Rose Aylmer, all were thine.

Rose Aylmer, whom these wakeful eyes
    May weep, but never see,
A night of memories and sighs
    I consecrate to thee.

573   *Ianthe*

FROM you, Ianthe, little troubles pass
    Like little ripples down a sunny river;
Your pleasures spring like daisies in the grass,
    Cut down, and up again as blithe as ever.

574   *Ianthe's Question*

'DO you remember me? or are you proud?'
    Lightly advancing thro' her star-trimm'd crowd,
Ianthe said, and look'd into my eyes.
'A *yes*, a *yes* to both: for Memory
Where you but once have been must ever be,
    And at your voice Pride from his throne must rise.'

575 *Verse*

PAST ruin'd Ilion Helen lives,
  Alcestis rises from the shades;
Verse calls them forth; 'tis verse that gives
  Immortal youth to mortal maids.

Soon shall Oblivion's deepening veil
  Hide all the peopled hills you see,
The gay, the proud, while lovers hail
  These many summers you and me.

576 *Proud Word you never spoke*

PROUD word you never spoke, but you will speak
  Four not exempt from pride some future day.
Resting on one white hand a warm wet cheek,
  Over my open volume you will say,
'This man loved *me*'—then rise and trip away.

577 *Mother, I cannot mind my Wheel*

MOTHER, I cannot mind my wheel;
  My fingers ache, my lips are dry:
O, if you felt the pain I feel!
  But O, who ever felt as I?

No longer could I doubt him true—
  All other men may use deceit;
He always said my eyes were blue,
  And often swore my lips were sweet.

578 *Of Clementina*

IN Clementina's artless mien
   Lucilla asks me what I see,
And are the roses of sixteen
        Enough for me?

Lucilla asks, if that be all,
   Have I not cull'd as sweet before:
Ah yes, Lucilla! and their fall
        I still deplore.

I now behold another scene,
   Where Pleasure beams with Heaven's own light,
More pure, more constant, more serene,
        And not less bright.

Faith, on whose breast the Loves repose,
   Whose chain of flowers no force can sever,
And Modesty who, when she goes,
        Is gone for ever.

579 *Alciphron and Leucippe*

AN ancient chestnut's blossoms threw
   Their heavy odour over two:
Leucippe, it is said, was one;
The other, then, was Alciphron.
'Come, come! why should we stand beneath
This hollow tree's unwholesome breath?'
Said Alciphron, 'here's not a blade
Of grass or moss, and scanty shade.
Come; it is just the hour to rove
In the lone dingle shepherds love;

There, straight and tall, the hazel twig
Divides the crookèd rock-held fig,
O'er the blue pebbles where the rill
In winter runs and may run still.
Come then, while fresh and calm the air,
And while the shepherds are not there.'

Leucippe. But I would rather go when they
Sit round about and sing and play.
Then why so hurry me? for you
Like play and song, and shepherds too.

Alciphron. I like the shepherds very well,
And song and play, as you can tell.
But there is play, I sadly fear,
And song I would not have you hear.

Leucippe. What can it be? What can it be?

Alciphron. To you may none of them repeat
The play that you have play'd with me,
The song that made your bosom beat.

Leucippe. Don't keep your arm about my waist.

Alciphron. Might you not stumble?

Leucippe.   Well then, do.
But why are we in all this haste?

Alciphron. To sing.

Leucippe.   Alas! and not play too?

580   *Dirce*

STAND close around, ye Stygian set,
   With Dirce in one boat convey'd!
Or Charon, seeing, may forget
   That he is old and she a shade.

581

On Catullus

TELL me not what too well I know
About the bard of Sirmio.
Yes, in Thalia's son
Such stains there are—as when a Grace
Sprinkles another's laughing face
With nectar, and runs on.

582

The Dragon-fly

LIFE (priest and poet say) is but a dream;
I wish no happier one than to be laid
Beneath a cool syringa's scented shade,
Or wavy willow, by the running stream,
Brimful of moral, where the dragon-fly,
Wanders as careless and content as I.
Thanks for this fancy, insect king,
Of purple crest and filmy wing,
Who with indifference givest up
The water-lily's golden cup,
To come again and overlook
What I am writing in my book.
Believe me, most who read the line
Will read with hornier eyes than thine;
And yet their souls shall live for ever,
And thine drop dead into the river!
God pardon them, O insect king,
Who fancy so unjust a thing!

583

Years

YEARS, many parti-colour'd years,
Some have crept on, and some have flown
Since first before me fell those tears
I never could see fall alone.

Years, not so many, are to come,
    Years not so varied, when from you
One more will fall: when, carried home,
    I see it not, nor hear *Adieu.*

584   *Finis*

I STROVE with none, for none was worth my strife.
    Nature I loved and, next to Nature, Art:
I warm'd both hands before the fire of life;
    It sinks, and I am ready to depart.

JOSEPH BLANCO WHITE

1775–1841

585   *To Night*

MYSTERIOUS Night! when our first parent knew
    Thee from report divine, and heard thy name,
Did he not tremble for this lovely frame,
This glorious canopy of light and blue?
Yet 'neath a curtain of translucent dew,
Bathed in the rays of the great setting flame,
Hesperus with the host of heaven came,
And lo! Creation widened in man's view.
Who could have thought such darkness lay concealed
Within thy beams, O sun! or who could find,
Whilst fly and leaf and insect stood revealed,
That to such countless orbs thou mad'st us blind!
    Why do we then shun death with anxious strife?
    If Light can thus deceive, wherefore not Life?

685

586 *A Wish*

MINE be a cot beside the hill;
　　A bee-hive's hum shall soothe my ear;
A willowy brook, that turns a mill,
　　With many a fall shall linger near.

The swallow oft beneath my thatch
　　Shall twitter from her clay-built nest;
Oft shall the pilgrim lift the latch
　　And share my meal, a welcome guest.

Around my ivied porch shall spring
　　Each fragrant flower that drinks the dew;
And Lucy at her wheel shall sing
　　In russet gown and apron blue.

The village church among the trees,
　　Where first our marriage vows were given,
With merry peals shall swell the breeze
　　And point with taper spire to Heaven.

CHARLES LAMB

587 *The Old Familiar Faces*

I HAVE had playmates, I have had companions,
　　In my days of childhood, in my joyful school-days—
All, all are gone, the old familiar faces.

I have been laughing, I have been carousing,
Drinking late, sitting late, with my bosom cronies—
All, all are gone, the old familiar faces.

I loved a Love once, fairest among women:
Closed are her doors on me, I must not see her—
All, all are gone, the old familiar faces.

I have a friend, a kinder friend has no man:
Like an ingrate, I left my friend abruptly;
Left him, to muse on the old familiar faces.

Ghost-like I paced round the haunts of my childhood,
Earth seem'd a desert I was bound to traverse,
Seeking to find the old familiar faces.

Friend of my bosom, thou more than a brother,
Why wert not thou born in my father's dwelling?
So might we talk of the old familiar faces—

How some they have died, and some they have left me,
And some are taken from me; all are departed—
All, all are gone, the old familiar faces.

588   *Hester*

WHEN maidens such as Hester die
      Their place ye may not well supply,
Though ye among a thousand try
         With vain endeavour.

A month or more hath she been dead,
Yet cannot I by force be led
To think upon the wormy bed
         And her together.

A springy motion in her gait,
A rising step, did indicate
Of pride and joy no common rate,
         That flush'd her spirit:

687

I know not by what name beside
I shall it call: if 'twas not pride,
It was a joy to that allied,
    She did inherit.

Her parents held the Quaker rule,
Which doth the human feeling cool;
But she was train'd in Nature's school;
    Nature had blest her.

A waking eye, a prying mind;
A heart that stirs, is hard to bind;
A hawk's keen sight ye cannot blind;
    Ye could not Hester.

My sprightly neighbour! gone before
To that unknown and silent shore,
Shall we not meet, as heretofore,
    Some summer morning—

When from thy cheerful eyes a ray
Hath struck a bliss upon the day,
A bliss that would not go away,
    A sweet forewarning?

589   *On an Infant dying as soon as born*

I SAW where in the shroud did lurk
  A curious frame of Nature's work;
A floweret crush'd in the bud,
A nameless piece of Babyhood,
Was in her cradle-coffin lying;
Extinct, with scarce the sense of dying:
So soon to exchange the imprisoning womb

For darker closets of the tomb!
She did but ope an eye, and put
A clear beam forth, then straight up shut
For the long dark: ne'er more to see
Through glasses of mortality.

Riddle of destiny, who can show
What thy short visit meant, or know
What thy errand here below?
Shall we say that Nature blind
Check'd her hand, and changed her mind,
Just when she had exactly wrought
A finish'd pattern without fault?
Could she flag, or could she tire,
Or lack'd she the Promethean fire
(With her nine moons' long workings sicken'd)
That should thy little limbs have quicken'd?
Limbs so firm, they seem'd to assure
Life of health, and days mature:
Woman's self in miniature!
Limbs so fair, they might supply
(Themselves now but cold imagery)
The sculptor to make Beauty by.
Or did the stern-eyed Fate descry
That babe or mother, one must die;
So in mercy left the stock
And cut the branch; to save the shock
Of young years widow'd, and the pain
When single state comes back again
To the lone man who, reft of wife,
Thenceforward drags a maimèd life?
The economy of Heaven is dark,
And wisest clerks have miss'd the mark,

Why human buds, like this, should fall,
More brief than fly ephemeral
That has his day; while shrivell'd crones
Stiffen with age to stocks and stones;
And crabbèd use the conscience sears
In sinners of an hundred years.

Mother's prattle, mother's kiss,
Baby fond, thou ne'er wilt miss:
Rites, which custom does impose,
Silver bells, and baby clothes;
Coral redder than those lips
Which pale death did late eclipse;
Music framed for infants' glee,
Whistle never tuned for thee;
Though thou want'st not, thou shalt have them,
Loving hearts were they which gave them.
Let not one be missing; nurse,
See them laid upon the hearse
Of infant slain by doom perverse.
Why should kings and nobles have
Pictured trophies to their grave,
And we, churls, to thee deny
Thy pretty toys with thee to lie—
A more harmless vanity?

THOMAS CAMPBELL 1774–1844
590 *Ye Mariners of England*

YE Mariners of England
  That guard our native seas!
Whose flag has braved a thousand years
  The battle and the breeze!

Your glorious standard launch again
   To match another foe;
And sweep through the deep,
   While the stormy winds do blow!
While the battle rages loud and long
   And the stormy winds do blow.

The spirits of your fathers
   Shall start from every wave—
For the deck it was their field of fame,
   And Ocean was their grave:
Where Blake and mighty Nelson fell
   Your manly hearts shall glow,
As ye sweep through the deep,
   While the stormy winds do blow!
While the battle rages loud and long
   And the stormy winds do blow.

Britannia needs no bulwarks,
   No towers along the steep;
Her march is o'er the mountain-waves,
   Her home is on the deep.
With thunders from her native oak
   She quells the floods below,
As they roar on the shore,
   When the stormy winds do blow!
When the battle rages loud and long,
   And the stormy winds do blow.

The meteor flag of England
   Shall yet terrific burn;
Till danger's troubled night depart
   And the star of peace return.
Then, then, ye ocean-warriors!

Our song and feast shall flow
To the fame of your name,
    When the storm has ceased to blow!
When the fiery fight is heard no more,
    And the storm has ceased to blow.

591   *The Battle of the Baltic*

OF Nelson and the North
    Sing the glorious day's renown,
When to battle fierce came forth
All the might of Denmark's crown,
And her arms along the deep proudly shone;
By each gun the lighted brand
In a bold determined hand,
And the Prince of all the land
Led them on.

Like leviathans afloat
Lay their bulwarks on the brine,
While the sign of battle flew
On the lofty British line:
It was ten of April morn by the chime:
As they drifted on their path
There was silence deep as death,
And the boldest held his breath
For a time.

But the might of England flush'd
To anticipate the scene;
And her van the fleeter rush'd
O'er the deadly space between:
'Hearts of oak!' our captains cried, when each gun

THOMAS CAMPBELL

From its adamantine lips
Spread a death-shade round the ships,
Like the hurricane eclipse
Of the sun.

Again! again! again!
And the havoc did not slack,
Till a feeble cheer the Dane
To our cheering sent us back;—
Their shots along the deep slowly boom:—
Then ceased—and all is wail,
As they strike the shatter'd sail,
Or in conflagration pale
Light the gloom.

Out spoke the victor then
As he hail'd them o'er the wave:
'Ye are brothers! ye are men!
And we conquer but to save:—
So peace instead of death let us bring:
But yield, proud foe, thy fleet,
With the crews, at England's feet,
And make submission meet
To our King.' . . .

Now joy, old England, raise!
For the tidings of thy might,
By the festal cities' blaze,
Whilst the wine-cup shines in light!
And yet amidst that joy and uproar,
Let us think of them that sleep
Full many a fathom deep,
By thy wild and stormy steep,
Elsinore!

THOMAS MOORE

1779–1852

592
The Young May Moon

THE young May moon is beaming, love,
The glow-worm's lamp is gleaming, love;
How sweet to rove
Through Morna's grove,
When the drowsy world is dreaming, love!
Then awake!—the heavens look bright, my dear,
'Tis never too late for delight, my dear;
And the best of all ways
To lengthen our days
Is to steal a few hours from the night, my dear!

Now all the world is sleeping, love,
But the Sage, his star-watch keeping, love,
And I, whose star
More glorious far
Is the eye from that casement peeping, love.
Then awake!—till rise of sun, my dear,
The Sage's glass we'll shun, my dear,
Or in watching the flight
Of bodies of light
He might happen to take thee for one, my dear!

593
The Light of Other Days

OFT, in the stilly night,
Ere slumber's chain has bound me,
Fond Memory brings the light
Of other days around me:
The smiles, the tears
Of boyhood's years,

694

The words of love then spoken;
　　The eyes that shone,
　　Now dimm'd and gone,
The cheerful hearts now broken!
Thus, in the stilly night,
　　Ere slumber's chain has bound me,
Sad Memory brings the light
　　Of other days around me.

When I remember all
　　The friends, so link'd together,
I've seen around me fall
　　Like leaves in wintry weather,
　　　　I feel like one
　　　　Who treads alone
　　Some banquet-hall deserted,
　　　　Whose lights are fled,
　　　　Whose garlands dead,
　　And all but he departed!
Thus, in the stilly night,
　　Ere slumber's chain has bound me,
Sad Memory brings the light
　　Of other days around me.

594　　　*At the Mid Hour of Night*

AT the mid hour of night, when stars are weeping, I fly
　To the lone vale we loved, when life shone warm in
　　thine eye;
　And I think oft, if spirits can steal from the regions of air
　To revisit past scenes of delight, thou wilt come to me there,
And tell me our love is remember'd even in the sky.

Then I sing the wild song it once was rapture to hear,
When our voices commingling breathed like one on the ear;
   And as Echo far off through the vale my sad orison rolls,
   I think, O my love! 'tis thy voice from the Kingdom of
      Souls
Faintly answering still the notes that once were so dear.

EDWARD THURLOW, LORD THURLOW

1781–1829

595   *May*

MAY! queen of blossoms,
   And fulfilling flowers,
With what pretty music
   Shall we charm the hours?
Wilt thou have pipe and reed,
Blown in the open mead?
Or to the lute give heed
   In the green bowers?

Thou hast no need of us,
   Or pipe or wire;
Thou hast the golden bee
   Ripen'd with fire;
And many thousand more
Songsters, that thee adore,
Filling earth's grassy floor
   With new desire.

Thou hast thy mighty herds,
   Tame and free-livers;
Doubt not, thy music too
   In the deep rivers;

And the whole plumy flight
Warbling the day and night—
Up at the gates of light,
  See, the lark quivers!

EBENEZER ELLIOTT

1781-1849

596 *Plaint*

DARK, deep, and cold the current flows
  Unto the sea where no wind blows,
Seeking the land which no one knows.

O'er its sad gloom still comes and goes
The mingled wail of friends and foes,
Borne to the land which no one knows.

Why shrieks for help yon wretch, who goes
With millions, from a world of woes,
Unto the land which no one knows?

Though myriads go with him who goes,
Alone he goes where no wind blows,
Unto the land which no one knows.

For all must go where no wind blows,
And none can go for him who goes;
None, none return whence no one knows.

Yet why should he who shrieking goes
With millions, from a world of woes,
Reunion seek with it or those?

Alone with God, where no wind blows,
And Death, his shadow—doom'd, he goes.
That God is there the shadow shows.

EBENEZER ELLIOTT

O shoreless Deep, where no wind blows!
And thou, O Land which no one knows!
That God is All, His shadow shows.

ALLAN CUNNINGHAM

1784-1842

597 *Hame, Hame, Hame*

HAME, hame, hame, O hame fain wad I be—
O hame, hame, hame, to my ain countree!

When the flower is i' the bud and the leaf is on the tree,
The larks shall sing me hame in my ain countree;
Hame, hame, hame, O hame fain wad I be—
O hame, hame, hame, to my ain countree!

The green leaf o' loyaltie 's beginning for to fa',
The bonnie White Rose it is withering an' a';
But I'll water 't wi' the blude of usurping tyrannie,
An' green it will graw in my ain countree.

O, there 's nocht now frae ruin my country can save,
But the keys o' kind heaven, to open the grave;
That a' the noble martyrs wha died for loyaltie
May rise again an' fight for their ain countree.

The great now are gane, a' wha ventured to save,
The new grass is springing on the tap o' their grave;
But the sun through the mirk blinks blythe in my e'e,
'I'll shine on ye yet in your ain countree.'

Hame, hame, hame, O hame fain wad I be—
O hame, hame, hame, to my ain countree!

1784-1859

598 *Abou Ben Adhem*

ABOU BEN ADHEM (may his tribe increase!)
  Awoke one night from a deep dream of peace,
And saw, within the moonlight in his room,
Making it rich, and like a lily in bloom,
An angel writing in a book of gold:—
Exceeding peace had made Ben Adhem bold,
And to the presence in the room he said,

'What writest thou?'—The vision rais'd its head,
And with a look made of all sweet accord,
Answer'd, 'The names of those who love the Lord.'

'And is mine one?' said Abou. 'Nay, not so,'
Replied the angel. Abou spoke more low,
But cheerly still; and said, 'I pray thee, then,
Write me as one that loves his fellow men.'

The angel wrote, and vanish'd. The next night
It came again with a great wakening light,
And show'd the names whom love of God had blest,
And lo! Ben Adhem's name led all the rest.

599 *The Fish, the Man, and the Spirit*

TO A FISH

YOU strange, astonished-looking, angle-faced,
  Dreary-mouthed, gaping wretches of the sea,
    Gulping salt-water everlastingly,
Cold-blooded, though with red your blood be graced,
And mute, though dwellers, in the roaring waste;
    And you, all shapes beside, that fishy be,—
    Some round, some flat, some long, all devilry,
Legless, unloving, infamously chaste:—

O scaly, slippery, wet, swift, staring wights,
　　What is't ye do? What life lead? eh, dull goggles?
How do ye vary your vile days and nights?
　　How pass your Sundays? Are ye still but joggled
In ceaseless wash? Still nought but gapes, and bites,
　　And drinks, and stares, diversified with boggles?

A FISH ANSWERS

Amazing monster! that, for aught I know,
　　With the first sight of thee didst make our race
For ever stare! O flat and shocking face,
Grimly divided from the breast below!
Thou that on dry land horribly dost go
　　With a split body and most ridiculous pace,
　　Prong after prong, disgracer of all grace,
Long-useless-finned, haired, upright, unwet, slow!

O breather of unbreathable, sword-sharp air,
　　How canst exist? How bear thyself, thou dry
And dreary sloth? What particle canst share
　　Of the only blessed life, the watery?
I sometimes see of ye an actual *pair*
　　Go by! linked fin by fin! most odiously.

THE FISH TURNS INTO A MAN, AND THEN INTO A SPIRIT, AND AGAIN SPEAKS

Indulge thy smiling scorn, if smiling still,
　　O man! and loathe, but with a sort of love;
　　For difference must its use by difference prove,
And, in sweet clang, the spheres with music fill.
One of the spirits am I, that at his will
　　Live in whate'er has life—fish, eagle, dove—
　　No hate, no pride, beneath nought, nor above,
A visitor of the rounds of God's sweet skill.

Man's life is warm, glad, sad, 'twixt loves and graves,
　　Boundless in hope, honoured with pangs austere,
Heaven-gazing; and his angel-wings he craves:—
　　The fish is swift, small-needing, vague yet clear,
A cold, sweet, silver life, wrapped in round waves,
　　Quickened with touches of transporting fear.

600　　　　*Jenny kiss'd Me*

JENNY kiss'd me when we met,
　　Jumping from the chair she sat in;
Time, you thief, who love to get
　　Sweets into your list, put that in!
Say I'm weary, say I'm sad,
　　Say that health and wealth have miss'd me,
Say I'm growing old, but add,
　　Jenny kiss'd me.

JOHN KENYON

1784-1856

601　　　*Champagne Rosée*

LILY on liquid roses floating—
　　So floats yon foam o'er pink champagne:
Fain would I join such pleasant boating,
　　And prove that ruby main,
　　And float away on wine!

Those seas are dangerous (greybeards swear)
　　Whose sea-beach is the goblet's brim;
And true it is they drown Old Care—
　　But what care we for him,
　　So we but float on wine?

And true it is they cross in pain
   Who sober cross the Stygian ferry:
But only make our Styx champagne,
   And we shall cross right merry,
      Floating away on wine!

Old Charon's self shall make him mellow,
   Then gaily row his boat from shore;
While we and every jovial fellow,
   Hear unconcern'd the oar
      That dips itself in wine!

THOMAS LOVE PEACOCK

1785–1866

602   *Love and Age*

I PLAY'D with you 'mid cowslips blowing,
   When I was six and you were four;
When garlands weaving, flower-balls throwing,
   Were pleasures soon to please no more.
Through groves and meads, o'er grass and heather,
   With little playmates, to and fro,
We wander'd hand in hand together;
   But that was sixty years ago.

You grew a lovely roseate maiden,
   And still our early love was strong;
Still with no care our days were laden,
   They glided joyously along;
And I did love you very dearly,
   How dearly words want power to show;
I thought your heart was touch'd as nearly;
   But that was fifty years ago.

Then other lovers came around you,
  Your beauty grew from year to year,
And many a splendid circle found you
  The centre of its glittering sphere.
I saw you then, first vows forsaking,
  On rank and wealth your hand bestow;
O, then I thought my heart was breaking!—
  But that was forty years ago.

And I lived on, to wed another:
  No cause she gave me to repine;
And when I heard you were a mother,
  I did not wish the children mine.
My own young flock, in fair progression,
  Made up a pleasant Christmas row:
My joy in them was past expression;
  But that was thirty years ago.

You grew a matron plump and comely,
  You dwelt in fashion's brightest blaze;
My earthly lot was far more homely;
  But I too had my festal days.
No merrier eyes have ever glisten'd
  Around the hearth-stone's wintry glow,
Than when my youngest child was christen'd;
  But that was twenty years ago.

Time pass'd. My eldest girl was married,
  And I am now a grandsire gray;
One pet of four years old I've carried
  Among the wild-flower'd meads to play.

In our old fields of childish pleasure,
    Where now, as then, the cowslips blow,
She fills her basket's ample measure;
    And that is not ten years ago.

But though first love's impassion'd blindness
    Has pass'd away in colder light,
I still have thought of you with kindness,
    And shall do, till our last good-night.
The ever-rolling silent hours
    Will bring a time we shall not know,
When our young days of gathering flowers
    Will be an hundred years ago.

603   *Three Men of Gotham*

SEAMEN three! What men be ye?
    Gotham's three wise men we be.
Whither in your bowl so free?
To rake the moon from out the sea.
The bowl goes trim. The moon doth shine.
And our ballast is old wine.—
And your ballast is old wine.

Who art thou, so fast adrift?
I am he they call Old Care.
Here on board we will thee lift.
No: I may not enter there.
Wherefore so? 'Tis Jove's decree,
In a bowl Care may not be.—
In a bowl Care may not be.

THOMAS LOVE PEACOCK

Fear ye not the waves that roll?
No: in charmèd bowl we swim.
What the charm that floats the bowl?
Water may not pass the brim.
The bowl goes trim. The moon doth shine.
And our ballast is old wine.—
And your ballast is old wine.

BRYAN WALLER PROCTER

1787–1874

604   *For a Fountain*

REST! This little Fountain runs
   Thus for aye:—It never stays
For the look of summer suns,
   Nor the cold of winter days.
Whosoe'er shall wander near,
   When the Syrian heat is worst,
Let him hither come, nor fear
   Lest he may not slake his thirst:
He will find this little river
Running still, as bright as ever.
Let him drink, and onward hie,
Bearing but in thought, that I,
Erotas, bade the Naiad fall,
And thank the great god Pan for all!

GEORGE GORDON BYRON, LORD BYRON

1788–1824

605   *When we Two parted*

WHEN we two parted
   In silence and tears,
Half broken-hearted
   To sever for years,

Pale grew thy cheek and cold,
　　Colder thy kiss;
Truly that hour foretold
　　Sorrow to this.

The dew of the morning
　　Sunk chill on my brow—
It felt like the warning
　　Of what I feel now.
Thy vows are all broken,
　　And light is thy fame:
I hear thy name spoken,
　　And share in its shame.

They name thee before me,
　　A knell to mine ear;
A shudder comes o'er me—
　　Why wert thou so dear?
They know not I knew thee,
　　Who knew thee too well:
Long, long shall I rue thee,
　　Too deeply to tell.

In secret we met—
　　In silence I grieve,
That thy heart could forget,
　　Thy spirit deceive.
If I should meet thee
　　After long years,
How should I greet thee?
　　With silence and tears.

606 *We'll go no more a-roving*

SO, we'll go no more a-roving
So late into the night,
Though the heart be still as loving,
And the moon be still as bright.

For the sword outwears its sheath,
And the soul wears out the breast,
And the heart must pause to breathe,
And love itself have rest.

Though the night was made for loving,
And the day returns too soon,
Yet we'll go no more a-roving
By the light of the moon.

607 *She walks in Beauty*

SHE walks in beauty, like the night
Of cloudless climes and starry skies;
And all that's best of dark and bright
Meet in her aspect and her eyes:
Thus mellow'd to that tender light
Which heaven to gaudy day denies.

One shade the more, one ray the less,
Had half impair'd the nameless grace
Which waves in every raven tress,
Or softly lightens o'er her face;
Where thoughts serenely sweet express
How pure, how dear their dwelling-place.

And on that cheek, and o'er that brow,
   So soft, so calm, yet eloquent,
The smiles that win, the tints that glow,
   But tell of days in goodness spent,
A mind at peace with all below,
   A heart whose love is innocent!

608　　　　　　　　*The Isles of Greece*

THE isles of Greece! the isles of Greece
   Where burning Sappho loved and sung,
Where grew the arts of war and peace,
   Where Delos rose, and Phœbus sprung!
Eternal summer gilds them yet,
But all, except their sun, is set.

The Scian and the Teian muse,
   The hero's harp, the lover's lute,
Have found the fame your shores refuse:
   Their place of birth alone is mute
To sounds which echo further west
Than your sires' 'Islands of the Blest.

The mountains look on Marathon—
   And Marathon looks on the sea;
And musing there an hour alone,
   I dream'd that Greece might still be free;
For standing on the Persians' grave,
I could not deem myself a slave.

A king sate on the rocky brow
   Which looks o'er sea-born Salamis;
And ships, by thousands, lay below,
   And men in nations;—all were his!

He counted them at break of day—
And when the sun set, where were they?

And where are they? and where art thou,
    My country? On thy voiceless shore
The heroic lay is tuneless now—
    The heroic bosom beats no more!
And must thy lyre, so long divine,
Degenerate into hands like mine?

'Tis something in the dearth of fame,
    Though link'd among a fetter'd race,
To feel at least a patriot's shame,
    Even as I sing, suffuse my face;
For what is left the poet here?
For Greeks a blush—for Greece a tear.

Must *we* but weep o'er days more blest?
    Must *we* but blush?—Our fathers bled.
Earth! render back from out thy breast
    A remnant of our Spartan dead!
Of the three hundred grant but three,
To make a new Thermopylæ!

What, silent still? and silent all?
    Ah! no;—the voices of the dead
Sound like a distant torrent's fall,
    And answer, 'Let one living head,
But one, arise,—we come, we come!'
'Tis but the living who are dumb.

In vain—in vain: strike other chords;
    Fill high the cup with Samian wine!
Leave battles to the Turkish hordes,
    And shed the blood of Scio's vine!

Hark! rising to the ignoble call—
How answers each bold Bacchanal!

You have the Pyrrhic dance as yet;
   Where is the Pyrrhic phalanx gone?
Of two such lessons, why forget
   The nobler and the manlier one?
You have the letters Cadmus gave—
Think ye he meant them for a slave?

Fill high the bowl with Samian wine!
   We will not think of themes like these!
It made Anacreon's song divine:
   He served—but served Polycrates—
A tyrant; but our masters then
Were still, at least, our countrymen.

The tyrant of the Chersonese
   Was freedom's best and bravest friend;
That tyrant was Miltiades!
   O that the present hour would lend
Another despot of the kind!
Such chains as his were sure to bind.

Fill high the bowl with Samian wine!
   On Suli's rock, and Parga's shore,
Exists the remnant of a line
   Such as the Doric mothers bore;
And there, perhaps, some seed is sown,
The Heracleidan blood might own.

Trust not for freedom to the Franks—
   They have a king who buys and sells;
In native swords and native ranks
   The only hope of courage dwells:

But Turkish force and Latin fraud
Would break your shield, however broad.

Fill high the bowl with Samian wine!
   Our virgins dance beneath the shade—
I see their glorious black eyes-shine;
   But gazing on each glowing maid,
My own the burning tear-drop laves,
To think such breasts must suckle slaves.

Place me on Sunium's marbled steep,
   Where nothing, save the waves and I,
May hear our mutual murmurs sweep;
   There, swan-like, let me sing and die:
A land of slaves shall ne'er be mine—
Dash down yon cup of Samian wine!

SIR AUBREY DE VERE
609   The Children Band

1788–1846

ALL holy influences dwell within
   The breast of Childhood: instincts fresh from God
Inspire it, ere the heart beneath the rod
Of grief hath bled, or caught the plague of sin.
How mighty was that fervour which could win
   Its way to infant souls!—and was the sod
Of Palestine by infant Croises trod?
Like Joseph went they forth, or Benjamin,
In all their touching beauty to redeem?
   And did their soft lips kiss the Sepulchre?
Alas! the lovely pageant as a dream
   Faded! They sank not through ignoble fear;
They felt not Moslem steel. By mountain, stream,
   In sands, in fens, they died—no mother near!

CHARLES WOLFE

1791-1823

610   *The Burial of Sir John Moore after*
Corunna

NOT a drum was heard, not a funeral note,
    As his corse to the rampart we hurried;
Not a soldier discharged his farewell shot
    O'er the grave where our hero we buried.

We buried him darkly at dead of night,
    The sods with our bayonets turning,
By the struggling moonbeam's misty light
    And the lanthorn dimly burning.

No useless coffin enclosed his breast,
    Not in sheet or in shroud we wound him;
But he lay like a warrior taking his rest
    With his martial cloak around him.

Few and short were the prayers we said,
    And we spoke not a word of sorrow;
But we steadfastly gazed on the face that was dead,
    And we bitterly thought of the morrow.

We thought, as we hollow'd his narrow bed
    And smooth'd down his lonely pillow,
That the foe and the stranger would tread o'er his head,
    And we far away on the billow!

Lightly they'll talk of the spirit that's gone,
    And o'er his cold ashes upbraid him—
But little he'll reck, if they let him sleep on
    In the grave where a Briton has laid him.

But half of our heavy task was done
  When the clock struck the hour for retiring;
And we heard the distant and random gun
  That the foe was sullenly firing.

Slowly and sadly we laid him down,
  From the field of his fame fresh and gory;
We carved not a line, and we raised not a stone,
  But we left him alone with his glory.

611   *To Mary*

IF I had thought thou couldst have died,
    I might not weep for thee;
But I forgot, when by thy side,
    That thou couldst mortal be:
It never through my mind had past
    The time would e'er be o'er,
And I on thee should look my last,
    And thou shouldst smile no more!

And still upon that face I look,
    And think 'twill smile again;
And still the thought I will not brook,
    That I must look in vain.
But when I speak—thou dost not say
    What thou ne'er left'st unsaid;
And now I feel, as well I may,
    Sweet Mary, thou art dead!

If thou wouldst stay, e'en as thou art,
    All cold and all serene—
I still might press thy silent heart,
    And where thy smiles have been.

CHARLES WOLFE

While e'en thy chill, bleak corse I have,
    Thou seemest still mine own;
But there—I lay thee in thy grave,
    And I am now alone!

I do not think, where'er thou art,
    Thou hast forgotten me;
And I, perhaps, may soothe this heart
    In thinking too of thee:
Yet there was round thee such a dawn
    Of light ne'er seen before,
As fancy never could have drawn,
    And never can restore!

PERCY BYSSHE SHELLEY

1792–1822

612   *Hymn of Pan*

FROM the forests and highlands
    We come, we come;
From the river-girt islands,
    Where loud waves are dumb,
Listening to my sweet pipings.
    The wind in the reeds and the rushes,
      The bees on the bells of thyme,
    The birds on the myrtle bushes,
      The cicale above in the lime,
And the lizards below in the grass,
Were as silent as ever old Tmolus was,
    Listening to my sweet pipings.

714

Liquid Peneus was flowing,
    And all dark Tempe lay
In Pelion's shadow, outgrowing
    The light of the dying day,
Speeded by my sweet pipings.
    The Sileni and Sylvans and Fauns,
        And the Nymphs of the woods and waves,
    To the edge of the moist river-lawns,
        And the brink of the dewy caves,
And all that did then attend and follow,
Were silent with love, as you now, Apollo,
    With envy of my sweet pipings.

    I sang of the dancing stars,
      I sang of the dædal earth,
And of heaven, and the giant wars,
    And love, and death, and birth.
And then I changed my pipings—
    Singing how down the vale of Mænalus
      I pursued a maiden, and clasp'd a reed:
Gods and men, we are all deluded thus;
    It breaks in our bosom, and then we bleed.
All wept—as I think both ye now would,
If envy or age had not frozen your blood—
    At the sorrow of my sweet pipings.

6r3   *The Invitation*

BEST and brightest, come away!
    Fairer far than this fair Day,
Which, like thee to those in sorrow,
Comes to bid a sweet good-morrow

To the rough Year just awake
In its cradle on the brake.
The brightest hour of unborn Spring,
Through the winter wandering,
Found, it seems, the halcyon Morn
To hoar February born.
Bending from heaven, in azure mirth,
It kiss'd the forehead of the Earth;
And smiled upon the silent sea;
And bade the frozen streams be free;
And waked to music all their fountains;
And breathed upon the frozen mountains;
And like a prophetess of May
Strew'd flowers upon the barren way,
Making the wintry world appear
Like one on whom thou smilest, dear.

Away, away, from men and towns,
To the wild wood and the downs—
To the silent wilderness
Where the soul need not repress
Its music lest it should not find
An echo in another's mind,
While the touch of Nature's art
Harmonizes heart to heart.
I leave this notice on my door
For each accustom'd visitor:—
'I am gone into the fields
To take what this sweet hour yields.
Reflection, you may come to-morrow;
Sit by the fireside with Sorrow.

You with the unpaid bill, Despair,—
You tiresome verse-reciter, Care,—
I will pay you in the grave,—
Death will listen to your stave.
Expectation too, be off!
To-day is for itself enough.
Hope, in pity, mock not Woe
With smiles, nor follow where I go;
Long having lived on your sweet food,
At length I find one moment's good
After long pain: with all your love,
This you never told me of.'

Radiant Sister of the Day,
Awake! arise! and come away!
To the wild woods and the plains;
And the pools where winter rains
Image all their roof of leaves;
Where the pine its garland weaves
Of sapless green and ivy dun
Round stems that never kiss the sun;
Where the lawns and pastures be,
And the sandhills of the sea;
When the melting hoar-frost wets
The daisy-star that never sets,
And wind-flowers, and violets
Which yet join not scent to hue,
Crown the pale year weak and new;
When the night is left behind
In the deep east, dun and blind,
And the blue noon is over us,
And the multitudinous

Billows murmur at our feet
Where the earth and ocean meet,
And all things seem only one
In the universal sun.

614 *Hellas*

THE world's great age begins anew,
  The golden years return,
The earth doth like a snake renew
  Her winter weeds outworn:
Heaven smiles, and faiths and empires gleam
Like wrecks of a dissolving dream.

A brighter Hellas rears its mountains
  From waves serener far;
A new Peneus rolls his fountains
  Against the morning star;
Where fairer Tempes bloom, there sleep
Young Cyclads on a sunnier deep.

A loftier Argo cleaves the main,
  Fraught with a later prize;
Another Orpheus sings again,
  And loves, and weeps, and dies;
A new Ulysses leaves once more
Calypso for his native shore.

O write no more the tale of Troy,
  If earth Death's scroll must be—
Nor mix with Laian rage the joy
  Which dawns upon the free,
Although a subtler Sphinx renew
Riddles of death Thebes never knew.

Another Athens shall arise,
    And to remoter time
Bequeath, like sunset to the skies,
    The splendour of its prime;
And leave, if naught so bright may live,
All earth can take or Heaven can give.

Saturn and Love their long repose
    Shall burst, more bright and good
Than all who fell, than One who rose,
    Than many unsubdued:
Not gold, not blood, their altar dowers,
But votive tears and symbol flowers.

O cease! must hate and death return?
    Cease! must men kill and die?
Cease! drain not to its dregs the urn
    Of bitter prophecy!
The world is weary of the past—
O might it die or rest at last!

615   *To a Skylark*

HAIL to thee, blithe spirit!
    Bird thou never wert—
That from heaven or near it
    Pourest thy full heart
In profuse strains of unpremeditated art.

Higher still and higher
    From the earth thou springest,
Like a cloud of fire;
    The blue deep thou wingest,
And singing still dost soar, and soaring ever singest.

In the golden light'ning
Of the sunken sun,
O'er which clouds are bright'ning,
Thou dost float and run,
Like an unbodied joy whose race is just begun.

The pale purple even
Melts around thy flight;
Like a star of heaven,
In the broad daylight
Thou art unseen, but yet I hear thy shrill delight—

Keen as are the arrows
Of that silver sphere
Whose intense lamp narrows
In the white dawn clear,
Until we hardly see, we feel that it is there.

All the earth and air
With thy voice is loud,
As, when night is bare,
From one lonely cloud
The moon rains out her beams, and heaven is overflow'd.

What thou art we know not;
What is most like thee?
From rainbow clouds there flow not
Drops so bright to see,
As from thy presence showers a rain of melody:—

Like a poet hidden
In the light of thought,
Singing hymns unbidden,
Till the world is wrought
To sympathy with hopes and fears it heeded not:

Like a high-born maiden
In a palace tower,
Soothing her love-laden
Soul in secret hour
With music sweet as love, which overflows her bower:

Like a glow-worm golden
In a dell of dew,
Scattering unbeholden
Its aërial hue
Among the flowers and grass which screen it from the view:

Like a rose embower'd
In its own green leaves,
By warm winds deflower'd,
Till the scent it gives
Makes faint with too much sweet these heavy-wingèd thieves:

Sound of vernal showers
On the twinkling grass,
Rain-awaken'd flowers—
All that ever was
Joyous and clear and fresh—thy music doth surpass.

Teach us, sprite or bird,
What sweet thoughts are thine:
I have never heard
Praise of love or wine
That panted forth a flood of rapture so divine.

Chorus hymeneal,
Or triumphal chant,
Match'd with thine would be all
But an empty vaunt—
A thing wherein we feel there is some hidden want.

What objects are the fountains
    Of thy happy strain?
What fields, or waves, or mountains?
    What shapes of sky or plain?
What love of thine own kind? what ignorance of pain?

    With thy clear keen joyance
        Languor cannot be:
    Shadow of annoyance
        Never came near thee:
Thou lovest, but ne'er knew love's sad satiety.

    Waking or asleep,
        Thou of death must deem
    Things more true and deep
        Than we mortals dream,
Or how could thy notes flow in such a crystal stream?

    We look before and after,
        And pine for what is not:
    Our sincerest laughter
        With some pain is fraught;
Our sweetest songs are those that tell of saddest thought.

    Yet, if we could scorn
        Hate and pride and fear,
    If we were things born
        Not to shed a tear,
I know not how thy joy we ever should come near.

    Better than all measures
        Of delightful sound,
    Better than all treasures
        That in books are found,
Thy skill to poet were, thou scorner of the ground!

Teach me half the gladness
That thy brain must know;
Such harmonious madness
From my lips would flow,
The world should listen then, as I am listening now.

616 *The Moon*

I

AND, like a dying lady lean and pale,
Who totters forth, wrapp'd in a gauzy veil,
Out of her chamber, led by the insane
And feeble wanderings of her fading brain,
The moon arose up in the murky east
A white and shapeless mass.

II

Art thou pale for weariness
Of climbing heaven and gazing on the earth,
Wandering companionless
Among the stars that have a different birth,
And ever changing, like a joyless eye
That finds no object worth its constancy?

617 *Ode to the West Wind*

I

O WILD West Wind, thou breath of Autumn's being
Thou from whose unseen presence the leaves dead
Are driven like ghosts from an enchanter fleeing,

Yellow, and black, and pale, and hectic red,
Pestilence-stricken multitudes! O thou
Who chariotest to their dark wintry bed

The wingèd seeds, where they lie cold and low,
　Each like a corpse within its grave, until
Thine azure sister of the Spring shall blow

　Her clarion o'er the dreaming earth, and fill
(Driving sweet buds like flocks to feed in air)
　With living hues and odours plain and hill;

Wild Spirit, which art moving everywhere;
Destroyer and preserver; hear, O hear!

II

Thou on whose stream, 'mid the steep sky's commotion,
　Loose clouds like earth's decaying leaves are shed,
Shook from the tangled boughs of heaven and ocean,

　Angels of rain and lightning! there are spread
On the blue surface of thine airy surge,
　Like the bright hair uplifted from the head

Of some fierce Mænad, even from the dim verge
　Of the horizon to the zenith's height,
The locks of the approaching storm. Thou dirge

　Of the dying year, to which this closing night
Will be the dome of a vast sepulchre,
　Vaulted with all thy congregated might

Of vapours, from whose solid atmosphere
Black rain, and fire, and hail, will burst: O hear!

III

Thou who didst waken from his summer dreams
　The blue Mediterranean, where he lay,
Lull'd by the coil of his crystalline streams,

　Beside a pumice isle in Baiæ's bay,
And saw in sleep old palaces and towers
　Quivering within the wave's intenser day,

All overgrown with azure moss, and flowers
  So sweet, the sense faints picturing them! Thou
For whose path the Atlantic's level powers

  Cleave themselves into chasms, while far below
The sea-blooms and the oozy woods which wear
  The sapless foliage of the ocean, know

Thy voice, and suddenly grow gray with fear,
And tremble and despoil themselves: O hear!

IV

If I were a dead leaf thou mightest bear;
  If I were a swift cloud to fly with thee;
A wave to pant beneath thy power, and share

  The impulse of thy strength, only less free
Than thou, O uncontrollable! if even
  I were as in my boyhood, and could be

The comrade of thy wanderings over heaven,
  As then, when to outstrip thy skiey speed
Scarce seem'd a vision—I would ne'er have striven

  As thus with thee in prayer in my sore need.
O! lift me as a wave, a leaf, a cloud!
  I fall upon the thorns of life! I bleed!

A heavy weight of hours has chain'd and bow'd
One too like thee—tameless, and swift, and proud.

V

Make me thy lyre, even as the forest is:
  What if my leaves are falling like its own?
The tumult of thy mighty harmonies

Will take from both a deep autumnal tone,
Sweet though in sadness. Be thou, Spirit fierce,
　My spirit! Be thou me, impetuous one!

Drive my dead thoughts over the universe,
　Like wither'd leaves, to quicken a new birth;
And, by the incantation of this verse,

　Scatter, as from an unextinguish'd hearth
Ashes and sparks, my words among mankind!
　Be through my lips to unawaken'd earth

The trumpet of a prophecy! O Wind,
If Winter comes, can Spring be far behind?

618　　　　*The Indian Serenade*

I ARISE from dreams of thee
　In the first sweet sleep of night,
When the winds are breathing low,
　And the stars are shining bright.
I arise from dreams of thee,
　And a spirit in my feet
Hath led me—who knows how?
　To thy chamber window, Sweet!

The wandering airs they faint
　On the dark, the silent stream—
And the Champak's odours [pine]
　Like sweet thoughts in a dream;
The nightingale's complaint,
　It dies upon her heart,
As I must on thine,
　O belovèd as thou art!

O lift me from the grass!
   I die! I faint! I fail!
Let thy love in kisses rain
   On my lips and eyelids pale.
My cheek is cold and white, alas!
   My heart beats loud and fast:
O press it to thine own again,
   Where it will break at last!

619　　　　　　　*Night*

SWIFTLY walk o'er the western wave,
     Spirit of Night!
Out of the misty eastern cave,—
Where, all the long and lone daylight,
Thou wovest dreams of joy and fear
Which make thee terrible and dear,—
     Swift be thy flight!

Wrap thy form in a mantle grey,
     Star-inwrought!
Blind with thine hair the eyes of Day;
Kiss her until she be wearied out.
Then wander o'er city and sea and land,
Touching all with thine opiate wand—
     Come, long-sought!

When I arose and saw the dawn
     I sigh'd for thee;
When light rode high, and the dew was gone,
And noon lay heavy on flower and tree,

727

And the weary Day turn'd to her rest,
Lingering like an unloved guest,
   I sigh'd for thee.

Thy brother Death came, and cried,
   'Wouldst thou me?'
Thy sweet child Sleep, the filmy-eyed,
Murmur'd like a noontide bee,
'Shall I nestle near thy side?
Wouldst thou me?'—And I replied,
   'No, not thee!'

Death will come when thou art dead,
   Soon, too soon—
Sleep will come when thou art fled.
Of neither would I ask the boon
I ask of thee, belovèd Night—
Swift be thine approaching flight,
   Come soon, soon!

620   *From the Arabic*

AN IMITATION

MY faint spirit was sitting in the light
  Of thy looks, my love;
It panted for thee like the hind at noon
  For the brooks, my love.
Thy barb, whose hoofs outspeed the tempest's flight,
  Bore thee far from me;
My heart, for my weak feet were weary soon,
  Did companion thee.

Ah! fleeter far than fleetest storm or steed,
 Or the death they bear,
The heart which tender thought clothes like a dove
 With the wings of care;
In the battle, in the darkness, in the need,
 Shall mine cling to thee,
Nor claim one smile for all the comfort, love,
 It may bring to thee.

621   *Lines*

WHEN the lamp is shatter'd,
 The light in the dust lies dead;
When the cloud is scatter'd,
The rainbow's glory is shed;
 When the lute is broken,
Sweet tones are remember'd not;
 When the lips have spoken,
Loved accents are soon forgot.

 As music and splendour
Survive not the lamp and the lute,
 The heart's echoes render
No song when the spirit is mute—
 No song but sad dirges,
Like the wind through a ruin'd cell,
 Or the mournful surges
That ring the dead seaman's knell.

 When hearts have once mingled,
Love first leaves the well-built nest;
 The weak one is singled
To endure what it once possest.

O Love, who bewailest
The frailty of all things here,
    Why choose you the frailest
For your cradle, your home, and your bier?

    Its passions will rock thee,
As the storms rock the ravens on high:
    Bright reason will mock thee,
Like the sun from a wintry sky.
    From thy nest every rafter
Will rot, and thine eagle home
    Leave thee naked to laughter,
When leaves fall and cold winds come.

622   *To ——*

ONE word is too often profaned
    For me to profane it;
One feeling too falsely disdain'd
    For thee to disdain it;
One hope is too like despair
    For prudence to smother;
And pity from thee more dear
    Than that from another.

I can give not what men call love:
    But wilt thou accept not
The worship the heart lifts above
    And the heavens reject not,
The desire of the moth for the star,
    Of the night for the morrow,
The devotion to something afar
    From the sphere of our sorrow?

730

The Question

I DREAM'D that, as I wander'd by the way,
  Bare Winter suddenly was changed to Spring;
And gentle odours led my steps astray,
  Mix'd with a sound of waters murmuring
Along a shelving bank of turf, which lay
  Under a copse, and hardly dared to fling
Its green arms round the bosom of the stream,
But kiss'd it and then fled, as thou mightest in dream.

There grew pied wind-flowers and violets;
  Daisies, those pearl'd Arcturi of the earth,
The constellated flower that never sets;
  Faint oxlips; tender bluebells, at whose birth
The sod scarce heaved; and that tall flower that wets—
  Like a child, half in tenderness and mirth—
Its mother's face with heaven-collected tears
When the low wind, its playmate's voice, it hears.

And in the warm hedge grew lush eglantine,
  Green cowbind and the moonlight-colour'd May,
And cherry-blossoms, and white cups whose wine
  Was the bright dew yet drain'd not by the day;
And wild roses, and ivy serpentine,
  With its dark buds and leaves wandering astray;
And flowers, azure, black, and streak'd with gold,
Fairer than any waken'd eyes behold.

And nearer to the river's trembling edge
  There grew broad flag-flowers, purple prank'd with white,
And starry river-buds among the sedge,
  And floating water-lilies, broad and bright,

Which lit the oak that overhung the hedge
    With moonlight beams of their own watery light;
And bulrushes, and reeds of such deep green
As soothed the dazzled eye with sober sheen.

Methought that of these visionary flowers
    I made a nosegay, bound in such a way
That the same hues which in their natural bowers
    Were mingled or opposed, the like array
Kept these imprison'd children of the Hours
    Within my hand;—and then, elate and gay,
I hasten'd to the spot whence I had come,
That I might there present it—O! to whom?

624   *Remorse*

AWAY! the moor is dark beneath the moon,
    Rapid clouds have drunk the last pale beam of even:
Away! the gathering winds will call the darkness soon,
    And profoundest midnight shroud the serene lights of
    heaven.
Pause not! the time is past! Every voice cries 'Away!'
    Tempt not with one last tear thy friend's ungentle mood:
Thy lover's eye, so glazed and cold, dares not entreat thy
    stay:
    Duty and dereliction guide thee back to solitude.

Away, away! to thy sad and silent home;
    Pour bitter tears on its desolated hearth;
Watch the dim shades as like ghosts they go and come,
    And complicate strange webs of melancholy mirth.

732

The leaves of wasted autumn woods shall float around thine
head,
    The blooms of dewy Spring shall gleam beneath thy feet:
But thy soul or this world must fade in the frost that binds the
dead,
    Ere midnight's frown and morning's smile, ere thou and
peace, may meet.

The cloud shadows of midnight possess their own repose,
    For the weary winds are silent, or the moon is in the deep;
Some respite to its turbulence unresting ocean knows;
    Whatever moves or toils or grieves hath its appointed sleep.
Thou in the grave shalt rest:—yet, till the phantoms flee,
    Which that house and heath and garden made dear to thee
erewhile,
Thy remembrance and repentance and deep musings are not
free
    From the music of two voices, and the light of one sweet
smile.

625   *Music, when Soft Voices die*

MUSIC, when soft voices die,
    Vibrates in the memory;
Odours, when sweet violets sicken,
Live within the sense they quicken.

Rose leaves, when the rose is dead,
Are heap'd for the belovèd's bed;
And so thy thoughts, when thou art gone,
Love itself shall slumber on.

733

JOHN KEBLE

1792–1866

626   *November*

RED o'er the forest peers the setting sun;
   The line of yellow light dies fast away
That crown'd the eastern copse; and chill and dun
   Falls on the moor the brief November day.

Now the tired hunter winds a parting note,
   And Echo bids good-night from every glade;
Yet wait awhile and see the calm leaves float
   Each to his rest beneath their parent shade.

How like decaying life they seem to glide
   And yet no second spring have they in store;
And where they fall, forgotten to abide
   Is all their portion, and they ask no more.

Soon o'er their heads blithe April airs shall sing,
   A thousand wild-flowers round them shall unfold,
The green buds glisten in the dews of Spring,
   And all be vernal rapture as of old.

Unconscious they in waste oblivion lie,
   In all the world of busy life around
No thought of them—in all the bounteous sky
   No drop, for them, of kindly influence found.

Man's portion is to die and rise again:
   Yet he complains, while these unmurmuring part
With their sweet lives, as pure from sin and stain
   As his when Eden held his virgin heart.

JOHN CLARE

1793–1864

627 *Written in Northampton County Asylum*

I AM! yet what I am who cares, or knows?
  My friends forsake me like a memory lost.
I am the self-consumer of my woes;
   They rise and vanish, an oblivious host,
Shadows of life, whose very soul is lost.
And yet I am—I live—though I am toss'd

Into the nothingness of scorn and noise,
   Into the living sea of waking dream,
Where there is neither sense of life, nor joys,
   But the huge shipwreck of my own esteem
And all that's dear. Even those I loved the best
Are strange—nay, they are stranger than the rest.

I long for scenes where man has never trod—
   For scenes where woman never smiled or wept—
There to abide with my Creator, God,
   And sleep as I in childhood sweetly slept,
Full of high thoughts, unborn. So let me lie,—
The grass below; above, the vaulted sky.

FELICIA DOROTHEA HEMANS

1793–1835

628 *Dirge*

CALM on the bosom of thy God,
  Fair spirit, rest thee now!
E'en while with ours thy footsteps trod,
  His seal was on thy brow.

Dust, to its narrow house beneath!
  Soul, to its place on high!
They that have seen thy look in death
  No more may fear to die.

JOHN GIBSON LOCKHART

1794–1854

629 *Lines*

WHEN youthful faith hath fled,
  Of loving take thy leave;
Be constant to the dead—
  The dead cannot deceive.

Sweet modest flowers of Spring,
  How fleet your balmy day!
And Man's brief life can bring
  No secondary May:

No earthly burst again
  Of gladness out of gloom,
Fond hope and vision vain,
  Ungrateful to the tomb.

But 'tis an old belief
  That on some solemn shore
Beyond the sphere of grief
  Dear friends shall meet once more:

Beyond the sphere of Time
  And Sin and Fate's control,
Serene in endless prime
  Of body and of soul.

That creed I fain would keep,
 That hope I'll not forgo—
Eternal be the sleep
 Unless to waken so!

JOHN KEATS

1795–1821

630   *Song of the Indian Maid*

FROM 'ENDYMION'

O SORROW!
 Why dost borrow
The natural hue of health, from vermeil lips?—
 To give maiden blushes
 To the white rose bushes?
Or is it thy dewy hand the daisy tips?

O Sorrow!
 Why dost borrow
The lustrous passion from a falcon-eye?—
 To give the glow-worm light?
 Or, on a moonless night,
To tinge, on siren shores, the salt sea-spry?

O Sorrow!
 Why dost borrow
The mellow ditties from a mourning tongue?—
 To give at evening pale
 Unto the nightingale,
That thou mayst listen the cold dews among?

630 sea-spry] sea-spray.

737

O Sorrow!
Why dost borrow
Heart's lightness from the merriment of May?—
A lover would not tread
A cowslip on the head,
Though he should dance from eve till peep of day—
Nor any drooping flower
Held sacred for thy bower,
Wherever he may sport himself and play.

To Sorrow
I bade good morrow,
And thought to leave her far away behind;
But cheerly, cheerly,
She loves me dearly;
She is so constant to me, and so kind:
I would deceive her,
And so leave her,
But ah! she is so constant and so kind.

Beneath my palm-trees, by the river side,
I sat a-weeping: in the whole world wide
There was no one to ask me why I wept,—
And so I kept
Brimming the water-lily cups with tears
Cold as my fears.
Beneath my palm-trees, by the river side,
I sat a-weeping: what enamour'd bride,
Cheated by shadowy wooer from the clouds,
But hides and shrouds
Beneath dark palm-trees by a river side?

And as I sat, over the light blue hills
There came a noise of revellers: the rills
Into the wide stream came of purple hue—
      'Twas Bacchus and his crew!
The earnest trumpet spake, and silver thrills
From kissing cymbals made a merry din—
      'Twas Bacchus and his kin!
Like to a moving vintage down they came,
Crown'd with green leaves, and faces all on flame;
All madly dancing through the pleasant valley,
      To scare thee, Melancholy!
O then, O then, thou wast a simple name!
And I forgot thee, as the berried holly
By shepherds is forgotten, when in June
Tall chestnuts keep away the sun and moon:—
      I rush'd into the folly!

Within his car, aloft, young Bacchus stood,
Trifling his ivy-dart, in dancing mood,
      With sidelong laughing;
And little rills of crimson wine imbrued
His plump white arms and shoulders, enough white
      For Venus' pearly bite;
And near him rode Silenus on his ass,
Pelted with flowers as he on did pass
      Tipsily quaffing.

'Whence came ye, merry Damsels! whence came ye,
So many, and so many, and such glee?
Why have ye left your bowers desolate,
      Your lutes, and gentler fate?'—
'We follow Bacchus! Bacchus on the wing,
      A-conquering!

Bacchus, young Bacchus! good or ill betide,
We dance before him thorough kingdoms wide:—
Come hither, lady fair, and joinèd be
      To our wild minstrelsy!'

'Whence came ye, jolly Satyrs! whence came ye,
So many, and so many, and such glee?
Why have ye left your forest haunts, why left
      Your nuts in oak-tree cleft?'—
'For wine, for wine we left our kernel tree;
For wine we left our heath, and yellow brooms,
      And cold mushrooms;
For wine we follow Bacchus through the earth;
Great god of breathless cups and chirping mirth!
Come hither, lady fair, and joinèd be
      To our mad minstrelsy!'

Over wide streams and mountains great we went,
And, save when Bacchus kept his ivy tent,
Onward the tiger and the leopard pants,
      With Asian elephants:
Onward these myriads—with song and dance,
With zebras striped, and sleek Arabians' prance,
Web-footed alligators, crocodiles,
Bearing upon their scaly backs, in files,
Plump infant laughers mimicking the coil
Of seamen, and stout galley-rowers' toil:
With toying oars and silken sails they glide,
      Nor care for wind and tide.

Mounted on panthers' furs and lions' manes,
From rear to van they scour about the plains;
A three days' journey in a moment done;

And always, at the rising of the sun,
About the wilds they hunt with spear and horn.
On spleenful unicorn.

I saw Osirian Egypt kneel adown
        Before the vine-wreath crown!
I saw parch'd Abyssinia rouse and sing
        To the silver cymbals' ring!
I saw the whelming vintage hotly pierce
        Old Tartary the fierce!
The kings of Ind their jewel-sceptres vail,
And from their treasures scatter pearlèd hail;
Great Brahma from his mystic heaven groans,
        And all his priesthood moans,
Before young Bacchus' eye-wink turning pale.
Into these regions came I, following him,
Sick-hearted, weary—so I took a whim
To stray away into these forests drear,
        Alone, without a peer:
And I have told thee all thou mayest hear.

        Young Stranger!
        I've been a ranger
In search of pleasure throughout every clime;
        Alas! 'tis not for me!
        Bewitch'd I sure must be,
To lose in grieving all my maiden prime.

        Come then, Sorrow,
        Sweetest Sorrow!
Like an own babe I nurse thee on my breast;
        I thought to leave thee,
        And deceive thee,
But now of all the world I love thee best.

There is not one,
No, no, not one
But thee to comfort a poor lonely maid;
Thou art her mother,
And her brother,
Her playmate, and her wooer in the shade.

631 *Ode to a Nightingale*

MY heart aches, and a drowsy numbness pains
My sense, as though of hemlock I had drunk,
Or emptied some dull opiate to the drains
One minute past, and Lethe-wards had sunk:
'Tis not through envy of thy happy lot,
But being too happy in thy happiness,
That thou, light-wingèd Dryad of the trees,
In some melodious plot
Of beechen green, and shadows numberless,
Singest of summer in full-throated ease.

O for a draught of vintage! that hath been
Cool'd a long age in the deep-delvèd earth,
Tasting of Flora and the country-green,
Dance, and Provençal song, and sunburnt mirth!
O for a beaker full of the warm South!
Full of the true, the blushful Hippocrene,
With beaded bubbles winking at the brim,
And purple-stainèd mouth;
That I might drink, and leave the world unseen,
And with thee fade away into the forest dim:

Fade far away, dissolve, and quite forget
   What thou among the leaves hast never known,
The weariness, the fever, and the fret
   Here, where men sit and hear each other groan;
Where palsy shakes a few, sad, last grey hairs,
    Where youth grows pale, and spectre-thin, and dies;
      Where but to think is to be full of sorrow
        And leaden-eyed despairs;
    Where beauty cannot keep her lustrous eyes,
      Or new Love pine at them beyond to-morrow.

Away! away! for I will fly to thee,
   Not charioted by Bacchus and his pards,
But on the viewless wings of Poesy,
   Though the dull brain perplexes and retards:
Already with thee! tender is the night,
    And haply the Queen-Moon is on her throne,
      Cluster'd around by all her starry Fays;
        But here there is no light,
    Save what from heaven is with the breezes blown
      Through verdurous glooms and winding mossy ways.

I cannot see what flowers are at my feet,
   Nor what soft incense hangs upon the boughs,
But, in embalmèd darkness, guess each sweet
   Wherewith the seasonable month endows
The grass, the thicket, and the fruit-tree wild;
    White hawthorn, and the pastoral eglantine;
      Fast-fading violets cover'd up in leaves;
        And mid-May's eldest child,
    The coming musk-rose, full of dewy wine,
      The murmurous haunt of flies on summer eves.

Darkling I listen; and for many a time
  I have been half in love with easeful Death,
Call'd him soft names in many a musèd rhyme,
  To take into the air my quiet breath;
Now more than ever seems it rich to die,
    To cease upon the midnight with no pain,
      While thou art pouring forth thy soul abroad
        In such an ecstasy!
    Still wouldst thou sing, and I have ears in vain—
      To thy high requiem become a sod.

Thou wast not born for death, immortal Bird!
  No hungry generations tread thee down;
The voice I hear this passing night was heard
  In ancient days by emperor and clown:
Perhaps the self-same song that found a path
    Through the sad heart of Ruth, when, sick for home,
      She stood in tears amid the alien corn;
        The same that ofttimes hath
    Charm'd magic casements, opening on the foam
      Of perilous seas, in faery lands forlorn.

Forlorn! the very word is like a bell
  To toll me back from thee to my sole self!
Adieu! the fancy cannot cheat so well
  As she is famed to do, deceiving elf.
Adieu! adieu! thy plaintive anthem fades
    Past the near meadows, over the still stream,
      Up the hill-side; and now 'tis buried deep
        In the next valley-glades:
    Was it a vision, or a waking dream?
      Fled is that music:—do I wake or sleep?

Ode on a Grecian Urn

THOU still unravish'd bride of quietness,
Thou foster-child of Silence and slow Time,
Sylvan historian, who canst thus express
A flowery tale more sweetly than our rhyme:
What leaf-fringed legend haunts about thy shape
Of deities or mortals, or of both,
In Tempe or the dales of Arcady?
What men or gods are these? What maidens loth?
What mad pursuit? What struggle to escape?
What pipes and timbrels? What wild ecstasy?

Heard melodies are sweet, but those unheard
Are sweeter; therefore, ye soft pipes, play on;
Not to the sensual ear, but, more endear'd,
Pipe to the spirit ditties of no tone:
Fair youth, beneath the trees, thou canst not leave
Thy song, nor ever can those trees be bare;
Bold Lover, never, never canst thou kiss,
Though winning near the goal—yet, do not grieve;
She cannot fade, though thou hast not thy bliss,
For ever wilt thou love, and she be fair!

Ah, happy, happy boughs! that cannot shed
Your leaves, nor ever bid the Spring adieu;
And, happy melodist, unwearièd,
For ever piping songs for ever new;
More happy love! more happy, happy love!
For ever warm and still to be enjoy'd,
For ever panting and for ever young;
All breathing human passion far above,
That leaves a heart high-sorrowful and cloy'd,
A burning forehead, and a parching tongue.

Who are these coming to the sacrifice?
　　To what green altar, O mysterious priest,
Lead'st thou that heifer lowing at the skies,
　　And all her silken flanks with garlands drest?
What little town by river or sea-shore,
　　Or mountain-built with peaceful citadel,
　　　Is emptied of its folk, this pious morn?
And, little town, thy streets for evermore
　　Will silent be; and not a soul, to tell
　　　Why thou art desolate, can e'er return.

O Attic shape! fair attitude! with brede
　　Of marble men and maidens overwrought,
With forest branches and the trodden weed;
　　Thou, silent form! dost tease us out of thought
As doth eternity. Cold Pastoral!
　　When old age shall this generation waste,
　　　Thou shalt remain, in midst of other woe
　　Than ours, a friend to man, to whom thou say'st,
'Beauty is truth, truth beauty,—that is all
　　　Ye know on earth, and all ye need to know.'

633　　*Ode to Psyche*

O GODDESS! hear these tuneless numbers, wrung
　　By sweet enforcement and remembrance dear,
And pardon that thy secrets should be sung
　　Even into thine own soft-conchèd ear:
Surely I dream'd to-day, or did I see
　　The wingèd Psyche with awaken'd eyes?
I wander'd in a forest thoughtlessly,
　　And, on the sudden, fainting with surprise,

Saw two fair creatures, couchèd side by side
   In deepest grass, beneath the whisp'ring roof
   Of leaves and trembled blossoms, where there ran
      A brooklet, scarce espied:
'Mid hush'd, cool-rooted flowers fragrant-eyed,
   Blue, silver-white, and budded Tyrian
They lay calm-breathing on the bedded grass;
   Their arms embracèd, and their pinions too;
   Their lips touch'd not, but had not bade adieu,
As if disjoinèd by soft-handed slumber,
And ready still past kisses to outnumber
   At tender eye-dawn of aurorean love:
      The wingèd boy I knew;
   But who wast thou, O happy, happy dove?
      His Psyche true!

O latest-born and loveliest vision far
   Of all Olympus' faded hierarchy!
Fairer than Phœbe's sapphire-region'd star,
   Or Vesper, amorous glow-worm of the sky;
Fairer than these, though temple thou hast none,
      Nor altar heap'd with flowers;
Nor Virgin-choir to make delicious moan
      Upon the midnight hours;
No voice, no lute, no pipe, no incense sweet
   From chain-swung censer teeming;
No shrine, no grove, no oracle, no heat
   Of pale-mouth'd prophet dreaming.

O brightest! though too late for antique vows,
   Too, too late for the fond believing lyre,
When holy were the haunted forest boughs,
   Holy the air, the water, and the fire;

Yet even in these days so far retired
  From happy pieties, thy lucent fans,
  Fluttering among the faint Olympians,
I see, and sing, by my own eyes inspired.
So let me be thy choir, and make a moan
      Upon the midnight hours;
Thy voice, thy lute, thy pipe, thy incense sweet
  From swingèd censer teeming:
Thy shrine, thy grove, thy oracle, thy heat
  Of pale-mouth'd prophet dreaming.

Yes, I will be thy priest, and build a fane
  In some untrodden region of my mind,
Where branchèd thoughts, new grown with pleasant **pain,**
  Instead of pines shall murmur in the wind:
Far, far around shall those dark-cluster'd trees
  Fledge the wild-ridgèd mountains steep by steep;
And there by zephyrs, streams, and birds, and bees,
  The moss-lain Dryads shall be lull'd to sleep;
And in the midst of this wide quietness
A rosy sanctuary will I dress
With the wreath'd trellis of a working brain,
  With buds, and bells, and stars without a name,
With all the gardener Fancy e'er could feign,
  Who, breeding flowers, will never breed the same:
And there shall be for thee all soft delight
      That shadowy thought can win,
A bright torch, and a casement ope at night,
      To let the warm Love in!

634 *To Autumn*

SEASON of mists and mellow fruitfulness!
  Close bosom-friend of the maturing sun;
Conspiring with him how to load and bless
  With fruit the vines that round the thatch-eaves run;
To bend with apples the moss'd cottage-trees,
  And fill all fruit with ripeness to the core;
    To swell the gourd, and plump the hazel shells
  With a sweet kernel; to set budding more,
And still more, later flowers for the bees,
Until they think warm days will never cease,
  For Summer has o'er-brimm'd their clammy cells.

Who hath not seen thee oft amid thy store?
  Sometimes whoever seeks abroad may find
Thee sitting careless on a granary floor,
  Thy hair soft-lifted by the winnowing wind,
Or on a half-reap'd furrow sound asleep,
  Drowsed with the fume of poppies, while thy hook
    Spares the next swath and all its twinèd flowers;
And sometimes like a gleaner thou dost keep
  Steady thy laden head across a brook;
  Or by a cider-press, with patient look,
    Thou watchest the last oozings hours by hours.

Where are the songs of Spring? Ay, where are they?
  Think not of them, thou hast thy music too,—
While barrèd clouds bloom the soft-dying day,
  And touch the stubble-plains with rosy hue;
Then in a wailful choir the small gnats mourn
  Among the river sallows, borne aloft
    Or sinking as the light wind lives or dies;
And full-grown lambs loud bleat from hilly bourn;

749

Hedge-crickets sing; and now with treble soft
The redbreast whistles from a garden-croft;
　　And gathering swallows twitter in the skies.

635　　　　　*Ode on Melancholy*

NO, no! go not to Lethe, neither twist
　　Wolf's-bane, tight-rooted, for its poisonous wine;
Nor suffer thy pale forehead to be kist
　　By nightshade, ruby grape of Proserpine;
Make not your rosary of yew-berries,
　　Nor let the beetle, nor the death-moth be
　　　Your mournful Psyche, nor the downy owl
A partner in your sorrow's mysteries;
　　For shade to shade will come too drowsily,
　　　And drown the wakeful anguish of the soul.

But when the melancholy fit shall fall
　　Sudden from heaven like a weeping cloud,
That fosters the droop-headed flowers all,
　　And hides the green hill in an April shroud;
Then glut thy sorrow on a morning rose,
　　Or on the rainbow of the salt sand-wave,
　　　Or on the wealth of globèd peonies;
Or if thy mistress some rich anger shows,
　　Emprison her soft hand, and let her rave,
　　　And feed deep, deep upon her peerless eyes.

She dwells with Beauty—Beauty that must die;
　　And Joy, whose hand is ever at his lips
Bidding adieu; and aching Pleasure nigh,
　　Turning to poison while the bee-mouth sips:

Ay, in the very temple of Delight
  Veil'd Melancholy has her sovran shrine,
    Though seen of none save him whose strenuous tongue
Can burst Joy's grape against his palate fine;
  His soul shall taste the sadness of her might,
    And be among her cloudy trophies hung.

636   *Fragment of an Ode to Maia*
          (*Written on May-Day, 1818*)

MOTHER of Hermes! and still youthful Maia!
      May I sing to thee
As thou wast hymnèd on the shores of Baiæ?
      Or may I woo thee
In earlier Sicilian? or thy smiles
Seek as they once were sought, in Grecian isles,
By bards who died content on pleasant sward,
  Leaving great verse unto a little clan?
O give me their old vigour! and unheard
  Save of the quiet primrose, and the span
      Of heaven, and few ears,
Rounded by thee, my song should die away
      Content as theirs,
Rich in the simple worship of a day.

637   *Bards of Passion and of Mirth*
Written on the Blank Page before Beaumont and Fletcher's
Tragi-Comedy 'The Fair Maid of the Inn'

BARDS of Passion and of Mirth,
  Ye have left your souls on earth!
Have ye souls in heaven too,
Doubled-lived in regions new?
Yes, and those of heaven commune

With the spheres of sun and moon;
With the noise of fountains wondrous,
And the parle of voices thund'rous;
With the whisper of heaven's trees
And one another, in soft ease
Seated on Elysian lawns
Browsed by none but Dian's fawns;
Underneath large blue-bells tented,
Where the daisies are rose-scented,
And the rose herself has got
Perfume which on earth is not;
Where the nightingale doth sing
Not a senseless, trancèd thing,
But divine melodious truth;
Philosophic numbers smooth;
Tales and golden histories
Of heaven and its mysteries.

Thus ye live on high, and then
On the earth ye live again;
And the souls ye left behind you
Teach us, here, the way to find you,
Where your other souls are joying,
Never slumber'd, never cloying.
Here, your earth-born souls still speak
To mortals, of their little week;
Of their sorrows and delights;
Of their passions and their spites;
Of their glory and their shame;
What doth strengthen and what maim.
Thus ye teach us, every day,
Wisdom, though fled far away.

Bards of Passion and of Mirth,
Ye have left your souls on earth!
Ye have souls in heaven too,
Double-lived in regions new!

638   *Fancy*

EVER let the Fancy roam,
   Pleasure never is at home:
At a touch sweet Pleasure melteth,
Like to bubbles when rain pelteth;
Then let wingèd Fancy wander
Through the thought still spread beyond her:
Open wide the mind's cage-door,
She'll dart forth, and cloudward soar.
O sweet Fancy! let her loose;
Summer's joys are spoilt by use,
And the enjoying of the Spring
Fades as does its blossoming:
Autumn's red-lipp'd fruitage too,
Blushing through the mist and dew,
Cloys with tasting: What do then?
Sit thee by the ingle, when
The sear faggot blazes bright,
Spirit of a winter's night;
When the soundless earth is muffled,
And the cakèd snow is shuffled
From the ploughboy's heavy shoon;
When the Night doth meet the Noon
In a dark conspiracy
To banish Even from her sky.

Sit thee there, and send abroad,
With a mind self-overawed,
Fancy, high-commission'd:—send her!
She has vassals to attend her:
She will bring, in spite of frost,
Beauties that the earth hath lost;
She will bring thee, all together,
All delights of summer weather;
All the buds and bells of May,
From dewy sward or thorny spray;
All the heapèd Autumn's wealth,
With a still, mysterious stealth:
She will mix these pleasures up
Like three fit wines in a cup,
And thou shalt quaff it:—thou shalt hear
Distant harvest-carols clear;
Rustle of the reapèd corn;
Sweet birds antheming the morn:
And, in the same moment—hark!
'Tis the early April lark,
Or the rooks, with busy caw,
Foraging for sticks and straw.
Thou shalt, at one glance behold
The daisy and the marigold;
White-plumed lilies, and the first
Hedge-grown primrose that hath burst;
Shaded hyacinth, alway
Sapphire queen of the mid-May;
And every leaf, and every flower
Pearlèd with the self-same shower.
Thou shalt see the fieldmouse peep
Meagre from its cellèd sleep;

And the snake all winter-thin
Cast on sunny bank its skin;
Freckled nest-eggs thou shalt see
Hatching in the hawthorn-tree,
When the hen-bird's wing doth rest
Quiet on her mossy nest;
Then the hurry and alarm
When the beehive casts its swarm;
Acorns ripe down-pattering
While the autumn breezes sing.

   O sweet Fancy! let her loose;
Every thing is spoilt by use:
Where's the cheek that doth not fade,
Too much gazed at? Where's the maid
Whose lip mature is ever new?
Where's the eye, however blue,
Doth not weary? Where's the face
One would meet in every place?
Where's the voice, however soft,
One would hear so very oft?
At a touch sweet Pleasure melteth
Like to bubbles when rain pelteth.
Let, then, wingèd Fancy find
Thee a mistress to thy mind:
Dulcet-eyed as Ceres' daughter,
Ere the God of Torment taught her
How to frown and how to chide;
With a waist and with a side
White as Hebe's, when her zone
Slipt its golden clasp, and down

Fell her kirtle to her feet,
While she held the goblet sweet,
And Jove grew languid.—Break the mesh
Of the Fancy's silken leash;
Quickly break her prison-string,
And such joys as these she'll bring.—
Let the wingèd Fancy roam,
Pleasure never is at home.

639 *Stanzas*

IN a drear-nighted December,
  Too happy, happy tree,
Thy branches ne'er remember
    Their green felicity:
The north cannot undo them,
With a sleety whistle through them;
Nor frozen thawings glue them
    From budding at the prime.

In a drear-nighted December,
    Too happy, happy brook,
Thy bubblings ne'er remember
    Apollo's summer look;
But with a sweet forgetting,
They stay their crystal fretting,
Never, never petting
    About the frozen time.

Ah! would 'twere so with many
    A gentle girl and boy!
But were there ever any
    Writhed not at passèd joy?

To know the change and feel it,
When there is none to heal it,
Nor numbèd sense to steal it,
    Was never said in rhyme.

640   *La Belle Dame sans Merci*

'O WHAT can ail thee, knight-at-arms,
    Alone and palely loitering?
The sedge is wither'd from the lake,
    And no birds sing.

'O what can ail thee, knight-at-arms,
    So haggard and so woe-begone?
The squirrel's granary is full,
    And the harvest's done.

'I see a lily on thy brow
    With anguish moist and fever dew;
And on thy cheek a fading rose
    Fast withereth too.'

'I met a lady in the meads,
    Full beautiful—a faery's child,
Her hair was long, her foot was light,
    And her eyes were wild.

'I made a garland for her head,
    And bracelets too, and fragrant zone;
She look'd at me as she did love,
    And made sweet moan.

'I set her on my pacing steed
   And nothing else saw all day long,
For sideways would she lean, and sing
    A faery's song.

'She found me roots of relish sweet,
   And honey wild and manna dew,
And sure in language strange she said,
    "I love thee true!"

'She took me to her elfin grot,
   And there she wept and sigh'd full sore;
And there I shut her wild, wild eyes
    With kisses four.

'And there she lullèd me asleep,
   And there I dream'd—Ah! woe betide!
The latest dream I ever dream'd
    On the cold hill's side.

'I saw pale kings and princes too,
   Pale warriors, death-pale were they all;
Who cried—"La belle Dame sans Merci
    Hath thee in thrall!"

'I saw their starved lips in the gloam
   With horrid warning gapèd wide,
And I awoke and found me here
    On the cold hill's side.

'And this is why I sojourn here
   Alone and palely loitering,
Though the sedge is wither'd from the lake,
    And no birds sing.'

641 *On first looking into Chapman's Homer*

MUCH have I travell'd in the realms of gold,
    And many goodly states and kingdoms seen;
Round many western islands have I been
Which bards in fealty to Apollo hold.
Oft of one wide expanse had I been told
    That deep-brow'd Homer ruled as his demesne:
    Yet did I never breathe its pure serene
Till I heard Chapman speak out loud and bold:
Then felt I like some watcher of the skies
    When a new planet swims into his ken;
Or like stout Cortez, when with eagle eyes
    He stared at the Pacific—and all his men
Look'd at each other with a wild surmise—
    Silent, upon a peak in Darien.

642 *When I have Fears that I may cease to be*

WHEN I have fears that I may cease to be
    Before my pen has glean'd my teeming brain,
Before high-pilèd books, in charact'ry,
Hold like rich garners the full-ripen'd grain;
When I behold, upon the night's starr'd face,
Huge cloudy symbols of a high romance,
And feel that I may never live to trace
Their shadows, with the magic hand of chance;
And when I feel, fair creature of an hour!
That I shall never look upon thee more,
Never have relish in the faery power
Of unreflecting love;—then on the shore
    Of the wide world I stand alone, and think,
    Till Love and Fame to nothingness do sink.

643 *To Sleep*

O SOFT embalmer of the still midnight!
  Shutting with careful fingers and benign
Our gloom-pleased eyes, embower'd from the light,
  Enshaded in forgetfulness divine;
O soothest Sleep! if so it please thee, close,
  In midst of this thine hymn, my willing eyes,
Or wait the amen, ere thy poppy throws
  Around my bed its lulling charities;
  Then save me, or the passèd day will shine
Upon my pillow, breeding many woes;
Save me from curious conscience, that still lords
  Its strength for darkness, burrowing like a mole;
Turn the key deftly in the oilèd wards,
  And seal the hushèd casket of my soul.

644 *Last Sonnet*

BRIGHT Star, would I were steadfast as thou art—
  Not in lone splendour hung aloft the night,
And watching, with eternal lids apart,
Like Nature's patient sleepless Eremite,
The moving waters at their priest-like task
Of pure ablution round earth's human shores,
Or gazing on the new soft-fallen mask
Of snow upon the mountains and the moors—
No—yet still steadfast, still unchangeable,
Pillow'd upon my fair love's ripening breast,
To feel for ever its soft fall and swell,
Awake for ever in a sweet unrest,
    Still, still to hear her tender-taken breath,
    And so live ever—or else swoon to death.

WILLIAM CULLEN BRYANT

1794–1878

645 *Thanatopsis*

TO him who in the love of Nature holds
  Communion with her visible forms, she speaks
A various language; for his gayer hours
She has a voice of gladness, and a smile
And eloquence of beauty, and she glides
Into his darker musings, with a mild
And healing sympathy, that steals away
Their sharpness, ere he is aware. When thoughts
Of the last bitter hour come like a blight
Over thy spirit, and sad images
Of the stern agony, and shroud, and pall,
And breathless darkness, and the narrow house,
Make thee to shudder and grow sick at heart;—
Go forth, under the open sky, and list
To Nature's teachings, while from all around—
Earth and her waters, and the depths of air—
Comes a still voice—Yet a few days, and thee
The all-beholding sun shall see no more
In all his course; nor yet in the cold ground,
Where thy pale form was laid with many tears,
Nor in the embrace of ocean, shall exist
Thy image. Earth, that nourish'd thee, shall claim
Thy growth, to be resolved to earth again,
And, lost each human trace, surrendering up
Thine individual being, shalt thou go
To mix for ever with the elements,
To be a brother to the insensible rock,

And to the sluggish clod, which the rude swain
Turns with his share, and treads upon. The oak
Shall send his roots abroad, and pierce thy mould.

Yet not to thine eternal resting-place
Shalt thou retire alone, nor couldst thou wish
Couch more magnificent. Thou shalt lie down
With patriarchs of the infant world—with kings,
The powerful of the earth—the wise, the good,
Fair forms, and hoary seers of ages past,
All in one mighty sepulchre. The hills
Rock-ribb'd and ancient as the sun,—the vales
Stretching in pensive quietness between;
The venerable woods; rivers that move
In majesty, and the complaining brooks
That make the meadows green; and, pour'd round all,
Old Ocean's grey and melancholy waste,—
Are but the solemn decorations all
Of the great tomb of man. The golden sun,
The planets, all the infinite host of heaven,
Are shining on the sad abodes of death,
Through the still lapse of ages. All that tread
The globe are but a handful to the tribes
That slumber in its bosom.—Take the wings
Of morning, pierce the Barcan wilderness,
Or lose thyself in the continuous woods
Where rolls the Oregon and hears no sound
Save his own dashings—yet the dead are there:
And millions in those solitudes, since first
The flight of years began, have laid them down
In their last sleep—the dead reign there alone.
So shalt thou rest: and what if thou withdraw

In silence from the living, and no friend
Take note of thy departure? All that breathe
Will share thy destiny. The gay will laugh
When thou art gone, the solemn brood of care
Plod on, and each one as before will chase
His favourite phantom; yet all these shall leave
Their mirth and their employments, and shall come
And make their bed with thee. As the long train
Of ages glide away, the sons of men,
The youth in life's green spring, and he who goes
In the full strength of years, matron and maid,
The speechless babe, and the grey-headed man—
Shall one by one be gathered to thy side
By those who in their turn shall follow them.

So live, that when thy summons comes to join
The innumerable caravan which moves
To that mysterious realm where each shall take
His chamber in the silent halls of death,
Thou go not, like the quarry-slave at night,
Scourged to his dungeon; but, sustain'd and soothed
By an unfaltering trust, approach thy grave,
Like one who wraps the drapery of his couch
About him, and lies down to pleasant dreams.

1795–1839

646　　*The Outlaw of Loch Lene*

FROM THE IRISH

O MANY a day have I made good ale in the glen,
　　That came not of stream or malt, like the brewing of
　　　　men:
My bed was the ground; my roof, the green-wood above;
And the wealth that I sought, one far kind glance from my Love.

Alas! on that night when the horses I drove from the field,
That I was not near from terror my angel to shield!
She stretch'd forth her arms; her mantle she flung to the wind,
And swam o'er Loch Lene, her outlaw'd lover to find.

O would that a freezing sleet-wing'd tempest did sweep,
And I and my love were alone, far off on the deep;
I'd ask not a ship, or a bark, or a pinnace, to save—
With her hand round my waist, I'd fear not the wind or the
　　wave.

'Tis down by the lake where the wild tree fringes its sides,
The maid of my heart, my fair one of Heaven resides:
I think, as at eve she wanders its mazes among,
The birds go to sleep by the sweet wild twist of her song.

WILLIAM SIDNEY WALKER

647　　　　　　　　　1795–1846

T OO solemn for day, too sweet for night,
　　Come not in darkness, come not in light;
But come in some twilight interim,
　　When the gloom is soft, and the light is dim.

764

GEORGE DARLEY

1795–1846

648 *The Phoenix*

O FAST her amber blood doth flow
 From the heart-wounded Incense Tree,
Fast as earth's deep-embosom'd woe
 In silent rivulets to the sea!

Beauty may weep her fair first-born,
 Perchance in as resplendent tears,
Such golden dewdrops bow the corn
 When the stern sickleman appears:

Büt O! such perfume to a bower
 Never allured sweet-seeking bee,
As to sip fast that nectarous shower
 A thirstier minstrel drew in me!

649 *The Solitary Lyre*

WHEREFORE, unlaurell'd Boy,
 Whom the contemptuous Muse will not inspire,
With a sad kind of joy
 Still sing'st thou to thy solitary lyre?

The melancholy winds
 Pour through unnumber'd reeds their idle woes,
And every Naiad finds
 A stream to weep her sorrow as it flows.

Her sighs unto the air
  The Wood-maid's native oak doth broadly tell,
And Echo's fond despair
  Intelligible rocks re-syllable.

Wherefore then should not I,
  Albeit no haughty Muse my heart inspire,
Fated of grief to die,
  Impart it to my solitary lyre?

650 *Song*

SWEET in her green dell the flower of beauty slumbers,
  Lull'd by the faint breezes sighing through her hair;
Sleeps she and hears not the melancholy numbers
  Breathed to my sad lute 'mid the lonely air.

Down from the high cliffs the rivulet is teeming
  To wind round the willow banks that lure him from above:
O that in tears, from my rocky prison streaming,
  I too could glide to the bower of my love!

Ah! where the woodbines with sleepy arms have wound her,
  Opes she her eyelids at the dream of my lay,
Listening, like the dove, while the fountains echo round her,
  To her lost mate's call in the forests far away.

Come then, my bird! For the peace thou ever bearest,
  Still Heaven's messenger of comfort to me—
Come—this fond bosom, O faithfullest and fairest,
  Bleeds with its death-wound, its wound of love for thee!

651

The Fallen Star

A STAR is gone! a star is gone!
    There is a blank in Heaven;
One of the cherub choir has done
    His airy course this even.

He sat upon the orb of fire
    That hung for ages there,
And lent his music to the choir
    That haunts the nightly air.

But when his thousand years are pass'd,
    With a cherubic sigh
He vanish'd with his car at last,
    For even cherubs die!

Hear how his angel-brothers mourn—
    The minstrels of the spheres—
Each chiming sadly in his turn
    And dropping splendid tears.

The planetary sisters all
    Join in the fatal song,
And weep this hapless brother's fall,
    Who sang with them so long.

But deepest of the choral band
    The Lunar Spirit sings,
And with a bass-according hand
    Sweeps all her sullen strings.

    From the deep chambers of the dome
        Where sleepless Uriel lies,
    His rude harmonic thunders come
        Mingled with mighty sighs.

The thousand car-borne cherubim,
     The wandering eleven,
All join to chant the dirge of him
     Who fell just now from Heaven.

HARTLEY COLERIDGE

1796–1849

652   *Song*

SHE is not fair to outward view
     As many maidens be,
Her loveliness I never knew
     Until she smiled on me;
O, then I saw her eye was bright,
A well of love, a spring of light!

But now her looks are coy and cold,
To mine they ne'er reply,
And yet I cease not to behold
     The love-light in her eye:
Her very frowns are fairer far
Than smiles of other maidens are.

653   *Early Death*

SHE pass'd away like morning dew
     Before the sun was high;
So brief her time, she scarcely knew
     The meaning of a sigh.

As round the rose its soft perfume,
     Sweet love around her floated;
Admired she grew—while mortal doom
     Crept on, unfear'd, unnoted.

Love was her guardian Angel here,
  But Love to Death resign'd her;
Tho' Love was kind, why should we fear
  But holy Death is kinder?

654 *Friendship*

WHEN we were idlers with the loitering rills,
    The need of human love we little noted:
  Our love was nature; and the peace that floated
On the white mist, and dwelt upon the hills,
To sweet accord subdued our wayward wills:
    One soul was ours, one mind, one heart devoted,
    That, wisely doting, ask'd not why it doted,
And ours the unknown joy, which knowing kills.
But now I find how dear thou wert to me;
    That man is more than half of nature's treasure,
Of that fair beauty which no eye can see,
    Of that sweet music which no ear can measure;
    And now the streams may sing for others' pleasure,
The hills sleep on in their eternity.

THOMAS HOOD
1798–1845

655 *Autumn*

I SAW old Autumn in the misty morn
  Stand shadowless like Silence, listening
To silence, for no lonely bird would sing
Into his hollow ear from woods forlorn,
Nor lowly hedge nor solitary thorn;—
Shaking his languid locks all dewy bright
With tangled gossamer that fell by night,
  Pearling his coronet of golden corn.

THOMAS HOOD

Where are the songs of Summer?—With the sun,
Oping the dusky eyelids of the South,
Till shade and silence waken up as one,
And Morning sings with a warm odorous mouth.
Where are the merry birds?—Away, away,
On panting wings through the inclement skies,
    Lest owls should prey
    Undazzled at noonday,
And tear with horny beak their lustrous eyes.

Where are the blooms of Summer?—In the West,
Blushing their last to the last sunny hours,
When the mild Eve by sudden Night is prest
Like tearful Proserpine, snatch'd from her flow'rs
    To a most gloomy breast.
Where is the pride of Summer,—the green prime,—
The many, many leaves all twinkling?—Three
On the moss'd elm; three on the naked lime
Trembling,—and one upon the old oak-tree!
    Where is the Dryad's immortality?—
Gone into mournful cypress and dark yew,
Or wearing the long gloomy Winter through
    In the smooth holly's green eternity.

The squirrel gloats on his accomplish'd hoard,
The ants have brimm'd their garners with ripe grain,
    And honey bees have stored
   The sweets of Summer in their luscious cells;
   The swallows all have wing'd across the main;
   But here the autumn Melancholy dwells,
    And sighs her tearful spells
   Amongst the sunless shadows of the plain.

THOMAS HOOD

Alone, alone,
Upon a mossy stone,
She sits and reckons up the dead and gone
With the last leaves for a love-rosary,
Whilst all the wither'd world looks drearily,
Like a dim picture of the drownèd past
In the hush'd mind's mysterious far away,
Doubtful what ghostly thing will steal the last
Into that distance, gray upon the gray.

O go and sit with her, and be o'ershaded
Under the languid downfall of her hair!
She wears a coronal of flowers faded
Upon her forehead, and a face of care;—
There is enough of wither'd everywhere
To make her bower,—and enough of gloom;
There is enough of sadness to invite,
If only for the rose that died, whose doom
Is Beauty's,—she that with the living bloom
Of conscious cheeks most beautifies the light:
There is enough of sorrowing, and quite
Enough of bitter fruits the earth doth bear,—
Enough of chilly droppings for her bowl;
Enough of fear and shadowy despair,
To frame her cloudy prison for the soul!

656 *Silence*

THERE is a silence where hath been no sound,
　　There is a silence where no sound may be,
　In the cold grave—under the deep, deep sea,
Or in wide desert where no life is found,
Which hath been mute, and still must sleep profound;
　　No voice is hush'd—no life treads silently,
　　But clouds and cloudy shadows wander free,
That never spoke, over the idle ground:
But in green ruins, in the desolate walls
　　Of antique palaces, where Man hath been,
Though the dun fox or wild hyæna calls,
　　And owls, that flit continually between,
Shriek to the echo, and the low winds moan—
There the true Silence is, self-conscious and alone.

657 *Death*

IT is not death, that sometime in a sigh
　　This eloquent breath shall take its speechless flight;
That sometime these bright stars, that now reply
　　In sunlight to the sun, shall set in night;
　　That this warm conscious flesh shall perish quite,
And all life's ruddy springs forget to flow;
　　That thoughts shall cease, and the immortal sprite
Be lapp'd in alien clay and laid below;
It is not death to know this—but to know
　　That pious thoughts, which visit at new graves
In tender pilgrimage, will cease to go
　　So duly and so oft—and when grass waves
Over the pass'd-away, there may be then
No resurrection in the minds of men.

658 *Fair Ines*

O SAW ye not fair Ines?
   She's gone into the West,
To dazzle when the sun is down,
   And rob the world of rest:
She took our daylight with her,
   The smiles that we love best,
With morning blushes on her cheek,
   And pearls upon her breast.

O turn again, fair Ines,
   Before the fall of night,
For fear the Moon should shine alone,
   And stars unrivall'd bright;
And blessèd will the lover be
   That walks beneath their light,
And breathes the love against thy cheek
   I dare not even write!

Would I had been, fair Ines,
   That gallant cavalier,
Who rode so gaily by thy side,
   And whisper'd thee so near!
Were there no bonny dames at home,
   Or no true lovers here,
That he should cross the seas to win
   The dearest of the dear?

I saw thee, lovely Ines,
   Descend along the shore,
With bands of noble gentlemen,
   And banners waved before;

And gentle youth and maidens gay,
   And snowy plumes they wore:
It would have been a beauteous dream,—
   If it had been no more!

Alas, alas! fair Ines,
   She went away with song,
With Music waiting on her steps,
   And shoutings of the throng;
But some were sad, and felt no mirth,
   But only Music's wrong,
In sounds that sang Farewell, farewell,
   To her you've loved so long.

Farewell, farewell, fair Ines!
   That vessel never bore
So fair a lady on its deck,
   Nor danced so light before,—
Alas for pleasure on the sea,
   And sorrow on the shore!
The smile that bless'd one lover's heart
   Has broken many more!

659   *Time of Roses*

IT was not in the Winter
   Our loving lot was cast;
It was the time of roses—
   We pluck'd them as we pass'd!

That churlish season never frown'd
   On early lovers yet:
O no—the world was newly crown'd
   With flowers when first we met!

'Twas twilight, and I bade you go,
  But still you held me fast;
It was the time of roses—
  We pluck'd them as we pass'd!

660   *Ruth*

SHE stood breast-high amid the corn,
  Clasp'd by the golden light of morn,
Like the sweetheart of the sun,
Who many a glowing kiss had won.

On her cheek an autumn flush,
Deeply ripen'd;—such a blush
In the midst of brown was born,
Like red poppies grown with corn.

Round her eyes her tresses fell,
Which were blackest none could tell,
But long lashes veil'd a light,
That had else been all too bright.

And her hat, with shady brim,
Made her tressy forehead dim;
Thus she stood amid the stooks,
Praising God with sweetest looks:—

Sure, I said, Heav'n did not mean,
Where I reap thou shouldst but glean,
Lay thy sheaf adown and come,
Share my harvest and my home.

661   *The Death-bed*

WE watch'd her breathing thro' the night,
        Her breathing soft and low,
As in her breast the wave of life
        Kept heaving to and fro.

So silently we seem'd to speak,
        So slowly moved about,
As we had lent her half our powers
        To eke her living out.

Our very hopes belied our fears,
        Our fears our hopes belied—
We thought her dying when she slept,
        And sleeping when she died.

For when the morn came dim and sad,
        And chill with early showers,
Her quiet eyelids closed—she had
        Another morn than ours.

662   *The Bridge of Sighs*

ONE more Unfortunate,
        Weary of breath,
Rashly importunate,
        Gone to her death!

Take her up tenderly
        Lift her with care;
Fashion'd so slenderly,
        Young, and so fair!

THOMAS HOOD

Look at her garments
Clinging like cerements;
Whilst the wave constantly
    Drips from her clothing;
Take her up instantly,
    Loving, not loathing.

Touch her not scornfully;
Think of her mournfully,
    Gently and humanly;
Not of the stains of her,
All that remains of her
    Now is pure womanly.

Make no deep scrutiny
Into her mutiny
    Rash and undutiful:
Past all dishonour,
Death has left on her
    Only the beautiful.

Still, for all slips of hers,
    One of Eve's family—
Wipe those poor lips of hers
    Oozing so clammily.

Loop up her tresses
    Escaped from the comb,
Her fair auburn tresses;
Whilst wonderment guesses
    Where was her home?

Who was her father?
    Who was her mother?

Had she a sister?
  Had she a brother?
Or was there a dearer one
Still, and a nearer one
  Yet, than all other?

Alas! for the rarity
Of Christian charity
  Under the sun!
O, it was pitiful!
Near a whole city full,
  Home she had none.

Sisterly, brotherly,
Fatherly, motherly
  Feelings had changed:
Love, by harsh evidence,
Thrown from its eminence;
Even God's providence
  Seeming estranged.

Where the lamps quiver
So far in the river,
  With many a light
From window and casement,
From garret to basement,
She stood, with amazement,
  Houseless by night.

The bleak wind of March
  Made her tremble and shiver;
But not the dark arch,
Or the black flowing river:

THOMAS HOOD

Mad from life's history,
Glad to death's mystery,
  Swift to be hurl'd—
Anywhere, anywhere
  Out of the world!

In she plunged boldly—
No matter how coldly
  The rough river ran—
Over the brink of it,
Picture it—think of it,
  Dissolute Man!
Lave in it, drink of it,
  Then, if you can!

Take her up tenderly,
  Lift her with care;
Fashion'd so slenderly,
  Young, and so fair!

Ere her limbs frigidly
Stiffen too rigidly,
  Decently, kindly,
Smooth and compose them;
And her eyes, close them,
  Staring so blindly!

Dreadfully staring
  Thro' muddy impurity,
As when with the daring
Last look of despairing
  Fix'd on futurity.

Perishing gloomily,
Spurr'd by contumely,

Cold inhumanity,
Burning insanity,
    Into her rest.—
Cross her hands humbly
As if praying dumbly,
    Over her breast!

Owning her weakness,
    Her evil behaviour,
And leaving, with meekness,
    Her sins to her Saviour!

ANONYMOUS

663   *The Canadian Boat Song*

LISTEN to me, as when ye heard our father
    Sing long ago the song of other shores—
Listen to me, and then in chorus gather
    All your deep voices as ye pull your oars:
        Fair these broad meads—these hoary woods are grand;
        But we are exiles from our fathers' land.

From the lone shieling of the misty island
    Mountains divide us, and the waste of seas—
Yet still the blood is strong, the heart is Highland,
    And we in dreams behold the Hebrides;
        Fair these broad meads, &c.

We ne'er shall tread the fancy-haunted valley,
    Where 'tween the dark hills creeps the small clear stream,
In arms around the patriarch banner rally,
    Nor see the moon on royal tombstones gleam:
        Fair these broad meads, &c.

780

When the bold kindred, in the time long-vanish'd,
  Conquer'd the soil and fortified the keep,—
No seer foretold the children would be banish'd,
  That a degenerate Lord might boast his sheep:
    Fair these broad meads, &c.

Come foreign rage—let Discord burst in slaughter!
  O then for clansmen true, and stern claymore—
The hearts that would have given their blood like water,
  Beat heavily beyond the Atlantic roar:
    Fair these broad meads—these hoary woods are grand;
    But we are exiles from our fathers' land.

WILLIAM THOM

1798–1848

664   *The Blind Boy's Pranks*

MEN grew sae cauld, maids sae unkind,
  Love kentna whaur to stay:
Wi' fient an arrow, bow, or string—
Wi' droopin' heart an' drizzled wing,
  He faught his lonely way.

'Is there nae mair in Garioch fair
  Ae spotless hame for me?
Hae politics an' corn an' kye
Ilk bosom stappit? Fie, O fie!
  I'll swithe me o'er the sea.'

He launch'd a leaf o' jessamine,
  On whilk he daur'd to swim,
An' pillow'd his head on a wee rosebud,
Syne laithfu', lanely, Love 'gan scud
  Down Ury's waefu' stream.

664 kentna] knew not.   wi fient an arrow] i.q. with deuce
an arrow.   swithe] hie quickly.   laithfu'] regretful.

The birds sang bonnie as Love drew near,
    But dowie when he gaed by;
Till lull'd wi' the sough o' monie a sang,
He sleepit fu' soun' and sail'd alang
    'Neath Heaven's gowden sky.

'Twas just whaur creeping Ury greets
    Its mountain cousin Don,
There wander'd forth a weelfaur'd dame,
Wha listless gazed on the bonnie stream,
As it flirted an' play'd with a sunny beam
    That flicker'd its bosom upon.

Love happit his head, I trow, that time
    The jessamine bark drew nigh,
The lassie espied the wee rosebud,
An' aye her heart gae thud for thud,
    An' quiet it wadna lie.

'O gin I but had yon wearie wee flower
    That floats on the Ury sae fair!'—
She lootit her hand for the silly rose-leaf,
But little wist she o' the pawkie thief
    That was lurkin' an' laughin' there!

Love glower'd when he saw her bonnie dark e'e,
    An' swore by Heaven's grace
He ne'er had seen nor thought to see,
Since e'er he left the Paphian lea,
    Sae lovely a dwallin'-place.

dowie] dejectedly.   weelfaur'd] well-favoured, comely.
happit] covered up.   lootit] lowered.   pawkie] sly.
glower'd] stared.

Syne first of a' in her blythesome breast
    He built a bower, I ween;
An' what did the waefu' devilick neist?
But kindled a gleam like the rosy east,
    That sparkled frae baith her e'en.

An' then beneath ilk high e'e-bree
    He placed a quiver there;
His bow? What but her shinin' brow?
An' O sic deadly strings he drew
    Frae out her silken hair!

Guid be our guard! Sic deeds waur deen
    Roun' a' our countrie then;
An' monie a hangin' lug was seen
'Mang farmers fat, an' lawyers lean,
    An' herds o' common men!

SIR HENRY TAYLOR

1800–1886

665   *Elena's Song*

QUOTH tongue of neither maid nor wife
    To heart of neither wife nor maid—
Lead we not here a jolly life
    Betwixt the shine and shade?

Quoth heart of neither maid nor wife
    To tongue of neither wife nor maid—
Thou wagg'st, but I am worn with strife,
    And feel like flowers that fade.

664 e'e-bree] eyebrow.   lug] ear.

THOMAS BABINGTON MACAULAY,
LORD MACAULAY

1800–1859

666 *A Jacobite's Epitaph*

TO my true king I offer'd free from stain
    Courage and faith; vain faith, and courage vain.
For him I threw lands, honours, wealth, away,
And one dear hope, that was more prized than they.
For him I languish'd in a foreign clime,
Gray-hair'd with sorrow in my manhood's prime;
Heard on Lavernia Scargill's whispering trees,
And pined by Arno for my lovelier Tees;
Beheld each night my home in fever'd sleep,
Each morning started from the dream to weep;
Till God, who saw me tried too sorely, gave
The resting-place I ask'd, an early grave.
O thou, whom chance leads to this nameless stone,
From that proud country which was once mine own,
By those white cliffs I never more must see,
By that dear language which I spake like thee,
Forget all feuds, and shed one English tear
O'er English dust. A broken heart lies here.

WILLIAM BARNES

1801–1886

667 *Mater Dolorosa*

I'D a dream to-night
    As I fell asleep,
O! the touching sight
    Makes me still to weep:

Of my little lad,
Gone to leave me sad,
Ay, the child I had,
   But was not to keep.

As in heaven high
   I my child did seek,
There in train came by
   Children fair and meek,
Each in lily white,
With a lamp alight;
Each was clear to sight,
   But they did not speak.

Then, a little sad,
   Came my child in turn,
But the lamp he had,
   O it did not burn!
He, to clear my doubt,
Said, half turn'd about,
'Your tears put it out;
   Mother, never mourn.'

668 *The Wife a-lost*

SINCE I noo mwore do zee your feäce,
   Up steärs or down below,
I'll zit me in the lwonesome pleäce,
   Where flat-bough'd beech do grow;
Below the beeches' bough, my love,
   Where you did never come,
An' I don't look to meet ye now,
   As I do look at hwome.

Since you noo mwore be at my zide,
  In walks in zummer het,
I'll goo alwone where mist do ride,
  Droo trees a-drippèn wet;
Below the raïn-wet bough, my love,
  Where you did never come,
An' I don't grieve to miss ye now,
  As I do grieve at hwome.

Since now bezide my dinner-bwoard
  Your vaïce do never sound,
I'll eat the bit I can avword
  A-vield upon the ground;
Below the darksome bough, my love,
  Where you did never dine,
An' I don't grieve to miss ye now,
  As I at hwome do pine.

Since I do miss your vaïce an' feäce
  In praÿer at eventide,
I'll praÿ wi' woone sad vaïce vor greäce
  To goo where you do bide;
Above the tree an' bough, my love,
  Where you be gone avore,
An' be a-waïtèn vor me now,
  To come vor evermwore.

669   *Evening, and Maidens*

NOW the shiades o' the elems da stratch muore an muore,
  Vrom the low-zinkèn zun in the west o' the sky;
An' the mâidens da stan out in clusters avore
The doors, var to chatty an' zee vo'ke goo by.

An' ther cuombs be a-zet in ther bunches o' hiair,
An' ther curdles da hang roun' ther necks lily-white,
An' ther cheäks tha be ruosy, ther shoulders be biare,
Ther looks tha be merry, ther lims tha be light.

An' the times have a-been—but tha cänt be noo muore—
When I, too, had my jây under evemen's dim sky,
When my Fanny did stan' out wi' others avore
Her door, var to chatty an' zee vo'ke goo by.

An' up there, in the green, is her own honey-zuck,
That her brother trâin'd up roun' her winder; an' there
Is the ruose an' the jessamy, where she did pluck
A flow'r var her buzom ar bud var her hiair.

An' zoo smile, happy mâidens! var every fiace,
As the zummers da come an' the years da roll by,
Wull soon sadden, ar goo vur awoy vrom the pliace,
Ar else, lik' my Fanny, wull wither an' die.

But when you be a-lost vrom the parish, some muore
Wull come on in y'ur pliazen to bloom an' to die;
An' zoo zummer wull always have mâidens avore
Ther doors, var to chatty an' zee vo'ke goo by.

Var dä'ters ha' marnen when mothers ha' night,
An' there's beauty alive when the fiairest is dead;
As when oon sparklèn wiave da zink down vrom the light,
Another da come up an' catch it instead.

Zoo smile on, happy mâidens! but I shall noo muore
Zee the mâid I da miss under evemen's dim sky;
An' my heart is a-touch'd to zee you out avore
The doors, var to chatty and zee vo'ke goo by.

curdles] curls.

1802-1839

The Vicar

SOME years ago, ere time and taste
 Had turn'd our parish topsy-turvy,
When Darnel Park was Darnel Waste,
 And roads as little known as scurvy,
The man who lost his way, between
 St. Mary's Hill and Sandy Thicket,
Was always shown across the green,
 And guided to the Parson's wicket.

Back flew the bolt of lissom lath;
 Fair Margaret, in her tidy kirtle,
Led the lorn traveller up the path,
 Through clean-clipt rows of box and myrtle;
And Don and Sancho, Tramp and Tray,
 Upon the parlour steps collected,
Wagg'd all their tails, and seem'd to say—
 'Our master knows you—you're expected.'

Uprose the Reverend Dr. Brown,
 Uprose the Doctor's winsome marrow;
The lady laid her knitting down,
 Her husband clasp'd his ponderous Barrow;
Whate'er the stranger's caste or creed,
 Pundit or Papist, saint or sinner,
He found a stable for his steed,
 And welcome for himself, and dinner.

If, when he reach'd his journey's end,
 And warm'd himself in Court or College,
He had not gained an honest friend
 And twenty curious scraps of knowledge,—

If he departed as he came,
  With no new light on love or liquor,—
Good sooth, the traveller was to blame,
  And not the Vicarage, nor the Vicar.

His talk was like a spring, which runs
  With rapid change from rocks to roses:
It slipped from politics to puns,
  It passed from Mahomet to Moses;
Beginning with the laws which keep
  The planets in their radiant courses,
And ending with some precept deep
  For dressing eels, or shoeing horses.

He was a shrewd and sound Divine,
  Of loud Dissent the mortal terror;
And when, by dint of page and line,
  He 'stablish'd Truth, or startled Error,
The Baptist found him far too deep;
  The Deist sigh'd with saving sorrow;
And the lean Levite went to sleep,
  And dream'd of tasting pork to-morrow.

His sermons never said or show'd
  That Earth is foul, that Heaven is gracious,
Without refreshment on the road
  From Jerome or from Athanasius:
And sure a righteous zeal inspired
  The hand and head that penn'd and plann'd them,
For all who understood admired,
  And some who did not understand them.

He wrote, too, in a quiet way,
   Small treatises, and smaller verses,
And sage remarks on chalk and clay,
   And hints to noble Lords—and nurses;
True histories of last year's ghost,
   Lines to a ringlet, or a turban,
And trifles for the *Morning Post*,
   And nothings for Sylvanus Urban.

He did not think all mischief fair,
   Although he had a knack of joking;
He did not make himself a bear,
   Although he had a taste for smoking;
And when religious sects ran mad,
   He held, in spite of all his learning,
That if a man's belief is bad,
   It will not be improved by burning.

And he was kind, and loved to sit
   In the low hut or garnish'd cottage,
And praise the farmer's homely wit,
   And share the widow's homelier pottage:
At his approach complaint grew mild;
   And when his hand unbarr'd the shutter,
The clammy lips of fever smiled
   The welcome which they could not utter.

He always had a tale for me
   Of Julius Caesar, or of Venus;
From him I learnt the rule of three,
   Cat's cradle, leap-frog, and *Quae genus*:

I used to singe his powder'd wig,
    To steal the staff he put such trust in,
And make the puppy dance a jig,
    When he began to quote Augustine.

Alack the change! in vain I look
    For haunts in which my boyhood trifled,—
The level lawn, the trickling brook,
    The trees I climb'd, the beds I rifled:
The church is larger than before;
    You reach it by a carriage entry;
It holds three hundred people more,
    And pews are fitted up for gentry.

Sit in the Vicar's seat: you'll hear
    The doctrine of a gentle Johnian,
Whose hand is white, whose tone is clear,
    Whose phrase is very Ciceronian.
Where is the old man laid?—look down,
    And construe on the slab before you,
'*Hic jacet GVLIELMVS BROWN,*
    Vir nullâ non donandus lauru.'

GERALD GRIFFIN

1803–1840

Eileen Aroon

671

WHEN like the rising day,
        Eileen Aroon!
Love sends his early ray,
        Eileen Aroon!
What makes his dawning glow,
Changeless through joy or woe?
Only the constant know:—
        Eileen Aroon!

I know a valley fair,
              Eileen Aroon!
I knew a cottage there,
              Eileen Aroon!
Far in that valley's shade
I knew a gentle maid,
Flower of a hazel glade,—
              Eileen Aroon! ...

Were she no longer true,
              Eileen Aroon!
What should her lover do?
              Eileen Aroon!
Fly with his broken chain
Far o'er the sounding main,
Never to love again,—
              Eileen Aroon!

JAMES CLARENCE MANGAN 1803–1849

672 *Dark Rosaleen*

O MY Dark Rosaleen,
  Do not sigh, do not weep!
The priests are on the ocean green,
  They march along the deep.
There's wine from the royal Pope,
  Upon the ocean green;
And Spanish ale shall give you hope,
  My Dark Rosaleen!
  My own Rosaleen!
Shall glad your heart, shall give you hope,
Shall give you health, and help, and hope,
  My Dark Rosaleen!

JAMES CLARENCE MANGAN

Over hills, and thro' dales,
  Have I roam'd for your sake;
All yesterday I sail'd with sails
  On river and on lake.
The Erne, at its highest flood,
  I dash'd across unseen,
For there was lightning in my blood,
  My Dark Rosaleen!
  My own Rosaleen!
O, there was lightning in my blood,
Red lightning lighten'd thro' my blood.
  My Dark Rosaleen!

All day long, in unrest,
  To and fro, do I move.
The very soul within my breast
  Is wasted for you, love!
The heart in my bosom faints
  To think of you, my Queen,
My life of life, my saint of saints,
  My Dark Rosaleen!
  My own Rosaleen!
To hear your sweet and sad complaints,
My life, my love, my saint of saints,
  My Dark Rosaleen!

Woe and pain, pain and woe,
  Are my lot, night and noon,
To see your bright face clouded so,
  Like to the mournful moon.
But yet will I rear your throne
  Again in golden sheen;

JAMES CLARENCE MANGAN

'Tis you shall reign, shall reign alone,
  My Dark Rosaleen!
  My own Rosaleen!
'Tis you shall have the golden throne,
'Tis you shall reign, and reign alone,
  My Dark Rosaleen!

Over dews, over sands,
  Will I fly, for your weal:
Your holy delicate white hands
  Shall girdle me with steel.
At home, in your emerald bowers,
  From morning's dawn till e'en,
You'll pray for me, my flower of flowers,
  My Dark Rosaleen!
  My fond Rosaleen!
You'll think of me through daylight hours,
My virgin flower, my flower of flowers,
  My Dark Rosaleen!

I could scale the blue air,
  I could plough the high hills,
O, I could kneel all night in prayer,
  To heal your many ills!
And one beamy smile from you
  Would float like light between
My toils and me, my own, my true,
  My Dark Rosaleen!
  My fond Rosaleen!
Would give me life and soul anew,
A second life, a soul anew,
  My Dark Rosaleen!

O, the Erne shall run red,
   With redundance of blood,
The earth shall rock beneath our tread,
   And flames wrap hill and wood,
And gun-peal and slogan-cry
   Wake many a glen serene,
Ere you shall fade, ere you shall die,
    My Dark Rosaleen!
    My own Rosaleen!
The Judgement Hour must first be nigh,
Ere you can fade, ere you can die,
    My Dark Rosaleen!

673   *To Amine*

VEIL not thy mirror, sweet Amine,
   Till night shall also veil each star!
Thou seest a twofold marvel there:
The only face so fair as thine,
The only eyes that, near or far,
Can gaze on thine without despair.

674   *The Nameless One*

ROLL forth, my song, like the rushing river,
   That sweeps along to the mighty sea;
God will inspire me while I deliver
      My soul of thee!

Tell thou the world, when my bones lie whitening
   Amid the last homes of youth and eld,
That once there was one whose veins ran lightning
      No eye beheld.

Tell how his boyhood was one drear night-hour,
　　How shone for him, through his griefs and gloom,
No star of all heaven sends to light our
　　　　　Path to the tomb.

Roll on, my song, and to after ages
　　Tell how, disdaining all earth can give,
He would have taught men, from wisdom's pages,
　　　　　The way to live.

And tell how trampled, derided, hated,
　　And worn by weakness, disease, and wrong,
He fled for shelter to God, who mated
　　　　　His soul with song.

—With song which alway, sublime or vapid,
　　Flow'd like a rill in the morning beam,
Perchance not deep, but intense and rapid—
　　　　　A mountain stream.

Tell how this Nameless, condemn'd for years long
　　To herd with demons from hell beneath,
Saw things that made him, with groans and tears, long
　　　　　For even death.

Go on to tell how, with genius wasted,
　　Betray'd in friendship, befool'd in love,
With spirit shipwreck'd, and young hopes blasted,
　　　　　He still, still strove;

Till, spent with toil, dreeing death for others
　　(And some whose hands should have wrought for him,
If children live not for sires and mothers),
　　　　　His mind grew dim;

And he fell far through that pit abysmal,
   The gulf and grave of Maginn and Burns,
And pawn'd his soul for the devil's dismal
        Stock of returns.

But yet redeem'd it in days of darkness,
   And shapes and signs of the final wrath,
When death, in hideous and ghastly starkness,
        Stood on his path.

And tell how now, amid wreck and sorrow,
   And want, and sickness, and houseless nights,
He bides in calmness the silent morrow,
        That no ray lights.

And lives he still, then? Yes! Old and hoary
   At thirty-nine, from despair and woe,
He lives, enduring what future story
        Will never know.

Him grant a grave to, ye pitying noble,
   Deep in your bosoms: there let him dwell!
He, too, had tears for all souls in trouble,
        Here and in hell.

THOMAS LOVELL BEDDOES

1803–1849

675   *Wolfram's Dirge*

IF thou wilt ease thine heart
  Of love and all its smart,
   Then sleep, dear, sleep;
And not a sorrow

Hang any tear on your eyelashes;
   Lie still and deep,
Sad soul, until the sea-wave washes
The rim o' the sun to-morrow,
   In eastern sky.

But wilt thou cure thine heart:
Of love and all its smart,
   Then die, dear, die;
'Tis deeper, sweeter,
   Than on a rose-bank to lie dreaming
     With folded eye;
   And there alone, amid the beaming
Of Love's stars, thou'lt meet her
   In eastern sky.

676   *Dream-Pedlary*

IF there were dreams to sell,
   What would you buy?
Some cost a passing bell;
   Some a light sigh,
That shakes from Life's fresh crown
Only a rose-leaf down.
If there were dreams to sell,
Merry and sad to tell,
And the crier rang the bell,
   What would you buy?

A cottage lone and still,
   With bowers nigh,
Shadowy, my woes to still,
   Until I die.

THOMAS LOVELL BEDDOES

Such pearl from Life's fresh crown
Fain would I shake me down.
Were dreams to have at will,
This would best heal my ill,
 This would I buy.

RALPH WALDO EMERSON

1803–1882

677   *Give All to Love*

GIVE all to love;
 Obey thy heart;
Friends, kindred, days,
Estate, good fame,
Plans, credit, and the Muse—
Nothing refuse.

'Tis a brave master;
Let it have scope:
Follow it utterly,
Hope beyond hope:
High and more high
It dives into noon,
With wing unspent,
Untold intent;
But it is a god,
Knows its own path,
And the outlets of the sky.

It was never for the mean;
It requireth courage stout,
Souls above doubt,
Valour unbending:

Such 'twill reward;—
They shall return
More than they were,
And ever ascending.

Leave all for love;
Yet, hear me, yet,
One word more thy heart behoved,
One pulse more of firm endeavour—
Keep thee to-day,
To-morrow, for ever,
Free as an Arab
Of thy beloved.

Cling with life to the maid;
But when the surprise,
First vague shadow of surmise,
Flits across her bosom young,
Of a joy apart from thee,
Free be she, fancy-free;
Nor thou detain her vesture's hem,
Nor the palest rose she flung
From her summer diadem.

Though thou loved her as thyself,
As a self of purer clay;
Though her parting dims the day,
Stealing grace from all alive;
Heartily know,
When half-gods go
The gods arrive.

Fore-runners

LONG I follow'd happy guides,
I could never reach their sides;
Their step is forth and, ere the day
Breaks, up their leaguer and away.
Keen my sense, my heart was young,
Right goodwill my sinews strung,
But no speed of mine avails
To hunt upon their shining trails.
On and away, their hasting feet
Make the morning proud and sweet;
Flowers they strew,—I catch the scent;
Or tone of silver instrument
Leaves on the wind melodious trace;
Yet I could never see their face.
On eastern hills I see their smokes
Mix'd with mist by distant lochs.
I met many travellers,
Who the road had surely kept;
They saw not my fine revellers—
These had cross'd them while they slept.
Some had heard their fair report
In the country or the court:
Fleetest couriers alive
Never yet could once arrive,
As they went or they return'd,
At the house where these sojourn'd.
Sometimes their strong speed they slacken
Though they are not overtaken;
In sleep their jubilant troop is near—
I tuneful voices overhear,

It may be in wood or waste—
At unawares 'tis come and past.
Their near camp my spirit knows
By signs gracious as rainbows.
I thenceforward and long after
Listen for their harplike laughter,
And carry in my heart, for days,
Peace that hallows rudest ways.

679   *Bacchus*

BRING me wine, but wine which never grew
In the belly of the grape,
Or grew on vine whose tap-roots, reaching through
Under the Andes to the Cape,
Suffer'd no savour of the earth to 'scape.

Let its grapes the morn salute
From a nocturnal root,
Which feels the acrid juice
Of Styx and Erebus;
And turns the woe of Night,
By its own craft, to a more rich delight.

We buy ashes for bread;
We buy diluted wine;
Give me of the true,
Whose ample leaves and tendrils curl'd
Among the silver hills of heaven
Draw everlasting dew;
Wine of wine,
Blood of the world,

RALPH WALDO EMERSON

Form of forms, and mould of statures,
That I intoxicated,
And by the draught assimilated,
May float at pleasure through all natures;
The bird-language rightly spell,
And that which roses say so well:

Wine that is shed
Like the torrents of the sun
Up the horizon walls,
Or like the Atlantic streams, which run
When the South Sea calls.

Water and bread,
Food which needs no transmuting,
Rainbow-flowering, wisdom-fruiting,
Wine which is already man,
Food which teach and reason can.

Wine which Music is,—
Music and wine are one,—
That I, drinking this,
Shall hear far Chaos talk with me;
Kings unborn shall walk with me;
And the poor grass shall plot and plan
What it will do when it is man.
Quicken'd so, will I unlock
Every crypt of every rock.
I thank the joyful juice
For all I know;
Winds of remembering
Of the ancient being blow,

And seeming-solid walls of use
Open and flow.

Pour, Bacchus! the remembering wine;
Retrieve the loss of me and mine!
Vine for vine be antidote,
And the grape requite the lote!
Haste to cure the old despair;
Reason in Nature's lotus drench'd—
The memory of ages quench'd—
Give them again to shine;
Let wine repair what this undid;
And where the infection slid,
A dazzling memory revive;
Refresh the faded tints,
Recut the agèd prints,
And write my old adventures with the pen
Which on the first day drew,
Upon the tablets blue,
The dancing Pleiads and eternal men.

680   *Brahma*

IF the red slayer think he slays,
    Or if the slain think he is slain,
They know not well the subtle ways
    I keep, and pass, and turn again.

Far or forgot to me is near;
    Shadow and sunlight are the same;
The vanish'd gods to me appear;
    And one to me are shame and fame.

RALPH WALDO EMERSON

They reckon ill who leave me out;
　　When me they fly, I am the wings;
I am the doubter and the doubt,
　　And I the hymn the Brahmin sings.

The strong gods pine for my abode,
　　And pine in vain the sacred Seven;
But thou, meek lover of the good!
　　Find me, and turn thy back on heaven.

RICHARD HENRY HORNE

1803-1884

681　　　　*The Plough*

A LANDSCAPE IN BERKSHIRE

ABOVE yon sombre swell of land
　　Thou see'st the dawn's grave orange hue,
With one pale streak like yellow sand,
　　And over that a vein of blue.

The air is cold above the woods;
　　All silent is the earth and sky,
Except with his own lonely moods
　　The blackbird holds a colloquy.

Over the broad hill creeps a beam,
　　Like hope that gilds a good man's brow;
And now ascends the nostril-stream
　　Of stalwart horses come to plough.

Ye rigid Ploughmen, bear in mind
　　Your labour is for future hours:
Advance—spare not—nor look behind—
　　Plough deep and straight with all your powers!

CHARLES WHITEHEAD

1804–1862

682 *The Lamp*

AS yonder lamp in my vacated room
　　With arduous flame disputes the darksome night,
And can, with its involuntary light,
But lifeless things, that near it stand, illume;
Yet all the while it doth itself consume,
　　And, ere the sun begins its heavenly height
　　With courier beams that meet the shepherd's sight,
There, whence its life arose, shall be its tomb—

So wastes my light away. Perforce confined
　　To common things, a limit to its sphere,
It shines on worthless trifles undesign'd
　　With fainter ray each hour imprison'd here.
Alas! to know that the consuming mind
　　Shall leave its lamp cold, ere the sun appear.

ROBERT STEPHEN HAWKER

1804–1875

683 *King Arthur's Waes-hael*

WAES-HAEL for knight and dame!
　　O merry be their dole!
Drink-hael! in Jesu's name
　　We fill the tawny bowl;
But cover down the curving crest,
Mould of the Orient Lady's breast.

ROBERT STEPHEN HAWKER

Waes-hael! yet lift no lid:
  Drain ye the reeds for wine.
Drink-hael! the milk was hid
  That soothed that Babe divine;
Hush'd, as this hollow channel flows,
He drew the balsam from the rose.

Waes-hael! thus glow'd the breast
  Where a God yearn'd to cling;
Drink-hael! so Jesu press'd
  Life from its mystic spring;
Then hush and bend in reverent sign
And breathe the thrilling reeds for wine.

Waes-hael! in shadowy scene
  Lo! Christmas children we:
Drink-hael! behold we lean
  At a far Mother's knee;
To dream that thus her bosom smiled,
And learn the lip of Bethlehem's Child.

FRANCIS MAHONY

1805-1866

684　　*The Bells of Shandon*

WITH deep affection,
  And recollection,
I often think of
  Those Shandon bells,
Whose sounds so wild would,
In the days of childhood,
Fling around my cradle
  Their magic spells.

FRANCIS MAHONY

On this I ponder
Where'er I wander,
And thus grow fonder,
 Sweet Cork, of thee;
With thy bells of Shandon,
That sound so grand on
The pleasant waters
 Of the River Lee.

I've heard bells chiming
Full many a clime in,
Tolling sublime in
 Cathedral shrine,
While at a glib rate
Brass tongues would vibrate—
But all their music
 Spoke naught like thine;
For memory, dwelling
On each proud swelling
Of the belfry knelling
 Its bold notes free,
Made the bells of Shandon
Sound far more grand on
The pleasant waters
 Of the River Lee.

I've heard bells tolling
Old Adrian's Mole in,
Their thunder rolling
 From the Vatican

FRANCIS MAHONY

And cymbals glorious
Swinging uproarious
In the gorgeous turrets
   Of Notre Dame;
But thy sounds were sweeter
Than the dome of Peter
Flings o'er the Tiber,
   Pealing solemnly—
O, the bells of Shandon
Sound far more grand on
The pleasant waters
   Of the River Lee.

There's a bell in Moscow,
While on tower and kiosk O!
In Saint Sophia
   The Turkman gets,
And loud in air
Calls men to prayer
From the tapering summits
   Of tall minarets.
Such empty phantom
I freely grant them;
But there's an anthem
   More dear to me,—
'Tis the bells of Shandon,
That sound so grand on
The pleasant waters
   Of the River Lee.

1806–1861

685   *Farewells from Paradise*

River-spirits

HARK! the flow of the four rivers—
        Hark the flow!
How the silence round you shivers,
While our voices through it go,
        Cold and clear.

A softer voice

Think a little, while ye hear,
        Of the banks
Where the willows and the deer
Crowd in intermingled ranks,
As if all would drink at once
Where the living water runs!—
Of the fishes' golden edges
Flashing in and out the sedges;
Of the swans on silver thrones,
Floating down the winding streams
With impassive eyes turned shoreward
And a chant of undertones,—
And the lotus leaning forward
To help them into dreams.
        Fare ye well, farewell!
The river-sounds, no longer audible,
        Expire at Eden's door.
        Each footstep of your treading

Treads out some murmur which ye heard before.
Farewell! the streams of Eden
Ye shall hear nevermore!

Bird-spirit

I am the nearest nightingale
That singeth in Eden after you;
And I am singing loud and true,
And sweet,—I do not fail.
I sit upon a cypress bough,
Close to the gate, and I fling my song
Over the gate and through the mail
Of the warden angels marshall'd strong,—
Over the gate and after you!
And the warden angels let it pass,
Because the poor brown bird, alas,
Sings in the garden, sweet and true.
And I build my song of high pure notes,
Note over note, height over height,
Till I strike the arch of the Infinite,
And I bridge abysmal agonies
With strong, clear calms of harmonies,—
And something abides, and something floats,
In the song which I sing after you.
Fare ye well, farewell!
The creature-sounds, no longer audible,
Expire at Eden's door.
Each footstep of your treading
Treads out some cadence which ye heard before
Farewell! the birds of Eden
Ye shall hear nevermore!

686 *Grief*

I TELL you, hopeless grief is passionless;
  That only men incredulous of despair,
  Half-taught in anguish, through the midnight air
Beat upward to God's throne in loud access
Of shrieking and reproach. Full desertness
  In souls as countries lieth silent-bare
  Under the blanching, vertical eye-glare
Of the absolute Heavens. Deep-hearted man, express
Grief for thy Dead in silence like to Death—
  Most like a monumental statue set
In everlasting watch and moveless woe
Till itself crumble to the dust beneath.
  Touch it; the marble eyelids are not wet:
If it could weep, it could arise and go.

687 *A Musical Instrument*

WHAT was he doing, the great god Pan,
  Down in the reeds by the river?
Spreading ruin and scattering ban,
Splashing and paddling with hoofs of a goat,
And breaking the golden lilies afloat
  With the dragon-fly on the river.

He tore out a reed, the great god Pan,
  From the deep cool bed of the river;
The limpid water turbidly ran,
And the broken lilies a-dying lay,
And the dragon-fly had fled away,
  Ere he brought it out of the river.

ELIZABETH BARRETT BROWNING

High on the shore sat the great god Pan,
   While turbidly flow'd the river;
And hack'd and hew'd as a great god can
With his hard bleak steel at the patient reed,
Till there was not a sign of the leaf indeed
   To prove it fresh from the river.

He cut it short, did the great god Pan
   (How tall it stood in the river!),
Then drew the pith, like the heart of a man,
Steadily from the outside ring,
And notch'd the poor dry empty thing
   In holes, as he sat by the river.

'This is the way,' laugh'd the great god Pan
   (Laugh'd while he sat by the river),
'The only way, since gods began
To make sweet music, they could succeed.'
Then dropping his mouth to a hole in the reed,
   He blew in power by the river.

Sweet, sweet, sweet, O Pan!
   Piercing sweet by the river!
Blinding sweet, O great god Pan!
The sun on the hill forgot to die,
And the lilies revived, and the dragon-fly
   Came back to dream on the river.

Yet half a beast is the great god Pan,
   To laugh as he sits by the river,
Making a poet out of a man:
The true gods sigh for the cost and pain—
For the reed which grows nevermore again
   As a reed with the reeds of the river.

688   *Sonnets from the Portuguese*

(*i*)

I THOUGHT once how Theocritus had sung
  Of the sweet years, the dear and wish'd-for years,
  Who each one in a gracious hand appears
To bear a gift for mortals old or young:
And, as I mused it in his antique tongue,
  I saw in gradual vision through my tears
  The sweet, sad years, the melancholy years—
Those of my own life, who by turns had flung
A shadow across me. Straightway I was 'ware,
  So weeping, how a mystic Shape did move
Behind me, and drew me backward by the hair;
  And a voice said in mastery, while I strove,
'Guess now who holds thee?'—'Death,' I said. But there
  The silver answer rang—'Not Death, but Love.'

689   (*ii*)

U NLIKE are we, unlike, O princely Heart!
  Unlike our uses and our destinies.
  Our ministering two angels look surprise
On one another, as they strike athwart
Their wings in passing. Thou, bethink thee, art
  A guest for queens for social pageantries,
  With gages from a hundred brighter eyes
Than tears even can make mine, to play thy part
Of chief musician. What hast thou to do
  With looking from the lattice-lights at me—
A poor, tired, wandering singer, singing through
  The dark, and leaning up a cypress tree?
The chrism is on thine head—on mine the dew—
  And Death must dig the level where these agree.

690   (*iii*)

GO from me. Yet I feel that I shall stand
 Henceforward in thy shadow. Nevermore
Alone upon the threshold of my door
Of individual life I shall command
The uses of my soul, nor lift my hand
 Serenely in the sunshine as before,
 Without the sense of that which I forbore—
Thy touch upon the palm. The widest land
Doom takes to part us, leaves thy heart in mine
 With pulses that beat double. What I do
And what I dream include thee, as the wine
 Must taste of its own grapes. And when I sue
God for myself, He hears that name of thine,
 And sees within my eyes the tears of two.

691   (*iv*)

IF thou must love me, let it be for naught
 Except for love's sake only. Do not say,
'I love her for her smile—her look—her way
Of speaking gently,—for a trick of thought
That falls in well with mine, and certes brought
 A sense of pleasant ease on such a day'—
 For these things in themselves, Belovèd, may
Be changed, or change for thee—and love, so wrought,
May be unwrought so. Neither love me for
 Thine own dear pity's wiping my cheeks dry:
A creature might forget to weep, who bore
 Thy comfort long, and lose thy love thereby!
But love me for love's sake, that evermore
 Thou mayst love on, through love's eternity.

692 (v)

WHEN our two souls stand up erect and strong,
   Face to face, silent, drawing nigh and nigher,
Until the lengthening wings break into fire
At either curving point,—what bitter wrong
Can the earth do us, that we should not long
   Be here contented? Think! In mounting higher,
   The angels would press on us, and aspire
To drop some golden orb of perfect song
Into our deep, dear silence. Let us stay
   Rather on earth, Belovèd—where the unfit
Contrarious moods of men recoil away
   And isolate pure spirits, and permit
A place to stand and love in for a day,
   With darkness and the death-hour rounding it.

FREDERICK TENNYSON

1807–1898

693 *The Holy Tide*

THE days are sad, it is the Holy tide.
   The Winter morn is short, the Night is long;
So let the lifeless Hours be glorified
   With deathless thoughts and echo'd in sweet song:
And through the sunset of this purple cup
   They will resume the roses of their prime,
And the old Dead will hear us and wake up,
   Pass with dim smiles and make our hearts sublime!

FREDERICK TENNYSON

The days are sad, it is the Holy tide:
  Be dusky mistletoes and hollies strown,
Sharp as the spear that pierced His sacred side,
  Red as the drops upon His thorny crown;
No haggard Passion and no lawless Mirth
  Fright off the solemn Muse,—tell sweet old tales,
Sing songs as we sit brooding o'er the hearth,
  Till the lamp flickers and the memory fails.

HENRY WADSWORTH LONGFELLOW

1807–1882

694   *My Lost Youth*

OFTEN I think of the beautiful town
    That is seated by the sea;
Often in thought go up and down
The pleasant streets of that dear old town,
    And my youth comes back to me.
        And a verse of a Lapland song
        Is haunting my memory still:
        'A boy's will is the wind's will,
And the thoughts of youth are long, long thoughts.'

I can see the shadowy lines of its trees,
    And catch, in sudden gleams,
The sheen of the far-surrounding seas,
And islands that were the Hesperides
    Of all my boyish dreams.
        And the burden of that old song,
        It murmurs and whispers still:
        'A boy's will is the wind's will,
And the thoughts of youth are long, long thoughts.'

I remember the black wharves and the slips,
   And the sea-tides tossing free;
And Spanish sailors with bearded lips,
And the beauty and mystery of the ships,
   And the magic of the sea.
      And the voice of that wayward song
      Is singing and saying still:
      'A boy's will is the wind's will,
And the thoughts of youth are long, long thoughts.'

I remember the bulwarks by the shore,
   And the fort upon the hill;
The sunrise gun with its hollow roar,
The drum-beat repeated o'er and o'er,
   And the bugle wild and shrill.
      And the music of that old song
      Throbs in my memory still:
      'A boy's will is the wind's will,
And the thoughts of youth are long, long thoughts.'

I remember the sea-fight far away,
   How it thunder'd o'er the tide!
And the dead sea-captains, as they lay
In their graves o'erlooking the tranquil bay
   Where they in battle died.
      And the sound of that mournful song
      Goes through me with a thrill:
      'A boy's will is the wind's will,
And the thoughts of youth are long, long thoughts.'

I can see the breezy dome of groves,
   The shadows of Deering's woods;
And the friendships old and the early loves

Come back with a Sabbath sound, as of doves
   In quiet neighbourhoods.
     And the verse of that sweet old song,
     It flutters and murmurs still:
     'A boy's will is the wind's will,
And the thoughts of youth are long, long thoughts.'

I remember the gleams and glooms that dart
   Across the schoolboy's brain;
The song and the silence in the heart,
That in part are prophecies, and in part
   Are longings wild and vain.
     And the voice of that fitful song
     Sings on, and is never still:
     'A boy's will is the wind's will,
And the thoughts of youth are long, long thoughts.'

There are things of which I may not speak;
   There are dreams that cannot die;
There are thoughts that make the strong heart weak,
And bring a pallor into the cheek,
   And a mist before the eye.
     And the words of that fatal song
     Come over me like a chill:
     'A boy's will is the wind's will,
And the thoughts of youth are long, long thoughts.'

Strange to me now are the forms I meet
   When I visit the dear old town;
But the native air is pure and sweet,
And the trees that o'ershadow each well-known street,
   As they balance up and down,

Are singing the beautiful song,
　　Are sighing and whispering still:
　　'A boy's will is the wind's will,
And the thoughts of youth are long, long thoughts.'

And Deering's woods are fresh and fair,
　　And with joy that is almost pain
My heart goes back to wander there,
And among the dreams of the days that were
　　I find my lost youth again.
　　And the strange and beautiful song,
　　The groves are repeating it still:
　　'A boy's will is the wind's will,
And the thoughts of youth are long, long thoughts.'

695　　*The Galley of Count Arnaldos*

AH! what pleasant visions haunt me
　　As I gaze upon the sea!
All the old romantic legends,
　　All my dreams, come back to me.

Sails of silk and ropes of sandal,
　　Such as gleam in ancient lore;
And the singing of the sailors,
　　And the answer from the shore!

Most of all, the Spanish ballad
　　Haunts me oft, and tarries long,
Of the noble Count Arnaldos
　　And the sailor's mystic song.

Telling how the Count Arnaldos,
　　With his hawk upon his hand,
Saw a fair and stately galley,
　　Steering onward to the land;—

How he heard the ancient helmsman
   Chant a song so wild and clear,
That the sailing sea-bird slowly
   Poised upon the mast to hear.

Till his soul was full of longing,
   And he cried, with impulse strong,—
'Helmsman! for the love of heaven,
   Teach me, too, that wondrous song!'

'Wouldst thou,'—so the helmsman answered,—
   'Learn the secret of the sea?
Only those who brave its dangers
   Comprehend its mystery!'

696   *Chaucer*

AN old man in a lodge within a park;
   The chamber walls depicted all around
   With portraitures of huntsman, hawk, and hound,
   And the hurt deer. He listeneth to the lark,
Whose song comes with the sunshine through the dark
   Of painted glass in leaden lattice bound;
   He listeneth and he laugheth at the sound,
   Then writeth in a book like any clerk.
He is the poet of the dawn, who wrote
   The Canterbury Tales, and his old age
   Made beautiful with song; and as I read
I hear the crowing cock, I hear the note
   Of lark and linnet, and from every page
   Rise odours of plough'd field or flowery mead.

697   *Dante*

OFT have I seen at some cathedral door
    A labourer, pausing in the dust and heat,
    Lay down his burden, and with reverent feet
    Enter, and cross himself, and on the floor
Kneel to repeat his paternoster o'er;
    Far off the noises of the world retreat;
    The loud vociferations of the street
    Become an undistinguishable roar.
So, as I enter here from day to day,
    And leave my burden at this minster gate,
    Kneeling in prayer, and not ashamed to pray,
The tumult of the time disconsolate
    To inarticulate murmurs dies away,
    While the eternal ages watch and wait.

JOHN GREENLEAF WHITTIER

1807–1892

698   *The Henchman*

MY lady walks her morning round,
    My lady's page her fleet greyhound,
My lady's hair the fond winds stir,
And all the birds make songs for her.

Her thrushes sing in Rathburn bowers,
And Rathburn side is gay with flowers;
But ne'er like hers, in flower or bird,
Was beauty seen or music heard.

JOHN GREENLEAF WHITTIER

Oh, proud and calm!—she cannot know
Where'er she goes with her I go;
Oh, cold and fair!—she cannot guess
I kneel to share her hound's caress!

The hound and I are on her trail,
The wind and I uplift her veil;
As if the calm, cold moon she were,
And I the tide, I follow her.

As unrebuked as they, I share
The licence of the sun and air,
And in a common homage hide
My worship from her scorn and pride.

No lance have I, in joust or fight,
To splinter in my lady's sight;
But, at her feet, how blest were I
For any need of hers to die!

CAROLINE ELIZABETH SARAH NORTON
1808–1876

699   *I do not love Thee*

I DO not love thee!—no! I do not love thee!
  And yet when thou art absent I am sad;
  And envy even the bright blue sky above thee,
Whose quiet stars may see thee and be glad.

I do not love thee!—yet, I know not why,
Whate'er thou dost seems still well done, to me:
  And often in my solitude I sigh
That those I do love are not more like thee!

CAROLINE ELIZABETH SARAH NORTON

I do not love thee!—yet, when thou art gone,
I hate the sound (though those who speak be dear)
    Which breaks the lingering echo of the tone
Thy voice of music leaves upon my ear.

I do not love thee!—yet thy speaking eyes,
With their deep, bright, and most expressive blue,
    Between me and the midnight heaven arise,
Oftener than any eyes I ever knew.

I know I do not love thee! yet, alas!
Others will scarcely trust my candid heart;
    And oft I catch them smiling as they pass,
Because they see me gazing where thou art.

CHARLES TENNYSON TURNER

1808–1879

700 *Letty's Globe*

WHEN Letty had scarce pass'd her third glad year,
    And her young artless words began to flow,
One day we gave the child a colour'd sphere
    Of the wide earth, that she might mark and know,
By tint and outline, all its sea and land.
    She patted all the world; old empires peep'd
Between her baby fingers; her soft hand
    Was welcome at all frontiers. How she leap'd,
    And laugh'd and prattled in her world-wide bliss;
But when we turn'd her sweet unlearnèd eye
On our own isle, she raised a joyous cry—
'Oh! yes, I see it, Letty's home is there!'
    And while she hid all England with a kiss,
Bright over Europe fell her golden hair.

EDGAR ALLAN POE

1809–1849

701 *To Helen*

HELEN, thy beauty is to me
    Like those Nicèan barks of yore
That gently, o'er a perfumed sea,
    The weary way-worn wanderer bore
    To his own native shore.

On desperate seas long wont to roam,
    Thy hyacinth hair, thy classic face,
Thy Naiad airs have brought me home
    To the glory that was Greece,
And the grandeur that was Rome.

Lo, in yon brilliant window-niche
    How statue-like I see thee stand,
    The agate lamp within thy hand,
Ah! Psyche, from the regions which
    Are holy land!

702 *For Annie*

THANK Heaven! the crisis—
    The danger is past,
And the lingering illness
    Is over at last—
And the fever called 'Living'
    Is conquer'd at last.

825

EDGAR ALLAN POE

Sadly, I know
   I am shorn of my strength,
And no muscle I move
   As I lie at full length:
But no matter—I feel
   I am better at length.

And I rest so composedly
   Now, in my bed,
That any beholder
   Might fancy me dead—
Might start at beholding me,
   Thinking me dead.

The moaning and groaning,
   The sighing and sobbing,
Are quieted now,
   With that horrible throbbing
At heart—ah, that horrible,
   Horrible throbbing!

The sickness—the nausea—
   The pitiless pain—
Have ceased, with the fever
   That madden'd my brain—
With the fever called 'Living'
   That burn'd in my brain.

And O! of all tortures
   That torture the worst
Has abated—the terrible
   Torture of thirst

For the naphthaline river
   Of Passion accurst—
I have drunk of a water
   That quenches all thirst.

—Of a water that flows,
   With a lullaby sound,
From a spring but a very few
   Feet under ground—
From a cavern not very far
   Down under ground.

And ah! let it never
   Be foolishly said
That my room it is gloomy,
   And narrow my bed;
For man never slept
   In a different bed—
And, to *sleep*, you must slumber
   In just such a bed.

My tantalized spirit
   Here blandly reposes,
Forgetting, or never
   Regretting its roses—
Its old agitations
   Of myrtles and roses:

For now, while so quietly
   Lying, it fancies
A holier odour
   About it, of pansies—

EDGAR ALLAN POE

A rosemary odour,
  Commingled with pansies—
With rue and the beautiful
  Puritan pansies.

And so it lies happily,
  Bathing in many
A dream of the truth
  And the beauty of Annie—
Drown'd in a bath
  Of the tresses of Annie.

She tenderly kiss'd me,
  She fondly caress'd,
And then I fell gently
  To sleep on her breast—
Deeply to sleep
  From the heaven of her breast.

When the light was extinguish'd,
  She cover'd me warm,
And she pray'd to the angels
  To keep me from harm—
To the queen of the angels
  To shield me from harm.

And I lie so composedly,
  Now, in my bed
(Knowing her love),
  That you fancy me dead—
And I rest so contentedly,
  Now, in my bed

(With her love at my breast),
    That you fancy me dead—
That you shudder to look at me,
    Thinking me dead.

But my heart it is brighter
    Than all of the many
Stars in the sky,
    For it sparkles with Annie—
It glows with the light
    Of the love of my Annie—
With the thought of the light
    Of the eyes of my Annie.

703   *To One in Paradise*

THOU wast all that to me, love,
    For which my soul did pine—
A green isle in the sea, love,
    A fountain and a shrine,
All wreathed with fairy fruits and flowers,
    And all the flowers were mine.

Now all my days are trances,
    And all my nightly dreams
Are where thy grey eye glances,
    And where thy footstep gleams—
In what ethereal dances,
    By what eternal streams!

EDWARD FITZGERALD

1809–1883

Old Song

T'IS a dull sight
　　To see the year dying,
When winter winds
　　Set the yellow wood sighing:
　　　Sighing, O sighing!

When such a time cometh
　　I do retire
Into an old room
　　Beside a bright fire:
　　　O, pile a bright fire!

And there I sit
　　Reading old things,
Of knights and lorn damsels,
　　While the wind sings—
　　　O, drearily sings!

I never look out
　　Nor attend to the blast;
For all to be seen
　　Is the leaves falling fast:
　　　Falling, falling!

But close at the hearth,
　　Like a cricket, sit I,
Reading of summer
　　And chivalry—
　　　Gallant chivalry!

EDWARD FITZGERALD

Then with an old friend
  I talk of our youth—
How 'twas gladsome, but often
  Foolish, forsooth:
    But gladsome, gladsome!

Or, to get merry,
  We sing some old rhyme
That made the wood ring again
  In summer time—
    Sweet summer time!

Then go we smoking,
  Silent and snug:
Naught passes between us,
  Save a brown jug—
    Sometimes!

And sometimes a tear
  Will rise in each eye,
Seeing the two old friends
  So merrily—
    So merrily!

And ere to bed
  Go we, go we,
Down on the ashes
  We kneel on the knee,
    Praying together!

Thus, then, live I
  Till, 'mid all the gloom,
By Heaven! the bold sun
  Is with me in the room
    Shining, shining!

Then the clouds part,
   Swallows soaring between;
The spring is alive,
   And the meadows are green!

I jump up like mad,
   Break the old pipe in twain,
And away to the meadows,
   The meadows again!

705   *From Omar Khayyam*

I

A BOOK of Verses underneath the Bough,
  A Jug of Wine, a Loaf of Bread—and Thou
Beside me singing in the Wilderness—
O, Wilderness were Paradise enow!

Some for the Glories of This World; and some
Sigh for the Prophet's Paradise to come;
  Ah, take the Cash, and let the Credit go,
Nor heed the rumble of a distant Drum!

Look to the blowing Rose about us—'Lo,
Laughing,' she says, 'into the world I blow,
  At once the silken tassel of my Purse
Tear, and its Treasure on the Garden throw.'

And those who husbanded the Golden grain
And those who flung it to the winds like Rain
  Alike to no such aureate Earth are turn'd
As, buried once, Men want dug up again.

832

EDWARD FITZGERALD

II

Think, in this batter'd Caravanserai
Whose Portals are alternate Night and Day,
   How Sultán after Sultán with his Pomp
Abode his destined Hour, and went his way.

They say the Lion and the Lizard keep
The Courts where Jamshyd gloried and drank deep:
   And Bahrám, that great Hunter—the wild Ass
Stamps o'er his Head, but cannot break his Sleep.

I sometimes think that never blows so red
The Rose as where some buried Cæsar bled;
   That every Hyacinth the Garden wears
Dropt in her Lap from some once lovely Head.

And this reviving Herb whose tender Green
Fledges the River-Lip on which we lean—
   Ah, lean upon it lightly! for who knows
From what once lovely Lip it springs unseen!

Ah, my Belovèd, fill the Cup that clears
To-day of past Regrets and Future Fears:
   To-morrow!—Why, To-morrow I may be
Myself with Yesterday's Sev'n thousand Years.

For some we loved, the loveliest and the best
That from his Vintage rolling Time hath prest,
   Have drunk their Cup a Round or two before,
And one by one crept silently to rest.

And we, that now make merry in the Room
They left, and Summer dresses in new bloom,
   Ourselves must we beneath the Couch of Earth
Descend—ourselves to make a Couch—for whom?

Ah, make the most of what we yet may spend,
Before we too into the Dust descend;
   Dust unto Dust, and under Dust to lie,
Sans Wine, sans Song, sans Singer, and—sans End!

III

Ah, with the Grape my fading Life provide,
And wash my Body whence the Life has died,
   And lay me, shrouded in the living Leaf,
By some not unfrequented Garden-side. . . .

Yon rising Moon that looks for us again—
How oft hereafter will she wax and wane;
   How oft hereafter rising look for us
Through this same Garden—and for *one* in vain!

And when like her, O Sákí, you shall pass
Among the Guests star-scatter'd on the Grass,
   And in your joyous errand reach the spot
Where I made One—turn down an empty Glass!

RICHARD MONCKTON MILNES, LORD HOUGHTON

1809–1885

706   *The Men of Old*

I KNOW not that the men of old
  Were better than men now,
Of heart more kind, of hand more bold,
  Of more ingenuous brow:
I heed not those who pine for force
  A ghost of Time to raise,
As if they thus could check the course
  Of these appointed days.

LORD HOUGHTON

Still it is true, and over true,
  That I delight to close
This book of life self-wise and new,
  And let my thoughts repose
On all that humble happiness
  The world has since forgone,
The daylight of contentedness
  That on those faces shone.

With rights, tho' not too closely scann'd,
  Enjoy'd as far as known;
With will by no reverse unmann'd,
  With pulse of even tone,
They from to-day and from to-night
  Expected nothing more
Than yesterday and yesternight
  Had proffer'd them before.

To them was Life a simple art
  Of duties to be done,
A game where each man took his part,
  A race where all must run;
A battle whose great scheme and scope
  They little cared to know,
Content as men-at-arms to cope
  Each with his fronting foe.

Man now his Virtue's diadem
  Puts on and proudly wears:
Great thoughts, great feelings came to them
  Like instincts, unawares.

Blending their souls' sublimest needs
    With tasks of every day,
They went about their gravest deeds
    As noble boys at play.

ALFRED TENNYSON, LORD TENNYSON
1809–1892

707   *Mariana*

WITH blackest moss the flower-plots
    Were thickly crusted, one and all:
The rusted nails fell from the knots
    That held the pear to the gable-wall.
The broken sheds look'd sad and strange;
    Unlifted was the clinking latch;
    Weeded and worn the ancient thatch
Upon the lonely moated grange.
      She only said, 'My life is dreary,
        He cometh not,' she said;
      She said, 'I am aweary, aweary,
        I would that I were dead!'

Her tears fell with the dews at even;
    Her tears fell ere the dews were dried;
She could not look on the sweet heaven,
    Either at morn or eventide.
After the flitting of the bats,
    When thickest dark did trance the sky,
    She drew her casement-curtain by,
And glanced athwart the glooming flats.
      She only said, 'The night is dreary,
        He cometh not,' she said;
      She said, 'I am aweary, aweary,
        I would that I were dead!'

Upon the middle of the night,
   Waking she heard the night-fowl crow:
The cock sung out an hour ere light:
   From the dark fen the oxen's low
Came to her: without hope of change,
   In sleep she seem'd to walk forlorn,
   Till cold winds woke the gray-eyed morn
About the lonely moated grange.
     She only said, 'The day is dreary,
       He cometh not,' she said;
     She said, 'I am aweary, aweary,
       I would that I were dead!'

About a stone-cast from the wall
   A sluice with blacken'd waters slept,
And o'er it many, round and small,
   The cluster'd marish-mosses crept.
Hard by a poplar shook alway,
   All silver-green with gnarlèd bark:
   For leagues no other tree did mark
The level waste, the rounding gray.
     She only said, 'My life is dreary,
       He cometh not,' she said;
     She said, 'I am aweary, aweary
       I would that I were dead!'

And ever when the moon was low,
   And the shrill winds were up and away,
In the white curtain, to and fro,
   She saw the gusty shadow sway.
But when the moon was very low,
   And wild winds bound within their cell,
   The shadow of the poplar fell

Upon her bed, across her brow.
    She only said, 'The night is dreary,
      He cometh not,' she said;
    She said, 'I am aweary, aweary,
      I would that I were dead!'

All day within the dreamy house,
    The doors upon their hinges creak'd;
The blue fly sung in the pane; the mouse
    Behind the mouldering wainscot shriek'd,
Or from the crevice peer'd about.
    Old faces glimmer'd thro' the doors,
    Old footsteps trod the upper floors,
Old voices call'd her from without.
    She only said, 'My life is dreary,
      He cometh not,' she said;
    She said, 'I am aweary, aweary,'
      I would that I were dead!'

The sparrow's chirrup on the roof,
    The slow clock ticking, and the sound
Which to the wooing wind aloof
    The poplar made, did all confound
Her sense; but most she loathed the hour
    When the thick-moted sunbeam lay
    Athwart the chambers, and the day
Was sloping toward his western bower.
    Then, said she, 'I am very dreary
      He will not come,' she said;
    She wept, 'I am aweary, aweary,
      O God, that I were dead!'

The Lady of Shalott

PART I

ON either side the river lie
   Long fields of barley and of rye,
That clothe the wold and meet the sky;
And thro' the field the road runs by
         To many-tower'd Camelot;
And up and down the people go,
Gazing where the lilies blow
Round an island there below,
         The island of Shalott.

Willows whiten, aspens quiver,
Little breezes dusk and shiver
Thro' the wave that runs for ever
By the island in the river
         Flowing down to Camelot.
Four gray walls, and four gray towers,
Overlook a space of flowers,
And the silent isle imbowers
         The Lady of Shalott.

By the margin, willow-veil'd,
Slide the heavy barges trail'd
By slow horses; and unhail'd
The shallop flitteth silken-sail'd
         Skimming down to Camelot:
But who hath seen her wave her hand?
Or at the casement seen her stand?
Or is she known in all the land,
         The Lady of Shalott?

Only reapers, reaping early
In among the bearded barley,
Hear a song that echoes cheerly
From the river winding clearly,
       Down to tower'd Camelot:
And by the moon the reaper weary,
Piling sheaves in uplands airy,
Listening, whispers ''Tis the fairy
       Lady of Shalott.'

Part II

There she weaves by night and day
A magic web with colours gay.
She has heard a whisper say,
A curse is on her if she stay
       To look down to Camelot.
She knows not what the curse may be,
And so she weaveth steadily,
And little other care hath she,
       The Lady of Shalott.

And moving thro' a mirror clear
That hangs before her all the year,
Shadows of the world appear.
There she sees the highway near
       Winding down to Camelot:
There the river eddy whirls,
And there the surly village-churls,
And the red cloaks of market girls,
       Pass onward from Shalott.

Sometimes a troop of damsels glad,
An abbot on an ambling pad,
Sometimes a curly shepherd-lad,
Or long-hair'd page in crimson clad,
      Goes by to tower'd Camelot;
And sometimes thro' the mirror blue
The knights come riding two and two:
She hath no loyal knight and true,
      The Lady of Shalott.

But in her web she still delights
To weave the mirror's magic sights,
For often thro' the silent nights
A funeral, with plumes and lights,
      And music, went to Camelot:
Or when the moon was overhead,
Came two young lovers lately wed;
'I am half sick of shadows,' said
      The Lady of Shalott.

Part III

A bow-shot from her bower-eaves,
He rode between the barley-sheaves,
The sun came dazzling thro' the leaves,
And flamed upon the brazen greaves
      Of bold Sir Lancelot.
A red-cross knight for ever kneel'd
To a lady in his shield,
That sparkled on the yellow field,
      Beside remote Shalott.

The gemmy bridle glitter'd free,
Like to some branch of stars we see
Hung in the golden Galaxy.
The bridle bells rang merrily
   As he rode down to Camelot:
And from his blazon'd baldric slung
A mighty silver bugle hung,
And as he rode his armour rung,
   Beside remote Shalott.

All in the blue unclouded weather
Thick-jewell'd shone the saddle-leather,
The helmet and the helmet-feather
Burn'd like one burning flame together,
   As he rode down to Camelot.
As often thro' the purple night,
Below the starry clusters bright,
Some bearded meteor, trailing light,
   Moves over still Shalott.

His broad clear brow in sunlight glow'd;
On burnish'd hooves his war-horse trode;
From underneath his helmet flow'd
His coal-black curls as on he rode,
   As he rode down to Camelot.
From the bank and from the river
He flash'd into the crystal mirror,
'Tirra lirra,' by the river
   Sang Sir Lancelot.

She left the web, she left the loom,
She made three paces thro' the room,

She saw the water-lily bloom,
She saw the helmet and the plume,
        She look'd down to Camelot.
Out flew the web and floated wide;
The mirror crack'd from side to side;
'The curse is come upon me!' cried
        The Lady of Shalott.

Part IV

In the stormy east-wind straining,
The pale yellow woods were waning,
The broad stream in his banks complaining,
Heavily the low sky raining
        Over tower'd Camelot;
Down she came and found a boat
Beneath a willow left afloat,
And round about the prow she wrote
        The Lady of Shalott.

And down the river's dim expanse—
Like some bold seer in a trance,
Seeing all his own mischance—
With a glassy countenance
        Did she look to Camelot.
And at the closing of the day
She loosed the chain, and down she lay;
The broad stream bore her far away,
        The Lady of Shalott.

Lying, robed in snowy white
That loosely flew to left and right—
The leaves upon her falling light—
Thro' the noises of the night
        She floated down to Camelot:

And as the boat-head wound along
The willowy hills and fields among,
They heard her singing her last song,
   The Lady of Shalott.

Heard a carol, mournful, holy,
Chanted loudly, chanted lowly,
Till her blood was frozen slowly,
And her eyes were darken'd wholly,
   Turn'd to tower'd Camelot;
For ere she reach'd upon the tide
The first house by the water-side,
Singing in her song she died,
   The Lady of Shalott.

Under tower and balcony,
By garden-wall and gallery,
A gleaming shape she floated by,
Dead-pale between the houses high,
   Silent into Camelot.
Out upon the wharfs they came,
Knight and burgher, lord and dame,
And round the prow they read her name,
   The Lady of Shalott.

Who is this? and what is here?
And in the lighted palace near
Died the sound of royal cheer;
And they cross'd themselves for fear,
   All the knights at Camelot:
But Lancelot mused a little space;
He said, 'She has a lovely face;
God in His mercy lend her grace,
   The Lady of Shalott.'

709 *The Miller's Daughter*

IT is the miller's daughter,
   And she is grown so dear, so dear,
That I would be the jewel
   That trembles in her ear:
For hid in ringlets day and night,
I'd touch her neck so warm and white.

And I would be the girdle
   About her dainty dainty waist,
And her heart would beat against me,
   In sorrow and in rest:
And I should know if it beat right,
I'd clasp it round so close and tight.

And I would be the necklace,
   And all day long to fall and rise
Upon her balmy bosom,
   With her laughter or her sighs:
And I would lie so light, so light,
I scarce should be unclasp'd at night.

710 *Song of the Lotos-Eaters*

THERE is sweet music here that softer falls
   Than petals from blown roses on the grass,
Or night-dews on still waters between walls
Of shadowy granite, in a gleaming pass;
Music that gentlier on the spirit lies,
Than tired eyelids upon tired eyes;
Music that brings sweet sleep down from the blissful skies.
Here are cool mosses deep,
And thro' the moss the ivies creep,

And in the stream the long-leaved flowers weep,
And from the craggy ledge the poppy hangs in sleep.

Why are we weigh'd upon with heaviness,
And utterly consumed with sharp distress,
While all things else have rest from weariness?
All things have rest: why should we toil alone,
We only toil, who are the first of things,
And make perpetual moan,
Still from one sorrow to another thrown:
Nor ever fold our wings,
And cease from wanderings,
Nor steep our brows in slumber's holy balm;
Nor harken what the inner spirit sings,
'There is no joy but calm!'—
Why should we only toil, the roof and crown of things?

Lo! in the middle of the wood,
The folded leaf is woo'd from out the bud
With winds upon the branch, and there
Grows green and broad, and takes no care,
Sun-steep'd at noon, and in the moon
Nightly dew-fed; and turning yellow
Falls, and floats adown the air.
Lo! sweeten'd with the summer light,
The full-juiced apple, waxing over-mellow,
Drops in a silent autumn night.
All its allotted length of days,
The flower ripens in its place,
Ripens and fades, and falls, and hath no toil,
Fast-rooted in the fruitful soil.

Hateful is the dark-blue sky,
Vaulted o'er the dark-blue sea.

LORD TENNYSON

Death is the end of life; ah, why
Should life all labour be?
Let us alone. Time driveth onward fast,
And in a little while our lips are dumb.
Let us alone. What is it that will last?
All things are taken from us, and become
Portions and parcels of the dreadful Past.
Let us alone. What pleasure can we have
To war with evil? Is there any peace
In ever climbing up the climbing wave?
All things have rest, and ripen toward the grave
In silence; ripen, fall and cease:
Give us long rest or death, dark death, or dreamful ease.

How sweet it were, hearing the downward stream,
With half-shut eyes ever to seem
Falling asleep in a half-dream!
To dream and dream, like yonder amber light,
Which will not leave the myrrh-bush on the height;
To hear each other's whisper'd speech;
Eating the Lotus day by day,
To watch the crisping ripples on the beach,
And tender curving lines of creamy spray;
To lend our hearts and spirits wholly
To the influence of mild-minded melancholy;
To muse and brood and live again in memory,
With those old faces of our infancy
Heap'd over with a mound of grass,
Two handfuls of white dust, shut in an urn of brass!

Dear is the memory of our wedded lives,
And dear the last embraces of our wives
And their warm tears: but all hath suffer'd change;

For surely now our household hearths are cold:
Our sons inherit us: our looks are strange:
And we should come like ghosts to trouble joy.
Or else the island princes over-bold
Have eat our substance, and the minstrel sings
Before them of the ten years' war in Troy,
And our great deeds, as half-forgotten things.
Is there confusion in the little isle?
Let what is broken so remain.
The Gods are hard to reconcile:
'Tis hard to settle order once again.
There *is* confusion worse than death,
Trouble on trouble, pain on pain,
Long labour unto agèd breath,
Sore task to hearts worn out with many wars
And eyes grown dim with gazing on the pilot-stars.

But propt on beds of amaranth and moly,
How sweet (while warm airs lull us, blowing lowly)
With half-dropt eyelids still,
Beneath a heaven dark and holy,
To watch the long bright river drawing slowly
His waters from the purple hill—
To hear the dewy echoes calling
From cave to cave thro' the thick-twinèd vine—
To watch the emerald-colour'd water falling
Thro' many a wov'n acanthus-wreath divine!
Only to hear and see the far-off sparkling brine,
Only to hear were sweet, stretch'd out beneath the pine.

The Lotos blooms below the barren peak:
The Lotos blows by every winding creek:
All day the wind breathes low with mellower tone:

Thro' every hollow cave and alley lone
Round and round the spicy downs the yellow Lotos-dust is
    blown.
We have had enough of action, and of motion we,
Roll'd to starboard, roll'd to larboard, when the surge was
    seething free,
Where the wallowing monster spouted his foam-fountains in
    the sea.
Let us swear an oath, and keep it with an equal mind,
In the hollow Lotos-land to live and lie reclined
On the hills like Gods together, careless of mankind.
For they lie beside their nectar, and the bolts are hurl'd
Far below them in the valleys, and the clouds are lightly curl'd
Round their golden houses, girdled with the gleaming world:
Where they smile in secret, looking over wasted lands,
Blight and famine, plague and earthquake, roaring deeps and
    fiery sands,
Clanging fights, and flaming towns, and sinking ships, and
    praying hands.
But they smile, they find a music centred in a doleful song
Steaming up, a lamentation and an ancient tale of wrong,
Like a tale of little meaning tho' the words are strong;
Chanted from an ill-used race of men that cleave the soil,
Sow the seed, and reap the harvest with enduring toil,
Storing yearly little dues of wheat, and wine and oil;
Till they perish and they suffer—some, 'tis whisper'd—down
    in hell
Suffer endless anguish, others in Elysian valleys dwell,
Resting weary limbs at last on beds of asphodel.
Surely, surely, slumber is more sweet than toil, the shore
Than labour in the deep mid-ocean, wind and wave and oar;
O rest ye, brother mariners, we will not wander more.

St. Agnes' Eve

DEEP on the convent-roof the snows
　　Are sparkling to the moon:
My breath to heaven like vapour goes:
　　May my soul follow soon!
The shadows of the convent-towers
　　Slant down the snowy sward,
Still creeping with the creeping hours
　　That lead me to my Lord:
Make Thou my spirit pure and clear
　　As are the frosty skies,
Or this first snowdrop of the year
　　That in my bosom lies.

As these white robes are soil'd and dark,
　　To yonder shining ground;
As this pale taper's earthly spark,
　　To yonder argent round;
So shows my soul before the Lamb,
　　My spirit before Thee;
So in mine earthly house I am,
　　To that I hope to be.
Break up the heavens, O Lord! and far,
　　Thro' all yon starlight keen,
Draw me, thy bride, a glittering star,
　　In raiment white and clean.

He lifts me to the golden doors;
　　The flashes come and go;
All heaven bursts her starry floors,
　　And strows her lights below,

And deepens on and up! the gates
   Roll back, and far within
For me the Heavenly Bridegroom waits,
   To make me pure of sin.
The sabbaths of Eternity,
   One sabbath deep and wide—
A light upon the shining sea—
   The Bridegroom with his bride!

712   *Blow, Bugle, blow*

THE splendour falls on castle walls
   And snowy summits old in story:
The long light shakes across the lakes,
   And the wild cataract leaps in glory.
Blow, bugle, blow, set the wild echoes flying,
Blow, bugle; answer, echoes, dying, dying, dying.

   O hark, O hear! how thin and clear,
     And thinner, clearer, farther going!
   O sweet and far from cliff and scar
     The horns of Elfland faintly blowing!
Blow, let us hear the purple glens replying:
Blow, bugle; answer, echoes, dying, dying, dying.

   O love, they die in yon rich sky,
     They faint on hill or field or river:
   Our echoes roll from soul to soul,
     And grow for ever and for ever.
Blow, bugle, blow, set the wild echoes flying,
And answer, echoes, answer, dying, dying, dying.

713 *Summer Night*

NOW sleeps the crimson petal, now the white;
Nor waves the cypress in the palace walk;
Nor winks the gold fin in the porphyry font:
The firefly wakens: waken thou with me.

Now droops the milk-white peacock like a ghost,
And like a ghost she glimmers on to me.

Now lies the Earth all Danaë to the stars,
And all thy heart lies open unto me.

Now slides the silent meteor on, and leaves
A shining furrow, as thy thoughts in me.

Now folds the lily all her sweetness up,
And slips into the bosom of the lake:
So fold thyself, my dearest, thou, and slip
Into my bosom and be lost in me.

714 *Come down, O Maid*

COME down, O maid, from yonder mountain height:
What pleasure lives in height (the shepherd sang),
In height and cold, the splendour of the hills?
But cease to move so near the Heavens, and cease
To glide a sunbeam by the blasted Pine,
To sit a star upon the sparkling spire;
And come, for Love is of the valley, come,
For Love is of the valley, come thou down
And find him; by the happy threshold, he,
Or hand in hand with Plenty in the maize,
Or red with spirted purple of the vats,

Or foxlike in the vine; nor cares to walk
With Death and Morning on the silver horns,
Nor wilt thou snare him in the white ravine,
Nor find him dropt upon the firths of ice,
That huddling slant in furrow-cloven falls
To roll the torrent out of dusky doors:
But follow; let the torrent dance thee down
To find him in the valley; let the wild
Lean-headed Eagles yelp alone, and leave
The monstrous ledges there to slope, and spill
Their thousand wreaths of dangling water-smoke,
That like a broken purpose waste in air:
So waste not thou; but come; for all the vales
Await thee; azure pillars of the hearth
Arise to thee; the children call, and I
Thy shepherd pipe, and sweet is every sound,
Sweeter thy voice, but every sound is sweet;
Myriads of rivulets hurrying thro' the lawn,
The moan of doves in immemorial elms,
And murmuring of innumerable bees.

715 *Maud*

COME into the garden, Maud,
    For the black bat, Night, has flown,
Come into the garden, Maud,
    I am here at the gate alone;
And the woodbine spices are wafted abroad,
    And the musk of the roses blown.

For a breeze of morning moves,
    And the planet of Love is on high,

853

Beginning to faint in the light that she loves
  On a bed of daffodil sky,
To faint in the light of the sun she loves,
  To faint in his light, and to die.

All night have the roses heard
  The flute, violin, bassoon;
All night has the casement jessamine stirr'd
  To the dancers dancing in tune;
Till a silence fell with the waking bird,
  And a hush with the setting moon.

I said to the lily, 'There is but one
  With whom she has heart to be gay,
When will the dancers leave her alone?
  She is weary of dance and play.'
Now half to the setting moon are gone,
  And half to the rising day;
Low on the sand and loud on the stone
  The last wheel echoes away.

I said to the rose, 'The brief night goes
  In babble and revel and wine.
O young lord-lover, what sighs are those
  For one that will never be thine?
But mine, but mine,' so I sware to the rose,
  'For ever and ever, mine.'

And the soul of the rose went into my blood,
  As the music clash'd in the hall;
And long by the garden lake I stood,
  For I heard your rivulet fall
From the lake to the meadow and on to the wood,
  Our wood, that is dearer than all;

From the meadow your walks have left so sweet
  That whenever a March-wind sighs
He sets the jewel-print of your feet
  In violets blue as your eyes,
To the woody hollows in which we meet
  And the valleys of Paradise.

The slender acacia would not shake
  One long milk-bloom on the tree;
The white lake-blossom fell into the lake,
  As the pimpernel dozed on the lea;
But the rose was awake all night for your sake,
  Knowing your promise to me;
The lilies and roses were all awake,
  They sigh'd for the dawn and thee.

Queen rose of the rosebud garden of girls,
  Come hither, the dances are done,
In gloss of satin and glimmer of pearls,
  Queen lily and rose in one;
Shine out, little head, sunning over with curls,
  To the flowers, and be their sun.

There has fallen a splendid tear
  From the passion-flower at the gate,
She is coming, my dove, my dear;
  She is coming, my life, my fate;
The red rose cries, 'She is near, she is near;'
  And the white rose weeps, 'She is late;'
The larkspur listens, 'I hear, I hear;'
  And the lily whispers, 'I wait'.

She is coming, my own, my sweet;
  Were it ever so airy a tread,
My heart would hear her and beat,
  Were it earth in an earthy bed;
My dust would hear her and beat,
  Had I lain for a century dead;
Would start and tremble under her feet,
  And blossom in purple and red.

716   *From 'In Memoriam'*

(ARTHUR HENRY HALLAM, MDCCCXXXIII)

LOVE is and was my Lord and King,
  And in his presence I attend
    To hear the tidings of my friend,
Which every hour his couriers bring.

Love is and was my King and Lord,
  And will be, tho' as yet I keep
    Within his court on earth, and sleep
Encompass'd by his faithful guard,

And hear at times a sentinel
  Who moves about from place to place,
    And whispers to the world of space,
In the deep night, that all is well.

717   *In the Garden at Swainston*

NIGHTINGALES warbled without,
  Within was weeping for thee:
Shadows of three dead men
  Walk'd in the walks with me:
  Shadows of three dead men, and thou wast one of the three.

Nightingales sang in the woods:
   The Master was far away:
Nightingales warbled and sang
    Of a passion that lasts but a day;
    Still in the house in his coffin the Prince of courtesy lay.

Two dead men have I known
   In courtesy like to thee:
Two dead men have I loved
    With a love that ever will be:
    Three dead men have I loved, and thou art last of the three.

718   *Crossing the Bar*

SUNSET and evening star,
   And one clear call for me!
And may there be no moaning of the bar,
   When I put out to sea,

But such a tide as moving seems asleep,
   Too full for sound and foam,
When that which drew from out the boundless deep
   Turns again home.

Twilight and evening bell,
   And after that the dark!
And may there be no sadness of farewell,
   When I embark;

For tho' from out our bourne of Time and Place
   The flood may bear me far,
I hope to see my Pilot face to face
   When I have crost the bar.

719 *O that 'twere possible*

O THAT 'twere possible
    After long grief and pain
To find the arms of my true love
Round me once again! . . .

A shadow flits before me,
Not thou, but like to thee:
Ah, Christ! that it were possible
For one short hour to see
The souls we loved, that they might tell us
What and where they be!

SIR SAMUEL FERGUSON

1810–1886

720 *Cashel of Munster*

FROM THE IRISH

I'D wed you without herds, without money or rich array,
    And I'd wed you on a dewy morn at day-dawn gray;
My bitter woe it is, love, that we are not far away
In Cashel town, tho' the bare deal board were our marriage-
    bed this day!

O fair maid, remember the green hill-side,
Remember how I hunted about the valleys wide;
Time now has worn me; my locks are turn'd to gray;
The year is scarce and I am poor—but send me not, love,
    away!

O deem not my blood is of base strain, my girl;
O think not my birth was as the birth of a churl;
Marry me and prove me, and say soon you will
That noble blood is written on my right side still.

My purse holds no red gold, no coin of the silver white;
No herds are mine to drive through the long twilight;
But the pretty girl that would take me, all bare tho' I be and lone,
O, I'd take her with me kindly to the county Tyrone!

O my girl, I can see 'tis in trouble you are;
And O my girl, I see 'tis your people's reproach you bear!
—*I am a girl in trouble for his sake with whom I fly,*
And, O, may no other maiden know such reproach as I!

721   *The Fair Hills of Ireland*

FROM THE IRISH

A PLENTEOUS place is Ireland for hospitable cheer,
                Uileacan dubh O!
Where the wholesome fruit is bursting from the yellow barley
      ear;
                Uileacan dubh O!
There is honey in the trees where her misty vales expand,
And her forest paths in summer are by falling waters fann'd,
There is dew at high noontide there, and springs i' the yellow
      sand,
                On the fair hills of holy Ireland.

Curl'd he is and ringleted, and plaited to the knee—
                Uileacan dubh O!
Each captain who comes sailing across the Irish Sea;
                Uileacan dubh O!
And I will make my journey, if life and health but stand,
Unto that pleasant country, that fresh and fragrant strand,
And leave your boasted braveries, your wealth and high
      command,
                For the fair hills of holy Ireland.

859

Large and profitable are the stacks upon the ground,
> *Uileacan dubh O!*
The butter and the cream do wondrously abound;
> *Uileacan dubh O!*
The cresses on the water and the sorrels are at hand,
And the cuckoo's calling daily his note of music bland,
And the bold thrush sings so bravely his song i' the forest
 grand,
> On the fair hills of holy Ireland.

SIR FRANCIS HASTINGS DOYLE
1810–1888

722 *The Private of the Buffs*

LAST night, among his fellow roughs,
 He jested, quaff'd, and swore;
A drunken private of the Buffs,
 Who never look'd before.
To-day, beneath the foeman's frown,
 He stands in Elgin's place,
Ambassador from Britain's crown
 And type of all her race.

Poor, reckless, rude, low-born, untaught,
 Bewilder'd, and alone,
A heart with English instinct fraught
 He yet can call his own.
Aye, tear his body limb from limb,
 Bring cord, or axe, or flame:
He only knows, that not through him
 Shall England come to shame.

Far Kentish hop-fields round him seem'd,
  Like dreams, to come and go;
Bright leagues of cherry-blossom gleam'd,
  One sheet of living snow;
The smoke above his father's door
  In grey soft eddyings hung:
Must he then watch it rise no more,
  Doom'd by himself, so young?

Yes, honour calls!—with strength like steel
  He put the vision by.
Let dusky Indians whine and kneel;
  An English lad must die.
And thus, with eyes that would not shrink,
  With knee to man unbent,
Unfaltering on its dreadful brink,
  To his red grave he went.

Vain, mightiest fleets of iron framed;
  Vain, those all-shattering guns;
Unless proud England keep, untamed,
  The strong heart of her sons.
So, let his name through Europe ring—
  A man of mean estate,
Who died, as firm as Sparta's king,
  Because his soul was great.

WILLIAM MAKEPEACE THACKERAY

1811–1863

723   *The Ballad of Bouillabaisse*

A STREET there is in Paris famous,
  For which no rhyme our language yields,
Rue Neuve des Petits Champs its name is—
  The New Street of the Little Fields;

WILLIAM MAKEPEACE THACKERAY

And here's an inn, not rich and splendid,
  But still in comfortable case;
The which in youth I oft attended,
  To eat a bowl of Bouillabaisse.

This Bouillabaisse a noble dish is—
  A sort of soup or broth, or brew,
Or hotchpotch, of all sorts of fishes,
  That Greenwich never could outdo;
Green herbs, red peppers, mussels, saffern,
  Soles, onions, garlic, roach, and dace;
All these you eat at Terré's tavern,
  In that one dish of Bouillabaisse.

Indeed, a rich and savoury stew 'tis;
  And true philosophers, methinks,
Who love all sorts of natural beauties,
  Should love good victuals and good drinks.
And Cordelier or Benedictine
  Might gladly, sure, his lot embrace,
Nor find a fast-day too afflicting
  Which served him up a Bouillabaisse.

I wonder if the house still there is?
  Yes, here the lamp is, as before;
The smiling red-cheek'd écaillère is
  Still opening oysters at the door.
Is Terré still alive and able?
  I recollect his droll grimace;
He'd come and smile before your table,
  And hope you liked your Bouillabaisse.

We enter—nothing's changed or older.
　'How's Monsieur Terré, waiter, pray?'
The waiter stares and shrugs his shoulder—
　'Monsieur is dead this many a day.'
'It is the lot of saint and sinner,
　So honest Terré's run his race!'
'What will Monsieur require for dinner?'
　'Say, do you still cook Bouillabaisse?'

'Oh, oui, Monsieur,' 's the waiter's answer;
　'Quel vin Monsieur désire-t-il?'
'Tell me a good one.'—'That I can, Sir:
　The Chambertin with yellow seal.'
'So Terré's gone,' I say, and sink in
　My old accustom'd corner-place;
'He's done with feasting and with drinking,
　With Burgundy and Bouillabaisse.'

My old accustom'd corner here is,
　The table still is in the nook;
Ah! vanish'd many a busy year is,
　This well-known chair since last I took.
When first I saw ye, *cari luoghi,*
　I'd scarce a beard upon my face,
And now a grizzled, grim old fogy,
　I sit and wait for Bouillabaisse.

Where are you, old companions trusty,
　Of early days, here met to dine?
Come, waiter! quick, a flagon crusty—
　I'll pledge them in the good old wine.

863

WILLIAM MAKEPEACE THACKERAY

The kind old voices and old faces
　My memory can quick retrace;
Around the board they take their places,
　And share the wine and Bouillabaisse.

There's Jack has made a wondrous marriage;
　There's laughing Tom is laughing yet;
There's brave Augustus drives his carriage;
　There's poor old Fred in the Gazette;
On James's head the grass is growing:
　Good Lord! the world has wagged apace
Since here we set the Claret flowing,
　And drank, and ate the Bouillabaisse.

Ah me! how quick the days are flitting!
　I mind me of a time that's gone,
When here I'd sit, as now I'm sitting,
　In this same place—but not alone.
A fair young form was nestled near me,
　A dear, dear face looked fondly up,
And sweetly spoke and smiled to cheer me
　—There's no one now to share my cup.

.　　.　　.　　.　　.　　.　　.　　.　　.

I drink it as the Fates ordain it.
　Come, fill it, and have done with rhymes:
Fill up the lonely glass, and drain it
　In memory of dear old times.
Welcome the wine, whate'er the seal is;
　And sit you down and say your grace
With thankful heart, whate'er the meal is.
　—Here comes the smoking Bouillabaisse!

724   *Persicos Odi*

DEAR Lucy, you know what my wish is,—
   I hate all your Frenchified fuss:
Your silly *entrées* and made dishes
   Were never intended for us.
No footman in lace and in ruffles
   Need dangle behind my arm-chair;
And never mind seeking for truffles,
   Although they be ever so rare.

But a plain leg of mutton, my Lucy,
   I pr'ythee get ready at three:
Have it smoking, and tender, and juicy,
   And what better meat can there be?
And when it has feasted the master,
   'Twill amply suffice for the maid;
Meanwhile I will smoke my canaster,
   And tipple my ale in the shade.

ROBERT BROWNING

1812–1889

725   *Song from 'Paracelsus'*

HEAP cassia, sandal-buds and stripes
   Of labdanum, and aloe-balls,
Smear'd with dull nard an Indian wipes
   From out her hair: such balsam falls
   Down sea-side mountain pedestals,
From tree-tops where tired winds are fain,
Spent with the vast and howling main,
To treasure half their island-gain.

And strew faint sweetness from some old
  Egyptian's fine worm-eaten shroud
Which breaks to dust when once unroll'd;
  Or shredded perfume, like a cloud
  From closet long to quiet vow'd,
With moth'd and dropping arras hung,
Mouldering her lute and books among,
As when a queen, long dead, was young.

726   *The Wanderers*

OVER the sea our galleys went,
  With cleaving prows in order brave
To a speeding wind and a bounding wave—
  A gallant armament:
Each bark built out of a forest-tree
  Left leafy and rough as first it grew,
And nail'd all over the gaping sides,
Within and without, with black bull-hides,
Seethed in fat and suppled in flame,
To bear the playful billows' game;
So, each good ship was rude to see,
Rude and bare to the outward view.

  But each upbore a stately tent
Where cedar pales in scented row
Kept out the flakes of the dancing brine,
And an awning droop'd the mast below,
In fold on fold of the purple fine,
That neither noontide nor star-shine
Nor moonlight cold which maketh mad,
  Might pierce the regal tenement.
When the sun dawn'd, O, gay and glad

We set the sail and plied the oar;
But when the night-wind blew like breath,
For joy of one day's voyage more,
We sang together on the wide sea,
Like men at peace on a peaceful shore;
Each sail was loosed to the wind so free,
Each helm made sure by the twilight star,
And in a sleep as calm as death,
We, the voyagers from afar,

    Lay stretch'd along, each weary crew
In a circle round its wondrous tent
Whence gleam'd soft light and curl'd rich scent,

    And with light and perfume, music too:
So the stars wheel'd round, and the darkness past,
And at morn we started beside the mast,
And still each ship was sailing fast!

Now, one morn, land appear'd—a speck
Dim trembling betwixt sea and sky—
'Avoid it,' cried our pilot, 'check

    The shout, restrain the eager eye!'
But the heaving sea was black behind
For many a night and many a day,
And land, though but a rock, drew nigh
So we broke the cedar pales away,
Let the purple awning flap in the wind.

    And a statue bright was on every deck!
We shouted, every man of us,
And steer'd right into the harbour thus,
With pomp and pæan glorious.

A hundred shapes of lucid stone!
    All day we built its shrine for each,

A shrine of rock for every one,
Nor paused till in the westering sun
   We sat together on the beach
To sing because our task was done;
When lo! what shouts and merry songs!
What laughter all the distance stirs!
A loaded raft with happy throngs
Of gentle islanders!
'Our isles are just at hand,' they cried,
   'Like cloudlets faint in even sleeping;
Our temple-gates are open'd wide,
   Our olive-groves thick shade are keeping
For these majestic forms'—they cried.
O, then we awoke with sudden start
From our deep dream, and knew, too late,
How bare the rock, how desolate,
Which had received our precious freight:
   Yet we call'd out—'Depart!
Our gifts, once given, must here abide:
   Our work is done; we have no heart
To mar our work,'—we cried.

727   *Thus the Mayne glideth*

THUS the Mayne glideth
   Where my Love abideth;
Sleep's no softer: it proceeds
On through lawns, on through meads,
On and on, whate'er befall,
Meandering and musical,
Though the niggard pasturage
Bears not on its shaven ledge

Aught but weeds and waving grasses
To view the river as it passes,
Save here and there a scanty patch
Of primroses too faint to catch
A weary bee. . . . And scarce it pushes
Its gentle way through strangling rushes
Where the glossy kingfisher
Flutters when noon-heats are near,
Glad the shelving banks to shun,
Red and steaming in the sun,
Where the shrew-mouse with pale throat
Burrows, and the speckled stoat;
Where the quick sandpipers flit
In and out the marl and grit
That seems to breed them, brown as they;
Naught disturbs its quiet way,
Save some lazy stork that springs,
Trailing it with legs and wings,
Whom the shy fox from the hill
Rouses, creep he ne'er so still.

728   *Pippa's Song*

THE year's at the spring,
   And day's at the morn;
Morning's at seven;
The hill-side's dew-pearl'd;
The lark's on the wing;
The snail's on the thorn;
God's in His heaven—
All's right with the world!

729 *Porphyria's Lover*

THE rain set early in to-night,
 The sullen wind was soon awake,
It tore the elm-tops down for spite,
 And did its worst to vex the lake:
 I listen'd with heart fit to break.
When glided in Porphyria; straight
 She shut the cold out and the storm,
And kneel'd and made the cheerless grate
 Blaze up, and all the cottage warm;
 Which done, she rose, and from her form
Withdrew the dripping cloak and shawl,
 And laid her soil'd gloves by, untied
Her hat and let the damp hair fall,
 And, last, she sat down by my side
 And call'd me. When no voice replied,
She put my arm about her waist,
 And made her smooth white shoulder bare,
And all her yellow hair displaced,
 And, stooping, made my cheek lie there,
 And spread, o'er all, her yellow hair,
Murmuring how she loved me—she
 Too weak, for all her heart's endeavour,
To set its struggling passion free
 From pride, and vainer ties dissever,
 And give herself to me for ever.
But passion sometimes would prevail,
 Nor could to-night's gay feast restrain
A sudden thought of one so pale
 For love of her, and all in vain:
 So, she was come through wind and rain.

ROBERT BROWNING

Be sure I look'd up at her eyes
  Happy and proud; at last I knew
Porphyria worshipp'd me; surprise
  Made my heart swell, and still it grew
  While I debated what to do.
That moment she was mine, mine, fair,
  Perfectly pure and good: I found
A thing to do, and all her hair
  In one long yellow string I wound
  Three times her little throat around,
And strangled her. No pain felt she;
  I am quite sure she felt no pain.
As a shut bud that holds a bee,
  I warily oped her lids: again
  Laugh'd the blue eyes without a stain.
And I untighten'd next the tress
  About her neck; her cheek once more
Blush'd bright beneath my burning kiss:
  I propp'd her head up as before,
  Only, this time my shoulder bore
Her head, which droops upon it still:
  The smiling rosy little head,
So glad it has its utmost will,
  That all it scorn'd at once is fled,
  And I, its love, am gain'd instead!
Porphyria's love: she guess'd not how
  Her darling one wish would be heard.
And thus we sit together now,
  And all night long we have not stirr'd,
And yet God has not said a word!

730 *The Laboratory*

[ANCIEN RÉGIME]

I

NOW that I, tying thy glass mask tightly,
   May gaze thro' these faint smokes curling whitely,
As thou pliest thy trade in this devil's-smithy—
Which is the poison to poison her, prithee?

II

He is with her; and they know that I know
Where they are, what they do: they believe my tears flow
While they laugh, laugh at me, at me fled to the drear
Empty church, to pray God in, for them!—I am here.

III

Grind away, moisten and mash up thy paste,
Pound at thy powder,—I am not in haste!
Better sit thus, and observe thy strange things,
Than go where men wait me and dance at the King's.

IV

That in the mortar—you call it a gum?
Ah, the brave tree whence such gold oozings come!
And yonder soft phial, the exquisite blue,
Sure to taste sweetly,—is that poison too?

V

Had I but all of them, thee and thy treasures,
What a wild crowd of invisible pleasures!
To carry pure death in an earring, a casket,
A signet, a fan-mount, a filligree-basket!

872

VI

Soon, at the King's, a mere lozenge to give
And Pauline should have just thirty minutes to live!
But to light a pastille, and Elise, with her head
And her breast and her arms and her hands, should drop dead!

VII

Quick—is it finished? The colour's too grim!
Why not soft like the phial's, enticing and dim?
Let it brighten her drink, let her turn it and stir,
And try it and taste, ere she fix and prefer!

VIII

What a drop! She's not little, no minion like me—
That's why she ensnared him: this never will free
The soul from those masculine eyes,—say, 'no!'
To that pulse's magnificent come-and-go.

IX

For only last night, as they whispered, I brought
My own eyes to bear on her so, that I thought
Could I keep them one half minute fixed, she would fall,
Shrivelled; she fell not; yet this does it all!

X

Not that I bid you spare her the pain!
Let death be felt and the proof remain;
Brand, burn up, bite into its grace—
He is sure to remember her dying face!

XI

Is it done? Take my mask off! Nay, be not morose
It kills her, and this prevents seeing it close:
The delicate droplet, my whole fortune's fee—
If it hurts her, beside, can it ever hurt me?

XI

Now, take all my jewels, gorge gold to your fill,
You may kiss me, old man, on my mouth if you will!
But brush this dust off me, lest horror it brings
Ere I know it—next moment I dance at the King's!

731   *Earl Mertoun's Song*

THERE's a woman like a dewdrop, she's so purer than
    the purest;
And her noble heart's the noblest, yes, and her sure faith's
    the surest:
And her eyes are dark and humid, like the depth on depth
    of lustre
Hid i' the harebell, while her tresses, sunnier than the wild-
    grape cluster,
Gush in golden-tinted plenty down her neck's rose-misted
    marble:
Then her voice's music . . . call it the well's bubbling, the
    bird's warble!

And this woman says, 'My days were sunless and my nights
    were moonless,
Parch'd the pleasant April herbage, and the lark's heart's out-
    break tuneless,
If you loved me not!' And I who (ah, for words of flame!)
    adore her,
Who am mad to lay my spirit prostrate palpably before her—
I may enter at her portal soon, as now her lattice takes me,
And by noontide as by midnight make her mine, as hers she
    makes me!

732 *In a Gondola*

THE moth's kiss, first!
  Kiss me as if you made me believe
You were not sure, this eve,
How my face, your flower, had pursed
Its petals up; so, here and there
You brush it, till I grow aware
Who wants me, and wide ope I burst.

The bee's kiss, now!
Kiss me as if you enter'd gay
My heart at some noonday,
A bud that dares not disallow
The claim, so all is render'd up,
And passively its shatter'd cup
Over your head to sleep I bow.

733 *Meeting at Night*

THE gray sea and the long black land;
  And the yellow half-moon large and low;
And the startled little waves that leap
In fiery ringlets from their sleep,
As I gain the cove with pushing prow,
And quench its speed i' the slushy sand.

Then a mile of warm sea-scented beach;
Three fields to cross till a farm appears;
A tap at the pane, the quick sharp scratch
And blue spurt of a lighted match,
And a voice less loud, thro' its joys and fears,
Than the two hearts beating each to each!

734 ## *Parting at Morning*

ROUND the cape of a sudden came the sea,
    And the sun look'd over the mountain's rim:
And straight was a path of gold for him,
And the need of a world of men for me.

735 ## *The Lost Mistress*

ALL's over, then: does truth sound bitter
    As one at first believes?
Hark, 'tis the sparrows' good-night twitter
    About your cottage eaves!

And the leaf-buds on the vine are woolly,
    I noticed that, to-day;
One day more bursts them open fully
    —You know the red turns gray.

To-morrow we meet the same then, dearest?
    May I take your hand in mine?
Mere friends are we,—well, friends the merest
    Keep much that I resign:

For each glance of the eye so bright and black,
    Though I keep with heart's endeavour,—
Your voice, when you wish the snowdrops back,
    Though it stay in my soul for ever!—

Yet I will but say what mere friends say,
    Or only a thought stronger;
I will hold your hand but as long as all may,
    Or so very little longer!

The Last Ride Together

I SAID—Then, dearest, since 'tis so,
Since now at length my fate I know,
Since nothing all my love avails,
Since all, my life seem'd meant for, fails,
   Since this was written and needs must be—
My whole heart rises up to bless
Your name in pride and thankfulness!
Take back the hope you gave,—I claim
Only a memory of the same,
—And this beside, if you will not blame;
   Your leave for one more last ride with me.

My mistress bent that brow of hers,
Those deep dark eyes where pride demurs
When pity would be softening through,
Fix'd me a breathing-while or two
   With life or death in the balance: right!
The blood replenish'd me again;
My last thought was at least not vain:
I and my mistress, side by side
Shall be together, breathe and ride,
So, one day more am I deified.
Who knows but the world may end to-night?

Hush! if you saw some western cloud
All billowy-bosom'd, over-bow'd
By many benedictions—sun's
And moon's and evening-star's at once—
   And so, you, looking and loving best,
Conscious grew, your passion drew
Cloud, sunset, moonrise, star-shine too,

Down on you, near and yet more near,
Till flesh must fade for heaven was here!—
Thus leant she and linger'd—joy and fear!
    Thus lay she a moment on my breast.

Then we began to ride. My soul
Smooth'd itself out, a long-cramp'd scroll
Freshening and fluttering in the wind.
Past hopes already lay behind.
    What need to strive with a life awry?
Had I said that, had I done this,
So might I gain, so might I miss.
Might she have loved me? just as well
She might have hated, who can tell!
Where had I been now if the worst befell?
    And here we are riding, she and I.

Fail I alone, in words and deeds?
Why, all men strive and who succeeds?
We rode; it seem'd my spirit flew,
Saw other regions, cities new,
    As the world rush'd by on either side.
I thought,—All labour, yet no less
Bear up beneath their unsuccess.
Look at the end of work, contrast
The petty done, the undone vast,
This present of theirs with the hopeful past!
    I hoped she would love me; here we ride.

What hand and brain went ever pair'd?
What heart alike conceived and dared?
What act proved all its thought had been?
What will but felt the fleshly screen?
    We ride and I see her bosom heave.

There's many a crown for who can reach.
Ten lines, a statesman's life in each!
The flag stuck on a heap of bones,
A soldier's doing! what atones?
They scratch his name on the Abbey-stones.
 My riding is better, by their leave.

What does it all mean, poet? Well,
Your brains beat into rhythm, you tell
What we felt only; you express'd
You hold things beautiful the best,
 And pace them in rhyme so, side by side.
'Tis something, nay 'tis much: but then,
Have you yourself what's best for men?
Are you—poor, sick, old ere your time—
Nearer one whit your own sublime
Than we who never have turn'd a rhyme?
 Sing, riding's a joy! For me, I ride.

And you, great sculptor—so, you gave
A score of years to Art, her slave,
And that's your Venus, whence we turn
To yonder girl that fords the burn!
 You acquiesce, and shall I repine?
What, man of music, you grown gray
With notes and nothing else to say,
Is this your sole praise from a friend?—
'Greatly his opera's strains intend,
But in music we know how fashions end!'
 I gave my youth: but we ride, in fine.

Who knows what's fit for us? Had fate
Proposed bliss here should sublimate

My being—had I sign'd the bond—
Still one must lead some life beyond,
　　Have a bliss to die with, dim-descried.
This foot once planted on the goal,
This glory-garland round my soul,
Could I descry such? Try and test!
I sink back shuddering from the quest.
Earth being so good, would heaven seem best?
　　Now, heaven and she are beyond this ride.

And yet—she has not spoke so long!
What if heaven be that, fair and strong
At life's best, with our eyes upturn'd
Whither life's flower is first discern'd,
　　We, fix'd so, ever should so abide?
What if we still ride on, we two
With life for ever old yet new,
Changed not in kind but in degree,
The instant made eternity,—
And heaven just prove that I and she
　　Ride, ride together, for ever ride?

737　　　*Love Among the Ruins*

I

WHERE the quiet-coloured end of evening smiles
　　Miles and miles
On the solitary pastures where our sheep
　　Half-asleep
Tinkle homeward thro' the twilight, stray or stop
　　As they crop—

880

II

Was the site once of a city great and gay,
　　(So they say)
Of our country's very capital, its prince
　　Ages since
Held his court in, gathered councils, wielding far
　　Peace or war.

III

Now—the country does not even boast a tree,
　　As you see,
To distinguish slopes of verdure, certain rills
　　From the hills
Intersect and give a name to, (else they run
　　Into one)

IV

Where the domed and daring palace shot its spires
　　Up like fires
O'er the hundred-gated circuit of a wall
　　Bounding all,
Made of marble, men might march on nor be prest,
　　Twelve abreast.

V

And such plenty and perfection, see, of grass
　　Never was!
Such a carpet as, this summer-time, o'erspreads
　　And embeds
Every vestige of the city, guessed alone,
　　Stock or stone—

VI

Where a multitude of men breathed joy and woe
　　Long ago;

Lust of glory pricked their hearts up, dread of shame
 Struck them tame;
And that glory and that shame alike, the gold
 Bought and sold.

VII

Now,—the single little turret that remains
 On the plains,
By the caper overrooted, by the gourd
 Overscored,
While the patching houseleek's head of blossom winks
 Through the chinks—

VIII

Marks the basement whence a tower in ancient time
 Sprang sublime,
And a burning ring, all round, the chariots traced
 As they raced,
And the monarch and his minions and his dames
 Viewed the games.

IX

And I know, while thus the quiet-coloured eve
 Smiles to leave
To their folding, all our many-tinkling fleece
 In such peace,
And the slopes and rills in undistinguished grey
 Melt away—

X

That a girl with eager eyes and yellow hair
 Waits me there
In the turret whence the charioteers caught soul
 For the goal,
When the king looked, where she looks now, breathless, dumb
 Till I come.

XI

But he looked upon the city, every side,
    Far and wide,
All the mountains topped with temples, all the glades,
    Colonnades,
All the causeys, bridges, aqueducts,—and then.
    All the men!

XII

When I do come, she will speak not, she will stand,
    Either hand
On my shoulder, give her eyes the first embrace
    Of my face,
Ere we rush, ere we extinguish sight and speech
    Each on each.

XIII

In one year they sent a million fighters forth
    South and North,
And they built their gods a brazen pillar high
    As the sky,
Yet reserved a thousand chariots in full force—
    Gold, of course.

XIV

Oh heart! oh, blood that freezes, blood that burns!
    Earth's returns
For whole centuries of folly, noise and sin!
    Shut them in,
With their triumphs and their glories and the rest.
    Love is best!

738   *Misconceptions*

THIS is a spray the Bird clung to,
    Making it blossom with pleasure,
Ere the high tree-top she sprung to,
    Fit for her nest and her treasure.
    O, what a hope beyond measure
Was the poor spray's, which the flying feet hung to,—
So to be singled out, built in, and sung to!

This is a heart the Queen leant on,
    Thrill'd in a minute erratic,
Ere the true bosom she bent on,
    Meet for love's regal dalmatic.
    O, what a fancy ecstatic
Was the poor heart's, ere the wanderer went on—
Love to be saved for it, proffer'd to, spent on!

739   *Home-thoughts, from Abroad*

O TO be in England
    Now that April's there,
And whoever wakes in England
Sees, some morning, unaware,
That the lowest boughs and the brushwood sheaf
Round the elm-tree bole are in tiny leaf,
While the chaffinch sings on the orchard bough
In England—now!

And after April, when May follows,
And the whitethroat builds, and all the swallows!
Hark, where my blossom'd pear-tree in the hedge
Leans to the field and scatters on the clover
Blossoms and dewdrops—at the bent spray's edge—
That's the wise thrush; he sings each song twice over,

Lest you should think he never could recapture
The first fine careless rapture!
And though the fields look rough with hoary dew,
All will be gay when noontide wakes anew
The buttercups, the little children's dower
—Far brighter than this gaudy melon-flower!

740   *Home-thoughts, from the Sea*

NOBLY, nobly Cape Saint Vincent to the North-west
    died away;
Sunset ran, one glorious blood-red, reeking into Cadiz Bay;
Bluish 'mid the burning water, full in face Trafalgar lay;
In the dimmest North-east distance dawn'd Gibraltar grand
    and gray;
'Here and here did England help me: how can I help Eng-
    land?'—say,
Whoso turns as I, this evening, turn to God to praise and
    pray,
While Jove's planet rises yonder, silent over Africa.

WILLIAM BELL SCOTT

1812–1890

741   *The Witch's Ballad*

O I hae come from far away,
    From a warm land far away,
A southern land across the sea,
With sailor-lads about the mast,
Merry and canny, and kind to me.

WILLIAM BELL SCOTT

And I hae been to yon town
   To try my luck in yon town;
Nort, and Mysie, Elspie too.
Right braw we were to pass the gate,
Wi' gowden clasps on girdles blue.

Mysie smiled wi' miminy mouth,
   Innocent mouth, miminy mouth;
Elspie wore a scarlet gown,
Nort's grey eyes were unco' gleg.
My Castile comb was like a crown.

We walk'd abreast all up the street,
   Into the market up the street;
Our hair with marigolds was wound,
Our bodices with love-knots laced,
Our merchandise with tansy bound.

Nort had chickens, I had cocks,
   Gamesome cocks, loud-crowing cocks;
Mysie ducks, and Elspie drakes,—
For a wee groat or a pound;
We lost nae time wi' gives and takes.

—Lost nae time, for well we knew,
   In our sleeves full well we knew,
When the gloaming came that night,
Duck nor drake, nor hen nor cock
Would be found by candle-light.

And when our chaffering all was done,
   All was paid for, sold and done,

miminy] prim, demure.   gleg] bright, sharp.

We drew a glove on ilka hand,
We sweetly curtsied, each to each,
And deftly danced a saraband.

The market-lassies look'd and laugh'd,
    Left their gear, and look'd and laugh'd;
They made as they would join the game,
But soon their mithers, wild and wud,
With whack and screech they stopp'd the same.

Sae loud the tongues o' randies grew,
    The flytin' and the skirlin' grew,
At all the windows in the place,
Wi' spoons or knives, wi' needle or awl,
Was thrust out every hand and face.

And down each stair they throng'd anon,
    Gentle, semple, throng'd anon:
Souter and tailor, frowsy Nan,
The ancient widow young again,
Simpering behind her fan.

Without a choice, against their will,
    Doited, dazed, against their will,
The market lassie and her mither,
The farmer and his husbandman,
Hand in hand dance a' thegither.

Slow at first, but faster soon,
    Still increasing, wild and fast,
Hoods and mantles, hats and hose,
Blindly doff'd and cast away,
Left them naked, heads and toes.

wud] mad.   randies] viragoes.   flytin'] scolding.
skirlin'] shrieking.   souter] cobbler.   doited] mazed.

887

They would have torn us limb from limb,
   Dainty limb from dainty limb;
But never one of them could win
Across the line that I had drawn
With bleeding thumb a-widdershin.

But there was Jeff the provost's son,
   Jeff the provost's only son;
There was Father Auld himsel',
The Lombard frae the hostelry,
And the lawyer Peter Fell.

All goodly men we singled out,
   Waled them well, and singled out,
And drew them by the left hand in;
Mysie the priest, and Elspie won
The Lombard, Nort the lawyer carle,
I mysel' the provost's son.

Then, with cantrip kisses seven,
   Three times round with kisses seven,
Warp'd and woven there spun we
Arms and legs and flaming hair,
Like a whirlwind on the sea.

Like a wind that sucks the sea,
   Over and in and on the sea,
Good sooth it was a mad delight;
And every man of all the four
Shut his eyes and laugh'd outright.

Laugh'd as long as they had breath,
   Laugh'd while they had sense or breath;

a-widdershin] the wrong way of the sun; or E. to W. through N.
waled] chose.   cantrip] magic.

WILLIAM BELL SCOTT

And close about us coil'd a mist
Of gnats and midges, wasps and flies,
Like the whirlwind shaft it rist.

Drawn up I was right off my feet,
   Into the mist and off my feet;
And, dancing on each chimney-top,
I saw a thousand darling imps
Keeping time with skip and hop.

And on the provost's brave ridge-tile,
   On the provost's grand ridge-tile,
The Blackamoor first to master me
I saw, I saw that winsome smile,
The mouth that did my heart beguile,
And spoke the great Word over me,
In the land beyond the sea.

I call'd his name, I call'd aloud,
   Alas! I call'd on him aloud;
And then he fill'd his hand with stour,
And threw it towards me in the air;
My mouse flew out, I lost my pow'r!

My lusty strength, my power were gone;
   Power was gone, and all was gone.
He will not let me love him more!
Of bell and whip and horse's tail
He cares not if I find a store.

But I am proud if he is fierce!
   I am as proud as he is fierce;

              stour] dust.

WILLIAM BELL SCOTT

I'll turn about and backward go,
If I meet again that Blackamoor,
And he'll help us then, for he shall know
I seek another paramour.

And we'll gang once more to yon town,
   Wi' better luck to yon town;
We'll walk in silk and cramoisie,
And I shall wed the provost's son
My lady of the town I'll be!

For I was born a crown'd king's child,
   Born and nursed a king's child,
King o' a land ayont the sea,
Where the Blackamoor kiss'd me first,
And taught me art and glamourie.

Each one in her wame shall hide
   Her hairy mouse, her wary mouse,
Fed on madwort and agramie,—
Wear amber beads between her breasts,
And blind-worm's skin about her knee.

The Lombard shall be Elspie's man,
   Elspie's gowden husband-man;
Nort shall take the lawyer's hand;
The priest shall swear another vow:
We'll dance again the saraband!

cramoisie] crimson.   ayont] beyond.   glamourie]
wizardry.

AUBREY DE VERE

1814–1902

742 *Serenade*

SOFTLY, O midnight Hours!
   Move softly o'er the bowers
Where lies in happy sleep a girl so fair!
   For ye have power, men say,
   Our hearts in sleep to sway,
And cage cold fancies in a moonlight snare.
   Round ivory neck and arm
   Enclasp a separate charm;
Hang o'er her poised, but breathe nor sigh nor prayer:
   Silently ye may smile,
   But hold your breath the while,
And let the wind sweep back your cloudy hair!
   Bend down your glittering urns,
   Ere yet the dawn returns,
And star with dew the lawn her feet shall tread;
   Upon the air rain balm,
   Bid all the woods be calm,
Ambrosial dreams with healthful slumbers wed;
   That so the Maiden may
   With smiles your care repay,
When from her couch she lifts her golden head;
   Waking with earliest birds,
   Ere yet the misty herds
Leave warm 'mid the gray grass their dusky bed.

743 *The County of Mayo*

FROM THE IRISH OF THOMAS LAVELLE

ON the deck of Patrick Lynch's boat I sat in woful plight,
   Through my sighing all the weary day and weeping
   all the night;
Were it not that full of sorrow from my people forth I go,
By the blessèd sun! 'tis royally I'd sing thy praise, Mayo!

When I dwelt at home in plenty, and my gold did much
   abound,
In the company of fair young maids the Spanish ale went
   round—
'Tis a bitter change from those gay days that now I'm forced
   to go
And must leave my bones in Santa Cruz, far from my own
   Mayo.

They are alter'd girls in Irrul now; 'tis proud they're grown
   and high,
With their hair-bags and their top-knots, for I pass their
   buckles by—
But it's little now I heed their airs, for God will have it so,
That I must depart for foreign lands and leave my sweet Mayo.

'Tis my grief that Patrick Loughlin is not Earl of Irrul still,
And that Brian Duff no longer rules as Lord upon the hill:
And that Colonel Hugh McGrady should be lying dead and
   low,
And I sailing, sailing swiftly from the county of Mayo.

744 *Stanza*

OFTEN rebuked, yet always back returning
   To those first feelings that were born with me,
And leaving busy chase of wealth and learning
   For idle dreams of things which cannot be:

To-day I will seek not the shadowy region;
   Its unsustaining vastness waxes drear;
And visions rising, legion after legion,
   Bring the unreal world too strangely near.

I'll walk, but not in old heroic traces,
   And not in paths of high morality,
And not among the half-distinguish'd faces,
   The clouded forms of long-past history.

I'll walk where my own nature would be leading:
   It vexes me to choose another guide:
Where the grey flocks in ferny glens are feeding,
   Where the wild wind blows on the mountain side.

745 *The Prisoner*

STILL let my tyrants know, I am not doom'd to wear
   Year after year in gloom and desolate despair;
A messenger of Hope comes every night to me,
And offers for short life, eternal liberty.

He comes with Western winds, with evening's wandering airs,
With that clear dusk of heaven that brings the thickest stars:
Winds take a pensive tone, and stars a tender fire,
And visions rise, and change, that kill me with desire.

893

Desire for nothing known in my maturer years,
When Joy grew mad with awe, at counting future tears:
When, if my spirit's sky was full of flashes warm,
I knew not whence they came, from sun or thunder-storm.

But first, a hush of peace—a soundless calm descends;
The struggle of distress and fierce impatience ends.
Mute music soothes my breast—unutter'd harmony
That I could never dream, till Earth was lost to me.

Then dawns the Invisible; the Unseen its truth reveals;
My outward sense is gone, my inward essence feels;
Its wings are almost free—its home, its harbour found,
Measuring the gulf, it stoops, and dares the final bound.

O dreadful is the check—intense the agony—
When the ear begins to hear, and the eye begins to see;
When the pulse begins to throb—the brain to think again—
The soul to feel the flesh, and the flesh to feel the chain.

Yet I would lose no sting, would wish no torture less;
The more that anguish racks, the earlier it will bless;
And robed in fires of hell, or bright with heavenly shine,
If it but herald Death, the vision is divine.

746 *The Old Stoic*

RICHES I hold in light esteem,
   And Love I laugh to scorn;
And lust of fame was but a dream
   That vanish'd with the morn:

And, if I pray, the only prayer
   That moves my lips for me
Is, 'Leave the heart that now I bear,
   And give me liberty!'

Yea, as my swift days near their goal,
    'Tis all that I implore:
In life and death a chainless soul,
    With courage to endure.

747   *Last Lines*

NO coward soul is mine,
    No trembler in the world's storm-troubled sphere:
I see Heaven's glories shine,
And faith shines equal, arming me from fear.

O God within my breast,
Almighty, ever-present Deity!
    Life—that in me has rest,
As I—undying Life—have power in Thee!

Vain are the thousand creeds
That move men's hearts: unutterably vain;
    Worthless as wither'd weeds,
Or idlest froth amid the boundless main,

To waken doubt in one
Holding so fast by Thine Infinity;
    So surely anchor'd on
The steadfast rock of immortality.

With wide-embracing love
Thy Spirit animates eternal years,
    Pervades and broods above,
Changes, sustains, dissolves, creates, and rears.

Though earth and man were gone,
And suns and universes ceased to be,
    And Thou were left alone,
Every existence would exist in Thee.

There is not room for Death,
Nor atom that his might could render void:
Thou—Thou art Being and Breath,
And what Thou art may never be destroyed.

CHARLES KINGSLEY

1819–1875

748   *Airly Beacon*

AIRLY Beacon, Airly Beacon;
  O the pleasant sight to see
Shires and towns from Airly Beacon,
    While my love climb'd up to me!

Airly Beacon, Airly Beacon;
  O the happy hours we lay
Deep in fern on Airly Beacon,
    Courting through the summer's day!

Airly Beacon, Airly Beacon;
  O the weary haunt for me,
All alone on Airly Beacon,
    With his baby on my knee!

ARTHUR HUGH CLOUGH

1819–1861

749   *Qua cursum ventus*

AS ships, becalm'd at eve, that lay
  With canvas drooping, side by side,
Two towers of sail at dawn of day
  Are scarce, long leagues apart, descried;

When fell the night, upsprung the breeze,
　And all the darkling hours they plied,
Nor dreamt but each the self-same seas
　By each was cleaving, side by side:

E'en so— but why the tale reveal
　Of those, whom year by year unchanged,
Brief absence join'd anew to feel,
　Astounded, soul from soul estranged?

At dead of night their sails were fill'd,
　And onward each rejoicing steer'd—
Ah, neither blame, for neither will'd,
　Or wist, what first with dawn appear'd!

To veer, how vain! On, onward strain,
　Brave barks! In light, in darkness too,
Thro' winds and tides one compass guides,—
　To that, and your own selves, be true.

But O blithe breeze! and O great seas,
　Though ne'er, that earliest parting past,
On your wide plain they join again,
　Together lead them home at last.

One port, methought, alike they sought,
　One purpose hold where'er they fare,—
O bounding breeze, O rushing seas,
　At last, at last, unite them there!

ARTHUR HUGH CLOUGH

750   *Say not the Struggle Naught availeth*

SAY not the struggle naught availeth,
    The labour and the wounds are vain,
The enemy faints not, nor faileth,
    And as things have been they remain.

If hopes were dupes, fears may be liars;
    It may be, in yon smoke conceal'd,
Your comrades chase e'en now the fliers,
    And, but for you, possess the field.

For while the tired waves, vainly breaking,
    Seem here no painful inch to gain,
Far back, through creeks and inlets making,
    Comes silent, flooding in, the main.

And not by eastern windows only,
    When daylight comes, comes in the light;
In front the sun climbs slow, how slowly!
    But westward, look, the land is bright!

WALT WHITMAN

1819-1892

751   *The Imprisoned Soul*

AT the last, tenderly,
    From the walls of the powerful, fortress'd house,
From the clasp of the knitted locks—from the keep of the
    well-closed doors,
Let me be wafted.

Let me glide noiselessly forth;
With the key of softness unlock the locks—with a whisper
Set ope the doors, O soul!

Tenderly! be not impatient!
(Strong is your hold, O mortal flesh!
Strong is your hold, O love!)

752   *O Captain! My Captain!*

O CAPTAIN! my Captain! our fearful trip is done,
     The ship has weather'd every rack, the prize we sought
     is won,
The port is near, the bells I hear, the people all exulting,
While follow eyes the steady keel, the vessel grim and daring;
          But O heart! heart! heart!
               O the bleeding drops of red!
                    Where on the deck my Captain lies,
                         Fallen cold and dead.

O Captain! my Captain! rise up and hear the bells;
Rise up—for you the flag is flung—for you the bugle trills,
For you bouquets and ribbon'd wreaths—for you the shores
     crowding,
For you they call, the swaying mass, their eager faces turning;
          Here, Captain! dear father!
               This arm beneath your head!
                    It is some dream that on the deck
                         You've fallen cold and dead.

My Captain does not answer, his lips are pale and still,
My father does not feel my arm, he has no pulse nor will;
The ship is anchor'd safe and sound, its voyage closed and
     done,
From fearful trip the victor ship comes in with object won;

WALT WHITMAN

Exult, O shores! and sing, O bells!
But I, with mournful tread,
  Walk the deck my Captain lies,
  Fallen cold and dead.

JOHN RUSKIN

1819–1900

753   *Trust Thou Thy Love*

TRUST thou thy Love: if she be proud, is she not sweet?
Trust thou thy Love: if she be mute, is she not pure?
Lay thou thy soul full in her hands, low at her feet;
Fail, Sun and Breath!—yet, for thy peace, She shall endure.

EBENEZER JONES

1820–1860

754   *When the World is burning*

WHEN the world is burning,
  Fired within, yet turning
    Round with face unscathed;
Ere fierce flames, uprushing,
O'er all lands leap, crushing,
    Till earth fall, fire-swathed;
Up amidst the meadows,
Gently through the shadows,
    Gentle flames will glide,
Small, and blue, and golden.
Though by bard beholden,
When in calm dreams folden,—
    Calm his dreams will bide.

EBENEZER JONES

Where the dance is sweeping,
Through the greensward peeping,
   Shall the soft lights start;
Laughing maids, unstaying,
Deeming it trick-playing,
High their robes upswaying,
   O'er the lights shall dart;
And the woodland haunter
Shall not cease to saunter
   When, far down some glade,
Of the great world's burning,
One soft flame upturning
Seems, to his discerning,
   Crocus in the shade.

ANONYMOUS

753   *Epitaph of Dionysia*

HERE doth Dionysia lie:
   She whose little wanton foot
Tripping (ah, too carelessly!)
   Touch'd this tomb and fell into 't.

.   .   .   .

Dionysia, o'er this tomb,
   Where thy buried beauties be, ·
From their dust shall spring and bloom
   Loves and graces like to thee.

MATTHEW ARNOLD

1822–1888

The Song of Callicles

THROUGH the black, rushing smoke-bursts,
   Thick breaks the red flame.
All Etna heaves fiercely
Her forest-clothed frame.

Not here, O Apollo!
Are haunts meet for thee.
But, where Helicon breaks down
In cliff to the sea.

Where the moon-silver'd inlets
Send far their light voice
Up the still vale of Thisbe,
O speed, and rejoice!

On the sward at the cliff-top,
Lie strewn the white flocks;
On the cliff-side, the pigeons
Roost deep in the rocks.

In the moonlight the shepherds,
Soft lull'd by the rills,
Lie wrapt in their blankets,
Asleep on the hills.

—What forms are these coming
So white through the gloom?
What garment out-glistening
The gold-flower'd broom?

MATTHEW ARNOLD

What sweet-breathing Presence
Out-perfumes the thyme?
What voices enrapture
The night's balmy prime?—

'Tis Apollo comes leading
His choir, The Nine.
—The Leader is fairest,
But all are divine.

They are lost in the hollows.
They stream up again.
What seeks on this mountain
The glorified train?—

They bathe on this mountain,
In the spring by their road.
Then on to Olympus,
Their endless abode.

—Whose praise do they mention:
Of what is it told?—
What will be for ever.
What was from of old.

First hymn they the Father
Of all things: and then,
The rest of Immortals,
The action of men.

The Day in his hotness,
The strife with the palm;
The Night in her silence,
The Stars in their calm.

MATTHEW ARNOLD

To Marguerite

YES: in the sea of life enisled,
　With echoing straits between us thrown,
Dotting the shoreless watery wild,
　We mortal millions live *alone*.
The islands feel the enclasping flow,
And then their endless bounds they know.

But when the moon their hollows lights,
　And they are swept by balms of spring,
And in their glens, on starry nights,
　The nightingales divinely sing;
And lovely notes, from shore to shore,
Across the sounds and channels pour;

O then a longing like despair
　Is to their farthest caverns sent!
For surely once, they feel, we were
　Parts of a single continent.
Now round us spreads the watery plain—
O might our marges meet again!

Who order'd that their longing's fire
　Should be, as soon as kindled, cool'd?
Who renders vain their deep desire?—
　A God, a God their severance ruled;
And bade betwixt their shores to be
The unplumb'd, salt, estranging sea.

Requiescat

STREW on her roses, roses,
　And never a spray of yew.
　　In quiet she reposes:
　　　Ah! would that I did too.

Her mirth the world required:
  She bathed it in smiles of glee.
But her heart was tired, tired,
  And now they let her be.

Her life was turning, turning,
  In mazes of heat and sound.
But for peace her soul was yearning,
  And now peace laps her round.

Her cabin'd, ample Spirit,
  It flutter'd and fail'd for breath.
To-night it doth inherit
  The vasty hall of Death.

759   *The Scholar-Gipsy*

GO, for they call you, Shepherd, from the hill;
  Go, Shepherd, and untie the wattled cotes:
  No longer leave thy wistful flock unfed,
Nor let thy bawling fellows rack their throats,
  Nor the cropp'd grasses shoot another head.
    But when the fields are still,
And the tired men and dogs all gone to rest,
  And only the white sheep are sometimes seen
  Cross and recross the strips of moon-blanch'd green;
Come, Shepherd, and again begin the quest.

Here, where the reaper was at work of late,
  In this high field's dark corner, where he leaves
  His coat, his basket, and his earthen cruise,
And in the sun all morning binds the sheaves,
    Then here, at noon, comes back his stores to use;
    Here will I sit and wait,

While to my ear from uplands far away
   The bleating of the folded flocks is borne,
     With distant cries of reapers in the corn—
All the live murmur of a summer's day.

Screen'd is this nook o'er the high, half-reap'd field,
   And here till sundown, Shepherd, will I be.
     Through the thick corn the scarlet poppies peep,
   And round green roots and yellowing stalks I see
     Pale pink convolvulus in tendrils creep:
       And air-swept lindens yield
   Their scent, and rustle down their perfumed showers
     Of bloom on the bent grass where I am laid,
     And bower me from the August sun with shade;
And the eye travels down to Oxford's towers:

And near me on the grass lies Glanvil's book—
   Come, let me read the oft-read tale again:
     The story of that Oxford scholar poor,
   Of pregnant parts and quick inventive brain,
     Who, tired of knocking at Preferment's door,
       One summer morn forsook
   His friends, and went to learn the Gipsy-lore,
     And roam'd the world with that wild brotherhood,
     And came, as most men deem'd, to little good,
But came to Oxford and his friends no more.

But once, years after, in the country lanes,
   Two scholars, whom at college erst he knew,
     Met him, and of his way of life inquired.
   Whereat he answer'd that the Gipsy-crew,
     His mates, had arts to rule as they desired
       The workings of men's brains;

And they can bind them to what thoughts they will:
    'And I,' he said, 'the secret of their art,
      When fully learn'd, will to the world impart:
But it needs Heaven-sent moments for this skill!'

This said, he left them, and return'd no more,
    But rumours hung about the country-side,
      That the lost Scholar long was seen to stray,
Seen by rare glimpses, pensive and tongue-tied,
    In hat of antique shape, and cloak of grey,
        The same the Gipsies wore.
Shepherds had met him on the Hurst in spring;
    At some lone alehouse in the Berkshire moors,
      On the warm ingle-bench, the smock-frock'd boors
Had found him seated at their entering,

But, 'mid their drink and clatter, he would fly:
    And I myself seem half to know thy looks,
      And put the shepherds, Wanderer, on thy trace;
And boys who in lone wheatfields scare the rooks
    I ask if thou hast pass'd their quiet place;
        Or in my boat I lie
Moor'd to the cool bank in the summer heats,
    'Mid wide grass meadows which the sunshine fills,
    And watch the warm green-muffled Cumner hills,
And wonder if thou haunt'st their shy retreats.

For most, I know, thou lov'st retirèd ground.
    Thee, at the ferry, Oxford riders blithe,
      Returning home on summer nights, have met
Crossing the stripling Thames at Bablock-hithe,
    Trailing in the cool stream thy fingers wet,
        As the slow punt swings round:

And leaning backwards in a pensive dream,
 And fostering in thy lap a heap of flowers
 Pluck'd in shy fields and distant Wychwood bowers.
And thine eyes resting on the moonlit stream:

And then they land, and thou art seen no more.
 Maidens who from the distant hamlets come
  To dance around the Fyfield elm in May,
 Oft through the darkening fields have seen thee roam,
  Or cross a stile into the public way.
   Oft thou hast given them store
 Of flowers—the frail-leaf'd, white anemone—
  Dark bluebells drench'd with dews of summer eves,
  And purple orchises with spotted leaves—
But none has words she can report of thee.

And, above Godstow Bridge, when hay-time's here
 In June, and many a scythe in sunshine flames,
  Men who through those wide fields of breezy grass
 Where black-wing'd swallows haunt the glittering Thames,
  To bathe in the abandon'd lasher pass,
   Have often pass'd thee near
 Sitting upon the river bank o'ergrown:
  Mark'd thine outlandish garb, thy figure spare,
  Thy dark vague eyes, and soft abstracted air;
But, when they came from bathing, thou wert gone.

At some lone homestead in the Cumner hills,
 Where at her open door the housewife darns,
  Thou hast been seen, or hanging on a gate
 To watch the threshers in the mossy barns.
  Children, who early range these slopes and late
   For cresses from the rills,

MATTHEW ARNOLD

Have known thee watching, all an April day,
  The springing pastures and the feeding kine;
  And mark'd thee, when the stars come out and shine,
Through the long dewy grass move slow away.

In autumn, on the skirts of Bagley Wood,
  Where most the Gipsies by the turf-edged way
  Pitch their smoked tents, and every bush you see
With scarlet patches tagg'd and shreds of gray,
  Above the forest-ground call'd Thessaly—
    The blackbird picking food
Sees thee, nor stops his meal, nor fears at all;
  So often has he known thee past him stray
  Rapt, twirling in thy hand a wither'd spray,
And waiting for the spark from Heaven to fall.

And once, in winter, on the causeway chill
  Where home through flooded fields foot-travellers go,
  Have I not pass'd thee on the wooden bridge
Wrapt in thy cloak and battling with the snow,
  Thy face towards Hinksey and its wintry ridge?
    And thou hast climb'd the hill
And gain'd the white brow of the Cumner range;
  Turn'd once to watch, while thick the snowflakes fall,
  The line of festal light in Christ Church hall—
Then sought thy straw in some sequester'd grange.

But what—I dream! Two hundred years are flown
  Since first thy story ran through Oxford halls,
  And the grave Glanvil did the tale inscribe
That thou wert wander'd from the studious walls
  To learn strange arts, and join a Gipsy-tribe:
    And thou from earth art gone

Long since, and in some quiet churchyard laid—
　　Some country nook, where o'er thy unknown grave
　　Tall grasses and white flowering nettles wave—
Under a dark red-fruited yew-tree's shade.

— No, no, thou hast not felt the lapse of hours.
　For what wears out the life of mortal men?
　　'Tis that from change to change their being rolls:
　'Tis that repeated shocks, again, again,
　　Exhaust the energy of strongest souls,
　　　And numb the elastic powers.
　Till having used our nerves with bliss and teen,
　　And tired upon a thousand schemes our wit,
　　To the just-pausing Genius we remit
　Our worn-out life, and are—what we have been.

Thou hast not lived, why shouldst thou perish, so?
　Thou hadst *one* aim, *one* business, *one* desire:
　　Else wert thou long since number'd with the dead!
　Else hadst thou spent, like other men, thy fire!
　　The generations of thy peers are fled,
　　　And we ourselves shall go;
　But thou possessest an immortal lot,
　　And we imagine thee exempt from age
　　And living as thou liv'st on Glanvil's page,
　Because thou hadst—what we, alas, have not!

For early didst thou leave the world, with powers
　Fresh, undiverted to the world without,
　　Firm to their mark, not spent on other things;
　Free from the sick fatigue, the languid doubt,
　　　Which much to have tried, in much been baffled, brings.
　　　O life unlike to ours!

Who fluctuate idly without term or scope,
   Of whom each strives, nor knows for what he strives,
   And each half lives a hundred different lives;
Who wait like thee, but not, like thee, in hope.

Thou waitest for the spark from Heaven! and we,
   Vague half-believers of our casual creeds,
   Who never deeply felt, nor clearly will'd,
Whose insight never has borne fruit in deeds,
   Whose weak resolves never have been fulfill'd;
     For whom each year we see
Breeds new beginnings, disappointments new;
   Who hesitate and falter life away,
   And lose to-morrow the ground won to-day—
Ah, do not we, Wanderer, await it too?

Yes, we await it, but it still delays,
   And then we suffer; and amongst us One,
   Who most has suffer'd, takes dejectedly
His seat upon the intellectual throne;
   And all his store of sad experience he
     Lays bare of wretched days;
Tells us his misery's birth and growth and signs,
   And how the dying spark of hope was fed,
   And how the breast was soothed, and how the head,
And all his hourly varied anodynes.

This for our wisest: and we others pine,
   And wish the long unhappy dream would end,
   And waive all claim to bliss, and try to bear,
With close-lipp'd Patience for our only friend,
   Sad Patience, too near neighbour to Despair:
     But none has hope like thine.

Thou through the fields and through the woods dost stray,
　　Roaming the country-side, a truant boy,
　　Nursing thy project in unclouded joy,
And every doubt long blown by time away.

O born in days when wits were fresh and clear,
　　And life ran gaily as the sparkling Thames;
　　　　Before this strange disease of modern life,
　　With its sick hurry, its divided aims,
　　　　Its heads o'ertax'd, its palsied hearts, was rife—
　　　　　　Fly hence, our contact fear!
　　Still fly, plunge deeper in the bowering wood!
　　　　Averse, as Dido did with gesture stern
　　　　From her false friend's approach in Hades turn,
　　Wave us away, and keep thy solitude.

Still nursing the unconquerable hope,
　　Still clutching the inviolable shade,
　　　　With a free onward impulse brushing through,
　　By night, the silver'd branches of the glade—
　　　　Far on the forest-skirts, where none pursue,
　　　　　　On some mild pastoral slope
　　Emerge, and resting on the moonlit pales,
　　　　Freshen thy flowers, as in former years,
　　　　With dew, or listen with enchanted ears,
　　From the dark dingles, to the nightingales.

But fly our paths, our feverish contact fly!
　　For strong the infection of our mental strife,
　　　　Which, though it gives no bliss, yet spoils for rest;
　　And we should win thee from thy own fair life,
　　　　Like us distracted, and like us unblest.
　　　　　　Soon, soon thy cheer would die,

Thy hopes grow timorous, and unfix'd thy powers,
  And thy clear aims be cross and shifting made:
  And then thy glad perennial youth would fade,
Fade, and grow old at last, and die like ours.

Then fly our greetings, fly our speech and smiles!
  —As some grave Tyrian trader, from the sea,
  Descried at sunrise an emerging prow
Lifting the cool-hair'd creepers stealthily,
  The fringes of a southward-facing brow
    Among the Ægean isles;
And saw the merry Grecian coaster come,
  Freighted with amber grapes, and Chian wine,
  Green bursting figs, and tunnies steep'd in brine;
And knew the intruders on his ancient home,

The young light-hearted Masters of the waves;
  And snatch'd his rudder, and shook out more sail,
  And day and night held on indignantly
O'er the blue Midland waters with the gale,
  Betwixt the Syrtes and soft Sicily,
    To where the Atlantic raves
Outside the Western Straits, and unbent sails
  There, where down cloudy cliffs, through sheets of foam,
  Shy traffickers, the dark Iberians come;
And on the beach undid his corded bales.

760 *Thyrsis*

HOW changed is here each spot man makes or fills!
  In the two Hinkseys nothing keeps the same;
  The village-street its haunted mansion lacks,
And from the sign is gone Sibylla's name,

And from the roofs the twisted chimney-stacks;
   Are ye too changed, ye hills?
See, 'tis no foot of unfamiliar men
   To-night from Oxford up your pathway strays!
   Here came I often, often, in old days;
Thyrsis and I; we still had Thyrsis then.

Runs it not here, the track by Childsworth Farm,
   Up past the wood, to where the elm-tree crowns
     The hill behind whose ridge the sunset flames?
The signal-elm, that looks on Ilsley Downs,
     The Vale, the three lone weirs, the youthful Thames?—
       This winter-eve is warm,
Humid the air; leafless, yet soft as spring,
    The tender purple spray on copse and briers;
    And that sweet City with her dreaming spires,
She needs not June for beauty's heightening,

Lovely all times she lies, lovely to-night!
   Only, methinks, some loss of habit's power
     Befalls me wandering through this upland dim;
Once pass'd I blindfold here, at any hour,
     Now seldom come I, since I came with him.
      That single elm-tree bright
Against the west—I miss it! is it gone?
    We prized it dearly; while it stood, we said,
    Our friend, the Scholar-Gipsy, was not dead;
While the tree lived, he in these fields lived on.

MATTHEW ARNOLD

Too rare, too rare, grow now my visits here!
But once I knew each field, each flower, each stick;
And with the country-folk acquaintance made
By barn in threshing-time, by new-built rick.
Here, too, our shepherd-pipes we first assay'd.
Ah me! this many a year
My pipe is lost, my shepherd's-holiday!
Needs must I lose them, needs with heavy heart
Into the world and wave of men depart,
But Thyrsis of his own will went away.

It irk'd him to be here, he could not rest.
He loved each simple joy the country yields,
He loved his mates; but yet he could not keep,
For that a shadow lower'd on the fields,
Here with the shepherds and the silly sheep.
Some life of men unblest
He knew, which made him droop, and fill'd his head.
He went; his piping took a troubled sound
Of storms that rage outside our happy ground;
He could not wait their passing, he is dead!

So, some tempestuous morn in early June,
When the year's primal burst of bloom is o'er,
Before the roses and the longest day—
When garden-walks, and all the grassy floor,
With blossoms, red and white, of fallen May,
And chestnut-flowers are strewn—
So have I heard the cuckoo's parting cry,
From the wet field, through the vext garden-trees,
Come with the volleying rain and tossing breeze:
The bloom is gone, and with the bloom go I.

Too quick despairer, wherefore wilt thou go?
  Soon will the high Midsummer pomps come on,
    Soon will the musk carnations break and swell,
  Soon shall we have gold-dusted snapdragon,
    Sweet-William with its homely cottage-smell,
      And stocks in fragrant blow;
  Roses that down the alleys shine afar,
    And open, jasmine-muffled lattices,
    And groups under the dreaming garden-trees,
  And the full moon, and the white evening-star.

He hearkens not! light comer, he is flown!
  What matters it? next year he will return,
    And we shall have him in the sweet spring-days,
  With whitening hedges, and uncrumpling fern,
    And blue-bells trembling by the forest-ways,
      And scent of hay new-mown.
  But Thyrsis never more we swains shall see!
    See him come back, and cut a smoother reed,
    And blow a strain the world at last shall heed—
  For Time, not Corydon, hath conquer'd thee.

Alack, for Corydon no rival now!—
  But when Sicilian shepherds lost a mate,
    Some good survivor with his flute would go,
  Piping a ditty sad for Bion's fate,
    And cross the unpermitted ferry's flow,
      And relax Pluto's brow,
  And make leap up with joy the beauteous head
    Of Proserpine, among whose crownèd hair
    Are flowers, first open'd on Sicilian air,
  And flute his friend, like Orpheus, from the dead.

916

O easy access to the hearer's grace
　When Dorian shepherds sang to Proserpine!
　　For she herself had trod Sicilian fields,
　She knew the Dorian water's gush divine,
　　She knew each lily white which Enna yields,
　　　Each rose with blushing face;
　She loved the Dorian pipe, the Dorian strain.
　　But ah, of our poor Thames she never heard!
　　Her foot the Cumner cowslips never stirr'd!
　And we should tease her with our plaint in vain.

Well! wind-dispers'd and vain the words will be,
　Yet, Thyrsis, let me give my grief its hour
　　In the old haunt, and find our tree-topp'd hill!
　Who, if not I, for questing here hath power?
　　I know the wood which hides the daffodil,
　　　I know the Fyfield tree,
　I know what white, what purple fritillaries
　　The grassy harvest of the river-fields,
　　Above by Ensham, down by Sandford, yields,
　And what sedg'd brooks are Thames's tributaries;

I know these slopes; who knows them if not I?—
　But many a dingle on the loved hill-side,
　　With thorns once studded, old, white-blossom'd trees,
　Where thick the cowslips grew, and, far descried,
　　High tower'd the spikes of purple orchises,
　　　Hath since our day put by
　The coronals of that forgotten time.
　　Down each green bank hath gone the ploughboy's team,
　　And only in the hidden brookside gleam
　Primroses, orphans of the flowery prime.

MATTHEW ARNOLD

Where is the girl, who, by the boatman's door,
  Above the locks, above the boating throng,
    Unmoor'd our skiff, when, through the Wytham flats,
  Red loosestrife and blond meadow-sweet among,
    And darting swallows, and light water-gnats,
      We track'd the shy Thames shore?
  Where are the mowers, who, as the tiny swell
    Of our boat passing heav'd the river-grass,
    Stood with suspended scythe to see us pass?—
  They are all gone, and thou art gone as well.

Yes, thou art gone! and round me too the night
  In ever-nearing circle weaves her shade.
    I see her veil draw soft across the day,
  I feel her slowly chilling breath invade
    The cheek grown thin, the brown hair sprent with grey;
      I feel her finger light
  Laid pausefully upon life's headlong train;
    The foot less prompt to meet the morning dew,
    The heart less bounding at emotion new,
  And hope, once crush'd, less quick to spring again.

And long the way appears, which seem'd so short
  To the unpractis'd eye of sanguine youth;
    And high the mountain-tops, in cloudy air,
  The mountain-tops where is the throne of Truth,
    Tops in life's morning-sun so bright and bare!
      Unbreachable the fort
  Of the long-batter'd world uplifts its wall.
    And strange and vain the earthly turmoil grows,
    And near and real the charm of thy repose,
  And night as welcome as a friend would fall.

But hush! the upland hath a sudden loss
  Of quiet;—Look! adown the dusk hill-side,
    A troop of Oxford hunters going home,
  As in old days, jovial and talking, ride!
    From hunting with the Berkshire hounds they come—
      Quick, let me fly, and cross
  Into yon further field!—'Tis done; and see,
    Back'd by the sunset, which doth glorify
    The orange and pale violet evening-sky,
  Bare on its lonely ridge, the Tree! the Tree!

I take the omen! Eve lets down her veil,
  The white fog creeps from bush to bush about,
    The west unflushes, the high stars grow bright,
  And in the scatter'd farms the lights come out.
    I cannot reach the Signal-Tree to-night,
      Yet, happy omen, hail!
  Hear it from thy broad lucent Arno vale
    (For there thine earth-forgetting eyelids keep
    The morningless and unawakening sleep
  Under the flowery oleanders pale),

Hear it, O Thyrsis, still our Tree is there!—
  Ah, vain! These English fields, this upland dim,
    These brambles pale with mist engarlanded,
  That lone, sky-pointing tree, are not for him.
    To a boon southern country he is fled,
      And now in happier air,
  Wandering with the great Mother's train divine
    (And purer or more subtle soul than thee,
    I trow, the mighty Mother doth not see!)
  Within a folding of the Apennine,

Thou hearest the immortal strains of old.
  Putting his sickle to the perilous grain
    In the hot cornfield of the Phrygian king,
  For thee the Lityerses song again
    Young Daphnis with his silver voice doth sing;
      Sings his Sicilian fold,
  His sheep, his hapless love, his blinded eyes;
    And how a call celestial round him rang
    And heavenward from the fountain-brink he sprang,
And all the marvel of the golden skies.

There thou art gone, and me thou leavest here
  Sole in these fields; yet will I not despair;
    Despair I will not, while I yet descry
  'Neath the soft canopy of English air
    That lonely Tree against the western sky.
      Still, still these slopes, 'tis clear,
  Our Gipsy-Scholar haunts, outliving thee!
    Fields where soft sheep from cages pull the hay,
    Woods with anemonies in flower till May,
Know him a wanderer still; then why not me?

A fugitive and gracious light he seeks,
  Shy to illumine; and I seek it too.
    This does not come with houses or with gold,
  With place, with honour, and a flattering crew;
    'Tis not in the world's market bought and sold.
      But the smooth-slipping weeks
  Drop by, and leave its seeker still untired;
    Out of the heed of mortals he is gone,
    He wends unfollow'd, he must house alone;
Yet on he fares, by his own heart inspired.

Thou too, O Thyrsis, on like quest wert bound,
  Thou wanderedst with me for a little hour;
    Men gave thee nothing, but this happy quest,
  If men esteem'd thee feeble, gave thee power,
    If men procured thee trouble, gave thee rest.
      And this rude Cumner ground,
  Its fir-topped Hurst, its farms, its quiet fields,
    Here cam'st thou in thy jocund youthful time,
    Here was thine height of strength, thy golden prime;
  And still the haunt beloved a virtue yields.

What though the music of thy rustic flute
  Kept not for long its happy, country tone,
    Lost it too soon, and learnt a stormy note
  Of men contention-tost, of men who groan,
    Which task'd thy pipe too sore, and tired thy throat—
      It fail'd, and thou wast mute;
  Yet hadst thou always visions of our light,
    And long with men of care thou couldst not stay,
    And soon thy foot resumed its wandering way,
  Left human haunt, and on alone till night.

Too rare, too rare, grow now my visits here!
  'Mid city-noise, not, as with thee of yore,
    Thyrsis, in reach of sheep-bells is my home!
  Then through the great town's harsh, heart-wearying roar,
    Let in thy voice a whisper often come,
      To chase fatigue and fear:
  Why faintest thou? I wander'd till I died.
    Roam on! the light we sought is shining still.
    Dost thou ask proof? Our Tree yet crowns the hill,
  Our Scholar travels yet the loved hillside.

Philomela

HARK! ah, the Nightingale!
 The tawny-throated!
Hark! from that moonlit cedar what a burst!
What triumph! hark—what pain!

O Wanderer from a Grecian shore,
Still, after many years, in distant lands,
Still nourishing in thy bewilder'd brain
That wild, unquench'd, deep-sunken, old-world pain—
 Say, will it never heal?
And can this fragrant lawn
With its cool trees, and night,
And the sweet, tranquil Thames,
And moonshine, and the dew,
To thy rack'd heart and brain
 Afford no balm?

 Dost thou to-night behold
Here, through the moonlight on this English grass,
The unfriendly palace in the Thracian wild?
 Dost thou again peruse
With hot cheeks and sear'd eyes
The too clear web, and thy dumb Sister's shame?
 Dost thou once more assay
Thy flight, and feel come over thee,
Poor Fugitive, the feathery change
Once more, and once more seem to make resound
With love and hate, triumph and agony,
Lone Daulis, and the high Cephissian vale?
  Listen, Eugenia—

9 22

How thick the bursts come crowding through the leaves!
  Again—thou hearest!
Eternal Passion!
Eternal Pain!

762   *Shakespeare*

OTHERS abide our question. Thou art free,
  We ask and ask: Thou smilest and art still,
Out-topping knowledge. For the loftiest hill
That to the stars uncrowns his majesty,
Planting his steadfast footsteps in the sea,
Making the heaven of heavens his dwelling-place,
Spares but the cloudy border of his base
To the foil'd searching of mortality;
And thou, who didst the stars and sunbeams know,
Self-school'd, self-scann'd, self-honour'd, self-secure,
Didst walk on earth unguess'd at. Better so!
All pains the immortal spirit must endure,
  All weakness that impairs, all griefs that bow,
  Find their sole voice in that victorious brow.

763   *From the Hymn of Empedocles*

IS it so small a thing
  To have enjoy'd the sun,
To have lived light in the spring,
  To have loved, to have thought, to have done;
To have advanced true friends, and beat down baffling foes;

  That we must feign a bliss
  Of doubtful future date,
  And while we dream on this

Lose all our present state,
And relegate to worlds yet distant our repose?

Not much, I know, you prize
What pleasures may be had,
Who look on life with eyes
Estranged, like mine, and sad:
And yet the village churl feels the truth more than you;

Who's loth to leave this life
Which to him little yields:
His hard-task'd sunburnt wife,
His often-labour'd fields;
The boors with whom he talk'd, the country spots he knew.

But thou, because thou hear'st
Men scoff at Heaven and Fate;
Because the gods thou fear'st
Fail to make blest thy state,
Tremblest, and wilt not dare to trust the joys there are.

I say, Fear not! life still
Leaves human effort scope.
But, since life teems with ill,
Nurse no extravagant hope.
Because thou must not dream, thou need'st not then despair.

764   *The Strayed Reveller to Ulysses*

THE Gods are happy.
They turn on all sides
Their shining eyes:
And see, below them,
The Earth, and men.

They see Tiresias
Sitting, staff in hand,
On the warm, grassy
Asopus' bank:
His robe drawn over
His old, sightless head:
Revolving inly
The doom of Thebes.

They see the Centaurs
In the upper glens
Of Pelion, in the streams,
Where red-berried ashes fringe
The clear-brown shallow pools;
With streaming flanks, and heads
Rear'd proudly, snuffing
The mountain wind.

They see the Indian
Drifting, knife in hand,
His frail boat moor'd to
A floating isle thick matted
With large-leav'd, low-creeping melon-plants,
And the dark cucumber.
He reaps, and stows them,
Drifting—drifting:—round him,
Round his green harvest-plot,
Flow the cool lake-waves:
The mountains ring them.

They see the Scythian
On the wide Stepp, unharnessing
His wheel'd house at noon.
He tethers his beast down, and makes his meal,

Mares' milk, and bread
Bak'd on the embers:—all around
The boundless waving grass-plains stretch, thick-starr'd
With saffron and the yellow hollyhock
And flag-leav'd iris flowers.
Sitting in his cart
He makes his meal: before him, for long miles,
Alive with bright green lizards,
And the springing bustard fowl,
The track, a straight black line,
Furrows the rich soil: here and there
Clusters of lonely mounds
Topp'd with rough-hewn,
Grey, rain-blear'd statues, overpeer
The sunny Waste.

They see the Ferry
On the broad, clay-laden
Lone Chorasmian stream: thereon,
With snort and strain,
Two horses, strongly swimming, tow
The ferry-boat, with woven ropes
To either bow
Firm-harness'd by the mane:—a Chief,
With shout and shaken spear
Stands at the prow, and guides them: but astern,
The cowering Merchants, in long robes,
Sit pale beside their wealth
Of silk-bales and of balsam-drops,
Of gold and ivory,
Of turquoise-earth and amethyst,
Jasper and chalcedony,

And milk-barr'd onyx stones.
The loaded boat swings groaning
In the yellow eddies.
The Gods behold them.

They see the Heroes
Sitting in the dark ship
On the foamless, long-heaving,
Violet sea:
At sunset nearing
The Happy Islands.

These things, Ulysses,
The wise Bards also
Behold and sing.
But oh, what labour!
O Prince, what pain!

They too can see
Tiresias:—but the Gods,
Who give them vision,
Added this law:
That they should bear too
His groping blindness,
His dark foreboding,
His scorn'd white hairs;
Bear Hera's anger
Through a life lengthen'd
To seven ages.

They see the Centaurs
On Pelion:—then they feel,
They too, the maddening wine
Swell their large veins to bursting: in wild pain

They feel the biting spears
Of the grim Lapithae, and Theseus, drive,
Drive crashing through their bones: they feel
High on a jutting rock in the red stream
Alcmena's dreadful son
Ply his bow:—such a price
The Gods exact for song;
To become what we sing.

They see the Indian
On his mountain lake:—but squalls
Make their skiff reel, and worms
In the unkind spring have gnaw'd
Their melon-harvest to the heart: They see
The Scythian:—but long frosts
Parch them in winter-time on the bare Stepp,
Till they too fade like grass: they crawl
Like shadows forth in spring.

They see the Merchants
On the Oxus' stream:—but care
Must visit first them too, and make them pale.
Whether, through whirling sand,
A cloud of desert robber-horse has burst
Upon their caravan: or greedy kings,
In the wall'd cities the way passes through,
Crush'd them with tolls: or fever-airs,
On some great river's marge,
Mown them down, far from home.

They see the Heroes
Near harbour:—but they share
Their lives, and former violent toil, in Thebes,

Seven-gated Thebes, or Troy;
Or where the echoing oars
Of Argo first
Startled the unknown Sea.

The old Silenus
Came, lolling in the sunshine,
From the dewy forest coverts,
This way, at noon.
Sitting by me, while his Fauns
Down at the water side
Sprinkled and smooth'd
His drooping garland,
He told me these things.

But I, Ulysses,
Sitting on the warm steps,
Looking over the valley,
All day long, have seen,
Without pain, without labour,
Sometimes a wild-hair'd Maenad;
Sometimes a Faun with torches;
And sometimes, for a moment,
Passing through the dark stems
Flowing-rob'd—the belov'd,
The desir'd, the divine,
Belov'd Iacchus.

Ah cool night-wind, tremulous stars!
Ah glimmering water—
Fitful earth-murmur—
Dreaming woods!
Ah golden-hair'd, strangely-smiling Goddess,

And thou, prov'd, much enduring,
Wave-toss'd Wanderer!
Who can stand still?
Ye fade, ye swim, ye waver before me.
The cup again!

Faster, faster,
O Circe, Goddess,
Let the wild thronging train,
The bright procession
Of eddying forms,
Sweep through my soul!

WILLIAM BRIGHTY RANDS   1823–1880

765
The Thought

INTO the skies, one summer's day,
   I sent a little Thought away;
Up to where, in the blue round,
The sun sat shining without sound.

Then my Thought came back to me.—
Little Thought, what did you see
In the regions whence you come?
And when I spoke, my Thought was dumb.

But she breathed of what was there,
In the pure bright upper air;
And, because my Thought so shone,
I knew she had been shone upon.

Next, by night a Thought I sent
Up into the firmament;
When the eager stars were out,
And the still moon shone about.

And my Thought went past the moon
In between the stars, but soon
Held her breath and durst not stir,
For the fear that covered her;
Then she thought, in this demur:

'Dare I look beneath the shade,
Into where the worlds are made;
Where the suns and stars are wrought?
Shall I meet another Thought?

'Will that other Thought have wings?
Shall I meet strange, heavenly things?
Thought of Thoughts, and Light of Lights,
Breath of Breaths, and Night of Nights?'

Then my Thought began to hark
In the illuminated dark,
Till the silence, over, under,
Made her heart beat more than thunder.

And my Thought, came trembling back,
But with something on her track,
And with something at her side;
Nor till she has lived and died,
Lived and died, and lived again,
Will that awful thing seem plain.

WILLIAM PHILPOT

1823–1889

766

Maritæ Suæ

I

OF all the flowers rising now,
   Thou only saw'st the head
Of that unopen'd drop of snow
   I placed beside thy bed.

In all the blooms that blow so fast,
    Thou hast no further part,
Save those the hour I saw thee last,
    I laid above thy heart.

Two snowdrops for our boy and girl,
    A primrose blown for me,
Wreathed with one often-play'd-with curl
    From each bright head for thee.

And so I graced thee for thy grave,
    And made these tokens fast
With that old silver heart I gave,
    My first gift—and my last.

II

I dream'd, her babe upon her breast,
Here she might lie and calmly rest
Her happy eyes on that far hill
That backs the landscape fresh and still.

I hoped her thoughts would thrid the boughs
Where careless birds on love carouse,
And gaze those apple-blossoms through
To revel in the boundless blue.

But now her faculty of sight
Is elder sister to the light,
And travels free and unconfined
Through dense and rare, through form and mind.

Or else her life to be complete
Hath found new channels full and meet—
Then, O, what eyes are leaning o'er,
If fairer than they were before!

WILLIAM (JOHNSON) CORY

1823–1892

Mimnermus in Church

YOU promise heavens free from strife,
　　Pure truth, and perfect change of will;
But sweet, sweet is this human life,
　　So sweet, I fain would breathe it still;
Your chilly stars I can forgo,
This warm kind world is all I know.

You say there is no substance here,
　　One great reality above:
Back from that void I shrink in fear,
　　And child-like hide myself in love:
Show me what angels feel. Till then
I cling, a mere weak man, to men.

You bid me lift my mean desires
　　From faltering lips and fitful veins
To sexless souls, ideal quires,
　　Unwearied voices, wordless strains:
My mind with fonder welcome owns
One dear dead friend's remember'd tones.

Forsooth the present we must give
　　To that which cannot pass away;
All beauteous things for which we live
　　By laws of time and space decay.
But Oh, the very reason why
I clasp them, is because they die.

WILLIAM (JOHNSON) CORY

768 *Heraclitus*

THEY told me, Heraclitus, they told me you were dead,
   They brought me bitter news to hear and bitter tears to
     shed.
I wept as I remember'd how often you and I
Had tired the sun with talking and sent him down the sky.

And now that thou art lying, my dear old Carian guest,
A handful of grey ashes, long, long ago at rest,
Still are thy pleasant voices, thy nightingales, awake;
For Death, he taketh all away, but them he cannot take.

COVENTRY PATMORE

1823–1896

769 *The Married Lover*

WHY, having won her, do I woo?
   Because her spirit's vestal grace
Provokes me always to pursue,
   But, spirit-like, eludes embrace;
Because her womanhood is such
   That, as on court-days subjects kiss
The Queen's hand, yet so near a touch
   Affirms no mean familiarness;
Nay, rather marks more fair the height
   Which can with safety so neglect
To dread, as lower ladies might,
   That grace could meet with disrespect;
Thus she with happy favour feeds
   Allegiance from a love so high
That thence no false conceit proceeds
   Of difference bridged, or state put by;

Because although in act and word
　　As lowly as a wife can be,
Her manners, when they call me lord,
　　Remind me 'tis by courtesy;
Not with her least consent of will,
　　Which would my proud affection hurt,
But by the noble style that still
　　Imputes an unattain'd desert;
Because her gay and lofty brows,
　　When all is won which hope can ask,
Reflect a light of hopeless snows,
　　That bright in virgin ether bask;
Because, though free of the outer court
　　I am, this Temple keeps its shrine
Sacred to Heaven; because, in short,
　　She's not and never can be mine.

770　　*Departure*

IT was not like your great and gracious ways!
　Do you, that have naught other to lament,
Never, my Love, repent
Of how, that July afternoon,
You went,
With sudden, unintelligible phrase,
And frighten'd eye,
Upon your journey of so many days
Without a single kiss, or a good-bye?
I knew, indeed, that you were parting soon;
And so we sate, within the low sun's rays,
You whispering to me, for your voice was weak,
Your harrowing praise.

935

Well, it was well
To hear you such things speak,
And I could tell
What made your eyes a growing gloom of love,
As a warm South-wind sombres a March grove.
And it was like your great and gracious ways
To turn your talk on daily things, my Dear,
Lifting the luminous, pathetic lash
To let the laughter flash,
Whilst I drew near,
Because you spoke so low that I could scarcely hear.
But all at once to leave me at the last,
More at the wonder than the loss aghast,
With huddled, unintelligible phrase,
And frighten'd eye,
And go your journey of all days
With not one kiss, or a good-bye,
And the only loveless look the look with which you pass'd:
'Twas all unlike your great and gracious ways.

771 *The Toys*

MY little Son, who look'd from thoughtful eyes
And moved and spoke in quiet grown-up wise,
Having my law the seventh time disobey'd,
I struck him, and dismiss'd
With hard words and unkiss'd,
—His Mother, who was patient, being dead.
Then, fearing lest his grief should hinder sleep,
I visited his bed,
But found him slumbering deep,

With darken'd eyelids, and their lashes yet
From his late sobbing wet.
And I, with moan,
Kissing away his tears, left others of my own;
For, on a table drawn beside his head,
He had put, within his reach,
A box of counters and a red-vein'd stone,
A piece of glass abraded by the beach.
And six or seven shells,
A bottle with bluebells,
And two French copper coins, ranged there with careful art,
To comfort his sad heart.
So when that night I pray'd
To God, I wept, and said:
Ah, when at last we lie with trancèd breath,
Not vexing Thee in death,
And Thou rememberest of what toys
We made our joys,
How weakly understood
Thy great commanded good,
Then, fatherly not less
Than I whom Thou hast moulded from the clay,
Thou'lt leave Thy wrath, and say,
'I will be sorry for their childishness.'

772   *Magna est Veritas*

HERE, in this little Bay,
    Full of tumultuous life and great repose,
Where, twice a day,
The purposeless, glad ocean comes and goes,
Under high cliffs, and far from the huge town,
I sit me down.

For want of me the world's course will **not fail;**
When all its work is done, the lie shall **rot;**
The truth is great, and shall prevail,
When none cares whether it prevail **or not.**

773   *A Farewell*

WITH all my will, but much against my heart,
   We two now part.
My Very Dear,
Our solace is, the sad road lies so clear.
It needs no art,
With faint, averted feet
And many a tear,
In our opposèd paths to persevere.
Go thou to East, I West.
We will not say
There's any hope, it is so far away
But, O, my Best,
When the one darling of our widowhead,
The nursling Grief,
Is dead,
And no dews blur our eyes
To see the peach-bloom come in evening skies,
Perchance we may,
Where now this night is day,
And even through faith of still averted feet,
Making full circle of our banishment,
Amazèd meet;
The bitter journey to the bourne so sweet
Seasoning the termless feast of our content
With tears of recognition never dry.

SYDNEY DOBELL

1824–1874

774 *The Ballad of Keith of Ravelston*

THE murmur of the mourning ghost
   That keeps the shadowy kine,
'O Keith of Ravelston,
   The sorrows of thy line!'

Ravelston, Ravelston,
   The merry path that leads
Down the golden morning hill,
   And thro' the silver meads;

Ravelston, Ravelston,
   The stile beneath the tree,
The maid that kept her mother's kine,
   The song that sang she!

She sang her song, she kept her kine,
   She sat beneath the thorn,
When Andrew Keith of Ravelston
   Rode thro' the Monday morn.

His henchmen sing, his hawk-bells ring,
   His belted jewels shine;
O Keith of Ravelston,
   The sorrows of thy line!

Year after year, where Andrew came,
   Comes evening down the glade,
And still there sits a moonshine ghost
   Where sat the sunshine maid.

Her misty hair is faint and fair,
  She keeps the shadowy kine;
O Keith of Ravelston,
  The sorrows of thy line!

I lay my hand upon the stile,
  The stile is lone and cold,
The burnie that goes babbling by
  Says naught that can be told.

Yet, stranger! here, from year to year,
  She keeps her shadowy kine;
O Keith of Ravelston,
  The sorrows of thy line!

Step out three steps, where Andrew stood—
  Why blanch thy cheeks for fear?
The ancient stile is not alone,
  'Tis not the burn I hear!

She makes her immemorial moan,
  She keeps her shadowy kine;
O Keith of Ravelston,
  The sorrows of thy line!

775   *A Chanted Calendar*

FIRST came the primrose,
  On the bank high,
Like a maiden looking forth
From the window of a tower
When the battle rolls below,
So look'd she,
And saw the storms go by.

Then came the wind-flower
In the valley left behind,
As a wounded maiden, pale
With purple streaks of woe,
When the battle has roll'd by
Wanders to and fro,
So totter'd she,
Dishevell'd in the wind.

Then came the daisies,
On the first of May,
Like a banner'd show's advance
While the crowd runs by the way,
With ten thousand flowers about them they came trooping
through the fields.
As a happy people come,
So came they,
As a happy people come
When the war has roll'd away,
With dance and tabor, pipe and drum,
And all make holiday.

Then came the cow-slip,
Like a dancer in the fair,
She spread her little mat of green,
And on it danced she.
With a fillet bound about her brow,
A fillet round her happy brow,
A golden fillet round her brow,
And rubies in her hair.

1824-1889

The Fairies

776

UP the airy mountain,
  Down the rushy glen,
We daren't go a-hunting
  For fear of little men;
Wee folk, good folk,
  Trooping all together;
Green jacket, red cap,
  And white owl's feather!

Down along the rocky shore
  Some make their home,
They live on crispy pancakes
  Of yellow tide-foam;
Some in the reeds
  Of the black mountain lake,
With frogs for their watch-dogs,
  All night awake.

High on the hill-top
  The old King sits;
He is now so old and gray
  He's nigh lost his wits.
With a bridge of white mist
  Columbkill he crosses,
On his stately journeys
  From Slieveleague to Rosses;

Or going up with music
    On cold starry nights
To sup with the Queen
    Of the gay Northern Lights.

They stole little Bridget
    For seven years long;
When she came down again
    Her friends were all gone.
They took her lightly back,
    Between the night and morrow,
They thought that she was fast asleep,
    But she was dead with sorrow.
They have kept her ever since
    Deep within the lake,
On a bed of flag-leaves,
    Watching till she wake.

By the craggy hill-side,
    Through the mosses bare,
They have planted thorn-trees
    For pleasure here and there.
If any man so daring
    As dig them up in spite,
He shall find their sharpest thorns
    In his bed at night.

Up the airy mountain,
    Down the rushy glen,
We daren't go a-hunting
    For fear of little men;

WILLIAM ALLINGHAM

Wee folk, good folk,
   Trooping all together;
Green jacket, red cap,
   And white owl's feather!

GEORGE MACDONALD

1824-1905

777   *That Holy Thing*

THEY all were looking for a king
   To slay their foes and lift them high:
Thou cam'st, a little baby thing
   That made a woman cry.

O Son of Man, to right my lot
   Naught but Thy presence can avail;
Yet on the road Thy wheels are not,
   Nor on the sea Thy sail!

My how or when Thou wilt not heed,
   But come down Thine own secret stair,
That Thou mayst answer all my need—
   Yea, every bygone prayer.

WALTER CHALMERS SMITH

1824–1908

778   *Glenaradale*

THERE is no fire of the crackling boughs
   On the hearth of our fathers,
There is no lowing of brown-eyed cows
   On the green meadows,
Nor do the maidens whisper vows
   In the still gloaming,
      Glenaradale.

WALTER CHALMERS SMITH

There is no bleating of sheep on the hill
  Where the mists linger,
There is no sound of the low hand-mill
  Ground by the women,
And the smith's hammer is lying still
  By the brown anvil,
    Glenaradale.

Ah! we must leave thee and go away
  Far from Ben Luibh,
Far from the graves where we hoped to lay
  Our bones with our fathers',
Far from the kirk where we used to pray
  Lowly together,
    Glenaradale.

We are not going for hunger of wealth,
  For the gold and silver,
We are not going to seek for health
  On the flat prairies,
Nor yet for the lack of fruitful tilth
  On thy green pastures,
    Glenaradale.

Content with the croft and the hill were we,
  As all our fathers,
Content with the fish in the lake to be
  Carefully netted,
And garments spun of the wool from thee,
  O black-faced wether
    Of Glenaradale!

No father here but would give a son
   For the old country,
And his mother the sword would have girded on
   To fight her battles:
Many's the battle that has been won
   By the brave tartans,
     Glenaradale.

But the big-horn'd stag and his hinds, we know,
   In the high corries,
And the salmon that swirls in the pool below
   Where the stream rushes
Are more than the hearts of men, and so
   We leave thy green valley,
     Glenaradale.

DANTE GABRIEL ROSSETTI 1828–1882
The Blessèd Damozel

779

THE blessèd damozel lean'd out
   From the gold bar of Heaven;
Her eyes were deeper than the depth
   Of waters still'd at even;
She had three lilies in her hand,
   And the stars in her hair were seven.

Her robe, ungirt from clasp to hem,
   No wrought flowers did adorn,
But a white rose of Mary's gift,
   For service meetly worn;
Her hair that lay along her back
   Was yellow like ripe corn.

DANTE GABRIEL ROSSETTI

Herseem'd she scarce had been a day
   One of God's choristers;
The wonder was not yet quite gone
   From that still look of hers;
Albeit, to them she left, her day
   Had counted as ten years.

(To one, it is ten years of years.
   . . . Yet now, and in this place,
Surely she lean'd o'er me—her hair
   Fell all about my face. . . .
Nothing: the autumn-fall of leaves.
   The whole year sets apace.)

It was the rampart of God's house
   That she was standing on;
By God built over the sheer depth
   The which is Space begun;
So high, that looking downward thence
   She scarce could see the sun.

It lies in Heaven, across the flood
   Of ether, as a bridge.
Beneath, the tides of day and night
   With flame and darkness ridge
The void, as low as where this earth
   Spins like a fretful midge.

Around her, lovers, newly met
   'Mid deathless love's acclaims,
Spoke evermore among themselves
   Their heart-remember'd names;
And the souls mounting up to God
   Went by her like thin flames.

And still she bow'd herself and stoop'd
　　Out of the circling charm;
Until her bosom must have made
　　The bar she lean'd on warm,
And the lilies lay as if asleep
　　Along her bended arm.

From the fix'd place of Heaven she saw
　　Time like a pulse shake fierce
Through all the worlds. Her gaze still strove
　　Within the gulf to pierce
Its path; and now she spoke as when
　　The stars sang in their spheres.

The sun was gone now; the curl'd moon
　　Was like a little feather
Fluttering far down the gulf; and now
　　She spoke through the still weather.
Her voice was like the voice the stars
　　Had when they sang together.

(Ah sweet! Even now, in that bird's song,
　　Strove not her accents there,
Fain to be hearkened? When those bells
　　Possess'd the mid-day air,
Strove not her steps to reach my side
　　Down all the echoing stair?)

'I wish that he were come to me:
　　For he will come,' she said.
'Have I not pray'd in Heaven?—on earth,
　　Lord, Lord, has he not pray'd?
Are not two prayers a perfect strength?
　　And shall I feel afraid?

'When round his head the aureole clings,
    And he is clothed in white,
I'll take his hand and go with him
    To the deep wells of light;
As unto a stream we will step down,
    And bathe there in God's sight.

'We two will stand beside that shrine,
    Occult, withheld, untrod,
Whose lamps are stirred continually
    With prayer sent up to God;
And see our old prayers, granted, melt
    Each like a little cloud.

'We two will lie i' the shadow of
    That living mystic tree,
Within whose secret growth the Dove
    Is sometimes felt to be,
While every leaf that His plumes touch
    Saith His Name audibly.

'And I myself will teach to him,
    I myself, lying so,
The songs I sing here; which his voice
    Shall pause in, hush'd and slow,
And find some knowledge at each pause,
    Or some new thing to know.'

(Alas! We two, we two, thou say'st!
    Yea, one wast thou with me
That once of old. But shall God lift
    To endless unity
The soul whose likeness with thy soul
    Was but its love for thee?)

'We two,' she said, 'will seek the groves
  Where the lady Mary is,
With her five handmaidens, whose names
  Are five sweet symphonies,
Cecily, Gertrude, Magdalen,
  Margaret and Rosalys.

'Circlewise sit they, with bound locks
  And foreheads garlanded;
Into the fine cloth white like flame
  Weaving the golden thread,
To fashion the birth-robes for them
  Who are just born, being dead.

'He shall fear, haply, and be dumb:
  Then will I lay my cheek
To his, and tell about our love,
  Not once abash'd or weak:
And the dear Mother will approve
  My pride, and let me speak.

'Herself shall bring us, hand in hand,
  To Him round whom all souls
Kneel, the clear-ranged unnumbered heads
  Bowed with their aureoles:
And angels meeting us shall sing
  To their citherns and citoles.

'There will I ask of Christ the Lord
  Thus much for him and me:—
Only to live as once on earth
  With Love,—only to be,
As then awhile, for ever now
  Together, I and he.'

She gazed and listen'd and then said,
  Less sad of speech than mild,—
'All this is when he comes.' She ceased.
  The light thrill'd towards her, fill'd
With angels in strong level flight.
  Her eyes prayed, and she smiled.

(I saw her smile.) But soon their path
  Was vague in distant spheres:
And then she cast her arms along
  The golden barriers,
And laid her face between her hands,
  And wept. (I heard her tears.)

780   *The Woodspurge*

THE wind flapped loose, the wind was still,
  Shaken out dead from tree and hill:
I had walk'd on at the wind's will,—
I sat now, for the wind was still.

Between my knees my forehead was,—
My lips, drawn in, said not Alas!
My hair was over in the grass,
My naked ears heard the day pass.

My eyes, wide open, had the run
Of some ten weeds to fix upon;
Among those few, out of the sun,
The woodspurge flower'd, three cups in one.

From perfect grief there need not be
Wisdom or even memory:
One thing then learnt remains to me,—
The woodspurge has a cup of three.

951

DANTE GABRIEL ROSSETTI

Soul's Beauty

UNDER the arch of Life, where love and death,
 Terror and mystery, guard her shrine, I saw
 Beauty enthroned; and though her gaze struck awe,
I drew it in as simply as my breath.
Hers are the eyes which, over and beneath,
 The sky and sea bend on thee,—which can draw,
 By sea or sky or woman, to one law,
The allotted bondman of her palm and wreath.

This is that Lady Beauty, in whose praise
 Thy voice and hand shake still,—long known to thee
 By flying hair and fluttering hem,—the beat
 Following her daily of thy heart and feet,
 How passionately and irretrievably,
In what fond flight, how many ways and days!

The Choice

THINK thou and act; to-morrow thou shalt die.
 Outstretch'd in the sun's warmth upon the shore,
 Thou say'st: 'Man's measured path is all gone o'er:
Up all his years, steeply, with strain and sigh,
Man clomb until he touch'd the truth; and I,
 Even I, am he whom it was destined for.'
 How should this be? Art thou then so much more
Than they who sow'd, that thou shouldst reap thereby?

Nay, come up hither. From this wave-wash'd mound
 Unto the furthest flood-brim look with me;
Then reach on with thy thought till it be drown'd.
 Miles and miles distant though the last line be,
And though thy soul sail leagues and leagues beyond,—
 Still, leagues beyond those leagues, there is more sea.

GEORGE MEREDITH

1828–1909

783   From '*Love in the Valley*'

UNDER yonder beech-tree single on the green-sward,
  Couch'd with her arms behind her golden head,
Knees and tresses folded to slip and ripple idly,
  Lies my young love sleeping in the shade.
Had I the heart to slide an arm beneath her,
  Press her parting lips as her waist I gather slow,
Waking in amazement she could not but embrace me:
  Then would she hold me and never let me go?

Shy as the squirrel and wayward as the swallow,
  Swift as the swallow along the river's light
Circleting the surface to meet his mirror'd winglets,
  Fleeter she seems in her stay than in her flight.
Shy as the squirrel that leaps among the pine-tops,
  Wayward as the swallow overhead at set of sun,
She whom I love is hard to catch and conquer,
  Hard, but O the glory of the winning were she won!

When her mother tends her before the laughing mirror,
  Tying up her laces, looping up her hair,
Often she thinks, were this wild thing wedded,
  More love should I have, and much less care.
When her mother tends her before the lighted mirror,
  Loosening her laces, combing down her curls,
Often she thinks, were this wild thing wedded,
  I should miss but one for many boys and girls.

Heartless she is as the shadow in the meadows
    Flying to the hills on a blue and breezy noon.
No, she is athirst and drinking up her wonder:
    Earth to her is young as the slip of the new moon.
Deals she an unkindness, 'tis but her rapid measure,
    Even as in a dance; and her smile can heal no less:
Like the swinging May-cloud that pelts the flowers with
      hailstones
    Off a sunny border, she was made to bruise and bless.

Lovely are the curves of the white owl sweeping
    Wavy in the dusk lit by one large star.
Lone on the fir-branch, his rattle-note unvaried,
    Brooding o'er the gloom, spins the brown evejar.
Darker grows the valley, more and more forgetting:
    So were it with me if forgetting could be will'd.
Tell the grassy hollow that holds the bubbling well-spring,
    Tell it to forget the source that keeps it fill'd.

Stepping down the hill with her fair companions,
    Arm in arm, all against the raying West,
Boldly she sings, to the merry tune she marches,
    Brave is her shape, and sweeter unpossess'd.
Sweeter, for she is what my heart first awaking
    Whisper'd the world was; morning light is she.
Love that so desires would fain keep her changeless;
    Fain would fling the net, and fain have her free.

Happy happy time, when the white star hovers
    Low over dim fields fresh with bloomy dew,
Near the face of dawn, that draws athwart the darkness,
    Threading it with colour, like yewberries the yew.

GEORGE MEREDITH

Thicker crowd the shades as the grave East deepens
   Glowing, and with crimson a long cloud swells.
Maiden still the morn is; and strange she is, and secret;
   Strange her eyes; her cheeks are cold as cold sea-shells.

       .   .   .

Mother of the dews, dark eye-lash'd twilight,
   Low-lidded twilight, o'er the valley's brim,
Rounding on thy breast sings the dew-delighted skylark,
   Clear as though the dewdrops had their voice in him.
Hidden where the rose-flush drinks the rayless planet,
   Fountain-full he pours the spraying fountain-showers.
Let me hear her laughter, I would have her ever
   Cool as dew in twilight, the lark above the flowers.

All the girls are out with their baskets for the primrose;
   Up lanes, woods through, they troop in joyful bands.
My sweet leads: she knows not why, but now she loiters,
   Eyes the bent anemones, and hangs her hands.
Such a look will tell that the violets are peeping,
   Coming the rose: and unaware a cry
Springs in her bosom for odours and for colour,
   Covert and the nightingale; she knows not why.

       .   .   .

Hither she comes; she comes to me; she lingers,
   Deepens her brown eyebrows, while in new surprise
High rise the lashes in wonder of a stranger;
   Yet am I the light and living of her eyes.
Something friends have told her fills her heart to brimming,
   Nets her in her blushes, and wounds her, and tames.—
Sure of her haven, O like a dove alighting,
   Arms up, she dropp'd: our souls were in our names.

Could I find a place to be alone with heaven,
    I would speak my heart out: heaven is my need.
Every woodland tree is flushing like the dogwood,
    Flashing like the whitebeam, swaying like the reed.
Flushing like the dogwood crimson in October;
    Streaming like the flag-reed South-West blown;
Flashing as in gusts the sudden-lighted whitebeam:
    All seem to know what is for heaven alone.

784   *Phœbus with Admetus*

WHEN by Zeus relenting the mandate was revoked,
    Sentencing to exile the bright Sun-God,
Mindful were the ploughmen of who the steer had yoked,
    Who: and what a track show'd the upturn'd sod!
Mindful were the shepherds, as now the noon severe
    Bent a burning eyebrow to brown evetide,
How the rustic flute drew the silver to the sphere,
    Sister of his own, till her rays fell wide.
            God! of whom music
            And song and blood are pure,
            The day is never darken'd
            That had thee here obscure.

Chirping none, the scarlet cicalas crouch'd in ranks:
    Slack the thistle-head piled its down-silk gray:
Scarce the stony lizard suck'd hollows in his flanks:
    Thick on spots of umbrage our drowsed flocks lay.
Sudden bow'd the chestnuts beneath a wind unheard,
    Lengthen'd ran the grasses, the sky grew slate:
Then amid a swift flight of wing'd seed white as curd,
    Clear of limb a Youth smote the master's gate.

956

GEORGE MEREDITH

God! of whom music
And song and blood are pure,
The day is never darken'd
That had thee here obscure.

Water, first of singers, o'er rocky mount and mead,
　First of earthly singers, the sun-loved rill,
Sang of him, and flooded the ripples on the reed,
　Seeking whom to waken and what ear fill.
Water, sweetest soother to kiss a wound and cool,
　Sweetest and divinest, the sky-born brook,
Chuckled, with a whimper, and made a mirror-pool
　Round the guest we welcomed, the strange hand shook.
God! of whom music
And song and blood are pure,
The day is never darken'd
That had thee here obscure.

Many swarms of wild bees descended on our fields:
　Stately stood the wheatstalk with head bent high:
Big of heart we labour'd at storing mighty yields,
　Wool and corn, and clusters to make men cry!
Hand-like rush'd the vintage; we strung the bellied skins
　Plump, and at the sealing the Youth's voice rose:
Maidens clung in circle, on little fists their chins;
　Gentle beasties through push'd a cold long nose.
God! of whom music
And song and blood are pure,
The day is never darken'd
That had thee here obscure.

GEORGE MEREDITH

Foot to fire in snowtime we trimm'd the slender shaft:
    Often down the pit spied the lean wolf's teeth
Grin against his will, trapp'd by masterstrokes of craft;
    Helpless in his froth-wrath as green logs seethe!
Safe the tender lambs tugg'd the teats, and winter sped
    Whirl'd before the crocus, the year's new gold.
Hung the hooky beak up aloft, the arrowhead
    Redden'd through his feathers for our dear fold.
            God! of whom music
            And song and blood are pure,
            The day is never darken'd
            That had thee here obscure.

Tales we drank of giants at war with Gods above:
    Rocks were they to look on, and earth climb'd air!
Tales of search for simples, and those who sought of love
    Ease because the creature was all too fair.
Pleasant ran our thinking that, while our work was good,
    Sure as fruits for sweat would the praise come fast.
He that wrestled stoutest and tamed the billow-brood
    Danced in rings with girls, like a sail-flapp'd mast.
            God! of whom music
            And song and blood are pure
            The day is never darken'd
            That had thee here obscure.

Lo, the herb of healing, when once the herb is known,
    Shines in shady woods bright as new-sprung flame,
Ere the string was tighten'd we heard the mellow tone,
    After he had taught how the sweet sounds came.

Stretch'd about his feet, labour done, 'twas as you see
   Red pomegranates tumble and burst hard rind.
So began contention to give delight and be
   Excellent in things aim'd to make life kind.
          God! of whom music
          And song and blood are pure,
          The day is never darken'd
          That day thee here obscure.

You with shelly horns, rams! and, promontory goats,
   You whose browsing beards dip in coldest dew!
Bulls, that walk the pastures in kingly-flashing coats!
   Laurel, ivy, vine, wreath'd for feasts not few!
You that build the shade-roof, and you that court the rays,
   You that leap besprinkling the rock stream-rent:
He has been our fellow, the morning of our days;
   Us he chose for housemates, and this way went.
          God! of whom music
          And song and blood are pure,
          The day is never darken'd
          That had thee here obscure.

785   *Love's Grave*

MARK where the pressing wind shoots javelin-like,
   Its skeleton shadow on the broad-back'd wave!
Here is a fitting spot to dig Love's grave;
Here where the ponderous breakers plunge and strike,
And dart their hissing tongues high up the sand:
In hearing of the ocean, and in sight
Of those ribb'd wind-streaks running into white.
If I the death of Love had deeply plann'd,

I never could have made it half so sure,
As by the unblest kisses which upbraid
The full-waked sense; or failing that, degrade!
'Tis morning: but no morning can restore
What we have forfeited. I see no sin:
The wrong is mix'd. In tragic life, God wot,
No villain need be! Passions spin the plot:
We are betray'd by what is false within.

786 *Lucifer in Starlight*

ON a starr'd night Prince Lucifer uprose.
  Tired of his dark dominion swung the fiend
 Above the rolling ball in cloud part screen'd,
Where sinners hugg'd their spectre of repose.
Poor prey to his hot fit of pride were those.
  And now upon his western wing he lean'd,
  Now his huge bulk o'er Afric's sands careen'd,
Now the black planet shadow'd Arctic snows.
Soaring through wider zones that prick'd his scars
  With memory of the old revolt from Awe,
He reach'd a middle height, and at the stars,
Which are the brain of heaven, he look'd, and sank.
Around the ancient track march'd, rank on rank,
  The army of unalterable law.

787 *Dirge in Woods*

A WIND sways the pines,
    And below
Not a breath of wild air;
Still as the mosses that glow
On the flooring and over the lines
Of the roots here and there.

GEORGE MEREDITH

The pine-tree drops its dead;
They are quiet, as under the sea.
Overhead, overhead
Rushes life in a race,
As the clouds the clouds chase;
  And we go,
And we drop like the fruits of the tree,
  Even we,
  Even so.

EMILY DICKINSON

1830–1886

788   *Parting*

MY life closed twice before its close;
 It yet remains to see
If Immortality unveil
 A third event to me

So huge, so hopeless to conceive,
 As these that twice befell.
Parting is all we know of heaven,
 And all we need of hell.

CHRISTINA GEORGINA ROSSETTI

1830–1894

789   *Bride Song*

FROM 'THE PRINCE'S PROGRESS'

TOO late for love, too late for joy,
 Too late, too late!
You loiter'd on the road too long,
 You trifled at the gate:

The enchanted dove upon her branch
    Died without a mate;
The enchanted princess in her tower
    Slept, died, behind the grate;
Her heart was starving all this while
    You made it wait.

Ten years ago, five years ago,
    One year ago,
Even then you had arrived in time,
    Though somewhat slow;
Then you had known her living face
    Which now you cannot know:
The frozen fountain would have leap'd.
    The buds gone on to blow,
The warm south wind would have awaked
    To melt the snow.

Is she fair now as she lies?
    Once she was fair;
Meet queen for any kingly king,
    With gold-dust on her hair.
Now there are poppies in her locks,
    White poppies she must wear;
Must wear a veil to shroud her face
    And the want graven there:
Or is the hunger fed at length,
    Cast off the care?

We never saw her with a smile
    Or with a frown;
Her bed seem'd never soft to her,
    Though toss'd of down;

She little heeded what she wore,
  Kirtle, or wreath, or gown;
We think her white brows often ached
  Beneath her crown,
Till silvery hairs show'd in her locks
  That used to be so brown.

We never heard her speak in haste:
  Her tones were sweet,
And modulated just so much
  As it was meet:
Her heart sat silent through the noise
  And concourse of the street.
There was no hurry in her hands,
  No hurry in her feet;
There was no bliss drew nigh to her,
  That she might run to greet.

You should have wept her yesterday,
  Wasting upon her bed:
But wherefore should you weep to-day
  That she is dead?
Lo, we who love weep not to-day,
  But crown her royal head.
Let be these poppies that we strew,
  Your roses are too red:
Let be these poppies, not for you
  Cut down and spread.

790 *A Birthday*

MY heart is like a singing bird
    Whose nest is in a water'd shoot;
My heart is like an apple-tree
    Whose boughs are bent with thick-set fruit;
My heart is like a rainbow shell
    That paddles in a halcyon sea;
My heart is gladder than all these,
    Because my love is come to me.

Raise me a daïs of silk and down;
    Hang it with vair and purple dyes;
Carve it in doves and pomegranates,
    And peacocks with a hundred eyes;
Work it in gold and silver grapes,
    In leaves and silver fleurs-de-lys;
Because the birthday of my life
    Is come, my love is come to me.

791 *Song*

WHEN I am dead, my dearest,
    Sing no sad songs for me;
Plant thou no roses at my head,
    Nor shady cypress tree:
Be the green grass above me
    With showers and dewdrops wet;
And if thou wilt, remember,
    And if thou wilt, forget.

I shall not see the shadows,
    I shall not feel the rain;
I shall not hear the nightingale
    Sing on, as if in pain;

And dreaming through the twilight
    That doth not rise nor set,
Haply I may remember,
    And haply may forget.

792   *Twice*

I TOOK my heart in my hand
    (O my love, O my love),
I said: Let me fall or stand,
    Let me live or die,
But this once hear me speak
    (O my love, O my love)—
Yet a woman's words are weak;
    You should speak, not I.

You took my heart in your hand
    With a friendly smile,
With a critical eye you scann'd,
    Then set it down,
And said, 'It is still unripe,
    Better wait awhile;
Wait while the skylarks pipe,
    Till the corn grows brown.'

As you set it down it broke—
    Broke, but I did not wince;
I smiled at the speech you spoke,
    At your judgement I heard:
But I have not often smiled
    Since then, nor question'd since,
Nor cared for cornflowers wild,
    Nor sung with the singing bird.

I take my heart in my hand,
  O my God, O my God,
My broken heart in my hand:
  Thou hast seen, judge Thou.
My hope was written on sand,
  O my God, O my God:
Now let thy judgement stand—
  Yea, judge me now.

This contemn'd of a man,
  This marr'd one heedless day,
This heart take thou to scan
  Both within and without:
Refine with fire its gold,
  Purge Thou its dross away—
Yea, hold it in Thy hold,
  Whence none can pluck it out.

I take my heart in my hand—
  I shall not die, but live—
Before Thy face I stand;
  I, for Thou callest such:
All that I have I bring,
  All that I am I give,
Smile Thou and I shall sing,
  But shall not question much.

793 *Uphill*

DOES the road wind uphill all the way?
  Yes, to the very end.
Will the day's journey take the whole long day?
  From morn to night, my friend.

But is there for the night a resting-place?
   A roof for when the slow, dark hours begin.
May not the darkness hide it from my face?
   You cannot miss that inn.

Shall I meet other wayfarers at night?
   Those who have gone before.
Then must I knock, or call when just in sight?
   They will not keep you waiting at that door.

Shall I find comfort, travel-sore and weak?
   Of labour you shall find the sum.
Will there be beds for me and all who seek?
   Yea, beds for all who come.

794   *Remember*

REMEMBER me when I am gone away,
   Gone far away into the silent land;
   When you can no more hold me by the hand,
Nor I half turn to go, yet turning stay.
Remember me when no more day by day
   You tell me of our future that you plann'd:
   Only remember me; you understand
It will be late to counsel then or pray.
Yet if you should forget me for a while
   And afterwards remember, do not grieve:
   For if the darkness and corruption leave
   A vestige of the thoughts that once I had,
Better by far you should forget and smile
   Than that you should remember and be sad.

795 *Aloof*

THE irresponsive silence of the land,
  The irresponsive sounding of the sea,
    Speak both one message of one sense to me:—
Aloof, aloof, we stand aloof, so stand
Thou too aloof, bound with the flawless band
    Of inner solitude; we bind not thee;
    But who from thy self-chain shall set thee free?
What heart shall touch thy heart? What hand thy hand?
And I am sometimes proud and sometimes meek,
    And sometimes I remember days of old
When fellowship seem'd not so far to seek,
    And all the world and I seem'd much less cold,
    And at the rainbow's foot lay surely gold,
And hope felt strong, and life itself not weak.

796 *Rest*

O EARTH, lie heavily upon her eyes;
  Seal her sweet eyes weary of watching, Earth;
    Lie close around her; leave no room for mirth
With its harsh laughter, nor for sound of sighs.
She hath no questions, she hath no replies,
    Hush'd in and curtain'd with a blessèd dearth
    Of all that irk'd her from the hour of birth;
With stillness that is almost Paradise.
Darkness more clear than noonday holdeth her,
    Silence more musical than any song;
Even her very heart has ceased to stir:
Until the morning of Eternity
Her rest shall not begin nor end, but be;
    And when she wakes she will not think it long.

797 *For Exmoor*

FOR Exmoor—
  For Exmoor, where the red deer run, my weary heart
    doth cry:
She that will a rover wed, far her feet shall hie.
Narrow, narrow, shows the street, dull the narrow sky.
    –Buy my cherries, whiteheart cherries, good my masters,
    buy!

For Exmoor—
O he left me, left alone, aye to think and sigh—
'Lambs feed down yon sunny coombe, hind and yearling shy
Mid the shrouding vapours walk now like ghosts on high.'
    —Buy my cherries, blackheart cherries, lads and lasses, buy!

For Exmoor—
Dear my dear, why did ye so? Evil day have I;
Mark no more the antler'd stag, hear the curlew cry,
Milking at my father's gate while he leans anigh.
    —Buy my cherries, whiteheart, blackheart, golden girls, O
    buy!

THOMAS EDWARD BROWN

798 *Salve!*

TO live within a cave—it is most good;
    But, if God make a day,
    And some one come, and say,
'Lo! I have gather'd faggots in the wood!'
    E'en let him stay,
And light a fire, and fan a temporal mood!

So sit till morning! when the light is grown
    That he the path can read,
    Then bid the man God-speed!
His morning is not thine: yet must thou own
They have a cheerful warmth—those ashes on the stone.

799   *Preparation*

HAST thou a cunning instrument of play,
  'Tis well; but see thou keep it bright,
And tuned to primal chords, so that it may
  Be ready day and night.
For when He comes thou know'st not, who shall say:—
  'These virginals are apt'; and try a note,
And sit, and make sweet solace of delight,
  That men shall stand to listen on the way,
And all the room with heavenly music float.

800   *My Garden*

A GARDEN is a lovesome thing, God wot!
  Rose plot,
    Fringed pool,
Fern'd grot—
    The veriest school
    Of peace; and yet the fool
Contends that God is not—
Not God! in gardens! when the eve is cool?
    Nay, but I have a sign;
    'Tis very sure God walks in mine.

RICHARD WATSON DIXON

1833–1900

Willow

801

The feathers of the willow
Are half of them grown yellow
    Above the swelling stream;
And ragged are the bushes,
And rusty now the rushes,
    And wild the clouded gleam.

The thistle now is older,
His stalk begins to moulder,
    His head is white as snow;
The branches all are barer,
The linnet's song is rarer,
    The robin pipeth now.

JAMES THOMSON

1834–1882

In the Train

802

AS we rush, as we rush in the Train,
    The trees and the houses go wheeling back,
But the starry heavens above the plain
    Come flying on our track.

All the beautiful stars of the sky,
    The silver doves of the forest of Night,
Over the dull earth swarm and fly,
    Companions of our flight.

We will rush ever on without fear;
    Let the goal be far, the flight be fleet!
For we carry the Heavens with us, dear,
    While the earth slips from our feet!

971

803 *Gifts*

GIVE a man a horse he can ride,
　Give a man a boat he can sail;
And his rank and wealth, his strength and health,
　On sea nor shore shall fail.

Give a man a pipe he can smoke,
　Give a man a book he can read:
And his home is bright with a calm delight,
　Though the room be poor indeed.

Give a man a girl he can love,
　As I, O my love, love thee;
And his heart is great with the pulse of Fate,
　At home, on land, on sea.

804 *The Vine*

THE wine of Love is music,
　And the feast of Love is song:
And when Love sits down to the banquet,
　Love sits long:

Sits long and arises drunken,
　But not with the feast and the wine;
He reeleth with his own heart,
　That great, rich Vine.

GEORGE LOUIS PALMELLA BUSSON DU MAURIER

1834–1896

805   *Music*

(AFTER SULLY PRUDHOMME)

KINDLY watcher by my bed, lift no voice in prayer,
    Waste not any words on me when the hour is nigh,
Let a stream of melody but flow from some sweet player,
And meekly will I lay my head and fold my hands to die.

Sick am I of idle words, past all reconciling,
Words that weary and perplex and pander and conceal,
Wake the sounds that cannot lie, for all their sweet beguiling;
The language one need fathom not, but only hear and feel.

Let them roll once more to me, and ripple in my hearing,
Like waves upon a lonely beach where no craft anchoreth:
That I may steep my soul therein, and craving naught, nor
    fearing,
Drift on through slumber to a dream, and through a dream
    to death.

WILLIAM MORRIS

1834–1896

806   *Summer Dawn*

PRAY but one prayer for me 'twixt thy closed lips,
    Think but one thought of me up in the stars.
The summer night waneth, the morning light slips
    Faint and gray 'twixt the leaves of the aspen, betwixt the
    cloud-bars,

That are patiently waiting there for the dawn:
   Patient and colourless, though Heaven's gold
Waits to float through them along with the sun.
Far out in the meadows, above the young corn,
   The heavy elms wait, and restless and cold
The uneasy wind rises; the roses are dun;
Through the long twilight they pray for the dawn
Round the lone house in the midst of the corn.
      Speak but one word to me over the corn,
      Over the tender, bow'd locks of the corn.

807   *Love is enough*

LOVE is enough: though the World be a-waning,
   And the woods have no voice but the voice of com-
      plaining,
   Though the sky be too dark for dim eyes to discover
The gold-cups and daisies fair blooming thereunder,
Though the hills be held shadows, and the sea a dark wonder
   And this day draw a veil over all deeds pass'd over,
Yet their hands shall not tremble, their feet shall not falter;
The void shall not weary, the fear shall not alter
   These lips and these eyes of the loved and the lover.

808   *Inscription for an Old Bed*

THE wind's on the wold
   And the night is a-cold,
And Thames runs chill
'Twixt mead and hill.
But kind and dear
Is the old house here

974

And my heart is warm
Midst winter's harm.
Rest then and rest,
And think of the best
'Twixt summer and spring,
When all birds sing
In the town of the tree,
And ye lie in me
And scarce dare move,
Lest the earth and its love
Should fade away
Ere the full of the day.
I am old and have seen
Many things that have been;
Both grief and peace
And wane and increase.
No tale I tell
Of ill or well,
But this I say:
Night treadeth on day,
And for worst or best
Right good is rest.

809   *The Nymph's Song to Hylas*

I KNOW a little garden-close
Set thick with lily and red rose,
Where I would wander if I might
From dewy dawn to dewy night,
And have one with me wandering.

975

And though within it no birds sing,
And though no pillar'd house is there,
And though the apple boughs are bare
Of fruit and blossom, would to God,
Her feet upon the green grass trod,
And I beheld them as before!

There comes a murmur from the shore,
And in the place two fair streams are,
Drawn from the purple hills afar,
Drawn down unto the restless sea;
The hills whose flowers ne'er fed the bee,
The shore no ship has ever seen,
Still beaten by the billows green,
Whose murmur comes unceasingly
Unto the place for which I cry.

For which I cry both day and night,
For which I let slip all delight,
That maketh me both deaf and blind,
Careless to win, unskill'd to find,
And quick to lose what all men seek.

Yet tottering as I am, and weak,
Still have I left a little breath
To seek within the jaws of death
An entrance to that happy place;
To seek the unforgotten face
Once seen, once kiss'd, once reft from me
Anigh the murmuring of the sea.

JOHN LEICESTER WARREN
LORD DE TABLEY

1835–1895

810 *Chorus from 'Medea'*

SWEET are the ways of death to weary feet,
Calm are the shades of men.
The phantom fears no tyrant in his seat,
The slave is master then.

Love is abolish'd; well, that this is so;
We knew him best as Pain.
The gods are all cast out, and let them go!
Who ever found them gain?

Ready to hurt and slow to succour these;
So, while thou breathest, pray.
But in the sepulchre all flesh has peace;
Their hand is put away.

811 *The Two Old Kings*

IN ruling well what guerdon? Life runs low,
As yonder lamp upon the hour-glass lies,
Waning and wasted. We are great and wise,
But Love is gone; and Silence seems to grow
Along the misty road where we must go.
From summits near the morning star's uprise
Death comes, a shadow from the northern skies,
As, when all leaves are down, there comes the snow.

JOHN LEICESTER WARREN

Brother and King, we hold our last carouse.
  One loving-cup we drain and then farewell.
    The night is spent: the crystal morning ray
Calls us, as soldiers laurell'd on our brows,
  To march undaunted while the clarions swell—
    Heroic hearts, upon our lonely way.

ALGERNON CHARLES SWINBURNE

1837-1909

812   *Chorus from 'Atalanta'*

WHEN the hounds of spring are on winter's traces,
  The mother of months in meadow or plain
Fills the shadows and windy places
  With lisp of leaves and ripple of rain;
And the brown bright nightingale amorous
Is half assuaged for Itylus,
For the Thracian ships and the foreign faces.
  The tongueless vigil, and all the pain.

Come with bows bent and with emptying of quivers,
  Maiden most perfect, lady of light,
With a noise of winds and many rivers,
  With a clamour of waters, and with might;
Bind on thy sandals, O thou most fleet,
Over the splendour and speed of thy feet;
For the faint east quickens, the wan west shivers,
  Round the feet of the day and the feet of the night.

Where shall we find her, how shall we sing to her,
  Fold our hands round her knees, and cling?
O that man's heart were as fire and could spring to her,
  Fire, or the strength of the streams that spring!

978

For the stars and the winds are unto her
As raiment, as songs of the harp-player;
For the risen stars and the fallen cling to her,
   And the southwest-wind and the west-wind sing.

For winter's rains and ruins are over,
   And all the season of snows and sins;
The days dividing lover and lover,
   The light that loses, the night that wins;
And time remember'd is grief forgotten,
And frosts are slain and flowers begotten,
And in green underwood and cover
   Blossom by blossom the Spring begins.

The full streams feed on flower of rushes,
   Ripe grasses trammel a travelling foot,
The faint fresh flame of the young year flushes
   From leaf to flower and flower to fruit;
And fruit and leaf are as gold and fire,
And the oat is heard above the lyre,
And the hoofed heel of a satyr crushes
   The chestnut-husk at the chestnut-root.

And Pan by noon and Bacchus by night,
   Fleeter of foot than the fleet-foot kid,
Follows with a dancing and fills with delight
   The Mænad and the Bassarid;
And soft as lips that laugh and hide
The laughing leaves of the trees divide,
And screen from seeing and leave in sight
   The god pursuing, the maiden hid.

The ivy falls with the Bacchanal's hair
    Over her eyebrows hiding her eyes;
The wild vine slipping down leaves bare
    Her bright breast shortening into sighs;
The wild vine slips with the weight of its leaves,
But the berried ivy catches and cleaves
To the limbs that glitter, the feet that scare
    The wolf that follows, the fawn that flies.

813   *Chorus from 'Atalanta'*

BEFORE the beginning of years
    There came to the making of man
Time, with a gift of tears;
    Grief, with a glass that ran;
Pleasure, with pain for leaven;
    Summer, with flowers that fell;
Remembrance fallen from heaven,
    And madness risen from hell;
Strength without hands to smite;
    Love that endures for a breath;
Night, the shadow of light,
    And life, the shadow of death.
And the high gods took in hand
    Fire, and the falling of tears,
And a measure of sliding sand
    From under the feet of the years;
And froth and drift of the sea;
    And dust of the labouring earth;
And bodies of things to be
    In the houses of death and of birth;

And wrought with weeping and laughter,
   And fashion'd with loathing and love,
With life before and after
   And death beneath and above,
For a day and a night and a morrow,
   That his strength might endure for a span
With travail and heavy sorrow,
   The holy spirit of man.

From the winds of the north and the south
   They gather'd as unto strife;
They breathed upon his mouth,
   They filled his body with life;
Eyesight and speech they wrought
   For the veils of the soul therein,
A time for labour and thought,
   A time to serve and to sin;
They gave him light in his ways,
   And love, and a space for delight,
And beauty and length of days,
   And night, and sleep in the night.
His speech is a burning fire;
   With his lips he travaileth;
In his heart is a blind desire,
   In his eyes foreknowledge of death;
He weaves, and is clothed with derision;
   Sows, and he shall not reap;
His life is a watch or a vision
   Between a sleep and a sleep.

Ave atque Vale

(IN MEMORY OF CHARLES BAUDELAIRE)

SHALL I strew on thee rose or rue or laurel,
    Brother, on this that was the veil of thee?
      Or quiet sea-flower moulded by the sea,
Or simplest growth of meadow-sweet or sorrel,
    Such as the summer-sleepy Dryads weave,
      Waked up by snow-soft sudden rains at eve?
Or wilt thou rather, as on earth before,
    Half-faded fiery blossoms, pale with heat
      And full of bitter summer, but more sweet
To thee than gleanings of a northern shore
    Trod by no tropic feet?

For always thee the fervid languid glories
    Allured of heavier suns in mightier skies;
      Thine ears knew all the wandering watery sighs
Where the sea sobs round Lesbian promontories,
    The barren kiss of piteous wave to wave
      That knows not where is that Leucadian grave
Which hides too deep the supreme head of song.
    Ah, salt and sterile as her kisses were,
      The wild sea winds her and the green gulfs bear
Hither and thither, and vex and work her wrong,
    Blind gods that cannot spare.

Thou sawest, in thine old singing season, brother,
    Secrets and sorrows unbeheld of us:
      Fierce loves, and lovely leaf-buds poisonous,
Bare to thy subtler eye, but for none other

Blowing by night in some unbreathed-in-clime
The hidden harvest of luxurious time,
Sin without shape, and pleasure without speech;
And where strange dreams in a tumultuous sleep
Make the shut eyes of stricken spirits weep;
And with each face thou sawest the shadow on each,
Seeing as men sow men reap.

O sleepless heart and sombre soul unsleeping,
That were athirst for sleep and no more life
And no more love, for peace and no more strife!
Now the dim gods of death have in their keeping
Spirit and body and all the springs of song,
Is it well now where love can do no wrong,
Where stingless pleasure has no foam or fang
Behind the unopening closure of her lips?
Is it not well where soul from body slips
And flesh from bone divides without a pang
As dew from flower-bell drips?

It is enough; the end and the beginning
Are one thing to thee, who art past the end.
O hand unclasp'd of unbeholden friend,
For thee no fruits to pluck, no palms for winning,
No triumph and no labour and no lust,
Only dead yew-leaves and a little dust.
O quiet eyes wherein the light saith naught,
Whereto the day is dumb, nor any night
With obscure finger silences your sight,
Nor in your speech the sudden soul speaks thought,
Sleep, and have sleep for light.

983

ALGERNON CHARLES SWINBURNE

Now all strange hours and all strange loves are over,
  Dreams and desires and sombre songs and sweet,
  Hast thou found place at the great knees and feet
Of some pale Titan-woman like a lover,
  Such as thy vision her solicited,
  Under the shadow of her fair vast head,
The deep division of prodigious breasts,
  The solemn slope of mighty limbs asleep,
  The weight of awful tresses that still keep
The savour and shade of old-world pine-forests
  Where the wet hill-winds weep?

Hast thou found any likeness for thy vision?
  O gardener of strange flowers, what bud, what bloom,
  Hast thou found sown, what gather'd in the gloom?
What of despair, of rapture, of derision,
  What of life is there, what of ill or good?
  Are the fruits gray like dust or bright like blood?
Does the dim ground grow any seed of ours,
  The faint fields quicken any terrene root,
  In low lands where the sun and moon are mute
And all the stars keep silence? Are there flowers
  At all, or any fruit?

Alas, but though my flying song flies after,
  O sweet strange elder singer, thy more fleet
  Singing, and footprints of thy fleeter feet,
Some dim derision of mysterious laughter
  From the blind tongueless warders of the dead,
  Some gainless glimpse of Proserpine's veil'd head,

Some little sound of unregarded tears
  Wept by effaced unprofitable eyes,
  And from pale mouths some cadence of dead sighs—
These only, these the hearkening spirit hears,
  Sees only such things rise.

Thou art too far for wings of words to follow,
  Far too far off for thought or any prayer.
  What ails us with thee, who art wind and air?
What ails us gazing where all seen is hollow?
  Yet with some fancy, yet with some desire,
  Dreams pursue death as winds a flying fire,
Our dreams pursue our dead and do not find.
  Still, and more swift than they, the thin flame flies,
  The low light fails us in elusive skies,
Still the foil'd earnest ear is deaf, and blind
  Are still the eluded eyes.

Not thee, O never thee, in all time's changes,
  Not thee, but this the sound of thy sad soul,
  The shadow of thy swift spirit, this shut scroll
I lay my hand on, and not death estranges
  My spirit from communion of thy song—
  These memories and these melodies that throng
Veil'd porches of a Muse funereal—
  These I salute, these touch, these clasp and fold
  As though a hand were in my hand to hold,
Or through mine ears a mourning musical
  Of many mourners roll'd.

I among these, I also, in such station
 As when the pyre was charr'd, and piled the sods,
 And offering to the dead made, and their gods,
The old mourners had, standing to make libation,
 I stand, and to the Gods and to the dead
 Do reverence without prayer or praise, and shed
Offering to these unknown, the gods of gloom,
 And what of honey and spice my seed-lands bear,
 And what I may of fruits in this chill'd air,
And lay, Orestes-like, across the tomb
 A curl of sever'd hair.

But by no hand nor any treason stricken,
 Not like the low-lying head of Him, the King,
 The flame that made of Troy a ruinous thing,
Thou liest and on this dust no tears could quicken.
 There fall no tears like theirs that all men hear
 Fall tear by sweet imperishable tear
Down the opening leaves of holy poet's pages.
 Thee not Orestes, not Electra mourns;
 But bending us-ward with memorial urns
The most high Muses that fulfil all ages
 Weep, and our God's heart yearns.

For, sparing of his sacred strength, not often
 Among us darkling here the lord of light
 Makes manifest his music and his might
In hearts that open and in lips that soften
 With the soft flame and heat of songs that shine.
 Thy lips indeed he touch'd with bitter wine,

And nourish'd them indeed with bitter bread;
    Yet surely from his hand thy soul's food came,
    The fire that scarr'd thy spirit at his flame
Was lighted, and thine hungering heart he fed
    Who feeds our hearts with fame.

Therefore he too now at thy soul's sunsetting,
    God of all suns and songs, he too bends down
    To mix his laurel with thy cypress crown,
And save thy dust from blame and from forgetting.
    Therefore he too, seeing all thou wert and art,
    Compassionate, with sad and sacred heart,
Mourns thee of many his children the last dead,
    And hallows with strange tears and alien sighs
    Thine unmelodious mouth and sunless eyes,
And over thine irrevocable head
    Sheds light from the under skies.

And one weeps with him in the ways Lethean,
    And stains with tears her changing bosom chill;
    That obscure Venus of the hollow hill,
That thing transform'd which was the Cytherean,
    With lips that lost their Grecian laugh divine
    Long since, and face no more call'd Erycine—
A ghost, a bitter and luxurious god.
    Thee also with fair flesh and singing spell
    Did she, a sad and second prey, compel
Into the footless places once more trod,
    And shadows hot from hell.

And now no sacred staff shall break in blossom,
    No choral salutation lure to light
    A spirit sick with perfume and sweet night
And love's tired eyes and hands and barren bosom.
    There is no help for these things; none to mend,
    And none to mar; not all our songs, O friend,
Will make death clear or make life durable.
    Howbeit with rose and ivy and wild vine
    And with wild notes about this dust of thine
At least I fill the place where white dreams dwell
    And wreathe an unseen shrine.

Sleep; and if life was bitter to thee, pardon,
    If sweet, give thanks; thou hast no more to live;
    And to give thanks is good, and to forgive.
Out of the mystic and the mournful garden
    Where all day through thine hands in barren braid
    Wove the sick flowers of secrecy and shade,
Green buds of sorrow and sin, and remnants gray,
    Sweet-smelling, pale with poison, sanguine-hearted,
    Passions that sprang from sleep and thoughts that
        started,
Shall death not bring us all as thee one day
    Among the days departed?

For thee, O now a silent soul, my brother,
    Take at my hands this garland, and farewell.
    Thin is the leaf, and chill the wintry smell,
And chill the solemn earth, a fatal mother,
    With sadder than the Niobean womb,
    And in the hollow of her breasts a tomb.

Content thee, howsoe'er, whose days are done;
    There lies not any troublous thing before,
    Nor sight nor sound to war against thee more,
For whom all winds are quiet as the sun,
    All waters as the shore.

815   *From 'Before the Mirror'*

GLAD, but not flush'd with gladness,
    Since joys go by;
Sad, but not bent with sadness,
    Since sorrows die;
Deep in the gleaming glass
She sees all past things pass,
    And all sweet life that was lie down and lie.

There glowing ghosts of flowers
    Draw down, draw nigh;
And wings of swift spent hours
    Take flight and fly;
She sees by formless gleams,
She hears across cold streams,
    Dead mouths of many dreams that sing and sigh.

Face fallen and white throat lifted,
    With sleepless eye
She sees old loves that drifted,
    She knew not why,
Old loves and faded fears
Float down a stream that hears
    The flowing of all men's tears beneath the sky.

BRET HARTE

1836–1902

What the Bullet sang

O JOY of creation,
  To be!
O rapture, to fly
  And be free!
Be the battle lost or won,
Though its smoke shall hide the sun,
I shall find my love—the one
  Born for me!

I shall know him where he stands
  All alone,
With the power in his hands
  Not o'erthrown;
I shall know him by his face,
By his godlike front and grace;
I shall hold him for a space
  All my own!

It is he—O my love!
  So bold!
It is I—all thy love
  Foretold!
It is I—O love, what bliss!
Dost thou answer to my kiss?
O sweetheart! what is this
  Lieth there so cold?

WILLIAM DEAN HOWELLS

1837–1920

817 *Earliest Spring*

TOSSING his mane of snows in wildest eddies and
   tangles,
  Lion-like March cometh in, hoarse, with tempestuous
   breath,
Through all the moaning chimneys, and 'thwart all the
   hollows and angles   [death.
  Round the shuddering house, threating of winter and

But in my heart I feel the life of the wood and the meadow
  Thrilling the pulses that own kindred with fibres that lift
Bud and blade to the sunward, within the inscrutable shadow,
  Deep in the oak's chill core, under the gathering drift.

Nay, to earth's life in mine some prescience, or dream, or
   desire   [goes—
  (How shall I name it aright?) comes for a moment and
Rapture of life ineffable, perfect—as if in the brier,
  Leafless there by my door, trembled a sense of the rose.

THOMAS HARDY

1840–1928

818 *The Darkling Thrush*

I LEANT upon a coppice gate
   When Frost was spectre-gray,
And Winter's dregs made desolate
   The weakening eye of day.

991

THOMAS HARDY

The tangled bine-stems scored the sky
    Like strings of broken lyres,
And all mankind that haunted nigh
    Had sought their household fires.

The land's sharp features seem'd to be
    The Century's corpse outleant,
His crypt the cloudy canopy,
    The wind his death-lament.
The ancient pulse of germ and birth
    Was shrunken hard and dry,
And every spirit upon earth
    Seem'd fervourless as I.

At once a voice arose among
    The bleak twigs overhead
In a full-hearted evensong
    Of joy illimited;
An aged thrush, frail, gaunt, and small,
    In blast-beruffled plume,
Had chosen thus to fling his soul
    Upon the growing gloom.

So little cause for carollings
    Of such ecstatic sound
Was written on terrestrial things
    Afar or nigh around,
That I could think there trembled through
    His happy good-night air
Some blessèd Hope, whereof he knew
    And I was unaware.

819   *She, to Him*

PERHAPS, long hence, when I have pass'd away,
    Some other's feature, accent, thought like mine,
Will carry you back to what I used to say,
And bring some memory of your love's decline.
Then you may pause awhile and think, 'Poor jade!'
And yield a sigh to me—as ample due,
Not as the tittle of a debt unpaid
To one who could resign her all to you—

And thus reflecting, you will never see
That your thin thought, in two small words convey'd,
Was no such fleeting phantom-thought to me,
But the Whole Life wherein my part was play'd;
And you amid its fitful masquerade
A Thought—as I in yours but seem to be.

820   '*I need not go*'

I NEED not go
    Through sleet and snow
To where I know
She waits for me;
She will tarry me there
Till I find it fair,
And have time to spare
From company.

When I've overgot
The world somewhat,
When things cost not

Such stress and strain,
Is soon enough
By cypress sough
To tell my Love
I am come again.

And if some day,
When none cries nay,
I still delay
To seek her side,
(Though ample measure
Of fitting leisure
Await my pleasure)
She will not chide.

What—not upbraid me
That I delay'd me,
Nor ask what stay'd me
So long? Ah, no!—
New cares may claim me.
New loves inflame me,
She will not blame me,
But suffer it so.

821   *Friends Beyond*

WILLIAM DEWY, Tranter Reuben, Farmer Ledlow
         late at plough,
     Robert's kin, and John's, and Ned's,
And the Squire, and Lady Susan, lie in Mellstock church-
         yard now!

994

'Gone,' I call them, gone for good, that group of local
hearts and heads;
Yet at mothy curfew-tide,
And at midnight when the noon-heat breathes it back
from walls and leads,
They've a way of whispering to me—fellow-wight who
yet abide—
In the muted, measured note
Of a ripple under archways, or a lone cave's stillicide:

'We have triumph'd: this achievement turns the bane to
antidote,
Unsuccesses to success,
Many thought-worn eves and morrows to a morrow free
of thought.

'No more need we corn and clothing, feel of old terrestrial
stress;
Chill detraction stirs no sigh;
Fear of death has even bygone us: death gave all that we
possess.'

W. D.—'Ye mid burn the old bass-viol that set I such value
by.'
Squire.—'You may hold the manse in fee,
You may wed my spouse, may let my children's memory
of me die.'

Lady.—'You may have my rich brocades, my laces; take each
household key;
Ransack coffer, desk, bureau;
Quiz the few poor treasures hid there, con the letters kept
by me.'

Far.—'Ye mid zell my favourite heifer, ye mid let the
    charlock grow,
      Foul the grinterns, give up thrift.'
Wife.—'If ye break my best blue china, children, I shan't
    care or ho.'

All.—'We've no wish to hear the tidings, how the people's
      fortunes shift;
      What your daily doings are;
Who are wedded, born, divided; if your lives beat slow
    or swift.

'Curious not the least are we if our intents you make or
      mar,
      If you quire to our old tune,
If the City stage still passes, if the weirs still roar afar.'

—Thus, with very gods' composure, freed those crosses
      late and soon
      Which, in life, the Trine allow
(Why, none witteth), and ignoring all that haps beneath
    the moon,

William Dewy, Tranter Reuben, Farmer Ledlow late at
    plough,
      Robert's kin, and John's, and Ned's,
And the Squire, and Lady Susan, murmur mildly to me
    now.

996

THOMAS HARDY

822   *In Time of 'The Breaking of Nations'*[1]

ONLY a man harrowing clods
    In a slow silent walk
With an old horse that stumbles and nods
    Half asleep as they stalk.

Only thin smoke without flame
    From the heaps of couch-grass;
Yet this will go onward the same
    Though Dynasties pass.

Yonder a maid and her wight
    Come whispering by:
War's annals will cloud into night
    Ere their story die.

WILFRID SCAWEN BLUNT

1840–1922

823   *The Desolate City*

DARK to me is the earth. Dark to me are the heavens.
    Where is she that I loved, the woman with eyes like
    stars?
Desolate are the streets. Desolate is the city.
    A city taken by storm, where none are left but the slain.

Sadly I rose at dawn, undid the latch of my shutters,
    Thinking to let in light, but I only let in love.
Birds in the boughs were awake; I listen'd to their chaunting.
    Each one sang to his love; only I was alone.

[1] Jer. li. 20.

This, I said in my heart, is the hour of life and of pleasure.
  Now each creature on earth has his joy, and lives in the sun,
Each in another's eyes finds light, the light of compassion,
  This is the moment of pity, this is the moment of love.

Speak, O desolate city! Speak, O silence in sadness!
  Where is she that I loved in my strength, that spoke to my
    soul?
Where are those passionate eyes that appeal'd to my eyes in
    passion?
  Where is the mouth that kiss'd me, the breast I laid to my
    own?

Speak, thou soul of my soul, for rage in my heart is kindled.
  Tell me, where didst thou flee in the day of destruction
    and fear?
See, my arms still enfold thee, enfolding thus all heaven,
  See, my desire is fulfill'd in thee, for it fills the earth.

Thus in my grief I lamented. Then turn'd I from the
    window,
  Turn'd to the stair, and the open door, and the empty
    street,
Crying aloud in my grief, for there was none to chide me,
  None to mock my weakness, none to behold my tears.

Groping I went, as blind. I sought her house, my belovèd's.
  There I stopp'd at the silent door, and listen'd and tried
    the latch.
Love, I cried, dost thou slumber? This is no hour for
    slumber,
  This is the hour of love, and love I bring in my hand.

I knew the house, with its windows barr'd, and its leafless
    fig-tree,
  Climbing round by the doorstep the only one in the street;
I knew where my hope had climb'd to its goal and there
    encircled
  All that those desolate walls once held, my belovèd's heart.

There in my grief she consoled me. She loved me when I
    loved not.
  She put her hand in my hand, and set her lips to my lips.
She told me all her pain and show'd me all her trouble.
  I, like a fool, scarce heard, hardly return'd her kiss.

Love, thy eyes were like torches. They changed as I beheld
    them.
  Love, thy lips were like gems, the seal thou settest on my
    life.
Love, if I loved not then, behold this hour thy vengeance;
  This is the fruit of thy love and thee, the unwise grown
    wise.

Weeping strangled my voice. I call'd out, but none answer'd;
  Blindly the windows gazed back at me, dumbly the door;
She whom I love, who loved me, look'd not on my yearning,
  Gave me no more her hands to kiss, show'd me no more
    her soul.

Therefore the earth is dark to me, the sunlight blackness,
  Therefore I go in tears and alone, by night and day;
Therefore I find no love in heaven, no light, no beauty,
  A heaven taken by storm where none are left but the slain!

WILFRID SCAWEN BLUNT

824 *With Esther*

HE who has once been happy is for aye
    Out of destruction's reach. His fortune then
Holds nothing secret; and Eternity,
    Which is a mystery to other men,
Has like a woman given him its joy.
    Time is his conquest. Life, if it should fret,
Has paid him tribute. He can bear to die,
    He who has once been happy! When I set
The world before me and survey its range,
    Its mean ambitions, its scant fantasies,
The shreds of pleasure which for lack of change
    Men wrap around them and call happiness,
The poor delights which are the tale and sum
Of the world's courage in its martyrdom;

When I hear laughter from a tavern door,
    When I see crowds agape and in the rain
Watching on tiptoe and with stifled roar
    To see a rocket fired or a bull slain,
When misers handle gold, when orators
    Touch strong men's hearts with glory till they weep,
When cities deck their streets for barren wars
    Which have laid waste their youth, and when I keep
Calmly the count of my own life and see
    On what poor stuff my manhood's dreams were fed
Till I too learn'd what dole of vanity
    Will serve a human soul for daily bread,
—Then I remember that I once was young
And lived with Esther the world's gods among.

825 *Gibraltar*

SEVEN weeks of sea, and twice seven days of storm
Upon the huge Atlantic, and once more
We ride into still water and the calm
Of a sweet evening, screen'd by either shore
Of Spain and Barbary. Our toils are o'er,
Our exile is accomplish'd. Once again
We look on Europe, mistress as of yore
Of the fair earth and of the hearts of men.

   Ay, this is the famed rock which Hercules
And Goth and Moor bequeath'd us. At this door
England stands sentry. God! to hear the shrill
Sweet treble of her fifes upon the breeze,
And at the summons of the rock gun's roar
To see her red coats marching from the hill!

826 *The Old Squire*

I LIKE the hunting of the hare
  Better than that of the fox;
I like the joyous morning air,
  And the crowing of the cocks.

I like the calm of the early fields,
  The ducks asleep by the lake,
The quiet hour which Nature yields,
  Before mankind is awake.

I like the pheasants and feeding things
  Of the unsuspicious morn;
I like the flap of the wood-pigeon's wings
  As she rises from the corn.

WILFRID SCAWEN BLUNT

I like the blackbird's shriek, and his rush
    From the turnips as I pass by,
And the partridge hiding her head in a bush
    For her young ones cannot fly.

I like these things, and I like to ride
    When all the world is in bed,
To the top of the hill where the sky grows wide,
    And where the sun grows red.

The beagles at my horse heels trot
    In silence after me;
There's Ruby, Roger, Diamond, Dot,
    Old Slut and Margery,—

A score of names well used, and dear,
    The names my childhood knew;
The horn, with which I rouse their cheer,
    Is the horn my father blew.

I like the hunting of the hare
    Better than that of the fox;
The new world still is all less fair
    Than the old world it mocks.

I covet not a wider range
    Than these dear manors give;
I take my pleasures without change,
    And as I lived I live.

I leave my neighbours to their thought;
    My choice it is, and pride,
On my own lands to find my sport,
    In my own fields to ride.

WILFRID SCAWEN BLUNT

The hare herself no better loves
    The field where she was bred,
Than I the habit of these groves,
    My own inherited.

I know my quarries every one,
    The meuse where she sits low;
The road she chose to-day was run
    A hundred years ago.

The lags, the gills, the forest ways,
    The hedgerows one and all,
These are the kingdoms of my chase,
    And bounded by my wall;

Nor has the world a better thing,
    Though one should search it round,
Than thus to live one's own sole king,
    Upon one's own sole ground.

I like the hunting of the hare;
    It brings me, day by day,
The memory of old days as fair,
    With dead men past away.

To these, as homeward still I ply
    And pass the churchyard gate
Where all are laid as I must lie,
    I stop and raise my hat.

I like the hunting of the hare;
    New sports I hold in scorn.
I like to be as my fathers were,
    In the days e'er I was born.

827   *A Garden Song*

HERE in this sequester'd close
Bloom the hyacinth and rose,
Here beside the modest stock
Flaunts the flaring hollyhock;
Here, without a pang, one sees
Ranks, conditions, and degrees.

All the seasons run their race
In this quiet resting-place;
Peach and apricot and fig
Here will ripen and grow big;
Here is store and overplus,—
More had not Alcinoüs!

Here, in alleys cool and green,
Far ahead the thrush is seen;
Here along the southern wall
Keeps the bee his festival;
All is quiet else—afar
Sounds of toil and turmoil are.

Here be shadows large and long
Here be spaces meet for song;
Grant, O garden-god, that I,
Now that none profane is nigh,—
Now that mood and moment please,—
Find the fair Pierides!

828   *Urceus Exit*

Triolet

I INTENDED an Ode,
   And it turn'd to a Sonnet
It began *à la mode*,
I intended an Ode;
But Rose cross'd the road
   In her latest new bonnet;
I intended an Ode;
   And it turn'd to a Sonnet.

829   *Fame and Friendship*

FAME is a food that dead men eat,—
   I have no stomach for such meat.
In little light and narrow room,
They eat it in the silent tomb,
With no kind voice of comrade near
To bid the feaster be of cheer.

But Friendship is a nobler thing,—
Of Friendship it is good to sing.
For truly, when a man shall end,
He lives in memory of his friend,
Who does his better part recall
And of his fault make funeral.

830 *In After Days*

Rondeau

IN after days when grasses high
   O'er-top the stone where I shall lie,
   Though ill or well the world adjust
   My slender claim to honour'd dust,
I shall not question nor reply.

I shall not see the morning sky;
I shall not hear the night-wind sigh;
   I shall be mute, as all men must
      In after days!

But yet, now living, fain would I
That some one then should testify,
   Saying—'He held his pen in trust
   To Art, not serving shame or lust.'
Will none?—Then let my memory die
      In after days!

HENRY CLARENCE KENDALL   1841–1882

831 *Mooni*

HE that is by Mooni now
   Sees the water-sapphires gleaming
Where the River Spirit, dreaming,
Sleeps by fall and fountain streaming
   Under lute of leaf and bough!—
Hears what stamp of Storm with stress is,
Psalms from unseen wildernesses
Deep amongst far hill-recesses—
   He that is by Mooni now.

HENRY CLARENCE KENDALL

Yea, for him by Mooni's marge
Sings the yellow-hair'd September,
With the face the gods remember,
When the ridge is burnt to ember,
    And the dumb sea chains the barge!
Where the mount like molten brass is,
Down beneath fern-feather'd passes
Noonday dew in cool green grasses
    Gleams on him by Mooni's marge.

Who that dwells by Mooni yet,
Feels in flowerful forest arches
Smiting wings and breath that parches
Where strong Summer's path of march is,
    And the suns in thunder set!
Housed beneath the gracious kirtle
Of the shadowy water-myrtle—
Winds may kiss with heat and hurtle,
    He is safe by Mooni yet!

Days there were when he who sings
(Dumb so long through passion's losses)
Stood where Mooni's water crosses
Shining tracks of green-hair'd mosses,
    Like a soul with radiant wings:
Then the psalm the wind rehearses—
Then the song the stream disperses—
Lent a beauty to his verses,
    Who to-night of Mooni sings.

HENRY CLARENCE KENDALL

Ah, the theme——the sad, gray theme!
Certain days are not above me,
Certain hearts have ceased to love me,
Certain fancies fail to move me,
    Like the effluent morning dream.
Head whereon the white is stealing,
Heart whose hurts are past all healing,
Where is now the first, pure feeling?
    Ah, the theme——the sad, gray theme!

Still to be by Mooni cool—
Where the water-blossoms glister,
And by gleaming vale and vista
Sits the English April's sister,
    Soft and sweet and wonderful!
Just to rest beneath the burning
Outer world—its sneers and spurning—
Ah, my heart—my heart is yearning
    Still to be by Mooni cool!

ARTHUR WILLIAM EDGAR O'SHAUGHNESSY

1844–1881

832 *Ode*

WE are the music-makers,
    And we are the dreamers of dreams,
Wandering by lone sea-breakers,
    And sitting by desolate streams;
World-losers and world-forsakers,
    On whom the pale moon gleams:
Yet we are the movers and shakers
    Of the world for ever, it seems.

With wonderful deathless ditties
We build up the world's great cities,
    And out of a fabulous story
    We fashion an empire's glory:
One man with a dream, at pleasure,
    Shall go forth and conquer a crown;
And three with a new song's measure
    Can trample an empire down.

We, in the ages lying
    In the buried past of the earth,
Built Nineveh with our sighing,
    And Babel itself with our mirth;
And o'erthrew them with prophesying
    To the old of the new world's worth;
For each age is a dream that is dying,
    Or one that is coming to birth.

833   *Song*

I MADE another garden, yea,
    For my new Love:
I left the dead rose where it lay
    And set the new above.
Why did my Summer not begin?
    Why did my heart not haste?
My old Love came and walk'd therein,
    And laid the garden waste.

She enter'd with her weary smile,
    Just as of old;
She look'd around a little while
    And shiver'd with the cold:

Her passing touch was death to all,
　　Her passing look a blight;
She made the white rose-petals fall,
　　And turn'd the red rose white.

Her pale robe clinging to the grass
　　Seem'd like a snake
That bit the grass and grounds, alas!
　　And a sad trail did make.
She went up slowly to the gate,
　　And then, just as of yore,
She turn'd back at the last to wait
　　And say farewell once more.

GERARD MANLEY HOPKINS

1844-1889

834　　　*Heaven-Haven*

A nun takes the veil

I HAVE desired to go
　　Where springs not fail,
To fields where flies no sharp and sided hail
And a few lilies blow.

And I have asked to be
　　Where no storms come,
Where the green swell is in the havens dumb,
　　And out of the swing of the sea.

835 *Pied Beauty*

GLORY be to God for dappled things—
　　For skies of couple-colour as a brinded cow;
　　　For rose-moles all in stipple upon trout that swim;
Fresh-firecoal chestnut-falls; finches' wings;
　　Landscape plotted and pieced—fold, fallow, and plough;
　　　And àll tràdes, their gear and tackle and trim.

All things counter, original, spare, strange;
　　Whatever is fickle, freckled (who knows how?)
　　　With swift, slow; sweet, sour; adazzle, dim;
He fathers-forth whose beauty is past change:
　　　　　Praise him.

836 *The Habit of Perfection*

ELECTED Silence, sing to me
　　And beat upon my whorlèd ear,
Pipe me to pastures still and be
The music that I care to hear.

Shape nothing, lips; be lovely-dumb:
It is the shut, the curfew sent
From there where all surrenders come
Which only makes you eloquent.

Be shellèd, eyes, with double dark
And find the uncreated light:
This ruck and reel which you remark
Coils, keeps, and teases simple sight.

Palate, the hutch of tasty lust,
Desire not to be rinsed with wine:
The can must be so sweet, the crust
So fresh that come in fasts divine!

Nostrils, your careless breath that spend
Upon the stir and keep of pride,
What relish shall the censers send
Along the sanctuary side!

O feel-of-primrose hands, O feet
That want the yield of plushy sward,
But you shall walk the golden street
And you unhouse and house the Lord.

And, Poverty, be thou the bride
And now the marriage feast begun,
And lily-coloured clothes provide
Your spouse not laboured-at nor spun.

837   *Felix Randal*

FELIX RANDAL the farrier, O he is dead then? my duty
    all ended,
Who have watched his mould of man, big-boned and hardy-
    handsome
Pining, pining, till time when reason rambled in it and
    some
Fatal four disorders, flesh'd there, all contended?

    1012

Sickness broke him. Impatient he cursed at first, but mended
Being anointed and all; though a heavenlier heart began some
Months earlier, since I had our sweet reprieve and ransom
Tender'd to him. Ah well, God rest him all road ever he
    offended!

This seeing the sick endears them to us, us too it endears.
My tongue had taught thee comfort, touch had quench'd thy
    tears,
Thy tears that touch'd my heart, child, Felix, poor Felix
    Randal;

How far from then forethought of, all thy more boisterous
    years,
When thou at the random grim forge, powerful amidst peers,
Didst fettle for the great grey drayhorse his bright and batter-
    ing sandal!

JOHN BOYLE O'REILLY

1844–1890

838   *A White Rose*

THE red rose whispers of passion,
  And the white rose breathes of love;
O, the red rose is a falcon,
  And the white rose is a dove.

But I send you a cream-white rosebud
  With a flush on its petal tips;
For the love that is purest and sweetest
  Has a kiss of desire on the lips.

ANDREW LANG

1844–1912

839 *The Odyssey*

AS one that for a weary space has lain
　　Lull'd by the song of Circe and her wine
In gardens near the pale of Proserpine,
Where that Ææan isle forgets the main,
And only the low lutes of love complain,
　　And only shadows of wan lovers pine—
　　As such an one were glad to know the brine
Salt on his lips, and the large air again—
So gladly from the songs of modern speech
　　Men turn, and see the stars, and feel the free
　　　　Shrill wind beyond the close of heavy flowers,
　　　　And through the music of the languid hours
They hear like Ocean on a western beach
　　The surge and thunder of the Odyssey.

ROBERT BRIDGES

1844–1930

840 *My Delight and Thy Delight*

MY delight and thy delight
　　Walking, like two angels white,
In the gardens of the night:

My desire and thy desire
Twining to a tongue of fire,
Leaping live, and laughing higher:

Thro' the everlasting strife
In the mystery of life.

1014

Love, from whom the world begun,
Hath the secret of the sun.

Love can tell, and love alone,
Whence the million stars were strewn,
Why each atom knows its own,
How, in spite of woe and death,
Gay is life, and sweet is breath:

This he taught us, this we knew,
Happy in his science true,
Hand in hand as we stood
'Neath the shadows of the wood,
Heart to heart as we lay
In the dawning of the day.

841 *Spirits*

ANGEL spirits of sleep,
White-robed, with silver hair,
In your meadows fair,
Where the willows weep,
And the sad moonbeam
On the gliding stream
Writes her scatter'd dream:

Angel spirits of sleep,
Dancing to the weir
In the hollow roar
Of its waters deep;

Know ye how men say
That ye haunt no more
Isle and grassy shore
With your moonlit play;
That ye dance not here,
White-robed spirits of sleep,
All the summer night
Threading dances light?

842   *Nightingales*

BEAUTIFUL must be the mountains whence ye come,
And bright in the fruitful valleys the streams, wherefrom
    Ye learn your song:
Where are those starry woods? O might I wander there,
  Among the flowers, which in that heavenly air
    Bloom the year long!

Nay, barren are those mountains and spent the streams:
Our song is the voice of desire, that haunts our dreams,
    A throe of the heart,
Whose pining visions dim, forbidden hopes profound,
  No dying cadence nor long sigh can sound,
    For all our art.

Alone, aloud in the raptured ear of men
We pour our dark nocturnal secret; and then,
    As night is withdrawn
From these sweet-springing meads and bursting boughs of
  May,
  Dream, while the innumerable choir of day
    Welcome the dawn.

843 *A Passer-by*

WHITHER, O splendid ship, thy white sails crowding,
    Leaning across the bosom of the urgent West,
That fearest nor sea rising, nor sky clouding,
    Whither away, fair rover, and what thy quest?
    Ah! soon, when Winter has all our vales opprest,
When skies are cold and misty, and hail is hurling,
    Wilt thou glide on the blue Pacific, or rest
In a summer haven asleep, thy white sails furling.

I there before thee, in the country that well thou knowest,
    Already arrived am inhaling the odorous air:
I watch thee enter unerringly where thou goest,
    And anchor queen of the strange shipping there,
    Thy sails for awnings spread, thy masts bare:
Nor is aught from the foaming reef to the snow-capp'd grandest
    Peak, that is over the feathery palms, more fair
Than thou, so upright, so stately and still thou standest.

And yet, O splendid ship, unhail'd and nameless,
    I know not if, aiming a fancy, I rightly divine
That thou hast a purpose joyful, a courage blameless,
    Thy port assured in a happier land than mine.
    But for all I have given thee, beauty enough is thine,
As thou, aslant with trim tackle and shrouding,
    From the proud nostril curve of a prow's line
In the offing scatterest foam, thy white sails crowding.

ROBERT BRIDGES

Pater Filio

SENSE with keenest edge unusèd,
  Yet unsteel'd by scathing fire;
Lovely feet as yet unbruisèd
  On the ways of dark desire;
Sweetest hope that lookest smiling
O'er the wilderness defiling!

Why such beauty, to be blighted
  By the swarm of foul destruction?
Why such innocence delighted,
  When sin stalks to thy seduction?
All the litanies e'er chaunted
Shall not keep thy faith undaunted.

I have pray'd the sainted Morning
  To unclasp her hands to hold thee;
From resignful Eve's adorning
  Stol'n a robe of peace to enfold thee;
With all charms of man's contriving
Arm'd thee for thy lonely striving.

Me too once unthinking Nature,
  —Whence Love's timeless mockery took me,—
Fashion'd so divine a creature,
  Yea, and like a beast forsook me.
I forgave, but tell the measure
Of her crime in thee, my treasure.

Winter Nightfall

THE day begins to droop,—
  Its course is done:
But nothing tells the place
  Of the setting sun.

The hazy darkness deepens,
  And up the lane
You may hear, but cannot see,
  The homing wain.

An engine pants and hums
  In the farm hard by:
Its lowering smoke is lost
  In the lowering sky.

The soaking branches drip,
  And all night through
The dropping will not cease
  In the avenue.

A tall man there in the house
  Must keep his chair:
He knows he will never again
  Breathe the spring air:

His heart is worn with work;
  He is giddy and sick
If he rise to go as far
  As the nearest rick:

He thinks of his morn of life,
  His hale, strong years;
And braves as he may the night
  Of darkness and tears.

846   *When Death to Either shall come*

WHEN Death to either shall come,—
  I pray it be first to me,—
Be happy as ever at home,
  If so, as I wish, it be.

Possess thy heart, my own;
  And sing to the child on thy knee,
Or read to thyself alone
  The songs that I made for thee.

847   *The Linnet*

I HEARD a linnet courting
  His lady in the spring:
His mates were idly sporting,
  Nor stayed to hear him sing
    His song of love.—
I fear my speech distorting
    His tender love.

The phrases of his pleading
  Were full of young delight;
And she that gave him heeding
  Interpreted aright
    His gay, sweet notes,—
So sadly marred in the reading,—
    His tender notes.

And when he ceased, the hearer
   Awaited the refrain,
Till swiftly perching nearer
   He sang his song again,
      His pretty song:—
Would that my verse spake clearer
   His tender song!

Ye happy, airy creatures!
   That in the merry spring
Think not of what misfeatures
   Or cares the year may bring;
      But unto love
Resign your simple natures,
   To tender love.

848   *Awake, my Heart, to be loved*

AWAKE, my heart, to be loved, awake, awake!
  The darkness silvers away, the morn doth break,
It leaps in the sky: unrisen lustres slake
The o'ertaken moon. Awake, O heart, awake!

She too that loveth awaketh and hopes for thee;
Her eyes already have sped the shades that flee,
Already they watch the path thy feet shall take:
Awake, O heart, to be loved, awake, awake!

And if thou tarry from her,—if this could be,—
She cometh herself, O heart, to be loved, to thee;
For thee would unashamèd herself forsake:
Awake to be loved, my heart, awake, awake!

Awake, the land is scattered with light, and see,
Uncanopied sleep is flying from field and tree:
And blossoming boughs of April in laughter shake;
Awake, O heart, to be loved, awake, awake!

Lo all things wake and tarry and look for thee:
She looketh and saith, 'O sun, now bring him to me.
Come more adored, O adored, for his coming's sake,
And awake my heart to be loved: awake, awake!'

849   *Elegy: On a Lady, whom Grief*
for the Death of her Betrothed killed

ASSEMBLE, all ye maidens, at the door,
  And all ye loves, assemble; far and wide
Proclaim the bridal, that proclaim'd before
Has been deferr'd to this late eventide:
     For on this night the bride,
    The days of her betrothal over,
  Leaves the parental hearth for evermore;
To-night the bride goes forth to meet her lover.

Reach down the wedding vesture, that has lain
Yet all unvisited, the silken gown:
Bring out the bracelets, and the golden chain
Her dearer friends provided: sere and brown
    Bring out the festal crown,
    And set it on her forehead lightly:
  Though it be wither'd, twine no wreath again;
This only is the crown she can wear rightly.

ROBERT BRIDGES

Cloke her in ermine, for the night is cold,
And wrap her warmly, for the night is long,
In pious hands the flaming torches hold,
While her attendants, chosen from among
       Her faithful virgin throng,
     May lay her in her cedar litter,
   Decking her coverlet with sprigs of gold,
Roses, and lilies white that best befit her.

Sound flute and tabor, that the bridal be
Not without music, nor with these alone;
But let the viol lead the melody,
With lesser intervals, and plaintive moan
       Of sinking semitone;
     And, all in choir, the virgin voices
   Rest not from singing in skill'd harmony
The song that aye the bridegroom's ear rejoices.

Let the priests go before, array'd in white,
And let the dark-stoled minstrels follow slow,
Next they that bear her, honour'd on this night,
And then the maidens, in a double row,
       Each singing soft and low,
     And each on high a torch upstaying:
   Unto her lover lead her forth with light,
With music, and with singing, and with praying.

'Twas at this sheltering hour he nightly came,
And found her trusty window open wide,
And knew the signal of the timorous flame,
That long the restless curtain would not hide

Her form that stood beside;
As scarce she dared to be delighted,
Listening to that sweet tale, that is no shame
To faithful lovers, that their hearts have plighted.

But now for many days the dewy grass
Has shown no markings of his feet at morn:
And watching she has seen no shadow pass
The moonlit walk, and heard no music borne
Upon her ear forlorn.
In vain has she looked out to greet him;
He has not come, he will not come, alas!
So let us bear her out where she must meet him.

Now to the river bank the priests are come:
The bark is ready to receive its freight:
Let some prepare her place therein, and some
Embark the litter with its slender weight:
The rest stand by in state,
And sing her a safe passage over;
While she is oar'd across to her new home,
Into the arms of her expectant lover.

And thou, O lover, that art on the watch,
Where, on the banks of the forgetful streams,
The pale indifferent ghosts wander, and snatch
The sweeter moments of their broken dreams,—
Thou, when the torchlight gleams,
When thou shalt see the slow procession,
And when thine ears the fitful music catch,
Rejoice, for thou art near to thy possession.

850   *Renouncement*

I MUST not think of thee; and, tired yet strong,
  I shun the thought that lurks in all delight—
    The thought of thee—and in the blue heaven's height,
And in the dearest passage of a song.
Oh, just beyond the sweetest thoughts that throng
    This breast, the thought of thee waits hidden yet bright;
But it must never, never come in sight;
  I must stop short of thee the whole day long.
But when sleep comes to close each difficult day,
    When night gives pause to the long watch I keep,
And all my bonds I needs must loose apart,
Must doff my will as raiment laid away,—
    With the first dream that comes with the first sleep
I run, I run, I am gather'd to thy heart.

851   *The Lady of the Lambs*

SHE walks—the lady of my delight—
  A shepherdess of sheep.
Her flocks are thoughts. She keeps them white;
  She guards them from the steep.
She feeds them on the fragrant height,
  And folds them in for sleep.

She roams maternal hills and bright,
  Dark valleys safe and deep.
Her dreams are innocent at night;
  The chastest stars may peep.
She walks—the lady of my delight—
  A shepherdess of sheep.

She holds her little thoughts in sight,
  Though gay they run and leap.
She is so circumspect and right;
  She has her soul to keep.
She walks—the lady of my delight—
  A shepherdess of sheep.

THE HON. EMILY LAWLESS

1845–1913

852   *After Aughrim*

SHE said, 'They gave me of their best,
  They lived, they gave their lives for me;
I tossed them to the howling waste,
And flung them to the foaming sea.'

She said, 'I never gave them aught,
Not mine the power, if mine the will;
I let them starve, I let them bleed,—
They bled and starved, and loved me still.

She said, 'Ten times they fought for me,
Ten times they strove with might and main,
Ten times I saw them beaten down,
Ten times they rose, and fought again.'

She said, 'I stayed alone at home,
A dreary woman, grey and cold;
I never asked them how they fared,
Yet still they loved me as of old.'

THE HON. EMILY LAWLESS

She said, 'I never called them sons,
I almost ceased to breathe their name,
Then caught it echoing down the wind,
Blown backwards from the lips of Fame.'

She said, 'Not mine, not mine that fame:
Far over sea, far over land,
Cast forth like rubbish from my shores,
They won it yonder, sword in hand.'

She said, 'God knows they owe me nought,
I tossed them to the foaming sea,
I tossed them to the howling waste,
Yet still their love comes home to me.'

WILLIAM ERNEST HENLEY

1849–1903

853   *Invictus*

OUT of the night that covers me,
Black as the pit from pole to pole,
I thank whatever gods may be
For my unconquerable soul.

In the fell clutch of circumstance
I have not winced nor cried aloud.
Under the bludgeonings of chance
My head is bloody, but unbow'd.

Beyond this place of wrath and tears
Looms but the Horror of the shade,
And yet the menace of the years
Finds and shall find me unafraid.

It matters not how strait the gate,
　　How charged with punishments the scroll,
I am the master of my fate:
　　I am the captain of my soul.

854　　　　　*Margaritæ Sorori*

A LATE lark twitters from the quiet skies:
　　And from the west,
Where the sun, his day's work ended,
Lingers as in content,
There falls on the old, gray city
An influence luminous and serene,
A shining peace.

The smoke ascends
In a rosy-and-golden haze. The spires
Shine and are changed. In the valley
Shadows rise. The lark sings on. The sun,
Closing his benediction,
Sinks, and the darkening air
Thrills with a sense of the triumphing night—
Night with her train of stars
And her great gift of sleep.

So be my passing!
My task accomplish'd and the long day done,
My wages taken, and in my heart
Some late lark singing,
Let me be gather'd to the quiet West,
The sundown splendid and serene,
Death.

855   *England, My England*

WHAT have I done for you,
   England, my England?
What is there I would not do,
   England, my own?
With your glorious eyes austere,
As the Lord were walking near,
Whispering terrible things and dear
   As the Song on your bugles blown,
      England—
   Round the world on your bugles blown!

Where shall the watchful sun,
   England, my England,
Match the master-work you've done,
   England, my own?
When shall he rejoice agen
Such a breed of mighty men
As come forward, one to ten,
   To the Song on your bugles blown,
      England—
   Down the years on your bugles blown?

Ever the faith endures,
   England, my England:—
'Take and break us: we are yours,
   England, my own!
Life is good, and joy runs high
Between English earth and sky:
Death is death; but we shall die

To the Song on your bugles blown,
   England—
To the stars on your bugles blown!'

They call you proud and hard,
   England, my England:
You with worlds to watch and ward,
   England, my own!
You whose mail'd hand keeps the keys
Of such teeming destinies,
You could know nor dread nor ease
   Were the Song on your bugles blown,
      England,
   Round the Pit on your bugles blown!

Mother of Ships whose might,
   England, my England,
Is the fierce old Sea's delight,
   England, my own,
Chosen daughter of the Lord,
Spouse-in-Chief of the ancient Sword,
There's the menace of the Word
   In the Song on your bugles blown,
      England—
   Out of heaven on your bugles blown!

SIR EDMUND GOSSE

1849–1928

856
Revelation

INTO the silver night
   She brought with her pale hand
The topaz lanthorn-light,
And darted splendour o'er the land:
   Around her in a band,

Ringstraked and pied, the great soft moths came flying,
    And flapping with their mad wings, fann'd
The flickering flame, ascending, falling, dying.

    Behind the thorny pink
        Close wall of blossom'd may,
    I gazed thro' one green chink
    And saw no more than thousands may,—
        Saw sweetness, tender and gay,—
Saw full rose lips as rounded as the cherry,
    Saw braided locks more dark than bay,
And flashing eyes decorous, pure, and merry.

    With food for furry friends
        She pass'd, her lamp and she,
    Till eaves and gable-ends
    Hid all that saffron sheen from me:
        Around my rosy tree
Once more the silver-starry night was shining,
    With depths of heaven, dewy and free,
And crystals of a carven moon declining.

    Alas! for him who dwells
        In frigid air of thought,
    When warmer light dispels
    The frozen calm his spirit sought;
        By life too lately taught
He sees the ecstatic Human from him stealing;
    Reels from the joy experience brought,
And dares not clutch what Love was half revealing.

1031

1849–1930

857 *A Meditation for Christmas*

CONSIDER, O my soul, what morn is this!
　Whereon the eternal Lord of all things made,
For us, poor mortals, and our endless bliss,
　　Came down from heaven; and, in a manger laid,
　　The first, rich, offerings of our ransom paid:
Consider, O my soul, what morn is this!

Consider what estate of fearful woe
　　Had then been ours, had He refused this birth;
From sin to sin toss'd vainly to and fro,
　　Hell's playthings, o'er a doom'd and helpless earth!
　　Had He from us withheld His priceless worth,
Consider man's estate of fearful woe!

Consider to what joys He bids thee rise,
　　Who comes, Himself, life's bitter cup to drain!
Ah! look on this sweet Child, whose innocent eyes,
　　Ere all be done, shall close in mortal pain,
　　That thou at last Love's Kingdom may'st attain:
Consider to what joys He bids thee rise!

Consider all this wonder, O my soul;
　　And in thine inmost shrine make music sweet!
Yea, let the world, from furthest pole to pole,
　　Join in thy praises this dread birth to greet;
　　Kneeling to kiss thy Saviour's infant feet!
Consider all this wonder, O my soul!

858 *Romance*

I WILL make you brooches and toys for your delight
Of bird-song at morning and star-shine at night.
I will make a palace fit for you and me,
Of green days in forests and blue days at sea.

I will make my kitchen, and you shall keep your room,
Where white flows the river and bright blows the broom,
And you shall wash your linen and keep your body white
In rainfall at morning and dewfall at night.

And this shall be for music when no one else is near,
The fine song for singing, the rare song to hear!
That only I remember, that only you admire,
Of the broad road that stretches and the roadside fire.

859 *Alcaics: to H. F. B.*

BRAVE lads in olden musical centuries
Sang, night by night, adorable choruses,
Sat late by alehouse doors in April
Chaunting in joy as the moon was rising.

Moon-seen and merry, under the trellises,
Flush-faced they play'd with old polysyllables
Spring scents inspired, old wine diluted:
Love and Apollo were there to chorus.

Now these, the songs, remain to eternity,
Those, only those, the bountiful choristers
Gone—those are gone, those unremember'd
Sleep and are silent in earth for ever.

1033

So man himself appears and evanishes,
So smiles and goes; as wanderers halting at
    Some green-embower'd house, play their music,
    Play and are gone on the windy highway.

Yet dwells the strain enshrined in the memory
Long after they departed eternally,
    Forth-faring tow'rd far mountain summits,
    Cities of men or the sounding Ocean.

Youth sang the song in years immemorial:
Brave chanticleer, he sang and was beautiful;
    Bird-haunted green tree-tops in springtime
    Heard, and were pleased by the voice of singing.

Youth goes and leaves behind him a prodigy—
Songs sent by thee afar from Venetian
    Sea-grey lagunes, sea-paven highways,
    Dear to me here in my Alpine exile.

860   *In the Highlands*

IN the highlands, in the country places,
  Where the old plain men have rosy faces,
    And the young fair maidens
        Quiet eyes;
Where essential silence cheers and blesses,
And for ever in the hill-recesses
    Her more lovely music
        Broods and dies—

O to mount again where erst I haunted;
Where the old red hills are bird-enchanted,
    And the low green meadows
      Bright with sward;
And when even dies, the million-tinted,
And the night has come, and planets glinted,
    Lo, the valley hollow
      Lamp-bestarr'd!

O to dream, O to awake and wander
There, and with delight to take and render,
    Through the trance of silence,
      Quiet breath!
Lo! for there, among the flowers and grasses,
Only the mightier movement sounds and passes;
    Only winds and rivers,
      Life and death.

861   *Wishes*

GO, little book, and wish to all
   Flowers in the garden, meat in the hall,
A bin of wine, a spice of wit,
A house with lawns enclosing it,
A living river by the door,
A nightingale in the sycamore.

862   *Requiem*

UNDER the wide and starry sky
   Dig the grave and let me lie:
Glad did I live and gladly die,
   And I laid me down with a will.

ROBERT LOUIS STEVENSON

This be the verse you grave for me:
Here he lies where he long'd to be;
Home is the sailor, home from sea,
And the hunter home from the hill.

FRANCIS WILLIAM BOURDILLON

1852–1921

863 *The Night has a Thousand Eyes*

THE night has a thousand eyes,
    And the day but one;
Yet the light of the bright world dies
    With the dying sun.

The mind has a thousand eyes,
    And the heart but one;
Yet the light of a whole life dies
    When love is done.

DORA SIGERSON

1866–1918

864 *Ireland*

'TWAS the dream of a God,
    And the mould of His hand,
That you shook 'neath His stroke,
That you trembled and broke
    To this beautiful land.

Here He loosed from His hold
    A brown tumult of wings,
Till the wind on the sea
Bore the strange melody
    Of an island that sings.

DORA SIGERSON

He made you all fair,
  You in purple and gold,
You in silver and green,
Till no eye that has seen
  Without love can behold.

I have left you behind
  In the path of the past,
With the white breath of flowers,
With the best of God's hours,
  I have left you at last.

MARGARET LOUISA WOODS

1856–1945

865   *Genius Loci*

PEACE, Shepherd, peace! What boots it singing on?
  Since long ago grace-giving Phœbus died,
  And all the train that loved the stream-bright side
Of the poetic mount with him are gone
Beyond the shores of Styx and Acheron,
  In unexplorèd realms of night to hide.
  The clouds that strew their shadows far and wide
Are all of Heaven that visits Helicon.
Yet here, where never muse or god did haunt,
  Still may some nameless power of Nature stray,
Pleased with the reedy stream's continual chant
  And purple pomp of these broad fields in May.
The shepherds meet him where he herds the kine,
And careless pass him by whose is the gift divine.

THOMAS WILLIAM ROLLESTON

1857–1920

866   *The Dead at Clonmacnois*

FROM THE IRISH OF ANGUS O'GILLAN

IN a quiet water'd land, a land of roses,
    Stands Saint Kieran's city fair;
And the warriors of Erin in their famous generations
    Slumber there.

There beneath the dewy hillside sleep the noblest
    Of the clan of Conn,
Each below his stone with name in branching Ogham
    And the sacred knot thereon.

There they laid to rest the seven Kings of Tara,
    There the sons of Cairbrè sleep—
Battle-banners of the Gael that in Kieran's plain of crosses
    Now their final hosting keep.

And in Clonmacnois they laid the men of Teffia,
    And right many a lord of Breagh;
Deep the sod above Clan Creidè and Clan Conaill,
    Kind in hall and fierce in fray.

Many and many a son of Conn the Hundred-Fighter
    In the red earth lies at rest;
Many a blue eye of Clan Colman the turf covers,
    Many a swan-white breast.

AGNES MARY FRANCES DUCLAUX
(ROBINSON-DARMESTETER)

1857–1944

867

Celia's Home-Coming

MAIDENS, kilt your skirts and go
Down the stormy garden-ways.
Pluck the last sweet pinks that blow,
Gather roses, gather bays,
Since our Celia comes to-day,
That has been so long away.

Crowd her chamber with your sweets—
Not a flower but grows for her!
Make her bed with linen sheets
That have lain in lavender:
Light a fire before she come,
Lest she find us chill at home.

Ah, what joy when Celia stands
By the leaping blaze at last,
Stooping low to warm her hands
All benumbèd with the blast,
While we hide her cloak away,
To assure us she shall stay!

Cyder bring and cowslip wine,
Fruits and flavours from the East,
Pears and pippins too, and fine
Saffron loaves to make a feast;
China dishes, silver cups,
For the board where Celia sups!

Then, when all the feasting's done,
    She shall draw us round the blaze,
Laugh, and tell us every one
    Of her far triumphant days—
Celia, out of doors a star,
By the hearth a holier Lar!

JOHN DAVIDSON

1857–1909

868   *Song*

THE boat is chafing at our long delay
    And we must leave too soon
The spicy sea-pinks and the inborne spray,
    The tawny sands, the moon.

Keep us, O Thetis, in our western flight!
    Watch from thy pearly throne
Our vessel, plunging deeper into night
    To reach a land unknown.

869   *A Runnable Stag*

WHEN the pods went pop on the broom, green broom,
    And apples began to be golden-skinn'd,
We harbour'd a stag in the Priory coomb,
  And we feather'd his trail up-wind, up-wind,
  We feather'd his trail up-wind—
    A stag of warrant, a stag, a stag,
    A runnable stag, a kingly crop,
    Brow, bay and tray and three on top,
    A stag, a runnable stag.

Then the huntsman's horn rang yap, yap yap,
  And 'Forwards' we heard the harbourer shout;
But 'twas only a brocket that broke a gap
  In the beechen underwood, driven out,
  From the underwood antler'd out
    By warrant and might of the stag, the stag,
    The runnable stag, whose lordly mind
    Was bent on sleep, though beam'd and tined
    He stood, a runnable stag.

So we tufted the covert till afternoon
  With Tinkerman's Pup and Bell-of-the-North;
And hunters were sulky and hounds out of tune
  Before we tufted the right stag forth,
  Before we tufted him forth,
    The stag of warrant, the wily stag,
    The runnable stag with his kingly crop,
    Brow, bay and tray and three on top,
    The royal and runnable stag.

It was Bell-of-the-North and Tinkerman's Pup
  That stuck to the scent till the copse was drawn.
'Tally ho! tally ho!' and the hunt was up,
  The tufters whipp'd and the pack laid on,
  The resolute pack laid on,
    And the stag of warrant away at last,
    The runnable stag, the same, the same,
    His hoofs on fire, his horns like flame,
    A stag, a runnable stag.

'Let your gelding be: if you check or chide
   He stumbles at once and you're out of the hunt;
For three hundred gentlemen, able to ride,
   On hunters accustom'd to bear the brunt,
   Accustom'd to bear the brunt,
      Are after the runnable stag, the stag,
      The runnable stag with his kingly crop,
      Brow, bay and tray and three on top,
      The right, the runnable stag.'

By perilous paths in coomb and dell,
   The heather, the rocks, and the river-bed,
The pace grew hot, for the scent lay well,
   And a runnable stag goes right ahead,
   The quarry went right ahead—
      Ahead, ahead, and fast and far;
      His antler'd crest, his cloven hoof,
      Brow, bay and tray and three aloof,
      The stag, the runnable stag.

For a matter of twenty miles and more,
   By the densest hedge and the highest wall,
Through herds of bullocks he baffled the lore
   Of harbourer, huntsman, hounds and all,
   Of harbourer, hounds and all—
      The stag of warrant, the wily stag,
      For twenty miles, and five and five,
      He ran, and he never was caught alive,
      This stag, this runnable stag.

When he turn'd at bay in the leafy gloom,
  In the emerald gloom where the brook ran deep
He heard in the distance the rollers boom,
  And he saw in a vision of peaceful sleep
  In a wonderful vision of sleep,
    A stag of warrant, a stag, a stag,
    A runnable stag in a jewell'd bed,
    Under the sheltering ocean dead,
    A stag, a runnable stag.

So a fateful hope lit up his eye,
  And he open'd his nostrils wide again,
And he toss'd his branching antlers high
  As he headed the hunt down the Charlock glen,
  As he raced down the echoing glen—
    For five miles more, the stag, the stag,
    For twenty miles, and five and five,
    Not to be caught now, dead or alive,
    The stag, the runnable stag.

Three hundred gentlemen, able to ride,
  Three hundred horses as gallant and free,
Beheld him escape on the evening tide,
  Far out till he sank in the Severn Sea,
  Till he sank in the depths of the sea—
    The stag, the buoyant stag, the stag
    That slept at last in a jewell'd bed
    Under the sheltering ocean spread,
    The stag, the runnable stag.

1858–1935

870 *Song*

APRIL, April,
     Laugh thy girlish laughter;
Then, the moment after,
Weep thy girlish tears!
April, that mine ears
Like a lover greetest,
If I tell thee, sweetest,
All my hopes and fears,
April, April,
Laugh thy golden laughter,
But, the moment after,
Weep thy golden tears!

871 *Ode in May*

LET me go forth, and share
     The overflowing Sun
  With one wise friend, or one
Better than wise, being fair,
Where the pewit wheels and dips
  On heights of bracken and ling,
And E.-th, unto her leaflet tips,
    Tingles with the Spring.

What is so sweet and dear
  As a prosperous morn in May,
  The confident prime of the day,
And the dauntless youth of the year,

When nothing that asks for bliss,
　Asking aright, is denied,
And half of the world a bridegroom is,
　And half of the world a bride?

The Song of Mingling flows,
　Grave, ceremonial, pure,
　As once, from lips that endure,
The cosmic descant rose,
When the temporal lord of life,
　Going his golden way,
Had taken a wondrous maid to wife
　That long had said him nay.

For of old the Sun, our sire,
　Came wooing the mother of men,
　Earth, that was virginal then,
Vestal fire to his fire.
Silent her bosom and coy,
　But the strong god sued and press'd;
And born of their starry nuptial joy
　Are all that drink of her breast.

And the triumph of him that begot,
　And the travail of her that bore,
　Behold they are evermore
As warp and weft in our lot.
We are children of splendour and flame,
　Of shuddering, also, and tears.
Magnificent out of the dust we came,
　And abject from the Spheres.

SIR WILLIAM WATSON

O bright irresistible lord!
   We are fruit of Earth's womb, each one,
   And fruit of thy loins, O Sun,
Whence first was the seed outpour'd.
To thee as our Father we bow,
   Forbidden thy Father to see,
Who is older and greater than thou, as thou
   Art greater and older than we.

Thou art but as a word of his speech;
   Thou art but as a wave of his hand;
   Thou art brief as a glitter of sand
'Twixt tide and tide on his beach;
Thou art less than a spark of his fire,
   Or a moment's mood of his soul:
Thou art lost in the notes on the lips of his choir
   That chant the chant of the Whole.

FRANCIS THOMPSON

1859–1907

872   *Daisy*

WHERE the thistle lifts a purple crown
   Six foot out of the turf,
And the harebell shakes on the windy hill—
   O the breath of the distant surf!—

The hills look over on the South,
   And southward dreams the sea;
And, with the sea-breeze hand in hand,
   Came innocence and she.

FRANCIS THOMPSON

Where 'mid the gorse the raspberry
   Red for the gatherer springs,
Two children did we stray and talk
   Wise, idle, childish things.

She listen'd with big-lipp'd surprise,
   Breast-deep 'mid flower and spine:
Her skin was like a grape, whose veins
   Run snow instead of wine.

She knew not those sweet words she spake,
   Nor knew her own sweet way;
But there's never a bird, so sweet a song
   Throng'd in whose throat that day!

O, there were flowers in Storrington
   On the turf and on the spray;
But the sweetest flower on Sussex hills
   Was the Daisy-flower that day!

Her beauty smooth'd earth's furrow'd face
   She gave me tokens three:—
A look, a word of her winsome mouth,
   And a wild raspberry.

A berry red, a guileless look,
   A still word,—strings of sand!
And yet they made my wild, wild heart
   Fly down to her little hand.

For, standing artless as the air,
   And candid as the skies,
She took the berries with her hand,
   And the love with her sweet eyes.

FRANCIS THOMPSON

The fairest things have fleetest end:
　　Their scent survives their close,
But the rose's scent is bitterness
　　To him that loved the rose!

She looked a little wistfully,
　　Then went her sunshine way:—
The sea's eye had a mist on it,
　　And the leaves fell from the day.

She went her unremembering way,
　　She went, and left in me
The pang of all the partings gone,
　　And partings yet to be.

She left me marvelling why my soul
　　Was sad that she was glad;
At all the sadness in the sweet,
　　The sweetness in the sad.

Still, still I seem'd to see her, still
　　Look up with soft replies,
And take the berries with her hand,
　　And the love with her lovely eyes.

Nothing begins, and nothing ends,
　　That is not paid with moan;
For we are born in other's pain,
　　And perish in our own.

873

In no Strange Land

'The Kingdom of God is within you.'

O WORLD invisible, we view thee,
  O world intangible, we touch thee,
O world unknowable, we know thee,
Inapprehensible, we clutch thee!

Does the fish soar to find the ocean,
The eagle plunge to find the air—
That we ask of the stars in motion
If they have rumour of thee there?

Not where the wheeling systems darken,
And our benumb'd conceiving soars!—
The drift of pinions, would we hearken,
Beats at our own clay-shutter'd doors.

The angels keep their ancient places;—
Turn but a stone, and start a wing!
'Tis ye, 'tis your estrangèd faces,
That miss the many-splendour'd thing.

But (when so sad thou canst not sadder)
Cry;—and upon thy so sore loss
Shall shine the traffic of Jacob's ladder
Pitched betwixt Heaven and Charing Cross.

Yea, in the night, my Soul, my daughter,
Cry,—clinging Heaven by the hems;
And lo, Christ walking on the water,
Not of Gennesareth, but Thames!

1859–1946

874 *An Autobiography*

WALES England wed; so I was bred. 'Twas merry
London gave me breath.
   I dreamt of love, and fame: I strove. But Ireland taught
me love was best:
   And Irish eyes, and London cries, and streams of Wales
may tell the rest.
What more than these I ask'd of Life I am content to have
from Death.

HENRY CHARLES BEECHING

1859–1919

875 *Prayers*

GOD who created me
  Nimble and light of limb,
In three elements free,
  To run, to ride, to swim:
Not when the sense is dim,
  But now from the heart of joy,
I would remember Him:
  Take the thanks of a boy.

Jesu, King and Lord,
  Whose are my foes to fight,
Gird me with Thy sword
  Swift and sharp and bright.
Thee would I serve if I might;
  And conquer if I can,
From day-dawn till night,
  Take the strength of a man.

Spirit of Love and Truth,
   Breathing in grosser clay,
The light and flame of youth,
   Delight of men in the fray,
Wisdom in strength's decay;
   From pain, strife, wrong to be free,
This best gift I pray,
   Take my spirit to Thee.

876   *Going down Hill on a Bicycle*

A BOY'S SONG

WITH lifted feet, hands still,
   I am poised, and down the hill
Dart, with heedful mind;
The air goes by in a wind.

Swifter and yet more swift,
Till the heart with a mighty lift
Makes the lungs laugh, the throat cry:—
'O bird, see; see, bird, I fly.

'Is this, is this your joy?
O bird, then I, though a boy,
For a golden moment share
Your feathery life in air!'

Say, heart, is there aught like this
In a world that is full of bliss?
'Tis more than skating, bound
Steel-shod to the level ground.

HENRY CHARLES BEECHING

Speed slackens now, I float
Awhile in my airy boat;
Till, when the wheels scarce crawl,
My feet to the treadles fall.

Alas, that the longest hill
Must end in a vale; but still,
Who climbs with toil, wheresoe'er,
Shall find wings waiting there.

ALFRED EDWARD HOUSMAN

1859–1936

877   *Epitaph on an Army of Mercenaries*

THESE, in the day when heaven was falling,
    The hour when earth's foundations fled,
Follow'd their mercenary calling
    And took their wages and are dead.

Their shoulders held the sky suspended;
    They stood, and earth's foundations stay;
What God abandon'd, these defended,
    And saved the sum of things for pay.

878   *Wenlock Edge*

ON Wenlock Edge the wood's in trouble;
    His forest fleece the Wrekin heaves;
The gale, it plies the saplings double,
    And thick on Severn snow the leaves.

'Twould blow like this through holt and hanger
    When Uricon the city stood:
'Tis the old wind in the old anger,
    But then it threshed another wood.

Then, 'twas before my time, the Roman
    At yonder heaving hill would stare:
The blood that warms an English yeoman,
    The thoughts that hurt him, they were there.

There, like the wind through woods in riot,
    Through him the gale of life blew high;
The tree of man was never quiet:
    Then 'twas the Roman, now 'tis I.

The gale, it plies the saplings double,
    It blows so hard, 'twill soon be gone:
To-day the Roman and his trouble
    Are ashes under Uricon.

879   *'Is My Team Ploughing?'*

'IS my team ploughing,
    That I was used to drive
And hear the harness jingle
    When I was man alive?'

Ay, the horses trample,
    The harness jingles now;
No change though you lie under
    The land you used to plough.

'Is football playing
    Along the river shore,
With lads to chase the leather,
    Now I stand up no more?'

ALFRED EDWARD HOUSMAN

Ay, the ball is flying,
  The lads play heart and soul,
The goal stands up, the keeper
  Stands up to keep the goal.

'Is my girl happy,
  That I thought hard to leave,
And has she tired of weeping
  As she lies down at eve?'

Ay, she lies down lightly,
  She lies not down to weep:
Your girl is well contented.
  Be still, my lad, and sleep.

'Is my friend hearty,
  Now I am thin and pine,
And has he found to sleep in
  A better bed than mine?'

Yes, lad, I lie easy,
  I lie as lads would choose;
I cheer a dead man's sweetheart,
  Never ask me whose.

BLISS CARMAN

1861-1929

A Northern Vigil

HERE by the grey north sea,
  In the wintry heart of the wild,
Comes the old dream of thee,
Guendolen, mistress and child.

BLISS CARMAN

The heart of the forest grieves
In the drift against my door;
A voice is under the eaves,
A footfall on the floor.

Threshold, mirror, and hall,
Vacant and strangely aware,
Wait for their soul's recall
With the dumb expectant air.

Here when the smouldering west
Burns down into the sea,
I take no heed of rest
And keep the watch for thee.

I sit by the fire and hear
The restless wind go by,
On the long dirge and drear,
Under the low bleak sky.

When day puts out to sea
And night makes in for land,
There is no lock for thee,
Each door awaits thy hand!

When the zenith moon is round,
And snow-wraiths gather and run,
And there is set no bound
To love beneath the sun,

O wayward will, come near
The old mad wilful way,
The soft mouth at my ear
With words too sweet to say!

BLISS CARMAN

Come, for the night is cold,
The ghostly moonlight fills
Hollow and rift and fold
Of the eerie Ardise hills!

The windows of my room
Are dark with bitter frost,
The stillness aches with doom
Of something loved and lost.

Outside, the great blue star
Burns in the ghostland pale,
Where giant Algebar
Holds on the endless trail.

Come, for the years are long
And silence keeps the door,
Where shapes with the shadows throng
The firelit chamber floor.

Come, for thy kiss was warm,
With the red embers' glare
Across thy folding arm
And dark tumultuous hair!

And though thy coming rouse
The sleep-cry of no bird,
The keepers of the house
Shall tremble at thy word.

Come, for the soul is free!
In all the vast dreamland
There is no lock for thee,
Each door awaits thy hand.

BLISS CARMAN

Ah, not in dreams at all,
Fleering, perishing, dim,
But thy old self, supple and tall,
Mistress and child of whim!

The proud imperious guise,
Impetuous and serene,
The sad mysterious eyes,
And dignity of mien!

Yea, wilt thou not return,
When the late hill-winds veer,
And the bright hill-flowers burn
With the reviving year?

When April comes, and the sea
Sparkles as if it smiled,
Will they restore to me
My dark Love, empress and child?

The curtains seem to part;
A sound is on the stair,
As if at the last . . . I start;
Only the wind is there.

Lo, now far on the hills
The crimson fumes uncurl'd,
Where the caldron mantles and spills
Another dawn on the world!

DOUGLAS HYDE

1861–1949

My Grief on the Sea

FROM THE IRISH

MY grief on the sea,
  How the waves of it roll!
For they heave between me
  And the love of my soul!

Abandon'd, forsaken,
  To grief and to care,
Will the sea ever waken
  Relief from despair?

My grief and my trouble!
  Would he and I were,
In the province of Leinster,
  Or County of Clare!

Were I and my darling—-
  O heart-bitter wound!—
On board of the ship
  For America bound.

On a green bed of rushes
  All last night I lay,
And I flung it abroad
  With the heat of the day.

And my Love came behind me,
  He came from the South;
His breast to my bosom,
  His mouth to my mouth.

1861–1907

882   *Blue and White*

BLUE is Our Lady's colour,
    White is Our Lord's.
To-morrow I will wear a knot
    Of blue and white cords,
That you may see it, where you ride
    Among the flashing swords.

.   .   .   .

O banner, white and sunny blue,
    With prayer I wove thee!
For love the white, for faith the heavenly hue,
And both for him, so tender-true,
    Him that doth love me!

883   *Our Lady*

MOTHER of God! no lady thou:
    Common woman of common earth
Our Lady ladies call thee now,
    But Christ was never of gentle birth;
    A common man of the common earth.

For God's ways are not as our ways:
    The noblest lady in the land
Would have given up half her days,
    Would have cut off her right hand,
    To bear the child that was God of the land.

Never a lady did He choose,
　　Only a maid of low degree,
So humble she might not refuse
　　The carpenter of Galilee:
　　A daughter of the people, she.

Out she sang the song of her heart.
　　Never a lady so had sung.
She knew no letters, had no art;
　　To all mankind, in woman's tongue,
　　Hath Israelitish Mary sung.

And still for men to come she sings,
　　Nor shall her singing pass away.
'He hath fillèd the hungry with good things' —
　　O listen, lords and ladies gay !—
　　'And the rich He hath sent empty away.'

884　　　　　*Punctilio*

O LET me be in loving nice,
　　Dainty, fine, and o'er precise,
That I may charm my charmèd dear
As tho' I felt a secret fear
To lose what never can be lost,—
Her faith who still delights me most !
So shall I be more than true,
Ever in my ageing new.
So dull habit shall not be
Wrongly call'd Fidelity.

885 *Unwelcome*

WE were young, we were merry, we were very very
    wise,
    And the door stood open at our feast,
When there pass'd us a woman with the West in her eyes,
    And a man with his back to the East.

O, still grew the hearts that were beating so fast,
    The loudest voice was still.
The jest died away on our lips as they pass'd,
    And the rays of July struck chill.

The cups of red wine turn'd pale on the board,
    The white bread black as soot.
The hound forgot the hand of her lord,
    She fell down at his foot.

Low let me lie, where the dead dog lies,
    Ere I sit me down again at a feast,
When there passes a woman with the West in her eyes,
    And a man with his back to the East.

886 *Gone*

ABOUT the little chambers of my heart
    Friends have been coming—going—many a year.
    The doors stand open there.
Some, lightly stepping, enter; some depart.

Freely they come and freely go, at will.
The walls give back their laughter; all day long
    They fill the house with song.
One door alone is shut, one chamber still.

1061

'Is it Nothing to You?'

WE were playing on the green together,
  My sweetheart and I—
O! so heedless in the gay June weather
  When the word went forth that we must die.
O! so merrily the balls of amber
  And of ivory toss'd we to the sky,
While the word went forth in the King's chamber
  That we both must die.

O! so idly straying thro' the pleasaunce
  Pluck'd we here and there
Fruit and bud, while in the royal presence
  The King's son was casting from his hair
Glory of the wreathen gold that crown'd it,
  And, ungirdling all his garments fair,
Flinging by the jewell'd clasp that bound it,
  With his feet made bare.

Down the myrtled stairway of the palace,
  Ashes on his head,
Came he, thro' the rose and citron alleys,
  In rough sark of sackcloth habited,
And in the hempen halter—O! we jested
  Lightly, and we laugh'd as he was led
To the torture, while the bloom we breasted
  Where the grapes grew red.

O! so sweet the birds, when he was dying,
  Piped to her and me—
Is no room this glad June day for sighing—
  He is dead, and she and I go free!

MAY PROBYN

When the sun shall set on all our pleasure
　　We will mourn him—What, so you decree
We are heartless? Nay, but in what measure
　　Do you more than we?

SIR GILBERT PARKER　　　　1862–1932

888　　　　　*Reunited*

WHEN you and I have play'd the little hour,
　　Have seen the tall subaltern Life to Death
Yield up his sword; and, smiling, draw the breath,
The first long breath of freedom; when the flower
Of Recompense hath flutter'd to our feet,
　　As to an actor's; and, the curtain down,
　　We turn to face each other all alone—
Alone, we two, who never yet did meet,
Alone, and absolute, and free: O then,
　　O then, most dear, how shall be told the tale?
Clasp'd hands, press'd lips, and so clasp'd hands again;
　　No words. But as the proud wind fills the sail,
　　　My love to yours shall reach, then one deep moan
　　　Of joy, and then our infinite Alone.

HENRY CUST　　　　1861–1917

889　　　　　*Non Nobis*

NOT unto us, O Lord,
　　Not unto us the rapture of the day,
The peace of night, or love's divine surprise,
High heart, high speech, high deeds 'mid honouring eyes;
For at Thy word
All these are taken away.

Not unto us, O Lord:
To us thou givest the scorn, the scourge, the scar,
The ache of life, the loneliness of death,
The insufferable sufficiency of breath;
And with Thy sword
Thou piercest very far.

Not unto us, O Lord:
Nay, Lord, but unto her be all things given—
May light and life and earth and sky be blasted—
But let not all that wealth of love be wasted:
Let Hell afford
The pavement of her Heaven!

SIR HENRY NEWBOLT

1862–1938

890　　*He fell among Thieves*

'YE have robb'd,' said he, 'ye have slaughter'd and made
    an end,
  Take your ill-got plunder, and bury the dead:
What will ye more of your guest and sometime friend?'
  'Blood for our blood,' they said.

He laugh'd: 'If one may settle the score for five,
  I am ready; but let the reckoning stand till day:
I have loved the sunlight as dearly as any alive.'
  'You shall die at dawn,' said they.

He flung his empty revolver down the slope,
  He climb'd alone to the Eastward edge of the trees;
All night long in a dream untroubled of hope
  He brooded, clasping his knees.

HENRY NEWBOLT

He did not hear the monotonous roar that fills
    The ravine where the Yassîn river sullenly flows;
He did not see the starlight on the Laspur hills,
    Or the far Afghan snows.

He saw the April noon on his books aglow,
    The wistaria trailing in at the window wide;
He heard his father's voice from the terrace below
    Calling him down to ride.

He saw the gray little church across the park,
    The mounds that hid the loved and honour'd dead;
The Norman arch, the chancel softly dark,
    The brasses black and red.

He saw the School Close, sunny and green,
    The runner beside him, the stand by the parapet wall,
The distant tape, and the crowd roaring between,
    His own name over all.

He saw the dark wainscot and timber'd roof,
    The long tables, and the faces merry and keen;
The College Eight and their trainer dining aloof,
    The Dons on the daïs serene.

He watch'd the liner's stem ploughing the foam,
    He felt her trembling speed and the thrash of her screw;
He heard the passengers' voices talking of home,
    He saw the flag she flew.

And now it was dawn. He rose strong on his feet,
    And strode to his ruin'd camp below the wood;
He drank the breath of the morning cool and sweet:
    His murderers round him stood.

Light on the Laspur hills was broadening fast,
    The blood-red snow-peaks chill'd to a dazzling white;
He turn'd, and saw the golden circle at last,
    Cut by the Eastern height.

'O glorious Life, Who dwellest in earth and sun,
    I have lived, I praise and adore Thee.'
                    A sword swept.
Over the pass the voices one by one
    Faded, and the hill slept.

891   *Clifton Chapel*

THIS is the Chapel: here, my son,
    Your father thought the thoughts of youth,
And heard the words that one by one
    The touch of Life has turn'd to truth.
Here in a day that is not far,
    You too may speak with noble ghosts
Of manhood and the vows of war
    You made before the Lord of Hosts.

To set the cause above renown,
    To love the game beyond the prize,
To honour, while you strike him down,
    The foe that comes with fearless eyes;
To count the life of battle good,
    And dear the land that gave you birth,
And dearer yet the brotherhood
    That binds the brave of all the earth.—

HENRY NEWBOLT

My son, the oath is yours: the end
 Is His, Who built the world of strife,
Who gave His children Pain for friend,
 And Death for surest hope of life.
To-day and here the fight's begun,
 Of the great fellowship you're free;
Henceforth the School and you are one,
 And what You are, the race shall be.

God send you fortune: yet be sure,
 Among the lights that gleam and pass,
You'll live to follow none more pure
 Than that which glows on yonder brass:
'*Qui procul hinc,*' the legend's writ,—
 The frontier-grave is far away—
'*Qui ante diem periit:
 Sed miles, sed pro patria.*'

EDEN PHILLPOTTS

1862–1960

892   *Man's Days*

A SUDDEN wakin', a sudden weepin',
 A li'l suckin', a li'l sleepin';
A cheel's full joys an' a cheel's short sorrows,
Wi' a power o' faith in gert to-morrows.

Young blood red-hot an' the love of a maid,
One glorious day as'll never fade;
Some shadows, some sunshine, some triumphs, some tears,
And a gatherin' weight o' the flyin' years.

EDEN PHILLPOTTS

Then old man's talk o' the days behind 'e,
Your darter's youngest darter to mind 'e;
A li'l dreamin', a li'l dyin':
A li'l lew corner o' airth to lie in.

KATHARINE TYNAN HINKSON

1861-1931

893   *Sheep and Lambs*

ALL in the April evening,
  April airs were abroad;
The sheep with their little lambs
  Pass'd me by on the road.

The sheep with their little lambs
  Pass'd me by on the road;
All in an April evening
  I thought on the Lamb of God.

The lambs were weary, and crying
  With a weak human cry,
I thought on the Lamb of God
  Going meekly to die.

Up in the blue, blue mountains
  Dewy pastures are sweet:
Rest for the little bodies,
  Rest for the little feet.

But for the Lamb of God
  Up on the hill-top green,
Only a cross of shame
  Two stark crosses between.

KATHARINE TYNAN HINKSON

All in the April evening,
    April airs were abroad;
I saw the sheep with their lambs,
    And thought on the Lamb of God.

ARTHUR CHRISTOPHER BENSON
1862–1925

894
The Phœnix

BY feathers green, across Casbeen
    The pilgrims track the Phœnix flown,
By gems he strew'd in waste and wood,
    And jewell'd plumes at random thrown:

Till wandering far, by moon and star,
    They stand beside the fruitful pyre,
Where breaking bright with sanguine light
    The impulsive bird forgets his sire.

Those ashes shine like ruby wine,
    Like bag of Tyrian murex spilt,
The claw, the jowl of the flying fowl
    Are with the glorious anguish gilt.

So rare the light, so rich the sight,
    Those pilgrim men, on profit bent,
Drop hands and eyes and merchandise,
    And are with gazing most content.

NORMAN GALE
1862–1942

895
The Country Faith

HERE in the country's heart
    Where the grass is green,
Life is the same sweet life
As it e'er hath been.

1069

NORMAN GALE

Trust in a God still lives,
    And the bell at morn
Floats with a thought of God
    O'er the rising corn.

God comes down in the rain,
    And the crop grows tall—
This is the country faith,
    And the best of all.

FRANCES BANNERMAN

896   *An Upper Chamber*

I CAME into the City and none knew me;
   None came forth, none shouted 'He is here!'
Not a hand with laurel would bestrew me,
    All the way by which I drew anear—
    Night my banner, and my herald Fear.

But I knew where one so long had waited
   In the low room at the stairway's height,
Trembling lest my foot should be belated,
    Singing, sighing for the long hours' flight
    Towards the moment of our dear delight.

I came into the City when you hail'd me
   Saviour, and again your chosen Lord:—
Not one guessing what it was that fail'd me,
    While along the way as they adored
    Thousands, thousands, shouted in accord.

FRANCES BANNERMAN

But through all the joy I knew—I only—
    How the hostel of my heart lay bare and cold,
Silent of its music, and how lonely!
    Never, though you crown me with your gold,
    Shall I find that little chamber as of old!

STEPHEN PHILLIPS

1864-1915

897   *The Apparition*

MY dead Love came to me, and said:
    'God gives me one hour's rest
To spend upon the earth with thee:
    How shall we spend it best?'

'Why, as of old,' I said, and so
    We quarrell'd as of old.
But when I turn'd to make my peace
    That one short hour was told.

RUDYARD KIPLING

1865-1936

898   *L'Envoi*

THERE's a whisper down the field where the year has
    shot her yield
    And the ricks stand gray to the sun,
Singing:—'Over then, come over, for the bee has quit the
    clover
    And your English summer's done.'

You have heard the beat of the off-shore wind
And the thresh of the deep-sea rain;
You have heard the song—how long! how long!
Pull out on the trail again!

Ha' done with the Tents of Shem, dear lass,
We've seen the seasons through,
And it's time to turn on the old trail, our own trail, the out
trail,
Pull out, pull out, on the Long Trail—the trail that is
always new.

It's North you may run to the rime-ring'd sun,
Or South to the blind Horn's hate;
Or East all the way into Mississippi Bay,
Or West to the Golden Gate;
Where the blindest bluffs hold good, dear lass,
And the wildest tales are true,
And the men bulk big on the old trail, our own trail, the
out trail,
And life runs large on the Long Trail—the trail that is
always new.

The days are sick and cold, and the skies are gray and old,
And the twice-breathed airs blow damp;
And I'd sell my tired soul for the bucking beam-sea roll
Of a black Bilbao tramp;
With her load-line over her hatch, dear lass,
And a drunken Dago crew,
And her nose held down on the old trail, our own trail, the
out trail,
From Cadiz Bar on the Long Trail—the trail that is always
new.

There be triple ways to take, of the eagle or the snake,
    Or the way of a man with a maid;
But the sweetest way to me is a ship's upon the sea
    In the heel of the North-East Trade.
Can you hear the crash on her bows, dear lass,
And the drum of the racing screw,
As she ships it green on the old trail, our own trail, the out
    trail,
As she lifts and 'scends on the Long Trail—the trail that is
    always new?

See the shaking funnels roar, with the Peter at the fore,
    And the fenders grind and heave,
And the derricks clack and grate, as the tackle hooks the
    crate,
    And the fall-rope whines through the sheave;
It's 'Gang-plank up and in,' dear lass,
It's 'Hawsers warp her through!'
And it's 'All clear aft' on the old trail, our own trail, the out
    trail,
We're backing down on the Long Trail—the trail that is
    always new.

O the mutter overside, when the port-fog holds us tied,
    And the sirens hoot their dread!
When foot by foot we creep o'er the hueless viewless deep
    To the sob of the questing lead!
It's down by the Lower Hope, dear lass,
With the Gunfleet Sands in view,
Till the Mouse swings green on the old trail, our own trail,
    the out trail,
And the Gull Light lifts on the Long Trail—the trail that
    is always new.

O the blazing tropic night, when the wake's a welt of light
  That holds the hot sky tame,
And the steady fore-foot snores through the planet-powder'd
    floors
  Where the scared whale flukes in flame!
Her plates are scarr'd by the sun, dear lass,
And her ropes are taut with the dew,
For we're booming down on the old trail, our own trail, the
    out trail,
We're sagging south on the Long Trail—the trail that is
  always new.

Then home, get her home, where the drunken rollers comb,
  And the shouting seas drive by,
And the engines stamp and ring, and the wet bows reel and
    swing,
  And the Southern Cross rides high!
Yes, the old lost stars wheel back, dear lass,
That blaze in the velvet blue.
They're all old friends on the old trail, our own trail, the
    out trail,
They're God's own guides on the Long Trail—the trail
    that is always new.

Fly forward, O my heart, from the Foreland to the Start—
  We're steaming all too slow,
And it's twenty thousand mile to our little lazy isle
  Where the trumpet-orchids blow!
You have heard the call of the off-shore wind
And the voice of the deep-sea rain;
You have heard the song—how long! how long!
  Pull out on the trail again!

The Lord knows what we may find, dear lass,
And the deuce knows what we may do—
But we're back once more on the old trail, our own trail,
    the out trail,
We're down, hull down on the Long Trail—the trail that
    is always new.

899   *The Way through the Woods*

THEY shut the road through the woods
    Seventy years ago.
Weather and rain have undone it again,
    And now you would never know
There was once a path through the woods
    Before they planted the trees,
It is underneath the coppice and heath,
    And the thin anemones.
    Only the keeper sees
That, where the ring-dove broods,
    And the badgers roll at ease,
There was once a road through the woods.

Yet, if you enter the woods
    Of a summer evening late,
When the night-air cools on the trout-ring'd pools
    Where the otter whistles his mate,
(They fear not men in the woods
    Because they see so few)
You will hear the beat of a horse's feet
    And the swish of a skirt in the dew,
    Steadily cantering through

The misty solitudes,
　As though they perfectly knew
The old lost road through the woods . . .
But there is no road through the woods.

900　　　　　*Recessional*

June 22, 1897

GOD of our fathers, known of old—
　Lord of our far-flung battle-line—
Beneath whose awful Hand we hold
　Dominion over palm and pine—
Lord God of Hosts, be with us yet,
Lest we forget, lest we forget!

The tumult and the shouting dies—
　The captains and the kings depart—
Still stands Thine ancient sacrifice,
　An humble and a contrite heart.
Lord God of Hosts, be with us yet,
Lest we forget, lest we forget!

Far-call'd our navies melt away—
　On dune and headland sinks the fire—
Lo, all our pomp of yesterday
　Is one with Nineveh and Tyre!
Judge of the Nations, spare us yet,
Lest we forget, lest we forget!

If, drunk with sight of power, we loose
　Wild tongues that have not Thee in awe—
Such boasting as the Gentiles use
　Or lesser breeds without the Law—
Lord God of Hosts, be with us yet,
Lest we forget, lest we forget!

For heathen heart that puts her trust
In reeking tube and iron shard—
All valiant dust that builds on dust,
And guarding calls not Thee to guard—
For frantic boast and foolish word,
Thy Mercy on Thy People, Lord!

WILLIAM BUTLER YEATS

1865–1939

901   *Where My Books go*

ALL the words that I utter,
And all the words that I write,
Must spread out their wings untiring,
And never rest in their flight,
Till they come where your sad, sad heart is,
And sing to you in the night,
Beyond where the waters are moving,
Storm-darken'd or starry bright.

902   *When You are Old*

WHEN you are old and gray and full of sleep
And nodding by the fire, take down this book,
And slowly read, and dream of the soft look
Your eyes had once, and of their shadows deep;

How many loved your moments of glad grace,
And loved your beauty with love false or true;
But one man loved the pilgrim soul in you,
And loved the sorrows of your changing face;

And bending down beside the glowing bars,
Murmur, a little sadly, how love fled
And paced upon the mountains overhead,
And hid his face amid a crowd of stars.

903   *The Lake Isle of Innisfree*

I WILL arise and go now, and go to Innisfree,
    And a small cabin build there, of clay and wattles made;
Nine bean rows will I have there, a hive for the honey bee,
    And live alone in the bee-loud glade.

And I shall have some peace there, for peace comes dropping
        slow,
Dropping from the veils of the morning to where the cricket
        sings;
There midnight's all a-glimmer, and noon a purple glow,
    And evening full of the linnet's wings.

I will arise and go now, for always night and day
I hear lake water lapping with low sounds by the shore;
While I stand on the roadway, or on the pavements gray,
    I hear it in the deep heart's core.

904   *Down by the Salley Gardens*

DOWN by the salley gardens my love and I did meet;
    She pass'd the salley gardens with little snow-white
        feet.
She bid me take love easy, as the leaves grow on the tree;
But I, being young and foolish, with her would not agree.

In a field by the river my love and I did stand,
And on my leaning shoulder she laid her snow-white hand.
She bid me take life easy, as the grass grows on the weirs;
But I was young and foolish, and now am full of tears.

905   *Aedh wishes for the Cloths of Heaven*

HAD I the heavens' embroider'd cloths,
  Enwrought with golden and silver light,
The blue and the dim and the dark cloths
Of night and light and the half light,
I would spread the cloths under your feet:
But I, being poor, have only my dreams;
I have spread my dreams under your feet;
Tread softly because you tread on my dreams.

HERBERT TRENCH

1865–1923

906   *She comes not when Noon is on the Roses*

SHE comes not when Noon is on the roses—
      Too bright is Day.
She comes not to the Soul till it reposes
      From work and play.

But when Night is on the hills, and the great Voices
      Roll in from Sea,
By starlight and by candlelight and dreamlight
      She comes to me.

907 *A Charge*

IF thou hast squander'd years to grave a gem
  Commission'd by thy absent Lord, and while
      'Tis incomplete,
Others would bribe thy needy skill to them—
    Dismiss them to the street!

Should'st thou at last discover Beauty's grove,
    At last be panting on the fragrant verge,
        But in the track,
Drunk with divine possession, thou meet Love—
    Turn at her bidding back.

When round thy ship in tempest Hell appears,
    And every spectre mutters up more dire
        To snatch control
And loose to madness thy deep-kennell'd Fears—
    Then to the helm, O Soul!

Last; if upon the cold green-mantling sea
    Thou cling, alone with Truth, to the last spar,
        Both castaway,
And one must perish—let it not be he
    Whom thou art sworn to obey!

RICHARD LE GALLIENNE   1866–1947

908 *Song*

SHE's somewhere in the sunlight strong,
  Her tears are in the falling rain,
She calls me in the wind's soft song,
    And with the flowers she comes again.

Yon bird is but her messenger,
  The moon is but her silver car;
Yea! sun and moon are sent by her,
  And every wistful waiting star.

LIONEL JOHNSON

1867–1902

909 *By the Statue of King Charles
  at Charing Cross*

SOMBRE and rich, the skies,
  Great glooms, and starry plains;
Gently the night wind sighs;
Else a vast silence reigns.

The splendid silence clings
Around me: and around
The saddest of all Kings,
Crown'd, and again discrown'd.

Comely and calm, he rides
Hard by his own Whitehall.
Only the night wind glides:
No crowds, nor rebels, brawl.

Gone, too, his Court: and yet,
The stars his courtiers are:
Stars in their stations set;
And every wandering star.

Alone he rides, alone,
The fair and fatal King:
Dark night is all his own,
That strange and solemn thing.

LIONEL JOHNSON

Which are more full of fate:
The stars; or those sad eyes?
Which are more still and great:
Those brows, or the dark skies?

Although his whole heart yearn
In passionate tragedy,
Never was face so stern
With sweet austerity.

Vanquish'd in life, his death
By beauty made amends:
The passing of his breath
Won his defeated ends.

Brief life, and hapless? Nay:
Through death, life grew sublime.
Speak after sentence? Yea:
And to the end of time.

Armour'd he rides, his head
Bare to the stars of doom;
He triumphs now, the dead,
Beholding London's gloom.

Our wearier spirit faints,
Vex'd in the world's employ:
His soul was of the saints;
And art to him was joy.

King, tried in fires of woe!
Men hunger for thy grace:
And through the night I go,
Loving thy mournful face.

LIONEL JOHNSON

Yet, when the city sleeps,
When all the cries are still,
The stars and heavenly deeps
Work out a perfect will.

GEORGE WILLIAM RUSSELL ('Æ')

1867-1935

910 *By the Margin of the Great Deep*

WHEN the breath of twilight blows to flame the misty skies,
All its vaporous sapphire, violet glow and silver gleam,
With their magic flood me through the gateway of the eyes;
    I am one with the twilight's dream.

When the trees and skies and fields are one in dusky mood,
Every heart of man is rapt within the mother's breast:
Full of peace and sleep and dreams in the vasty quietude,
    I am one with their hearts at rest.

From our immemorial joys of hearth and home and love
Stray'd away along the margin of the unknown tide,
All its reach of soundless calm can thrill me far above
    Word or touch from the lips beside.

Aye, and deep and deep and deeper let me drink and draw
From the olden fountain more than light or peace or dream,
Such primæval being as o'erfills the heart with awe,
    Growing one with its silent stream.

GEORGE WILLIAM RUSSELL ('Æ')

911 *The Great Breath*

ITS edges foam'd with amethyst and rose,
  Withers once more the old blue flower of day:
There where the ether like a diamond glows,
    Its petals fade away.

A shadowy tumult stirs the dusky air;
Sparkle the delicate dews, the distant snows;
The great deep thrills—for through it everywhere
    The breath of Beauty blows.

I saw how all the trembling ages past,
Moulded to her by deep and deeper breath,
Near'd to the hour when Beauty breathes her last
    And knows herself in death.

912 *Germinal*

CALL not thy wanderer home as yet
  Though it be late.
Now is his first assailing of
  The invisible gate.
Be still through that light knocking. The hour
  Is throng'd with fate.

To that first tapping at the invisible door
  Fate answereth.
What shining image or voice, what sigh
  Or honied breath,
Comes forth, shall be the master of life
  Even to death.

GEORGE WILLIAM RUSSELL ('Æ')

Satyrs may follow after. Seraphs
  On crystal wing
May blaze. But the delicate first comer
  It shall be King.
They shall obey, even the mightiest,
  That gentle thing.

All the strong powers of Dante were bow'd
  To a child's mild eyes,
That wrought within him that travail
  From depths up to skies,
Inferno, Purgatorio
  And Paradise.

Amid the soul's grave councillors
  A petulant boy
Laughs under the laurels and purples, the elf
  Who snatch'd at his joy,
Ordering Caesar's legions to bring him
  The world for his toy.

In ancient shadows and twilights
  Where childhood had stray'd,
The world's great sorrows were born
  And its heroes were made.
In the lost boyhood of Judas
  Christ was betray'd.

Let thy young wanderer dream on:
  Call him not home.
A door opens, a breath, a voice
  From the ancient room,
Speaks to him now. Be it dark or bright
  He is knit with his doom.

ERNEST DOWSON

913   *Non sum qualis eram bonae*
              sub regno Cynarae

LAST night, ah, yesternight, betwixt her lips and mine
    There fell thy shadow, Cynara! thy breath was shed
Upon my soul between the kisses and the wine;
And I was desolate and sick of an old passion,
    Yea, I was desolate and bow'd my head:
I have been faithful to thee, Cynara! in my fashion.

All night upon mine heart I felt her warm heart beat,
Night-long within mine arms in love and sleep she lay;
Surely the kisses of her bought red mouth were sweet;
But I was desolate and sick of an old passion,
    When I awoke and found the dawn was gray:
I have been faithful to thee, Cynara! in my fashion.

I have forgot much, Cynara! gone with the wind,
Flung roses, roses, riotously with the throng,
Dancing, to put thy pale lost lilies out of mind;
But I was desolate and sick of an old passion,
    Yea, all the time, because the dance was long:
I have been faithful to thee, Cynara! in my fashion.

I cried for madder music and for stronger wine,
But when the feast is finish'd and the lamps expire,
Then falls thy shadow, Cynara! the night is thine;
And I am desolate and sick of an old passion,
    Yea, hungry for the lips of my desire:
I have been faithful to thee, Cynara! in my fashion.

ERNEST DOWSON

914   *Vitae summa brevis spem nos vetat*
incohare longam

THEY are not long, the weeping and the laughter,
  Love and desire and hate:
I think they have no portion in us after
    We pass the gate.

They are not long, the days of wine and roses:
    Out of a misty dream
Our path emerges for a while, then closes
    Within a dream.

LAURENCE BINYON

1869–1943

915   *Invocation to Youth*

COME then, as ever, like the wind at morning!
  Joyous, O Youth, in the agèd world renew
Freshness to feel the eternities around it,
    Rain, stars and clouds, light and the sacred dew.
        The strong sun shines above thee:
        That strength, that radiance bring!
        If Winter come to Winter,
        When shall men hope for Spring?

916   *O World, be Nobler*

O WORLD, be nobler, for her sake!
  If she but knew thee what thou art,
What wrongs are borne, what deeds are done
In thee, beneath thy daily sun,
  Know'st thou not that her tender heart
For pain and very shame would break?
O World, be nobler, for her sake!

917 *The Statues*

TARRY a moment, happy feet,
  That to the sound of laughter glide!
O glad ones of the evening street,
Behold what forms are at your side!

You conquerors of the toilsome day
Pass by with laughter, labour done;
But these within their durance stay;
Their travail sleeps not with the sun.

They, like dim statues without end,
Their patient attitudes maintain;
Your triumphing bright course attend,
But from your eager ways abstain.

Now, if you chafe in secret thought,
A moment turn from light distress,
And see how Fate on these hath wrought,
Who yet so deeply acquiesce.

Behold them, stricken, silent, weak,
The maim'd, the mute, the halt, the blind,
Condemn'd amid defeat to seek
The thing which they shall never find.

They haunt the shadows of your ways
In masks of perishable mould:
Their souls a changing flesh arrays,
But they are changeless from of old.

Their lips repeat an empty call,
But silence wraps their thoughts around.
On them, like snow, the ages fall;
Time muffles all this transient sound.

LAURENCE BINYON

When Shalmaneser pitch'd his tent
By Tigris, and his flag unfurl'd,
And forth his summons proudly sent
Into the new unconquer'd world;

Or when with spears Cambyses rode
Through Memphis and her bending slaves,
Or first the Tyrian gazed abroad
Upon the bright vast outer waves;

When sages, star-instructed men,
To the young glory of Babylon
Foreknew no ending; even then
Innumerable years had flown

Since first the chisel in her hand
Necessity, the sculptor, took,
And in her spacious meaning plann'd
These forms, and that eternal look;

These foreheads, moulded from afar,
These soft, unfathomable eyes,
Gazing from darkness, like a star;
These lips, whose grief is to be wise.

As from the mountain marble rude
The growing statue rises fair,
She from immortal patience hew'd
The limbs of ever-young despair.

There is no bliss so new and dear,
It hath not them far-off allured.
All things that we have yet to fear
They have already long endured.

Nor is there any sorrow more
Than hath ere now befallen these,
Whose gaze is as an opening door
On wild interminable seas

O Youth, run fast upon thy feet,
With full joy haste thee to be fill'd,
And out of moments brief and sweet
Thou shalt a power for ages build.

Does thy heart falter? Here, then, seek
What strength is in thy kind! With pain
Immortal bow'd, these mortals weak
Gentle and unsubdued remain.

918 *For the Fallen*

WITH proud thanksgiving, a mother for her children,
England mourns for her dead across the sea.
Flesh of her flesh they were, spirit of her spirit,
Fallen in the cause of the free.

Solemn the drums thrill: Death august and royal
Sings sorrow up into immortal spheres.
There is music in the midst of desolation
And a glory that shines upon our tears.

They went with songs to the battle, they were young,
Straight of limb, true of eye, steady and aglow.
They were staunch to the end against odds uncounted,
They fell with their faces to the foe.

They shall grow not old, as we that are left grow old:
Age shall not weary them, nor the years condemn.
At the going down of the sun and in the morning
We will remember them.

They mingle not with their laughing comrades again;
They sit no more at familiar tables of home;
They have no lot in our labour of the day-time;
They sleep beyond England's foam.

But where our desires are and our hopes profound,
Felt as a well-spring that is hidden from sight,
To the innermost heart of their own land they are known
As the stars are known to the Night;

As the stars that shall be bright when we are dust,
Moving in marches upon the heavenly plain,
As the stars that are starry in the time of our darkness,
To the end, to the end, they remain.

LORD ALFRED DOUGLAS
1870–1945

919 *Impression de Nuit*
LONDON

SEE what a mass of gems the city wears
  Upon her broad live bosom! row on row
    Rubies and emeralds and amethysts glow.
See! that huge circle, like a necklace, stares
With thousands of bold eyes to heaven, and dares
    The golden stars to dim the lamps below.
    And in the mirror of the mire I know
The moon has left her image unawares.

That's the great town at night: I see her breasts,
    Prick'd out with lamps they stand like huge black towers,
      I think they move! I hear her panting breath.
And that's her head where the tiara rests.
    And in her brain, through lanes as dark as death,
    Men creep like thoughts . . . The lamps are like pale
      flowers.

920 *To Olive*

I HAVE been profligate of happiness
    And reckless of the world's hostility,
    The blessêd part has not been given to me
Gladly to suffer fools, I do confess
I have enticed and merited distress,
    By this, that I have never bow'd the knee
    Before the shrine of wise Hypocrisy,
Nor worn self-righteous anger like a dress.

Yet write you this, sweet one, when I am dead:
    'Love like a lamp sway'd over all his days
        And all his life was like a lamp-lit chamber,
Where is no nook, no chink unvisited
    By the soft affluence of golden rays,
        And all the room is bathed in liquid amber.'

921 *Green River*

I KNOW a green grass path that leaves the field,
    And like a running river, winds along
    Into a leafy wood where is no throng
Of birds at noon-day, and no soft throats yield
Their music to the moon. The place is seal'd,
    An unclaim'd sovereignty of voiceless song,
    And all the unravish'd silences belong
To some sweet singer lost or unreveal'd.

So is my soul become a silent place.
    Oh may I wake from this uneasy night
        To find a voice of music manifold.
Let it be shape of sorrow with wan face,
    Or Love that swoons on sleep, or else delight
        That is as wide-eyed as a marigold.

922 *A Duet*

'FLOWERS nodding gaily, scent in air,
  Flowers posied, flowers for the hair,
Sleepy flowers, flowers bold to stare——'
        'O pick me some!'

'Shells with lip, or tooth, or bleeding gum,
Tell-tale shells, and shells that whisper *Come*,
Shells that stammer, blush, and yet are dumb——'
        'O let me hear.'

'Eyes so black they draw one trembling near,
Brown eyes, caverns flooded with a tear,
Cloudless eyes, blue eyes so windy clear——'
        'O look at me!'

'Kisses sadly blown across the sea,
Darkling kisses, kisses fair and free,
Bob-a-cherry kisses 'neath a tree——'
        'O give me one!'

Thus sang a king and queen in Babylon.

923 *Sent from Egypt with a Fair Robe of*
     Tissue to a Sicilian Vinedresser

                B.C. 276

PUT out to sea, if wine thou wouldest make
  Such as is made in Cos: when open boat
May safely launch, advice of pilots take;
And find the deepest bottom, most remote

From all encroachment of the crumbling shore,
Where no fresh stream tempers the rich salt wave,
Forcing rash sweetness on sage ocean's brine;
As youthful shepherds pour
Their first love forth to Battos gnarl'd and grave,
Fooling shrewd age to bless some fond design.

Not after storm! but when, for a long spell,
No white-maned horse has raced across the blue,
Put from the beach! lest troubled be the well—
Less pure thy draught than from such depth were due.
Fast close thy largest jars, prepared and clean!
Next weight each buoyant womb down through the flood,
Far down! when, with a cord the lid remove,
And it will fill unseen,
Swift as a heart Love smites sucks back the blood:—
This bubbles, deeper born than sighs, shall prove.

If thy bow'd shoulders ache, as thou dost haul—
Those groan who climb with rich ore from the mine;
Labour untold round Ilion girt a wall;
A god toil'd that Achilles' arms might shine;
Think of these things and double knit thy will!
Then, should the sun be hot on thy return,
Cover thy jars with piles of bladder weed,
Dripping, and fragrant still
From sea-wolds where it grows like bracken-fern:
A grapnel dragg'd will soon supply thy need.

Home to a tun convey thy precious freight!
Wherein, for thirty days, it should abide,
Closed, yet not quite closed from the air, and wait
While, through dim stillness, slowly doth subside

1094

Thick sediment. The humour of a day,
Which has defeated youth and health and joy,
Down, through a dreamless sleep, will settle thus,
Till riseth maiden gay,
Set free from all glooms past—or else a boy
Once more a school-friend worthy Troilus.

Yet to such cool wood tank some dream might dip:
Vision of Aphrodite sunk to sleep,
Or of some sailor let down from a ship,
Young, dead, and lovely, while across the deep
Through the calm night his hoarse-voiced comrades chaunt—
So far at sea, they cannot reach the land
To lay him perfect in the warm brown earth.
Pray that such dreams there haunt!
While, through damp darkness, where thy tun doth stand,
Cold salamanders sidle round its girth.

Gently draw off the clear and tomb it yet,
For other twenty days, in cedarn casks!
Where through trance, surely, prophecy will set;
As, dedicated to light temple-tasks,
The young priest dreams the unknown mystery.
Through Ariadne, knelt disconsolate
In the sea's marge, so well'd back warmth which throbb'd
With nuptial promise: she
Turn'd; and, half-choked through dewy glens, some great,
Some magic drone of revel coming sobb'd.

Of glorious fruit, indeed, must be thy choice!
Such as has fully ripen'd on the branch,
Such as due rain, then sunshine, made rejoice,
Which, pulp'd and colour'd, now deep bloom doth blanch!

Clusters like odes for victors in the games,
Strophe on strophe globed, pure nectar all!
Spread such to dry! if Helios grant thee grace,
Exposed unto his flames
Two days, or, if not, three, or, should rain fall,
Stretch them on hurdles in the house four days!

Grapes are not sharded chestnuts, which the tree
Lets fall to burst them on the ground, where red
Rolls forth the fruit, from white-lined wards set free,
And all undamaged glows 'mid husks it shed;
Nay, they are soft and should be singly stripp'd
From off the bunch, by maiden's dainty hand,
Then dropp'd through the cool silent depth to sink
(Coy, as herself hath slipp'd,
Bathing, from shelves in caves along the strand)
Till round each dark grape water barely wink;

Since some nine measures of sea-water fill
A butt of fifty, ere the plump fruit peep,
Like sombre dolphin shoals when nights are still,
Which penn'd in Proteus' wizard circle sleep,
And 'twixt them glinting curves of silver glance
If Zephyr, dimpling dark calm, counts them o'er.
Let soak thy fruit for two days thus, then tread!
While bare-legg'd bumpkins dance,
Bright from thy bursting press arch'd spouts shall pour,
And gurgling torrents towards thy vats run red.

Meanwhile the maidens, each with wooden rake,
Drag back the skins and laugh at aprons splash'd;
Or youths rest, boasting how their brown arms ache,
So fast their shovels for so long have flash'd,

Baffling their comrades' legs with mounting heaps.
Treble their labour! still the happier they,
Who, at this genial task, wear out long hours,
Till vast night round them creeps,
When soon the torch-light dance whirls them away;
For gods, who love wine, double all their powers.

Iacchus is the always grateful god!
His vineyards are more fair than gardens far;
Hanging, like those of Babylon, they nod
O'er each Ionian cliff and hill-side scar!
While Cypris lends him saltness, depth, and peace;
The brown earth yields him sap for richest green;
And he has borrow'd laughter from the sky;
Wildness from winds; and bees
Bring honey.—Then choose casks which thou hast seen
Are leakless, very wholesome, and quite dry!

That Coan wine the very finest is,
I do assure thee, who have travell'd much
And learn'd to judge of diverse vintages.
Faint not before the toil! this wine is such
As tempteth princes launch long pirate barks;—
From which may Zeus protect Sicilian bays,
And, ere long, me safe home from Egypt bring,
Letting no black-sail'd sharks
Scent this king's gifts, for whom I sweeten praise
With those same songs thou didst to Chloë sing!

I wrote them 'neath the vine-cloak'd elm, for thee.
Recall those nights! our couches were a load
Of scented lentisk; upward, tree by tree,
Thy father's orchard sloped, and past us flow'd

A stream sluiced for his vineyards; when, above,
The apples fell, they on to us were roll'd,
But kept us not awake,—O Laco, own
How thou didst rave of love!
Now art thou staid, thy son is three years old;
But I, who made thee love-songs, live alone.

Muse thou at dawn o'er thy yet slumbering wife!—
Not chary of her best was Nature there,
Who, though a third of her full gift of life
Was spent, still added beauties still more rare;
What calm slow days, what holy sleep at night,
Evolved her for long twilight trystings fraught
With panic blushes and tip-toe surmise:
And then, what mystic might—
All, with a crowning boon, through travail brought!
Consider this and give thy best likewise!

Ungrateful be not! Laco, ne'er be that!
Well worth thy while to make such wine 'twould be:
I see thy red face 'neath thy broad straw hat,
I see thy house, thy vineyards, Sicily!—
Thou dost demur, good, but too easy, friend:
Come put those doubts away! thou hast strong lads,
Brave wenches; on the steep beach lolls thy ship,
Where vine-clad slopes descend,
Sheltering our bay, that headlong rillet glads,
Like a stripp'd child fain in the sea to dip.

924 *Song*

INVITING THE INFLUENCE OF A YOUNG LADY UPON THE
OPENING YEAR

YOU wear the morning like your dress
And are with mastery crown'd;
When as you walk your loveliness
Goes shining all around:
Upon your secret, smiling way
Such new contents were found,
The Dancing Loves made holiday
On that delightful ground.
Then summon April forth, and send
Commandment through the flowers;
About our woods your grace extend,
A queen of careless hours.
For O! not Vera veil'd in rain,
Nor Dian's sacred Ring,
With all her royal nymphs in train
Could so lead on the Spring.

925 *The Night*

MOST Holy Night, that still dost keep
The keys of all the doors of sleep,
To me when my tired eyelids close
Give thou repose.

And let the far lament of them
That chaunt the dead day's requiem
Make in my ears, who wakeful lie,
Soft lullaby.

HILAIRE BELLOC

Let them that guard the hornèd Moon
By my bedside their memories croon.
So shall I have new dreams and blest
    In my brief rest.

Fold thy great wings about my face,
Hide day-dawn from my resting-place,
And cheat me with thy false delight,
    Most Holy Night.

WILLIAM HENRY DAVIES

1871–1940

926   *The Kingfisher*

IT was the Rainbow gave thee birth,
  And left thee all her lovely hues;
And, as her mother's name was Tears,
  So runs it in thy blood to choose
For haunts the lonely pools, and keep
In company with trees that weep.

Go you and, with such glorious hues,
  Live with proud peacocks in green parks;
On lawns as smooth as shining glass,
  Let every feather show its marks;
Get thee on boughs and clap thy wings
Before the windows of proud kings.

Nay, lovely Bird, thou art not vain;
  Thou hast no proud, ambitious mind;
I also love a quiet place
  That's green, away from all mankind;
A lonely pool, and let a tree
Sigh with her bosom over me.

927 *Money*

WHEN I had money, money, O!
 I knew no joy till I went poor;
For many a false man as a friend
 Came knocking all day at my door.

Then felt I like a child that holds
 A trumpet that he must not blow
Because a man is dead; I dared
 Not speak to let this false world know.

Much have I thought of life, and seen
 How poor men's hearts are ever light;
And how their wives do hum like bees
 About their work from morn till night.

So, when I hear these poor ones laugh,
 And see the rich ones coldly frown—
Poor men, think I, need not go up
 So much as rich men should come down.

When I had money, money, O!
 My many friends proved all untrue;
But now I have no money, O!
 My friends are real, though very few.

928 *Leisure*

WHAT is this life if, full of care,
 We have no time to stand and stare?—

No time to stand beneath the boughs
And stare as long as sheep or cows:

WILLIAM HENRY DAVIES

No time to see, when woods we pass,
Where squirrels hide their nuts in grass:

No time to see, in broad daylight,
Streams full of stars, like skies at night:

No time to turn at Beauty's glance,
And watch her feet, how they can dance:

No time to wait till her mouth can
Enrich that smile her eyes began?

A poor life this if, full of care,
We have no time to stand and stare.

JOHN SWINNERTON PHILLIMORE

1873-1926

929   *In a Meadow*

THIS is the place
     Where far from the unholy populace
The daughter of Philosophy and Sleep
          Her court doth keep,
Sweet Contemplation. To her service bound
          Hover around
The little amiable summer airs,
          Her courtiers.

          The deep black soil
Makes mute her palace-floors with thick trefoil;
The grasses sagely nodding overhead
          Curtain her bed;

JOHN SWINNERTON PHILLIMORE

And lest the feet of strangers overpass
   Her walls of grass,
Gravely a little river goes his rounds
   To beat the bounds.

   —No bustling flood
To make a tumult in her neighbourhood,
But such a stream as knows to go and come
   Discreetly dumb.
Therein are chambers tapestried with weeds
   And screen'd with reeds;
For roof the waterlily-leaves serene
   Spread tiles of green.

   The sun's large eye
Falls soberly upon me where I lie;
For delicate webs of immaterial haze
   Refine his rays.
The air is full of music none knows what,
   Or half-forgot;
The living echo of dead voices fills
   The unseen hills.

   I hear the song
Of cuckoo answering cuckoo all day long;
And know not if it be my inward sprite
   For my delight
Making remember'd poetry appear
   As sound in the ear:
Like a salt savour poignant in the breeze
   From distant seas.

JOHN SWINNERTON PHILLIMORE

Dreams without sleep,
And sleep too clear for dreaming and too deep;
And Quiet very large and manifold
    About me roll'd;
Satiety, that momentary flower,
    Stretch'd to an hour:
These are her gifts which all mankind may use,
    And all refuse.

GILBERT KEITH CHESTERTON

1872-1936

930   *The Rolling English Road*

BEFORE the Roman came to Rye or out to Severn strode,
   The rolling English drunkard made the rolling English
   road.
A reeling road, a rolling road, that rambles round the shire,
And after him the parson ran, the sexton and the squire;
A merry road, a mazy road, and such as we did tread
The night we went to Birmingham by way of Beachy Head.

I knew no harm of Bonaparte and plenty of the Squire,
And for to fight the Frenchman I did not much desire;
But I did bash their baggonets because they came array'd
To straighten out the crooked road an English drunkard
   made,
Where you and I went down the lane with ale-mugs in our
   hands,
The night we went to Glastonbury by way of Goodwin
   Sands.

His sins they were forgiven him; or why do flowers run
Behind him; and the hedges all strengthening in the sun?
The wild thing went from left to right and knew not which
    was which,
But the wild rose was above him when they found him in the
    ditch.
God pardon us, nor harden us; we did not see so clear
The night we went to Bannockburn by way of Brighton Pier.

My friends, we will not go again or ape an ancient rage,
Or stretch the folly of our youth to be the shame of age,
But walk with clearer eyes and ears this path that wandereth,
And see undrugg'd in evening light the decent inn of death;
For there is good news yet to hear and fine things to be seen,
Before we go to Paradise by way of Kensal Green.

931   *The Donkey*

WHEN fishes flew and forests walk'd
    And figs grew upon thorn,
Some moment when the moon was blood
    Then surely I was born;

With monstrous head and sickening cry
    And ears like errant wings,
The devil's walking parody
    On all four-footed things.

The tatter'd outlaw of the earth,
    Of ancient crooked will;
Starve, scourge, deride me: I am dumb,
    I keep my secret still.

GILBERT KEITH CHESTERTON

Fools! For I also had my hour;
    One far fierce hour and sweet:
There was a shout about my ears,
    And palms before my feet.

RALPH HODGSON

1872–1962

932   *The Bells of Heaven*

'TWOULD ring the bells of Heaven
    The wildest peal for years,
If Parson lost his senses
And people came to theirs,
And he and they together
Knelt down with angry prayers
For tamed and shabby tigers,
And dancing dogs and bears,
And wretched, blind pit ponies,
And little hunted hares.

WALTER DE LA MARE

1873–1956

933   *An Epitaph*

HERE lies a most beautiful lady,
    Light of step and heart was she:
I think she was the most beautiful lady
    That ever was in the West Country.
But beauty vanishes; beauty passes;
    However rare, rare it be;
And when I crumble who shall remember
    This lady of the West Country?

The Listeners

'IS there anybody there?' said the Traveller,
    Knocking on the moonlit door;
And his horse in the silence champ'd the grasses
    Of the forest's ferny floor:
And a bird flew up out of the turret,
    Above the Traveller's head:
And he smote upon the door again a second time;
    'Is there anybody there?' he said.
But no one descended to the Traveller;
    No head from the leaf-fringed sill
Lean'd over and look'd into his grey eyes,
    Where he stood perplex'd and still.
But only a host of phantom listeners
    That dwelt in the lone house then
Stood listening in the quiet of the moonlight
    To that voice from the world of men:
Stood thronging the faint moonbeams on the dark stair,
    That goes down to the empty hall,
Hearkening in an air stirr'd and shaken
    By the lonely Traveller's call.
And he felt in his heart their strangeness,
    Their stillness answering his cry,
While his horse moved, cropping the dark turf,
    'Neath the starr'd and leafy sky;
For he suddenly smote on the door, even
    Louder, and lifted his head:—
'Tell them I came, and no one answer'd,
    That I kept my word,' he said.
Never the least stir made the listeners,
    Though every word he spake

Fell echoing through the shadowiness of the still house
　From the one man left awake:
Ay, they heard his foot upon the stirrup,
　And the sound of iron on stone,
And how the silence surged softly backward,
　When the plunging hoofs were gone.

935　　　　　　*Fare Well*

WHEN I lie where shades of darkness
　　Shall no more assail mine eyes,
Nor the rain make lamentation
　　When the wind sighs;
How will fare the world whose wonder
Was the very proof of me?
Memory fades, must the remember'd
　　Perishing be?

Oh, when this my dust surrenders
Hand, foot, lip, to dust again,
May these loved and loving faces
　　Please other men!
May the rusting harvest hedgerow
Still the Traveller's Joy entwine,
And as happy children gather
　　Posies once mine.

Look thy last on all things lovely,
Every hour. Let no night
Seal thy sense in deathly slumber
　　Till to delight

Thou have paid thy utmost blessing;
Since that all things thou wouldst praise
Beauty took from those who loved them
      In other days.

GORDON BOTTOMLEY

1874–1948

936   *To Iron-Founders and Others*

WHEN you destroy a blade of grass
  You poison England at her roots:
Remember no man's foot can pass
Where evermore no green life shoots.

You force the birds to wing too high
Where your unnatural vapours creep:
Surely the living rocks shall die
When birds no rightful distance keep.

You have brought down the firmament
And yet no heaven is more near;
You shape huge deeds without event,
And half-made men believe and fear.

Your worship is your furnaces,
Which, like old idols, lost obscenes,
Have molten bowels; your vision is
Machines for making more machines.

O, you are busied in the night,
Preparing destinies of rust;
Iron misused must turn to blight
And dwindle to a tetter'd crust.

GORDON BOTTOMLEY

The grass, forerunner of life, has gone,
But plants that spring in ruins and shards
Attend until your dream is done:
I have seen hemlock in your yards.

The generations of the worm
Know not your loads piled on their soil;
Their knotted ganglions shall wax firm
Till your strong flagstones heave and toil.

When the old hollow'd earth is crack'd,
And when, to grasp more power and feasts,
Its ores are emptied, wasted, lack'd,
The middens of your burning beasts

Shall be raked over till they yield
Last priceless slags for fashionings high,
Ploughs to wake grass in every field,
Chisels men's hands to magnify.

JOHN ALEXANDER CHAPMAN

b. 1875

937   *Gipsy Queen*

GIPSY queen of the night, wraith of the fire-lit dark,
   Glittering eyes of ice, sharp as glacier green,
Lisping falling kisses, syllabled flakes of snow,
Down on the stubble fields, over my eyes and hair;
If on my mouth one falls, it is tasteless and light and cold—
She mocks you, gipsy queen, the brown-eyed child of earth;
As berry that grew from flower, she, as grape of the vine,
Is warm and sweet for man; the wine, in herself, and cup.
Why do you haunt me then? Are you for me, not she?

1110

JOHN ALEXANDER CHAPMAN

Am I a leafless branch, bowed with a load of snow;
Not for warm hands to pluck, but alone in the world of cold;
Black against pale-washed sky, grey never vein'd with red?
But so the better for you, cold shape of the dark outside;
You banish'd from rose too red for ice-green eyes to see;
Chased before lambing time, ere even the snowdrops come,
Poor gipsy-wraith of the snow, but knowing your brother,
　　and come
To him? Then come to me. I will give you a cold, cold kiss.
My roses are dead, they too. My lips are grey. My eyes
Have neither iris nor pupil. They died, and now all is white;
White in a face of stone. Sister, cold lover, come.

JOHN MASEFIELD   1878–1967

938　　　　*Cargoes*

QUINQUIREME of Nineveh from distant Ophir
　Rowing home to haven in sunny Palestine,
With a cargo of ivory,
And apes and peacocks,
Sandalwood, cedarwood, and sweet white wine.

Stately Spanish galleon coming from the Isthmus,
Dipping through the Tropics by the palm-green shores,
With a cargo of diamonds,
Emeralds, amethysts,
Topazes, and cinnamon, and gold moidores.

Dirty British coaster with a salt-caked smoke stack
Butting through the Channel in the mad March days,
With a cargo of Tyne coal,
Road-rail, pig-lead,
Firewood, iron-ware, and cheap tin trays.

939   *Captain Stratton's Fancy*

OH some are fond of red wine, and some are fond of white,
    And some are all for dancing by the pale moonlight:
But rum alone's the tipple, and the heart's delight
    Of the old bold mate of Henry Morgan.

Oh some are fond of Spanish wine, and some are fond of
    French,
And some'll swallow tay and stuff fit only for a wench;
But I'm for right Jamaica till I roll beneath the bench,
    Says the old bold mate of Henry Morgan.

Oh some are for the lily, and some are for the rose,
But I am for the sugar-cane that in Jamaica grows;
For it's that that makes the bonny drink to warm my copper
    nose,
    Says the old bold mate of Henry Morgan.

Oh some are fond of fiddles, and a song well sung,
And some are all for music for to lilt upon the tongue;
But mouths were made for tankards, and for sucking at the
    bung,
    Says the old bold mate of Henry Morgan.

Oh some are fond of dancing, and some are fond of dice,
And some are all for red lips, and pretty lasses' eyes;
But a right Jamaica puncheon is a finer prize
    To the old bold mate of Henry Morgan.

Oh some that's good and godly ones they hold that it's a sin
To troll the jolly bowl around, and let the dollars spin;
But I'm for toleration and for drinking at an inn,
    Says the old bold mate of Henry Morgan.

Oh some are sad and wretched folk that go in silken suits,
And there's a mort of wicked rogues that live in good reputes;
So I'm for drinking honestly, and dying in my boots,
   Like an old bold mate of Henry Morgan.

940   *The Passing Strange*

OUT of the earth to rest or range
   Perpetual in perpetual change,
The unknown passing through the strange.

Water and saltness held together
To tread the dust and stand the weather,
And plough the field and stretch the tether,

To pass the wine-cup and be witty,
Water the sands and build the city,
Slaughter like devils and have pity,

Be red with rage and pale with lust,
Make beauty come, make peace, make trust,
Water and saltness mixed with dust;

Drive over earth, swim under sea,
Fly in the eagle's secrecy,
Guess where the hidden comets be;

Know all the deathy seeds that still
Queen Helen's beauty, Caesar's will,
And slay them even as they kill;

Fashion an altar for a rood,
Defile a continent with blood,
And watch a brother starve for food:

JOHN MASEFIELD

Love like a madman, shaking, blind,
Till self is burnt into a kind
Possession of another mind;

Brood upon beauty, till the grace
Of beauty with the holy face
Brings peace into the bitter place;

Prove in the lifeless granites, scan
The stars for hope, for guide, for plan;
Live as a woman or a man;

Fasten to lover or to friend,
Until the heart break at the end:
The break of death that cannot mend;

Then to lie useless, helpless, still,
Down in the earth, in dark, to fill
The roots of grass or daffodil.

Down in the earth, in dark, alone,
A mockery of the ghost in bone,
The strangeness, passing the unknown.

Time will go by, that outlasts clocks,
Dawn in the thorps will rouse the cocks,
Sunset be glory on the rocks:

But it, the thing, will never heed
Even the rootling from the seed
Thrusting to suck it for its need.

.   .   .   .   .   .

JOHN MASEFIELD

Since moons decay and suns decline,
How else should end this life of mine?
Water and saltness are not wine.

But in the darkest hour of night,
When even the foxes peer for sight,
The byre-cock crows; he feels the light.

So, in this water mixed with dust,
The byre-cock spirit crows from trust
That death will change because it must;

For all things change, the darkness changes,
The wandering spirits change their ranges,
The corn is gathered to the granges.

The corn is sown again, it grows;
The stars burn out, the darkness goes;
The rhythms change, they do not close.

They change, and we, who pass like foam,
Like dust blown through the streets of Rome,
Change ever, too; we have no home,

Only a beauty, only a power,
Sad in the fruit, bright in the flower,
Endlessly erring for its hour,

But gathering, as we stray, a sense
Of Life, so lovely and intense,
It lingers when we wander hence,

That those who follow feel behind
Their backs, when all before is blind,
Our joy, a rampart to the mind.

1878–1957

941   *The Plum Tree by the House*

IN morning light my damson show'd
Its airy branches oversnow'd
On all their quickening fronds,
That tingled where the early sun
Was flowing soft as silence on
Palm trees by coral ponds.
Out of the dark of sleep I come
To find the clay break into bloom,
The black boughs all in white!
I said, I must stand still and watch
This glory, strive no more to match
With similes things fair.
I am not fit to conjure up
A bird that's white enough to hop
Unstain'd in such a tree;
Nor crest him with the bloom to come
In purple glory on the plum.
Leave me alone with my delight
To store up joy against the night,
This moment leave to me!
Why should a poet strain his head
To make his mind a marriage bed;
Shall Beauty cease to bear?
There must be things which never shall
Be match'd or made symmetrical
On Earth or in the Air;
Branches that Chinese draughtsmen drew,
Which none may find an equal to,
Unless he enter there

Where none may live—and more's the pity!—
The Perfect, the Forbidden City,
That's built—ah, God knows where!
Then leave me while I have the light
To fill my mind with growths of white,
Think of them longer than
Their budding hour, their springing day,
Until my mind is more than May;
And, maybe, I shall plan
To make them yet break out like this
And blossom where their image is,
More lasting and more deep
Than coral boughs in light inurn'd,
When they are to the earth return'd;
And I am turn'd to sleep.

942 *The Image-Maker*

HARD is the stone, but harder still
The delicate preforming will
That guided by a dream alone,
Subdues and moulds the hardest stone,
Making the stubborn jade release
The emblem of eternal peace.

If but the will be firmly bent,
No stuff resists the mind's intent;
The adamant abets his skill
And sternly aids the artist's will,
To clothe in perdurable pride
Beauty his transient eyes descried.

1878–1963

943   *Chant for Reapers*

WHY do you hide, O dryads! when we seek
      Your healing hands in solace?
Who shall soften like you the places rough?
Who shall hasten the harvest?

Why do you fly, O dryads! when we pray
      For laden boughs and blossom?
Who shall quicken like you the sapling trees?
Who shall ripen the orchards?

Bare in the wind the branches wave and break,
      The hazel nuts are hollow.
Who shall garner the wheat if you be gone?
Who shall sharpen his sickle?

Wine have we spilt, O dryads! on our knees
      Have made you our oblation.
Who shall save us from dearth if you be fled?
Who shall comfort and kindle?

Sadly we delve the furrows, string the vine
      Whose flimsy burden topples.
Downward tumble the woods if you be dumb,
Stript of honey and garland.

Why do you hide, O dryads! when we call,
      With pleading hands up-lifted?
Smile and bless us again that all be well;
Smile again on your children.

944

The New House

NOW first, as I shut the door,
  I was alone
In the new house; and the wind
  Began to moan.

Old at once was the house,
  And I was old;
My ears were teased with the dread
  Of what was foretold,

Nights of storm, days of mist, without end;
  Sad days when the sun
Shone in vain: old griefs and griefs
  Not yet begun.

All was foretold me; naught
  Could I foresee;
But I learn'd how the wind would sound
  After these things should be.

945

Adlestrop

YES. I remember Adlestrop—
The name, because one afternoon
Of heat the express-train drew up there
Unwontedly. It was late June.

The steam hiss'd. Some one clear'd his throat.
No one left and no one came
On the bare platform. What I saw
Was Adlestrop—only the name

And willows, willow-herb, and grass,
And meadowsweet, and haycocks dry,
No whit less still and lonely fair
Than the high cloudlets in the sky.

And for that minute a blackbird sang
Close by, and round him, mistier,
Farther and farther, all the birds
Of Oxfordshire and Gloucestershire.

ALFRED NOYES

1880–1958

946

Art

(*i*)

YES! Beauty still rebels!
Our dreams like clouds disperse:
 She dwells
In agate, marble, verse.

No false constraint be thine!
But, for right walking, choose
 The fine,
The strict cothurnus, Muse.

Vainly ye seek to escape
The toil! The yielding phrase
 Ye shape
Is clay, not chrysoprase.

And all in vain ye scorn
That seeming ease which ne'er
 Was born
Of aught but love and care.

Take up the sculptor's tool!
Recall the gods that die
    To rule
In Parian o'er the sky.

(ii)

Poet, let passion sleep
Till with the cosmic rhyme
    You keep
Eternal tone and time,

By rule of hour and flower,
By strength of stern restraint
    And power
To fail and not to faint.

The task is hard to learn
While all the songs of Spring
    Return
Along the blood and sing.

Yet hear—from her deep skies,
How Art, for all your pain,
    Still cries
Ye must be born again!

Reject the wreath of rose,
Take up the crown of thorn
    That shows
To-night a child is born.

The far immortal face
In chosen onyx fine
    Enchase,
Delicate line by line.

ALFRED NOYES

Strive with Carrara, fight
With Parian, till there steal
    To light
Apollo's pure profile.

Set the great lucid form
Free from its marble tomb
    To storm
The heights of death and doom.

Take up the sculptor's tool!
Recall the gods that die
    To rule
In Parian o'er the sky.

HERBERT EDWARD PALMER 1880–1961

947 *Ishmael*

'*And God was with the lad; and he grew, and dwelt in the
vilderness and became an archer.*'—Genesis xxi. 20.

AND Ishmael crouch'd beside a crackling briar
    Blinded with sand, and madden'd by his thirst,
A derelict, though he knew not why accursed.
And lo! One saw, and strung the dissonant lyre,
Made firm his bow unto the arrow's spire,
And gave him dates and wine. Then at the first
Flushings of dawn Ishmael arose, and burst
To triumphing freedom, ran, and eased desire.

His domain was the desert. None tamed him.
None bought nor sold his spirit, though his hand
Dripp'd red against the dawn and sunset stain.

'Thrones melted, kingdoms pass'd to the world's rim.
But Ishmael scourged the lion in Paran land,
And kept his faith with God. And he will reign.

948   *Woodworker's Ballad*

ALL that is moulded of iron
   Has lent to destruction and blood;
But the things that are honour'd of Zion
Are most of them made from wood.

Stone can be chisell'd to Beauty,
And iron shines bright for Defence;
But when Mother Earth ponder'd her duty
She brought forth the forest, from whence

Come tables, and chairs, and crosses,
Little things that a hot fire warps,
Old ships that the blue wave tosses,
And fiddles for music, and harps;

Oak boards where the carved ferns mingle,
Monks' shrines in the wilderness,
Snug little huts in the dingle,
All things that the sad poets bless.

King Arthur had a wood table;
And Our Lord blessed wood; for, you see,
He was born in a wooden stable,
And He died on a wooden tree;

And He sailed in a wooden vessel
On the waters of Galilee,
And He work'd at a wooden trestle
At His wonderful carpentry.

Oh, all that is moulded of iron
Has lent to destruction and blood;
But the things that are honour'd of Zion
Are most of them made from wood.

LASCELLES ABERCROMBIE

1881–1938

949   *Hymn to Love*

WE are thine, O Love, being in thee and made of thee,
    As thóu, Lóve, were the déep thought
And we the speech of the thought; yea, spoken are we,
        Thy fires of thought out-spoken:

But burn'd not through us thy imagining
    Like fiérce móod in a sóng cáught,
We were as clamour'd words a fool may fling,
        Loose words, of meaning broken.

For what more like the brainless speech of a fool,—
    The lives travelling dark fears,
And as a boy throws pebbles in a pool
        Thrown down abysmal places?

Hazardous are the stars, yet is our birth
    And our journeying time theirs;
As words of air, life makes of starry earth
        Sweet soul-delighted faces;

LASCELLES ABERCROMBIE

As voices are we in the worldly wind;
    The great wind of the world's fate
Is turn'd, as air to a shapen sound, to mind
    And marvellous desires.

But not in the world as voices storm-shatter'd,
    Not borne down by the wind's weight;
The rushing time rings with our splendid word
    Like darkness fill'd with fires.

For Love doth use us for a sound of song,
    And Love's meaning our life wields,
Making our souls like syllables to throng
    His tunes of exultation.

Down the blind speed of a fatal world we fly,
    As rain blown along earth's fields;
Yet are we god-desiring liturgy,
    Sung joys of adoration;

Yea, made of chance and all a labouring strife,
    We go charged with a strong flame;
For as a language Love hath seized on life
    His burning heart to story.

Yea, Love, we are thine, the liturgy of thee,
    Thy thought's golden and glad name,
The mortal conscience of immortal glee,
    Love's zeal in Love's own glory.

PADRAIC COLUM

1881–1972

950   *An Old Woman of the Roads*

O, TO have a little house!
 To own the hearth and stool and all!
The heap'd-up sods upon the fire,
 The pile of turf against the wall!

To have a clock with weights and chains
 And pendulum swinging up and down!
A dresser filled with shining delph,
 Speckled with white and blue and brown!

I could be busy all the day
 Clearing and sweeping hearth and floor;
And fixing on their shelf again
 My white and blue and speckled store!

I could be quiet there at night
 Beside the fire and by myself,
Sure of a bed and loth to leave
 The ticking clock and the shining delph!

Och! but I'm weary of mist and dark,
 And roads where there's never a house or bush,
And tired I am of bog and road
 And the crying wind and the lonesome hush!

And I am praying to God on high,
 And I am praying Him night and day,
For a little house—a house of my own—
 Out of the wind's and the rain's way.

JAMES JOYCE
1882–1941

951
Bid adieu to Maidenhood

BID adieu, adieu, adieu,
  Bid adieu to girlish days,
Happy Love is come to woo
  Thee and woo thy girlish ways—
The zone that doth become thee fair,
The snood upon thy yellow hair,

When thou hast heard his name upon
  The bugles of the cherubim
Begin thou softly to unzone
  Thy girlish bosom unto him
And softly to undo the snood
That is the sign of maidenhood.

JAMES STEPHENS
1882–1950

952
The Watcher

A ROSE for a young head,
  A ring for a bride,
Joy for the homestead
Clean and wide—
  Who's that waiting
  In the rain outside?

A heart for an old friend,
A hand for the new:
Love can to earth lend
Heaven's hue—
  Who's that standing
  In the silver dew?

A smile for the parting,
A tear as they go,
God's sweethearting
Ends just so—
   Who's that watching
   Where the black winds blow?

He who is waiting
In the rain outside,
He who is standing
Where the dew drops wide,
He who is watching
In the wind must ride
   (Tho' the pale hands cling)
   With the rose
   And the ring
   And the bride,
     Must ride
With the red of the rose,
And the gold of the ring,
And the lips and the hair of the bride.

953   *The Rivals*

I HEARD a bird at dawn
  Singing sweetly on a tree,
That the dew was on the lawn,
And the wind was on the lea;
But I didn't listen to him,
For he didn't sing to me!

I didn't listen to him,
For he didn't sing to me
That the dew was on the lawn,
And the wind was on the lea!
I was singing at the time,
Just as prettily as he!

I was singing all the time,
Just as prettily as he,
About the dew upon the lawn,
And the wind upon the lea!
So I didn't listen to him,
As he sang upon a tree!

JAMES ELROY FLECKER

1884–1915

954 *Rioupéroux*

HIGH and solemn mountains guard Rioupéroux
—Small untidy village where the river drives a mill—
Frail as wood anemones, white and frail were you,
And drooping a little, like the slender daffodil.

O I will go to France again, and tramp the valley through,
And I will change these gentle clothes for clog and corduroy,
And work with the mill-hands of black Rioupéroux,
And walk with you, and talk with you, like any other boy.

955 *Hassan's Serenade*

HOW splendid in the morning glows
the lily; with what grace he throws
His supplication to the rose:
    do roses nod the head, Yasmin?

JAMES ELROY FLECKER

But when the silver dove descends
    I find the little flower of friends
Whose very name that sweetly ends
    I say when I have said 'Yasmin'.

The morning light is clear and cold,
    I dare not in that light behold
A deeper light, a deeper gold
    a glory too far shed, Yasmin.
But when the deep red eye of day
    is level with the lone highway,
And some to Mecca turn to pray,
    and I toward thy bed, Yasmin,

Or when the wind beneath the moon
    is drifting like a soul aswoon,
And harping planets talk love's tune
    with milky wings outspread, Yasmin,
Shower down thy love, O burning bright!
    for one night or the other night
Will come the Gardener in white,
    and gathered flowers are dead, Yasmin!

CHARLES WILLIAMS   1886–1945

Night Song for a Child!

SLEEP, our lord, and for thy peace
  Let thy mother's softer voice
Pray thy patrons to increase
  Freedom from all light and noise
Hark, her invocation draws
To thy guard those princely Laws!

CHARLES WILLIAMS

Prince of Fire, in favour quench
  Moonlight upon wall and floor,
And with gentle shadow drench
  Candles entering at the door;
Michael, round about his bed
Be thy great protection shed.

Prince of Air, lest winds rush by
  Blustering about the park
Of this night, with watchful eye
  Keep the palings of the dark;
Raphael, round about his bed
Be thy great protection shed.

Prince of Water, if thy rains
  Must to-night prevent our dearth,
Keep them from the window-panes;
  Softly let them bless the earth;
Gabriel, round about his bed
Be thy great protection shed.

Prince of Earth, beneath our tread
  And above each doubtful board
Be thy silent carpet spread;
  Let thy stillness hush our lord;
Auriel, round about his bed
Be thy great protection shed.

Let your vast quaternion,
  Earth and Water, Fire and Air,
Friend him as he goes upon
  His long journey, out to where,
Princes, round his final bed
Be your great protection shed.

957 *A Dream*

NO more in any house can I be at peace,
  Because of a house that waits, far off or near,
  To-morrow or (likelier) after many a year,
  Where a room and a door are that shall fulfil my fear.

For last night, dreaming, I stood in a house and saw
  Softly the room door open, and one came in,
  Its owner, and as round the edge his evil grin
  Peep'd ere he pass'd, I knew him for visible Sin.

Unwash'd, unshaven, frowsy, abominable,
  In a green greasy hat, a green greasy coat,
  Loose-mouth'd, with silent tread and the smell of the goat,
  He stole in, and helplessness stifled rage in my throat.

For this was he who came long since to my heart,
  This was he who enter'd the house of my soul long ago;
  Now he possesses imagination, and O
  I shall meet him yet in some brick-built house, I know.

He shall come, he shall turn from the long parch'd street he
    treads
  For ever, shuffling, hand rubb'd over hand unclean,
  Servile yet masterful, with satiate spleen
  Watching his houses, and muttering of things obscene.

He shall come to my flesh as he came last night to my dream;
  Eyes shall know him as soul and insight have known;
  Though all the world be there, I shall stand alone
  Watching him peer and enter and find out his own.

Noisier he shall not move, nor loudlier speak,
   Than the first sly motion of lewd delight in me
   Long since—which then I shall know none other than he,
   Now visible, aged, and filled with monstrous glee.

Therefore now in terror I enter all houses, all rooms
   Enter in dread, and move among them in fear,
   Watching all doors, saying softly 'It draws more near
   Daily; and here shall it be in the end—or here?'

SIEGFRIED SASSOON

1886–1967

958 *In Me, Past, Present, Future meet*

IN me, past, present, future meet
   To hold long chiding conference.
My lusts usurp the present tense
And strangle Reason in his seat.
My loves leap through the future's fence
To dance with dream-enfranchised feet.

In me the cave-man clasps the seer,
And garlanded Apollo goes
Chanting to Abraham's deaf ear.
In me the tiger sniffs the rose.
   Look in my heart, kind friends, and tremble,
   Since there your elements assemble.

959 *Everyone Sang*

EVERYONE suddenly burst out singing;
   And I was fill'd with such delight
As prison'd birds must find in freedom
Winging wildly across the white
Orchards and dark-green fields; on; on; and out of sight.

1133

Everyone's voice was suddenly lifted,
And beauty came like the setting sun.
My heart was shaken with tears; and horror
Drifted away . . . O but every one
Was a bird; and the song was wordless; the singing will
    never be done.

RUPERT BROOKE

1887–1915

960   *The Soldier*

IF I should die, think only this of me:
  That there's some corner of a foreign field
That is for ever England. There shall be
  In that rich earth a richer dust conceal'd;
A dust whom England bore, shaped, made aware,
  Gave, once, her flowers to love, her ways to roam,
A body of England's, breathing English air,
  Wash'd by the rivers, blest by suns of home.
And think, this heart, all evil shed away,
  A pulse in the eternal mind, no less
    Gives somewhere back the thoughts by England given;
Her sights and sounds; dreams happy as her day;
  And laughter, learnt of friends; and gentleness,
    In hearts at peace, under an English heaven.

961   *Clouds*

DOWN the blue night the unending columns press
  In noiseless tumult, break and wave and flow,
  Now tread the far South, or lift rounds of snow
Up to the white moon's hidden loveliness.

Some pause in their grave wandering comradeless,
 And turn with profound gesture vague and slow,
 As who would pray good for the world, but know
Their benediction empty as they bless.

They say that the Dead die not, but remain
 Near to the rich heirs of their grief and mirth.
 I think they ride the calm mid-heaven, as these,
In wise majestic melancholy train,
  And watch the moon, and the still-raging seas,
 And men, coming and going on the earth.

JULIAN GRENFELL

1888-1915

962 *Into Battle*

THE naked earth is warm with spring,
 And with green grass and bursting trees
Leans to the sun's gaze glorying,
 And quivers in the sunny breeze;
And life is colour and warmth and light,
 And a striving evermore for these;
And he is dead who will not fight;
 And who dies fighting has increase.

The fighting man shall from the sun
 Take warmth, and life from the glowing earth;
Speed with the light-foot winds to run,
 And with the trees to newer birth;
And find, when fighting shall be done,
 Great rest, and fullness after dearth.

JULIAN GRENFELL

All the bright company of Heaven
　　Hold him in their high comradeship,
The Dog-Star, and the Sisters Seven,
　　Orion's Belt and sworded hip.

The woodland trees that stand together,
　　They stand to him each one a friend;
They gently speak in the windy weather;
　　They guide to valley and ridge's end.

The kestrel hovering by day,
　　And the little owls that call by night,
Bid him be swift and keen as they,
　　As keen of ear, as swift of sight.

The blackbird sings to him, 'Brother, brother,
　　If this be the last song you shall sing,
Sing well, for you may not sing another;
　　Brother, sing.'

In dreary, doubtful, waiting hours,
　　Before the brazen frenzy starts,
The horses show him nobler powers;
　　O patient eyes, courageous hearts!

And when the burning moment breaks,
　　And all things else are out of mind,
And only joy of battle takes
　　Him by the throat, and makes him blind,

Through joy and blindness he shall know,
　　Not caring much to know, that still
Nor lead nor steel shall reach him, so
　　That it be not the Destin'd Will.

JULIAN GRENFELL

The thundering line of battle stands,
  And in the air Death moans and sings:
But Day shall clasp him with strong hands,
  And Night shall fold him in soft wings.

WILFRID OWEN

1893–1918

963   *Anthem for Doomed Youth*

WHAT passing-bells for these who die as cattle?
  Only the monstrous anger of the guns.
Only the stuttering rifles' rapid rattle
Can patter out their hasty orisons.
No mockeries for them from prayers or bells,
  Nor any voice of mourning save the choirs,—
The shrill, demented choirs of wailing shells;
  And bugles calling for them from sad shires.

What candles may be held to speed them all?
  Not in the hands of boys, but in their eyes
Shall shine the holy glimmers of good-byes.
  The pallor of girls' brows shall be their pall;
Their flowers the tenderness of silent minds,
And each slow dusk a drawing-down of blinds.

CHARLES HAMILTON SORLEY

1895–1915

964   *The Song of the Ungirt Runners*

WE swing ungirded hips,
  And lighten'd are our eyes,
The rain is on our lips,
We do not run for prize.

We know not whom we trust
Nor whitherward we fare,
But we run because we must
   Through the great wide air.

The waters of the seas
Are troubled as by storm.
The tempest strips the trees
And does not leave them warm.
Does the tearing tempest pause?
Do the tree-tops ask it why?
So we run without a cause
   'Neath the big bare sky.

The rain is on our lips,
We do not run for prize.
But the storm the water whips
And the wave howls to the skies.
The winds arise and strike it
And scatter it like sand,
And we run because we like it
   Through the broad bright land.

EDMUND BLUNDEN

1896–1974

965   *Forefathers*

HERE they went with smock and crook,
Toil'd in the sun, loll'd in the shade,
Here they muddled out the brook
   And here their hatchet clear'd the glade:
Harvest-supper woke their wit,
Huntsman's moon their wooings lit.

EDMUND BLUNDEN

From this church they led their brides,
    From this church themselves were led
Shoulder-high; on these waysides
    Sat to take their beer and bread.
Names are gone—what men they were
These their cottages declare.

Names are vanish'd, save the few
    In the old brown Bible scrawl'd;
These were men of pith and thew
    Whom the city never call'd;
Scarce could read or hold a quill,
Built the barn, the forge, the mill.

On the green they watch'd their sons
    Playing till too dark to see,
As their fathers watch'd them once,
    As my father once watch'd me;
While the bat and beetle flew
On the warm air webb'd with dew.

Unrecorded, unrenown'd,
    Men from whom my ways begin,
Here I know you by your ground
    But I know you not within—
There is silence, there survives
Not a moment of your lives.

Like the bee that now is blown
    Honey-heavy on my hand,
From his toppling tansy-throne
    In the green tempestuous land—
I'm in clover now, nor know
Who made honey long ago.

966

The Survival

TO-DAY'S house makes to-morrow's road;
I knew these heaps of stone
When they were walls of grace and might,
The country's honour, art's delight
That over fountain'd silence show'd
Fame's final bastion.

Inheritance has found fresh work,
Disunion union breeds;
Beauty the strong, its difference lost,
Has matter fit for flood and frost.
Here's the true blood that will not shirk
Life's new-commanding needs.

With curious costly zeal, O man,
Raise orrery and ode;
How shines your tower, the only one
Of that especial site and stone!
And even the dream's confusion can
Sustain to-morrow's road.

1825–1900

967 *Dominus Illuminatio Mea*

IN the hour of death, after this life's whim,
When the heart beats low, and the eyes grow dim,
And pain has exhausted every limb—
The lover of the Lord shall trust in Him.

When the will has forgotten the lifelong aim,
And the mind can only disgrace its fame,
And a man is uncertain of his own name—
The power of the Lord shall fill this frame.

When the last sigh is heaved, and the last tear shed,
And the coffin is waiting beside the bed,
And the widow and child forsake the dead—
The angel of the Lord shall lift this head.

For even the purest delight may pall,
And power must fail, and the pride must fall,
And the love of the dearest friends grow small—
But the glory of the Lord is all in all.

INDEX OF FIRST LINES

INDEX OF FIRST LINES

INDEX OF FIRST LINES

INDEX OF FIRST LINES

INDEX OF FIRST LINES

INDEX OF FIRST LINES

INDEX OF FIRST LINES

INDEX OF FIRST LINES

INDEX OF FIRST LINES

INDEX OF FIRST LINES

INDEX OF FIRST LINES

INDEX OF FIRST LINES

INDEX OF FIRST LINES

INDEX OF FIRST LINES

INDEX OF FIRST LINES

INDEX OF FIRST LINES

INDEX OF FIRST LINES

INDEX OF FIRST LINES

INDEX OF FIRST LINES

INDEX OF FIRST LINES

INDEX OF FIRST LINES

INDEX OF FIRST LINES

INDEX OF FIRST LINES

INDEX OF FIRST LINES